# INTER...
## PUBLIC I ...

### AND

## PUBLIC DIPLOMACY

This book is part of the Peter Lang Media and Communication list.
Every volume is peer reviewed and meets
the highest quality standards for content and production.

PETER LANG
New York • Bern • Frankfurt • Berlin
Brussels • Vienna • Oxford • Warsaw

# INTERNATIONAL
# PUBLIC RELATIONS
## AND
# PUBLIC DIPLOMACY

## COMMUNICATION AND ENGAGEMENT

GUY J. GOLAN,
SUNG-UN YANG,
DENNIS F. KINSEY,
EDITORS

PETER LANG
New York • Bern • Frankfurt • Berlin
Brussels • Vienna • Oxford • Warsaw

**Library of Congress Cataloging-in-Publication Data**

International public relations and public diplomacy: communication and engagement /
edited by Guy J. Golan, Sung-Un Yang, Dennis F. Kinsey.
pages cm
Includes bibliographical references and index.
1. Public relations and politics. 2. Diplomacy. 3. International relations.
I. Golan, Guy J. II. Yang, Sung-un. III. Kinsey, Dennis F.
JF1525.P8I57   327.1'1—dc23   2014031261
ISBN 978-1-4331-2688-8 (hardcover)
ISBN 978-1-4331-2687-1 (paperback)
ISBN 978-1-4539-1432-8 (e-book)


Bibliographic information published by **Die Deutsche Nationalbibliothek**.
**Die Deutsche Nationalbibliothek** lists this publication in the "Deutsche
Nationalbibliografie"; detailed bibliographic data are available
on the Internet at http://dnb.d-nb.de/.

The paper in this book meets the guidelines for permanence and durability
of the Committee on Production Guidelines for Book Longevity
of the Council of Library Resources.

© 2015 Peter Lang Publishing, Inc., New York
29 Broadway, 18th floor, New York, NY 10006
www.peterlang.com

Printed in the United States of America

# Contents

## Global Issues & Challenges

## Conclusion

# 1. *Introduction: The Integrated Public Diplomacy Perspective*

GUY J. GOLAN & SUNG-UN YANG

Research on public diplomacy serves as the intellectual meeting point of various academic disciplines, including international public relations, mass communication, international relations, strategic studies, and diplomatic studies (Gilboa, 2008). Since Edmund Gullion, dean of the Fletcher School of Law and Diplomacy at Tufts University, coined the term *public diplomacy* in 1965 (Cull, 2009), the field of public diplomacy has increasingly attracted attention from international professionals and scholars alike. Despite the growing body of scholarship on public diplomacy, there is still much confusion about what the term actually means and how it differs from international public relations. The current book aims to clear some of the confusion regarding the perceptual intersection between the two fields. Based on Golan (2013)'s integrated public diplomacy model, our book aims to provide a comprehensive perspective on what often seems like a complex and multilayered area of scholarship and practice.

Public relations is most commonly referred to as management of communication between an organization and its publics (e.g., J. E. Grunig & Hunt, 1984). To be more specific, public relations has been defined as "the management function that establishes and maintains mutually beneficial relationships between an organization and the publics on whom its success or failure depends" (Cutlip, Center, & Broom, 2000, p. 6). As such, international public relations can be understood as the relationship management function in its global sense.

In the past, communication scholars and researchers, especially those studying international public relations, have tried to identify the convergence between public relations and public diplomacy (e.g., Gilboa, 2008; Manheim, 1994; Signitzer & Coombs, 1992; Signitzer & Wasmer, 2006;

Wang & Chang, 2004). Among them, Signitzer and Wasmer (2006) viewed public diplomacy as a specific governmental function of public relations, and explained that a matrix of goals in public diplomacy can be intertwined with those in public relations. Signitzer and Wasmer (2006) maintained that these key objectives of public relations can be applied to communication management between a sovereign nation and its strategic foreign publics in an international or diplomatic situation.

Public diplomacy essentially deals with the *management of communication* among diplomatic actors, including nations and non-state actors, which have specific informational or motivational objectives toward reaching the foreign publics through various channels of communication to promote national interest. Above all, in contemporary public diplomacy, the focus has shifted from conventional diplomatic means and goals for promotion to *relationship cultivation with key foreign publics* (e.g., Kruckeberg & Vujnovic, 2005; Snow, 2009).

The focus of earlier development within public diplomacy was on media diplomacy or political information for advocacy, including international broadcasting: i.e., one-way transmission of information to foreign publics to "influence the behavior of a foreign government by influencing the attitudes of its citizens" (Malone, 1988, p. 3). In recent years, key changes in conceptualizing contemporary public diplomacy have shifted the focus to the roles of non-state actors and the nature of their global relationships (Yun, 2012; Yun & Toth, 2009) in their cultivation of substantial relationships or *genuine* contact. Also, *The New Public Diplomacy* (Melissen, 2005) emphasizes the *relational* role of non-state diplomatic actors, the inter-connectedness of foreign/domestic publics on multiple layers, and the two-way engagement of publics through the use of "soft power" (Nye, 2008) as the key leverage to attract foreign publics.

Consequently, rather than a one-way transmission of information for one-sided persuasion from a nation to foreign publics, contemporary public diplomacy now emphasizes ways to establish and foster mutual understanding and two-way exchanges of information on the basis of the *soft power* of a nation. Examples of these changes are the emergence of cultural and educational exchange in terms of *cultural* diplomacy (e.g., Melissen, 2005; Schneider, 2003; Snow, 2008). Along the same line, Snow (2009) called for the need for "rethinking public diplomacy" (pp. 3–11) in order to conceptualize a *relationship*-centered public diplomacy, calling for the adoption of public relations' two-way symmetrical communication[1] (J. E. Grunig, 2001) in public diplomacy (p. 10).

A key area of differentiation between international public relations and public diplomacy can be identified in its ultimate goal. While international public relations between any organization and foreign publics may focus on mutual beneficial relationship for the sake of long term ends of consumerism or philanthropy, public diplomacy's ultimate aim is to gather international support for a nation's foreign policy.

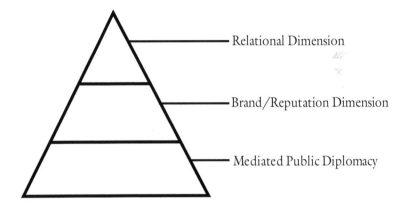

*Figure 1.1.* The Integrated Public Diplomacy Model.

## Introduction

*International Public Relations and Public Diplomacy* provides a collection of chapters that integrate research on public diplomacy with research on public relations. Unlike traditional public diplomacy research largely focused on soft power programs such as educational or cultural exchanges, our volume accepts the argument presented by many scholars for the/regarding the appropriateness of studying public diplomacy from a public relations perspective (Fitzpatrick, 2007; Signitzer and Coombs, 1992; L'Etang, 2009). We posit that public diplomacy should be examined as a strategic management approach (Grunig and Repper, 1992) and therefore should apply key lessons from public relations literature. This book includes chapters by scholars who synthesize and argue for the suitability of such public relations functions as relationship management (Ki), crisis communication (Kim), advocacy (Vibber and Kim), stewardship (Gilmore and Waters) and campaign evaluation (Pamment) to the field of public diplomacy. In addition, the chapters discuss how governments (Schneider), corporations (Kochhar and Molleda) and NGOs

(Zatepilina-Monacell; Yang) apply various public relations tactics to build and maintain relationships with foreign publics.

When viewed holistically, the current book presents an integrated approach to public diplomacy scholarship (in this chapter, I will refer to this approach as **integrated public diplomacy**) that combines both the short, medium and long termed perspectives on public diplomacy. The relational perspective focuses on the long term relationship management efforts of government, corporations and NGOs to build and maintain mutually beneficial relationships with foreign publics. Such efforts traditionally focus on such soft power programs as aid, development and exchange programs. The mediated public diplomacy approach (Entman, 2008) is focused on government attempts to shape and influence its framing in the global news media and, therefore, constitutes a short term perspective. As global governments compete to shape international debate regarding global conflict and salient international relations issues (Sheafer and Gabay, 2009; Sheafer and Shenhav, 2009), the success or failure of mediated public diplomacy efforts can have direct consequences regarding global public opinion (Manheim, 1994; Wanta, Golan, Lee, 2004). Mediated public diplomacy is under-invested by scholars but is likely to gain much attention from both scholars and public diplomacy practitioners considering the powerful impact of such satellite broadcast channels as Al Jazeera and Al Arabyia on political events around the world (Powers and Samuel-Azran, in this book). Representing a more tactical approach that is meant to produce long term results, government nation branding efforts extend the attempt to link issues and attributes to nations through public relations and marketing tactics (Wang, 2006; Kaneva, 2011; Rasmussen and Merkelsen, 2012). However, it is these efforts that may ultimately shape long term relational outcomes and therefore play an important element bridging between the short term mediated public diplomacy and the longer term relational public diplomacy.

It is important to note that a full understanding of public diplomacy cannot be attained through either the relational, nation branding or mediated perspectives alone. The long term success of relationship building and stewardship is often contingent on the success or failure of organizations to communicate their values, culture or policies to their target audiences. As such only the **integrated public diplomacy** approach to public diplomacy (as illustrated in Figure 1.1) can provide a meaningful understanding of the field that can guide both academics and professionals.

The current chapter will outline the soft power approach as the theoretic framework of previous public diplomacy scholarship. Next, it will discuss the mediated public diplomacy approach and its centrality to the success of American public diplomacy efforts abroad. Finally, the chapter will argue for the **integrated public diplomacy** concept and argue for a new approach to the practice of public diplomacy that draws upon the political campaign model as the most appropriate operational perspective for achieving both the short, medium and long term public diplomacy outcomes.

In this introductory chapter, the authors will explain the convergence between public diplomacy and public relations, followed by a brief overview of two key public relations perspectives, *relational* public diplomacy and *mediated* public diplomacy.

Regarding the convergence between public diplomacy and public relations, there have been at least two distinctive perspectives. One is the view of public diplomacy as a field of *relational* public diplomacy, involving key foreign publics by means of cultural exchange or other forms of public engagement and utilizing two-way communication, which can bring out mutual benefits between a nation and its publics (e.g., Yun, 2006, 2012; Yun & Toth, 2009).

The other is the view of public diplomacy's primary role in the context of *mediated* public diplomacy (e.g., Entman, 2003; Sheafer & Gabay, 2009; Sheafer & Shenhav, 2009) by which a nation attempts to strategically promote its agenda and frames, through strategically selected mass media efforts, in order to impact opinions held by targeted foreign audiences (Manheim, 1994; Wang & Chang, 2004; Wanta, Golan & Lee, 2004). Whereas the first perspective has emerged from the field of public relations, particularly influenced by relationship management (e.g., Ledingham & Bruning, 2000), the later has stemmed from researchers in the field of public opinion and political communication.

Recognizing the importance of both the mediated and relational public diplomacy perspectives, the current book provides a comprehensive approach to what Golan (2013) referred to as the integrated public diplomacy perspective. Key to this perspective is the understanding that the focus of public diplomacy is contingent upon the context in which governments and or non-state actors operate. As explained by Golan, the mediated public diplomacy approach may be best suited for short to medium term public diplomacy objectives. On the other hand, reputation management and relational diplomacy may be best suited for medium to long term objectives.

Recognizing that no model provides a one size fits all solution to public diplomacy, we contend that different nations and non-state actors will focus on either or both the mediated or the relational approaches to public diplomacy, depending on the internal and external factors that may impact their stakeholder relationships. The purpose of the current edited book is to

provide an intellectual bridge that connects public relations and public diplomacy scholarship with the hopes of clarifying the conceptual overlaps and
academic commonalities between the disciplines.

## Mediated Public Diplomacy

The perspective of mediated public diplomacy has considered public diplomacy as the field of strategic management of communication *content* that is
able to effectively pursue favorable image cultivation through media coverage
on international affairs (Sheafer & Gabay, 2009). Typically, this field of public diplomacy touches upon governmental attempts to issue-manage through
mass communication outlets in times of crisis or international competition
over issue framing. Entman (2008) defines mediated public diplomacy as
a government's strategic attempts to exert control over the framing of the
country's policy in foreign media (p. 89). Foreign publics often have limited
global awareness of and direct experience with foreign nations; therefore,
mass media have become suitable in shaping foreign publics' images of foreign countries (Entman, 2004; Kunczik, 1997; Leonard, Stead & Smewing,
2002). For such reasons, some countries have garnered and enhanced favorable national images through strategic implementation of public relations
campaigns to influence international media coverage (Manheim, 1994).

Wanta, Golan, and Lee (2004) tested the extent to which international
media coverage influences public perceptions of foreign nations. They argued
that the study found supportive first-level and second-level agenda-setting
effects (McCombs & Shaw, 1972). Wang and Chang (2004) analyzed the
relationship between Chinese public diplomacy efforts and American news
coverage of China during the Chinese president's visit to the United States
in 1997. Wang and Chang found that, despite the significant public relations efforts for strategic communication of head-of-state visits, the image
of China in the local press coverage had not improved. Additionally, Sheafer
and Gabay (2009) recently analyzed agenda and frame building in foreign
media on Israel's disengagement from Gaza and the general elections in the
Palestinian Authority. Accordingly, Sheafer and Gabay considered mediated
public diplomacy efforts as *strategic contests* over international agenda building and frame building where various public diplomacy actors need to *compete*
to promote their own agenda and frames to influence foreign policy. In the
current book Powers and Samuel-Azran discuss the global significance of international broadcasting in the realm of public diplomacy. They contend that
actors use international broadcasting to promote an ideological perspective
that the audience is hopefully willing to "buy" with attention. Over time, as

an individual consumes more information, that individual becomes increasingly loyal to both the medium and that actor's ideological perspective.

## National Branding and Country Reputation

Unlike the media-centered mediated public diplomacy, governmental and/or organizational attempts to shape and define their reputation or brand has been an area of great interest to both scholars of international public relations and public diplomacy. While definitions of nation branding and country reputation may depend on the intellectual perspective of the researchers, there are many lessons from the area of public relations that are applicable to this area of inquiry. Several of the chapters in the current book deal with these topics from a variety of perspectives. For example, Hung's chapter builds upon the topic of how countries utilize information subsidies, such as speeches, to establish and promote a nation brand. Their research finds that information subsidies were often used as part of a one-way communication approach but can be applied to new media that lend themselves to a more relationship-based communication approach. This shift would ultimately better engage the global audience and would more effectively help a nation in their nation branding and perception management. Hung's chapter further builds upon the topic of nation branding by examining China's use of advertisements in their global engagement efforts. Looking at the success of China's "Made with China" ad campaign, Hung argues that countries can re-brand themselves more effectively if they are able to build their credibility through advertising.

Discussing the problematic nature of the nation branding area of scholarship, Anholt presents his concept of competitive identity. The author defines competitive identity as the way in which a nation holistically presents itself to other nations, taking into account all aspects of how a country develops its image. This image, or "brand," is then applied to public diplomacy, which is said to "wield" the soft power created by a nation's competitive identity.

## Relational Public Diplomacy

Recently, especially with the influence of the field of public relations, there has been a notable shift to relationship-centered endeavors in the study of public diplomacy (e.g., Fitzpatrick, 2007; Yun, 2006; Yun & Toth, 2009). To advance issues facing contemporary public diplomacy, Fitzpatrick (2007), for example, suggested that the relationship management theories from the public relations field can be a useful framework in public diplomacy:

[by] defining public diplomacy's central purpose as relationship management, unifying the functions under one overarching concept, adopting a management (rather than communication) mindset, and recognizing the importance of diplomatic deeds that support communication practices, practitioners will be better equipped to conduct public diplomacy effectively. (p. 187)

The quality of first-hand, substantial relationships management will be the key basis of excellence in public diplomacy. This can be enhanced by effective two-way communication and public engagement that connect governments and various non-state actors with key foreign publics through an exchange of information, ideas, education, and culture. Emphasizing inter-organizational relationships, Zatepilina-Monacell, one of our contributors, also suggested that public diplomacy can enhance its effectiveness through the role of non-governmental organizations (NGOs) by creating a quality *relationship* between state and non-state actors with similar values.

Despite such increasing connection to public diplomacy, public relations has been sometimes criticized as a mere tool to "sell democracy." For example, "In many op-eds and addresses before Congress, the public relations industry is singled out as the main culprit in why U.S. public diplomacy efforts have failed" (Snow, 2009, p. 9). Those critiques often relegate public relations to being propaganda or unilateral persuasion to manipulate public opinion; Grunig has called this *asymmetrical* communication. Regarding this ethical dilemma facing public relations, Grunig (1993) explained:

As noted earlier, the asymmetrical models can be ethical if their practitioners can be certain they know what is best for the publics they try to influence. In contrast, the two-way symmetrical model is inherently ethical because it opens the question of right and wrong to dialogue, collaboration, and compromise. In practice, the asymmetrical models almost always present ethical problems. (p. 160)

The book chapter by Jiang on public diplomacy ethics, calls for the direction of public diplomacy to reflect the theories of public relations, including two-way symmetrical communication (J. E. Grunig, 2001) and community-building (Kruckeberg & Vujnovic, 2005). The latter theory recognizes overseas audiences as *publics* with whom public diplomatic actors cultivate quality relationships for mutually beneficial outcomes rather than as "markets" to sell foreign policies (Kruckeberg & Vujnovic, 2005, p. 303). In a recent book, *Excellent Public Relations and Effective Organizations*, L. Grunig et al. (2002) concluded that effective organizations build quality relationships with key publics by management of *symmetrical* communication, which allow those organizations to sustain ethical practice.

Therefore, public relations should not be considered as the manipulation of the image or reputation that foreign publics hold of a nation. Rather, favorable images or country reputations must be conceptualized as a byproduct of *quality actions* and related information, which includes foreign policies and exchange of values and cultures to cultivate quality relationships with foreign publics. To accomplish this, effective management of communication is essential to signal the quality of diplomacy actions to key foreign publics.

A relevant example of relational diplomacy addresses growing diaspora communities. Citing Salter and Teger's (1975) differentiation of people contact to *genuine contact* and *superficial contact*, Yun and Toth (2009) called for *relational* public diplomacy to enhance quality genuine contact among global migrants. Accordingly, "a country's soft power resources are nakedly exposed to migrants' living experiences" (p. 500); through (diplomatic) actions to sustain the quality of relationships, migrants themselves can be a more conducive channel of communication to overseas publics than "messages and information abroad on the attractiveness of its soft power resources" (p. 500). Likewise, in terms of relational public diplomacy efforts to emphasize the role of transnational communities (Yun, 2012), Bravo, in her chapter, suggests that *diaspora* communities should be considered strategic publics for public diplomacy actors. Diaspora communities, as permanent migrants, are unique and important as strategically intervening publics that connect home and host countries.

The chapter by Ki, introduces the relationship management theory in the context of public diplomacy. She contends that nation-states employ public diplomacy to create and maintain the relationship between a nation-state and foreign publics. The shift of public diplomacy's focus from one-way communication to managing networks of relationships (Riordan, 2003) is largely attributed to new communication technologies, such as the Internet, which have placed heavier emphasis on developing relationships.

## *Conclusion*

To summarize, this edited book aims to demonstrate aspects of both relational public diplomacy and mediated public diplomacy in conceptualizing contemporary public diplomacy through the integrated public diplomacy perspective. The collection of chapters collectively aim to bridge between research on international public relations and public diplomacy. Goals of public diplomacy can range widely, from short-term to long-term, between the various vehicles that exist to influence foreign publics' perceptions of, attitudes toward, and behaviors towards a nation, corporation or any other non-state actor. These vehicles include personal/relational experience, interpersonal influence, strategic communication delivered through traditional mass communication or social media platforms. Therefore, rather than focusing on each perspective separately, our edited book intends to provide readers with those competing perspectives to understand the study and practice of contemporary public diplomacy. While the diplomacy fields have many differences between them, we posit that they also share many commonalities. Based on the strategic communication functions of the mediated public diplomacy perspective and the organizational-stakeholder functions of reputation management and relational diplomacy, we believe the integrated public diplomacy perspective fits well into the political public relations approach (Strömbäck and Kiousis, 2011) with the requirement of global organization-public engagement.

## Note

1. Symmetrical communication is a model of public relations/communication management between organization and publics, in which the outcomes of communication process is mutually beneficial between organizations and their key publics, rather than unilateral/asymmetrical persuasion to change publics' opinions and behaviors for the interests of organizations.

## Bibliography

Cull, N. J. (2009). Public diplomacy before Gullion. In N. Snow & P. M. Taylor (Eds.), *Routledge handbook of public diplomacy* (pp. 19–23). New York: Routledge.

Cutlip, S. M., Center, A. H., & Broom, G. M. (2000). *Effective public relations* (8th ed.). Upper Saddle River, NJ: Prentice Hall.

Entman, R. M. (2003). Cascading activation: Contesting the White House's frame after 9/11. *Political Communication, 20,* 425–432.

Entman, R. M. (2008). Theorizing mediated public diplomacy: The US case. *The International Journal of Press/Politics, 13*(2), 87–102.

———. (2004). *Projections of power: Framing news, public opinion, and US foreign policy.* Chicago: University of Chicago Press.

Fitzpatrick, K. R. (2007). Advancing the new public diplomacy: A public relations perspective. *The Hague Journal of Diplomacy, 2,* 187–221.

Gilboa, E. (2008). Searching for a theory of public diplomacy. *The ANNALS of the American Academy of Political and Social Science, 616,* 55–77. doi: 10.1177/0002716207312142

Golan, G. J. (2013). An Integrated Approach to Public Diplomacy. *American Behavioral Scientist, 57*(9), 1251–1255.

Grunig, J. E. (1993). Public relations and international affairs: Effects, ethics and responsibility. *Journal of International Affairs, 47*(1), 138–162.

———. (2001). Two-way symmetrical public relations: Past, present, and future. In R. L. Heath (Ed.), *Handbook of Public Relations* (pp. 11–32). Thousand Oaks, CA: Sage.

Grunig, J. E., & Hunt, T. (1984). *Managing public relations.* New York: Holt, Rinehart, & Winston.

Grunig, J. E., & Repper, F. C. (1992). Strategic management, publics, and issues. In J. E. Grunig (Ed.), Excellence in public relations and communication management (pp. 117–157). Hillsdale, NJ: Lawrence Erlbaum Associates.

Grunig, L. A., Grunig, J. E., & Dozier, D. M. (2002). *Excellent public relations and effective organizations: A study of communication management in three countries.* Mahwah, NJ: Lawrence Erlbaum Associates.

Kaneva, N. (2011). Nation branding: Toward an agenda for critical research. *International Journal of Communication, 5,* 117–141.

Kruckeberg, D., & Vujnovic, M. (2005). Public relations, not propaganda, for US public diplomacy in a post-911 1 world: Challenges and opportunities. *Journal of Communication Management, 9,* 296–304.

Kunczik, M. (1997). *Images of nations and international public relations.* Mahwah, NJ: Lawrence Erlbaum Associates.

Ledingham, J. A., & Bruning, S. D. (Eds.). (2000). *Public relations as relationship management: A relational approach to the study and practice of public relations.* Mahwah, NJ: Lawrence Erlbaum.

Leonard, M., Stead, C., & Smewing, C. (2002). *Public diplomacy.* London: Foreign Policy Centre.

L'Etang, J. (2009). Public relations and diplomacy in a globalized world: An issue of public communication. *American Behavioral Scientist, 53*(4), 607–626.

Malone, G. D. (1988). *Political advocacy and cultural communication. Organizing the nation's public diplomacy.* Lanham, MD: University Press of America.

Manheim, J. (1994). *Strategic public diplomacy and American foreign policy: The evolution of influence.* New York: Oxford University Press.

McCombs, M. E., & Shaw, D. L. (1972). The agenda-setting function of mass media. *Public Opinion Quarterly, 36,* 176–187.

Melissen, J. (2005). *The new public diplomacy: Softpower in international relations.* New York: Palgrave Macmillan.

Nye, J. S. (2008). Public diplomacy and soft power. *The ANNALS of the American Academy of Political and Social Science, 616,* 94–109. doi: 10.1177/0002716207311699

Rasmussen, R. K., & Merkelsen, H. (2012). The new PR of states: How nation branding practices affect the security function of public diplomacy. *Public Relations Review, 38*(5), 810–818.

Riordan, S. (2003). *The new diplomacy.* Blackwell Publishing.

Salter, C. A., & Teger, A. I. (1975). Change in attitudes toward other nations as a function of the type of international contact. *Sociometry,* 213–222.

Schneider, C. (2003). *Diplomacy that works: Best practices in cultural diplomacy.* Washington, DC: Center for Arts and Culture.

Sheafer, T., & Gabay, I. (2009). Mediated public diplomacy: A strategic contest over international agenda building and frame building. *Political Communication, 26,* 447–467.

Sheafer, T., & Shenhav, S. R. (2009). Mediated public diplomacy in a new era of warfare. *The Communication Review, 12,* 272–283.

Signitzer, B. H., & Coombs, T. (1992). Public relations and public diplomacy: Conceptual covergences. *Public Relations Review, 18*(2), 137–147.

Signitzer, B. H., & Wasmer, C. (2006). Public diplomacy: A specific government public
    relations function. In I. C. H. Botan & V. Hazelton (Eds.), *Public relations theory II*
    (pp. 435–464). Mahwah, NJ: Lawrence Erlbaum Associates.
Snow, N. (2008). International Exchanges and the U.S. Image. *The ANNALS
    of the American Academy of Political and Social Science, 616,* 198–222. doi:
    10.1177/0002716207311864
Strömbäck, J., & Kiousis, S. (Eds.). (2011). *Political public relations. Principles and appli-
    cations.* New York, NY: Routledge.
———. (2009). Rethinking public diplomacy. In N. Snow & P. M. Taylor (Eds.), *Rout-
    ledge handbook of public diplomacy* (pp. 3–11). New York: Routledge.
Wang, J. (2006). Localising public diplomacy: The role of sub-national actors in nation
    branding. *Place Branding, 2*(1), 32–42.
Wang, J., & Chang, T.-K. (2004). Strategic public diplomacy and local press: How a
    high-profile "head-of-state" visit was covered in America's heartland. *Public Relations
    Review, 30,* 11–24.
Wanta, W., Golan, G., & Lee, C. (2004). Agenda setting and international news: Media
    influence on public perceptions of foreign nations. *Journalism & Mass Communica-
    tion Quarterly, 81,* 364–377.
Yun, S. H. (2006). Toward public relations theory-based study of public diplomacy: Test-
    ing the applicability of the Excellence study. *Journal of Public Relations Research, 18,*
    278–312.
———. (2012). Relational public diplomacy: The perspective of sociological globalism.
    *International Journal of Communication, 6,* 2199–2219.
Yun, S. H., & Toth, E. (2009). Future sociological public diplomacy and the role of public
    relations: Evolution of public diplomacy. *American Behavioral Scientist, 53*(4), 493–503.

# *Foundations*

# 2. U.S. Public Diplomacy Since 9–11: The Challenges of Integration

Michael D. Schneider

The narrative of U.S. public diplomacy in the past decade weaves together a revolution in communication, world-wide demographic changes and a number of serious threats to U.S. national security. Trans-national non-state actors play a far greater part in global affairs than in the past. With mobile devices, Wi-fi zones and broadband spreading almost exponentially, information flows ever faster and threatens to overwhelm our absorptive capacity. These and other elements of the new communications have greatly expanded participation in decision making. Even in the authoritarian nations, leaders can neither ignore nor easily dominate publics. Paradoxically, the new communication can fragment as well as mobilize, confuse as well as enlighten, harden as well as challenge values and customs. So long as the pace of change accelerates, societies seem to have little time or capacity to consolidate all the changes. U.S. statecraft has struggled to adopt to the new realities.

## Post-9/11 PD Realities

Among the many challenges of post-9–11, U.S. leaders faced the need to gain worldwide public support for a global war on terrorism. Initially key publics rallied to support the U.S. In many languages people said, "We're all Americans!" As the focus of U.S. diplomacy shifted to the Middle East, Afghanistan and Pakistan as well as a few other "frontline states, the Bush Administration warned that other governments must side with the U.S. or be considered tantamount to opponents. However, with the U.S. invasion of Iraq, public support dropped rapidly. New lows persisted throughout the central zone of contention in the Middle East and in Pakistan. European approval of U.S. policies dropped significantly (Kull, 2007).[1]

While America initially rallied to the Bush Administration, as the Bush team pressed for international action against Saddam Hussein, and as the subsequent successful invasion turned into a highly contentious occupation, domestic opinion turned against the Administration. Over the past decade domestic opinion has remained highly divided over the wars in Iraq and Afghanistan, with increasing calls for scaling down and removing our forces from the conflict (Dao, 2011). The 9–11 terror attack also brought home with a vengeance historic demographic and technological changes as well as myriad unresolved tensions in Islamic societies. A "youth bulge" in the Middle East and Africa underlies other influences on public opinion. The accelerating digital revolution has opened new lifestyles centering on individual freedom and material aspirations denied previous generations and empowered far more people throughout societies. Others have sought more violent answers as recruits for al Qaeda and its various offshoots (Venhaus, 2010).

## State's Public Communication Response

While the Department has been well served by a fine corps of highly energetic, intelligent and devoted public servants here and around the globe, it has lacked the communications capacity, funding and staff levels to respond to the new challenges. Only in recent years has the Department strengthened its communications.

The Department was saddled with mid-20th century telecommunications in the face of 21st century challenges. Not until Colin Powell became secretary of state did the Department aggressively modernize its public communication capacities with the large-scale purchase of new systems. As one senior officer commented, "State was in the dark ages in that regard and Powell was committed to bring them into the 21st century" (Senior State Department Official, personal communication, August 16, 2012).

Gradually State shifted toward more universal unclassified Internet connectivity and the increased use of email rather than the traditional, slow cable system. The merger of USIA into State brought experience with contemporary communication technologies, but the Department wasn't able to draw on that experience as fully as it should.

Beyond the tools of communication, Public Diplomacy (PD) needed more strategic focus. PD professionals in Washington and abroad had suffered from a decade of budget cuts, indecisive leadership, and the awkward absorption of USIA into State. Field posts had fewer U.S. Foreign Service and indigenous foreign national employees. A number of libraries and cultural centers had closed or reduced their service. The corps of Foreign and Civil

Service officers previously involved in public diplomacy through USIA were disheartened by the loss of autonomy inherent in their agency's merger with State. Between 2001 and 2013 seven individuals served as under secretary for Public Diplomacy and Public Affairs, none staying much more than two years. The position was vacant almost 40 percent of the time, according to several accounts.

In early 2001, Secretary Powell selected Charlotte Beers to be under secretary of state for Public Diplomacy and Public Affairs. Ms. Beers, a leading advertising executive, called for a PD response to 9–11and beyond that portrayed values of life, family, religion and community that Muslim communities shared with American society. In mid-2002 she told a Congressional Committee: "We have to be able to enter the Information Revolution aggressively to build a larger presence—what I'd call a larger 'share of voice' engaged in discussing shared ideas and values." She accepted the need to speak with government officials and elites but argued

> At the same time, we must improve considerably our communication with the mainstream of young adults, especially in the Middle East and South and Southeast Asia...We have to meet this expanded target on their terms and in their channels of distribution.

Ms. Beers wanted to employ more public opinion research as well. She emphasized the role of exchanges in leading to "transformations" in personal understanding by foreign visitors to America (Beers 2002).

While her concepts wisely played for the mid- to- long run, her approach could not meet the immediate negativity in the Arab World and Europe. Critics thought a campaign to stress commonly held American and Islamic values was artificial and forced. Some argued that the U.S. needed to deal with the hard, immediate policy issues more forcefully. In the face of rising dissent at home over the invasion of Iraq and strong opposition from media and publics abroad, it is not likely that any public diplomacy campaign would have gained supporters for the Bush Administration between 2003 and 2008. Frustrated by negative reaction abroad and in the American press to her values campaign, and also by the slowness of bureaucracy to act and the lack of funds, Ms. Beers resigned her position in early March 2003. "The gap between who we are and how we wish to be seen and how we are in fact seen is frighteningly wide," she testified before the Senate Foreign Relations Committee the week before (Beers, 2002).

Ms. Beers' successors, Margaret Tutwiler, Karen Hughes and James Glassman, also stayed too briefly in the State Department to upgrade public diplomacy. Drawing on her experience as ambassador to Morocco,

Ms. Tutwiler emphasized improved and increased exchanges, but stayed on the job for only three months. (Tutwiler, 2004). In the face of skeptical publics abroad, Karen Hughes conducted heralded "listening tours." However to the press and other observers she seemed to do most of the talking in her meetings abroad. (Weisman, 2005). Her emphasis on "the diplomacy of deeds" seemed a passing flourish rather than a serious endeavor. Neither Ms. Tutwiler nor Ms. Hughes seemed to use their political prominence to significantly shape any particular U.S. foreign policy direction at State or in their relations with the president. Nor was Mr. Glassman able to achieve much in his six months' tenure at the end of the Bush Administration. He worked quickly, however, and brought to State from his tenure as chair of the Broadcasting Board of Governors, a concept of "Public Diplomacy 2.0." This idea emphasized the use of social media and Internet interactivity. He also focused on what appeared to be a re-make of the ideological battle of the Cold War in his own war of ideas against radical Islam (Glassman, 2008).

By the end of the Bush Administration, the State Department was technically better equipped for public diplomacy. While Congress had provided significantly more funding for exchanges, it had not provided adequate funds to rebuild staff levels in the field nor to handle the expanding exchange program. In DC and abroad public diplomats had lost autonomy and organizational clout through the merger of USIA and State. Only slight changes occurred in the operational culture of the Department. Political appointees stayed too briefly, had some useful ideas but were not able to see them through. The potential for public diplomacy to broaden and deepen change at State remained unfulfilled.

## The Department of Defense Response: The Rise of "Strategic Communication"

Officials in the U.S. Department of Defense had long developed concepts of strategic influence. Shortly after 9–11, with direction from the White House, the Department initiated a comprehensive approach for addressing international audiences in response to terrorists' propaganda (Gough, 2003). The Department relied on massive increases in funding and experimentation in information operations, psychological operations and media relations, especially in Iraq and Afghanistan. In the absence of adequate civilian USG capacity to assist media and affect public opinion in conflict zones, the Pentagon stepped in with varied programs, at one point totaling close to $1 billion (Cary, 2010).[2]

The Department understood Strategic Communication not only as a way to affect the perceptions and behavior of audiences in conflict zones, but also in societies where extremists or terrorists could flourish. Arguing that "every action, image and word sends a message," the 2008 paper, "Principles of Strategic Communication" asserted:

> Communication no longer has boundaries, in time or space. All players are communicators, wittingly or not. Everything the Joint Force says, does, or fails to do and say, has intended and unintended consequences. Every action, word, and image sends a message, and every team member is a messenger, from the 18-year-old rifleman to the commander.

For the Department of Defense the Global War on Terrorism became a Global War on All Forms of Extremism, and our involvement in Iraq and Afghanistan validated an expanded program of strategic communication. These include, among others, a few notable initiatives:

> The Department staffed some 21 Military Information Support Teams (MIST) assigned to work for U.S. embassies. These teams have provided printing and radio-TV/video support, and supplement the more limited media outreach of the embassies. A number of these teams operate under embassy direction in Africa (Cary, 2010).

Since 2010, in part for the optics, the DoD extended the reach of its psyops assets beyond immediate conflict zones, and retitled psyops MISO–Military Information Support Operations. "Psyops" has long posed a problem in the eyes of civilian PD practitioners abroad who fear association will affect the credibility of State Department public and cultural affairs officers as well as non-governmental organizations working to build media capacity and other elements of democratic governance abroad (Cary, 2010).

In Afghanistan DoD has partnered with State PD and USAID to help build communications capacity in Afghanistan. With annual budgets as high as approximately $120 million, the PD shop in the U.S. embassy in Kabul benefited greatly from DoD and USAID transfers.

In a late 2009 report to Congress, the Defense Department summarized its efforts and philosophy. Strategic communication "is the process of integrating issues of audience and stakeholder perception into policy-making, planning, and operations at every level." The report also stressed the importance of "active listening and sustained engagement with relevant stakeholders." The DoD report stressed another essential consideration:

> A key lesson...is that processes intended to develop separate and distinct strategic communication priorities, plans or organizations are ineffective when divorced from other planning processes. Strategic communication must instead

be integrated into existing and time-tested policy-making and planning processes (Department of Defense, 2009)

DoD concepts are reflected in the 2006 U.S. National Strategy for Public Diplomacy and Strategic Communication, and the 2010 National Framework for Strategic Communication, published by the National Security Staff for the White House.

Both documents emphasized the importance of "synchronization" and integration of communication with policy and action. Ultimately, inter-agency consultation helped the White House in both the Bush and Obama Administrations promulgate reports to Congress that sanctioned concepts of strategic communication as an over-arching "whole of government" endeavor abroad (The White House, 2010).[3]

## State's Vision: The QDDR and the PD Strategic Framework at State

More recently public diplomacy in the State Department evolved within the broader effort to develop a Quadrennial Diplomacy and Development Review (QDDR). Aware of the DoD Quadrennial Defense Review and frustrated by the slowness of change at State, Secretary of State Clinton saw the opportunity to achieve several goals with a new QDDR. It would better integrate development and diplomacy, gain greater support in Congress, strengthen State's competitive position with DoD and other federal agencies with stakes in international affairs. Overall, it would better prepare State for leadership in the national security community. As much as the exercise and resulting document were an attempt to integrate USAID and State and restructure responsibilities, it was also an attempt to modernize State (W. Burke-White, personal communication, n. d.).

Secretary Clinton encapsulated the new spirit,

> We will also pursue new ways of doing business that help us bring together like-minded people and nations to solve the pressing problems we all face. We will reform and update international institutions, and we'll use 21st century statecraft to extend the reach of our diplomacy beyond the halls of government office buildings. (U.S. State Department, 2010).[4]

Section III of the QDDR, "Engaging Beyond the State" dealt with public diplomacy and related concerns. It recognized the increased prominence of non-state actors in international affairs, and promised three broad, new orientations: to engage through expanded private-public partnerships; to enhance public diplomacy through new communication technologies and expanded people-to-people relationships; and to "incorporate women and girls into all our public-engagement efforts" (U.S. State Department, 2010).

The report asserted:

> as much as civilian power derives from the combined resources and expertise of all U.S. government agencies, it is also the power of the public—of NGOs, corporations, civil society groups, and individuals around the world who share our goals and interests. Making the most of civilian power requires connecting with these actors and designing programs, projects and partnerships with them to advance America's security, prosperity and values around the world. (U.S. State Department, 2010)

To achieve these goals, the QDDR briefly recommended that State strengthen its public affairs relations with international media, employ new technologies, expand English language teaching, combat extremism through an innovative inter-Agency Center for Strategic Counter-Terrorism Communication, and improve 21st century statecraft through "community diplomacy" and public-private partnerships (U.S. State Department, 2010).

While PD was underplayed in the document, the QDDR's commitment to a new culture, new approaches, greater involvement in the public sector, public-private partnerships and new communication technologies paved the way for important enhancements in public diplomacy.

## *The State PD Strategic Framework: A Road Map to Innovation*

The QDDR deferred to the Strategic Framework for Public Diplomacy, issued by Judith McHale in February 2010. With the blessings of Secretary Clinton, Under Secretary Judith McHale, formerly CEO of Discovery Communication and a talented group of experienced pros and newcomers with management experience developed a plan to revitalize public diplomacy and its instrumentalities in State. Their late February 2010 report, "Public Diplomacy: Strengthening U.S. Engagement with the World—A Strategic Approach for the 21st Century," provided a detailed roadmap.[5]

The Framework developed ideas for how public diplomacy could respond to key transnational demographic, communications and political changes. Beginning with one important premise in the document, the Framework argued that "Traditional bilateral diplomacy cannot address the full range of actors now engaged on global issues."

The document went on to highlight the competing influences in the public domain and the complex global challenges, as well as a few states that pose special concerns for the U.S. These reflect the broad policy concerns of the United States.

In five broad "Strategic Imperatives for 21st Century Public Diplomacy" the Framework recognized the necessity to: (a) shape the narrative; (b) expand and strengthen people-to-people relationships; (c) combat violent extremism; (d) better inform policy-making, and (e) deploy resources in line with current priorities. The strategy called for a series of reforms, innovations or improvements, ranging from the very specific to very global in nature. Among them were:

- Add a deputy assistant secretary in each of the regional bureaus to better infuse policy considerations with the public perspective. Such an addition would make it possible to bring more public and cultural expertise into policy discussions.
- Designate a deputy assistant secretary to head international media relations within the Bureau of Public Affairs and hence to strengthen the ability of State/PA to broaden its responsiveness beyond the American press corps in Washington, D.C.
- Improve State's ability to reach out through social media and respond to new communication technologies.
- Increase the ability of posts to engage more quickly by giving the front-line staff more flexible guidelines and greater operational freedom in clearance processes.
- Broaden audiences in order to respond to political and cultural realities around the globe.
- Expand English language instruction, exchange programs, and activities that help attract increased numbers of foreign students to the U.S. and encourage more Americans to study abroad.[6]

## PD Initiatives: Achievements and Challenges

Specific programs and initiatives following the Framework's prescriptions reveal the works in progress and attendant challenges.

### The CSCC: The Challenge of Moving Youth Away from Extremism

State and DoD created an unusual cooperative endeavor, the Center for Strategic Counter-terrorism Communication (CSCC), to seek out those youth especially vulnerable to terrorist recruitment.[7] Housed at State, the $5–6 million includes some 40 representatives from the intelligence community, DoD strategic communications, State PD and political affairs officers— a mix of Foreign Service, Military and Civil Service officials.[8] The CSCC reports to the PD Under Secretary but works closely with the new Bureau of Counter-Terrorism.

White House Executive Order of September 9, 2011 defined the new arrangement. The Executive Order identified audiences vaguely as "...those who may be susceptible to radicalization and recruitment by terrorist organizations." The challenge as described in the Executive Order is to draw together diverse governmental and private analytic sources, integrate efforts to counter extremism among federal national security agencies, and

> provide thematic guidance for strategic counterterrorism narrative and policies and to respond to and rebut extremist messaging and narratives when communicating to audiences outside the United States, as informed by a wide variety of government and non-government sources, including government organizations, academic sources, and finished intelligence created by the intelligence community

The CSCC engages with al Qaeda and other extremist groups in Arabic, Urdu and Somali, primarily on websites and social media. A digital team provides all the text, poster art, video and other necessary digital support. All materials are attributed. Native language speakers produce the varied items for varied social media. The State teams use humor and satire as well as efforts to create empathy for innocent victims of al Qaeda violence. While some would argue that making AQ violence salient will only lend support to the intimidation of local populace, CSCC leaders believe the opposite. Thus CSCC output will talk of the violence the AQ organizations bring to innocent civilians. This, too, seems to be a risk worth taking, but surely merits careful evaluation.

The hybrid organization links to the National Counterterrorism Center, and seeks to integrate and coordinate efforts among involved federal agencies. This is a tall order for any organization that neither controls the assets involved in such enterprises nor has a great deal of funding to lead the way. Even with the White House endorsement, such coordination is difficult (Obama, 2011).

As to the challenge of communicating with potentially hostile audiences, there is a paucity of definitive models or typologies to ferret out potential terrorists. Nor is it easy to claim success when someone *doesn't* do something. However the cost to the taxpayer is very low. Careful evaluation over time will be needed to tell whether the CSCC is successful.

## *Academic Exchanges: The Challenge of Planning and Prioritization*

Since 9–11 funding has roughly doubled for academic and citizen exchanges, international visitor programs and educational and cultural activities of the

Department. Congress, especially individual Congressional leaders, had special programs that they urged on State, or wrote into legislation as earmarks. In the past decade, expanded exchanges focused on the Middle East, Afghanistan and Pakistan and other frontline states.

Along the way, ECA has developed very creative responses to new trends or needs, including an array of social media and new programs abroad. One new initiative, the English Access Micro-scholarship Program, since 2004 has helped more than 70,000 high school students from disadvantaged sectors in 85 nations develop basic English skills through after-school and summer programs. These students are better prepared to compete for scholarships and otherwise attend college in the U.S. and to contribute to their own nation's growth.[9]

To accomplish the demanding agenda and set priorities for the future, ECA has developed a strategic plan that should better relate, if not integrate exchange activities with the work of other elements of the Department. Its time has come. ECA will benefit from at least a three-year look forward to better understand trends here and abroad that might be addressed. A 2011 State Department inspection report also pointed to the need to reduce stove-piping, improve communication both internally and externally, improve program flexibility and foster greater decision making responsibility lower down in the hierarchy (U.S. Department of State, 2012).

## American Spaces: The Challenge of Accessibility

Earlier known as libraries and cultural centers, these physical venues have been, for the past 75 years, the bedrock of U.S. informational and cultural activities abroad, a vital image of American representation around the globe, a common meeting ground for students, scholars, writers, all those who praise and criticize our policies and our society. American libraries and cultural or binational centers have a rich history, and their decline in the past 25 years attests to the decline in U.S. PD presence abroad.

For more than a decade, the Bureau of International Information Programs has been experimenting with new configurations that surmount the limitations of reduced staffs and budgets and increased security concerns. The answers are 498 American Corners and ten science corners around the world. These supplement 183 Information Resource Centers in U.S. embassies and 30 independently located American Centers. Additionally the field posts provide financial, technical and informational resources to 129 binational centers, sponsored by indigenous organizations. New digital technologies are playing an increasing part in the IIP mix of approaches and providing more content for the updated American Spaces. The Spaces vary greatly from very small corners in a university library or indigenous cultural center to the flagship center run by the U.S. embassy in Jakarta, built at a cost of $5 million and administered for $3 million a year. The Jakarta center, titled "@america," showcases the latest in multi-media technology. Eighty iPads, e-readers, and other electronic equipment connect visitors to information resources available via the Internet (McCall, personal communication, n.d.). The mix of outreach to groups in their spaces, the use of virtual spaces and U.S. facilities is evolving. Meanwhile, embassy facilities are not likely to fulfill the need for mutually appealing meeting grounds. Indeed, the fortified embassies of the new era of insecurity inhibit contact with audiences.[10]

## New Technologies: The Challenge of Finding an Effective Mix

The International Information Programs Bureau (IIP) has started to catch up with the non-governmental sector in innovative communication. IIP leadership has been justifiably proud of new starts in the employment of communication technologies. With a marketing campaign in 2011–12, the Bureau gained about two million users for each of four websites, on environmental issues ("Global Conversations: Our Planet") representative governance ("Democracy Challenge") entrepreneurial change (Innovation Generation") and American life and times ("eJournal USA"). These sites are potentially lively ways to reach significant numbers of younger people. As they evolve they will need to develop the spontaneity and authenticity of sites initiated from within a movement or a community. To help target younger people in the host country, IIP provides informational, technical and management support to PD field posts for their Facebook sites. These show greater engagement and appeal. With 600 million Facebook friends and more than half the world with cell phones, audiences of two million for State's pages are modest and relatively undefined. IIP set a goal of doubling and then re-doubling the number of visitors in coming years (McCall, personal communication, n.d.). However, this might be not only difficult but unnecessary.

As mobile phone apps and hybrid phone/tablets continue to offer new ways of communication State/IIP will require micro- or meta- audience identification and the skill to condense information and structure it in levels of complexity. Even as broadband and Wi-fi zones spread across the globe, expanding the use of imagery and speeding the flow of data, State will continue to need better analytics to assess which ideas are being conveyed, to what effect, with which publics and opinion leaders. The IIP role, especially in view of the multiple IBB platforms with far larger audiences, might be to focus on carefully defined opinion leaders or active groups in cooperation with U.S. Missions and not compete with sites that will continue to command far larger audiences.

The International Informational Bureau also conducted a pilot program in 2011 to employ Kindles and other e-readers to the field. An initial round deployed 2,300 units to American Spaces in 169 countries and 3,800 to support ECA's English Access Microscholarship program in 17 countries. More than 300,000 e-books have been wirelessly disseminated abroad. This approach provides a range of fiction and non-fiction, biography, reference materials and English language learning titles to readers around the globe, and has promise for future expansion.

## *The Advisory Role of Public Diplomacy: The Challenge of Integrating PD into Decision Making*

By recommending a deputy assistant secretary of state for public diplomacy in each geographic bureau, State intended to assure closer ties between PD and policy. With mixed results, experienced PD professionals have served in this capacity for the past three-plus years. Depending on their background and experience, different individuals have brought different skills and relationships with colleagues. The mix has ranged from the daily policy grind to the more strategic dimensions. Based on multiple interviews, there is room for more significant PD inputs across the range of concerns confronting the geographic bureaus, from involvement in policy decisions to long-term planning. Several interviewees essentially argued that serious advice from PD practitioners in the regional bureaus has been pasted on top of other core functions, not fully integrated. This is not the first time such an experiment could dissipate without the benefit for U.S. diplomacy.

Similarly, the policy role of the under secretary for public diplomacy and public affairs, after a decade-plus, remains unfulfilled. This is not surprising; even the director of the independent U.S. Information Agency rarely was able, or enabled, to contribute to senior-level National Security Council policy considerations. Other players have looked to USIA, and PD in State, for help on the policy outputs, not inputs. The policy advice of public affairs officers to their country teams has traditionally been more important, depending on personal relationships, but rarely filtered up to the top in D.C. Excellent public opinion and international media analyses continue to provide useful information on the public dimension of U.S. global concerns, but merit more consistent use by policy makers.

The under secretary can do more than propose the orchestration of policy support. S/he can draw on the experience of public diplomacy officers at home and abroad, and should have access to senior counterparts in the White House, National Security staff and the InterAgency. With the available research tools and corps of expertise, the under secretary and staff can make a difference in national security policy coordinating groups when they consider the public dimension of policy choices.. However, realistically, the under secretary must stay long enough to build credibility as a policy adviser, and know which issues are most significant for the special expertise of public diplomacy.

## Unfinished Business for Public Diplomacy

Any analysis of U.S. Public Diplomacy must include consideration of the role and future of U.S. funded international broadcasting, a major element of American global engagement.

### The Need to Update Broadcasting

Just as libraries and cultural centers have been traditional venues for outreach to publics abroad, so also has U.S. broadcasting held a valued long-term place in U.S. Public Diplomacy. U.S. Government-funded broadcasting is grappling with an historic set of ambitious changes. Under the leadership of *Time Magazine* editor and prize-winning author, Walter Isaacson, the Board of Broadcasting Governors (BBG) in early January, 2012, released a far-reaching plan that would: combine administrative and technical facilities; create a central news service; assign special roles to different entities in the complex of radio and TV systems under its purview, and dramatically improve use of social media and varied communication platforms (Broadcasting Board of Governors, 2012).

Elements of the BBG initiative are controversial, involving significant organizational changes, consolidations, possibly staff reductions and program decisions. Authors of the new strategy saw a need for dramatic changes in the broadcasting complex in order to respond to equally dramatic changes in the ways in which audiences gain information, and to achieve the goal of reaching an audience of 216 million people by 2016. (By early 2014 the total stood at 206 million.) Unfortunately, Isaacson and two other supportive BBG members resigned several months after issuance of the strategic plan. Resistance to elements of the plan, possible budget cutbacks, and other obstacles have slowed progress. However the BBG with new members has begun to work on changes, especially a process to select a CEO, urgently needed to give the system active leadership.

By far the largest percentage of audiences in most parts of the world continue to gain information and knowledge of the world via radio and TV (Broadcasting Board of Governors [BBG], 2012). Changing technologies and audience habits have resulted in the decline of short-wave radio and increases in local FM stations, TV channels, cable and satellite-delivered programming. In the digital era sources of entertainment and information will proliferate and find multiple outlets that include mobile phones and hybrid mobile devices allowing people to move from home to car or mass transit to office or countryside and stay tuned in. USG Broadcasting has accepted the idea of ongoing interaction with and among audiences, and is searching for modalities to sustain the process. Multiple experiments with cross-platform content distribution, audience engagement, and integration of mobile technologies are among the several innovations. The challenge will be to find the maximal mix of platforms in a time of rapid introduction of new approaches.

The BBG has begun to take advantage of Congressional approval for changes in the 1948 Smith-Mundt Act that in part prohibited the use of public funds for Public Diplomacy communication with the American public. BBG leaders believe that diaspora groups in the U.S. are valuable international audiences to engage, and argue that there is no way to restrict the flow of information through the social media. Careful consideration will be needed to implement the updated Smith-Mundt to allow more flexibility yet not divert broadcasting—or other public diplomacy resources—toward influencing American audiences.

Although the social media comprise a very small percentage of BBG international broadcasting audiences, trends in the industrialized nations suggest rising engagement of younger people through social media, in tandem with popular broadcasts. A number of exciting BBG social media platforms are important responses to the growing youth demographic. The challenge will be to sustain such engagement along with the generational change into adulthood.[11]

Senior BBG policy officials work closely with counterparts in State and the interagency policy coordinating committee for strategic communication. There are also many opportunities for State Department public diplomacy and USAID in particular to work closely with BBG staff in educational and informational activities. There are shared concerns and past cooperation in developing programming on a large number of topics relevant to development, civil society, public health, environment, energy and economic growth. Officials at VOA and State, especially in the Bureau of African Affairs, have mentioned past endeavors and acknowledged there is room for more regular interaction of staffers who pursue similar interests, although with somewhat different responsibilities.

Such cooperation can be achieved without threatening the necessity for the broadcasting entities to retain their independence. The model of integrated public diplomacy should continue to call for U.S. funded broadcasting to collaborate with the national security policy community when mutual interests are served – just like any non-governmental organization—while keeping the news function totally free of interference. The credibility of news is crucial to keep the trust of international audiences.

## *The Need for Additional Support for the Field*

One third of PD assets are vested in the field posts and Foreign Service and Foreign National employees around the world. They have been shortchanged for years, and should gain restored support. In the current period of austerity this will be difficult to achieve, but every effort is needed to add staff abroad, including to administer the many exchange programs of a beefed-up ECA. By wisely challenging old ongoing allocations, Judith McHale's staff shifted resources to nations that are today more critical to U.S. interests and concerns. Additional funds for "patching" staffing deficiencies are needed, including a "ready reserve" to help posts during crises. Greater flexibility should be allowed in moving civil servants to posts for extended tours. At some point as the nation works through the looming budget deficit, a major campaign should begin to convince the Administration and the Congress to increase, not cut, field personnel.[12]

## **Looking Ahead**

Looking ahead, several cross-cutting concerns or opportunities merit ongoing consideration:

## *Green vs. Red Lines in the Whole of Government Approach*

There is a compelling need for inter-Agency and Congressional agreement on how the Department of Defense and State Department will engage with publics abroad. Strategic Communication has encroached—in part by State's default—on issue areas and audiences that State PD and embassies abroad should handle. Neither the Department of Defense nor its Congressional oversight committees are likely to accept a permanent reduction of funds authorized to DoD in favor of the Department of State. Cooperation remains imperative. The cooperative arrangements in Afghanistan have shown the promise, as has the CSCC. An annual review by the under secretary with the under secretary of Defense for Policy, the Joint Chiefs staff and representatives of the Combatant Commands might identify national security issues in which DoD and State responsibilities overlap and civilian audiences that State/PD and posts should deal with, rather than DoD by default, and, with Congressional oversight, transfer funds for this purpose.

## Short- Versus Long-Term Needs: The Urgent Versus the Important

In the future, one major challenge for the Department will be the degree to which ECA (and USAID) are able to maintain long-term institutional linkages, collaboration and capacity building programs rather than see resources siphoned off to meet urgent crises or immediate demands of U.S. foreign policy. Few, for example, would dispute the potential value of hosting newly minted Tunisian parliamentarians here for brief visits, or helping a significant number of Syrian students caught in the diaspora study in the U.S. But from which pot of money will any new or expanded initiative come? Who should pay, and who decides? With no significant cushion for emergencies, the Department has faced difficulties in balancing current demands with long-term needs. It has not been able to afford being strategic. Conversely, when ECA is challenged to respond creatively to unusual opportunities or needs, a modest revolving contingency fund might help deal with an immediate crisis of unforeseen opportunity.[13]

## Educational Exchange: A Benefit or a Necessity?

Although the Strategic Framework highlighted the importance of higher education in U.S. global engagement, the sector deserved more attention, particularly in the QDDR. The sector is not only a valued partner in international affairs, it is a vital component of the American economy, a major export earner, a conduit for recruiting talent and the construction of new enterprise, for filling gaps in our own talent base. International students in American community colleges, colleges and universities enrich our culture and add depth to every phase of our national life. The new ECA strategic plan might help fill a much-needed gap in thinking about higher education, and make routine partnerships with higher education and related organizations more strategic.[14] Going beyond the QDDR and PD Framework, the Department, with the Department of Education, should consider a biennial summit with educational associations. What are the level and extent of their communication and exchange activities? Where are there gaps and needs? How can the

Department and USAID, and other USG agencies, in partnership with university professional councils and national associations, facilitate or help catalyze activities that could draw on support available from the private sector, American philanthropy and citizenry? What more can State and USAID do to foster independent commitments? Is there need for the strategic plan involving higher education to examine long-term national needs in various sectors and how public and private institutions, through international exchanges and other collaboration, promote long-term national needs?

## *American Understanding of a Changing World: Region to Region*

Strategic planning and consultation with others can also help State deal with one of the important unmet needs of U.S. public diplomacy, the degree to which American citizens and institutions understand and are prepared to deal knowledgably with a rapidly changing world. America is ever more a nation of nations and relates more comprehensively to multiple global trends. Our economy depends on a globally knowledgeable public and institutions that can compete effectively in the world arena. Our society and culture are enriched by such interaction, and we find answers to some of our domestic concerns in learning from others. In the decades to come our society will rely all the more on international talent, on young men and women who study and stay here or go back to their home countries with a network of American links. Beyond national-level consideration, almost every metropolitan region and state actively pursues commercial, cultural and ethnic contacts with counterparts abroad. These should be enhanced.

In the mid-70s USIA leadership developed the concept of a "second mandate" to help Americans learn more about the world. Perhaps ahead of its time, the concept became a left-right political hot potato, and suffered a rapid demise when the conservative Reagan team replaced the liberal Carter team in 1981. Nevertheless, the so-called "American learning process" embedded in the second mandate is important to the national interest, and should be viewed as a non-partisan necessity to strengthen national competitiveness as well as a benefit for American society and culture.

## *Messaging Versus Dialogue: Tactics Versus Strategy*

Pro-active public affairs and rapid response will always be vital in the ever-more contentious global public arena. Yet, the best tactics can't make up for wrong-headed policies and the absence of strategic vision. Even with the most modern technologies and up-to-date staffs, the USG will not be able to control the larger flow of messages, information or communication worldwide. The digital revolution has made this abundantly clear. The Arab Spring, the rise of "citizen journalism" and "crowd sourcing" show the capacity of transnational non-state actors to command the world public agenda. State can't effectively "de marche" public opinion which is far more active and effective a driver of decisions than ever before. The challenge will be to step back, better analyze and understand the multiple transnational forces, and shape public strategies that help better position the U.S. This applies most importantly to the global quest for economic opportunity, fair play, social justice and human dignity. These struggles underlie conflict around the world. Public Diplomacy is best suited to help Americans, from policy makers to citizens, understand and adapt to global challenges. The next generation of State employees is already filling the void in communications technology, and is prepared to seek out the important long-term concerns of young people around the world. Even if they ruffle some feathers in taking policy risks, younger State Department employees should be empowered to recommend new modalities for State. There needs to be even more latitude for experimentation in overseas missions and in Washington. The field can feed ideas to a panel of young officers in DC designed to be in touch with those who start the next "....Spring" or mash-up or inspire new ways to build community.

## Prospects for Integration: Closing the Concept-Practice Gap

The prospects for integration of public diplomacy with other elements of statecraft are better today than a decade ago, in part because the public dimension of world affairs is so clearly more significant, and in part because leadership through the QDDR and the Public Diplomacy Strategic Framework has recognized the need for reform. As State becomes more public in its orientation it will be challenged to provide more support and greater flexibility for its communicators abroad.

A stronger public diplomacy advisory function at every step in the policy process, would help political leadership develop wise and effective policies, and help Americans better understand international concerns.

Likewise sustained focus on building relations pertains not just to the conduct and mission of exchanges. In all phases of U.S. diplomacy and development assistance, it will be vital to build the personal, organizational or sectoral relations that maximize cooperation and minimize conflict with the U.S. This realization was expressed by the QDDR and the Public Diplomacy Strategic Framework, and should become doctrine for all who serve our nation.

## *Notes*

1. World Public Opinion has studies throughout the past decade that document the decline in support for the U.S.
2. Reports of the Defense Science Board contributed significantly to the Department's consideration. See DSB '04 report with '07 and '08 updates.
3. There is need for more research into the recent evolution of strategic communication doctrine and practices. As Cary (2010) points out, Gates, Admiral Mullen, and several Congressional leaders and staff expressed concern at the excessive and unclear spending in this field.
4. Senior Department leaders chaired four task forces with 11 working groups and additional sub-groups. For details of the QDDR's many proposals see http://www.state.gov/documents/organization/153142.pdf
5. For additional details see pp. 59–70 of the QDDR.
6. The PD Strategic Framework is essentially an extended PowerPoint presentation, a clever way to encapsulate complex ideas and focus attention on key initiatives. See also critique in Seib (2010) Mountain Runner.
7. The CSCC succeeded a smaller unit, the Counter-Terrorism Communication Center created by Under Secretary Hughes.
8. See: http://www.state.gov/r/cscc/
9. ECA has begun to integrate use of social media with regular exchange programs. Exchange Connect, its website, has spawned a number of interactive outreach activities.
10. Some of the best examples of field post creativity are described in the annual awards of the Public Diplomacy Alumni Association, available online.
11. A few examples of outstanding VOA/BBG use of social media platforms include:

    - **Podelis**, an interactive Russian-language program from VOA, which encourages and integrates audience participation;
    - **Congo Story** is a crowdsourced journalism & social awareness campaign.
    - **#EgyptDecides** was a crowdsourcing and citizen journalism initiative for the 2012 Egyptian election.
    - **OMG! Meiyu**, an "interactive social media platform," that helps mainly youthful audiences in China learn colloquial American slang and encourages dialogue through Facebook and Weibo.

12. The QDDR mention of an overseas contingency budget, modeled on the approach to unusual and unforeseen costs by DoD, merits consideration.
13. Open to question are the number and mix of students, and the degree to which American universities should focus on in-country training and institutional development vs. more expensive study and visits here.
14. Regional bureaus and the field posts also came in with ideas, and funding, along with foundation support, for new starts, for example, the East Asia Pacific Affairs Bureau proposed the "100,000 Strong" project to dramatically expand American student study in China.

## *Bibliography*

Ambassador Hughes, K. P. (2007, April). *Presentation to U.S. House of Representatives Committee on Appropriations Subcommittee on State, Foreign Operations, and Related Programs* [PowerPoint Presentation]. Washington, D.C.

BBC. (2011, March 7). View of US Continues to Improve in 2011. Retrieved from Globe Scan: http://www.globescan.com/images/images/pressreleases/bbc2011_countries/bbc2011_countries_release.pdf

Beers, C. (2002, June 11). *Statement before the senate foreign relations committee.* Washington, DC. Retrieved from: http://2001–2009.state.gov/r/us/12170.htm

Broadcasting Board of Governors. (2012, February). Impact through innovation and integration: BBG Strategic Plan 2012–2016. Retrieved from: http://www.bbg.gov/wp-content/media/2012/02/BBGStrategicPlan_2012–2016_OMB_Final.pdf

Cary, P. (2010, November 23). *The pentagon, information operations, and international media development.* Washington, D.C. Retrieved from the Center for International Media Assistance (CIMA): http://cima.ned.org/publications/research-reports/pentagon-information-operations-and-international-media-development

Dao, J. (2011, June 7). Public opinion on the wars? New polls offer conflicting evidence. *The New York Times.* Retrieved from: http://atwar.blogs.nytimes.com/2011/06/07/public-opinion-on-the-wars-new-polls-offer-conflicting-evidence/

Defense Science Board. (2008, January). Task force on strategic communication. Retrieved from: http://www.acq.osd.mil/dsb/reports/ADA476331.pdf

Gallup. (2010). World citizens' views on U.S. leadership, pre- and post-Obama. Retrieved from: http://www.gallup.com/poll/121991/world-citizens-views-leadership-pre-post-obama.aspx

———. (2010, May 25). Sub-Saharan Africa leads world in U.S. approval. Retrieved from: http://www.gallup.com/poll/134102/Sub-Saharan-Africa-Leads-World-Approval.aspx

Glassman, J. (2008, December 1). *Public diplomacy 2.0.: A new approach to global engagement.* Washington, DC: New America Foundation. Retrieved from: http://2001–2009.state.gov/r/us/2008/112605.htm

Gough, S. (2003, April 7). The Evolution of Strategic Influence [Unpublished Research Paper]. Carlisle Barracks, PA.: U.S. Army War College.

Kull, S. (2007, March 6). America's Image in the World [Testimony]. Retrieved from the House Committee on Foreign Affairs: http://www.worldpublicopinion.org/pipa/articles/views_on_countriesregions_bt/326.php?lb=btvoc&pnt=326 & nid=&id.

Lord, K. M., Nagl, J. A. & Rosen, S. D. (2009, June). *Beyond bullets: A pragmatic strategy to combat violent Islamist extremism.* Washington, DC: Center for a New American Security.

McHale, J. A. (2011, June 21). Strengthening U.S. engagement with the world: A review of U.S. public diplomacy. Open remarks presented at the Council on Foreign Relations, New York, NY. Retrieved from: http://www.state.gov/r/remarks/2011/166596.htm

Obama, B. (2011, September 9). *Executive order 13584—Developing an integrated strategic counterterrorism communications initiative.* Washington, DC. Retrieved from:

http://www.whitehouse.gov/the-press-office/2011/09/09/executive-order-1358
4-developing-integrated-strategic-counterterrorism-c

Office of the Under Secretary for Public Diplomacy and Public Affairs, U.S. Department
of State (2010, February). *Public diplomacy: Strengthening U.S. engagement with the
world.* Washington, DC. Retrieved from: http://uscpublicdiplomacy.org/pdfs/PD_
US_World_Engagement.pdf

Office of Inspections, U.S. Department of State. (2012, February). *Inspection of the bureau of educational and cultural affairs.* Washington, DC. Retrieved from: http://
oig.state.gov/documents/organization/217892.pdf

Pew Research Center (2010, June 17). Obama more popular abroad than at home,
global image of U.S. continues to benefit. Retrieved from: http://www.pewglobal.
org/2010/06/17/ obama-more-popular-abroad-than-at-home/

———. Global Attitudes Project. (2012, June 13). Drone strikes widely opposed: Global
opinion of Obama slips, international policies faulted. Retrieved from: http://www.
pewglobal.org/2012/06/13/global-opinion-of-obama-slips-international-policies-
faulted/

———. (2013). Global indicators database. Retrieved from: http://www.pewglobal.org/
database/?indicator=1

Seib, P. (2010, March 8). U.S. public diplomacy's flimsy framework. *Huffington Post.*
Retrieved from: http://www.huffingtonpost.com/philip-seib/us-public-diploma
cys-flim_b_490972.html

———. (2009). *America's new approach to Africa: AFRICOM and public diplomacy.* Los
Angeles, CA: Figueroa Press. Retrieved from: http://uscpublicdiplomacy.org/CPD_
Perspectives.pdf

Sonenshine, T. (n.d.) *Confirmation testimony.* Washington, DC: Cross Continental Cooperation. Retrieved from: http://www.state.gov/r/pa/ei/biog/187350.htm

The White House. (2010). National framework for strategic communication. Retrieved from
http://fas.org/man/eprint/pubdip.pdf

Tutwiler, M. (2004, February 4). *Testimony to house appropriations committee.* Retrieved from:
http://www.iwar.org.uk/psyops/resources/public-diplomacy-programs/margaret_tut-
wiler_testimony.pdf

U.S. Department of Defense. (2009, December). *Report on strategic communication.*
Washington, DC: U.S. Government Printing Office.

———. (2008, August) *Principles of strategic communication.* Washington, DC. Retrieved
from: http://www.carlisle.army.mil/DIME/documents/Principles%20of%20SC%20
(22%20Aug%2008)%20Signed%20versn.pdf

———. (2007, September 12). *Strategic communication plan for Afghanistan* (unclassified). Washington, DC: U.S. Government Printing Office.

———. (n.d.). *Office of support to public diplomacy* [PowerPoint Presentation]. Washington, DC.

U.S. Department of State. (2010). *Leading through civilian power—The first quadrennial
diplomacy and development review.* Washington, DC. Retrieved from: http://www.
state.gov/s/dmr/qddr/index.htm

———. (2012, February). *Report: Inspection of the bureau of educational and cultural
affairs.* Washington, DC. Retrieved from: http://oig.state.gov/documents/organi
zation/186048.pdf

U.S. General Accounting Office (2010, July). *Engaging foreign audiences: Assessment of public diplomacy platforms could help improve state department plans to expand engagement.* Washington, DC. Retrieved from: http://www.gao.gov/products/GAO-10-767

————. (2009, May). U.S. *public diplomacy: Key issues for Congressional oversight.* Washington, DC. Retrieved from http://www.gao.gov/products/GAO-09-679SP

U.S. House of Representatives., 105th Congress 2nd Session. (1998, March 10). *Foreign affairs reform and reconstructing act.* (Report 105–432, to accompany HR 1757). Washington, DC: U.S. Government Printing Office.

Venhaus, J. M., U.S. Army (2010, May). *Why youth join al-Qaeda* (U.S. Institute of Peace: Special Report 236). Washington, DC: U.S. Government Printing Office.

Weisman, S. R. (2005, September 30). On Mideast 'listening tour,' the question is who's hearing. *The New York Times.* Retrieved from: http://www.nytimes.com/2005/09/30/international/middleeast/30hughes.html?_r=1

# 3. *Public Diplomacy in NGOs*

Olga Zatepilina-Monacell

An integrated, strategic approach to public diplomacy entails not only engaging in mediated communication, nation branding or relationship management (Golan, 2013), but also integrating the efforts of both state and non-state actors for a nation's global outreach mission that is based on national values and aligned with foreign policy goals. However, such integration does not necessarily call for bureaucratization or government oversight of global outreach. On the contrary, the integration of a nation's public diplomacy efforts might mean preserving the autonomy of its non-state actors' engagement with global publics. Drawing on the findings from a research study that explains why U.S. NGOs have a stake in the U.S. standing abroad (Zatepilina, 2010; Zatepilina-Monacell, 2012), strategic public diplomacy in nongovernmental organizations (NGOs) and NGOs' contribution to a nation's integrated public diplomacy are discussed in this chapter.

## *NGOs in International Relations and Non-State Public Diplomacy*

Non-state actors are entities other than governments (e.g., for-profit and not-for-profit organizations, or formal and informal groups of individuals) that interact in both domestic and world affairs (Taylor, 1994). Increasingly, non-state actors such as NGOs affect political outcomes within one or more states or within international institutions (Atack, 1999; Josselin and Wallace, 2001; Taylor, 1994; Ripinsky and Van den Bossche, 2007). For instance, development NGOs seek to influence national and multilateral development policies (Atack, 1999; McCleary, 2009). Inevitably, non-state actors also engage with their counterparts and other publics in other countries.

Such interactions are sometimes described as people-to-people engagement or citizen diplomacy, but more often than not, as public diplomacy. Notwithstanding the occasional voices opposing the acceptance of people-to-people engagement or citizen diplomacy as part of public diplomacy, scholars and practitioners recognize that non-state actors—such as business corporations, nonprofit organizations, private think-tanks, religious missionary groups, transnational diasporas, and social networking communities—enhance the government-to-people initiatives (Cowan & Cull, 2008; Cull, 2010; Gregory, 2011; Leonard, Stead, & Smewing, 2002; Lord & Fontaine, 2010; Melissen, 2005, 2011; Snow & Taylor, 2009; Zaharna, 2010; Zatepilina, 2009, 2010; Zatepilina-Monacell, 2012). By definition, a nation's outreach to the world is a multi-stakeholder effort: The establishment alone does not make a nation, whereas non-state actors have an agency in both what a nation is and how it is regarded in the world (Golan, 2013; U.S. Advisory Commission on Public Diplomacy, 2010; Zatepilina, 2010).

Historically, the human and monetary resources devoted to public diplomacy by the U.S. Government have lagged behind what non-state actors such as multinational corporations, media and private foundations brought to the table (Arndt, 2005; Lord, 2008; Nye, 2004; 2008; Richmond, 2008; U.S. Government Accountability Office, 2009, May). Non-state actors such as NGOs have tended to enjoy greater credibility among international stakeholders than state actors (Leonard et al., 2002; Nye, 2004, 2008; Zaharna, 2010; Zatepilina, 2009, 2010; Zatepilina-Monacell, 2012). For instance, representatives of the U.S. development community see American NGOs as equal players within the context of the U.S. public diplomacy and want the government's public diplomacy messages to incorporate the achievements of development NGOs (Zatepilina, 2009).

As the case studies described in this chapter demonstrate, the public diplomacy efforts of U.S. NGOs are not a government-orchestrated "program." Even if an NGO is funded by the U.S. Government, it has its own voice—commonly, a dissenting one—and its own way of engaging with global publics, on behalf of its stakeholders and on behalf of its country of origin. In other words, public diplomacy in NGOs is a separate, albeit complementary effort to a nation's public diplomacy.

## Conceptual and Operational Definitions of a U.S. NGO

Although the term NGO may be used interchangeably with the terms civil society organizations and non-state actors, the latter two are broader concepts, both inclusive of NGOs (Atack, 1999; Edwards, 2000; Florini, 2000;

O'Connell, 2000; Lewis, 2005). The literature defines NGOs as all the formally registered entities except governments, political parties, and businesses that are (a) self-governing; (b) producing public goods; (c) raising revenues from voluntary donations; (d) employing both paid staff and volunteers; (e) exempt from paying income taxes; and (f) not distributing profits to members (Lewis; 2005; Ripinsky and Van den Bossche, 2007; Salamon, 1994; United Nations, 2003).

Furthermore, in the context of the United States, the term nonprofit organization (NPO) is often used interchangeably with the term NGO (Vakil, 1997). NPOs traditionally highlight the exempt status of NGOs under the U.S. Tax Code (Internal Revenue Service, 2008, June, and 2009, January). In addition, NGOs in the United States are collectively referred to as the independent sector, the third sector, or the nonprofit sector. The NGOs examined in this chapter are headquartered in the United States and, therefore, could be described as both NGOs and nonprofits (NPOs).

NGOs and NPOs differ in size, political opinions, strategies and tactics. The United Nations (2003) distinguishes two major types of NGOs, operational and advocacy. Other typologies identify nongovernmental organizations by geographical reach (e.g., community-based, national, international, or transnational); purpose (e.g., welfare, development, advocacy, education or research); or guiding principles (e.g., faith-based or secular) (Internal Revenue Service, 2008, June, and 2009, January; McCleary, 2009; Ripinsky & Van den Bossche, 2007; Vakil, 1997). In this chapter, different types of NGOs such as operational or advocacy, and faith-based or secular are compared and contrasted in the context of their engagement in public diplomacy.

Finally, it is worth mentioning that the literature does not offer a clear-cut distinction between international NGOs and transnational NGOs (McCleary, 2009). In this chapter, the term international describes NGOs that are based in their country of origin but operate globally, whereas the term transnational refers to NGOs that have more than one national headquarters in countries other than the country of their origin. Examples of transnational NGOs include organizations such as Amnesty International or Médecins sans Frontières. The organizations examined in this chapter are conceptually and operationally defined as U.S.-based, international NGOs.

## *Overview of the Case Studies*

Of the five NGOs in the multiple-case study described in Zatepilina (2010) and Zatepilina-Monacell (2012), the examples of four nonprofits are discussed in this chapter: American Jewish Committee (AJC), American Jewish

World Service (AJWS), DKT International (DKT), and Episcopal Relief and Development (ERD).[1] These NGOs are headquartered in the United States and registered under §501(c)(3) of the U.S. Internal Revenue Code.

AJC is an advocacy NGO focusing on civil rights (American Jewish Committee, 2010b). AJWS could be described as both an operational and advocacy NGO; its programs range from international development to human rights support (American Jewish World Service, 2010b). Both DKT and ERD are operational NGOs. DKT focuses on family planning and HIV/AIDS prevention through social marketing programs (DKT International, 2010). The focus of ERD is reflected in its name—the NGO is engaged in disaster relief and international development (Episcopal Relief & Development, 2010).

At the time the executive interviews and textual analysis of corporate documentation were conducted (i.e., in 2010), two of the four NGOs received less than one fifth of their revenue from government funds (i.e., DKT and ERD), whereas the other two were funded only from private sources (i.e., AJC and AJWS) (American Jewish Committee, 2010a; American Jewish World Service, 2010a; DKT International, 2010; Episcopal Relief & Development, 2009). In addition, DKT generated most of its profits from sales of contraceptives (DKT International, 2010).

Three NGOs (i.e., AJC, AJWS, and ERD) describe themselves as faith-based, albeit only one is closely affiliated with a religious institution, the Episcopal Church. Although ERD does not raise money from individuals in the secular world, most recipients of the organization's services are not Christian or religious. The other two NGOs define their connection to faith as a shared Jewish worldview. In addition to describing their organizations as faith-based, the interviewed executives of both AJC and AJWS referred to their groups as ethnicity based, and emphasized that their fundraising efforts reach out to donors from both the religious and ethnic Jewish communities around the United States. Similarly to ERD, however, most recipients of AJC's and AJWS's services are not necessarily Jewish.

Although all four NGOs engage in international programs and interact with various foreign publics, only two (i.e., AJC and DKT) operate their own field offices overseas, whereas the other two provide grants, technical assistance, and volunteer support to indigenous civil society organizations (i.e., implementing partners) in host countries. DKT's operations are decentralized, and its headquarters-based executives delegate decision-making responsibilities to the field-office management—represented by U.S., host-country or third-country nationals. Neither AJWS nor ERD employ fulltime staff to work overseas. "We really believe in building capacities of local partners," explained one of ERD's representatives. Although AJWS has no offices abroad, most of its volunteers are American and Jewish. With regard to hiring policies for their overseas offices, both AJC and DKT look for individuals who possess cultural sensitivity and are immersed in the countries where they work, but are not necessarily U.S. nationals.

In-depth interviews with two or three executives from each NGO, as well as an analysis of corporate texts such as websites, blogs, annual reports and newsletters, provided a comprehensive picture of how these four NGOs interact with global publics and generate goodwill among their domestic and international stakeholders. Although each case offered insights into the organizational practices and discourses of an individual nonprofit organization, the theoretical replication across cases revealed several parallels. These four NGOs consciously engage in both symbolic (i.e., identity-based) and behavioral reputation management (Yang, 2007; Yang & Grunig, 2005; Zatepilina, 2010). The identity-based aspect of NGOs' reputation management involves seeing themselves (and wanting to be seen by others) as having complex identities that represent the NGO's domestic and global stakeholders and are grounded in the NGO's country of origin and its core values. The behavioral aspect of NGOs' reputation management involves commitment to excellence in serving stakeholders, relationship-building premised on stakeholder empowerment, and responsibility for addressing stakeholders' concerns.

## *Country-of-Origin Is Intrinsic to NGOs' Corporate Identities*

The complex organizational identities (i.e., corporate selves) of the four NGOs were studied on two levels: (a) the organizational (i.e., by examining various corporate texts such as websites, blogs, annual reports, newsletters etc.), and (b) individual (i.e., by interviewing NGOs' executives). Notably, the first aspect of these NGOs' corporate selves denotes their country of origin. As their top executives explained, each of these NGOs positions itself as foremost American, although with various degrees of emphasis on the country of origin. With the exception of DKT, each of these NGOs identifies with a specific segment of the U.S. society by representing its members, donors and volunteers. In addition, for the two Jewish organizations (i.e., AJC and AJWS), American is part of their names. The name of ERD also alludes to its country of origin, albeit somewhat more subtly: Although the Episcopal Church has members in several countries, it is best known as a part of the Anglican Church in the United States. While DKT does not particularly highlight its country of origin, its executives explained that social marketing, which is part of the NGO's organizational identity, has distinct American roots.

Another aspect of these NGOs' identities refers to their main beliefs. For AJC, universal human rights and democracy are constituents of the NGO's corporate self. The organizational identities of both AJWS and ERD emphasize their faith (i.e., Judaism's pursuit of justice, and the Episcopal Church's compassion, dignity, and generosity). As mentioned earlier, DKT relies on marketing principles to address social problems and achieve a humanitarian impact. Interestingly, most interviewed executives described the underlying principles that guide their NGOs' work in the international arena as inherently American.

The third aspect of each NGO's identity is conveyed through its global presence and sense of global responsibility. NGOs see themselves as voices of both their domestic and international stakeholders before the U.S. government, foreign governments, and international intergovernmental organizations. For AJC, those stakeholders are Jewish minority populations in the United States and around the world. AJWS stresses humility in advocating for grassroots human-rights organizations from the world's poorest countries. DKT aspires to bring accessibility and affordability of family planning and HIV prevention to the developing world. ERD seeks to spotlight the role of indigenous religious and civil society organizations in providing disaster response and strengthening communities around the world.

Regardless of whether an NGO operates through its own overseas offices or through counterpart civil society groups in host countries, and whether an NGO is represented in a host country by a U.S. national or a third-country national, all four NGOs strive for consistency of organizational values and philosophies. NGOs' headquarters in the country of origin safeguard those values and philosophies without restricting difference of opinion. Instances of disagreement between a U.S.-based NGO and its host country's counterpart organization are not uncommon. While the U.S. NGO does not control the message on the ground, it expects the implementing partner to speak on its own behalf. According to most interviewed executives, while both sides are free to make public their differing positions, the U.S. NGOs would definitely detach themselves from the counterpart if the latter's position goes counter to the core beliefs of the former.

When operating in the regions or countries known for their anti-American sentiment, an NGO might downplay its American identity to avoid putting its staff members, volunteers or implementing partners at risk. Nevertheless, most interviewed executives said that, while they don't "flaunt" or "trumpet" their country of origin, NGOs don't distance themselves intentionally from their country of origin either.

Moreover, these NGOs believe that their corporate selves each add a facet to projecting outward the multifaceted U.S. state identity. NGOs see themselves as having agency in the U.S. state identity by representing the values and interests of their stakeholders, and by seeking to shape U.S. and non-U.S. government policies. Representatives from AJC, AJWS, and ERD expressly asserted their NGOs' agency in the U.S. state identity. Both the faith-based nature (i.e., strong connections to their respective religious communities) and makeup of their donor base (i.e., heavy reliance on donor contributions from individual U.S. citizens) could explain why these NGOs appear more proactive in assuming ownership of the U.S. state identity. In addition, by virtue of their focus on advocacy, both AJC and AJWS play active parts in U.S. foreign affairs and, thus, strongly identify with the United States.

## *Quality, Stakeholder Empowerment, and Issues Management*

While recognizing the value of a unique and consistent organizational identity, NGOs understand that their behaviors, rather than their identities, generate the credibility, trust, and loyalty among NGOs' stakeholders both domestically and internationally. Nearly all interviewed executives agreed that, although corporate reputation is in the eyes of the beholder (i.e., the organization's stakeholders and publics), its management is not out of the organization's control. Therefore, the four NGOs take a strategic approach to building their reputational capital both in the United States and abroad. As mentioned earlier, some of the reputational strategies NGOs employ include: (a) commitment to quality of the services they provide directly to stakeholders and projects they fund through implementing partners; (b) relationship-building grounded in the empowerment of host-country stakeholders; and (c) thought-out management of issues concerning stakeholders at home and abroad.

NGOs believe that the quality of what they do is one of the building blocks of a good reputation—from lobbying the government on human rights issues (e.g., AJC) to selling family planning products in low-income communities (e.g., DKT), and from offering volunteer services to grassroots community-based human rights organizations (e.g., AJWS) to supporting micro-finance initiatives in the developing countries (e.g., ERD). Moreover, NGOs working through host-country civil society organizations (e.g., AJWS and ERD) expect their implementing partners on the ground to use the funding provided by NGOs effectively.

DKT focuses on promoting its family planning and reproductive health products and services rather than the organization. According to the interviewed executives, DKT's brands have gained recognition in the developing world for their safety and affordability. The NGO delegates responsibility for marketing contraceptives to its country-office managers who understand both the politics and markets in their respective host countries. Although the establishment in some host countries may not approve of family planning programs, DKT seeks to comply with local customs and foster long-term partnerships with national governments and civil societies. Such autonomy and flexibility of operations in each country allows DKT to be accepted as a natural part of the commercial landscape and become a key player in the area of family planning. Frequently, host-country governments and international aid agencies either buy the NGO's products or award grants to DKT for implementing family and HIV/AIDS prevention programs in those countries. As a result of a growing demand for its brands, DKT generates most of its revenues from sales, thus reducing its dependency on grants or donations. "I think we do care about how we are perceived, but we spend more time trying to get our job done," noted a DKT executive.

Another reputational strategy by NGOs involves building and maintaining relationships both domestically and internationally with such stakeholder groups as members and donors in the United States, host-country civil society organizations, and governments. Most NGOs earn the trust of their counterparts in host countries by strengthening local capacities and encouraging local initiative.

In its relationships with grassroots organizations in poor countries, AJWS avoids throwing its weight around. The grant-making NGO wants its grantees and project partners to have a say in how to use the funding for effective community development. AJWS is also aware that its volunteers (i.e., predominantly U.S. citizens) might draw unwanted attention to their host organizations, which often represent marginalized populations or work on human rights issues that aren't supported by local authorities. Because media coverage might jeopardize the safety of both the volunteer and local staff, AJWS's volunteers are not allowed to speak with the press or blog about their experiences in the host country without the New York City-based headquarters' permission.

A DKT executive underscored humility in interactions and respect for host-country stakeholders. The executive cautioned against making the beneficiaries of assistance "feel an obligation that can never be repaid." DKT wants its employees to remember that the NGO's stakeholders should be given a choice to accept or reject the assistance, "They are the ones who can choose to improve their lives."

ERD's philosophy is to "leave no footprints" and empower the implementing partners on the ground "to be active agents of change." In addition to providing financial support, ERD encourages those local organizations to grow and eventually generate other sources of revenue. For the most part, ERD's implementing partners are known in their countries for providing services the respective governments don't provide. Nevertheless, the NGO monitors how its relief and development funds are spent. ERD believes it enjoys a favorable reputation by ensuring that the implementing partners in host countries live up to the organization's principles and methods of providing services. ERD's executive said, "Our corporate reputation is also dependent on the quality of the work carried out in our name. And it is why we establish vigorous monitoring and evaluation standards."

AJC's relationship with its stakeholders such as U.S.-based members and donors, as well as Jewish communities around the world, is premised on the understanding of their needs and expectations. The NGO engages in opinion research to identify the issues of concern for the Jewish minorities. AJC's relationship-building efforts also involve finding a common ground with those stakeholder groups that might not share the same ideologies and beliefs (e.g., building alliances with Catholic and Muslim institutions in the United States and overseas). Furthermore, AJC generates intangible reputational capital by nurturing connections with the U.S. political, business, and cultural elites and by encouraging its board, management and staff to engage in the civic and political life of the United States. The interviewed executives believe that being associated with the American establishment enhances the effectiveness of AJC's advocacy work with U.S. and foreign governments on behalf of the NGO's domestic and international stakeholders. When AJC disagrees with U.S. or foreign government policies vis-à-vis the Jewish people or universal human rights, the NGO can capitalize on its connections to power to "take on the government directly or indirectly, publicly or privately," thus establishing itself as a credible representative of its constituents.

One more component of NGOs' reputational strategies is addressing the issues that might affect them or their stakeholders. As expected, for the two advocacy organizations (i.e., AJC and AJWS), issues management is more than a reputational strategy, it is also what they do. Guided by a sense of urgency for constituents and the availability of adequate resources, advocacy NGOs identify decision-makers, build coalitions with allies and map out the advocacy strategies. AJC manages issues both reactively and proactively. An AJC executive explained that the NGO responds to the news and to visits of government officials to and from the United States as opportunities to catalyze its human rights agenda. "We are sensitive to a particular role that our government may play in advancing our agenda," added the interviewed executive. Part of AJC's issue management requires years of proactive work on Capitol Hill to influence a particular piece of legislation (e.g., on Israel and Palestine or on immigration in the United States).

AJWS engages in both direct and grassroots lobbying. The NGO tries to influence those policy issues that might affect its worldwide projects (e.g., global funding for AIDS, debt forgiveness for developing countries, or the U.S. foreign assistance reform). According to an interviewed executive, Americans ought to know more about the hope that U.S. NGOs-sponsored development projects bring to small communities in developing countries, but the U.S. news media do not cover those issues frequently. "Most of our projects are in urban slums or in rural areas, and the press is not actually walking around, looking for quotes.... This isn't the type of thing the *New York Times* looks to write about," said an AJWS executive. Therefore, AJWS encourages its volunteers returning to the United States to speak and write about their experiences in the developing countries and advocate for global justice at home. "The best way to get involved with us locally is to be an advocate for all kinds of social change," explained an AJWS executive.

An ERD executive mentioned that a controversy in the church, such as the debate within the Anglican Community on the ordination of gay bishops, would be one of those issues that might affect the organization and its relationships with stakeholders. The NGO's implementing partners in host countries might disagree with the position that the Episcopal Church in the United States takes. In those instances, ERD finds a common ground with host-country counterparts and diplomatically shifts the focus from ideology to disaster relief or development projects. "We have a lot of things we can agree about," an interviewed executive said. At the same time, the NGO seeks to demonstrate to its donor base in the United States its ability to work out disagreements with host-country partners and direct its support to those in need regardless of their beliefs.

## NGOs' Autonomy and Pluralism as U.S. Reputational Assets

The findings from these case studies suggest that NGOs contribute to strengthening the United States' global standing by being epitomes of the autonomy and pluralism of the U.S. civil society. Nearly all interviewed executives underscored that their NGOs' relationships with the U.S. Government are based on equality and autonomy. Inspired by the U.S. values of democracy and freedom, these four NGOs reserve the right to disagree with government policies and openly share their dissenting position with domestic and international stakeholders and publics.

According to an AJC executive, generally, the NGO works with the government, not against it. However, as another executive pointed out, being an advocacy organization requires that the NGO challenge the official U.S. policies when those contravene the NGO's values or fail to meet its stakeholders' expectations. When the U.S. Congress and Administration have different positions on the issues of importance for AJC (e.g., immigration reform or protection of the rights of asylum seekers), the NGO capitalizes on this difference of opinions by allying with those in government who share its stance on these issues. AJC's executives argued that other U.S. faith-based international NGOs (e.g., Evangelical, Catholic and other Jewish groups) are equally unconstrained in their speech.

AJWS, DKT and ERD frequently oppose the U.S. government's foreign aid policies. Most interviewed executives argued that U.S. development assistance programs prioritize national interests over global development needs. An executive explained that, because of such disagreement, AJC is not only reluctant to pursue government funding, but also actively advocates for a policy reform. According to a DKT executive, disagreement with official U.S. foreign aid policies would not prevent the organization either from applying for government contracts or from making its dissenting voice heard. Likewise, being a recipient of government funding, does not deter ERD from expressing its opposing views.

The interviewed executives argued that their NGOs' global stakeholders and publics make a distinction between the U.S. government and U.S. NGOs. In those instances when U.S. NGOs might be perceived by some publics as agents of the U.S. government, NGOs' source of funding (i.e., whether or not the NGO receives funds from the U.S. government) appears to play little or no role. By and large, however, in the international arena these NGOs tend to be perceived as agents of U.S. civil society. By virtue of representing specific segments of U.S. society (e.g., American Jews or American Episcopalians) and sharing inherent American values (e.g., pursuit of justice or social marketing), the four NGOs bring to light the plurality of U.S. civil society and assume ownership in the U.S. national identity.

Furthermore, while these cases studies reflect only NGOs' own views on their corporate reputations, NGOs' interactions with their stakeholders and publics in host countries appear to be connected with the U.S. standing in those host countries. The four NGOs recognize that the U.S. reputation in host countries either facilitates or impedes U.S. NGOs' operations in those countries. Likewise, these NGOs are cognizant of how their corporate behaviors in host countries affect the overall perception about the United States and, in turn, impact the operating environments in those countries for all types of U.S. organizations. As a result, while U.S. NGOs may not be engaging in strategic reputation management on behalf of the United States, the outcomes of their own reputation management go beyond their corporate interests. In addition, because of their explicit country-of-origin identities, the four NGOs have an intrinsic interest in improving the U.S. standing overseas. Therefore, U.S. NGOs share responsibility for the U.S. reputation and add to the nation's global outreach efforts.

Finally, although the examples reviewed in this chapter ostensibly emphasize the American identity of U.S. NGOs and First Amendment-based freedoms of expression, association and petition, the argument for non-state actors' global outreach applies in the context of other nations as well. One of the interviewed executives suggested that American NGOs are more likely to challenge the U.S. government's foreign policies whereas, for example, comparable European NGOs tend to limit their advocacy before respective European governments to domestic issues. Such a subjective generalization may not reflect the reality of European NGOs, and U.S. NGOs' inherent dissent may not be uniquely American after all. Notwithstanding the degree of independence from their respective governments, civil society groups such as NGOs represent a range of opinions and play a role in formation of public opinion in their own countries and abroad (Cohen & Arato, 1992; Habermas, 1989). This fundamental aspect of civil society implies that none of the three layers of a nation's of public diplomacy (i.e., mediated, reputational or relational) (Golan, 2013) can succeed unless it embraces the nation's NGOs—those with close government ties, those in opposition, and all those in between.

## Note

1. The top executives interviewed for the study in 2010 gave permission for the names of their organizations to be disclosed.

## Bibliography

American Jewish Committee (2010a). *Impact: AJC 2009 Annual Report.* New York: AJC.
———. (2010b). *Who We Are,* retrieved April 22, 2010 from http://www.ajc.org/site/c. ijITI2PHKoG/b.789093/k.124/Who_We_Are.htm
American Jewish World Service (2010a). *AJWS 2008 Financial Statements.* Retrieved April 27, 2010 from http://www.ajws.org/who_we_are/financial.html
———. (2010b). *Who we are.* Retrieved April 22, 2010 from http://ajws.org/who_we_are/.
Arndt, R.T. (2005). *The first resort of kings: American cultural diplomacy in the twentieth century.* Washington, DC: Potomac Books.

Atack, I. (1999). Four criteria of development NGO legitimacy. *World Development, 27*(5), 864–885.

Cohen, J.L., & Arato, A. (1992). *Civil society and political theory.* Cambridge, MA: MIT Press.

Cowan, G., & Cull. N. (2008). Public diplomacy in a changing world. *The Annals of the American Academy of Political and Social Science, 616*(1).

Cull, N.J. (2010). Public diplomacy: Seven lessons for its future from its past. *Place branding and Public Diplomacy,* 6, 11–17.

DKT International (2010). *About DKT.* Retrieved April 22, 2010, from http://www.dktinternational.org/index.php?section=10

Edwards, M. (2000). *NGO rights and responsibilities: A new deal for global governance.* London: Foreign Policy Centre and NCVO.

Episcopal Relief & Development (2010). *Who we are.* Retrieved April 22, 2010 from http://www.er-d.org/WhoWeAre/

———. (2009). *Annual summary 2008.* New York: Episcopal Relief & Development.

Florini, A.M. (ed.) (2000). *The third force: The rise of transnational civil society.* Washington, DC: Carnegie Endowment for International Peace.

Golan, G. J. (2013). Introduction: An Integrated Approach to Public Diplomacy. *American Behavioral Scientist. 57*(9): 1251–1255.

Gregory, B. (2011). American public diplomacy: Enduring characteristics, elusive transformation. *The Hague Journal of Diplomacy, 6*(3/4), 351–372.

Habermas, J. (1989). *Jurgen Habermas on society and politics: A reader.* Boston: Beacon Press.

Internal Revenue Service. (2009, January). Exempt purposes: Internal Revenue Code Section 501(c)(3). Unites States Department of the Treasury. Retrieved November 12, 2009 from http://www.irs.gov/charities/charitable/article/0,,id=175418,00.html

———. (2008, June). Tax-exempt status for your organization. Publication 557. United Stated Department of the Treasury. Retrieved November 12, 2009 from http://www.irs.gov/pub/irs-pdf/p557.pdf

Josselin, D., & Wallace, W. (eds.) (2001). *Non-state actors in world politics.* London: Palgrave.

Leonard, M., Stead C., & Smewing, C. (2002). *public diplomacy.* London: The Foreign Policy Centre.

Lewis, L. (2005). The civil society sector: Review of critical issues and research agenda for organization communication scholars. *Management Communication Quarterly, 19*(2), 238–267.

Lord, K.M. (2008). *Voices of America: U.S. public diplomacy for the 21$^{st}$ century.* Washington, DC: Brookings Institution.

Lord, K.M., & Fontaine, R. (2010). *Managing 21$^{st}$ century diplomacy: Lessons from global corporations.* Center for New American Security. Retrieved February 4, 2011 from http://www.cnas.org/files/documents/publications/CNAS_Managing%20 21st-Century%20Diplomacy_LordFontaine.pdf.

McCleary, R.M. (2009). *Global compassion: Private voluntary organizations and U.S. foreign policy since 1939.* New York: Oxford University Press.

Melissen, J. (2005). The new public diplomacy: Between theory and practice. In J. Melissen (ed.), *The new public diplomacy: Soft power in international relations,* pp. 3–27. New York: Palgrave Macmillan.

Melissen, J. (2011, October). Beyond the new public diplomacy. *Clingendael Papers No. 3*. The Hague: Netherlands Institute of International Relations 'Clingendael.'

Nye, J.S. (2008). *The powers to lead.* New York: Oxford University Press.

———. (2004). *Soft power: The means to succeed in world politics.* New York: Public Affairs.

O'Connell, B. (2000). Civil society: Definitions and descriptions. *Nonprofit and Voluntary Sector Quarterly, 29*(3), 471–478.

Richmond, Y. (2008). *Practicing public diplomacy: A cold war odyssey.* New York, Oxford: Berghahn Books.

Ripinsky, S. & Van den Bossche, P. (2007). *NGO involvement in international organizations: A legal analysis.* London: British Institute of International and Comparative Law.

Salamon, L. (1994). The rise of the nonprofit sector. *Foreign Affairs, 73*, 109–122.

Snow, N., & Taylor, P.M. (Eds.). (2009). *The Routledge handbook of public diplomacy.* New York and London: Routledge Taylor & Francis Group.

Taylor, P. (1994). *Nonstate actors in international politics: From transregional to substate organizations.* Boulder, CO, London: Westview Press.

United Nations. (2003). *Handbook on non-profit institutions in the system of national accounts.* New York: United Nations.

U.S. Advisory Commission on Public Diplomacy. (2010). *Assessing U.S. public diplomacy: A national model.* Retrieved on January 2, 2014 from http://www.state.gov/documents/organization/149966.pdf.

U.S. Government Accountability Office. (2009, May). *U.S. public diplomacy: Key issues for Congressional oversight.* Report to Congressional Committees. Retrieved November 09, 2009 from http://www.gao.gov/new.items/d09679sp.pdf.

Vakil, A.C. (1997). Confronting the classification problem: Toward a taxonomy of NGOs, *World Development, 25*(12), 2057–2070.

Yang, S. (2007). An integrated model of organization-public relational outcomes, organizational reputation, and their antecedents. *Journal of Public Relations Research,* 19(2), 91–211.

Yang, S. U., & Grunig, J. E. (2005). The effects of organization-public relationships outcomes on cognitive representations of organizations and overall evaluations of organizational performance. *Journal of Communication Management, 9*(4), 305–326.

Zaharna, R.S. (2010). *Battles to bridges: U.S. strategic communication and public diplomacy after 9/11.* London: Palgrave Macmillan.

Zatepilina, O. (2010). *Why U.S.-based nonprofit organizations have a stake in the U.S. standing: A case study in public diplomacy.* (Unpublished doctoral dissertation). Syracuse University. ProQuest Dissertation & Theses database.

———. (2009). Non-state ambassadors: NGOs' contribution to America's public diplomacy. *Place Branding and Public Diplomacy, 5*(2), 156–168.

Zatepilina-Monacell, O. (2012). High stakes: U.S. nonprofit organizations and the U.S. standing abroad. *Public Relations Review,* 38(3), 471–476.

# 4. The Evolving Links Between International Public Relations and Corporate Diplomacy

SARABDEEP K. KOCHHAR & JUAN-CARLOS MOLLEDA

Today's global business comprises a complex web of linkages across a spectrum of governments and communities. The nature of business is more politicized and humanized than ever before (Moore & Sullivan, 2011), which requires a wider set of academic theories and different models of practice, for multinational corporations (MNCs) either looking to engage, or those that have already established themselves, in host countries. Moreover, the advent of globalization has made it challenging for organizations and nations to gain global recognition. The challenge of global recognition demands that nations endlessly eliminate any negative perceptions among their stakeholders so they gain legitimate power and a voice on the world stage.

Organizations today constantly remain in the public eye and under shareholders, media, and activists' scrutiny (Meznar, Johnson, & Mizzi, 2006). The challenges for organizations arise from a multitude of stakeholders, diverse sociopolitical issues, and persistent focus on building and maintaining legitimacy (Drogendijk, 2004). The stakeholder pressures are significantly shaped by global public opinion (Berg & Holtbrugge, 2001) and the use of mediated and personal communications.

The mediated public diplomacy approach that focuses on government-to-citizen engagement through the third-party mediators has been a strategic global communications effort (Golan, 2013). The need to create a favorable reputation among foreign publics and the media coverage as a prerequisite for achieving that reputation have been explored earlier (Nye, 2004). Prakash (2002) cited globalization of media as a reason for why local nonmarket issues get global dimension immediately. He further added that MNCs are increasingly threatened by "supranational actors who oppose them, supranational regimes that govern their behavior and global media that scrutinize them" (p. 15).

Further advancing the mediated public diplomacy approach, Golan (2013) conceptualized the integrated model of public diplomacy. The model presents mediated public diplomacy as a part of the bigger picture and is seen as a short-to-medium term approach to public diplomacy efforts. The medium-to-long term approach builds country reputation and even helps in nation branding. The long-term approach to public diplomacy is relational in its perspective. The long-term perspective seems more strategic and also characterizes the engagement efforts of MNCs, as influential, political non-state actors, to build and cultivate beneficial relationships with governments and communities worldwide, which is the focus of this chapter.

Countries around the world have their own public diplomacy mechanisms which shape and refine public attitudes overseas. There are many examples of issues and crises where the attitudes of host publics play a determining role in the nation's ability to pursue its foreign policies. There are also other examples of nations branding themselves in a unique way. In a one-of-its-kind initiative of public diplomacy, the U.S. Department of State launched an Arabic-language Twitter account in 2011, declaring that they recognize the critical role played by social media in the Arab world and that the United States desires to be a part of it.

Public diplomacy has generated a substantial body of critical discourse from both the professional and academic worlds. The current chapter is a significant inquiry into the future of public and, in particular, corporate diplomacy by situating it within a broader international public relations context. The main purpose of this chapter is to argue that corporate diplomacy comprises many distinct yet related concepts in international public relations.

Specifically, the chapter delves into the realm of public diplomacy and how it is interlinked with corporate diplomacy. The chapter also analyzes the concept of corporate diplomacy by identifying key concepts of international public relations, such as staged and perceived authenticity, localization, cross-national conflict shifts or transnational crises, corporate social responsibility, and multi-sector partnerships. Finally, the chapter provides some insight into concepts of public relations, particularly legitimacy and stakeholder theory, offering some propositions and recommendations for the practice of corporate diplomacy from a relational public diplomacy perspective.

## *Dimensions of Public Diplomacy*

Public diplomacy literature emphasizes the increasing awareness of the importance of a nation's image and reputation as "state's strategic equity" in global affairs (van Ham, 2008). Wang (2006) stated how a nation's reputation capital impacts the nation's ability to accomplish international political objectives and an increase in their foreign investment and tourism. Public diplomacy is defined as a governmental process of "communicating with foreign publics in an attempt to bring about understanding for its nation's ideas and ideals, its institutions and culture, as well as its national goals and current policies" (Tuch, 1990, p. 3). Communication thus becomes a critical component of public diplomacy. Leonard, Stead, and Smewing (2002) laid emphasis on relationship building as a part of the public diplomacy process, which relates to the relational approach of Golan's integrated model (2013). Wang (2006) outlined three main objectives of public diplomacy: promoting nation-states' goals and policies, communicating their values and ideals, and developing common understanding and mutual trust among countries and peoples.

The phrase "public diplomacy" reflects multiple viewpoints and ideas and, hence, does not possess a unique, well-established conceptualization (Payne, 2009). Yet, in simple words public diplomacy is the influence of a nation on foreign audiences (Ordeix-Rigo & Duarte, 2009). Public diplomacy may also be defined as "direct communication with foreign peoples, with the aim of affecting their thinking and, ultimately, that of their governments" (Taylor, 2008, p. 12). Hence, public diplomacy can be thought of as a process of a nation listening and understanding the needs of other countries and communicating its viewpoint to eventually build relationships.

Public diplomacy is based on the identity and reputation of a nation that is dictated by many factors: political, social, economic, and cultural. Trust has been highlighted as the most important factor necessary to initiate a conversation, sustain a dialogue, and build relationships (Iivonen, Sonnenwald, Parma, & Poole-Kober, 1998; Payne, 2009). The focus on developing relationships is also indicated in the definition of public diplomacy as "the process by which direct relations are pursued with a country's people to advance the interests and extend the values of those being represented" (Sharp, 2007, p. 106). Molleda (2011) also highlighted engagement and dialogue as key indicators of developing relationships in public diplomacy. Payne (2009) explained that "Effective public diplomacy is a two-way street with reciprocal influence on both the source and receiver involved in the ongoing communication process" (p. 582). The ongoing communication process leads to developing lasting relationships with a foreign audience that bestows nations with soft power. Soft power is an advantage in world affairs and incites admiration and respect in other parts of the world.

In the context of international relations theory, Nye (2004) defined the term "soft power" as "an intangible attraction that persuades us to go along with others' purposes without any explicit threat or exchange taking place" (p. 7). The soft power of a country is defined by three factors: its culture, political values, and foreign policies (Nye, 2004). All these factors rest primarily on its ability to shape preferences of others by using strategic communications skills. But for Nye (2010), public diplomacy is not a public relations campaign, instead it "involves building long-term relationships that create an enabling environment for government policies" (p. 31). China is one such example of the benefits of a soft-power portfolio. With China's focus on strengthening energy relationships in the Middle East, Africa, and Latin America, Chinese leaders aim to deepen relationships with these nations and thereby increase influence on them. The strategy adopted by China, as articulated by Hu Jintao, China's 2003–2013 president, is in response to international hostile forces and the fact that China is under assault by western soft power (Jintao, 2012).

Public diplomacy is, to a significant extent, concerned with identity, reputation, and mutual relations between nations and individuals that require trust and build nations' brands or the way *the world sees the world* (Anholt, 2000). Factors such as people or human capital determine how people of a nation are perceived by the rest of the world. For example, the Colombian government attempted to improve its reputation abroad by conducting a national and international campaign called *Colombia is passion*, which communicated positive claims about Colombia and Colombians. Likewise, the Israeli Ministry of Public Diplomacy and Diaspora Affairs launched a website in 2010 in an effort to enable every single citizen to become an ambassador. The website, *Together, we can change the picture,* provides information on Israel's achievements, its global contributions, and tips for Israeli citizens abroad to practice public diplomacy. The efficacy of the nation's branding initiative by Israel is particularly interesting as the Gallup research (2012) indicated an increase in the United States' favorability towards Israel as a result of the campaign (71% in 2012 as compared to 68% in 2011).

These examples of public diplomacy using social media, global citizen diplomacy, creating platforms for networked communications, etc., emphasize the need for nations to keep up with the challenges and demands of globalization, which is defined by an increasingly interdependent and interconnected world economically, environmentally, politically, and socially or demographically. It is also important to identify and acknowledge the growing impact of non-state actors on the practice of public diplomacy. Public diplomacy is no longer restricted to governmental efforts, but also incorporates non-state actors, which have redefined its concepts and understanding. The role and potential of non-state actors in shaping foreign public opinion need more focused attention. In this chapter, non-state actors include multilateral organizations, corporations, media, nongovernmental groups, and activists. As Zakaria (2011) said:

> Functions that were once controlled by governments are now shared with international bodies like the World Trade Organization and the European Union. Nongovernmental groups are mushrooming every day on every issue in every country. Corporations and capital are moving from place to place, finding the best location in which to do business, rewarding some governments while punishing others. [...] Power is shifting away from nation-states, up, down, and sideways. (p. 5)

## The Shift of Power: From Country Power to Corporate Power

In today's world MNCs can greatly influence the lives of people in more ways than what any government can possibly do. The focal point of political power no longer rests with the state and national government alone (Bolewski, 2007), but also rests in the hands of MNCs. Muldoon (2004) stated how MNCs command a crucial position in the world economy and are "active participants in global political and economic affairs" (p. 341). The power and reach of MNCs are a reality that has drawn enhanced critical analysis from media and NGOs worldwide. Globalization is one of the main reasons for a shift in power between government and organizations (Scherer & Palazzo, 2007). Globalization has promoted mutual reliance between countries and has given MNCs the ability to shape global trade, production, and financial transactions.

Rothkopf (2012) detailed how top companies on the *Forbes Global* 2000 list stack up against many countries around the globe. Examples range from HSBC Bank that has 300,000 employees worldwide (more than Germany's number of active military troops) to ExxonMobil that produces 2.4 million barrels a day of crude oil and natural gas liquids (more than the 2.2 million barrels produced in the entire European Union). The ICBC Asia made profits of $18.8 billion in 2011, which is more than Syria's annual budget expenditures. Citigroup does business in more than 140 countries, more than Italy has embassies in the world. Corporate power has the ability to create and redefine the global perception of a nation.

MNCs progressively are adopting a global perspective to survive in a complex environment shaped by dynamic political, economic, and social factors. For example, the government of China has always made the operation for firms in the financial and internet-communication technology sectors difficult ("China loses," 2014). A significant rise in the number of MNCs from emerging economies is projected in the coming years. India is expected to overtake China and become a world leader in the number of new MNCs. More than 2,200 Indian companies are projected to start operations worldwide from 2014 onward, owing to an increase in investment, government support, and trade policies (PwC, 2010).

Public diplomacy and corporate diplomacy are closely linked as the reputation of a nation helps organizations sell its products the world over and, likewise, the organizations' products and services reinforce the nation's reputation and heritage. MNCs shape international relations and can even enhance the national reputation of their respective countries in many ways. The organization and country are seen as dependent and integrated in everyday operations and specific objectives (Eskew, 2006). For example, the Chinese-manufactured products quality crisis of 2007 gained extensive international notoriety, deeply affecting the nation's trade with long-term ramifications on its national brand and reputation. Corporate diplomacy is, therefore, crucial to the credibility of an organization in developing a unique position, voice, and influence in shaping public opinion and policies in the host country.

The concept of corporate diplomacy was originally suggested in 1966 by Christian A. Herter, the former general manager of the government relations department at Socony Mobil Oil Company. Herter emphasized the need for corporate diplomacy, especially after WWII, due to the global competition, mistrust towards Western nations, and the majority of the European corporations being state owned (Molleda, 2011). Corporate diplomacy is defined as "a complex process of commitment towards society, and in particular with its public institutions, whose main added value to the corporation is a greater degree of legitimacy or 'license-to-operate,' which in turn, improves its power within a given social system" (Ordeix-Rigo & Duarte, 2009, p. 549). This definition focuses on corporate legitimacy, with which an organization will gain better acceptance in the host country. However, the expectations of stakeholders are changing as organizations are evaluated more from a morally-legitimate perspective than a financially practical one. The foundation of success in effective corporate diplomacy is to understand the multifarious agendas and alignments of home and host stakeholders.

Steger (2003) in his book described corporate diplomacy as "an attempt to manage systematically and professionally the business environment in such a way as to ensure that business is done smoothly basically with an unquestioned license to operate and an interaction that leads to mutual adaptation between corporations and society" (p. 6). Salzmann, Ionsecu-Somers, and Steger (2006) defined the term 'license to operate' as "the degree of match between stakeholders' individual expectations of corporate behavior and companies' actual behavior" (p. 4). Corporate diplomacy, therefore, focuses on the strategic choices that MNCs make in their host environments to maintain and strengthen their corporate reputation and function easily. Corporate diplomacy is built on the key concepts of relationship and dialogue and shares these with public relations (Macnamara, 2012).

Edelman (2009) termed corporate diplomacy as "private-sector diplomacy" that refers to the initiatives organizations implement to connect with their stakeholders in the environments where they operate. Grupp (2008) defined corporate diplomacy to include two things: firstly, a focus on "collaboration" on the part of organization with its stakeholders, and secondly, addressing everything that can impact the organization directly or indirectly. These definitions briefly point out how organizations and stakeholders will have differences in their objectives, issues, and agendas, and hence it is for the organizations to strategically and tactfully deal with and reconcile those differences (Amann, Khan, Salzmann, Steger, and Ionescu-Somers, 2007). Steger (2003) also emphasized that conflicts of interest and differences in priorities often arise between organizations and their stakeholders and corporate diplomacy can help settle these differences. Corporate diplomacy is, thus, defined as a strategic function that relates to creating and seizing business opportunities, safeguarding the reputation of the firm, affecting the making of rules, and preventing conflicts.

The role of organizations as political non-state actors is analyzed through a deeper understanding of corporate social responsibility (CSR) by Scherer and Palazzo (2007) and Palazzo and Scherer (2008). Scherer and Palazzo (2007) mentioned the importance of governments in defining the function of an organization within a society; i.e., the politicization of corporations. A similar idea of social responsibility is articulated by Amann et al. (2007) who defined corporate diplomacy as "the attempt to manage the business environment systematically and professionally, to ensure that business is done smoothly, with an unquestioned license to operate and an interaction that leads to mutual adaptation between corporations and society in a sense of coevolution" (p. 34).

Corporate diplomacy is not merely the participation of organizations in the public diplomacy initiatives (Ordeix-Rigo & Duarte, 2009). Rather, the challenge is for organizations to connect the corporate diplomacy initiatives with the public diplomacy initiatives. The concept of building trust and long-term relationships is shared between public and corporate diplomacy. Conglomerates like Coca-Cola, Embraer, General Electric, Lenovo, McDonald's, Samsung, Tata Motors, and Toyota, are symbols of their home country, its people, its culture, and legacy. Using corporate diplomacy, organizations are able to leverage their power and legitimacy (Ordeix-Rigo & Duarte, 2009) across their various stakeholders. A comprehensive communication strategy that embraces all stakeholders, facilitates dialogue, and measures the reach and effectiveness of the message and engagement systems is needed to ensure the effectiveness and success of corporate diplomacy campaigns.

## *Who Really Matters? Addressing Stakeholders in Corporate Diplomacy*

Previous discussion on public and corporate diplomacy reiterated the importance of public perceptions and attitudes about a nation or organization. Various definitions and examples indicated the need to establish legitimacy in the minds and hearts of foreign publics. The role of the public in the process of diplomacy needs no further mention, but needs greater understanding, especially from a corporate diplomacy perspective. The various stakeholders of an organization have been studied in the form of stakeholder theory that describes the relationship an organization holds with its various constituency groups, including customers, employees, and investors (Donaldson & Preston, 1995). According to stakeholder theory, an organization must be receptive to various stakeholders in order to facilitate its long-term success.

Similarly in corporate diplomacy, identifying stakeholders is important as organizations need to ensure that their organizational decisions are globally accepted. Friedman (2006) defined an organization as a set of various stakeholders with the prime aim of maintaining their respective varied interests and viewpoints. Maignan and Ferrell (2004) defined stakeholders as those that are motivated to participate in organizational activities by various interests. Overall, stakeholder theory describes an organization "as an open and flexible system made up of diverse actors and active in a network or relationships with various other actors" (Maignan & Ferrell, 2004, p. 5). An organization has interest in communicating with the stakeholders it serves, and the messages are expected to address topics of interest to those stakeholders. In corporate diplomacy, addressing stakeholders can be approached as a two-step process of "who" to engage and "how" to engage.

The growing threats and risks faced by MNCs have led to an even greater necessity to find, establish, and strengthen political and social support for their operations (Henisz, Dorobantu, & Nartey, 2011). Hart and Sharma (2004, p. 8) stated that MNCs "need a new capability focused on engaging the stakeholders necessary for managing disruptive change and creating competitive imagination." Relationships with a government agency or another regulatory agency are termed as long-term activities that influence the decisions an organization would take (Hillman & Wan, 2005). The example of Walmart in India illustrates this point. Walmart's investment in Bharti, India, has come under a scanner amid allegations that the global retail chain may have entered India's front-end multi-brand retail business two-and-a-half years before the government actually lifted the ban on foreign investors in the sector last year ("Walmart set to buy," 2013). Indian authorities including the Enforcement Directorate, which tracks money-laundering deals, are probing charges against Walmart's investment of $100 million in March 2010. Bharti Walmart suspended five executives as part of an ongoing investigation against alleged corrupt practices that the U.S. retail giant has launched globally including in China, Brazil, and Mexico ("Walmart set to buy," 2013). The Walmart case is an example of dependence on political factors as crucial for organizational success.

Johanson and Vahlne (2009) explained how the business environment is viewed as a web of relationships, a network, rather than as a neoclassical market with many independent suppliers and customers. MNCs interact and build relations with a wide range of stakeholders specific to the host country to include even the public opinion (Hillman & Wan, 2005). The dependence on stakeholders is termed as stakeholder capital by Dorobantu, Henisz, and Nartey (2012) and defined as the "level of mutual recognition, understanding and trust established by the firm with its stakeholders" (p. 2). Stakeholder capital can help an organization retain the 'social license to operate' during critical times. The critical times are the instances when "the firm's actions and operations are being challenged by opponents" (Dorobantu et al., 2012, p. 2). The benefits of stakeholder capital are also reflected through the support of the stakeholders who are more likely to defend organizational activities in challenging times (Dorobantu et al., 2012). Investment in stakeholder capital by organizations is considered as an insurance, which will provide relief after adverse events.

Pfeffer and Salancik (1978) evaluated the priorities in relationship building to suggest evaluating the critical dependence of an MNC on different stakeholders. The relational view given by Dyer and Singh (1998) argued that organizations need to pay attention to a select few important stakeholders at a given point of time. The relational view highlights that an organization is at times unable to cope with the global competition and should cooperate and develop relational networks in the international market for mobilizing its resources. Windsor (2005) stated that the external environment of business will continue to become more global and effectively mobilize more stakeholders and has to address the interface between a corporation and its environment.

## The Emerging Definitions of Global Success: Authenticity and Localization

With so many brands, products, and services to choose from, publics and consumers are making choices based on what seems to be original, sincere, or what can be called authentic. Authenticity defines the success of an organization and its brands by giving publics and customers a sense of safety, certainty, and meaning in the ideas and brands they chose to support. "Organizations are being pressured by societies demanding greater transparency, clarity, and responsibility from organizations and their spokespeople," stated Molleda (2009, p. 87). Hence, authenticity needs to be at the core of every organization's interaction with the stakeholders.

Molleda (2010a) defined that organizations, in order to be authentic, need to be "faithful to their true self and the core values embedded in corporate identities, offerings, and promises they make to targeted stakeholders" (p. 224). He also noted that authenticity requires a combination of action and communication. Authenticity as a construct was tested in a nation's branding study done by Molleda and Roberts (2008). The five genres of authenticity (natural, original, exceptional, referential, and influential) were used to analyze the case study of Juan Valdez as the Colombian coffee ambassador. The five genres originally given by Gilmore and Pine (2007) reflect how organizations should articulate and communicate authenticity to influence the perceptions of its stakeholders.

Camilleri (2008) also used a case study to explain the primary role of trust in communicating authenticity. She clarified that "the less time there is for consumers to choose for themselves and evaluate the trustworthiness of certain brands, the more important it is for brands to be authentically trustworthy" (p. 58). Molleda and Jain (2011, 2013) tested a perceived authenticity index in the case of Xcaret. They established that authenticity is a construct that is continuously defined and redefined by exchange of experiences and messages (negotiation of meanings) between an organization and its stakeholders.

The constant flux of customer experiences makes it challenging for organizations to identify corporate diplomacy efforts. Corporate diplomacy works on basic variables, indicators, and goals (Ordeix-Rigo & Duarte, 2009). The initial steps are defined as a basic acquaintance with the host country and the creation of positive, preliminary perceptions about the organization and the home country. The next step is the acceptance of the organization in the host country by the stakeholders, and the final step is engagement of the corporation with various stakeholders as a good employer, responsible corporate citizen, and trustworthy business partner (Ordeix-Rigo & Duarte, 2009).

Studies have shown that organizations undergoing mergers or acquisitions abroad continue to keep the local/domestic brand for some time before rebranding (Moss, 2002). Rigby and Vishwanath (2006) explained in the *Harvard Business Review* that "success for retailers and product manufacturers now hinges on their ability to cater to local differences while maintaining scale efficiencies" (p. 82). Molleda, Kochhar, and Wilson (2012) defined localization in international public relations "as the process of adapting standardized corporate communication to address political regulations, cultural differences, media expectations, and stakeholders' self-interests in host countries where TNCs have operations" (p. 11).

Daniels, Radebaugh, and Sullivan (2007) identified four macro-level strategies used to address the complexities of global business and emphasized the need for localization. International strategy focuses on a company's core competency and allows for limited localization, multi-domestic strategy adapts products, services, and business operations to meet the needs of countries or regions, global strategy emphasized standardization and consistency and transnational strategy attempts to find a balance between global effectiveness through standardization and local responsiveness in different countries.

Lim (2010) identified five environmental factors that can be addressed to achieve local public relations effectiveness: 1) policies and regulations, 2) culture and language, 3) local activism, 4) local hostility and skepticism, and 5) relationships with local media. The adherence to these rules can help organizations practice effective corporate diplomacy. As described by Sewpaul (2006), "the potential to dilute or even annihilate local cultures and traditions and to deny context specific realities the effect of dominant global discourses can cause individual and cultural displacement" (p. 419). Doing effective global corporate diplomacy requires local knowledge, competencies, and tools for implementing strategic communications to deal effectively with foreign publics and handle crisis situations.

## Handling a Crisis in a Transnational Environment

The age of transparency and the diversity of the world media system have revolutionized the business world. Organizations can no longer evade talking about an issue that concerns and is visible to shareholders, customers, employees, partners, and society. Incidences and conflicts are also not isolated in the country from which they originate (Molleda & Quinn, 2004). The world of internet, social media, and blogging has compelled organizations to rethink their business principles and values. Globalization and the development of emergent communication technologies have added to the challenge for MNCs in managing crises, conflicts, and issues in multiple locations. As one of the main outcomes of globalization, corporations are involved and affected by transnational incidents or challenging situations (Wakefield, 2001). An action, policy, or decision by a MNC that is rapidly made public via these technologies may negatively affect a multitude of publics and can damage an organization's credibility in the home and host country (Molleda & Quinn, 2004) and can lead to a crisis. As Freitag (2002) described, "thanks to Internet, a regional issue can become an international crisis" (p. 240).

The term "transnational crisis" was borrowed from the international strategic and business management disciplines and introduced to the public relations field by Molleda and Connolly-Ahern (2002). The term "transnational crisis" within global public relations is known as "cross-national conflict shifting" (CNCS) and is defined as "crises or troublesome situations that transnational organizations face either at 'home,' where they have their headquarters, or in 'host' countries, where they operate and engage in commercial and/or institutional activities" (Molleda, 2010b, p. 680). Simply, a CNCS occurs when a crisis originates in one country and, subsequently, spreads to other countries where the MNC has operations (Molleda, 2010b, 2011). Molleda and Connolly-Ahern (2002) developed a series of propositions regarding CNCS to study crisis management in an international context which restates how a transnational crisis in a country can move and impact other places in the world (Kim & Molleda, 2005; Molleda & Quinn, 2004).

The Foxconn employee suicide outbreak of 2010 was one such example of CNCS with serious implications in the home and host countries. With a series of suicide attempts inside Foxconn factories, the company faced criticism about their improper treatment of laborers and this, in turn, affected its international clients, such as Apple and Dell.

The literature on CNCS or transnational crisis also addresses the importance of localization. Conflicts that affect TNC operations in multiple countries require coordination among subsidiaries and with home offices; however, responses to the crises in individual locations require a localized response that takes into account local expectations, perceptions, and regulations and stakeholders (Molleda, 2010b, 2011). Addressing stakeholders in CNCS, Molleda and Laskin (2009) explained the involvement of "a variety of publics at various geographical levels, namely, host, home, and transnational publics (e.g., NGOs and activist groups, global media outlets, international news agencies, pan-regional media, shareholders)" (p. 333).

CNCS has serious implications for corporate diplomacy as both the increasingly advanced communication technology and the proliferation of global and national news media play an important role in informing home, host, and transnational publics about the issues. "Without delay, a news event will be published and discussed with great interest where it has some or high resonance," Molleda wrote (2010b, p. 679). Freitag's (2002) study about international media coverage of the Firestone tire recall case reinforced the power of media as one of the potentially determining factors in crisis planning and response models. Developing an international and intercultural sense and sensibility enables corporate diplomacy practitioners to predict, anticipate, and address unique dimensions of crises subject to international exposure (Freitag, 2002). The threat to corporate reputation can be managed in several ways; one of which is defined as the moral way of doing business in today's competitive world.

## CSR and Partnerships for Global Development

In today's global marketplace, organizations are members of the worldwide community, rather than merely members of their respective country or city of origin (Maignan & Ferrell, 2004). The change in the global scenario has made CSR all the more important for organizations today. Organizations have begun to invest millions in CSR initiatives, with the end goals of increasing reputation and improving connections with organizational stakeholders (McDonald & Rundle-Thiele, 2007). Interest in CSR has been promoted by increased sensitivity to ethical issues among individuals and organizations. Husted and Allen (2006) explained that "institutional pressures, rather than strategic analysis of social issues and stakeholders, are guiding decision-making with respect to CSR" (p. 838).

The role of MNCs in society has been understood as central, if not paramount, in achieving the economic, social, and environmental aspirations of governments and people worldwide. Globalization has blurred national borders, and has moved CSR from the margins to the mainstream of business practices (Grayson & Hodges, 2004). This is evident in an organization's level of commitment to CSR, which is influenced by individual, organizational, national, and transnational actors and agencies (Aguilera, Rupp, & Williams, 2005). "Globalization has had significant political and cultural effects, raising major PR [public relations] issues and corporate social responsibility challenges," L'Etang explained (2009, p. 610).

Thus CSR practiced by organizations is essential and presents an easy alternative to using corporate power as a catalyst for social intervention and change. The interests of development agencies and nonprofit organizations lead to added pressure on organizations to address the issues most relevant to their stakeholders in home and host countries. Also, the development agencies in the public sector have observed the challenges in effectively solving societal issues in a unilateral manner. Hence, these agencies are working to determine and prioritize sectors where development challenges meet business opportunities, thus forming strategic alliances and partnerships to achieve substantial outcomes.

According to Miller (2010), globalization mobilized the growing complexity of social problems and challenges, which are global in scope. Miller (2010) also noted the necessity of increased partnerships for social change to achieve a sustainable impact on development issues and further lead to community building.

Hallahan (2004) explained that the focus on community building shifts the organizational emphasis from cold treatment of impersonal, often adversarial publics, to a warmer, more enlightened emphasis on collaboration and cooperation with them. Hallahan (2004) described three levels of community building from an organizational perspective: community involvement, community nurturing, and community organizing. Molleda, Martínez, and Suárez (2008) suggested that "to achieve broader solutions and improved quality of life it is necessary to capture the experiences of community members, work together toward common goals, and facilitate participation by diverse groups" (p. 106). The process of community building through multi-sector partnerships is studied as a continuous improvement in the communities to collectively accomplish goals.

In general, Bud (2001) explained how times are changing, with international affairs becoming prevalent in every nation and the significance placed on how an organization's social responsibility matches stakeholder expectations. The emphasis for any organization is to maintain corporate integrity abroad, which can be achieved by being a good corporate citizen. Moreover, increased attention should be given to a relational approach to multi-sector partnerships and engagement with the community whose issues are being addressed through the partnership. This particular emphasis on relationship cultivation and participation is an area corporate diplomacy practitioners should understand further. Hardy, Lawrence, and Phillips (2006) defined the "first step in managing effective collaboration is to ensure that stakeholders move beyond feelings of indifference concerning the particular issue and develop an interest in engaging in conversation about it" (p. 103).

According to Hallahan (2004), community building involves "the integration of people and the organizations they create into a functional collectivity that strives toward common or compatible goals" (p. 259). Both public relations and, in particular, community building are concerned with the development and maintenance of symbiotic relationships that establish the connection between the two strategic partners. The function of corporate diplomacy should aim to find ways to collaborate with other sectors and influence the growth and development of the home and the host societies where they operate.

## Putting the Pieces Together: Propositions for Corporate Diplomacy

The consonance between diplomacy and public relations work adds to a broader understanding of the strategic communication role internationally, nationally, and culturally as part of power relations. Scholars in public diplomacy (Snow & Taylor, 2008; Zaharna, 2009) have noticed a growing interest in public diplomacy literature for dialogue, transparency, trust, and commitment. Zaharna (2009) also highlighted that "public diplomacy is as much a communication phenomenon as a political one" (p. 86).

Van Dyke and Vercic (2009) stated that, "for decades, scholars and practitioners have debated the issues of separation or convergence between public relations and public diplomacy" (p. 832). L'Etang (2009) found strong connections and similarities between public relations and diplomacy. Both public relations and public diplomacy are responsible for communications with other organizations, maintaining relations with multiple stakeholders, and shaping public opinion (L'Etang, 2009). Signitzer and Wamser (2006) rationalized public relations and public diplomacy as, "strategic communicative function of either organizations or nation-states, that typically deal with the reciprocal consequences a sponsor and its publics have upon each other" (p. 441). Analyzing the relationship between the two fields and summarizing the international public relations literature, the following propositions can inform the practice of corporate diplomacy.

Proposition 1: Corporate diplomacy efforts by organizations in host countries will identify, respond, and monitor all stakeholders based on their association, traits, and participation with the organization to maximize its legitimacy, influence, and power.

Proposition 2: Corporate diplomacy efforts by organizations in host countries in the form of communication and action will be representative and authentic of the organization's core values to be accepted and authenticated by its stakeholders.

Proposition 3: Corporate diplomacy efforts by organizations in host countries will be responsive to adjust and adapt according to the local political, economic, social, cultural, and legal conditions.

Proposition 4: Corporate diplomacy efforts by organizations in host countries will focus and be proactive in their transnational crisis management efforts addressing the type of economy, industry, issue, and stakeholders involved.

Proposition 5: Corporate diplomacy efforts by organizations in host countries will display increased sensitivity and responsibility across all corporate functions and exhibit socially responsible practices.

Proposition 6: Corporate diplomacy efforts by organizations in host countries will create alliances and partnerships with multiple sectors to sustain social and long-term community change and to reinforce its corporate reputation.

In conclusion, special focus in the practice of corporate diplomacy must be placed on developing strategic communications for host nations including government, NGOs, local influencers, and specialized news media; in creating and maintaining a brand reputation through corporate advocacy programs for environment; and developing rapid response crisis communication strategies. The chapter restates the requirement of a comprehensive, strategic communications plan to execute successful corporate diplomacy efforts.

The chapter acknowledges the importance of understanding both the grassroots and the elites of the population an organization engages with in order to convey authentic, consistent, and targeted message and engagement systems. The need to engage with the stakeholders for mutual respect and mutual interest is also signified as a precursor to long-term relationships, which is at the core of the integrated public diplomacy model (Golan, 2013). The chapter also specified new roles and responsibilities for corporate diplomacy practitioners and outlined numerous international public relations theoretical concepts to contribute to the understanding of corporate diplomacy as a political function of MNCs.

## Bibliography

Aguilera, R. V., Rupp, D. E., Williams, C. A., & Ganapathi, J. (2005). Putting the S back in corporate social responsibility: A multi-level theory of social change in organizations. *Academy of Management Review, 32*(3), 836–863.

Amann, W., Khan, S., Salzmann, O., Steger, U. & Ionescu-Somers, A. (2007). Managing external pressures through corporate diplomacy. *Journal of General Management, 33*(1), 33–49.

Anholt, S. (2000). *Nation Brands Index.* Retrieved June 11, 2012, from http://www.simonanholt.com/Research/research-introduction.aspx

Berg, N., & Holtbrugge, D. (2001). Public affairs management activities of German multinational corporations in India. *Journal of Business Ethics, 30*, 105–119.

Bolewski, W. (2007). *Diplomacy and international law in globalized relations.* Berlin: Springer.

Bud, J. F. Jr. (2001). Opinion foreign policy acumen needed by global CEOs. *Public Relations Review, 27*(2), 123–134.

Camilleri, C. S. (2008). True blue: Authenticity and Yalumba's journey of discovery. *Australian Journal of Communication, 35*(3), 41–67.

China loses its allure. (2014, January 25–31). *The Economist, 410*(8871), p. 9.

Daniels, J., Radebaugh, L. H., and Sullivan, D. P. (2007). *International business: Environments and operations.* Upper Saddle River, NJ: Pearson Prentice Hall.

Donaldson, T., and Preston, L. (1995). The stakeholder theory of the corporation: Concepts, evidence, and implications. *The Academy of Management Review, 20*(1), 65–91.

Dorobantu, S., Henisz, W. J., & Nartey, L. (2012). Stakeholder capital and performance in tough times. Working Paper.

Drogendijk, R. (2004). The public affairs of internationalisation: Balancing pressures from multiple environments. *Journal of Public Affairs, 4*(1), 44–55.

Dyer, J. H., & Singh, H. (1998). The relational view: Cooperative strategy and sources of interorganizational competitive advantage. *Academy of Management Review, 23*(4), 660–679.

Edelman, R. (2009). *A 'New Paradigm': The Private Sector and Public Diplomacy.* Retrieved on June 13, 2012 from http://uscpublicdiplomacy.org/index.php/newswire/cpd blog_detail/070201_a_new_paradigm_the_private_sector_and_public_diplomacy

Eskew, M. (2006). Corporate diplomacy. *Leadership Excellence, 23*(4), 5–6.

Freitag, A. (2002). International media coverage of the Firestone tyre recall. *Journal of Communication Management, 6*(3), 239–256.

Friedman, T. (2006). *The world is flat: The globalized world in the twenty-first century.* London: Penguin.

Gallup (2012, February 16). *Americans give record-high ratings to several U.S. allies.* Retrieved June 12, 2012, from http://www.gallup.com/poll/152735/americans-give-record-high-ratings-several-allies.aspx

Gilmore, J. H., & Pine, B. J., Jr. (2007). *Authenticity: What consumers really want.* Boston, MA: Harvard Business School Press.

Golan, G. J. (2013). An integrated approach to public diplomacy. *American Behavioral Scientist, 57*(9), 1251–1255.

Grayson, D., and Hodges A. (2004). *Corporate social opportunity.* Newcastle, UK: Green Leaf Publishers.

Grupp, B. (2008), Bob Grupp: *Corporate Diplomacy in Action*. Retrieved from: www.insti
tuteforpr.org/digest_entry/bob_grupp_corporate_diplomacy_in_action/ (accessed 12
September 2013).

Hallahan, K. (2004). "Community" as a foundation for public relations theory and practice. *Communication Yearbook, 28*(1), 233–280

Hardy, C., Lawrence, T. B., & Phillips, N. (2006). Swimming with sharks: Creating strategic change through multi-sector collaboration. *International Journal of Strategic
Change Management, 1*(1), 96–112.

Hart, S. L., & Sharma, S. (2004). Engaging fringe stakeholders for competitive imagination. *The Academy of Management Executive, 18*(1), 7–18.

Henisz, W. J., Dorobantu, S., & Nartey, L. (2011, January). Spinning gold: The financial
returns to external stakeholder engagement. In *Academy of Management Proceedings*
(Vol. 2011, No. 1, pp. 1–6). Academy of Management.

Hillman, A., & Wan, W. P. (2005). The determinants of MNE subsidiaries' political strategies: Evidence of institutional duality. *Journal of International Business Studies, 36*,
322–340.

Husted, B. W. & Allen, D. B. (2006). Corporate social responsibility in the multinational
enterprise: Strategic and institutional approaches. *Journal of International Business
Studies, 37*, 838–849.

Iivonen, M., Sonnenwald, D. H., Parma, M., & Poole-Kober, E. (1998). *Analyzing and
understanding cultural differences: Experiences from education in library and information studies.* Paper presented at the 1998 International Federation of Library Associations and Institutions Annual Conference, Amsterdam, North Holland.

Jintao, H. (2012, January 17). Why China is weak on soft power. *The New York Times.*
Retrieved June 12, 2012, from http://www.nytimes.com

Johanson, J., & Vahlne, J. (2009). The Uppsala internationalization process model revisited: From liability of foreignness to liability of outsidership. *Journal of International
Business Studies, 40*, 1411–1431.

Kim, R. J., & Molleda, J. C. (2005). *Cross-national conflict shifting and crisis management: an analysis of Halliburton's bribery probe case in Nigeria.* Paper presented at the
8th International Public Relations Research Conference, Miami, FL.

L'Etang, J. (2009). Public relations and diplomacy in a globalized world: An issue of public communication. *American Behavioral Scientist, 53*(4) 607–626.

Leonard, M., Stead, C., & Smewing, C. (2002). *Public diplomacy.* Foreign Policy Centre,
New York.

Lim, S.L. (2010). Global integration or local responsiveness? Multinational corporation's
public relations strategies and cases. In G.J. Golan, T.J. Johnson, & W. Wanta (Eds.),
*International media communication in a global age* (pp. 299–318). New York, NY:
Routledge.

Macnamara, J. (2012). Corporate and organizational diplomacy: An alternative paradigm
to PR. *Journal of Communication Management, 16*(3). 312–325.

Maignan, I., & Ferrell, O. C. (2004). Corporate social responsibility and marketing: An
integrative framework. *Journal of the Academy of Marketing Science, 32*(1), 3–19.

McDonald, L. M. & Rundle-Thiele, S. (2007). Corporate social responsibility and bank
customer satisfaction. *International Journal of Bank Marketing, 26*(3), 170–182.

Meznar, M. B., Johnson, J. H., & Mizzi, P. J. (2006). No news is good news? Press coverage and corporate public affairs management. *Journal of Public Affairs, 6*(1), 58–68.

Miller, J. (2010). *Private sector emerges as key partner in food aid.* Devex website. Retrieved March 21, 2012, from http://www.devex.com/en/news/private-sector-emerges-as-key-partner-in-food-aid/70759.

Molleda, J. C. (2009). The construct and dimensions of authenticity in strategic communication research. *Anagramas, 8*(15), 85–97.

Molleda, J. C. (2010a). Authenticity and the construct's dimensions in public relations and communication research. *Journal of Communication Management, 14*(3), 223–236.

Molleda, J. C. (2010b). Cross-national Conflict Shifting: A transnational crisis perspective in global public relations. In R. L. Heath, *The Sage Handbook of Public Relations* (pp. 679–688). Thousand Oaks, CA: Sage Publications.

Molleda, J. C. (2011). Advancing the theory of cross-national conflict shifting; A case discussion and quantitative content analysis of a transnational crisis' newswire coverage. *International Journal of Strategic Communication, 5,* 49–70.

Molleda, J. C., & Connolly-Ahern, C. (2002). *Cross-national conflict shifting: Conceptualization and expansion in an international public relations context.* A paper presented at the meeting of the Association for Education in Journalism and Communication, Miami, FL.

Molleda, J. C., & Jain, R. (2011, October). *Testing a perceived authenticity index with triangulation research: The case of Xcaret in Mexico.* Paper presented at the Public Relations Society of America (PRSA) Educators Academy International Conference, Orlando, FL.

Molleda, J. C., & Jain, R. (2013). Testing a perceived authenticity index with triangulation research: The case of Xcaret in Mexico. *International Journal of Strategic Communication, 7,* 1–20.

Molleda, J. C., Kochhar, S., & Wilson, C. (2012, August). *Theorizing the global-local paradox: Comparative research on information subsidies' localization by U.S.-based multinational corporations.* Paper presented at the Association for Education in Journalism and Mass Communication's 100th Annual Convention, Division of Public Relations, Chicago, IL.

Molleda, J. C., & Laskin, A. (2009). Coordination and control of global public relations to manage cross-national conflict shifts: A multidisciplinary perspective for research and practice. In G. J. Golan, T. J. Johnson, & W. Wanta (Eds.), *International media communication in a global age* (pp. 319–344). New York, NY: Routledge.

Molleda, J. C., Martínez, B., & Suárez, A. M. (2008). Building multi-sector partnerships for progress with strategic, participatory communication: A case study from Colombia. *Anagramas, 6*(12), 105–125.

Molleda, J. C., & Quinn, C. (2004). Cross-national conflict shifting: A global public relations dynamic. *Public Relations Review, 30,* 1–9.

Molleda, J. C., & Roberts, M. (2008). The value of "authenticity" in "global" strategic communication: The new Juan Valdez campaign. *International Journal of Strategic Communication, 2*(3), 154–174.

Moore, J., & Sullivan, K. (2011). Business, diplomacy and frontier markets. Best practice for business leaders. *Reflections from Practice.* Retrieved from http://fletcher.tufts.edu/CEME/publications/reflections/~/media/Fletcher/Microsites/CEME/pubs/reflections/MooreSullivanBizDip.pdf

Muldoon, J. P. (2004). *The architecture of global governance: an introduction to the study of international organizations.* Westview Pr.

Moss, D. (2002). *Public relations cases, international perspective.* London: Routledge.

Nye, J. (2010). The new public diplomacy. *Project Syndicate.*

Nye, J. S. (2004). The decline of America's soft power. *Foreign Affairs, 83,* 16–20.

Ordeix-Rigo, E., & Duarte, J. (2009). From public diplomacy to corporate diplomacy: Increasing corporations' legitimacy and influence. *American Behavioral Scientist, 53*(4), 549–564.

Palazzo, G., & Scherer, A. G. (2008). Corporate social responsibility, democracy, and the politicization of the corporation. *Academy of Management Review, 33*(3), 773–775.

Payne, J. G. (2009). Reflections on public diplomacy: People-topeople communication. *American Behavioral Scientist, 53*(4), 579–606.

Pfeffer, J., & Salancik, G. (1978). *The external control of organizations.* New York: Harper & Row.

Prakash, A. (2002). Beyond Seattle: Globalization, the nonmarket environment and corporate strategy. *Review of International Political Economy, 9*(3), 513–537.

PWC. (April 29, 2010). *India to produce 2219 new multinational companies between 2010–2024.* Retrieved June 12, 2012, from http://www.pwc.com/in/en/press-releases/press-releases-2010.jhtml

Rawlins, Brad L. (2006). *Prioritizing stakeholders for public relations.* Retrieved from http://www.instituteforpr.org/research_single/prioritizing_stakeholders. Published by the Institute for Public Relations, www.instituteforpr.org.

Rigby, D. K., & Vishwanath, V. (2006, May). Localization: The revolution in consumer markets. *Harvard Business Review, 87*(5), 82–92.

Rothkopf, D. (2012, March). *Supercitizens and semistates.* The global elites that really run the world. Retrieved June 12, 2012, from http://www.foreignpolicy.com/articles/2012/02/27/Supercitizens_and_Semistates

Salzmann, O., Ionescu-Somers, A., & Steger, U. (2006). Corporate License to Operate (LTO)–Review of the Literature and Research Options. *20International Institute for Management Development,* 2011.

Scherer, A. G., & Palazzo, G. (2007). Toward a political conception of corporate responsibility: Business and society seen from a Habermasian perspective. *Academy of Management Review, 32*(4), 1096–1120.

Sewpaul, V. (2006). The global-local dialectic: Challenges for Africa scholarship and social work in a post-colonial world. *British Journal of Social Work, 36,* 419–434.

Sharp, P. (2007). Revolutionary states, outlaw regimes and the techniques of public diplomacy. In J. Melissen (Ed.), *The new public diplomacy: Soft power in international relations* (pp. 106–123). London, UK: Palgrave Macmillan.

Signitzer, B., & Wamser, C. (2006). Public diplomacy: A specific governmental *public relations function. Public relations theory II,* 435–464.

Snow, N., & Taylor, P. M. (Eds.). (2008). *Routledge handbook of public diplomacy.* Routledge.

Steger, U. (2003). *Corporate diplomacy: The strategy for a volatile, fragmented business environment.* Wiley.com.

Taylor, M. (2008, November). *Toward a relational of public diplomacy.* Paper presented at the annual meeting of the 94th Annual National Communication Association, San Diego, CA.

Tuch, H. N. (1990). *Communicating with the world: US public diplomacy overseas.* New York: St. Martin's Press.

Van Dyke, M., & Vercic, D. E. J. A. N. (2009). Public relations, public diplomacy and strategic communication: An international model of conceptual convergence. *Global Public Relations Handbook: Theory, Research and Practice.* New York: Routledge.

Van Ham, P. (2008). Place branding: the state of the art. *The ANNALS of the American Academy of Political and Social Science, 616*(1), 126–149.

Wal-Mart set to buy 49% in Bharti Retail subsidiary (May 29, 2013). *Hindustan Times,* Retrieved from http://www.hindustantimes.com/business-news/wal-mart-set-to-buy-49-in-bharti-retail-subsidiary/article1-1067968.aspx

Wakefield, R. I. (2001). Effective public relations in the multinational organization. In R. L. Heath (Ed.), *Handbook of Public Relations* (pp. 639–658). Thousand Oaks, CA: Sage.

Wang, J. (2006). Public diplomacy and global business. *Journal of Business Strategy, 27*(3), 41–49.

Windsor, D. (2005). "Theories" and theoretical roots of public affairs. In P. Harris, & C. Fleisher (Eds.), *The handbook of public affairs.* (pp. 401–418). London: Sage Publications Ltd.

Yun, S. (2006). Toward public relations theory-based study of public diplomacy: Testing the applicability of the excellence study. *Journal of Public Relations Research, 18*(4), 287–312.

Zaharna, R. S. (2009). *Battles to bridges: US strategic communication and public diplomacy after 9/11.* Palgrave Macmillan.

Zakaria, F. (2011). *The post-American world: Release 2.0.* New York: W.W. Norton & Company.

# 5. *Public Diplomacy and Public Relations: Will the Twain Ever Meet?*

Nancy Snow

The integrated model of public diplomacy, which is introduced in this book, employs a strategic communication approach that constitutes a merging of public relations practice and techniques with public diplomacy goals and outcomes. One of the three layers of the integrated model, mediated public diplomacy, implores governments to engage foreign publics through third party mediators such as global media (global satellite networks, international broadcasting) and international social media influencers. The mediated public diplomacy layer is a recognition of 21st century realities for public diplomacy: namely, that the whole world is watching what governments say and do and not only writing and reporting on their talk and actions, but also utilizing the opinions and evaluations of those third party influencers like bloggers and digital activists who are talking back at their governments like never before.

The other two layers, nation branding/country reputation and relational public diplomacy, inclusively medium and long-term strategies, position public relations perspectives and practitioners at the forefront of implementing effective public diplomacy outcomes. The majority of contributors to this volume, including the editors who introduce the integrated model of public diplomacy, argue that public relations should lead, and not follow, in public diplomacy research and applications. The present author is a former federal government official employed by a public diplomacy agency, the United States Information Agency, which was formally abolished in 1999 as an independent foreign affairs agency of the United States. One of USIA's most famous directors was the legendary CBS journalist, Edward R. Murrow, who served as USIA director during the Kennedy administration. In his capacity as director of USIA, Murrow (1961) referred to himself as a government propagandist and not as public relations executive, but he acknowledged a

familial connection between public diplomacy and public relations in a speech
he gave to the Public Relations Society of America:

> I know that I am among friends this morning. For the U.S. Information Agency
> and the Public Relations Society, like the Colonel's Lady and Judy O'Grady, are
> sisters under the skin. We both work for others—you for clients and firms; my
> Agency for 180 million Americans. We both are in the business of persuasion—
> for you, the American public; for us, peoples everywhere abroad.

Murrow's kindred spirit is evident in those words, but the purpose of
this chapter is to offer a more critical communications dimension to the integration of public relations with public diplomacy as proposed by the integrated model of public diplomacy. Two fundamental questions are addressed:
Is public relations closely allied to public diplomacy? And if so, is the field of
public relations in need of its own makeover in both public perception and
media framing?

Public diplomacy, whose purpose may not be completely understood by
the lay public, does not suffer the same source credibility problems as does
public relations (e.g., Stauber & Rampton, 1995; Callison, 2001; National Credibility Index, 1999). Of the two disciplines examined in this book,
public relations suffers more from a persistent image problem while public
diplomacy suffers more from a persistent funding problem (e.g., Murrow,
1961; Coombs, 1964; Duffey, 1995; Callison, 2004; Defense Science Board,
2004, O'Brien, 2005; GAO, 2006). This suggests that the integration of
public diplomacy and public relations is not yet on solid footing. There is a
greater need "that public relations needs more public relations" (L'Etang,
1997, p. 34) than there is a need for public diplomacy to need more public
diplomacy, at least from a credibility stance. Nevertheless, public diplomacy
has been widely examined from the perspective of theorists and practitioners
in public relations (Galboa, 2008; Signitzer and Coombs, 1992; Signitzer
and Wasmer, 2006), and the more modern interpretations of two-way symmetrical approaches to public relations (Grunig, 1993; Grunig, 2001) reflect
the relationship-driven rethinking in public diplomacy strategies that have
greatly evolved from the more self-serving, self-preservation approaches of
press agentry and public information (Snow, 2009).

To be sure, American public diplomacy and public relations uniquely differ in their semantic and reputational contexts than public diplomacy and
public relations campaigns in other countries. An Austrian immigrant to the
United States wrote the first public relations texts (Bernays, 1928, 1929)
and the involvement of eminent political communication scholars (Lasswell,
1927; Lippmann, 1922) in World War I and World War II advanced the

study and application of public relations to national conflict outcomes, therein setting the historical foundation for a future integration of public relations with public diplomacy campaigns. While there are some studies (Johnson, 2005) that show a natural evolution from one-way directional propaganda approaches to strategic communication with other countries' own public relations in the United States, this chapter is focused exclusively on the relational ties between U.S.-based persuasion initiatives in public diplomacy, traditionally a foreign affairs strategy in the public domain, and public relations, traditionally a non-governmental strategy in the private sector.

In a U.S. context, there has been a long history of promoting the concepts of truth and openness as they relate to organizational credibility, especially during the Cold War era (1945–1991). Before his appointment as director of the United States Information Agency, former CBS News legend Edward R. Murrow told the Senate Foreign Relations Committee that the aims of the public diplomacy agency he was about to lead were simple:

> We shall operate on the basis of truth. Being convinced that we are engaged in hot and implacable competition with communist forces around the world, we will not be content to counter their lies and distortions. We shall constantly reiterate our faith in freedom. (Whitton, 1963, p. 5)

In May 1963 when Murrow was requesting additional appropriations for the U.S. Information Agency, he reinforced to members of Congress that U.S. credibility in the world was directly linked to truth and transparency since they stood in contrast to the ideology and praxis of the Soviet Union:

> American traditions and the American ethic require us to be truthful, but the most important reason is that truth is the best propaganda and lies are the worst. To be persuasive we must be believable; to be believable we must be credible; to be credible we must be truthful. It is as simple as that. (Snow, 2013)

In today's post-September 11 environment where public diplomacy is featured prominently in information and image war contests, problems of American credibility remain, especially as they relate to the public perceptions of public relations practitioners. Callison (2004) notes that public relations problems stem not from the organizational management level but from the practitioner level. When labeled as public relations specialists or company spokespersons in news stories, practitioners are often perceived as holding vested interests in preserving the reputation of their client companies, which leads to a "perceived reporting bias" that causes doubt in the minds of the reader on questions of credibility and trustworthiness. As Callison explained:

> With all text held constant across message condition other than identification of the information source as either a public relations specialist or a more nondescript

company spokesperson, analyses revealed that participants were much more critical of the public relations source and the organization employing the source than
his or her unlabeled counterpart and accompanying organization. More precisely, the public relations source was perceived as less likely to be telling the truth,
more dishonest, and less trustworthy (p. 372).

In an effort to devise an answer to these questions of relational parallels
between public diplomacy and public relations, this chapter analyzes the way
public relations has been framed in the debate and discourse of failures of
U.S. public diplomacy since 9/11. Such writings have often centered their
criticism on the failure of strategies to persuade through attempts to "sell" a
positive image of the United States to the rest of the world. This selling strategy, a failure to "tell" America's story to the world (USIA's motto) in favor
of selling or hyping a positive image of America (Snow, 2010), is presented
as a one-way asymmetrical public relations approach, which leaves out an entire discourse and debate on public relations strategies that may prove useful
to a more complete public diplomacy toolbox. The often overlooked public
relations strategies, those which could help explain, clarify and possibly improve the image of public relations within the public diplomacy community,
include two-way symmetrical communication strategies, relationship building
and influence models, all of which will be presented as cases where strategic
communications efforts prevail over antiquated one-way asymmetrical public
relations campaigns.

The possibility for a smoother integration of public relations and public
diplomacy may rest with a critical assessment of the context, merits or ends to
which these communicative practices are applied (e.g., Snow, 2009; Weaver
et al., 2004, p. 2). The twain between the two fields of PR (public relations)
and PD (public diplomacy) may meet on firmer ground if one rejects the
strongly held belief that propaganda always operates counter to the public
interest while public relations necessarily works for the public interest. One
may have to recognize, as pointed out by Weaver et al. (2004) that since "Edward Bernays first introduced the term 'public relations counsel' in his 1923
publication, *Crystallizing Public Opinion*, public relations, although widely
practiced by corporations and governments alike, has monumentally failed
to establish itself of positive utility and benefit" (p. 2). To make these distant
cousins more aligned, public relations may need more PR to increase the
public's understanding of its role and function in society.

Certainly public relations is a tool for social and political power in some
hands, but can also become a tool for those who seek to challenge such
power. Two-way symmetrical communication in public relations theory and

practice—which includes public opinion research mixed with engagement in stakeholder dialogue to establish organizational objectives—suggests a distinction for public relations from propaganda. Given the explosive growth in the public relations profession (from 1992–2001 the industry grew by 220% and revenues at the top 50 firms grew by 12%) and the popularity of public relations study in university communication programs where it is becoming one of the fastest-growing majors, there is no question that the influence and involvement of public relations in public diplomacy strategies will increase (Wang, 2004). Wang cites Ketchum Public Relations chairman, David Drobis, who has said that relationship building is the public relations profession.

There is no question that public relations' cousin in the post-9/11 environment is public diplomacy. The question remains whether or not this is a naturally close relationship or one derived from external crisis circumstances that gave rise to such integration. After September 11, 2001, when outside terrorists attacked U.S. financial and military centers, the U.S. government immersed itself in a global information war to promote the interests, values, and image of the United States. Not since the Cold War had the government so engaged its persuasion industries (advertising, public relations) to combat stereotypes, target enemy populations, and single out particular regions like the Middle East for widespread broadcast information campaigns to overcome negative perceptions and attitudes toward the United States. Within the matrix of this new information war campaign, a number of terms were resurrected to describe the U.S. effort, most notably propaganda, public relations, and public diplomacy. Public relations received a universal definition almost forty years ago when a group of sixty-five public relations leaders took 472 definitions and came up with an eighty-eight-word sentence to describe what they do:

> Public relations is a distinctive management function which helps establish and maintain mutual lines of communications, understanding, acceptance, and cooperation between an organization and its publics; involves the management of problems or issues; helps management to keep informed on and responsive to public opinion; defines and emphasizes the responsibility of management to serve the public interest; helps management keep abreast of and effectively utilize change, serving as an early warning system to help anticipate trends; and uses research and sound and ethical communication techniques as its principal tools (Harlow, 1976, 36).

Similarly, in 1980, the Public Relations Society of America came up with two short definitions that have remained popular to this day: "Public relations helps an organization and its publics adapt mutually to each other" and

"Public relations is an organization's efforts to win cooperation of groups of people" (Seitel, 2001).

Embedded in the longer and shorter definitions of public relations is an emphasis on process, mutuality, and building credibility (e.g., Grunig, 1993, 2001; Signitzer and Coombs, 1992), all of which overlap with the goals and strategies of public diplomacy managers involved in the information wars since 9/11. The challenge is that to many laypersons public relations amounts at times to nothing more than "spin," where words, facts, and images are twisted in order to better the outcome of the client; a public diplomacy campaign to the Middle East may suffer the same characterization—as really nothing more than propaganda with a happy face. This may explain why public relations officials denounce the characterization of what they do as spinmeistering, while public diplomacy officials tend to eschew the word "propaganda" as a euphemism for what they do. Outside the United States, these delineations and defenses are not always accepted. In many circles, public relations, advertising, and marketing are used interchangeably with propaganda and do not carry the same negative, false assumptions.

How is what public relations professionals do that much different from the international persuasion campaigns we call public diplomacy? The difference may be just semantic, over which scholars and practitioners continue to debate. Former United States Information Agency (USIA)/ WorldNet TV Service Director Alvin Snyder said that during the Cold War "the U.S. government ran a full-service public relations organization, the largest in the world, about the size of the twenty biggest U.S. commercial PR firms combined," and "the biggest branch of this propaganda machine is called the United States Information Agency" (1995, xi). What Snyder identified as propaganda then is preferably referred to today as public diplomacy, defined by USIA's successors at the U.S. State Department as that which "seeks to promote the national interest and the national security of the United States through understanding, informing, and influencing foreign publics and broadening dialogue between American citizens and institutions and their counterparts abroad" (USIAAA, 2002). The U.S. State Department has an under secretary for Public Diplomacy and Public affairs, with former advertising executive Charlotte Beers serving in that position from just after 9/11 until the start of the war in Iraq in March 2003.

Like the term propaganda's tenuous tie to public diplomacy, the public relations industry continues to carry negative associations whenever it is associated only with one-way asymmetrical communication such as a publicist who generates favorable publicity and flacks for one's client. A case in point is the testimony of Joseph Duffey, who served as the final director of the USIA before its integration into the State Department. He told the U.S. Senate Foreign Relations Committee that American public diplomacy must always be distinguished from American public relations:

> Let me just say a word about public diplomacy. It is not public relations. It is not flacking for a Government agency or even flacking for America. It is trying to relate beyond government-to-government relationships the private institutions, the individuals, the long-term contacts, the accurate understanding, the full range of perceptions of America to the rest of the world, both to those who are friendly or inclined to be our partners or allies from one issue to another to those who are hostile, with some credibility or impartiality (Duffey, 1995).

What Joseph Duffey was describing is an ongoing definitional problem for public diplomacy in the twenty-first century: it is often defined, rightly or wrongly, in terms of what it is not. This volume is likely to help to overcome the difficulty that agency directors like Duffey have had in their understanding of what it is that public relations professionals and public diplomacy managers do in real world contexts and how often their communicative practices overlap.

What does distinguish public diplomacy from public relations is that while public relations is still primarily linked to corporate communications and business management models, public diplomacy theory and practice are linked to foreign affairs and the national interest. It sits squarely in the midst of national security objectives and promoting national security interests. Generally accepted definitions of public diplomacy include the following: (1) Public diplomacy seeks to promote the national interest of the United States through understanding, informing and influencing foreign audiences; and (2) Public diplomacy is as important to the national interest as military preparedness (Wallin, 2012).

The U.S. Information and Educational Exchange Act of 1948, also known as the Smith-Mundt Act, is one of the linchpins of U.S. public diplomacy. It has two-way communication strategies in its language:

> The objectives of this Act are to enable the Government of the United States to correct the misunderstandings about the United States in other countries, which constituted obstacles to peace, and to promote mutual understanding between the peoples of the United States and other countries, which is one of the essential foundations of peace.

One of its authors, Karl Mundt, clearly viewed the act more as a one-way informational counterpropaganda to Soviet propaganda. He wrote:

Immediately following the close of World War II when we realized that we were leaving a hot war only to enter a cold war, many of us recognized the importance of fashioning programs to meet effectively the non-military challenge confronting us. It was out of this era that the Smith-Mundt Act emerged. These Cold War weapons of words were needed because the United States faced "an alien force which seeks our total destruction" (Mundt, quoted in Glander, 2000, 61).

The other U.S. public diplomacy linchpin, the Fulbright-Hays Act of 1961, incorporated provisions of Senator J. William Fulbright's amendment in 1946 and the Smith-Mundt Act to establish a new educational and cultural exchange policy to increase mutual understanding between the people of the United States and the people of other countries by means of educational and cultural exchange; to strengthen the ties which unite us with other nations by demonstrating the educational and cultural interests, developments, and achievements of the people of the United States and other nations, and the contributions being made toward a peaceful and more fruitful life for people throughout the world; to promote international cooperation for educational and cultural advancement; and thus to assist in the development of friendly, sympathetic, and peaceful relations between the United States and the other countries of the world. (Smith-Mundt Act, quoted in Snow, 1998, 619) This view of mutual understanding and mutuality in public diplomacy would likely emphasize very different approaches and measures of effectiveness than one placing public diplomacy squarely in the midst of a national crisis.

Over the last fifty years, no single consensus has emerged to define the direction of U.S. public diplomacy aside from the goals and whims of the incumbent executive branch of the U.S. government. As Michael Holtzman (2003) observed in *The New York Times*:

United States public diplomacy is neither public nor diplomatic. First, the government—not the broader American public—has been the main messenger to a world that is mightily suspicious of it. Further, the State Department, which oversees most efforts, seems to view public diplomacy not as a dialogue but as a one-sided exercise...America speaking to the world.

Holtzman's criticism reflects that same criticism surrounding the public relations school that says the best public relations is the least visible. Holtzman asserts that U.S. public diplomacy has failed because it has not adhered to the school of thought advanced at by both Senator J. William Fulbright and Edward R. Murrow. What I have referred to as both "rethinking public diplomacy" and "public diplomacy as if publics mattered," (Snow, 2006, 2009, 2010) suggests a far wider array of participants, practitioners, and perspectives than just those seen or heard in the armed forces or Foreign Service or inside the Washington beltway. As Murrow himself defined the field fifty years ago when serving as director of the USIA in 1963:

> Public diplomacy differs from traditional diplomacy in that it involves interaction not only with governments but primarily with non-governmental individuals and organizations. Furthermore, public diplomacy activities often present many differing views represented by private American individuals and organizations in addition to official government views.

Murrow's definition suggests that public diplomacy in practice is as much at home in corporate boardrooms, pop concerts, and peace rallies as it is inside the halls of Congress. Nevertheless, U.S. public diplomacy today is still often assumed to be linked with traditional diplomatic goals of national governments. As Christopher Ross, former U.S. State Department special coordinator for public diplomacy and public affairs, writes:

> The practitioners of traditional diplomacy engage the representatives of foreign governments in order to advance the national interests articulated in their own government's strategic goals in international affairs. Public diplomacy, by contrast, engages carefully targeted sectors of foreign publics in order to develop support for those same strategic goals (2002, 75).

Whenever public diplomacy definitions are overtly linked to official outcomes of national governments (e.g., in the Bush Administration's War on Terror), this tends to connote a more negative interpretation linked to propaganda outcomes. In December 2004, the U.S.-based science and technology firm Battelle released a list of the top ten innovations for the war on terror. One innovation forecast to emerge in the following decade (2005–2014) was twenty-first-century public diplomacy that requires nontechnical skills development in intercultural communication and advanced strategic communication. Battelle's team of experts included retired generals from the U.S. Army, Air Force, and Marine Corps as well as Ohio State University faculty. The team linked public diplomacy innovations directly to the U.S.-led War on Terror as well as modern public relations:

> The war against terrorism is, in part, a war with extremists whose culture, world view, and values conflict with those of the West. There are economic, religious, political, and ideological tensions between the Middle East and the West. As such, any discussion of tools for combating terrorism must include deploying mass communication to break down these barriers. The first step will be gaining a fuller understanding of opposing cultures and values so that the United States and its allies can develop more effective strategies to prevent terrorism. America needs to project a more balanced image of Western culture through strategic, positive communication. This could be achieved by communicating the Western message through targeted use of mass media, developing a next-generation Voice

of America approach, perhaps supported with distribution of inexpensive, dispos-
able TVs. (Battelle, 2004)

While acknowledging the obvious strains in policy and projected images
between the Middle East and the West, this definition of twenty-first-century
public diplomacy offers primarily an asymmetric information model of public
relations that seeks to break down barriers in the Middle East to a Western
worldview, message, and values. Western tension with the Middle East is caus-
ally linked to combating terrorism and overcoming oppositional cultures and
values, but not linked to specific foreign policy disagreements with the United States. Gaining understanding of another culture is concerned primarily
with comprehension in order to combat terrorism, not with building mutual
understanding that may improve the foreign relations of the United States, its
people, and its government with other nations and peoples.

The Battelle definition of twenty-first-century public diplomacy is an accepted dimension of public diplomacy, one identified in U.S. history as the
tough-minded, Cold War–centric government information model whereby
public diplomacy is defined as "the way in which both government and private individuals and groups influence directly or indirectly those public attitudes and opinions which bear directly on another government's foreign
policy decisions" (Signitzer & Coombs, 1992, 138). The Battelle version belongs to the political information side of public diplomacy that advocates the
U.S. case in particular and the Western civilization model in general. Within
this school of thought, it is most important that international publics gain a
better understanding of the United States and its culture, values, and institutions, primarily for securing U.S. foreign policy ends and defending national
security objectives.

The best public diplomacy, like the best public relations, uses multifaceted approaches to global communication, including an intercultural communication dimension of public diplomacy identified earlier, to foster "mutual
understanding between the people of the United States and the people of
other countries" as advocated in the Fulbright-Hays Act. In this framework,
cultural comprehension is also sought, but not primarily for unilateral advantage and outcome (which by definition stresses fast media such as radio and
television). Rather, long-term strategies for mutual benefit and mutual trust
are emphasized, including slower media such as films, exhibitions, and educational and cultural exchanges (e.g., Fulbright scholars, International Visitors
Leadership Program).

As noted earlier, both public relations and public diplomacy can and do
emphasize relationship-building practices. It very much depends on the intended outcome of the information campaign whether or not the relationship

is tilted more to the sponsoring organization's needs or to both the sponsor and the intended recipient. A widely accepted definition of international public relations is "the planned and organized effort of a company, institution, or government to establish mutually beneficial relations with the publics of other nations" (Wilcox, 1989, 395). This definition allows for two-way symmetric tactics of persuasion to be included in communication outcomes.

Going forward, the intercultural communication dimension in public diplomacy and public relations should be distinguished from the more tough-minded battlefield tactics associated with counterterrorism. The calamitous events of 9/11 centered U.S. public diplomacy and public relations strategies around strategic communication efforts to combat terrorism as defined by and advocated primarily by the U.S. government generally, and the White House in particular. These government efforts were criticized by the Defense Science Board (2004), a federal task force comprised of an independent group of both academic and private sector advisers that reports directly to the secretary of defense:

> We must understand that the United States is engaged in a generational and global struggle about ideas, not a war between the West and Islam....This approach will build on in-depth knowledge of other cultures and factors that motivate human behavior. It will adapt techniques of skillful political campaigning, even as it avoids slogans, quick fixes, and mindsets of winners and losers. It will search out credible messengers and create message authority. It will seek to persuade within news cycles, weeks, and months. It will engage in a respectful dialogue of ideas that begins with listening and assumes decades of sustained effort. (Defense Science Board 2004, 2)

The Defense Science Board report concluded that U.S. credibility in the Middle East was at an all-time low and that American intervention in the Muslim world has increased the power and reputation of the most radical Islamists. These Islamists, despite President Bush's claims, do not "hate our freedoms" or hate "freedom-loving peoples" but rather hate very specific policies, namely, what they perceive as uncritical, imbalanced support for Israel over Palestinian sovereignty and support for tyrannical regimes such as those in Egypt, Saudi Arabia, Jordan, and Pakistan, all of which receive varying levels of U.S. military and economic aid.

Mark Leonard (Leonard et al., 2002, 8) of the London-based Foreign Policy Centre identifies three dimensions of public diplomacy: (1) news management; (2) strategic communications; and (3) relationship-building. These three dimensions may apply to domestic, bilateral, and global public diplomacy efforts. All three have dimensions that overlap with what public relations and public diplomacy officials do at varying times and intensities.

News management is cited as the first dimension of public diplomacy and involves management of day-to-day communication issues. News management or media relation is also cited as the most common strategy of effective public relations. Examples include the White House Office of Global Communications or the Coalition Information Centers (CICs) during the Afghanistan war period of 2001 and 2002. News management is reactive in minutes and hours and is mostly handled by traditional diplomacy institutions. In wartime, this dimension may operate at multiple levels, as pointed out by General Colin Powell during Operation Desert Storm:

> Remember when you are out there on television, communicating instantaneously around the world, we're talking to five audiences. One, the reporters who ask the question—important audience. Second audience, the American people who are watching. The third audience, 170 capitals who may have an interest in what the subject is. Fourth, you are talking to your enemy. It was a unique situation to know that your enemy was getting the clearest indication of your intentions by watching you on television at the same time you were giving that message. And fifth, you are talking to the troops. Their lives are on the line. (Leonard et al., 2002, pp. 12–13)

A more recent term that unites public diplomacy and public relations is strategic communications, which refers to the totality of communications used to promote positive messages about the country—including those from government, business, tourism, finance sectors, and cultural institutions. While news management is more political and military in emphasis and has a reactive stance, strategic communications operates more in an economic realm and is proactive in process and purpose. All countries are interested in having a global competitive advantage that separates them from their competition. A country's reputation and national identify affect the bottom line where trading partners will buy services and goods. Strategic communications requires proactive campaigns that are refined and developed over weeks and months and those create a stake or buy-in for all public diplomacy institutions. Examples include the Shared Values Campaign of Charlotte Beers's tenure that used ninety-second advertisements called "mini-documentaries" of five Muslim Americans in an attempt to open dialogue with the Muslim world and Muslims in the United States. Strategic communications seems to be old wine in new bottles and is more often associated today with the public affairs and information operations at the Pentagon (Brooks, 2012).

The best public relations in the service of good public diplomacy will enhance or detract from a country's reputation. No country can get its way politically, economically or culturally unless it is favorably perceived in the global environment. Countries are wise to play upon their strengths: The national image for Germany to play up might be brand quality and luxury, as signified in BMW and Mercedes. Great Britain is known for tradition, which helps heritage brands that stress the past. Norway, home to the Nobel Peace Prize, has a national reputation in international mediation, which signals to countries involved in civil conflict that it can be a neutral and honest broker.

The Pew Global Attitudes Surveys that have measured attitudes toward the United States since 2001 show that while many foreign publics condemn U.S. government action in the world, there is strong support for U.S. values of technical expertise, entrepreneurialism, and openness. While these value traits are indeed positive, they may not be effective if the values are not associated with the sponsoring country due to an overarching negative image or brand—that of the world's sole military, economic, and cultural superpower. This is why relationship-building among nongovernmental actors is the most long term of the three dimensions of public diplomacy and the one most oriented toward mutuality and exchange among peers and equal partners. Further, relationship-building is by far the most closely aligned dimension of public diplomacy associated with public relations.

A two-way symmetric model of public diplomacy is characterized by international exchanges, cultural diplomacy, international conferences and seminars, and face-to-face and virtual networks. Examples include the International Visitor Leadership Program (IVLP) and Fulbright exchange programs in the United States, the Japan Exchange and Teaching (JET) program in Japan, Sister Cities International, Rotary International, and exchange programs of the British Council.

Relationship-building in public diplomacy places an emphasis on engaging populations rather than winning arguments or selling a brand. Engaging requires that your public diplomacy strategy increase contact and interaction impacts that enhance others' appreciation for one's country in the long term. This includes strengthening educational, scientific, and sports ties and increasing tourism, international study, trade, and support for your values. Relationship-building will not be measured in terms of weeks or months but years. This dimension is the most public-targeted and public-involved of the three dimensions. As Mark Leonard writes:

> Public diplomacy is about building relationships: understanding the needs of other countries, cultures and peoples; communicating our points of view; correcting misperceptions; looking for areas we can find in common cause. The difference between public and traditional diplomacy is that public diplomacy involves a much broader group of people on both sides, and a broader set of interests that go beyond those of the government of the day. Public diplomacy

is based on the premise that the image and reputation of a country are public goods which can create an enabling or a disabling environment for individual transactions. (Leonard et al., 2002, pp. 8–9)

Signitzer and Coombs note a distinction in public diplomacy between the so-called tough-minded who "hold that the purpose of public diplomacy is to exert an influence on attitudes of foreign audiences using persuasion and 'propaganda' and the 'tender-minded' school, which 'argues that information and cultural programs must bypass current foreign policy goals to concentrate on the highest long-range national objectives.' The goal is to create a climate of mutual understanding" (Signitzer & Coombs, 1992, 140). Neither school of thought can stand entirely on its own; they must be synthesized. A further breakdown from tough and tender is what practitioners of public diplomacy engage in on two tracks: political communication, is administered by a section of the foreign ministry, embassy, or (in the U.S. context) State Department; and cultural communication, which may be administered not only by a cultural section of the foreign ministry, embassy, or State Department but also by quasi-governmental or nongovernmental bodies (e.g., the British Council, Sister Cities International, or National Council of International Visitors). Signitzer and Coombs also distinguish between two types of cultural communication: cultural diplomacy, which aims to present a favorable national image abroad; and cultural relations, which have mutual information exchange and no unilateral objective in mind, just "an honest picture of each country rather than a beautified one" (1992, 140).

U.S. foreign policy makers are frequently criticized for being intransigent on core policies, for example, unfailing support for Israel, with no evidence that dialogue about policy is even possible. While the U.S. policy of supporting Israel is not going to change, there is certainly room for U.S. policy makers to show more sympathy for Palestinian deaths as often as the United States condemns the killing of Israelis. The avenues by which goodwill and dialogue can be strengthened are through citizen diplomacy and international exchanges. While the ultimate purpose of official U.S. public diplomacy and the government marketing campaign to foreign publics is to present U.S. foreign policy and national security objectives in the best light, an important secondary source for America's public diplomacy campaign is citizen diplomacy. This calls on the American public to play its part and not watch foreign policy making from the sidelines. For too long, and perhaps in part due to our incredible comparative advantage in communications technology, the United States has emphasized amplification over active listening, telling America's story to the world over promoting international dialogue. Anti-Americanism and general ill will toward the United States has been driven by perceptions that the United States is quick to talk and explain but last to listen or understand. For a change, it wouldn't take much for the United States to listen first and talk second. It certainly wouldn't make things worse if we tried harder to be citizen-diplomats in our relations with our overseas counterparts.

There is so much we still don't know, and we need to unite partnerships among government, the private sector, and universities to study social influence, changes in mindsets, how to teach tolerance and mutual respect, and methodologies that will measure current public diplomacy programs in an effort to find best practices. We could start by undertaking efforts to identify the best public diplomacy and public relations practices used by other countries. Some of the world's leaders in so-called soft power diplomacy (as opposed to hard power military domination) include the Scandinavian countries such as Denmark and Norway, as well as the Netherlands, Japan, and the United Kingdom.

Whether or not we choose to call it public diplomacy or public relations campaigns, to have a lasting and effective public diplomacy that places mutual understanding at its core, the United States must consider its legacy of strategies of truth. The short-lived and ill-conceived Office of Strategic Influence (OSI) was a here-today, gone-tomorrow debacle in 2002, at least in the public's mind, but there remains plenty of concern that some within the Department of Defense would just as soon continue to use such strategies of deception under the "whatever works" rubric. It is one thing to use deception against the enemy, but the OSI sought to use deception to plant false stories in reputable overseas news markets. Any approach based on falsehoods and deception will not have long-lasting, enduring outcomes but only short-term, tactical advantages.

The more transparent and genuine U.S. public diplomacy strategies are, the better off long-term strategic and mutual interests will be, both from government and public perspectives. The United States learned from the Soviets and others that psychological operations based on falsehoods can be effective, but in the long run are likely to damage a country's credibility in the eyes of the world. John Arquilla and David Ronfeldt argue that "an approach based on falsehoods will more likely have only short-term, or tactical effects—not enduring strategic ones. Therefore, truth must be the polestar of American strategic public diplomacy, and uses of information as 'propaganda' must be eschewed" (1999, 65). Practitioners of public relations and public diplomacy may wish to take heed of this last recommendation as they seek to adopt and use each other's strategies and tools in their efforts to build influence, trust, and credibility among their international customers, clients, and publics.

## *Bibliography*

Arquilla, J., & Ronfeldt, D. (1999). *The emergence of Noopolitik: Toward an American information strategy.* Santa Monica, CA: Rand.

Barrett, E. W. (1955). *Truth is our weapon.* New York: Funk & Wagnalls.

Battelle. (2004). Battelle panel's top ten innovations for the war on terror headed by technology advances to support better intelligence, decision-making: Scientists, academicians also call for non-technical advance-communication to foster cultural understanding. May 10. Retrieved June 7, 2005, from http://www.battelle.org/news/04/5-1004TopTenTerrorInnova.stm

Bernays, E. L. (1928). *Propaganda.* New York: Liveright.

———. (1929). *Crystallizing Public Opinion.* New York: Liveright.

Brooks, R. (2012). Confessions of a strategic communicator: Tales from inside the Pentagon's message machine. *Foreign Policy.* December 6.

Callison, C. (2001). Do PR practitioners have a PR problem?: The effect of associating a source with public relations and client-negative news on audience perception of credibility. *Journal of Public Relations Research, 13,* 219–234.

———. (2004). The good, the bad and the ugly: Perceptions of public relations practitioners. *Journal of Public Relations Research, 16,* 4, 371–389.

Coombs, P. H. (1964). *The fourth dimension of foreign policy: Education and cultural affairs.* New York: Harper and Row.

Defense Science Board. 2004. Report of the Defense Science Board Task Force on Strategic Communication. September. Washington, DC: Office of the Under Secretary of Defense for Acquisition, Technology, and Logistics. Available at http://www.acq.osd.mil/dsb/reports/2004-09-Strategic Communication.pdf (accessed June 8, 2005).

Duffey, J. 1995. Comments before the U.S. Senate Committee on Foreign Relations, Subcommittee on International Operations. Reorganization and revitalization of America's foreign affairs institution. Senate Hearing 104–215. 104th Congress, 1st session. March 23.

Gilboa, E. (2008). Searching for a theory of public diplomacy. *The ANNALS of the American Academy of Political and Social Science, 616*(1), 55–77.

Glander, T. (2000). *Origins of mass communications research during the American Cold War: Educational effects and contemporary implications.* Mahwah, NJ: Lawrence Erlbaum Associates.

Government Accountability Office (2006). U.S. Public Diplomacy: State Department Efforts Lack Certain Communication Elements and Face Persistent Challenges. GAO-06-707T.

Grunig, J. E. (1993). Public relations and international affairs: Effects, ethics and responsibility. *Journal of International Affairs, 47,* 1, 138–162.

———. (2001). Two-way symmetrical public relations: Past, present and future. In R. L. Heath, (Ed). *Handbook of public relations* (pp. 11–32), Thousand Oaks, CA: Sage.

Harlow, R. F. (1976). Building a public relations definition. Public Relations Review, 4, 2, 34–42.

Holtzman, M. (2003). Washington's sour sales pitch. *The New York Times.* October 4.

Johnson, M. A. (2005). Five decades of Mexican public relations in the United States: From propaganda to strategic counsel. *Public Relations Review, 31,* 11–20.

Kruckeberg, D. & Vujnovic, M. (2005). Public relations, not propaganda, for US public diplomacy in a post-9/11 world: Challenges and opportunities. *Journal of Communication Management, 9*, 4, 296–304.

Kunczik, M. (1997). *Images of nations and international public relations.* Mahwah, NJ: Lawrence Erlbaum Associates.

Lasswell, H. D. (1927) *Propaganda technique in the world war.* Gloucester, MA: Peter Smith.

Leonard, M., Stead, C. & Smewing, C. (2002). Public Diplomacy. London: Foreign Policy Centre.

L'Etang, J. (1997) Public relations and the rhetorical dilemma: Legitimate 'perspectives', persuasion, or pandering? *Australian Journal of Communication, 24*, 2, 33–53.

Lippmann, W. (1922). *Public opinion.* New York: Harcourt, Brace.

Manheim, J. B. (1994). *Strategic public diplomacy and American foreign policy: The evolution of influence.* New York: Oxford University Press.

Manheim, J. B., & Albritton, R. B. (1984). Changing national images: International public relations and media agenda setting. *The American Political Science Review, 78*, 641–657.

Murrow, E.R. (1961). Speech at the Public Relations Society of America, Houston, Texas, November 16. Folder ERM, "Speeches, 1961," Box 20, E1069, RG306, National Archives.

National Credibility Index, The. (1999). Retrieved December 23, 2012, from http://www.prsa.org/searchresults/view/2d-0007/0/national_credibility_index_new_survey_measures_who

O'Brien, T. L. (2005). Spinning Frenzy: PR's Bad Press. *The New York Times,* February 13.

Pew Global Attitudes Project. (2003). Anti-Americanism: Causes and Characteristics. December 10. Washington, D.C.: Pew Research Center. Retrieved December 3, 2012 from http://www.pewglobal.org/2003/12/10/anti-americanism-causes-and-characteristics/

Pratkanis, A., & Aronson, E. (1992). *Age of propaganda.* New York: W. H. Freeman & Co.

Public Relations Society of America. (1999). *National Credibility Index: New Survey Measures Who The Public Believes On Major Issues.* New York.

Ross, Christopher. (2002). Public diplomacy comes of age. *Washington Quarterly, 25*, 2, 75–83.

Seitel, F. (2001). *The practice of public relations.* 8th Edition. Upper Saddle River, NJ: Prentice-Hall.

Signitzer, B. H., and Coombs, T. (1992). Public relations and public diplomacy: Conceptual convergences. *Public Relations Review*, 18, 2, 137–47.

Signitzer, B., & Wasmer, C. (2006). Public diplomacy: A specific government public relations function. In C. H. Botan & V. Hazelton, (Eds.), *Public relations theory II* (pp. 435–464). Mahwah, NJ: Lawrence Erlbaum Associates.

Snow, N. (1998). The Smith-Mundt Act of 1948. *Peace Review 10*, 4, 619–24.

———. (2006). *The arrogance of American power: What U.S. leaders are doing wrong and why it's our duty to dissent.* Lanham, MD: Rowman & Littlefield.

———. (2008). International Exchanges and the U.S. Image. *The ANNALS of the American Academy of Political and Social Science, 616*, 198–222. doi: 10.1177/0002716207311864

————. (2009). Rethinking public diplomacy. In N. Snow & P. M. Taylor (Eds.), *Routledge handbook of public diplomacy* (pp. 3–11). New York: Routledge.

————. (2010). *Propaganda, Inc.: Selling America's culture to the world*. Third Edition. New York: Seven Stories Press.

————. (2013). *Truth is the best propaganda: Edward R. Murrow's speeches in the Kennedy years*. McLean, VA: Miniver Press.

Snyder, A. A. (1995). *Warriors of disinformation: American propaganda, Soviet lies, and the winning of the Cold War*. New York: Arcade.

Stauber, J. & Rampton, S. (1995). *Toxic sludge is good for you! Lies, damn lies, and the public relations industry*. Monroe, ME: Common Courage Press.

————. (2013). *Truth is the best propaganda: Edward R. Murrow's speeches in the Kennedy years*. McLean, VA: Miniver Press.

Taylor, M. & Kent, M. L. (2006). Nation-building: Public relations theory and practice. In V. Hazelton, & C. H. Botan (Eds.), Public Relations Theory II (pp. 341–360). Hillsdale, NJ: Lawrence Erlbaum Associates.

Toth, E. L. (2006). Building public affairs theory. In C. H. Botan & V. Hazelton, (Eds.), Public relations theory II (pp. 499–522).

U.S. General Accounting Office. (2006). Staffing and foreign language shortfalls persist despite initiatives to address gaps. Washington, DC, Report 06–894.

U.S. Information Agency Alumni Association. 2002. What is public diplomacy? Retrieved June 7, 2005 from http://www.publicdiplomacy.org/1.htm

Wallin, M. (2012). The new public diplomacy imperative: America's vital need to communicate strategically. White Paper. American Security Project, Washington, DC.

Wang, J. (2004). "Building a Winning Public Relations Education Program: Developing the Next Generation of PR Professionals. Paper presented at the International Communication Association 54th Annual Conference. New Orleans, LA.

Wang, Z., & Chang, T-K. (2004). Strategic public diplomacy and local press: How a high-profile "head-of-state" visit was covered in America's heartland. *Public Relations Review, 30*, 1, 11–24.

Weaver, C. K, Motion, J. & Roper, J. (2004). Truth, power and public interest: A critical theorising of propaganda and public relations. Paper presented at the International Communication Association 54th Annual Conference. New Orleans, LA.

Whitton, J. B. (1963). *Propaganda and the Cold War: A Princeton University symposium*. Washington, DC: Public Affairs Press.

Wilcox, D. L., Ault, P. H. & Agee, W. K. (1989). *Public relations: Strategies and tactics*. Second edition. New York: Harper and Row.

Yun, S. H. (2006). Toward public relations theory-based study of public diplomacy: Testing the applicability of the excellence study. *Journal of Public Relations Research, 18*, 287–312.

# The Functions of International Public Relations and Public Diplomacy

# 6. *Application of Relationship Management to Public Diplomacy*

Eyun-Jung Ki

The advancement of communication technologies has helped the world become more united than ever before. Today, approximately one third of organizations in the United States deal with global stakeholders (Wilcox & Cameron, 2012). About one third of the public relations fees billed by large public relations firms in the US are collected from other countries (Wilcox & Cameron, 2012). Thanks to communication technologies, global publics participate more actively in communication with organizations as well as foreign governments.

This global village fostered by communication technologies has inspired the need to build and cultivate relationships between organizations or governments and their respective publics. For instance, the Obama administration stated that currently, it is vital that America pursues a public diplomacy policy "that connects with, listens to, and builds upon long-term relationships with key stakeholders" (Biden, 2009, p. 4). This goal represents the crossroads of public relations, in particular where relationship management and public diplomacy meet.

Anticipating the benefits of overlaps between public relations and public diplomacy, several scholars have proposed the idea of convergence of these two domains. For example, Signitzer and Coombs (1992) encouraged public relations scholars to undertake empirical research on public diplomacy, drawing upon public relations theories. Similarly, L'Etang (2008) specified that public relations is an area of diplomacy responsible for managing international communications and media relations in order to improve relationships between a nation-state and its foreign publics. He further noted that diplomacy (political, economic, information, cultural) represents strategic public relations and that skills of diplomacy are essential for effective public relations

(L'Etang, 2008). Moreover, in the integrated public diplomacy model, Golan (2013) identifies long-term relational public diplomacy as one of three essential elements. Responding to these calls for convergence, this chapter intends to fill the theoretical gap in public diplomacy research by proposing the application of a framework which links relationship outcomes, attitudes, and behaviors to the context of public diplomacy.

## Theoretical Background

### Definitions of Public Diplomacy and Public Relations

Public diplomacy has typically been rooted and primarily researched in the area of international relations, which has categorized diplomacy into two types—traditional diplomacy and public diplomacy. *Traditional diplomacy* deals with "conducting negotiations between governments" (Deutsch, 1996, p. 81). This type of diplomacy deals with government-to-government negotiations or nation-to-nation negotiations, which are often performed by government leaders and appointed diplomats, such as ambassadors.

The other type, *public diplomacy*, also referred to as *media diplomacy* or *cultural diplomacy*, represents a contemporary form of diplomacy. Public diplomacy is a term used to describe "the efforts by nations to win support and a favorable image among the general public of other countries, usually by way of news management and carefully planned initiatives designed to foster positive impressions" (McQuail, 2010, p. 568). The term is also associated with being "concerned with the management of *relations* between states and other actors[1]" (Barston, 1997, p. 1). A majority of literature in public diplomacy demonstrated that all forms of diplomacy are concerned with and restricted to "the *relationships* [emphasis added] among the world's national governments" (Goldstein, 1994, p. 1). As demonstrated through popular definitions and the literature of public diplomacy, contemporary diplomacy highlights the importance of *relationships*.

Like the scholarship of diplomacy, contemporary public relations research has also highlighted the key concept of *relationships*. A widely adopted definition of public relations reflects this paradigm. Public relations is defined as "the management function that establishes and maintains mutually beneficial relationships between an organization and the publics on whom its success or failure depends" (Cutlip, Center, & Broom, 1994, p. 2). Focusing on relationship management would thus render public relations a more valuable practice (J. E. Grunig & Hunt, 1984).

## Nexus of Public Relations and Public Diplomacy

Emphasizing the importance of relationships in both public relations and public diplomacy, a number of scholars (Fitzpatrick, 2007; L'Etang, 2008; Signitzer, 2008; Signitzer & Coombs, 1992; Signitzer & Wamser, 2006) have compared these two domains and discussed their common grounds in terms of practice and goals.[2] First, both areas are viewed in terms of their strategic communicative functions of an organization or a nation [or a state] (Macnamara, 2012; Signitzer & Wamser, 2006). Professionals in both fields actively distribute information, advocate with a view toward persuasion, and cultivate relationships (Macnamara, 2012). Signitzer and Wamser (2006) described public diplomacy as "a specific governmental public relations function" (p. 435).

Second, the individuals or groups that are dealt with in these two domains represent another commonality in public relations and public diplomacy. In public relations, the terms *publics* or *stakeholders* are used to refer to the group (Hon & Grunig, 1999), while public diplomacy typically uses the terms *political actors* or *social collectives* to refer to these groups (Habermas, 2006). Third, the role of professionals in both these domains is boundary-spanning, because they serve as liaisons between the organization [nation or state] and the outside groups and individuals (J. E. Grunig & Hunt, 1984; L'Etang, 1996).

Keeping in mind the similarities of these two domains, a few scholars in public relations applied the concept of new public diplomacy to various public relations theories including Excellence Theory and Relationship Management (Fitzpatrick, 2007; L'Etang, 1996, 2008; Signitzer & Wamser, 2006; Yun, 2006). For example, Yun (2006) empirically tested the applicability of Excellence Theory to public diplomacy theory. Excellence Theory is a normative theory in public relations that explains the factors that make public relations most effective within an organization. Yun (2006) proved that public relations frameworks are applicable to conceptualizing and measuring behaviors and excellence in public diplomacy. The framework would be more applicable to new public diplomacy, as it is normative and demonstrates ideal approaches to modern public diplomacy.

Signitzer and Wamser (2006) applied J. E. Grunig and Hunt's (1984) model of the public relations function in an organization to public diplomacy. The model outlined the role and necessity of public relations department in an organization as a boundary-spanner between top management and its strategic publics who have reciprocal consequences. They demonstrated that this model could be useful for solving public diplomacy problems, because a public diplomacy department fulfills the same function as a public relations department does for an organization.

Macnamara (2012) analyzed the two areas of public diplomacy and public relations according to Excellence Theory, relationship theory, dialogic theory, strategic communication theory, and postmodern theory. His analysis revealed the six commonalities of the two fields as follows: 1) recognize a need to understand the environment (gained through intelligence, monitoring environmental scanning, etc.), 2) viewed as strategic communication, 3) prioritize relationship cultivation, 4) see dialogue as a core activity, 5) deal with a diversity of interests and sometimes conflicts, and 6) deal with multiple groups of "political actors," "social collectives," "publics," and "stakeholders," including the government and organizations (p. 318). Macnamara urged that the field of public relations should accept more diverse concepts and principles, including ethical public diplomacy and new diplomacy (corporate or organizational diplomacy) in order to develop new perspectives and practices rather than making territorial claims.

Echoing several public diplomacy studies, Golan (2013) highlights the importance of relationship in his integrated public diplomacy model. The integrated public diplomacy model illustrates a structure consisting of three components of public diplomacy—1) "short- to medium-term mediated public diplomacy," 2) "the medium- to long-term nation building and country reputation," and 3) "the long-term relational public diplomacy" (p. 2). He emphasizes that each of the three components in this model is differentiated according to the stakeholder engagement level, but governments are more likely to research long-term engagement outcomes through the integration of all three components.

In a similar vein, by recognizing that the public relations field involves both non-profit and for-profit organizations as well as government, Fitzpatrick (2007) claimed that application of relationship management theory to public diplomacy could help to advance the scholarship and practice of public diplomacy for several reasons. First, the application of relational perspective delineates a conceptual grounding of public diplomacy. Second, as relational theory represents a holistic approach, applying the theory offers a fundamental framework for analyzing the strategic dimensions of public diplomacy. Third, adopting management perspectives acknowledges the importance of diplomatic behaviors and supports the communication practices of public diplomatic professionals. Finally, applying a relational theory would enhance contemporary public diplomacy by transitioning from a normative to a more realistic perspective.

In the scholarship of public relations, quality relationships with publics were found to yield more tangible outcomes for organizations, such as supportive attitudes and behaviors toward those organizations (L. A. Grunig, Grunig, & Dozier, 2002; Ledingham, 2003). Although the aforementioned scholars attempted to apply the relational perspective to public diplomacy, they have not stretched their perspective enough to evaluate the effects of relationship on more tangible outcomes of relationship. Therefore, this chapter aims to apply a theoretical framework of relationship management for public diplomacy and expand it by linking relationship outcomes, attitudes, and behaviors.

## A Theoretical Framework of Relationship Management for Public Diplomacy

Relationship management, a primary program of research in public relations has developed a conceptual and measurement framework to characterize and measure public relations practices over the past two decades. Ferguson (1984) initiated the idea that relationships between an organization and its strategic publics should act as the central unit of analysis for public relations scholarship and its practice. Since then, numerous scholars have embraced this new direction and made the discipline more relationship focused (Broom, Casey, & Ritchey, 2000; Bruning & Ledingham, 1999, 2000; Coombs, 2000; Cutlip et al., 1994; Ferguson, 1984; J. E. Grunig & Huang, 2000; Ki & Hon, 2007a; Ledingham, 2003; Wilson, 2001). Ledingham (2003) evidenced that relationship management is a general theory in public relations that provides a valuable framework for the study, instruction, and practice of public relations.

Greater numbers of public diplomacy scholars have also identified the importance of relationship building. Specifically, Riordan (2003) stated that public diplomacy has transformed its focus from mere communication with foreign people into managing networks of relationships. Nye (2004) identified the three key dimensions of public diplomacy as 1) daily communication to explain the context of foreign policy decisions, 2) strategic communication involving symbolic events and branding activities to advance specific government policies, and 3) relationship-building with key individuals over the course of many years.

As such, both fields have emphasized relationships, and the application of a theoretical framework of relationship management from a public relations perspective to the public diplomacy domain would benefit the scholarship and practice in both fields.

## Relationship Perspective

Prior to introducing relationship dimensions, it is necessary to define the concept of a relationship. Scholars have differed slightly in their definitions of the term relationship. For example, Ledingham and Bruning (1998a) defined organization-public relationships as "the state which exists between an organization and its key publics, in which the actions of either can impact the economic, social, cultural or political well being of the other" (p. 63). Broom et al. (2000) conceptualized them as follows:

> Organization-public relationships are represented by the patterns of interaction, transaction, exchange, and linkage between an organization and its publics. These relationships have properties that are distinct from the identities, attributes, and perceptions of the individuals and social collectivities in the relationships. Though dynamic in nature, organization-public relationships can be described at a single point in time and tracked over time. (p. 18).

These definitions highlight interactions between and impacts on the parties involved in the relationship.

Relationship dimensions determine the state or characteristics of a relationship. Because the concept of a relationship is intangible and abstract, public relations scholars have endeavored to quantify it (Hon & Grunig, 1999; Huang, 2001a; Jo, 2006; Ki & Hon, 2007b; Kim, 2001; Ledingham & Bruning, 1998b). In the scholarship, approximately two dozen relationship dimensions have been developed (Ki & Shin, 2006). Two groups of these dimensions are worth discussing. Ledingham and Bruning (1998b) developed a relationship dimension including trust, openness, involvement, investment, and commitment. They evidenced that these dimensions could act as predictors of a public's perceptions of overall satisfaction with an organization as well as their behaviors toward that organization (Ledingham & Bruning, 1998b). They also categorized organization-public relationships as either professional, personal, and community relationships (Ledingham & Bruning, 1998b).

Hon and J. E. Grunig (1999) also developed another widely used dimension that includes control mutuality, satisfaction, trust, and commitment. In the discipline, the four relationship dimensions have served as the fundamental measure of relationship status and have proven to be reliable and valid across studies (Huang, 2001a; Jo, 2006; Ki & Hon, 2007b; Kim, 2001). Furthermore, scholars have found three dimensions—satisfaction, trust, and commitment—to be essential relationship indicators in cross-cultural settings (Huang, 2001a; Jo, 2006). Jo (2006) described these three dimensions as a global measure. A brief description of each dimension and its applicability to public diplomacy follows below.

*Control mutuality.* This dimension is related to the degree of control in the decision making process and the extent to which the opinion of each party is reflected in the final decision (Hon & Grunig, 1999). Scholars have noted that some imbalance of power may exist, but in a well-established relationship, the parties involved need to feel some degree of control over one another (Hon & Grunig, 1999). Relational cultivation strategies of access, positivity, shared tasks and assurances were found to predict control mutuality (Ki & Hon, 2009).

In public diplomacy literature, *mutuality* (Rose & Wadham-Smith, 2004), *trust-building* (Leonard, Small, & Rose, 2005), and *power balance* (Fry, Goldstein, & Langhome, 2004) are echoed by control mutuality. In the new public diplomacy, power balance, a concept similar to control mutuality, is defined as "the situation in international relations when there is stability between competing forces" (Fry et al., 2004). In an ideal situation, power balance prevents any party (state or nation) from being strong enough to force its will upon the rest (Waltz, 1979). In reality, however, power imbalance often naturally exists.

Control mutuality or power balance could act as a key dimension in the context of public diplomacy for a couple of reasons. First, this dimension was found to be important in relationships with high political involvement (Huang, 2001b). In the context of public diplomacy, high political involvement naturally exists. Second, control mutuality could motivate the opposing public to identify an innovative and mutually beneficial resolution to deal with a conflict.

*Satisfaction.* Huang (2001a) noted that it is essential to consider satisfaction when evaluating relationships. Satisfaction refers to the degree to which parties engaged in a relationship are satisfied with one another and the relationship between them. One party perceives a relational satisfaction when the other party makes an effort to sustain a positive relationship (Hosmer, 1996). The level of satisfaction is often believed to increase with rewards received and decreases with the costs incurred to maintain the relationship (Jo, Hon, & Brunner, 2004). The level of satisfaction is calculated by the extent to which the advantages of the relationship surpass both parties' expectations. Satisfaction is a significant predictor of trust in the relationship as well as the overall relationship quality (Ki & Hon, 2007b).

Like any type of relationship, satisfaction would act as a pillar in the relationship between a nation (state) and its foreign publics. Specifically, in the context of public diplomacy, level of satisfaction would be increased when members of foreign publics are assured that a nation or state is listening and that they have been heard in the communication process (Fisher & Ury, 1991). As perceived satisfaction is often considered as prerequisite to other relationship indicators including relational commitment and long-term investment in the relationship (Stafford & Canary, 1991), it would be pivotal that a nation demonstrates great efforts to cultivate relationships with the foreign publics. This dimension would be useful for evaluating satisfaction levels of foreign publics toward a particular nation in a public diplomacy context.

*Trust.* This dimension represents a focal concept to both the domains of public relations and public diplomacy. In public relations, trust is explained as "a feeling that those in the relationship can rely on the other" (Ledingham & Bruning, 1998b). Huang (2001a) describes trust as the degree of confidence that parties engaged in a relationship have in each other and their willingness to open themselves up to the other party through symmetrical, open and ethical communication. For public relations practitioners in the international arena, trust is even more fundamental to building positive relationships (Hung, 2000).

Credibility, a concept similar to trust, has been identified as a pillar of public diplomacy. Trust plays a key role in maintaining a nation's faultless reputation and positive image in the world of nations (F. I. Nye, 2008). In contemporary public diplomacy and international relations, governments tend to compete for their country's reputation by establishing credibility (F. I. Nye, 2008). In a similar vein, a nation's level of credibility corresponds with its image (Anholt, 2008).

Gass and Seiter (2009) explicated credibility as a multi-dimensional concept, indicating the following three primary dimensions of credibility in the context of public diplomacy:

> 1) expertise, competence, or qualifications (all of which refer to the source, who could be the president or one of a nation's top officials, as well as the media that carry the message); 2) trustworthiness of the source that carry the message; and 3) goodwill of all actors engaged in the international relationship.

L'Etang (2006) examined the concepts of trust, credibility, and reputation from the perspectives of public relations and public diplomacy. The researcher concluded that the overlapping area of trust in both domains is obvious, particularly when personnel of either organizations or governments actively engage the concept of trust and associated relevant strategies when explaining their activities to their target publics (L'Etang, 2006).

*Commitment.* This dimension is a key component for successful and long-term relationships (Morgan & Hunt, 1994). Huang (2001a) explained commitment as the extent to which the parties involved in the relationship feel connected to each other and engaged in the relationship itself as well as their level of desire to maintain the relationship. Two underlying dimensions of commitment are continuance commitment, which refers to a certain line of action, and affective commitment, which represents an emotional orientation or psychological attachment. Commitment was found to be a significant predictor of supportive behavior toward an organization (Ki & Hon, 2007a, 2007b).

Commitment is often described as "the extent to which an organization gives itself over to *dialogue*, interpretation, and understanding in its interactions with publics" (Kent & Taylor, 2002, p. 24). When considering commitment, Ross (2002) placed an emphasis on *dialogue and exchange* as one of the six pillars of public diplomacy—the other five are policy advocacy, context, credibility, tailored messages, and alliances and partnerships. Ross (2002) further noted that government commitment to engaging in dialogue with publics in another country results in the enhancement of that country's society and culture. In his view, commitment in relationship with foreign publics is a process of avoiding stereotypes and providing opportunities for feedback. J. S. Nye (2004) also echoed the importance of relational commitment and demonstrated that public diplomacy "involves building long-term relationships that create an enabling environment for government policies" (p. 107).

Commitment would be vital as contemporary public diplomacy aims to build long-term relationships with key publics, the importance of which has been emphasized by the Obama Administration (Biden, 2009) and other scholars (J. S. Nye, 2004; Ross, 2002). More importantly, as commitment is closely associated with one of public diplomacy's primary goals, namely, to garner key stakeholders' support of the organization (state, nation or government), relational commitment in the context of public diplomacy would be requisite.

## Linking Relationship, Attitude and Behavior

As relationships have been considered to produce more tangible outcomes, scholars endeavored to evaluate the effects of relationships on relationship outcomes, including attitudinal and behavior outcomes. Through evaluations of publics' perceptions of certain relationships (Hon & Grunig, 1999), a few recent studies attempted to link relationship perception, attitude, and behavior (Ki & Hon, 2007a, 2012; Seltzer & Zhang, 2010).

Ki and Hon (2007a) tested a model linking relationship perception, attitude, and behavior by applying a theory of hierarchy of effects in the context of a university-student relationship. They found that students' positive relationship perceptions of their university act as a significant predictor of supportive attitudes toward the university and the students' intentions to participate in supportive behaviors. Seltzer and Zhang (2010) investigated whether publics' relationship perceptions of their political parties correlated with favorable attitudes and supportive behaviors toward those parties. Though they determined that healthy relationship perceptions did indeed yield more positive attitudes among the publics, they did not identify any significant link between publics' relationship perceptions and behavior.

The scholarship of public relations posits that effectively managed organization-public relationships yield positive attitudes, evaluations, and behaviors of key publics (Bruning, Castle, & Schrepfer, 2004). In contemporary public diplomacy, it is even more essential to effectively manage relationships with foreign publics, which would in turn influence more favorable attitudes and supportive behaviors toward a nation or government involved in the relationship.

## Attitude

In the public relations domain, the evaluation of publics' attitudes is regarded as synonymous with the measurement of public relations program effectiveness, as a primary goal of a program is often to inspire a positive view of an organization or positive public opinion. Likewise, in the context of public diplomacy, evaluating the attitudes of foreign publics would be essential, as their public opinion might influence international political processes and outcomes. The importance of influencing the attitudes of foreign publics is reflected well in the following popular definition of public diplomacy. Public diplomacy is referred to as "the way in which both government and private individuals and group influence directly or indirectly those public attitudes and opinions which bear directly on another government's foreign policy decisions" (Delaney, 1968, p. 3). Signitzer and Wamser (2006) claimed that a goal of public diplomacy should be to establish a public's favorable reaction or opinion toward a state (nation or government). For this goal to be actualized, foreign publics must either transform their negative attitudes or maintain and strengthen positive ones toward their state (nation or government).

## Behavior

A substantial number of studies have confirmed the causal link between attitude and behavior in the process of persuasion (Fishbein & Ajzen, 1975; Hale, Householder, & Greene, 2002; Sheeran, Abraham, & Orbell, 1999).

In public relations, measuring and evaluating attitude and behavior change have often been regarded as a measurement of public relations program effectiveness aimed at determining the success of the persuasive communication message.

It would also be essential to measure behavior or behavioral intention in public diplomacy as there is a general consensus among scholars that a goal of public diplomacy is "to influence the behavior of a foreign government by influencing the attitudes of its citizens" (Malone, 1988, p. 3). Behavior indicates that a public changes or maintains their action according to a goal of an organization (state/nation/government) (Signitzer & Wamser, 2006). To induce the target publics to act according to the organizational goal is often considered difficult, as only those publics who have changed or maintained their attitude in support of the organization are willing to actively influence other publics to support the organization (state/nation/government) as well.

An important issue in measuring the outcome of a public diplomacy program is to identify which evaluative construct is key to predicting behavioral intention of a target public, namely a foreign public. It is important to evaluate the public's behavioral intentions in an effort to assess their potential to remain engaged with or oppose the organization (state, nation, or government). By applying the theory of hierarchy of effect (cognition → attitude → behavior (conative)) or persuasion process and relationship management perspective to public diplomacy, this chapter proposes to treat relationship quality as a perception. Furthermore, this discussion tests the effects of relationship quality perception on attitude and behavior in the context of public diplomacy in order to evaluate the effectiveness of a public diplomacy program.

## Discussion and Research Agenda

Public diplomacy is not about image cultivation, but rather relationship building (Signitzer & Wamser, 2006; Yun, 2006). Indeed, a primary role of a public diplomat is managing and cultivating good relationships between nation-states and overseas publics. With new communication technologies, more emphasis has been placed on *relationship*. This chapter delineates the commonalities of public diplomacy and public relations in order to suggest the applicability of relationship management to public diplomacy. Specifically, this chapter proposes the idea of testing a causal linkage among relationship, attitude, and behavior in a public diplomacy context. As scholars claimed (Signitzer & Coombs, 1992; Yun, 2006), the relational approach to understanding public diplomacy that acts as the foundation for this chapter has yielded a useful framework for advancing public relations as well as public diplomacy.

The convergence of relationship management and public diplomacy has been suggested in prior scholarship (Fitzpatrick, 2007; Signitzer & Wamser, 2006; Yun, 2006). Golan (2013) proposed the positive consequences of long-term relational public diplomacy in his integrated model of public diplomacy. However, empirical evidence of the convergence between public diplomacy and relationship management has yet to be documented. Therefore, scholars should consider empirically testing the effectiveness of the convergence in these two arenas. Hopefully, this chapter brings more attention to the convergence of public diplomacy and relationship management.

Multiple research ideas should be considered for exploring the convergence as previously discussed. First, as proposed in this chapter, future research is needed to empirically document evidence of the linkages between/among relationship quality outcomes, attitudes, and behaviors in the public diplomacy environment. Second, the three elements—antecedents, cultivation strategies, and relationship outcomes—are considered as primary components in the organization-public relationship literature (Broom et al., 2000). Antecedents are the reasons that publics and organizations initiate relationships. Cultivation strategies are the communications and behaviors that occur between an organization and its publics in the cultivation of relationships. Relationship outcome refers to the perceptions of relationship quality held by each party involved in a given relationship. This chapter addresses only the portion of relationship outcomes. Therefore, future research is needed to apply antecedents and cultivation strategies to public diplomacy. Third, the proposed model should be tested across countries to achieve generalizability. Last, given that public diplomats deal with oversea publics, it would be necessary to test the effect of culture in cultivating relationships with these foreign publics.

## Notes

1. Actors include inter- and nongovernmental organizations, and sub-state actors and they increasingly also become transnational actors and individuals (Barston, 1997).
2. For further comparison of public relations and public diplomacy, refer to the following two articles. Macnamara, J. (2012). Corporate and organisational diplomacy: an alternative paradigm to PR. *Journal of Communication Management, 16* (3), 312–325. Signitzer, B., & Wamser, C. (2006). Public diplomacy: A specific governmental public relations function. In C. H. Botan & V. Hazleton (Eds.), *Public relations theory II*, (pp. 435–464). Mahwah, NJ: Lawrence Erlbaum.

## Bibliography

Anholt, S. (2008). The importance of national reputation. In J. Welsh & D. Fearn (Eds.), *Engagement: Public diplomacy in a globalized world* (pp. 30–43). London: Foreign and Commonwealth Office.

Barston, R. (1997). *Modern diplomacy* (2nd ed.). London: Longman.

Biden, J. R. (2009). *The White House.* Retrieved from http://www.fas.org/man/eprint/pubdip.pdf

Broom, G. M., Casey, S., & Ritchey, J. (2000). Toward a concept and theory of organization-public relationships: An update. In J. A. Ledingham & S. D. Bruning (Eds.), *Public relations as relationship management: A relational approach to public relations* (pp. 3–22). Mahwah, NJ: Lawrence Erlbaum Associates.

Bruning, S. D., Castle, J. D., & Schrepfer, E. (2004). Building relationships between organization and publics: Examining the linkage between organization-public relationships, evaluation of satisfaction, and behavioral intent. *Communication Studies, 55*(3), 435–446.

Bruning, S. D., & Ledingham, J. A. (1999). Relationships between organizations and publics: Development of a multi-dimensional organization-public relationship scale. *Public Relations Review, 25,* 157–170.

Bruning, S. D., & Ledingham, J. A. (2000). Perceptions of relationships and evaluations of satisfaction: An exploration of interaction. *Public Relations Review, 26*(1), 85–95.

Coombs, W. T. (2000). Crisis management advantages of a relational perspective. In J. A. Ledingham & S. D. Bruning (Eds.), *Public relations as relationship management: A relational approach to the study and practice of public relations* (pp. 73–93). Mahwah, NJ: Erlbaum.

Cutlip, S. M., Center, A. H., & Broom, G. M. (1994). *Effective public relations.* Englewood Cliffs, NJ: Prentice Hall.

Delaney, R. F. (1968). Introduction. In A. S. Hoffman (Ed.), *International communication and the new diplomacy.* Bloomington, IN: Indiana University Press.

Deutsch, K. (1996). *Nationalism and social communication: An inquiry into the foundations of nationality.* Cambridge, MA: MIT Press.

Ferguson, M. A. (1984). *Building theory in public relations: Interorganizational relationships.* Paper presented at the meeting of Association for Education in Journalism and Mass Communication, Gainesville, FL.

Fishbein, M., & Ajzen, I. (1975). *Belief, attitude, intention and behavior: An introduction to theory and research.* Reading, MA: Addison-Wesley.

Fisher, R., & Ury, W. L. (1991). *Getting to yes: Negotiating agreement without giving in.* New York: Penguin Books.

Fitzpatrick, K. R. (2007). Advancing the new public diplomacy: A public relations perspective. *The Hague Journal of Diplomacy, 2*(3), 187–211.

Fry, M. G., Goldstein, E., & Langhome, R. (2004). *Guide to international relations and diplomacy.* New York, NY: Continuum International Publishing Corp.

Gass, R. H., & Seiter, J. S. (2009). Credibility and public diplomacy. In N. Snow & T. Philip (Eds.), *Routledge handbook of public diplomacy* (pp. 154–165). New York, NY: Routledge.

Golan, G. (2013). Introduction: An integrated approach to public diplomacy. *American Behavioral Science, 57*, 1251–1255.

Goldstein, J. (1994). *International relations.* New York, NY: Harper Collins College.

Grunig, J. E., & Huang, Y.-H. (2000). From organizational effectiveness to relationship indicators: Antecedents of relationships, public relations strategies, and relationship outcomes. In J. A. Ledingham & S. D. Bruning (Eds.), *Public relations as relationship management: A relational approach to the study and practice of public relations* (pp. 23–53). Mahwah, NJ: Erlbaum.

Grunig, J. E., & Hunt, T. (1984). *Managing public relations.* New York: Holt, Rinehart & Winston.

Grunig, L. A., Grunig, J. E., & Dozier, D. M. (2002). *Excellent public relations and effective organizations: A study of communication management in three countries.* Mahwah, NJ: Erlbaum.

Habermas, J. (2006). Political communication in media society: Does democracy still enjoy an epistemic dimension? The impact of normative theory on empirical research. *Communication Theory, 16*(4), 411–426.

Hale, J., Householder, B. J., & Greene, K. L. (2002). The theory of reasoned action. In J. P. Dillard & M. Pfau (Eds.), *The persuasion handbook: Developments in theory and practice* (pp. 259–286). Thousand Oaks, CA: Sage.

Hon, L. C., & Grunig, J. E. (1999). *Guidelines for measuring relationships in public relations.* Gainesville: Institution for Public Relations.

Hosmer, L. T. (1996). Research notes and communications: Responses to 'Do good ethics always make for good business?'. *Strategic Management Journal, 17*(6), 501.

Huang, Y.-H. (2001a). OPRA: A cross-cultural, multiple-item scale for measuring organization-public relationships. *Journal of Public Relations Research, 13*, 61–90.

———. (2001b). Values of public relations: Effects on organization-public relationships mediating conflict resolution. *Journal of Public Relations Research, 13*(4), 265–301.

Hung, C. J. (2000). *Organization-public relationships, relationship maintenance strategies, and relationship outcomes.* Paper presented at the Educator's Academy, Public Relations Society of America, Miami, FL.

Jo, S. (2006). Measurement of organization-public relationships: Validation of measurement using a manufacturer-retailer relationship. *Journal of Public Relations Research, 18*(3), 225–248.

Jo, S., Hon, L. C., & Brunner, B. R. (2004). Organization-public relationships: Measurement validation in a university setting. *Journal of Communication Management, 9*(1), 14–27.

Kent, M. L., & Taylor, M. (2002). Toward a dialogic theory of public relations. *Public Relations Review, 28*, 21–37.

Ki, E. -J., & Hon, L. C. (2007a). Testing the linkages among the organization-public relationship and attitude and behavioral intentions. *Journal of Public Relations Research, 17*(1), 1–23.

———. (2007b). Validation of relationship quality outcome measurement. *Journalism & Mass Communication Quarterly, 84*(3), 419–438.

———. (2009). The causal linkages between/among relationship cultivation strategies and relationship quality outcomes. *International Journal of Strategic Communication, 3*, 1–22.

———. (2012). Causal linkages among relationship quality perception, attitude, and behavior intention in a membership organization. *Corporate Communication: An International Journal, 17,* 187–208.

Ki, E. -J., & Shin, J.-H. (2006). The status of organization-public relationship research from an analysis of published articles, 1985–2004. *Public Relations Review, 32*(2), 194–195.

Kim, Y. (2001). Searching for the organization-public relationship: A valid and reliable instrument. *Journalism and Mass Communication Quarterly, 78,* 799–815.

L'Etang, J. (1996). Public relations as diplomacy. In J. L'Etang & M. Pieczka (Eds.), *Critical perspectives in public relations* (pp. 14–34). London: International Thomson Business.

———. (2006). Public relations as public diplomacy. In J. L'Etang & M. Pieczka (Eds.), *Public relations: Critical debates and contemporary practice* (pp. 373–388). Mahwah, NJ: Lawrence Erlbaum Associates.

———. (2008). *Public relations: Concepts, practice and critique.* London and Thousand Oaks, CA: Sage.

Ledingham, J. A. (2003). Explicating relationship management as a general theory of public relations. *Journal of Public Relations Research, 15*( 2), 181–198.

Ledingham, J. A., & Bruning, S. D. (1998a). *Community relations and relationship dimensions: Measuring the impact of a managed communication program.* Paper presented at the International Interdisciplinary Research Conference, College Park, MD.

———. (1998b). Relationship management in public relations: Dimensions of an organization-public relationship. *Public Relations Review, 24,* 55–65.

Leonard, M., Small, A., & Rose, M. (2005). *British public diplomacy in the Age of Schisms.* London: The Foreign Policy Centre.

Macnamara, J. (2012). Corporate and organisational diplomacy: An alternative paradigm to PR. *Journal of Communication Management, 16*(3), 312–325.

Malone, G. D. (1988). *Political advocacy and cultural communication. Organizing the nation's public diplomacy.* Lanham, MD: University Press of America.

McQuail, D. (2010). *McQuail's mass communication theory* (6th ed.). London: Sage.

Morgan, R. M., & Hunt, S. D. (1994). The commitment-trust theory of relationship marketing. *Journal of Marketing, 58*(3), 20–38.

Nye, F. I. (2008). Public diplomacy and soft power. *ANNALS, American Academy of Political and Social Science, 616*(1), 94–109.

Nye, J. S. (2004). *Soft power: The means to success in world politics.* New York: Public Affairs.

Riordan, S. (2003). *The new diplomacy.* Cambridge, UK: Polity.

Rose, M., & Wadham-Smith, N. (2004). *Mutuality, trust and cultural relations.* London: British Council.

Ross, C. (2002). Public diplomacy comes of age. *Washington Quarterly, 25*(2), 75–83.

Seltzer, T., & Zhang, W. (2010). Toward a model of political organization-public relationships: Antecedent and cultivation strategy influence on citizens' relationships with political parties. *Journal of Public Relations Research, 23,* 24–45.

Sheeran, P., Abraham, C., & Orbell, S. (1999). Psychosocial correlates of hetero-sexual condom use: A meta-analysis. *Psychological Bulletin, 125,* 90–132.

Signitzer, B. (2008). Public relations and public diplomacy: Some conceptual explorations. In A. Zerfass, B. van Ruler & K. Sriramesh (Eds.), *Public relations research:*

*European and international perspectives* (pp. 205–218). Wiesbaden: Verlag fur sozial-wissenschaft.

Signitzer, B., & Coombs, T. (1992). Public relations and public diplomacy: Conceptual convergences. *Public Relations Review, 18*(2), 137–147.

Signitzer, B., & Wamser, C. (2006). Public diplomacy: A specific governmental public relations function. In C. H. Botan & V. Hazleton (Eds.), *Public relations theory II* (pp. 435–464). Mahwah, NJ: Lawrence Erlbaum.

Stafford, L., & Canary, D. J. (1991). Maintenance strategies and romantic relationship type, gender, and relational characteristics. *Journal of Social and Personal Relationships, 8,* 217–242.

Waltz, K. N. (1979). *Theory of international politics.* New York: Random House.

Wilcox, D. L., & Cameron, G. T. (2012). *Public relations: Strategies and tactics.*

Wilson, L. J. (2001). Relationships within communities: Public relations for the new century. In R. L. Heath (Ed.), *Handbook of public relations* (pp. 521–526). Thousand Oaks, CA: Sage.

Yun, S. H. (2006). Toward public relations theory-based study of public diplomacy: Testing the applicability of the excellence study. *Journal of Public Relations Research, 18,* 287–312.

# 7. Application of Issues and Crisis Management to Public Diplomacy

Jangyul Robert Kim

National governments consistently face issues and fall into situations of crisis. These issues and crises are typically unwelcome and unexpected, and can have any number of causes. Some arise from internal domestic causes, while others are caused by external influences such as conflict with neighboring countries or flux in the world economy. In some cases, an individual's faults or mistakes lead to a crisis, while a national government's policy can also lead to an inevitable occurrence. Some crises are caused by wars or natural disasters.

Some issues can be anticipated or found via environmental scanning, allowing time for preparation. Conversely, some issues are entirely unpredictable and, even if predicted, might be unavoidable. However, it is believed that in general, issues and crises can be detected and prevented.

Although different in the size and character, a corporation, like a national government, consistently faces crises, and is swept by issues that need to be prevented or solved. The crises and issues that face a corporation are generally smaller in scale. However, many multinational corporations exceed the size of some nations' economies and their business areas cover the entire world (Signitzer & Wamser, 2006).

In particular, a national government and corporations in that country hold symbiotic relationships, given that they both have to deal with the same international publics. Take a look at governments today. A national government supports its national corporations on the international level, and in turn, these corporations share important information with the government. For instance, former President Lee Myung-Bak of South Korea has personally travelled to UAE to support a Korean company's bidding for construction of a nuclear powerhouse. The fact that high-ranking officials from the South

Korean government visit the United States to seek restriction on American beef (USA Today, 2008) shows the coherent and complementary relationship between a national government and its corporations. A strong corporation aids the government, and a strong nation supports corporations. Conversely, governmental turmoil negatively affects its corporations. The recent tsunami and resulting nuclear leakage in Japan not only affected Japan as a nation, but also on the performance and reputation of Japanese corporations internationally. Companies such as McDonald's and Coca-Cola often become the victims of boycotts against the United States, simply for being representatives of America (BBC News, 2009).

The reality is that, as long as a national government and its corporations continue to build relationships with other governments and international publics, it is inevitable that issues will surface and crises will occur. While national governments have previously performed "elite diplomacy" with foreign governments and officials, corporations have performed international public relations, targeting international publics and stakeholders, and have accumulated expertise and developed systems that strategically deal with issues and crisis management. Thus, to understand how a national government should undertake issues and crisis management, it is worthwhile to look at how corporations handle them.

Regarding public diplomacy research, it is mainly influenced by Nye (1990, 2008) who coined the term, *soft power*, as opposed to *hard power*. A national government may deploy soft power programs to build long-term friendly relationships with citizens (international publics) in other countries via educational and cultural exchange programs. On the other hand, some scholars (Entman, 2004; Sheafer & Gabay, 2009; Sheafer & Shenhav, 2010) focused on mediated public diplomacy research, which deals with a national government's efforts to engage international citizens in favor of it by leveraging global news media. Recently, Golan (2013) proposed an *integrated model of public diplomacy*, which classified public diplomacy into three layers of terms and objectives: *mediated public diplomacy* (short/medium term), *nation branding* and *country reputation* (medium/long term), and *relational public diplomacy* (long term).

Among these layers, issues and crisis management research fall into short- to medium-termed mediated public diplomacy as they deal with current issues and crisis that need immediate attention and follow-ups. Therefore, this chapter first offers a literature review on issues and crisis management in corporations. In particular, by focusing on definitions and crisis management strategies, this chapter attempts to apply a corporation's crisis management frame to public diplomacy; and suggests a direction on how issues and crisis management research can be best utilized in mediated public diplomacy programs.

Before applying issues and crisis communications as functions of organizational communications to public diplomacy, operational definitions of issues management, crisis, and crisis management are required. These definitions will first be examined then be revised to fit public diplomacy.

## Issue Management and Public Diplomacy

### Conceptualization

Out of the numerous existing definitions of issues management for corporate communications, two represent the general characteristics of issues management. The first is that of Coates and his associates (1986) where they define issues management as the "organized activity of identifying emerging trends, concerns, or issues likely to affect an organization in the next few years, and developing a wider and more positive range of organizational responses toward the future" (Coates, Coates, Jarratt, & Heinz, 1986, p. ix). Wilcox and Cameron (2009) defined issues management as "a proactive and systematic approach to predict problems, anticipate threats, minimize surprises, resolve issues, and prevent crises" (p. 9).

Applying these to public diplomacy, it can be defined that "issues management in public diplomacy is a proactive and systematic approach of a national government and its agencies to identify emerging trends, concerns, or issues among the international publics[1] likely to affect a nation in the near future, minimize surprises, resolve issues and prevent crises." A corporation's issues management and that of a national government differ in that, while a corporation's issues management deals with direct and indirect stakeholders (domestic and international), issues management in public diplomacy deals with the general and specific publics in other targeted countries, as well as foreigners in a host territory. Furthermore, the time frame that issues management should cover is broader. It includes not only issues foreseen in the long-term, but also issues that could surface within the span of a week. In particular, in a world with rapid movement via social media, more immediate and elaborated issues management is a necessity. Take a look at the Arab Spring across North Africa and the Middle East; mass demonstrations for democracy did not take place over a long period of time. Instead, following the spark of first protests in Tunisia, it quickly spread to Egypt, Libya, Yemen, Bahrain, and Syria. A national government learned that it must be prompt in responding to such issues, and that it should have strategic issues management systems (The Guardian, 2011).

According to Wilcox and Cameron (2009), issues management goes through five stages; issue identification, issue analysis, strategy options, an action plan, and the evaluation of results. For an effective issues management, two-way communication, formal environmental scanning, and active sense-making strategies are required. Similarly, a national government can plan and undertake issues management in the same manner (i.e., identify issues through careful environmental scanning, analyze searched issues, develop response strategies and undertake issues management programs). Through this, a national government may either thwart the issue from developing into a crisis or appropriately solve the problem, save on budget and resources, and position itself as a stronger nation with a better reputation, just like a corporation.

Issues management in a national government lies across greater scale and has more complexity potential than corporate issues management. Issues can also emerge, not only from economics, but from a variety of sectors such as safety, education, sciences, technology, and so forth. The impact of an issue is greater, too. In particular, issues management targeting international publics cannot simply be carried out successfully through government level diplomacy via elite diplomats, but should effectively utilize existing resources from government, corporations, grassroots, education, culture and many others.

*On the publics.* Here, it may help to review the categorized publics by public relations scholars (Grunig, 1997; Grunig & Hunt, 1984; Hallahan, 2000, 2001) and apply them to public diplomacy to undertake a more sophisticated issues management. Grunig and Hunt (1984) categorized publics as *non-publics, latent publics, aware publics* and *active publics.* Later, Grunig (1997) categorized the publics into *all-issue publics, apathetic publics, single issue-publics,* and *hot-issue publics,* depending on *problem recognition, constraint recognition,* and *level of involvement.* Hallahan (2000, 2001) also categorized publics into *inactive publics, aroused publics, aware publics, active publics* and *nonpublics,* depending on the *level of knowledge* and *level of involvement.* Proposing a different method for each type of public, Hallahan (2001) proposed education-based strategies (alliance building, media advocacy, lobbying) for *aware publics,* negotiation-based strategies (avoidance, acknowledgment, concession, bargaining) for *active publics,* prevention-based strategies (poll-taking/market monitoring, performance/quality assurance, ingratiation, reputation enhancement) for *inactive publics,* and intervention-based strategies (monitoring, outreach/cooperation, inquiry handling, co-optation, containment) for *aroused publics* (Figure 7.1). Applying these typologies to public diplomacy, one can categorize publics and formulate respective issues management strategies.

Another particularity of the publics categorized above is that their characters are not static, but prone to change depending on the issue and the given environment. According to Hallahan (2001), members of "inactive publics identify problematic situations" (p. 36) and became aroused publics, "aroused publics organize to seek solutions, [and] became active [publics]" (p. 39), and "uninvolved publics became aware of issues and might become active [publics]" (p. 40). This typology is highly demonstrated via the American government and its troops stationed in Afghanistan. As they were demolishing the Taliban regime, the Afghan publics responded in varying degrees. Some were aware publics (high knowledge but low involvement) or aroused publics (high involvement and low knowledge). Some may have been inactive publics (low knowledge and low involvement) due to their personal preferences. However, when the Afghan publics became knowledgeable of American soldiers burning the Qur'an, and as the issue instantly became less distant and more personal, they immediately transformed into active publics (high knowledge and high involvement).

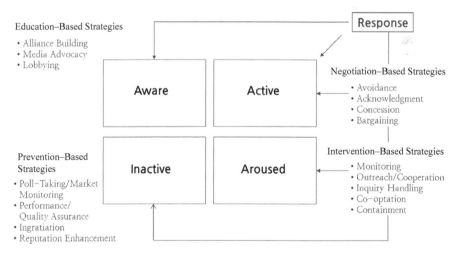

*Figure 7.1.* Hallahan's issue response process. (Hallahan, 2001, p. 43)

This typology, of course, cannot guarantee the comprehension of all publics regarding an issue. Furthermore, some issues may not be prevented or be managed even when they are grasped. In this case, the unresolved issues may develop to a crisis, and it is the next step for a national government to cope with the crisis so that it can mitigate and prevent it from further developing into a larger crisis, and terminate the crisis situation with least damage.

For these reasons, it is necessary to understand crisis management. A general agreement on the difference between issues management and crisis management is that while issues management is a *proactive* method, crisis management is about an organization's (and a national government's) *reactive* response to a crisis (Gaunt & Ollenburger, 1995). Similar to that of a corporation, a national government's management of a crisis changes a nation's reputation and image among international publics.

## Crisis Management and Public Diplomacy

Many scholars and professionals have conducted research on crisis communication and crisis response strategies. Among these, this chapter seeks to apply the works of Coombs and Holladay (2002, 2012) and Fearn-Banks (2011) that researched theory and practice.

### Conceptualization

According to Fearn-Banks (2011), a crisis is "a major occurrence with a potentially negative outcome affecting the organization, company, or industry, as well as its publics, products, services, or good name" (p. 2). Coombs and Holladay (2012) concluded from looking at the many works of crisis management scholars that "crisis" cannot be defined in simple terms. Nonetheless, a common viewpoint holds that a crisis can result in positive or negative outlooks depending on how it is managed (p. 18). They argue that crises can be predicted, and some among these can be managed through preparation and strategic response. When crisis management is handled well, it can transform danger into opportunity.

Fearn-Banks (2011) also defined crisis management and crisis communication, saying, "Crisis management is a process of strategic planning for a crisis or negative turning points, a process that removes some of the risk and uncertainty from the negative occurrence and thereby allows the organization to be in greater control of its own destiny" (p. 2). And she defined crisis communications as, "the dialog between the organization and its public(s) prior to, during, and after the negative occurrence. The dialog details strategies and tactics designed to minimize damage to the image of the organization" (p. 2).

As both Coombs and Holladay and Fern-Banks argued, the key to crisis management is appropriate preparation beforehand to prevent a crisis from occurring or to minimize its damage once a crisis occurs. In order to achieve this, it is not enough to depend on well-executed communications; a properly designed system must be put in place in advance of the crisis. In other words, there must be a system to anticipate and analyze a crisis and a well-prepared crisis management program (including a crisis management manual) that should be used as a guideline for effective communications in times of crisis. In reality, numerous multinational corporations and *Fortune 500* companies have these crisis communications management systems and carry out crisis management with the aid of outside crisis communication professionals and consultants. Crisis management, furthermore, should not be a one-time treatment, but continuously be managed and modified.

In his book, Coombs (2011) attempts to understand crisis management by *pre, during,* and *post stages,* and suggests necessary crisis management preparation and response strategies in each stage. Fink (1986) also divides crisis into a *prodromal stage, acute stage, chronic stage,* and *resolution stage* according to their occurrence in the crisis life cycle model. In general, the quintessence of crisis management is to detect a signal of a crisis, and take necessary prevention measures during the prodromal stage, so that the crisis moves directly to the resolution stage, skipping the acute and chronic stages, and minimize the damage even if the crisis develops through the various stages (Figure 7.2).

Then, how can crisis management and crisis communications be applied to public diplomacy? The following definitions were developed and modified based on several existing definitions (Coombs & Holladay, 2002, 2012; Fearn-Banks; 2011). First, a crisis in public diplomacy can be defined as "a major occurrence with a potentially negative outcome affecting reputation of a nation and its government among the international publics." *Crisis management,* in turn, is "a process of strategic planning for a crisis or negative turning points; a process that removes some of the risk and uncertainty from a negative occurrence and thereby allows a national government to be in control of the situation." Finally, *crisis communication* is "the dialog between a national government and its international publics prior to, during, and after the negative occurrence. The dialog details strategies and tactics designed to minimize damage to the reputation and image of the country and its government."

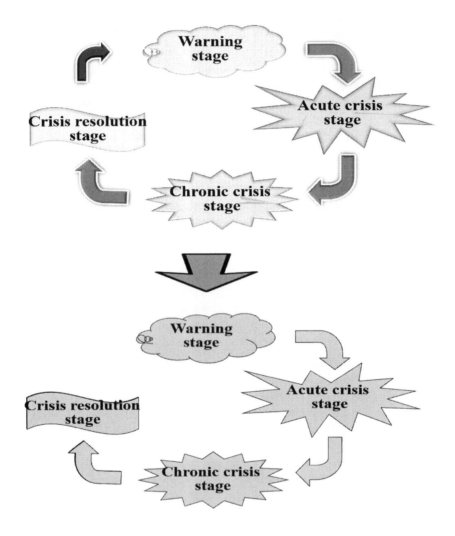

*Figure 7.2.* Crisis Life Cycle (Fink, 1986) vs. the objective of crisis management.

In public diplomacy, the targets of crisis management and crisis communication are the publics in other (targeted) countries as well as foreigners in that country. Here, "other countries" could be one or more countries or regions depending on the crisis type, involvement with the affected nations, and the proximity. Because the results of a crisis situation not only affect a nation's reputation, but also its economy and culture, it is critical for a national government to develop strategic crisis communication plans and to undertake them promptly and relevantly when a crisis occurs. Furthermore, as the publics are located in foreign countries with different cultural backgrounds, a national government should consider these characteristics to ensure an effective and relevant crisis management and crisis communication process.

## Research on Crisis Response Strategies

Coombs (2006) argued that existing literature on crisis response strategies can largely be categorized into research on *form* and research on *content*. Research on form looks at "what should be done" before, during and after a crisis, while research on content analyzes "what is actually said in the messages" (p. 171). This chapter takes Coombs's study further and expands the frame of crisis management research to public diplomacy.

*Research on form.* After analyzing previous literature on *form*, Coombs (2006) suggested three principles that a corporation should follow in times of crisis: *be quick, be consistent,* and *be open.*

The foremost crisis response principle is quick response in order to control information. A corporation should announce its position within the first two hours of crisis, and the first 24 to 48 hours are most crucial. If not executed properly, a corporation may lose control of information and may not be able to effectively manage a crisis due to incorrect information and rumors.

This applies to the crisis response strategies for a national government as well. Today, with the Internet, where information is instantly disseminated through social media such as Facebook and Twitter, quick response to a crisis is even more important. While previous crisis management was at the mercy of media deadlines, a national government's response to crisis today is under a tighter watch in real time. The government must release its position as early as possible and immediately undertake necessary follow-up activities.

Secondly, a corporation should disseminate consistent messages to raise its trustworthiness and to effectively control information. Generally referred to as a *one-voice rule,* one view advocates for the use of only one spokesperson–typically a CEO–to increase the credibility and consistency of a message, while another view says the consistency of a message matters more, thus multiple spokespersons are allowed (Coombs, 2011). In reality, it is difficult to appoint only one spokesperson to represent a multinational corporation, therefore the corporation may choose multiple spokespersons depending on the region and the issue, and still maintain consistency of messages through media training and communication efforts.

Thirdly, when a corporation releases information during a crisis, it should reveal *complete* information. It should carefully consider whether or not full disclosure is the best strategy. The decision should be ethical and beneficial to both the corporation and the publics. In reality, depending on issues and situations, full disclosure of information is not always achievable (Table 7.1).

*Table 7.1.* Crisis response principles (Coombs, 2006) and application to public diplomacy.

| Principle | Crisis response principle–Corporation | Crisis response principle–National government | Application example (to public diplomacy) *Case: Afghan-based American soldiers burning the Qur'an* |
|---|---|---|---|
| Be quick | A corporation should respond quickly when a crisis occurs | A national government should respond quickly when a crisis occurs, targeting international publics | When Afghanistan-based American soldiers burnt the Qur'an, the American government should have responded immediately–do apologize |
| Be consistent | Consistent messages will increase credibility of a corporation | Consistent messages will increase credibility of a national government | The American government's position should remain the same regardless of the situation |
| Be open | A corporation should disclose full information for the benefit of both the corporation and its publics | A national government may disclose full information as long as it does not hurt the nation's profit | As demonstrated in the case of WikiLeaks, full disclosure may not be the best policy for the benefit of a nation and international publics |

***Research on content.*** Coombs (2006) maintains that most research on crisis communication and crisis management employed case analysis and experimental studies based on attribution theory. In the study on content, the crisis response strategy is of utmost importance, for it is posited that a certain type of crisis response strategy is more effective in a specific crisis situation (Benson, 1988).

According to Coombs (2006), literature on crisis response strategies looks at the following three areas: *corporate apologia, corporate impression management,* and *image restoration theory.*

First, corporate apologia says during a time of crisis, a corporation must develop various advocacy strategies acceptable to each stakeholder. A corporation must aim to persuade its stakeholders as an individual strives to persuade others to understand his or her position. Ice (1991) lists *denial, bolstering, differentiation*, and *transcendence* as general strategies of advocacy. Further developing these, Hobbs (1995) suggested four types of apologia strategies by combining each strategy, focusing on the improvement of relationships: (1) *absolution, differentiation, denial*; (2) *vindication, denial, transcendence*; (3) *explanation, bolstering, differentiation*; and (4) *justification, bolstering, transcendence*. While scholars vary on the specifics of corporate apologia, it can largely be divided into whether a corporation acknowledges its mistake and apologizes, or denies its responsibility to the crisis.

Similar to a corporation, a national government may take two different stances on a crisis such as accepting responsibility and apologizing (and further compensating the victims), or denying its responsibility depending on the level of responsibility. In many cases, it is not possible to dichotomize the response strategies in such manner as there are various internal and external variables that affect the national government's position. A basic rule is that the government should analyze the crisis situation and determine the best strategy based on strict ethical standards for the benefit of both its national and international publics.

Historically, however, there have been numerous cases where a national government denied its responsibility in a case despite its fair share of blame, thus exacerbating and escalating a crisis. Similar to a corporation, the unethical consideration of government officials or politicians can sway the outcome of a crisis situation in a negative way. In the case of a corporation, its pursuit of profits and responsibility to stakeholders may lead to unethical decisions. Likewise, a national government taking into account voters' opinions (votes) and the political dynamics with other nations may lead to similar outcomes. For instance, it has been historically proven that during the early 20th century, the Japanese government forcefully took women from its colonies including Korea, China and several Southeast Asian countries in order to make them "comfort women" (Japanese military sexual slavery) for its soldiers (Memory and Reconciliation in the Asia-Pacific, 2012). The Japanese government asserts that these women "volunteered" to be "comfort women," despite such proof that it is unethical and incorrect. Consequently, while the Japanese government may win the right-wing votes domestically, it may not escape the negative consequences of its unethical past internationally, especially in contrast to the apologetic position of the German government on the Holocaust. It is shown that denying responsibility, such as the position of the Japanese government, leads to more losses than benefits in the unfolding of public diplomacy. Recently, the U.S. Secretary of State Hillary Clinton called the term "comfort women" to be wrong, and that they should be referred to as "enforced sex slaves" (Lee, 2012).

Second, corporate impression management and third, image restoration theory further develop corporate apologia as a crisis management strategy. Coombs (2006) differentiates corporate impression management and image restoration theory, but there seems to be little difference.

There are several theories on this, with the most inclusive image restoration theory being that of Benoit and Brinson (Benoit, 1995; Brinson & Benoit, 1999). According to Benoit (1995), a corporation can choose any crisis response strategy proportional to the level of responsibility, from *denial* (least responsibility) to *evasion of responsibility, reducing offensiveness of the event, corrective action* or *mortification* (most responsibility). Brinson and Benoit (1999) later added *separation* to this list. Separation is not simply the denial of a corporation in its part in crisis, but acknowledging responsibility while choosing a scapegoat to overcome the crisis. Applying these response strategies to public diplomacy, examples of how a national government may respond to the actual case of Afghanistan-based American soldiers burning the Qur'an are shown in Table 7.2.

In particular, in their situational crisis communication theory (SCCT), Coombs and Holladay (2002) specifically sought to combine corporate apologia, impression management, and image restoration theory. For this, Coombs placed type of crisis into three categories by the level of crisis responsibility in the minds of stakeholders. They are:

(1) *Stakeholders hold strong attributions of organizational crisis responsibility*, such as organizational misdeeds (an organization purposefully places stakeholders at risk), human breakdown product recall (recall caused by human error), and human breakdown accident (industrial accident caused by human error);

(2) *Stakeholders hold moderate attributions of organizational crisis responsibility*, such as technical breakdown product recall, technical breakdown accident, mega damage (significant environmental damage from a technical error), and challenge (confronted by stakeholders who claim the organization is operating in an inappropriate manner);

(3) *Stakeholders hold weak attributions of organizational crisis responsibility*, such as rumors, natural disasters, malevolence/product tampering and workplace violence (attack by an employee or former employee against co-workers and/or customers) (Coombs, 2006, p. 183).

To manage crisis effectively, a corporation should understand which crisis belongs in which category, then based on attribution theory, considering its performance history and crisis severity, it should evaluate the "*modifiers*: variables that can alter attributions generated by the crisis type" (Coombs, 2006, p. 182). Finally, a corporation should develop a crisis response strategy depending on the level of crisis responsibility.

According to SCCT, "as attributions of crisis responsibility increase, the crisis managers should use crisis response strategies that progressively accept more responsibility for the crisis" (p. 187). The crisis management response strategy must vary by the level of responsibility acceptance, from *full apology* (very high acceptance) to corrective action, ingratiation, justification, excuse, denial or attack (no acceptance). As shown in Table 7.3, such outcomes are also applicable to public diplomacy.

## Conclusion

Hiebert (2005) asserts that, with the development of technology such as satellite television and the Internet, people are able to see what was previously unseen and therefore can focus on the hidden truth behind images. For example, while the American government tried to control the information regarding the Iraq War to gain public support, people in the world, including American citizens, were able to access information through other media channels on the atrocities abroad, leading to a greater distrust of the American government.

*Table 7.2.* Image restoration strategies (Benoit, 1995; Brinson & Benoit, 1999) and application to public diplomacy.

| | Crisis response strategies– Corporation | Crisis response strategies– National government | Application example (to public diplomacy)–*Case: Afghan-based American soldiers burning the Qur'an* |
|---|---|---|---|
| Denial | Organization claims there is no crisis | National government claims there is no crisis | |
| Evasion of responsibility | Organization attempts to reduce responsibility for the crisis | National government attempts to reduce responsibility for the crisis | |
| Reducing offensiveness of the event | Organization makes the crisis appear more positive | National government makes the crisis appear more positive | While the burning of the Qur'an remains true, it was unintentional and resulted from a mistake (alcohol, carelessness, etc.). The soldiers are deeply regretting such incident, thus it is unnecessary to escalate the matter |

| | Crisis response strategies– Corporation | Crisis response strategies– National government | Application example (to public diplomacy)–*Case: Afghan-based American soldiers burning the Qur'an* |
|---|---|---|---|
| Corrective action | Organization takes steps to solve the problem and/ or prevent a repetition of the crisis | National government takes steps to solve the problem and/or prevent a repetition of the crisis | Prevent any future wrongdoings by Afghanistan-based American soldiers via education, and ensure strict punishment to those soldiers and officials who violate such rules |
| Mortification | Organization accepts responsibility and apologizes | National government accepts responsibility and apologizes | The Qur'an burning by Afghanistan-based American soldiers resulted from the lack of proper education and control of action (was not able to prevent it from happening); accepts responsibility and apologizes on behalf of the United States |
| Separation | Organization explains that the act violated its policies, identifies a separate scapegoat within the organization, and initiates corrective action | National government explains that the act violated its policies, identifies a separate scapegoat from the relative government parties, and initiates corrective action | The identified Afghanistan-based American soldiers are responsible for the burning of Qur'an. The United States (government and military) respects the culture and religion of Afghanistan and took necessary educational measures to prevent any acts originated from misunderstanding. In addition, the American government will strengthen its efforts to prevent such violation of policies from taking place in the future |

*Table 7.3.* Crisis response strategies by level of responsibility acceptance (Coombs, 2006, 2011) and application to public diplomacy.

| Crisis response strategy | Content | Level of responsibility acceptance | Application to public diplomacy |
|---|---|---|---|
| **Full apology** | Organization takes full responsibility for the crisis and request forgiveness from stakeholders. It can also include some form of compensation. | Very high acceptance | National government takes full responsibility for the crisis and request forgiveness from the international publics. It can also include some form of compensation to victims and related stakeholders. |
| **Corrective action** | Organization takes steps to repair the crisis damage and/or prevent a recurrence of the crisis. | High acceptance | National government takes steps to repair the crisis damage and/or prevent a recurrence of the crisis. |
| **Ingratiation** | Organization reminds stakeholders of past good works by the organization or praises the stakeholders in some fashion | Mild acceptance | National government reminds international publics of past good works by the national government or the friendly relationship between countries. |
| **Justification** | Organization tries to minimize the perceived damage related to the crisis. Includes claiming that the damage was minimal or that the victim deserved it. | Mild acceptance | National government tries to minimize the perceived damage related to the crisis. Includes claiming that the damage was minimal or that the victim deserved it. |
| **Excuse** | Organization tries to minimize its responsibility for the crisis. Includes denying intent or control over the crisis event. | Mild acceptance | National government tries to minimize its responsibility for the crisis. Includes denying intent or control over the crisis event. |

| Crisis response strategy | Content | Level of responsibility acceptance | Application to public diplomacy |
|---|---|---|---|
| **Denial** | Organization maintains that no crisis occurred. The response may include efforts to explain why there was no crisis. | No acceptance | National government maintains that no crisis occurred. The response may include efforts to explain why there was no crisis. |
| **Attack** | Organization confronts the people or group who say that a crisis exists. The response may include a threat such as lawsuit. | No acceptance | National government confronts the people or group who claim that a crisis exists. The response may include a threat such as international lawsuit. |

The recent release of confidential information from WikiLeaks has raised controversial debates on public access to national government's confidential information, i.e., national security versus freedom of speech (Hirshman, 2011). As these contents are not limited to domestically confidential information, but reach far greater to international affairs, each governmental response was to affect the perception of international publics and of its citizens. Each government had to decide its position considering all possible responses and counter-responses.

International relations have inarguably become more complex and intertwined. In particular, thanks to the Internet and social media, the international publics are not only more informed and empowered, but they also affect the decisions regarding a national government's international policy through group alliances and social networking sites. To cope with this phenomenon, public diplomacy has emerged as an indispensable area that can complement existing elite diplomacy. Consequently, because of the complex and uncertain nature of public diplomacy, issues and crisis management is becoming more important as national governments communicate with international publics.

Despite the similarities, applying the issues management and crisis management used by corporations to public diplomacy is a challenging task. While issues management and crisis management for corporations focus on managing direct influential stakeholders mainly for economic reasons, public diplomacy is more related to international publics who are more diverse, loosely tied, remote, and different in characteristics, culture and perspectives. However, as issues management and crisis management research developed in the area of international public relations, it is worthwhile to attempt to apply these frames to public diplomacy, i.e., the issues and crisis communication and management for a national government targeting international publics who reside both in other countries and in the host territory.

In public diplomacy, the basic assumption of issues and crisis management is not different from that of a corporation, that issues and crisis can be detected, and therefore, can be prevented or at least managed through close preparation and well-prepared issues and crisis management programs. More specifically, issues management is based on a national government's finding issues through environmental scanning and solving/preventing the issue before it occurs. Crisis management is no different. The key for a national government is to detect signs of a crisis through systematic monitoring systems, eliminate the cause or the crisis itself in advance or prevent it from intensifying, and mitigate or minimize the negative effects of an unfolding crisis. Furthermore, a system that can track and prevent any recurrence of such a crisis is necessary.

Comprehensive and versatile crisis response strategies should be established that can work most effectively, depending on the type and severity of a crisis and the level of responsibility of a national government. The basic principle is that a national government should take more apologetic and corrective strategies as the level of its responsibility increases, and may choose denial strategies as the level decreases. Still, not all crises can be managed this way.

For instance, the level of responsibility may not be initially apparent. As the crisis escalates or new information is uncovered, however, the level of responsibility attributed to a national government may increase. Conversely, some crises may have started with large speculation of governmental responsibility, where later the government is proven to be the victim. Some crisis, despite the level of responsibility, may still require compensative action on the part of the national government due to the severity of the crisis or its negative past history. Optimal response strategies should not only focus on minimizing damage, but on what is most favorable for all, including a national government and international publics in other nations. Most of all, its crisis response strategies should be based on strong ethical consideration.

Crisis response strategies may begin at national government level, but its scope may soon be expanded to the regional level (e.g., the European Union) depending on the nature and severity of the crisis.

## *Suggestions for Future Research*

This chapter attempts to define issues and crisis management from the perspective of public diplomacy, and apply them to public diplomacy scholarship and practices. Even though issues management and crisis management were developed as part of organizational communication strategy, it is worthwhile to apply these concepts and cases to public diplomacy, more specifically, to mediated public diplomacy as a short- to medium-termed communication strategy that will lead to better nation branding and country reputation in the long term. However, this chapter is only a kindling attempt. Further research on issues and crisis management will enhance issues and crisis communication scholarship and will facilitate interdisciplinary research on both sides. Some research idea suggestions follow:

1.  *Use of international opinion to persuade its own citizens.* In general, a national government utilizes public diplomacy to inform and change perception of the international publics. Issues and crisis management can be a critical part to its public diplomacy. Conversely, a national government may utilize an issue or crisis of its own or of another nation to its benefit by persuading its citizens and drawing out their supports. The different viewpoint on the death of Kim Jong-Il of North Korea is an example. People in South Korea were concerned of the possibility of invasion and an unfortunate war, initiated by leaderless and cornered North Korea. On the other hand, pro-North Korean Chinese government saw utmost importance in maintaining stability in North Korea by acknowledging Kim Jong-Eun as a new legitimate leader. The international community kept a concerned eye on this incident and on the security of the Korean Peninsula. Amidst such concerns, the South Korean government may need to advocate the situation as normal and stable to the world, especially to those governments and corporations in trade with South Korea as well as to current and potential tourists. Internally, the South Korean government may need to urge its citizens to engage in their works without apprehension and support/trust of the government policies by strengthening public communication with them. Here, a possible crisis management card that the Korean government could play is to inform and ask the Korean people about how people in other nations would perceive the situation, and how Korean people should act in such situation.

    These situations are not simple portrayals of issues or crisis management, but are examples of how a national government may leverage the viewpoint of international publics (i.e., what news is covered on international media and what information is shared via social media websites, etc.) in persuading its own citizens, which is opposite to normal public diplomacy practices. Further research on the subject would illustrate how public diplomacy could benefit from issues and crisis management.

2.  *Public diplomacy from the perspective of traditionalists*: Public diplomacy and public relation can be viewed from the perspectives of *behavioralists* and *traditionalists* (Signitzer & Wamser, 2006, p. 445). These viewpoints may apply to public diplomacy and crisis management as well. Behavioralists assert that a crisis can be managed with prior preparation and relevant crisis response strategies. As L'Etang (1996) declared, "all assumptions should be clearly spelt out and only empirically verifiable hypotheses should be produced" (p. 27). This viewpoint is portrayed in the study of Coombs (2011), Coombs & Holladay (2002, 2012), and Fearn-Banks (2011). On the other hand, traditionalists view a crisis to be unpredictable in essence and disprove the credibility of a crisis management program because a national government cannot prevent all crises or escape from these crises. Including Seeger (2002) who asserted, "precise, accurate and unequivocal communication about the behavior of complex systems is inherently inaccurate" (p. 332), some scholars (Gilpin & Murphy, 2006; Murphy, 1996, 2001; Seeger, 2002) advocate this view based on chaos theory or complexity theory. Follow up research on these viewpoints and review on how crisis management can be applied to public diplomacy would bestow justification on this attempt, and help strategize issues and crisis management as part of public diplomacy planning and deployment.

3.  *Public diplomacy and crisis management*: Crisis management today is not exclusively dependent on mainstream media such as television and newspapers. As the terms public diplomacy or cultural diplomacy represent, future crisis management depends on how it can best utilize social media via the Internet. How will a national government carry out crisis management using social media? This question calls for future research on social media as a critical communication tool for issues and crisis management in public diplomacy. Looking at the recent Arab Spring movement that swept the regions of North Africa and the Middle East, most of these national governments fell short of reading the wave of democratic revolution (although they share a long history of dictatorship). From these dictators' point of view, they failed to predict the crisis, but from a broader lens, they failed to read the trend that is the yearning for democracy. Their largest

mistake is overlooking or underestimating the uncontrollability of information sharing on the Internet, propagation of news through the Internet, and above all, the power of social media, in particular, Twitter and Facebook.

4. *Public diplomacy and international public relations*. Although not thoroughly covered in this chapter, international public relations and public diplomacy have many similarities. In fact, they are rather parallel in nature. Given the character of public diplomacy as an activity that deals with international publics, further research is required on how differences in culture, history, geography, language and perception affect the practices of international public relations, issues and crisis management and how they can be applied to public diplomacy–the causal relationships or correlations among them.

## Notes

1. International publics include the publics and stakeholders in other nations as well as foreign people in a host country. They may include travelers, businessmen, diplomats, students, residents and non-residents with foreign nationalities.

## Bibliography

BBC News (2009). Gaza prompts boycott in Malaysia. *BBC News*. Retrieved January 28, 2014, http://news.bbc.co.uk/2/hi/asia-pacific/7819561.stm

Benoit, W. L. (1995). *Accounts, excuses, and apologies: A theory of image restoration*. Albany, NY: State University of New York Press.

Benson, J. A. (1988). Crisis revisited: An analysis of the strategies used by Tylenol in the second tampering episode. *Central State Speech Journal, 39*, 49–66.

Brinson, S. L., & Benoit W. L. (1999). The tarnished star: Restoring Texaco's damaged public image. *Management Communication Quarterly, 12*, 481–510.

Coates, J. F., Coates, V. T., Jarratt, J., & Heinz, L. (1986). *Issues management: How you can plan, organize and manage for the future*. Mt. Airy, MD: Lomond.

Coombs, W. T. (1995). Choosing the right words: The development of guidelines for the selection of the "appropriate" crisis response strategies. *Management Communication Quarterly, 8*, 211–227.

Coombs, W. T. (2006). Crisis management: A communicative approach. In C. Botan & V. Hazleton (Eds.), *Public relations theory II* (pp. 171–197). Mahwah, NJ: Lawrence Erlbaum Associates.

Coombs, W. T. (2011). *Ongoing crisis communication: Planning, managing, and responding*. Thousand Oaks, CA: Sage.

Coombs, W. T., & Holladay, S. J. (2002). Helping managers protect reputational assets: Initial tests of the situational crisis communication theory. *Management Communication Quarterly, 16,* 165–186.

Coombs, W. T., & Holladay, S. J. (2012). *The handbook of crisis communication.* Malden, MA: Blackwell Publishing.

Entman, R. M. (2004). *Projections of power: Framing news, public opinion, and foreign policy.* Chicago, IL: University of Chicago Press.

Fearn-Banks, K. (2011). *Crisis communications: A casebook approach.* New York, NY: Routledge.

Fink, S. (1986). *Crisis management: Planning for the inevitable.* New York, NY: American Management Association.

Gaunt, P., & Ollenburger, J. (1995). Issues management revisited: A tool that deserves another look. *Public Relations Review, 21*(3), 199–210.

Gilpin, D., & Murphy, P. (2006). Reframing crisis management through complexity. In C. Botan & V. Hazleton (Eds.), *Public relations theory II* (pp. 375–392). Mahwah, NJ: Lawrence Erlbaum Associates.

Golan, G. J. (2013). Introduction: An integrated approach to public diplomacy. *American Behavioral Science, 57*(9), 1251–1255

Grunig, J. E. (1997). A situational theory of publics: Conceptual history, recent challenges, and new research. In D. Moss, T. MacManus, & D. Verčič. (Eds.), *Public relations research: An international perspective* (pp.3–48). London: International Thomson Business Press.

Grunig, J. E., & Hunt, T. (1984). *Managing public relations.* New York: Holt, Rinehart and Winston.

Guardian(2011).RetrievedMay18,2012,http://www.guardian.co.uk/world/interactive/2011/mar/22/middle-east-protest-interactive-timeline.

Hallahan, K. (2000). Inactive publics: The forgotten publics in public relations. *Public Relations Review, 26*(4), 499–515.

Hallahan, K. (2001). The dynamics of issues activation and response: An issues process model. *Journal of Public Relations Research, 13*(1), 27–59.

Hiebert, R. E. (2005). Commentary: New technologies, public relations, and democracy. *Public Relations Review, 31*(1), 1–9.

Hirshman, R. (2011). WikiLeaks controversy raises questions about freedom of speech, the nature of journalism and the conduct of diplomacy. *Quinnipiac Law, 17*(1), 12–15.

Hobbs, J. D. (1995). Treachery by any other name: A case study of the Toshiba public relations crisis. *Management Communication Quarterly, 8,* 323–346.

Ice, R. (1991). Corporate publics and rhetorical strategies: The case of Union Carbide's Bhopal crisis. *Management Communication Quarterly, 4,* 341–362.

Lee, S. (2012, July 12). Ending the 'comfort women' euphemism. *Stars and Stripes.* Retrieved from http://www.stripes.com/news/pacific/ending-the-comfort-women-euphemism-1.182823.

L'Etang, J. (1996). Public relations as diplomacy. In J. L'Etang & M. Pieczka (Eds.), *Critical perspectives in public relations* (pp. 14–34). London: International Thomson Business Press.

Memory and Reconciliation in the Asia-Pacific (2012). Retrieved June 11, 2012, http://www.gwu.edu/~memory/research/bibliography/comfortwomen.html.

Murphy, P. (1996). Chaos theory as a model for managing issues and crises. *Public Relations Review, 22*(2), 95–113.

Murphy, P. (2001). Symmetry, contingency, complexity: Accommodating uncertainty in public relation theory. *Public Relations Review, 26*(4), 447–462.

Nye, J. S., Jr. (1990). Soft power. *Foreign Policy*, 153–171.

Nye, J. S., Jr. (2008). Public diplomacy and soft power. *ANNALS of the American Academy of Political and Social Science, 616*, 94–109.

Seeger, M. W. (2002). Chaos and crisis: Propositions for a general theory of crisis communication. *Public Relations Review, 28*(4), 329–337.

Sheafer, T., & Gabay, I. (2009). Mediated public diplomacy: A strategic contest over international agenda building and frame building. *Political Communication, 26*, 447–467.

Sheafer, T., & Shenhav, S. R. (2010). Mediated public diplomacy in a new era of warfare. *Communication Review, 12*, 272–283.

Signitzer, B., & Wamser, C. (2006). Public diplomacy: A specific governmental public relations function. In C. Botan & V. Hazleton (Eds.), *Public relations theory II* (pp. 435–464). Mahwah, NJ: Lawrence Erlbaum Associates.

USA Today (2008). Retrieved June 19, 2012, http://www.usatoday.com/news/world/2008-06-12-korea-usbeef_N.htm.

Wilcox, D. L., & Cameron, G. T. (2009). *Public relations: Strategies and tactics.* Boston, MA: Allyn & Bacon.

# 8. Diplomacy in a Globalized World: Focussing Internally to Bulid Relationships Externally

KELLY VIBBER & JEONG-NAM KIM

As we entered the 21st century the onslaught of round the clock news coverage and the dramatic increase in the number of democracies worldwide made public diplomacy not only necessary but also crucial (Graffy, 2009). Emerging communication technologies as well as the development and expansion of transportation networks are reprioritizing the traditional order of strategies in public diplomacy. Historically, major sources and determinants of public diplomacy and international relations included power, resources, state-to-state level interactions, and military strength (Doyle, 1997; Morgenthau, 1978). More recently the concepts of soft power (Nye, 2004) and smart power (Nye, 2008) have come to the forefront. Nye's concepts highlight the importance of two-way interaction and the need for diplomatic efforts to be directed towards citizens of other countries and not just governments. In addition, Nye highlights the important shift to influencing others through likeability, attraction, and relationship as opposed to the traditional tactics of power, force, and coercion. Payne (2009) has similarly argued that, "At the heart of any successful public diplomacy initiative is meeting the challenge of understanding, respecting, and appreciating cross-cultural differences as well as similarities" (p. 490). A recent movement to sociological globalism affirms this, positing that direct person-to-person interactions are one of the more important, if not the most important approach in building and maintaining a nation's soft power (Kim & Ni, 2011; Yun & Kim, 2008; Yun, 2012; Yun & Toth, 2009; Yun & Vibber, 2012).

The movement of immigrants, refugees, sojourners, students, business people, and travelers has increased steadily over the last several years making this sociological approach to diplomacy even more critical to consider.

According to the United Nations Department of Economic and Social Affairs (2013) there are an estimated 232 million international migrants worldwide, which means approximately 3.2% of the world's population or one in every 31 people is an international migrant. The number has increased substantially since 2000 when there were 175 million international migrants. This movement of individuals around the world is creating more direct person-to-person global interaction and areas of highly diverse populations. According to the United Nations' data from 2013, the United States remains the most popular destination with 45.8 million international immigrants. These numbers all serve to reiterate that the *within border, foreign publics* are not small, nor are they shrinking. Further, it is important to understand the potential they have to impact their host countries and the way public diplomacy is enacted.

This chapter identifies and presents the role of communicative actions by internal foreign publics, relational factors that trigger their positive or negative communicative actions about various issues related to their host countries, and how their communicative actions could have impacts on public diplomacy outcomes such as "soft power" for their host countries. We conceptually frame the contextual variables of the relationships between the host country and the internal foreign publics, as well as the communicative actions of these publics and what social consequences are likely among their personal social networks (e.g., friends and family). It is this last perspective that makes the connection between technological development, the individual, activism, and diplomacy most clear. It highlights both the importance of sociological public diplomacy for within border, foreign publics as well as the potential impact of the communicative activism of these publics through digital media and social networks.

## The International Public Inside the Border

Public and international diplomacy is something that has long been seen as a function of the government. However it has become obvious that traditional government oriented approaches to diplomacy are not as functional in today's world and as a result grassroots approaches to public diplomacy are rising (Payne, 2009). Individuals, academia, business, and nongovernmental organizations have all approached this issue of public diplomacy and how it might be used to "heal the great divides globally and locally" (Payne, 2009, p. 487).

The concept of sociological public diplomacy, or how direct interpersonal contact through people flow around the world impacts the soft power of a nation, has been explored by several scholars (Kim & Ni, 2011; Yun, 2012; Yun & Kim, 2008; Yun & Toth, 2009; Yun & Vibber, 2012). Sociological public diplomacy emphasizes the role of direct interaction or people-to-people contact and necessitates governmental policy efforts to facilitate and protect freer and open interaction (e.g., visa or immigration regulation, monitoring and preventing xenophobia, nationalism, or ethnocentrism) among its citizens and individuals from foreign countries. It prioritizes people-to-people interaction and affirmative governmental action for diasporas and foreign publics over mediated messages and the role of governmental propagandistic campaigns. These prioritized actions are seen as having a greater influence on what shapes an individual's view of a host country or impacts their perceived relationship with it (Yun & Toth, 2009). From this perspective, having a society that is open to foreign publics and interacts positively with them could do more for that country's soft power and diplomatic efforts (cf. "behavioral, strategic management paradigm in public relations") than governmental campaigns and nation branding campaigns to implant positive images among foreign publics (cf. "symbolic, interpretive paradigm in public relations") (Kim, Hung-Baesecke, Yang, & Grunig, 2013; Kim & Ni, 2010; Grunig & Kim, 2011).

Yun and Toth (2009) predicted that under the framework of soft power, "sociological globalism will be a new background of future public diplomacy" (p. 493). This new background would in turn dictate another shift in the focus of diplomacy; that "sociological public diplomacy will become domesticated toward 'inside border' foreign publics as part of government's public affairs" (Yun & Toth, 2009, p. 493). This awareness of within border internationals is critical if one believes in sociological public diplomacy, because just as your own citizens will have a greater impact on this public's view of your country, the internal, foreign public will also interact with others from their home country or other countries and impact their views of your country. Recent developments in communication technology have accelerated the rate at which this sort of opinion or experience sharing can occur.

## Advocates vs. Adversaries: Positive and Negative Megaphoning of Hosted Publics

The advent of many developments in digital communication technology places within border, foreign publics in a unique position to engage in active communication behaviors either for or against their host countries. New conceptualizations of public diplomacy have reflected these changes. Terms such as participation, exchange, and dialogue have entered the conversation about what diplomacy is and what it looks like as "people expect a more interactive and participatory role" (Zaharna, 2005, p. 2; Vickers, 2004). Active communication behavior by the internal, yet foreign, public now travels larger distances faster than ever before and may spread exponentially through "shares," "retweets," and "likes" on a variety of social networks.

Wellman (2002) framed the implications of this digital age by developing the concept of networked individualism. Within the framework of networked individualism, "each person separately operates his networks to obtain information, collaboration, order, support, sociability, and a sense of belonging" (Wellman, 2002, p. 16). As such, the individual becomes the portal and is essentially always connected to and has access to create messages of influence and information via cell phones, smartphones, computers, etc. This provides the within border, foreign public with an instant medium and audience for their positive or negative communicative action about their host country, a behavior that can be called *megaphoning* (Kim & Rhee, 2011). In addition, the people in their networks are essentially wired into receiving the megaphoning messages when they are sent, provided they have access to some form of digital communication. These received messages can then be shared again through their own networks, creating a chain effect of megaphoning.

Kim and Rhee (2011) introduced the concept of megaphoning as an application of *information forwarding* and *information sharing*, both of which were developed in the communicative action part of the problem solving model (CAPS) (Kim, Grunig, & Ni, 2010) and the situational theory of problem solving (STOPS) (Kim & Grunig, 2011). Originally, megaphoning was conceptualized as a form of employee communication behavior where employees spread positive or negative information about the organization to members of the external publics (Kim & Rhee, 2011). However, it is also possible to extend this role and action to within border foreign publics, if we juxtapose organizations with a government or hosting society and employees with internationals within borders (Kim, 2012). These within border foreign publics have insider experience with the country, its people, and the government, which makes them more credible to their audiences. In addition, they have external publics (e.g., friends and family in their home country) who are listening to them and perhaps even waiting to hear from them. These combined factors strategically position within border foreigners to be able to execute/create potential activism.

According to the situational theory of problem solving (STOPS), individuals who identify a problem will organize to resolve it provided that they feel involved with the issue, motivated to act, and feel they can do something about it (Kim & Grunig, 2011; Kim & Krishna, 2014). When these things are true, the public, and the individuals who make up the public, are likely to engage in communicative action or activism to attempt to solve the problem or correct the issue. These active behaviors could include information forwarding, information seeking, and information forefending (Kim, Grunig, & Ni, 2010). Information forwarding is the active sharing or passing on of information related to the problem or issue. Information seeking is the active searching for information or resources to help with the issue, and information forefending is the active selective attending to and rejecting of different information based on how it fits a set of criteria (e.g. validity, consistency with beliefs or goals).

It is important here to acknowledge that the availability of digital communication technologies has in some ways altered the *constraint recognition*—perceived obstacles in addressing problematic states—that individuals and publics feel. Kim and Ni (2010) have noted that active publics exploit online communication space because these media allow them to feel more powerful, as well as more empowered to share their thoughts. Also it is critical to highlight that neither communicative action in problem solving (Kim, Grunig, & Ni, 2010) nor the situational theory of problem solving (Kim & Grunig, 2011) dictates that the issue must be negative (e.g., some publics may arise around a positive issue to secure beneficial consequences from a management decision or policy). Furthermore, the concepts of positive and negative megaphoning are both situational and cross-situational communicative actions. This means that they may be situational—increasing for a short time related to a hot issue such as a hostile immigration law—or may be dormant or chronic—continuing and reappearing even after the situational motivation has declined, such as when a person asks them about their experiences with the country. In the latter case, the way publics view previous experiences with the host country is mediated through their perceived relationship quality (e.g., trust, control mutuality) and type of relationship (i.e., communal vs. exchange relationship) with the country. These perceived relationships in turn influence the direction (i.e., positive or negative) and the amount of communicative actions the publics take (Kim, 2012). Thus it is possible that activism and megaphoning behavior can take on either a positive or negative tone, as well as potentially becoming a continuous or recurrent behavior that would be strong enough to trigger information flows in communicators' social networks. This positions internal, foreign publics as potential advocates or adversaries for their host country and essentially *micro-diplomats* or spokespersons to their social networks and members of their home country. Recent work by Yun and Vibber (2012) did find some support for the idea that students abroad would at least attempt to act as advocates or adversaries on behalf of their host country when communicating with people in their home country.

## Impetus for Communicative Activism

The relationship between a foreign public and its host country serves as the impetus for any communicative action they may take for or against the host country. This relationship is twofold and extends beyond the individual or diaspora within the host country to those in their social networks. When reconceptualizing the communicative action of publics, Kim, Grunig, and Ni, (2010) outlined the potential of communicative action to spread from the focal communicant, the one directly involved and high in communicative action, to the peripheral communicants, members of the focal communicant's network who received the message or megaphoning. In turn, these peripheral communicants with medium levels of communicative action may share these messages with their own networks reaching a still more peripheral communicant (Kim, Grunig, & Ni, 2010).

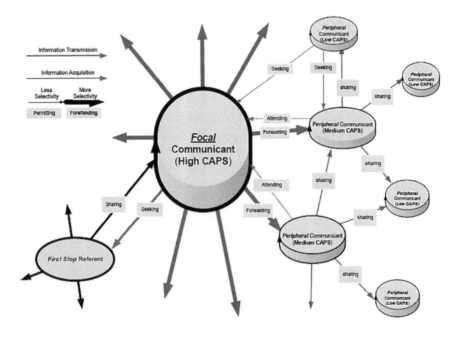

*Figure 8.1.* Illustration of intercommunication using the communicative action model variables. (reprinted from Kim, Grunig, & Ni, 2010)

Within the context of sociological diplomacy, the first part of this relationship is the direct relationship between the individual (focal communicant) and the host country. This perceived relationship is based on the direct interaction or sociological public diplomacy between the foreigner and people of the host country. It is a *behavioral relationship* in that it is contextual, sociological, and based on actual interactions (Grunig & Kim, 2011; Kim et al., 2014). The second part of the relationship involves members of the social network (peripheral communicants) of the individual who has a direct relationship with the host country. These individuals have an indirect and tangential *reputational relationship* with the country (Grunig & Kim, 2011; Kim, Hung-Baesecke, Yang, & Grunig, 2013). For example, parents who perceived a positive relationship when choosing to send their children to school in the United States may feel differently if their child is treated unfairly or experiences racism. There may also be individuals who experience both levels of the relationship, such as immigrants who left their home country based on a positive reputational relationship with a host country and then experienced a behavioral relationship with the people and the country that may or may not confirm the reputational relationship. Either of these situations may influence publics or individuals at the first or second level to engage in communicative activism. Activism that engages social networks can spread quickly and affect the host country's soft power. Negative megaphoning and word of mouth may more easily damage soft power because this power essentially relies on the country's appeal and attractiveness to others through its culture, ideologies, and institutions (Nye, 2004). Stories of others' negative or positive experiences can more immediately impact others' views of that country, thus directly impacting the attractiveness of that country to others and in turn the power or influence that country has.

## *Framing the Relationship: Major Contextual Factors of Perceived Relationships Among Foreign Publics*

Work by a variety of scholars has attempted to conceptualize the major sources of soft power that influence the perceived relationships, both behavioral and reputational, that foreign publics have with their host country (Kim & Ni, 2011; Yun & Kim, 2008; Yun & Toth, 2009; Pratt, 1989). Kim and Ni (2011) summarize the three antecedents of soft power as follows: political and economic interactions; people-to-people interactions; and cultural interactions. It is important to note that only the first of these functions at an institutional/governmental level. The second construct more immediately impacts the direct or behavioral relationship with a country.

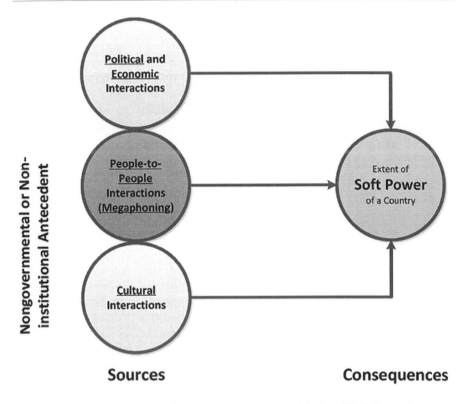

*Figure 8.2.* Antecedents of soft power: A positive model. (modified from Kim & Ni, 2011)

Although the construct of people-to-people interactions reflects socio-logical public diplomacy and interpersonal interaction, Kim and Ni (2011) also acknowledge the role of information technology in making this type of interaction cheaper and more accessible to many even though it may not always reflect actual face-to-face interaction. The third antecedent, cultural interactions, reflects more immediately on the indirect reputational relation-ship with a country. This antecedent reflects the individualized consumption of cultural products such as music, literature, art, and films. This consump-tion can lead to the development and amplification of a perception about the cultural products and the country of origin (Kim & Ni, 2011). It is re-cent developments such as globalization of economies, social media, and new media technology which have allowed for greater individual participation in international relations making these types of cultural and media diplomacy possible (Signitzer & Wamser, 2006). These have in turn impacted the factors that most directly shape individuals' relations with foreign countries and the ways in which they can impact the soft power of those nations as a result of their relationships.

Taking a slightly different approach to soft power, Yun and Kim (2008) developed a regression model with three predicting variables: ethnic relations, between country relationship quality, and normative performance (reputation) of the country. Ethnic relations, like in the constructs of Kim and Ni (2011), were based on sociological globalism and interaction with members of other ethnicities. Relationship quality was a measure of the relationship between the individual's home country and the host country or other country in question. This is similar to the construct of political and economic interactions from Kim and Ni (2011). Yun and Kim (2008) found that relationship quality had the most significant influence on soft power and that ethnic relations had a sizeable and significant effect as well. Normative performance had a weak and insignificant impact on soft power.

Examining these two studies, it seems consistent that although the role of the institution and government in forming relationships and soft power with other publics has not been eliminated, it is also no longer the main factor. The relationship between one's country and another country in terms of politics, policies, and economy does impact the relationship citizens perceive with that country (e.g. hostile vs. friendly). However, the increased access to cultural products as well as direct or digital interaction with individuals who are from or have been to these countries has changed and continues to change the way in which individuals' relationships with countries are shaped.

## The Process and Outcomes of Migrants' Communicative Activism

Increased accessibility of information, communication technologies, and global networking are making the voice of the individual perhaps more important to public diplomacy than ever before. Locke, Levine, Searls, and Weinberger (1999) contend that the Internet has reinstated the value of the individual's voice and that people want to hear and believe in individuals more than they do corporations and organizations. After a long period driven by mass marketing, what is currently valued is personal voice and interaction with real people. This theory in conjunction with the ideas of sociological diplomacy and communicative activism (megaphoning) highlights the potential impact of these within border, foreign publics: their personal accounts of what they experience are likely to be valued, believed, and prioritized over official government statements or national news. According to Kim and Ni (2011):

> Because migrants have more substantial, direct, and natural, rather than super-
> ficial, indirect, and artificial interaction and contact with the hosting countries,
> their experiences and perceptions are more credible with people in their home
> countries. And because migrants still have connections with people back home,
> they can more easily enhance or destroy the hosting countries' reputation or the
> resources of soft power. (pp. 140–141)

As previously highlighted, the advent of social networking sites and the
development of communication technology have made it possible for their
megaphoning to be disseminated quickly and then echoed, reverberating
through "shares," "retweets," and "likes" that may then echo again through
the next set of networks and the next (cf. the informative behavioral interactions between focal communicants and peripheral communicants in Figure
8.1). In this way social networks do part of the activist work for the user placing their information into the newsfeeds of the users' network and allowing
them to easily forward the message with minimal effort.

The important message here is that of contagious relational quality in
that there is a two-step flow of influence through communicative actions (i.e.,
megaphoning) from the direct behavioral relationship holders to the indirect
reputational holders. Because of the technological developments discussed
here, their connections are now more portable, accessible, and immediate,
positioning both types of relationship holders to embrace communicative action. As a result, communicating with within border foreigners "is no longer
a means to an end but an end itself," reshaping the way we think about public
diplomacy and the importance of person-to-person contact (Kim & Ni, 2011,
p. 141). These individuals with direct behavioral relationships are not only
well positioned but also contextually legitimized as micro-diplomats, relating
their experiences abroad to members of their home country and acting as
local representatives of their native country in their host residence.

It is noteworthy that the very vehicle that connects concrete, first-hand
experiences (relationship) to superficial, second-hand opinion (reputation)
among foreign publics is the communicative actions of members of foreign
publics (see Figure 8.1). The motivated communicative actions of behavioral
relationship holders become the engine or social cognitive mills to produce
the direction and amount of information related to the hosting country that is
shared and amplified over socio-communicative networks among foreign publics. More importantly, the communicative activism by the first-hand, behavioral relationship holding foreign publics would earn priority or added-weight
when the information from the hosting country itself and the information
from the foreign publics in that country are inconsistent (e.g., positive media
image vs. negative witness from family about the given country). In this vein,

communicative activism is an under-studied aspect in conceptualizing the process and outcomes of public diplomacy and has increasingly more salient theoretical linkages among the key factors and outcomes of public diplomacy. Public diplomacy theory and practice should pay attention to these threats and opportunities in the positive and negative megaphoning of within border foreign publics.

## *Strategic Public Diplomacy: The Opportunities and Threats of Communicative Activism by Behavioral, Relationship Holding Foreign Publics*

This new face of diplomacy comes with both great benefits and also potential threats. On the plus side, the value of word of mouth has a long history both in that it provides good marketing and reputation building without tangible cost and that others find it more believable than if the organization had promoted itself. However, on the negative side, sociological diplomacy is much harder to control. It is based more on individual actions and responses than systematic or planned communication campaigns. A country cannot control how individual citizens act in all situations, or prevent all foreigners from encountering racism or prejudice. Should a country or its individuals do something that others find offensive or wrong, these individuals only have to access their social networks to start gathering support from individuals and groups domestically and abroad. Despite a variety of countries attempting to control digital information flow both into as well as out of their country, the resourcefulness of citizens, revolutionaries, and activists has prevailed repeatedly connecting these individuals with the information they were seeking and providing an audience for their voice so that they could mobilize support, awareness, and activism. These actions have often resulted in severe damage to a country's soft power or complete social revolution.

Because of both the potential opportunities as well as the risks in this approach to diplomacy, it is important to approach the relationship with within border foreign publics in a symmetrical way and to attempt to achieve balance of interests among related parties (Grunig, 2009). Symmetrical communication has been shown to be more effective than an asymmetrical approach in relationship building, particularly long-term relationship building between organizations and publics (Grunig & Huang, 2000; Hon & Grunig, 1999). Kim and Ni (2011) have highlighted the need for diplomacy to not only be one sided in seeking soft power to secure one's own nation's interests, but also to be "soft empowering" to those countries who may be less culturally powerful or attractive to other nations. There is a need to open the dialogue and to learn from and understand each other in order to build successful and enduring soft power; otherwise a nation runs the risk of being revealed as only seeking its own interests through cultural and social interactions. If this happens, the nation will in turn lose some of its soft power, as manipulation and exploitation are not viewed as factors that increase one's attractiveness to others but may only further increase active information behaviors against the country among foreign publics.

Here again the role of the individual and grassroots movements is critical in developing effective and enduring soft power. As previously mentioned, their messages have the benefit of being seen as unbiased and authentic. As a result of recent developments in communication technology and social networking, within border foreign publics can spread their legitimized voice quickly and efficiently at a very low or no cost to the country. Thus making these publics a country's greatest ally or enemy in the realm of diplomacy. By extension of this idea, Kim and Ni (2011) highlight that a country might even reap benefits or losses from its own citizens interacting as diasporas or visitors within other countries. As a result it may be advantageous to cultivate cultural awareness and respect for diversity among one's citizens in order for them to act as assets to a nation's soft power both at home and abroad.

Furthermore, if governments embrace a role of facilitating instead of attempting to censor or limit the exchange of cultural products and information among social members internally and externally, they may encourage more creativity among cultural producers who can enact the role of positive diplomats on behalf of the nation (Kim & Ni, 2011). Lastly, governmental policy efforts to foster and secure open and egalitarian grassroots interactions will be critical to maximize positive communicative actions and temper negative communicative activism. The efforts of social institutions to create inclusive culture, tolerance for foreign values, and mutual respect for within border, foreign publics will also be important in encouraging positive communicative actions among these strategically positioned publics. Despite the shift to a more person-to-person approach, as dictated by sociological globalism, the role of the government in diplomacy has not been completely revoked. However, it has been drastically altered and it is important that governments acknowledge this and adjust their approaches and policies to help mobilize the resources already available through their citizens and social organizations.

In today's globalizing society some of the strongest potential advocates and adversaries of a nation and its diplomacy are no longer in the state offices and municipal buildings, but in the grocery store, the bar, and on Facebook. These groups and individuals have the potential to be the most believable and affordable allies in building a nation's soft power, but the relationship a nation cultivates with its within border foreign public is critical in determining whether or not this potential is realized. This chapter has provided a discussion of major factors that influence that relationship as well as predictors of communicative action, the types of activism likely to be enacted, and important considerations in developing these relationships. As we move forward in this age of globalization and digital technology it is likely that our networks and connections will only become more advanced and interconnected. Nations would do well to recognize the importance and value of relationships with those key publics inside their borders and work to develop them to the best of their ability, not only to benefit relations within their borders but also to in turn bolster relationships with constituents abroad.

## Bibliography

Doyle, M. W. (1997). *Ways of war and peace.* New York: W. W. Norton & Company.

Graffy, C. (2009). Public diplomacy: A practitioner's perspective. *American Behavioral Scientist, 52*(5), 791–796.

Grunig, J. E. (2009). Paradigms of global public relations in an age of digitalization. *Prism, 6*(2), http://praxis.massey.ac.nz./prism_on-line_journ.html

Grunig, J. E., & Huang, Y. H. (2000). From organizational effectiveness to relationship indicators: Antecedents of relationships, public relations strategies, and relationship outcomes. In J. A. Ledingham & S. D. Bruning (Eds.), *Public relations as relationship management: A relational approach to the study and practice of public relations* (pp. 23–53). Mahwah, NJ: Lawrence Erlbaum Associates.

Grunig, J. E., & Kim, J.-N. (2011). Actions speak louder than words: How a strategic management approach to public relations can shape a company's brand and reputation through relationships. *Insight Train, 1*(1), 36–51.

Hon, L. C., & Grunig, J. E. (1999). *Guidelines for measuring relationships in public relations.* Gainesville, FL: The Institute for Public Relations, Commission on PR Measurement and Evaluation.

Kim, J. -N. (2012). From organizational decisions to constituencies' communicative actions: Linking two phenomena for strategic communication fields. *International Journal of Strategic Communication, 6*(1), 1–6.

———. (2011). Problem solving and communicative action: A situational theory of problem solving. *Journal of Communication, 61,* 120–149.

Kim, J. -N., Grunig, J. E., & Ni, L. (2010). Reconceptualizing public's communicative action: Acquisition, selection, and transmission of information in problematic situations. *International Journal of Strategic Communication, 4,* 126–154.

Kim, J. -N. & Krishna, A. (2014). A situational theory of problem solving: A review of the theory, intellectual origins, and new research. *Communication Yearbook 38.*

———. (2014). Publics and lay informatics: A review of the situational theory of problem solving. *Communication Yearbook 38,* 71–105.

Kim, J. -N., & Ni, L. (2010). Seeing the forest through the trees. In R. Heath (Ed.). *The Sage handbook of public relations* (second edition) (pp. 35–57). Thousand Oaks: Sage Publications.

———. (2011). The nexus between Hallyu and soft power: Cultural public diplomacy in the era of sociological globalism. In D. K. Kim & M. -S. Kim (Eds.) *Hallyu: Influence of Korean popular culture in Asia and beyond* (pp. 131–154).

Kim, J. -N., & Rhee, Y. (2011). Strategic thinking about employee communication behavior (ECB) in public relations: Testing the models of megaphoning and scouting effects in Korea. *Journal of Public Relations Research, 23,* 1–268.

Kim, J. -N., Hung-Baesecke, C. -J., Yang, S-U., & Grunig, J. E. (2013). A strategic management approach to reputation, relationships, and publics: The research heritage of the Excellence Theory. In C. Carroll (Ed.), *Handbook of communication and corporate reputation* (pp. 197–212). New York: Wiley-Blackwell.

Locke, C., Levine, R., Searls, D., & Weinberger, D. (1999). The Cluetrain Manifesto. Retrieved from http://www.cluetrain.com/book/index.html

Morgenthau, H. J. (1978). *Politics among nations: The struggle for power and peace* (5th ed.). New York: Alfred A. Knopf.

Nye, J. S. (2004). *Soft power: The means to success in world politics.* New York: PublicAffairs.

———. (2008). Security and smart power. *American Behavioral Scientist, 51*(9), 1351–1356.

Payne, J. G. (2009). Trends in global public relations and grassroots diplomacy. *American Behavioral Scientist, 53*(4), 487–492.

Pratt, C. (Ed.). (1989). *Internationalism under strain: The North-South policies of Canada, the Netherlands, Norway, and Sweden.* Toronto, Ontario, Canada: University of Toronto Press.

Signitzer, B. & Wamser, C. (2006). Public diplomacy: A specific governmental public relations function. In C. H. Botan & V. Hazleton (Eds.), *Public Relations Theory* (pp. 435–464). Mahwah, NJ: Lawrence Erlbaum Associates.

UNESCO (2010). *Global Education Digest 2010.* Montreal: UNESCO Institute for Statistics.

United Nations Department of Economic and Social Affairs (2013). 232 million international migrants living abroad worldwide—new UN global migration statistics revealed. Retrieved from http://esa.un.org/unmigration/wallchart2013.htm

Vickers, R. (2004). The new public diplomacy: Britain and Canada compared. *British Journal of Politics & International Relations, 6,* 182–194.

Wellman, B. (2002). Little boxes, glocalization, and networked individualism. Digital cities II: Computational and sociological approaches: Kyoto, 18–20 October 2001, revised papers. Kyoto workshop on digital cities No. 2, Kyoto, JAPON (18/10/2001) 2002, vol. 2362, 10–25.

Yun, S-H. (2012). Relational public diplomacy: The perspective of sociological globalism. *International Journal of Communication, 6,* 2199–2219.

Yun, S-H. & Kim, J-N. (2008). Soft power: From ethnic attraction to national attraction in sociological globalism. *International Journal of Intercultural Relations, 32,* 565–577.

Yun, S-H. & Toth, E. (2009). Future sociological public diplomacy and the role of public relations: Evaluation of public diplomacy. *American Behavioral Scientist, 53*(4), 493–503.

Yun, S-H., & Vibber, K. (2012). The strategic values and communicative actions of Chinese students for Korean sociological diplomacy. *International Journal of Strategic Communication, 6*(1), 77–92.

Zaharna, R. S. (2005). The network paradigm of strategic public diplomacy. *Foreign Policy in Focus Policy Brief, 10*(1). Retrieved from http://www.fpif.org/briefs/vol10/v10n01pubdip.html

# 9. Stewardship and the Political Process: Improving the Political Party-Constituent Relationship Through Public Relations

Kristi S. Gilmore & Richard D. Waters

Voter satisfaction and confidence in politicians and political parties are at an all-time low in the United States. Despite popular movements on the left and right of the political spectrum, constituents are increasingly describing their political beliefs as independent and moving away from the two main political parties. Ultimately, this creates a scenario where political party leadership has a vested interest in strengthening party relationships with voters in order to boost their respective party's political prowess and chances for policy change.

This chapter looks at the deteriorating relationship between political parties and constituents and explores how, through the relationship management paradigm, effective stewardship can be used by political parties to strengthen that vital connection. In addition, it considers how similar stewardship efforts could be effective in relational public diplomacy between the United States and other countries as "soft power" or relationship-building becomes more accepted in the field of public diplomacy.

The relationship management paradigm of public relations provides a framework to analyze the political party-constituent relationship and suggests ways in which the four stewardship strategies—reciprocity, responsibility, reporting, and relationship nurturing—can be realized as an effective means to strengthen relationships between organizations/nations and their important constituencies.

## Introduction

### Voter Confidence Down

In April 2012, the Harris Poll released its annual confidence index after surveying more than 2,000 Americans to assess their trust and satisfaction with various branches of government, the for-profit sector, and the media. Following years of declining approval, Congress was ranked last with only 6 percent of respondents saying they had a great amount of confidence and nearly 52 percent reporting having hardly any confidence at all (Price, 2012). The continued decline in trust and satisfaction, as expressed by confidence and approval ratings, for Congress has been attributed to backroom dealings made by party leaders and a general feeling among the constituency that the parties are no longer looking out for the public, but are more interested in self-preservation of their political power (Wolak & Palus, 2010).

Lindaman and Haider-Markel (2002) noted that individuals who have self-identified as a member of the Republican or Democratic Party have started turning away from party labels because they feel the parties have lost their way and are disconnected from those that they serve. Despite increases in favorable evaluation of government entities in wake of the terrorist attacks of Sept. 11, 2001, continued scandal and the global financial crisis have caused that confidence to fade (Gross, Brewer, & Aday, 2009) and the number of independent voters has steadily been increasing (Petrocik, 2009). Mayer (2008) notes that the number of independent voters has risen to nearly 40 percent and that the increased number of voters willing to embrace candidates from either of the major political parties is making it more difficult to accurately poll and predict election results. The increasing dissatisfaction with the two main parties, combined with the increasing number of third-party candidates who have won elections at local and state contests, has been noted by party leaders who feel that the parties must do something to reconnect with their base (Lee, 2011).

The relationship management paradigm of public relations provides a framework to analyze the political party-constituent relationship and suggests ways in which the four stewardship strategies—reciprocity, responsibility, reporting, and relationship nurturing—can be realized as an effective means to strengthen relationships between organizations and their important constituencies.

Public relations scholarship provides a theoretical framework for this situation by allowing the political parties to improve their relationship with their constituents. The relationship management paradigm of public relations focuses on the creation and growth of relationships between an organization and its public, or, in this case, a political party and its supporters. This cultivation cannot be done superficially. Rather, there must be a legitimate attempt to develop the mutually-beneficial relationship. For most political parties, the mutually-beneficial dimension of the relationship is logical; by helping constituents with their overall fiscal and social well-being, the constituents are more likely to support the party in future elections (Gunther & Diamond, 2003). However, critics have argued that today's political parties have started to shift away from that mutually-beneficial focus.

## Stewardship

The public relations concept of stewardship, the pursuit of ongoing relationships with stakeholders rather than a focus on short-term campaign goals, has been identified through literature as a key strategy to foster relationship growth in the organization-public relationships. However, it has largely only been examined within the nonprofit sector. This study seeks to expand the horizons of this public relations concept by measuring the perception of stewardship usage by political party constituents; examining how stewardship can be used by political parties to bolster their relationship with constituents; and discussing how those lessons of stewardship can be translated into the application of soft power in public diplomacy to achieve the same results.

## Soft Power

While the study highlighted here is specific to political party/constituent relationships in the United States, there are striking similarities between the relationship-building efforts in public relations through stewardship and Nye's soft power perspective in public diplomacy (2008), which introduces the concept of relationship-building between countries by developing credibility and creating mutually-beneficial relationships. This "soft power" approach is one of the three primary components or "layers" of the integrated approach to public diplomacy (Golan, 2013), which focuses on the development of long-term, ongoing relationships and is likely to benefit from the use of stewardship strategies. The potential implications for these strategies in public diplomacy will be discussed here.

## **Literature Review**

In public relations, the definition and conceptualization of the organization-public relationship (OPR) are contested. Broom, Casey, and Ritchey (1997) defined OPR as a representation created through "the patterns of interaction, transaction, exchange, and linkage between an organization and its publics" (p. 18). Ledingham and Bruning (1998) coined this definition of organization-public relationships: "the state that exists between an organization and its key publics that provides economic, social, political, and/or cultural benefits to all parties involved, and is characterized by mutual positive regard" (p. 62). Hon and Grunig (1999) posited that an organization-public relationship occurs when both parties—the organization and the public—face outcomes and repercussions based on the other's behavior. After considering the limitations of these definitions (too broad, too neglectful of the communication effort needed in the communication process), Rhee (2007) interpreted organization-public relationships as "a connection or association between an organization and a public that results from behavioral consequences an organization or a public has on the other and that necessitates repeated communication" (p. 109).

Public diplomacy is similarly defined by Nye (2008) as "an instrument that governments use to mobilize resources to communicate with and attract the publics of other countries, rather than merely their governments" (p. 94). Signitzer and Coombs (1992) emphasize the similarities between public relations and public diplomacy as they seek similar objectives and employ similar tools. They defined public diplomacy as "the way in which both government and private individuals and groups influence directly or indirectly those public attitudes and opinions which bear directly on another government's foreign policy decisions" (p. 138). And, Gilboa (2008) claims that the Signitzer and Coombs's definition "abolishes the distinction between public diplomacy and PR" (p. 57). Consequently, the focus both OPR and public diplomacy place on relationship-building, long-term maintenance of relationships or "stewardship," and the ability to effectively communicate and persuade publics through attraction and persuasion provides an opportunity to examine the application of effective dimensions of successful relationships in one area or another.

## Dimensions of Organizational-Public Relationships

Botan and Taylor (2004) noted that "the scholars researching OPR have delved into interpersonal communication theory and research, all in an effort to better understand relationship building, including the construct of trust, often seen as an important part of the relationship between publics and organizations" (p. 652).

Initially, Ferguson (1984) detailed several attributes for defining and measuring organization-public relations: dynamic nature of the relationship, level of openness, degree of satisfaction for both parties, distribution of power, the extent of mutuality of understanding and agreement, and consensus. Pulling from interpersonal theory, the foundational critique by Ferguson (1984), and from concept explications on OPR (see Broom, Casey, & Ritchey, 1997), Hon and Grunig (1999) identified trust, control mutuality, relational satisfaction, and relational commitment as the indicators for a quality relationship.

*Trust.* According to Ni (2007), trust is a matter of "confidence in the other party and the willingness of one to open himself or herself to the other party" (p. 54). Hon and Grunig (1999) considered the following three dimensions as fundamental to trust: (a) integrity: "the belief that an organization is fair and just," (b) dependability: "the belief that an organization will do what it says it will do," and (c) competence: "the belief that an organization has the ability to do what it says it will do" (p. 19).

*Control mutuality.* Hon and Grunig (1999) defined control mutuality as "the degree to which parties agree on who has rightful power to influence one another" (p. 13). At the core of this dimension are power and reciprocity (Yang, 2007). The imbalances and balances of power between the organization and its publics, per Bortree and Waters (2008), influence "the perceptions and actualities of an individual's relationship with an organization" (p. 3). Reciprocity is a crucial component of "stable and quality organization–public relationships even if power asymmetry is inevitable in any relationship" (Yang, 2007, p. 94).

*Satisfaction.* Hon and Grunig (1999) believed satisfaction is the relationship component that is reinforced through positive interactions. Grunig wrote, "A satisfying relationship occurs when each party believes the other is engaging in positive steps to maintain the relationship" (1999, p. 2). Stafford and Canary (1991) approached satisfaction from a social exchange perspective, thus defining the concept as occurring when "the distribution of rewards is equitable and the relations rewards outweigh the cost" (p. 225). Ledingham and Bruning (2000) proposed that if organizations infuse resources and time into the growth of established relationships, individuals' level of satisfaction could increase.

*Commitment.* Scholars have reiterated the importance of commitment as an element of loyalty (e.g., Morgan & Hunt, 1994; Yang, 2007) or as Ni (2007) put it, "an enduring desire to maintain a relationship because it is valued" (p. 55). Morgan and Hunt (1994) interpreted commitment as "an exchange partner believing that an ongoing relationship with another is so important as to warrant maximum efforts at maintaining it; that is, the committed party believes the relationship is worth working on to ensure that it endures indefinitely" (p. 23). Grunig (2002) considered commitment as "the extent to which both parties believe and feel that the relationship is worth spending energy on to maintain and promote" (p. 2). Because of the loyalty aspects attached to commitment, this dimension can hint to future behaviors and intentions toward the organization (Bortree & Waters, 2008).

Ki and Hon (2007) found that publics' perceptions of control mutuality and satisfaction best predicted a positive relationship with the organization. Their proposed model supported that the building and sustaining of positive OPR should be the public relations function's primary aim. These quality relationships have been assumed to drive supportive attitudes and behaviors toward the organization among strategic constituencies.

Given that the four relationship outcomes serve as the foundation for understanding the OPR, the first research question was created to provide the baseline evidence for the political party-constituent relationship. Without asking this basic question, research into the topic is stymied:

**RQ1:** To what extent do constituents value their relationship with the political party with which they most identify?

## Stewardship and the Organization-Public Relationship

The public relations literature suggests that organizations can improve relationships by engaging cultivation strategies (Hon & Grunig, 1999). Writing about nonprofit organizations' relationship cultivation practices, Kelly (1998) proposed four stewardship strategies that she conceptualized based on theory and professional experience. Her work has application outside of nonprofit organizations as well and has the potential to be implemented in the field of public diplomacy. As Hon and Grunig (1999) acknowledge, stewardship is the "final but missing step in popular formulas for describing the public relations process" (p. 17). Other scholars have focused on how core dimensions of stewardship, including responsibility, can contribute to the employee relationship and lead to greater support for the organization (Ledingham & Bruning, 1998).

The construct of stewardship consists of four dimensions, as proposed by Kelly (2001)—reciprocity, responsibility, reporting, and relationship nurturing. The first dimension, reciprocity, is the imperative that organizations show gratitude toward their publics for the contributions they make. Showing gratitude for stakeholder involvement is a way to demonstrate respect for stakeholders and their contributions to the organization. According to Gouldner (1960), from the sociological perspective, "those whom you have helped have an obligation to help you" (p. 173). Political parties can show respect for their constituents through acts of appreciation and by simply saying "thank you." But, simply saying "thank you" during an election-night victory speech is not enough. Politicians and the parties they represent must make sure that voters know their gratitude is lasting and genuine. Recognizing the support given to the candidate by constituents "shows good stewardship. It says you're thoughtful, attentive, and caring" (Ryan, 1994, p. 64). This can be a powerful motivator for future support.

When organizations fulfill their obligations to stakeholders they demonstrate the second component of stewardship, responsibility. Responsible organizations keep promises to their publics and act in a "socially responsible manner to[ward] publics that have supported the organization and its goals in the past" (Kelly, 2001, p. 285). It is often difficult for political parties to keep all of the promises made to constituents, given the government processes in place, but they can work toward those promises and make decisions that are best for the voters.

Not only should organizations be responsible for their actions, but they need to inform stakeholders of the decisions they make and the actions they take. This is the third dimension of stewardship, reporting. The act of reporting improves the accountability of an organization and provides general information that can lead to a positive perception of the organization (Ledingham, 2001). As the Harris Poll noted (Price, 2012), the continued lack of confidence by the public in the political parties and Congress is largely due to the broken promises that are made each year in regard to lower spending and policy reform when all indicators point to increased expenditures and continued abuse of government policies and regulations.

The fourth stewardship strategy, relationship nurturing, focuses on the care taken by an organization in building and maintaining an ongoing relationship with a public (Kelly, 2001). This includes engaging with stakeholders by inviting publics to give input on organizational direction, making decisions with publics' best interest in mind, and creating dialogue with stakeholders. According to Kelly (2001), organizations engage in relationship nurturing when they "accept the importance of supportive publics and keep them at the forefront of the organization's conscience" (p. 286). Culbertson, Jeffers, Stone, and Terrell (1993) illustrate the importance of organizational involvement with publics by stating, "There is reason to believe that involvement enhances genuine, long-term behavioral support" (p. 98). Turning to individual voters, research has shown that constituents who take the time to attend town hall meetings and participate in community-sponsored civic and political events are much more likely to support the sponsor in the future, including in upcoming elections (McLeod, Scheufele, & Moy, 1999).

To fully understand the role stewardship plays, two final research questions were created. The study's second research question provides a framework for understanding the extent to which constituents perceive stewardship strategies being used by their respective political parties while the third research question attempts to determine whether using the stewardship strategies can impact an individual's involvement with their political party:

> **RQ 2:** To what extent do individuals see stewardship being used to cultivate the political party-constituent relationship?
>
> **RQ 3:** Can stewardship be used to strengthen constituents' involvement with the political party they most identify with?

## Dimensions of Soft Power in Public Diplomacy

In today's global economy, politicians and their respective political parties must also look beyond their internal constituencies to build mutually-beneficial relationships with the larger global population. The dimensions of trust, control mutuality, relational satisfaction, and relational commitment as indicators for a quality relationship in organizational-public relations are equally applicable to quality relationships in public diplomacy. The importance of good relationships in the public diplomacy arena is emphasized by the concept of "soft power," a term coined by Nye in the 1980s (Keohane & Nye, 1998). In contrast to the forceful or reward driven "power" gained by governments over other governments in the past, soft power is "the ability to achieve goals through attraction rather than coercion" (Keohane & Nye, 1998, p. 86). In other words, rather than acquire power in a relationship through force or rewards, the organization can achieve and maintain a position of power by developing relationships with publics and persuading them to see things from the same perspective or to share common goals. This soft power is viewed as a valuable tool for building and maintaining relationships in public diplomacy and has become even more important in an increasingly digital, more interconnected world.

With the proliferation of technology and influx of non-government-generated information available to foreign publics, Keohane and Nye (1998) describe "a world in which security and force matter less and countries are connected by multiple social and political relationships" (p. 83). With the influx of information, people must decide on who and what to believe and "information power flows to those who can edit and credibly validate information to sort out what is both correct and important" (p. 89). In other words, credibility is a vital dimension in the successful use of soft power and parallels the literature in organizational-public relationships, a fact reiterated by Nye (2003) as he states, "soft power is the ability to get what you want by attracting and persuading others to adopt your goals. ...Attraction depends on credibility."

L'Etang (2009) emphasizes the role of stewardship in public diplomacy and the increased focus on building and maintaining mutually beneficial relationships between parties. And, the concept is becoming more and more evident in other public diplomacy literature. For example, Wang (2006) points to a British report that states, "...public diplomacy is not merely about advocating and promoting political and economic goals to the international public; it is, instead, about relationship building between nations and cultures through better communication" (p. 93). Likewise, Fitzpatrick (2007) indicates that relationship management is part of the central purpose of public diplomacy, and Kelly (2010) alludes to the need for building multi-layer relationships in his discussion about the "new diplomacy."

As noted earlier, there is an assumption that quality relationships between any two parties are built on the factors identified by Hon and Grunig (1999): trust, control mutuality, relational satisfaction, and relational commitment. This is in sharp contrast to the one-way communication techniques that were used for years in public diplomacy and are, to a large degree, still prevalent today. Cowan and Arsenault (2008) recognize a place for one-way communication, but argue that the goal should be two-way, mutually beneficial relationships, saying,

> One-way communication strategies are important at critical moments and for day-to-day explanations about policy. Sometimes they can also help to build credibility, as the BBC, Voice of America, and other international broadcasters have done for years with reports that are truthful, even when describing embarrassing facts about the nation and/or government that sponsors the broadcasts. But it is at least as important for countries to develop communication techniques that focus on relationship building of the kind that only dialogues and collaborations can achieve. (p. 16)

This need for developing and maintaining long-term, mutually beneficial relationships between parties is essential in public diplomacy and the same factors that impact a successful relationship between political parties and their constituencies can be applied to this more global arena.

## *Method*

This project utilized intercept surveys in heavily trafficked downtown streets surrounding a major park, shopping plazas, and business offices that were administered by a supervised research team in one major metropolitan technology center in the Southeastern United States. Of the 1,200 adults invited to participate in the study, 282 completed the study in its entirety, resulting in a 23.5 percent completion rate.

The survey designed for this study used Hon and Grunig's (1999) four relational outcome scales (trust, control mutuality, satisfaction, and commitment). These questions were used to evaluate the relationship participants had with their employer along with newly created scales for the four stewardship dimensions. These scales were created after modifying Waters (2009) stewardship scales, which focused exclusively on the nonprofit sector. After reviewing literature and discussing the constructs with public relations scholars, the revised scales were created and pretested to ensure reliability and validity. The relationship outcomes and stewardship items were measured using a modified 9-point Likert scale ranging from strongly disagree (1) to strongly agree (9). The survey had six measures for trust; five each for commitment and satisfaction; four measures for control mutuality; each of the four stewardship dimensions were measured with four items. The eight scales were deemed to be reliable as Cronbach alpha values ranged from a low of $\alpha = .78$ for control mutuality to a high of $\alpha = .96$ for trust and commitment.

Additionally, respondents answered six semantic differential scale questions to gauge their involvement with their employer. These questions represent the abbreviated version of Zaichkowsky's (1985) original scale, and were found to be reliable ($\alpha = .97$). Participants also anonymously provided information about their demographics, including gender, age, race, and major.

### Results

Of the 282 participants, the majority were female ($n = 175$, 62.1%) and Caucasian ($n = 181$, 64.2%). The remaining participants represented a wide spectrum of ethnic backgrounds, including African American/Black ($n = 34$, 12.1%), Asian ($n = 19$, 6.7%), Hispanic/Latino ($n = 24$, 8.5%), and Native American ($n = 10$, 3.5%). Fourteen participants chose not to answer this question (4.9%). The average age of the participants was 32.41 years ($SD = 14.21$ years), and the participants' ages ranged from 18 to 73. Their educational background was reflective of the metropolitan area as the participants had varying levels of college education. The largest group had earned a bachelor's degree ($n = 121$, 42.9%), followed by those who had some college classes ($n = 98$, 34.8%) and those with a graduate degree ($n = 27$, 9.6%). Participants who earned a high school diploma but did not enter college ($n = 21$, 7.4%) represented the smallest participant group though 15 participants did not answer this question (5.3%).

The first research question sought to determine how these 282 voters viewed the relationship with the political party with which they most identified. For 163 voters, this party was the Democratic Party (57.8%) while 108 voters most identified with the Republican Party (38.3%). The remaining 11 voters (3.9%) most identified with a third party, largely represented by the Libertarian ($n$ = 6, 2.1%) and Green ($n$ = 3, 1.1%) parties. Overall, the voters in this study were mildly pleased with the relationships they had with their political parties as all four relationship outcome mean scores were above the neutral point on the 9-point scale. Commitment ($M$ = 6.54, $SD$ = 2.24) and trust ($M$ = 6.22, $SD$ = 2.08) were higher than control mutuality ($M$ = 5.89, $SD$ = 2.09) and satisfaction ($M$ = 5.60, $SD$ = 1.71). Table 9.1 presents the results of a one-way ANOVA that shows there were no statistical differences between the mean scores for these four relationship measures across party identification lines. Although it appears that voters who identify with parties that are not the Democratic or Republican Party are more content with their political parties, the small number of respondents resulted in a lack of statistical significance for that comparison. However, Table 9.1 shows a marked difference between third-party identifiers and those identifying with the two main American political parties.

*Table 9.1.* One-way ANOVA on Relationship Outcome Measures by Political Party Identification.

| | Democrat ($n$ = 163) $M$ (SD) | Republican ($n$ = 108) | Third-Party ($n$ = 11) | F (2,280) | p-value |
|---|---|---|---|---|---|
| Trust | 6.29 (2.19) | 5.95 (2.03) | 7.82 (0.97) | 1.96 | .14 |
| Commitment | 6.59 (2.32) | 6.29 (2.23) | 7.05 (1.10) | 1.54 | .22 |
| Satisfaction | 5.70 (1.81) | 5.32 (1.66) | 6.87 (0.94) | 1.88 | .16 |
| Control Mutuality | 5.95 (2.19) | 5.64 (2.02) | 7.43 (1.65) | 1.73 | .17 |

Using Zaichkowsky's (1985) measure of involvement allows the researcher to determine whether an individual's involvement with a political party is related to their evaluation of the relationship with that political party. The participants in this study report moderate levels of participation overall ($M$ = 4.34, $SD$ = 1.97). There was little difference in the levels for Democrats ($M$ = 4.35, $SD$ = 1.91), Republicans ($M$ = 4.26, $SD$ = 2.15), and third-party identifiers ($M$ = 5.03, $SD$ = .83). A one-way ANOVA determined that these differences were not statistically different ($F$ 2, 2800 = 0.75, $p$ = .47). However, when Pearson's correlation is used to determine whether there was a relationship between an individual's involvement with a political party and their evaluation of the relationship, findings were significantly for trust ($r = .81$, $p < .001$), commitment ($r = .80$, $p < .001$), satisfaction ($r = .82$, $p < .001$), and control mutuality ($r = .76$, $p < .001$).

Turning to stewardship and the role it can play in relationship cultivation with political parties, the second question sought to determine whether the voters perceived that the four stewardship strategies were being used by political parties. The survey participants were less enthusiastic about the extent to which they perceived the political parties were using stewardship; however, third-party identifiers continued to rate their parties higher than the two mainstream American parties. Overall, constituents felt that the parties reported back to them ($M = 5.62$, $SD = 1.99$) more than any of the other stewardship strategies. Reciprocity, or demonstrating gratitude, was the only other strategy that scored above the neutral point on the 9-point scale ($M = 5.06$, $SD = 1.62$). The two remaining strategies—responsibility ($M = 4.98$, $SD = 1.54$) and relationship nurturing ($M = 4.46$, $SD = 1.32$) scored below the neutral point on the 9-point scale.

Table 9.2 presents the results of a one-way ANOVA to compare the mean scores by the three political party groupings. Following trends similar to the relationship outcomes, third-party identifiers had the highest mean scores followed by those who identified with the Democratic Party and lastly those identifying with the Republican Party. This trend held true for all four stewardship variables just as with the four relationship outcomes; these differences continued to show no statistical difference.

*Table 9.2.* One-way ANOVA on Perceptions of Stewardship Usage by Political Party Identification.

| | Democrat (n = 163) M (SD) | Republican (n = 108) | Third-Party (n = 11) | F(2,280) | p-value |
|---|---|---|---|---|---|
| Reciprocity | 5.18 (1.71) | 4.77 (1.58) | 6.14 (1.04) | 1.74 | .18 |
| Responsibility | 5.06 (1.64) | 4.75 (1.48) | 6.11 (1.01) | 1.61 | .20 |
| Reporting | 5.67 (2.07) | 5.42 (1.95) | 6.68 (1.89) | 0.95 | .39 |
| Relationship Nurturing | 4.41 (1.37) | 4.39 (1.26) | 5.81 (1.74) | 1.99 | .14 |

To answer the third research question, a series of regression analyses were run using the four dimensions of stewardship as the independent variables and the individual's level of involvement with the political party as the dependent variables. Results suggested that relationship nurturing ($\beta = .31$, $p < .001$) and responsibility ($\beta = .29$, $p = .019$) were significant predictors of involvement ($R^2 = .64$, $F(3, 273) = 119.44$, $p < .001$). Although they were perceived to be used more by the political parties, neither reciprocity ($\beta = .08$, $p = .43$) nor reporting ($\beta = .15$, $p = .17$) were found to be significant influencers on an individual's level of involvement. These findings demonstrate that political parties can use specific stewardship strategies to boost their constituencies' feelings of trust, satisfaction, commitment, and control mutuality.

## Discussions

### Stewardship Strategies Can Be Successful

This study found that the relationship management paradigm from public relations can have positive results when applied to the political parties and their constituencies and suggests implications for other applications. Ultimately, the study found that stewardship strategies, as outlined by Kelly (2001), have a positive influence on an individual's involvement with political parties, which ultimately boosts their overall evaluation of the political party-constituent relationship. While all four of the strategies have been suggested to have positive benefits for organizations, linear regression results demonstrated that the responsibility and relationship nurturing were the two that had the most significant impact on involvement with political parties.

### Promises Broken/Credibility

And, at its core, the responsibility construct boils down to simply keeping promises and being credible. Especially during election seasons, politicians and parties make countless campaign promises and pledges to meet various constituents' demands; however, upon winning elections, the realities of fulfilling those promises are often a difficult, uphill battle. Christensen and Lægreid (2005) found that the decline in public confidence in elected officials and political parties is largely attributed to the nonchalance with which they respond and react to the promises that were made during the campaign. Voters have become accustomed to political discourse that promises change and reform during the campaign season and then continues to carry on with the status quo during the political term (Damore, Waters, & Bowler, 2011). They are unhappy with their political choices, dissatisfied with their political parties, and increasingly uninterested in public policy and diplomacy based on continued declining voter turnout rates.

Woon (2009) cautions political parties and candidates that they should not make extreme campaign promises they cannot deliver. In assessing President Barack Obama's social change policies shortly after his election in 2008, Woon (2009) predicted that promises made to niche voter blocs, such as the LGBT and Hispanic/Latino communities, would be difficult to achieve because of political realities facing the administration and the Democratic Party. However, as noted by Matland and Walker (2011), campaign audiences rarely heard messages of the struggle and difficult roads in store for political policy reform by the Obama campaign; instead, hope and change messages were greeted with the "Yes, we can!" rallying cry by campaign supporters. The fervor that surrounded these campaign promises and constituent thoughts were not tempered with the reality of the contemporary political system.

Likewise, conservatives and supporters of the Republican Party's "Tea Party" movement were largely disappointed with the realities of the 2011 debt ceiling debates (Williamson, Skocpol, & Coggin, 2011). The emotional attachment to promises made by political candidates only serves to hurt the politicians and parties who make those promises when they cannot be kept. Druckman (2010) encourages political candidates and parties to tone down their campaign rhetoric in regard to constituency promises, but he does not suggest abandoning them altogether. The promises made by political parties benefit candidates, but constituents have to be made aware of potential obstacles to political change. When voters are presented a realistic picture of the scenario candidates and parties face, they are more likely to respect the players involved, despite the failure to keep their promises (President, 2004).

As candidates extend their campaigns past the U.S. borders, they also need to be aware of the promises they make to larger, global audiences. For example, in 2008, Obama's trip to Germany was heralded by the German press with headlines such as, "Lincoln, Kennedy, Obama" (Kulish, 2008). The potential impact of this was noted by Kulish (2008), "Mr. Obama's new-found popularity among Germans underscores not only the breadth of his appeal but also the opportunity he might have as president—though far from even his party's nomination—to mend fences abroad." This is a prime example of stewardship in public diplomacy through the use of soft power.

Therefore, political party leaders are encouraged to revisit the discussion of stewardship and discover ways that these strategies can become a permanent fixture in the messaging and behaviors of politicians and party leaders. It also lends itself to public diplomacy as these same strategies build trust and credibility in a relationships between nation states and foreign publics, a key component in gaining and effectively utilizing Nye's "soft power" to persuade publics by attraction. As Kelman (2005) noted, "Trust is a central requirement for the peaceful and effective management of all relationships—between individuals, between groups, and between individuals or groups and the organizations and societies to which they belong" (p. 640).

## Responsibility and Reporting

Based on public relations' conceptualization of stewardship, responsibility and reporting go hand in hand. As Kelly (2001) noted, it is not enough for organizations to make promises to their stakeholders, they also have to report back to them what has been done to keep those promises. In this case, politicians and political parties have to keep their constituents informed of the progress made toward their policy promises. The participants in the current study indicated that reporting was the stewardship strategy they perceived being used most often by political parties; however, it was only slightly above the neutral point of the continuum. Generally speaking, voters report being satisfied with the amount of information they receive from politicians but are confused with the doublespeak and jargon used to sidestep direct questions by journalists during news interviews and by their fellow constituents during townhall meetings (Savigny & Temple, 2010).

Political parties can use direct communication and strategies to make political messages more relevant to their constituencies; however, one-sided messaging—even when echoed in various media outlets—has limited effects on today's voters (Bennett & Iyengar, 2008). Instead, political parties have to increase their constituencies' involvement with the party both online and offline. This involvement is at the center of the relationship nurturing strategy of stewardship. Kelly (2001) argues that organizations must do everything they can to ensure that stakeholders know they are valued. For political parties, this translates into keeping voters involved in the political process even when the campaign season has ended.

## Long-Term Involvement

Relationship nurturing was one of the two stewardship variables that had a key influence on boosting involvement with the party. Looking at the specific measures for that scale, it is clear to see that long-term involvement is the key—not just turning to voters during times of need (e.g., campaigns). This construct was measured by asking participants to respond to whether the political party was more concerned with its own well-being than with relationships with constituents, whether constituents only hear from the parties when they need something from them, whether they receive personalized attention, and whether they are invited to participate in non-campaign events.

Each of these measures focuses on non-election actions. Political parties have fallen into the trap of turning to their constituents during election years, but often fail to turn to them at other points during the political process. Political parties must actively attempt to engage audiences directly to ensure their longevity. However, the attempt to increase participation will likely not be easy. Savigny and Temple (2010) claim that voters have grown weary of Congressmen's weekend trips back to Congressional districts to interact with constituents and that automated replies via email have turned voters away from attempting to communicate directly with their elected officials.

However, there is hope as Meredith (2009) found that individuals who were more connected to partisan causes and political parties during non-campaign cycles were more likely to vote and contribute to the parties' political candidates during election cycles. These findings echo the urgings of scholars who have said that to boost the participation rates of the American public in the political system, change had to occur not just during election cycles but throughout the entire spectrum of American politics (Dalton, 2008). Fortunately, the relationship management paradigm of public relations offers several strategies, such as stewardship, to help foster relationship growth with key stakeholders. Political parties just have to be motivated enough to take the first step to move in the direction of mutually beneficial relationships and make legitimate attempts to motivate people to become involved in American politics for the long term.

It is the targeted focus on developing long-term relationships in the "nurturing" variable that makes stewardship particularly promising for those focused on public diplomacy. While the integrated approach identified in Golan (2013) touches on the need for short and mid-term diplomacy, the model is not complete without the "relational public diplomacy" that requires a long-term, relationship-building focus or the "long-termed nation-branding campaigns aimed at the reshifting of public opinion regarding a nation's global reputation" (p. 1254).

## Conclusion, Limitations, Future Research

This study found that implementing stewardship strategies, especially building credibility, nurturing and the constructs of responsibility and reporting can be an essential part of an ongoing, relationship-building effort. This is essential in developing mutually beneficial, long-term relationships, which is key to our understanding of the relationship management paradigm and suggests applications that this paradigm might have in the fields of public relations, political science and public diplomacy.

Though this chapter provided one of the first examples of using public relations theory to measure relationships in the political environment, its results provide several new avenues of study for like-minded scholars. For example, although trends emerged with these participants in terms of clear patterns of relationship evaluation among Democratic, Republican, and Third-Party identifiers, does that pattern transfer to other domains? While the study included a large number of participants, there were some limitations to the way the data were gathered that could impact the generalizability of the findings. Additionally, the geographic collection sites are not representative of the entire nation's suburban and rural areas. Relationships with political parties in those regions may be vastly different based on environmental and cultural factors which the relationship with the political party. Therefore the results cannot be generalized beyond the current participants. Finally, it is important to acknowledge that this is the first time the stewardship scales were tested in a setting that did not focus on nonprofit organizations or nation-building efforts. Although the scales were developed so that they could be applied universally, this is the first time they have been applied. Also, in order to validate the generalization of these finding to other fields, additional work must be done.

## Bibliography

Barnhurst, K. G. (2011). The new "media affect" and the crisis of representation for political communication. *The International Journal of Press/Politics, 16*(4), 573–593.

Bennett, W. L, & Iyengar, S. (2008). A new era of minimal effects? The changing foundations of political communication. *Journal of Communication, 58*(4), 707–731.

Bortree, D., & Waters, D. (2008). Admiring the organization: A study of the relational quality outcomes of the nonprofit organization-volunteer relationship. *Public Relations Journal, 2*, 1–17.

Botan, C. H., & Taylor, M. (2004). Public relations: State of the field. *Journal of Communication, 54*(4), 645–661.

Broom, G., Casey, S., & Ritchey, J. (1997). Toward a concept and theory of organization-public relationships. *Journal of Public Relations Research, 9*(2), 83–98.

Christensen, T., & Lægreid, P. (2005). Trust in government: The relative importance of service satisfaction, political factors, and demography. *Public Performance & Management Review, 28*(4), 487–511.

Cowen, G. & Arsenault, A. (2008). Moving from monologue to dialogue to collaboration: The three layers of public diplomacy. *The ANNALS of the American Academy of Political and Social Science, 616*, 10–30.

Culbertson, H. M, Jeffers, D. W., Stone, D. B., & Terrell, M. (1993). *Social, political, and economic concepts and contexts in public relations: Theory and cases.* Hillsdale, NJ: Lawrence Erlbaum.

Dalton, R. J. (2008). Citizenship norms and the expansion of political participation. *Political Studies, 56*(1), 76–98.

Damore, D. F., Waters, M. M., & Bowler, S. (2011). Unhappy, uninformed, or uninterested? Understanding "none of the above" voting. Published first online: doi:10.1177/1065912911424286

Druckman, J. N. (2010). Competing frames in a political campaign. In B. F. Schaffer & Sellers, P. J. (Eds.), *Winning with words: The origins and impact of political framing* (pp. 101–120). New York: Routledge.

Ellison, N. B., Steinfield, C., & Lampe, C. (2011). Connection strategies: Social capital implications of Facebook-enabled communication practices. *New Media & Society, 13*(6), 873–892.

Ferguson, M. A. (1984, August). Building theory in public relations: Interorganizational relationships. Paper presented at the Association for Education in Journalism and Mass Communication, Gainesville, FL.

Fitzpatrick, K. R. (2007). Advancing the new public diplomacy: A public relations perspective. *The Hague Journal of Diplomacy, 2*(3), 187–211.

Gilboa, E. (2008). Searching for a theory of public diplomacy. *The ANNALS of the American Academy of Political and Social Science, 616,* 55–76.

Golan, Guy J. (2013). Introduction: An integrated approach to public diplomacy. *American Behavioral Scientist, 57*(9), 1251–1255.

Gouldner, A. W. (1960). The norm of reciprocity: A preliminary statement. *American Sociological Review, 25*(2), 161–178.

Gross, K., Brewer, P. R., & Aday, S. (2009). Confidence in government and emotional responses to terrorism after September 11, 2011. *American Politics Research, 37*(1), 107–128.

Grunig, J. E. (2002). Qualitative methods for assessing relationships between organizations and publics. Gainesville, FL: The Institute for Public Relations, Commission on PR Measurement and Evaluation.

Gunther, R. & Diamond, L. (2003). Species of political parties: A new typology. *Party Politics, 9*(2), 167–199.

Heath, R. L. (1997). *Strategic issues management: Organizations and public policy challenges.* Thousand Oaks, CA: Sage Publications, Inc.

Hon, L. C., & Grunig, J. E. (1999). Guidelines for measuring relationships in public relations. Gainesville, FL: The Institute for Public Relations, Commission on PR Measurement and Evaluation.

Kelly, J. R. (2010). The new diplomacy: Evolution of a revolution. *Diplomacy & Statecraft, 21,* 286–305.

Kelly, K. S. (1998). *Effective fund-raising management.* Mahwah, NJ: Lawrence Erlbaum.

———. (2001). Stewardship: The missing step in the public relations process, in R. L. Heath (Ed.), *Handbook of public relations*. Thousand Oaks, CA: Sage.

Kelman, H. C. (2005). Building trust among enemies: The central challenge for international conflict resolution. *International Journal of Intercultural Relations, 29*, 639–650.

Keohane, R. O. & Nye, J. S., Jr. (1998). Power and interdependence in the information age. *Foreign Affairs, 77*(5), 81–94.

Ki, E.-J., & Hon, L. C. (2007). Testing the linkages among the organization-public relationship and attitude and behavioral intentions. *Journal of Public Relations Research, 19*, 1–23.

Kulish, N. (2008, January 6). Germany's got a crush on Obama. *New York Times*, Retrieved from http://thecaucus.blogs.nytimes.com/2008/01/06/germanys-got-a-crush-on-obama/

Ledingham, J. A. (2001). Government-community relationships: Extending the relational theory of public relations. *Public Relations Review, 27*(3), 285–295.

Ledingham, J. & Bruning, S. (Eds.) (2000). *Public relations as relationship management. A relational approach to the study and practice of public relations.* Mahwah: Lawrence Erlbaum Associates.

———. (1998). Relationship management in public relations: Dimensions of an organization-public relationship. *Public Relations Review, 24*, 55–65.

Lee, D. J. (2011). Anticipating entry: Major party positioning and third party threat. *Political Research Quarterly.* Published online first: doi:10.1177/1065912910391476.

Leonard, M. & Alakeson, V. (2000). Going public: Diplomacy for the information society. *Progressive Thinking for a Global Age.* Retrieved from the Foreign Policy Centre website, http://fpc.org.uk/publications/going-public

L'Etang, J. (2009). Public relations and diplomacy in a globalized world: An issue of public communication. *American Behavioral Scientist, 53*, 607–626.

Lindaman, K., & Haider-Markel, D. P. (2002). Issue evolution, political parties, and the culture wars. *Political Research Quarterly, 55*(1), 91–110.

Matland, R. E., & Walker, A. L. (2011). Obama and social policy: Acclamation or alienation among women, minorities, and gays? In S. E. Schier (Ed.), *Transforming America: Barack Obama in the White House* (pp. 189–210). Lanham, MD: Rowman & Littlefield Publishers.

Mayer, W. G. (2008). *The swing voter in American politics*. Washington, D.C.: The Brookings Institution.

McLeod, J. M., Scheufele, D. A., & Moy, P. (1999). Community, communication, and participation: The role of mass media and interpersonal discussion in local political participation. *Political Communication, 16*(3), 315–336.

Meredith, M. (2009). Persistence in political participation. *Quarterly Journal of Political Science, 4*(3), 187–209.

Morgan, R. M., & Hunt, S. D. (1994). The commitment-trust theory of relationship marketing. *Journal of Marketing, 58*(3), 20–38.

Ni, L. (2007). Redefined understanding of perspectives on employee-organization relationships. *Journal of Communication Management, 11,* 53–70.

Nye, J. S., Jr. (2003, January 10). Propaganda isn't the way: Soft power. *International Herald Tribune.* Retrieved from http://www.nytimes.com/2003/01/10/opin ion/10iht-ednye_ed3_.html

———. (2004). The decline of America's soft power. *Foreign Affairs, 83*(3), 16–20.

———. (2008). Public diplomacy and soft power. *The ANNALS of the American Academy of Political and Social Science, 616,* 94–109.

Petrocik, J. R. (2009). Measuring party support: Leaners are not independents. *Electoral Studies, 28*(4), 562–572.

President, C. G. (2004). Democracy promotion: the relationship of political parties and civil society. *Democratization, 11*(3), 27–35.

Price, K. (2012, May 21). Public confidence in Congress remains at all time low. *U.S. Daily Review.* Retrieved online July 2, 2012: http://usdailyreview.com/public-confi dence-in-congress-remains-at-all-time-low

Rhee, Y. (2007). Interpersonal communication as an element of symmetrical public relations: A case study. In Toth, E.L. (Ed.), *The future of excellence in public relations and communication management* (pp. 103–117). Mahwah, NJ: Lawrence Erlbaum.

Ryan, J. P. (1994, March). Thanks a million: You need strong recognition programs to foster healthy donor relations. *CASE Currents,* 64.

Savigny, H., & Temple, M. (2010). Political marketing models: The curious incident of the dog that doesn't bark. *Political Studies, 58*(5), 1049–1064.

Signitzer, B. & Coombs, T. (1992). Public relations and public diplomacy: Conceptual divergence. *Public Relations Review, 18*(2), 137–147.

Stafford, L., & Canary, D. J. (1991). Maintenance strategies and romantic relationship type, gender, and relational characteristics. *Journal of Social and Personal Relationships, 8,* 217–242.

Wang, J. (2006). Managing national reputation and international relations in the global era: Public diplomacy revisited. *Public Relations Review, 32,* 91–96.

Waters, R. D. (2009). Measuring stewardship in public relations: A test exploring impact on the fundraising relationship. *Public Relations Review, 35*(2), 113–119.

Williamson, V., Skocpol, T., & Coggin, J. (2011). The Tea Party and the remaking of Republican conservatism. *Perspectives on Politics, 9*(1), 25–43.

Wolak, J., & Palus, C. K. (2010). The dynamics of public confidence in U.S. state and local government. *State Politics & Policy Quarterly, 10*(4), 421–445.

Woon, J. (2009). Change we can believe in? Using political science to predict policy change in the Obama presidency. *PS: Political Science & Politics, 42,* 329–333.

Yang, S.-U. (2007). An integrated model for organization-public relational outcomes, organizational reputation, and their antecedents. *Journal of Public Relations Research, 19,* 91–121.

Zaichkowsky, J. L. (1985). Measuring the involvement construct. *Journal of Consumer Research 12*(3), 341–353.

# 10. Ethical Visions for Public Diplomacy as International Public Relations

Hua Jiang

This chapter reviews prior studies on the conceptualization of public diplomacy, the similarities and convergences between public diplomacy and international public relations, and the ethical values, philosophies, and approaches guiding public diplomacy practices.

Scholars have discussed multiple approaches or perspectives from which public diplomacy is conceptualized. Several dominant definitions of public diplomacy are public diplomacy (1) as one-way persuasive communication with an attempt to influence international public opinions, (2) as two-way symmetrical communication focused on promoting mutual understanding and cultivating long-term trusting relationships with audiences including governments, corporations and nongovernmental organizations, citizens of foreign countries alike, and (3) as a multifaceted system that integrates three layers of public diplomacy (i.e., mediated public diplomacy, nation branding and reputation management, and relational public diplomacy) (Golan, 2013).

In this chapter, the author defines public diplomacy as a form or a function of international public relations. It denotes how state (e.g., governments and countries) and non-state actors (e.g., nongovernmental organizations, transnational organizations, multinationals, and many other non-state groups) engage their strategic publics in an international setting, through mediated (global news media and social media) and personal dialogic means of communication.

A review of ethical public diplomacy literature indicates both deontology- and utilitarianism-based philosophies are practiced in public diplomacy programs. Theorists and practitioners are still debating the applicability of these moral philosophies across cultures and in various contextualized diplomacy programs. Suggestions for future ethical public diplomacy scholarship are made: (1) go beyond the normative approach of examining ethical visions for public diplomacy and consider cultural nuances; (2) explore ethical considerations for a diversified public diplomacy audience; (3) examine the ethical dilemmas that different diplomacy actors face and the ethical guidelines they can follow in different cultures; and (4) investigate the ethical insights that new technologies can potentially bring into the field of public diplomacy.

## Conceptualizations of Public Diplomacy

Traditional diplomacy has been widely conceptualized as the elitist and well-staged activities of a state administration (Zöllner, 2006). It is an integral part of a nation's formal government-level affairs with other nations (Berridge, Keens-Soper, & Otte, 2001; Eban, 1998; Gilboa, 2000, 2002; Ziegler, 2000). Public diplomacy is represented through the promotional communication of a nation's values, culture, language, history, and politics (Fortner, 1993; Signitzer & Coombs, 1992). In a broader sense, public diplomacy actually denotes the global engagement between governments, nongovernmental organizations, corporations, and their foreign publics, with the purpose of reaching agreements and understanding via key tools such as academic lectures and language programs, cultural exchange festivals, print materials, on-line websites of musical events, movies, radio and television programs (Golan, 2013; Zöllner, 2006).

### Major Approaches/Perspectives in Conceptualizing Public Diplomacy

Public diplomacy has gained much attention from communication scholars (Cull, 2008). Based on previous literature, Zöllner (2006) summarized the following major approaches in defining public diplomacy: (1) public diplomacy as a communication function from the systems-theory perspective (Signitzer & Coombs, 1992); (2) public diplomacy as a government-sponsored program, aiming to inform and influence public opinion in a broader cultural sphere yet from a top-down angle (US Department of State, 1987; Napoli & Fejeran, 2004); and (3) public diplomacy as engagement between a nation and its publics, from a more progressive dialogic viewpoint (Zöllner, 2006, pp. 163–164). From the systems-theory approach, researchers defined it as a state's diplomatic communication focused on promoting foreign policies. Apparently, the conceptualization of public diplomacy, from the top-down approach, is rooted in one-way asymmetrical persuasion, intended to manipulate or influence public opinion that sides with the interests of the sponsoring nation. A much needed dialogic approach is imperative for us to examine how engaging this process can be via both mediated and personal communication efforts (Zöllner, 2006).

Likewise, based on a plethora of previous studies, researchers (e.g., Zhang & Swartz, 2009) identified key dimensions in conceptualizing public diplomacy. First of all, most definitions of public diplomacy stress it as a one-way advocacy function that centers on *building national identity* or *nation branding* (Taylor, 1997). Practicing this model of public diplomacy, a country would use one-way persuasive techniques (e.g., information or message dissemination) to build a favorable national image or manipulate desirable world public opinions (Kunczik, 2001). Second, public diplomacy has also been conceptualized as a communication means to *promote national interests* (Zhang & Swartz, 2009). Government agencies and policy-making organizations can use various programs to inform their targeted publics, promote understanding of their objectives, and influence foreign audiences to satisfy national interests or interests of the public diplomacy sponsoring organizations (see USIAAA, 2012). The above two dimensions are synonymous to the first two approaches that Zöllner (2006) proposed: public diplomacy as an image-building function centered on informing, influencing, and persuading by using one-way communication. Third, some scholars have defined public diplomacy as international communication to achieve relational goals—*promoting dialogue* and *achieving mutual understanding* (Tuch, 1990), which is equivalent to the engaging and dynamic interaction approach that Zöllner (2006) suggested. To facilitate the formation and execution of foreign policies, governments and non-state units use public diplomacy programs to create an open and transparent communication environment, involve target audiences overseas in dialogue and interactions, and smooth over the misconceptions and misunderstanding that may complicate the relationships between the sponsoring organizations and their constituents (Zhang & Swartz, 2009). Finally, public diplomacy includes an integral function of promoting Global Public Goods (GPG) (Zhang & Swartz, 2009). It refers to the issues of global concern, such as global warming, human rights, ethnic freedom, poverty, peace and security, financial stability, and health issues. All these issues demand collective international actions (Cornes, 2008; Kaul, Grunberg, & Stern, 1999; Long & Woolley, 2009; Sandler, 1999; Smith, Woodward, Acharya, Beaglehole, & Drager, 2004).

## A Broader Definition of Public Diplomacy

As evident in the above reviewed approaches and dimensions, public diplomacy nowadays is no longer merely a government-level communication function.

A lot of non-state players have been practicing their diplomacy programs. Seib (2010) proposed a broader definition—the sponsoring organizations of public diplomacy programs include both state administrations and non-state actors such as nongovernmental organizations, religious proselytizers, and transnational media organizations, as long as they use public diplomacy programs to communicate with their foreign audiences. News organizations and social media have also become critical public diplomacy players. On one hand, for countries who attempt to wield their soft power, news organizations and social media provide opportunities that go beyond information dissemination. On the other hand, media do not act as "merely an arm of a state but rather devising and advancing its own political perspective" (p. 743). Furthermore, as governments increasingly engage their foreign publics through "global media and international social media influencers," (Golan, 2013, p. 1252), scholars argued for the need to examine public diplomacy from an integrated approach: short/medium term public diplomacy using mediated communication, medium/long term public diplomacy centered on nation branding/country reputation, and long term public diplomacy focused on relationship cultivation.

## Public Diplomacy and International Public Relations: Similarities and Convergences

Public relations scholars (e.g., J. E. Grunig, 1993; L'Etang, 1996; Signitzer & Coombs, 1992; Signitzer & Wamser, 2006) have discussed the convergences between public relations and public diplomacy. Several trends in this body of literature (Petersone, 2008) are summarized as follows: (1) the comparison between the four models of public relations (J. E. Grunig & Hunt, 1984) and Peisert's (1978) goals of cultural diplomacy (Signitzer & Coombs, 1992; Signitzer & Wamser, 2006); (2) the similarities among various levels of analysis in public relations and public diplomacy research (Signitzer & Wamser, 2006); (3) the common functions of public diplomacy and public relations (L'Etang, 1996); and (4) the similarities between the behaviors of public diplomats and public relations professionals (J. E. Grunig, 1993; Yun, 2006).

According to Signitzer and Coombs (1992) and Signitzer and Wamser (2006), the press-agentry model (i.e., propaganda and persuasion) is synonymous to one-way cultural diplomacy that aims to influence or change other countries' cultural values. The public information model is equivalent to the goal of cultural diplomats to self-portray and showcase the strengths of their home cultural values. The two-way asymmetrical model has its roots in advanced research-based persuasion, which is similar to cultural image advertising. Finally, the two-way symmetrical model is compatible with the cultural diplomacy goals of cultivating relationships and maintaining collaboration between nations (J. E. Grunig & Hunt, 1984; Peisert, 1978; Petersone, 2008).

Moreover, researchers have discussed the similarities among different levels of analysis in public diplomacy and public relations research (Petersone, 2008; Signitzer & Wamser, 2006). Based on Ronneberger and Rühl's (1992) public relations levels and Goldstein's (1994) levels of international relations, Signitzer and Wamser (2006) analyzed four overlapping levels of analysis. First of all, on the macro level (global public relations and international relations), scholars are interested to know the way their disciplines influence global changes. Second, on the micro level, public relations researchers examine how various interests of different publics intersect and contradict. International studies scholars, however, are concerned about relationship building between nations within the same state system. Third, on the organizational (domestic) level, public relations explains how the communication function contributes to an organization's effectiveness. For international studies, it focuses more on how domestic organizations or groups, such as governmental, nongovernmental, and special interests organizations, impact a nation's international behaviors. Finally, on the individual level, public relations and public diplomacy are both interested in studying the behaviors of individual human beings as publics or constituents.

In addition, L'Etang (1996) identified three common functions of public relations and public diplomacy: (1) the representational function to protect the interests of represented organizations or states in an attempt to inform, influence, and persuade their target audiences; (2) the negotiation and peacemaking function in which public relations and public diplomacy rely on dialogic communication to engage their target audiences; and (3) the advisory function that involves counseling the management of organizations or government officials.

Based on the Excellence study (L. A. Grunig, J. E. Grunig, & Dozier, 2002), Yun (2006) argued that excellent public diplomacy involves two-way symmetrical communication (J. E. Grunig, 1993), focused on scientific research, symmetrical internal communication, ethical participatory decision making, inclusion of public diplomacy in a government's strategic external relationship management, and so forth. Symmetrical communication connects public relations and public diplomacy in a sense that symmetry, as the ethical and socially responsible way of practicing public diplomacy programs, helps nations and non-state actors "promote mutual understanding and collaborate on conflict resolution" (Yun, 2006).

Based on the above trends existing in the extant research, it is safe to argue that public diplomacy can be seen as a form or a function of international public relations. It is concerned with how state administrations and non-state actors communicate with their constituents in the international setting through both mass-mediated and interpersonal means.

## A Review of Ethical Visions for Public Diplomacy as International Public Relations

### Key Values, Philosophies, and Models of Ethics for Public Diplomacy

Scholars have been discussing the ethical principles associated with international relations since the 1980s (Harbour, 1998). Similarly, it is critical to examine the ethical choices that public diplomacy practitioners make and the moral consequences of their decisions (Zhang & Swartz, 2009). Some examples of the ethical decisions include those related to nuclear monopoly and nuclear weapons, hunger and poverty, population policy, human rights, health issues such as avian influenza pandemic, HIV/AIDS, breast cancer, and heart disease (Zhang & Swartz, 2009).

Researchers have identified various values, philosophies, and models that may guide decision making in public diplomacy. Five most critical ethical values for public diplomacy professionals to abide by are credibility, dialogue, openness, respect, and truthfulness (Fitzpatrick, 2006; Fitzpatrick & Gauthier, 2001). Apart from the ethical values, researchers also identified two normative moral philosophies relevant to public diplomacy practices: (1) deontology and (2) utilitarianism (Zhang & Swartz, 2009).

Deontology, conceived by Immanuel Kant (1724–1804), emphasizes duty, respect for others, rationality, and moral obligations of human beings (Bowen, 2004a, 2004b, 2005; Crawley & Sinclair, 2003; De George, 2006; Harshman & Harshman, 1999; Martinson, 1994; Smudde, 2005; Sullivan, 1994). *Autonomy*, as one of the primary theoretical concepts of Kantian deontology, denotes that rationality enables decision makers to make moral judgments autonomously (Bowen & Heath, 2005; Sullivan, 1989). Being autonomous, human beings can make morally right decisions that are not biased by the interests or advantages of any individual or organization (De George, 1999, 2006; Sullivan, 1989).

Deontological philosophers also use *the principle of universality* to assess an ethical behavior. As Kant (1785/1964) stated, "act only on that maxim through which you can at the same time will that it should become a universal law" (p. 88). Universality stipulates that rational and objective human beings should apply the maxims of ethical reasoning that are generic across time, culture, and social norms (Bowen, 2004a, 2005; De George, 1999). Moreover, universality also indicates the reciprocity of moral obligations between people (Sullivan, 1994). It is the moral *duty* of human beings to reason and make ethical judgments based on universal moral maxims (Bowen, 2004a, 2004b, 2005). *Dignity and respect for others* are also embedded in the Kantian philosophy—"Act in such a way that you always treat humanity, whether in your own person or in the person of any other, never simply as a means, but always at the same time as an end" (Kant, 1785/1964, p. 96). All human beings should be seen as "an end in themselves" rather than "a means to an end" (Bowen, 2005, p. 197).

Finally, *a morally good will*, as the last key imperative of deontology, suggests that autonomous and objective human beings make ethical decisions based on their moral duty rather than prudential or selfish concerns (Paton, 1967; Sullivan, 1994). The impact of deontology on public diplomacy is considerable (Brown, 1992). For instance, public diplomacy programs focused on human rights should be deontological (Harbour, 1998).

Utilitarianism, on the other hand, is cconsequence oriented (Derek, 1986; Zhang & Swartz, 2009). Basically, the adopted means are justified by the ends they can lead to. Classic examples of utilitarian public diplomacy were the U.S. policy toward the International Criminal Court (ICC) and the international environment treaty the Kyoto Protocol (Zhang & Swartz, 2009, p. 384). The U.S. government rejected both treaties because of their consequences for national security and economic interests. Nevertheless, most of the world nations expressed assent and approved the treaties (Zhang & Swartz, 2009). The moral framework that overseas publics used to assess these public diplomacy programs was deontological—the treaties should have been ratified because they preserved the environment and protected human rights. As a consequence, the national image of the United States was tarnished. In conclusion, public diplomacy programs based on the moral philosophy of utilitarianism cannot help cultivate national reputation or secure mutual understanding (Zhang & Swartz, 2009).

In addition to the two dominant moral philosophies, the ethics models for public relations can also be applied in public diplomacy practices (Fitzpatrick & Gauthier, 2001; Zhang & Swartz, 2009). Researchers identified the following four models of ethical public relations. First, *the attorney/advocacy model* indicates that public relations professionals play the role of an attorney and are expected to advocate for the interests of their organizations (Zhang & Swartz, 2009). Second, in *the responsible advocacy model,* professionals should protect the interests of their clients at large and strive to serve the interests of their clients' publics or the society as a whole (Fitzpatrick & Gauthier, 2001). Third, *the two-way communication model* argues that in order to practice public relations ethically, professionals should engage publics of their client organizations in dialogic communication, use open communication to negotiate with them to resolve conflicts if there are any, achieve mutual understanding between organizations and their publics, and cultivate long-term, trusting organization-public relationships (Zhang & Swartz, 2009). Finally, *the enlightened self-interest model* suggests that public relations practitioners and their client organizations should act to promote the interests of others (e.g., their internal and external stakeholders) or the interests of a bigger group they belong to because what they do will ultimately serve their own self-interests (Schultz, Yunus, Khosla, Scher, & Gladwell, 2012; Zhang & Swartz, 2009).

The idea of public diplomacy as image cultivation is compatible with the responsible advocacy model—to maintain a favorable national image of a country, its public diplomacy programs need to serve the interests of its overseas audiences while promoting its self-interests. The definition of public diplomacy as international communication to promote dialogue and achieve mutual understanding dictates two-way communication to resolve potential conflicts and build mutually beneficial relationships between public diplomacy sponsoring organizations and their publics. Finally, the function of public diplomacy to promote Global Public Goods (GPG) fits into the model of enlightened self-interest. To devote its public diplomacy programs to advance global welfare, organizations will ultimately benefit from their altruistic endeavors (Zhang & Swartz, 2009). Two-way communication distinguishes public diplomacy from propaganda (Izadi, 2009). As Melissen (2005) argued, "public diplomacy is similar to propaganda in that it tries to persuade people what to think, but it is fundamentally different from propaganda in the sense that public diplomacy also listens to what people have to say" (p. 18). To achieve genuine dialogue, public diplomacy should adopt two-way symmetrical public relations rather than relying on one-way flow of information and manipulative image management. Two-way symmetrical communication should be adopted as a viable framework for ethical public diplomacy (Izadi, 2009). Two-way symmetrical communication is proposed as the most ethical way of practicing public relations because its collaborative/symmetrical nature enables organizations to accomplish their goals and simultaneously to take into consideration the needs of their strategic publics (Botan, 1993; J. E. Grunig, 1992, 2001). By practicing two-way symmetrical communication, organizations disseminate open and honest information and actively seek feedback from their targeted audiences (Smudde, 2005). Two-way symmetry in public diplomacy means that both parties (the sponsoring organization of a public diplomacy program and its publics) should be involved in dialogic interactions and be open to changes if they further the interests of both parties (Izadi, 2009).

## *(Un)ethical Cases of Public Diplomacy in International Public Relations*

Public diplomacy has been widely conceptualized as a symbolic process of interactions in which nations actively negotiate and construct their image through various public relations strategies targeted toward their audiences (Cai, Lee, & Pang, 2009; Hiebert, 2005; Zhang, 2006). Scholars have discussed cases about how nations rebuilt their image after crises and identified insights for ethical public diplomacy.

In 2003, the Chinese government faced a severe onslaught from the international society because of its refusal to open lines of communication and its ignorance of the perceptions and emotions of its strategic publics during the Severe Acute Respiratory Syndrome (SARS) crisis (Pang, Jin, & Cameron, 2004). In 2007, a "Made in China" crisis exploded with a report submitted to the United States Food and Drug Administration (FDA), in which a Canadian-based manufacturer informed China that its pet food products were unsafe (Cai et al., 2009; Coghlan, 2007). The crisis escalated into a bigger one when more consumer products (e.g., toothpastes, toys, candies, and pajamas) came within the range of recalls and bans (Cai et al., 2009). Having learned lessons from its 2003 SARS crisis, China adopted a series of corrective actions and responded to the accusations coherently and consistently (see Benoit, 1997, 2004; Lu, 1994). Several tenets of ethics were visible in the Chinese government's public diplomacy efforts: (1) *open and interactive communication* (Cai et al., 2009); (2) *speaking with one consistent voice in various media outlets* (Cai et al., 2009; Choong, 2009; Lawrence, 2007; Signitzer & Coombs, 1992); and (3) *credible messaging* (Hiebert, 2005; Van Dyke & Verčič, 2008; Yun, 2006).

Drawing upon Habermas's (1984) *Theory of Communicative Action*, Zöllner (2006) proposed "dialogue" as the ethical basis of the public diplomacy efforts of German government via media communication with the Arabic world after the 9/11 attack (p. 160). Dialogue was also projected as the underlying national value and myth of new, post-Nazi Germany. *The Theory of Communicative Action* implies that, in order to achieve understanding as the goal of public diplomacy, a nation needs to assure that:

1. The statements [that a nation] made are true [i.e., *truth*];
2. The [communication] act, with respect to an existing normative context, is right (and that this normative context is legitimate) [i.e., *rightness*];
3. The manifest intention of [the nation] is meant as it is expressed [i.e., *sincerity*]. (Zöllner, 2006, p. 168; based on Habermas, 1984, p. 99)

For the principle of *truth for statements*, Germany needs to provide *valid* public diplomacy activities (e.g., lectures, youth, academic and sport exchanges, cultural and art exhibitions, language training, radio, television and online programs) to inform the Arabic world about Germany's political, cultural, and economic affairs and to build a *true* image of the new, post-Nazi Germany (based on Zöllner, 2006, pp. 168–171). The *validity* and *truthfulness* lie in the conditions under which the objective image of the nation can connect with what is acceptable in the Arabic world (based on Zöllner, 2006, p. 168). Second, as for *the rightness* for legitimately administered public diplomacy programs, the best thing that Germany can do is to make sure all its communication programs in the Arabic world are right in relation to the socially prescribed rules, norms, and regulations in the society (based on Zöllner, 2006, p. 168). Lastly, the *sincerity* of Germany's public diplomacy programs is determined by the correspondence between what the German government actually means to achieve and its expressed intention for reaching *dialogue and understanding* (based on Zöllner, 2006, p. 168).

Scholars have called for a shift of public diplomacy's focus from *information dissemination* (one-way communication) and *control of communication environment* (one-way communication) to *network* and *engagement* (two-way communication) (Izadi, 2009; Zaharna, 2005). The traditional public diplomacy follows a "hierarchical state-centric model" of international communication; whereas, new public diplomacy functions in a "network [engagement] environment" where target audiences of public diplomacy programs participate in receiving information as well as generating feedback and content (Izadi, 2009, p. 37; Zaharna, 2005, p. 12). The top-down mentality for information dissemination ought to be replaced by *dialogic engagement* (Fitzpatrick, 2007). New public diplomacy programs should be characterized by a more equal distribution of resources and more coordinated communication between target audiences and state administrations (or non-state actors such as nongovernmental organizations) (Hocking, 2005). For achieving credibility, genuine dialogue, integrity, authenticity, shared meanings and values underlying new public diplomacy, public diplomacy professionals are expected to listen to the concerns of other parties and respect their opinions, via both actual behavioral interactions and mediated communication (global news media and social media) (Riordan, 2005).

Charlotte Beers, the former chief of public diplomacy under U.S. Secretary of State Colin Powell, developed the "Shared Values" initiatives/campaign targeted toward Muslim countries (Plaisance, 2005, p. 250). Based on the theories of propaganda, Plaisance (2005) analyzed the ethical shortcomings of the campaign. The campaign, in general, treated its Muslim publics as a means to its end—"to serve [the United States'] broader policy objectives," rather than taking into consideration the needs and preferences of the target audiences or engaging them in dynamic interactions (p. 250).

Similar to all the other human communication acts, public diplomacy programs are subject to high standards of ethical assessment (Black, 2001; Cunningham, 1992, 2002). The "Shared Values" public diplomacy campaign raised serious ethical concerns (Plaisance, 2005). First of all, as Altheide and Johnson (1980) and Postman (1985) argued, propaganda, as a special mode of organizational communication, is deeply rooted in the *utilitarian* philosophy of selective truth and information dissemination. To build its national image of being "credible" and "trustworthy," a nation's public diplomacy programs (when propaganda is central) may choose to present part of realities in various mass media communication narratives—the statements are all true, but not the whole truth. This is obviously subject to ethical questioning—the nature of communication is then "disfigur[ed]" if truth is "instrumentaliz[ed]" (Cunningham, 2002, p. 141). *Truth and truthfulness* remain as a pivotal ethical standard to evaluate public diplomacy programs (Plaisance, 2005). In particular, *truth and truthfulness* denote *accuracy, clarity, correctness, validity*, and *disproval of any forms of falsity, incompleteness, and distortion* (Cunningham, 2002). The "Shared Values" campaign violated the above-mentioned ethical principle:

> The American Muslims featured in the videos certainly may be truthful in their claims about American egalitarianism *as they have experienced it*. The videos offer these claims as proof of a larger truth: that persecution does not exist in this country. A less blatant "instrumentalization" of truth, however, might directly address the simultaneous realities of the post-Sept. 11 incarceration of more than 700 uncharged Muslims and the new, controversial policy of the U.S. Immigration and Naturalization Service (renamed the Bureau of Citizenship and Immigration Services) that requires Middle Easterners to register with the government (Immigration and Naturalization Service News Release, 2003). This

is not to criticize administration antiterror policy, but to point out the selective depiction of reality in a message campaign. (Plaisance, 2005, p. 263)

By presenting merely part of the truth about American egalitarianism, the practitioners of the public diplomacy campaign subjugated themselves to projecting the United States as credible and trustworthy, but lost sight of higher epistemic values including contemplating, reflecting, understanding, critiquing, and reasoning (Cunningham, 2002; Plaisance, 2005).

Secondly, based on *deontology*, Cunningham (2002) suggested that the constituents or publics of public diplomacy programs are not means to an end but the end itself. In propaganda, truth is very often reduced to statements that are conducive to reaching the desired ends (Ellul, 1981; Snow, 2003). Apart from the blurred distinction between truth and credibility, another questionable ethical facet of the "Shared Values" campaign is "Who or what is the means to which end?" (Plaisance, 2005, p. 263). Overall, the campaign treated its target audiences as *means* rather than *ends*—the selective portrayal of America's egalitarianism in the campaign messages was not meant to achieve engaging dialogue or interactions enhancing mutual understanding between the United States and Muslims, but to accomplish the intended partisan advocacy, i.e., to influence the public opinions of Muslim audiences (Brancaccio, 2003).

Finally, modern propaganda programs adopt "influence talk[s]" that enable target audiences to associate simple statements or storylines with their everyday lives (Combs & Nimmo, 1993, p. 86). Unfortunately, this "influence talk" is not *genuine communication* because it is actually "the language of authority" short of "the logic of scientific proof" and "the logic of rhetorical argument" (Plaisance, 2005, p. 264). The "Shared Values" campaign was reduced to merely non-genuine communication, due to the fact that it only presented an idyllic vision of American egalitarianism and failed to depict the truth of historical and perpetuating inequality and discrimination in American society (Black, 2001; Plaisance, 2005).

Likewise, due to the perceived commonality between propaganda and public diplomacy, the U.S. public diplomacy programs in Iraq and Arab-speaking countries have been widely criticized (Seib, 2009, p. 772). Seib (2009) argued that *objectivity, accuracy, openness,* and *transparency* as critical ethical standards should be firmly held by public diplomacy practitioners. To implement these standards in their practices, public diplomacy proponents should resist to plentiful temptations to stray from the ethical criteria— "spreading false information, using communication tools to defame or provoke, interfering with transparency, and other tampering with the foundations of honesty" (p. 772).

The true public diplomacy that the United States practices should rely not only on political theories and international relations theories, but also on public relations theories focused on two-way symmetrical communication and community building (Kruckeberg & Vujnovic, 2005, p. 296). A propaganda worldview centers the United States at the hub of its communication and relationships that radiates outward to the rest of the world; in contrast, a public relations or community-building model situates America as part of the global social system that recognizes other nations as *constituents* or *publics* it needs to engage and cultivate long-term trusting relationships with (Kruckeberg & Vujnovic, 2005, p. 296).

## Conclusions and Future Research

As in many other related disciplines (e.g., public relations, international studies), ethical public diplomacy needs to be constantly revisited and informed by perpetuating impediments and changing events (see Wang, 2006). Ethical challenges for public diplomacy vary across cultures too. They can be largely influenced by many societal factors, such as economic development, political systems, and levels of activism in foreign nations. Based on the present review of previous scholarship, the author identified several ethical implications for public diplomacy that are to be further examined in public diplomacy theory building and practices.

First, managing public diplomacy programs in an international setting is not just about adopting one-way persuasive communication tactics to influence international public opinions, but rather negotiating mutual understanding and arriving at consensus with target audiences abroad, through symmetrical dialogic interactions characterized by credibility, respect, openness, truthfulness, sincerity, rightness, and genuineness (Guth, 2008). Many previous studies have discussed ethical public diplomacy from a normative approach—What is the most ethical way of practicing public diplomacy? How should it be practiced? More research is needed to further explore how it is actually practiced today, especially in various *cross-cultural settings* (Xifra, 2009). In particular, what are the obstacles that public diplomacy practitioners face in applying the deontology-based ethical tenets? For example, what is the role those entrenched US foreign policy norms play in interfering with the current implementation of *engagement* as the dominant principle of US public diplomacy (Comor & Bean, 2012)?

Second, more research efforts are demanded to investigate the increasing scope of public diplomacy audiences (Wise, 2009). With more and more civic engagement and public opinions emerged from all over the world, the scope of the audiences for public diplomacy programs is much broader than before (Wang, 2006). If public diplomacy is about cultivating relationships and negotiating understanding with different nations, organizations, groups, and individual human beings, it is important for us to develop ethical grounds for communication with every single one of them and take into consideration cultural nuances.

The third implication for research and practices is that government is no longer the only sponsor category for public diplomacy programs (with more and more nongovernmental, transgovernmental organizations, and multinationals leading public diplomacy programs). For example, in late 2003 through 2004, the Saudi American Exchange conducted an exchange program (as an example of applied, grassroots public diplomacy) aiming to promote intercultural communication between Arab and U.S. graduate and undergraduate students (Hayden, 2009, p. 533). More studies are needed to examine the ethical dilemmas that these types of actors face in conducting their public diplomacy programs. Moreover, the credibility and trustworthiness of governments, as the primary sponsor or communicator of public diplomacy, are very often suspect because publics tend to perceive a government's public diplomacy programs as manipulative propaganda (Wang, 2006). Therefore, public diplomacy researchers and practitioners face the challenge to redefine the ethical and socially responsible role of a sponsoring organization.

The final research implication relates to new communication technologies (social media) and ethical diplomacy (Milam & Avery, 2012; Wang, 2006). More research is needed to study whether the prevalent combination of mass media (along with social media) and personal communication behaviors, such as cultural and educational exchanges in public diplomacy is sufficient now (Brookings Institution, 2004). This paves a fertile ground for future scholarship about the role of new communication technologies (Internet, social media, and so on) in public diplomacy, especially for those public diplomacy programs targeted to the younger global publics (Wang, 2006). For instance, in 2010 the U.S. State Department funded an "Apps4Africa" contest to promote the development of "socially conscious mobile applications" for Africa, which marked a significant new adventure for public diplomacy efforts (Milam & Avery, 2012, p. 328). Now, there is a glaring absence of scholarship studying the insights that new communication technologies may shed on ethical visions for public diplomacy.

## Bibliography

Altheide, D. L., & Johnson, J. M. (1980). *Bureaucratic propaganda*. Boston: Allyn and Bacon.

Benoit, W. L. (1997). Hugh Grant's image restoration discourse: An actor apologizes. *Communication Quarterly, 45*, 251–268.

Benoit, W. L. (2004). Image restoration discourse and crisis communication. In D. P. Millar & R. Heath (Eds.), *Responding to crisis: A rhetorical approach to crisis communication* (pp. 263–280). Mahwah, NJ: Lawrence Erlbaum Associates.

Berridge, G. R., Keens-Soper, M., & Otte, T. G. (2001). *Diplomatic theory from Machiavelli to Kissinger*. Hampshire: Palgrave Macmillan.

Black, J. (2001). The semantics and ethics of propaganda. *Journal of Mass Media Ethics, 16*, 121–137.

Botan, C. (1993). A human nature approach to image and ethics in international public relations. *Journal of Public Relations Research, 5*, 71–81.

Bowen, S. A. (2004a). Expansion of ethics as the tenth generic principle of public relations excellence: A Kantian theory and model for managing ethical issues. *Journal of Public Relations Research, 16*, 65–92.

———. (2004b). Organizational factors encouraging ethical decision making: An exploration into the case of an exemplar. *Journal of Business Ethics, 52*, 311–324.

———. (2005). A practical model for ethical decision making in issues management and public relations. *Journal of Public Relations Research, 17*, 191–216.

Bowen, S. A., & Heath, R. L. (2005). Issues management, systems, and rhetoric: Exploring the distinction between ethical and legal guidelines at Enron. *Journal of Public Affairs, 5*, 84–98.

Brancaccio, D. (2003, March 5). *U.S. marketing of its image overseas* [Radio broadcast]. Minnesota Public Radio.

Brookings Institution. (2004). *The need to communicate: How to improve U.S. public diplomacy with the Islamic world*. Washington, DC: The Saban Center for Middle East Policy at the Brookings Institution.

Brown, C. (1992). *International relations theory: New normative approaches*. Hemel, Hempstead: Harvester Wheatsheaf.

Cai, P., Lee, P. T., & Pang, A. (2009). Managing a nation's image during crisis: A study of the Chinese government's image repair efforts in the "Made in China" controversy. *Public Relations Review, 35*, 213–218.

Choong, W. (2009, May 15). Chinese navy needs a PR frontman. *The Straits Times*, A16.

Coghlan, A. (2007, May 2). *Melamine suspected of killing hundreds of US pets*. Retrieved from http://www.newscientist.com/article.ns?id=mg19426023.600

Combs, J. E., & Nimmo, D. (1993). *The new propaganda: The dictatorship of palaver in contemporary politics*. New York: Longman.

Comor, E., & Bean, H. (2012). America's 'engagement' delusion: Critiquing a public diplomacy consensus. *International Communication Gazette, 74*, 203–220. doi: 10.1177/1748048511432603

Cornes, R. (2008). Global public goods and commons: Theoretical challenges for a changing world. *International Tax and Public Finance, 15*, 353–360.

Crawley, A., & Sinclair, A. (2003). Indigenous human resource practices in Australian mining companies: Towards an ethical model. *Journal of Business Ethics, 45*, 361–373.

Cull, N. (2008). Public diplomacy: Taxonomies and histories. *ANNALS of The American Academy of Political and Social Science, 616*, 31.

Cunningham, S. B. (1992). Sorting out the ethics of propaganda. *Communication Studies, 43*, 233–245.

———. (2002). *The idea of propaganda: A reconstruction*. Westport, CT: Praeger.

De George, R. T. (1999). *Business ethics* (5th ed.). Englewood Cliffs, NJ: Pearson Prentice Hall.

———. (2006). *Business ethics* (6th ed.). Upper Saddle River, NJ: Pearson Prentice Hall.

Derek, P. (1986). *Reasons and persons*. Oxford: Oxford University Press.

Eban, A. (1998). *Diplomacy for the next century*. New Haven, CT: Yale University Press.

Ellul, J. (1981). The ethics of propaganda: Propaganda, innocence and amorality. *Communication, 6*, 159–175.

Fitzpatrick, K. R. (2006, March). *The ethics of "soft power": Examining the moral dimensions of U.S. public diplomacy*. Paper presented at the annual meeting of the International Studies Association, San Diego, CA.

———. (2007). Advancing the new public diplomacy: A public relations perspective. *The Hague Journal of Diplomacy, 2*, 187–211.

Fitzpatrick, K. R., & Gauthier, C. (2001). Toward a professional responsibility theory. *Journal of Mass Media Ethics, 16*, 193–212.

Fortner, R. S. (1993). *International communication: History, conflict, and control of the global metropolis*. Belmont, CA: Wadsworth.

Gilboa, E. (2000). Mass communication and diplomacy: A theoretical framework. *Communication Theory, 10*, 275–309.

———. (2002). Global communication and foreign policy. *Journal of Communication, 52*, 731–748.

Golan, G. (2013). An integrated approach to public diplomacy. *American Behavioral Scientist, 57*(9), 1251–1255. doi: 10.1177/0002764213487711

Goldstein, J. S. (1994). *International relations*. New York: HarperCollins College.

Grunig, J. E. (Ed.). (1992). *Excellence in public relations and communication management*. Hillsdale, NJ: Lawrence Erlbaum Associates.

———. (1993). Public relations and international affairs: Effects, ethics, and responsibility. *Journal of International Affairs, 47*, 137–162.

———. (2001). Two-way symmetrical public relations: Past, present, and future. In R. L. Heath (Ed.), *Handbook of public relations* (pp. 11–30). Thousand Oaks, CA: Sage.

Grunig, J. E., & Grunig, L. A. (1992). Models of public relations and communication. In J. E. Grunig, L. A. Grunig, & D. M. Dozier (Eds.), *Excellence in public relations and communication management* (pp. 285–326). Hillsdale, NJ: Lawrence Erlbaum Associates.

Grunig, L. A., Grunig, J. E., & Dozier, D. M. (2002). *Excellent public relations and effective organizations: A study of communication management in three countries.* Mahwah, NJ: Lawrence Erlbaum Associates.

Grunig, J. E., & Hunt, T. (1984). *Managing public relations.* New York: Holt, Rinehart & Winston.

Guth, D. W. (2008) Black, white, and shades of gray: The sixty-year debate over propaganda versus public diplomacy. *Journal of Promotion Management, 14,* 309–325. doi: 10.1080/10496490802624083

Habermas, J. (1984). *The theory of communicative action. Volume 1: Reason and the rationalization of society,* trans. T. McCarthy. London: Heinemann.

Harbour, F. (1998). *Thinking about international ethics: Moral theory and cases from American foreign policy.* Boulder, CO: Westview Press.

Harshman, E. F., & Harshman, C. L. (1999, March). Communicating with employees: Building on an ethical foundation. *Journal of Business Ethics, 19,* 3–19.

Hayden, C. (2009). Applied public diplomacy: A marketing communications exchange program in Saudi Arabia. *American Behavioral Scientist, 53,* 533–548. doi: 10.1177/0002764209347629

Hiebert, R. E. (2005). Commentary: Challenges for Arab and American public relations and public diplomacy in a global age. *Public Relations Review, 31,* 317–322.

Hocking, B. (2005, February). *Multistakeholder diplomacy: Foundations, forms, functions and frustrations.* Paper presented at the International Conference on Multistakeholder Diplomacy, Malta.

Izadi, F. (2009, May). *U.S. public diplomacy: A theoretical treatise.* Paper presented at the annual convention of the International Communication Association, Chicago, IL.

Kant, I. (1785/1964). *Groundwork of the metaphysic of morals* (H. J. Paton, Trans.). New York: Harper & Row. (Original publication 1785)

Kaul, I., Grunberg, I., & Stern, M. (Eds.). (1999). *Global public goods: International cooperation in the 21st century.* New York: Oxford University Press.

Kruckeberg, D., & Vujnovic, M. (2005). Public relations, not propaganda, for US public diplomacy in a post-9/11 world: Challenges and opportunities. *Journal of Communication Management, 9,* 296–304.

Kunczik, M. (2001, July). *Globalization: News media, images of nations and the flow of international capital with special reference to the role of rating agencies.* Paper presented at the IAMCR conference, Singapore.

Lawrence, D. (2007, August 24). *China begins four-month campaign to enhance quality.* Retrieved from http://www.bloomberg.com/apps/news?pid=20601080&sid=aV zYIFyYGNIY & refer=asia

L'Etang, J. (1996). Public relations as diplomacy. In J. L'Etang & M. Pieczka (Eds.), *Critical perspectives in public relations* (pp. 14–34). London: International Thomson Business Press.

Long, D., & Woolley, F. (2009). Global public goods: Critique of a UN discourse. *Global Governance, 15*(1), 107–123.

Lu, X. (1994). The theory of persuasion in Han Fei Tzu and its impact on Chinese communication behaviors. *Howard Journal of Communication, 5*, 108–122.

Martinson, D. L. (1994). Enlightened self-interest fails as an ethical baseline in public relations. *Journal of Mass Media Ethics, 9*, 100–108.

Melissen, J. (2005). The new public diplomacy: Between theory and practice. In J. Melissen (Ed.), *The new public diplomacy: Soft power in international relations* (pp. 3–27). New York: Palgrave Macmillan.

Milam, L., & Avery, E. J. (2012). Apps4Africa: A new State Department public diplomacy initiative. *Public Relations Review, 38*, 328–335. doi:10.1016/j.pubrev.2011.12.013

Napoli, J. J., & Fejeran, J. (2004). Of two minds: U.S. public diplomacy and the Middle East. *Global Media Journal, 3*(5). Retrieved from http://lass.calumet.purdue.edu/cca/gmj/SubmittedDocuments/archivedpapers/Fall2004/refereed/napoli.htm

Pang, A., Jin, Y., & Cameron, G. T. (2004, March). *If we can learn some lessons in the process: A contingency approach to analyzing the Chinese Government's management of the perception and emotion of its multiple publics during the Severe Acute Respiratory Syndrome (SARS) crisis.* Miami, FL: International Public Relations Research Conference (IPRRC).

Paton, H. J. (1967). *The categorical imperative: A study in Kant's moral philosophy.* New York: Harper & Row.

Peisert, H. (1978). *Die auswärtige Kulturpolitik der Bundesrepublik Deutschland: Sozialwissenschaftliche Analysen und Planungmodelle.* Stuttgart: Klett-Cotta.

Petersone, B. (2008, May). *Increasing a nation's diplomatic capabilities through relationship management: Public relations contributes to middle power diplomacies.* Paper presented at the annual convention of the International Communication Association, Montreal, Quebec, Canada.

Plaisance, P. L. (2005). The propaganda war on terrorism: An analysis of the United States' "Shared Values" public-diplomacy campaign after September 11, 2001. *Journal of Mass Media Ethics, 20*, 250–268.

Postman, N. (1985). *Amusing ourselves to death: Public discourse in the age of show business.* New York: Penguin.

Riordan, S. (2005). Dialogue-based public diplomacy: A new foreign policy paradigm. In J. Melissen (Ed.), *The new public diplomacy: Soft power in international relations* (pp. 180–195). New York: Palgrave Macmillan.

Ronneberger, F., & Rühl, M. (1992). *Theorie der Public Relations: Ein Entwurf.* Opladen, Germany: Westdeutscher Verlag.

Sandler, T. (1999). Intergenerational public goods: Strategies, efficiency and institutions. In I. Kaul, I. Grunberg, & M. Stern (Eds.), *Global public goods: International cooperation in the 21st century* (pp. 20–50). New York: Oxford University Press.

Schultz, H., Yunus, M., Khosla, V., Scher, L., & Gladwell, M. (2012). *How to do well by doing good.* Retrieved from http://money.cnn.com/popups/2006/biz2/howtosuc ceed_dowell/

Seib, P. (2009). Public diplomacy and journalism: Parallels, ethical issues, and practical concerns. *American Behavioral Scientist, 52,* 772–786.

———. (2010). Transnational journalism, public diplomacy, and virtual states. *Journalism Studies, 11,* 734–744. doi:10.1080/1461670X.2010.503023

Signitzer, B. H., & Coombs, W. T. (1992). Public relations and public diplomacy: Conceptual convergences. *Public Relations Review, 18,* 137–147.

Signitzer, B. H., & Wamser, C. (2006). Public diplomacy: A specific governmental public relations function. In C. H. Botan & V. Hazleton (Eds.), *Public relations theory II* (pp. 435–464). Mahwah, NJ: Lawrence Erlbaum Associates.

Smith, R., Woodward, D., Acharya, A., Beaglehole, B., & Drager, N. (2004). Communicable disease control: A "Global Public Good" perspective. *Health Policy and Planning, 19,* 271–278.

Smudde, P. M. (2005, Fall). Blogging, ethics and public relations: A proactive and dialogic approach. *Public Relations Quarterly,* 34–38.

Snow, N. (Speaker). (2003, January 3). Analysis: History, methods and current use of propaganda [Radio broadcast]. *Talk of the nation.* Washington, DC: National Public Radio.

Sullivan, R. J. (1989). *Immanuel Kant's moral theory.* Cambridge: Cambridge University Press.

———. (1994). *An introduction to Kant's ethics.* New York: Holt, Rinehart & Winston.

Taylor, M. (1997). *Global communications, international affairs and the media since 1945.* London: Routledge.

Tuch, H. (1990). *Communicating with the world.* New York: St. Martin's Press.

US Department of State. (1987). *Dictionary of international relations terms.* Washington, DC: Department of State Library.

USIAAA. (2012). *About U.S. public diplomacy: What public diplomacy is and is not.* Retrieved from http://www.publicdiplomacy.org/1.htm

Van Dyke, M. A., & Verčič, D. (2008, March). Public relations, public diplomacy and soft power: *Conceptual convergence or credibility crisis?* Miami, FL: International Public Relations Research Conference (IPRRC).

Wang, J. (2006). Managing national reputation and international relations in the global era: Public diplomacy revisited. *Public Relations Review, 32,* 91–96. doi:10.1016/j. pubrev.2005.12.001

Wise, K. (2009). Public relations and health diplomacy. *Public Relations Review, 35,* 127–129. doi:10.1016/j.pubrev.2009.01.003

Xifra, J. (2009). Catalan public diplomacy, soft power, and noopolitik: A public relations approach to Catalonia's governance. *Catalan Journal of Communication & Cultural Studies, 1,* 67–85. doi:10.1386/cjcs.1.1.67/1

Yun, S. (2006). Toward public relations theory-based study of public diplomacy: Testing the applicability of the excellence study. *Journal of Public Relations Research, 18* (4), 287–312.

Zaharna, R. (2005). The network paradigm of strategic public diplomacy. *Foreign Policy in Focus: Policy Brief, 1.* Retrieved from http://www.fpif.org/pdf/vol10/v10n01pub dip.pdf

Zhang, J. (2006). Public diplomacy as symbolic interactions: A case study of Asian tsunami relief campaigns. *Public Relations Review, 32,* 26–32.

Zhang, J., & Swartz, B. C. (2009). Public diplomacy to promote Global Public Goods (GPG): Conceptual expansion, ethical grounds, and rhetoric. *Public Relations Review, 35,* 382–387. doi:10.1016/j.pubrev.2009.08.001

Ziegler, D. W. (2000). *War, peace, and international politics.* New York: Longman.

Zöllner, O. (2006). A quest for dialogue in international broadcasting: Germany's public diplomacy targeting Arab audiences. *Global Media and Communication, 2,* 160–182. doi:10.1177/1742766506061817

*Nation Brands and Country Reputation*

# 11. Public Diplomacy and Competitive Identity: Where's the Link?

Simon Anholt

This chapter focuses on the connection between public diplomacy and the less well understood discipline of Competitive Identity (or, as it is usually and, for reasons which I will shortly explain, misleadingly called "nation branding"). How should we distinguish between them? Are they two versions of the same idea—one seen from an international relations perspective and the other from a more commercial angle—or are they entirely different concepts? And if different, to what extent are they linked or compatible?

I first wrote about an idea I called *nation brand* in 1998 (Anholt,1998), and claimed that the reputations of countries, cities and regions are just as critical to their progress and prosperity as the brand images of products are to the companies that own them. A powerful, positive national image makes it relatively cheap and easy to attract immigrants, tourists, investors, talent and positive media coverage, and to export products, services, ideas and culture. A weak or negative image usually means spending more to achieve less.

In the busy and crowded global marketplace, most people don't have time to learn about what other places or their populations are really like. We navigate through the complexity of our world armed with a few simple clichés, and they form the background of our opinions, even if we aren't fully aware of this and don't always admit it to ourselves: Paris is about style, Japan about technology, Tuscany about the good life, and most African nations about poverty, corruption, war, famine and disease. Few of us form complete, balanced, and informed views about seven billion other people and nearly two hundred other countries. We make do with summaries for the vast majority of people and places—the ones we will probably never know or visit—and only start to expand and refine these impressions when for some reason we acquire a particular interest in them. When you haven't got time to read a book, you judge it by its cover.

These clichés and stereotypes—whether they are positive or negative, true or untrue—fundamentally affect our behavior towards places and their people and products. So all responsible governments, on behalf of their populations, their institutions and their companies, need to measure and monitor the world's perception of their nation, and to develop a strategy for managing it. It is a critical part of their job to try to earn and maintain a national standing that is fair, true, powerful, attractive, genuinely useful to their economic, political and social aims, and honestly reflects the spirit, the genius and the will of the people. This huge task has become one of the primary skills of administrations in the 21st century.

Unfortunately, the phrase I coined back in 1998, *nation brand,* soon become distorted, mainly by a combination of ambitious consulting firms and gullible or impatient governments, into *nation branding:* a dangerously misleading phrase which seems to contain a promise that the images of countries can be directly manipulated using the techniques of commercial marketing communications. Yet despite repeatedly calling for it over the last 15 years, I have never seen a shred of evidence to suggest that this is possible—or, indeed, any very convincing arguments in favor of it. I conclude that countries are judged by what they do, not by what they say, as they have always been; yet the notion that a country can simply advertise its way into a better reputation has proved to be a pernicious and surprisingly resilient one.

The message is clear: if a country is serious about enhancing its international image, it should concentrate on the "product" rather than chase after the chimera of "branding." There are no short cuts. Only a consistent, coordinated and unbroken stream of useful, noticeable, world-class and above all *relevant* ideas, products and policies can, gradually, enhance the reputation of the country that produces them.

Of course, the promotion of individual national sectors, products and services is a different matter, and much confusion is created by the conflation of sectoral marketing with national image. The confusion isn't helped by the fact that people who are responsible for marketing places as investment, study or tourism destinations often describe their work as "branding." However, the distinction is really quite clear: when you're selling a product or service (such as holidays, investment opportunities, exported goods or even—at a stretch— culture) then of course advertising and marketing are legitimate and necessary. Your competitors are doing it, and consumers accept it: the underlying message ("buy this, it's good") is fundamentally honest and straightforward. Nation "branding," on the other hand, has nothing to sell, and the underlying message ("please change your mind about my country") is government propaganda, which investors and most other people rightly ignore.

Thus, in one way or another, the term "nation brand(ing)" has become, at least for my tastes, fatally contaminated, and I no longer care to use it. In an effort to steer the discourse away from propaganda and messaging, and to encourage administrations to understand that national standing needs to be earned, I coined the rather inelegant phrase "Competitive Identity" (which was also the title of a book I published in 2007) (Anholt, 2007). For the purposes of this chapter, then, I will only use the term "nation brand(ing)" in order to specify the kind of communications-based approach which I do *not* endorse; otherwise, I will stick to "Competitive Identity."

I have usually contended that public diplomacy is in fact a subset of Competitive Identity. I always intended Competitive Identity to consider how the nation *as a whole* engages, presents and represents itself to other nations, whereas public diplomacy appears to concentrate exclusively on the presentation and representation of *government policy* to other publics: in other words, the international equivalent of what is usually known as public affairs, or a type of diplomacy where the interlocutor is society at large rather than other diplomats or ministers. Public diplomacy is generally practiced only by Ministries of Foreign Affairs, and although it intersects in many cases with cultural relations and trade promotion, its native area of interest is clearly that of government policy.

According to my theory of Competitive Identity, government policy is simply one point of the "hexagon" of national image; one-sixth of the picture that nations habitually paint of themselves, whether by accident or by design. From this point of view, public diplomacy is clearly a component of Competitive Identity: it is concerned with presenting one aspect of national activity—foreign policy—while Competitive Identity attempts to harmonise policy, people, sport and culture, exports, tourism, trade and investment promotion and talent recruitment.

However, my initial contention that public diplomacy is a subset of Competitive Identity was, I later realized, based on a rather conventional interpretation of public diplomacy as a *means of presentation and representation* of the national interest: in other words, that it was primarily concerned with the communication of policies rather than with their execution or conception. This now seems to me to be doing the discipline a disservice, even if there are as yet few examples of public diplomacy rising above its conventional role of press and public affairs agency to the Ministry of Foreign Affairs.

Potentially, I believe, public diplomacy truly is the "master discipline" of international relations for developed and prominent countries, just as

Competitive Identity is potentially the "master discipline" of economic development for emerging and less well known countries.

Ironically, my initially rather narrow view of public diplomacy was precisely analogous to the interpretation of Competitive Identity against which I have been battling for the last fifteen years: the idea that "brand management" for a nation (or city or region) is simply a matter of marketing or promoting the place more expensively, creatively and noisily.

During this period I have advanced many arguments for why this is often neither wise, effective, nor even possible, and that the huge expenditures by governments on national promotional campaigns are, more often than not, a waste of taxpayers' or donors' money. National image, I have argued, is like a juggernaut without wheels, and imagining that it can really be shifted by so weak an instrument as marketing communications is an extravagant delusion. People don't change their views about countries—views they may have held for decades—simply because a marketing campaign tells them to. Most publics today, I have always maintained, are simply too well inoculated against advertising and too savvy about the media to believe mere government propaganda.

Similar arguments have often been levied against conventional public diplomacy by its wiser practitioners. When Edward R. Murrow, the "father" of American public diplomacy and first head of the United States Information Agency (USIA) found out about the CIA's botched attempt to invade Cuba at the Bay of Pigs in April 1961, he was "spitting mad," as the then Voice of America director, Henry Loomis, recalls. "They expect us to be in on the crash landings," Murrow said to Loomis. "We had better be in on the takeoffs [too]" (Anholt & Hildreth, 2004)

President Kennedy apparently took this advice, for in January 1963 his administration issued the USIA new orders. Its role would no longer be merely to inform and explain U.S. objectives; it would be "to help achieve United States foreign policy objectives by...influencing public attitudes in other nations." This explicitly shifted the mission from information provision to persuasion, and from commentator (or apologist) to actor. The USIA would also have responsibility for "advising the President, his representatives abroad, and the various departments and agencies on the implications of foreign opinion for present and contemplated United States policies, programs and official statements."

The debate continues to this day, and Karen Hughes, a former undersecretary for public diplomacy at the U.S. State Department, frequently stressed that her job should not be limited to the communication of government policy; "being in at the takeoffs" means having an influence over the formation of those policies too. Her close relationship with President George W. Bush was initially taken as an encouraging sign by the public diplomacy community that her department stood a real chance of achieving its aims, since it was in a better position to have some influence over the way the 'takeoffs' were planned: "As 'counselor to the President'—Bush created the position unique-ly for her—she sat in on every meeting, oversaw the offices of press secretary, communications and speechwriting, and had the communications directors of every department reporting directly to her" (Flanders, 2004).

However, the main challenge to Hughes's work may not, after all, have had much to do with her closeness to the former president or the influence she wielded over U.S. foreign policy. In the end it was more likely to be the image, credibility and reputation of the country whose policies she sought to justify.

If the purpose of public diplomacy is simply to promote government poli-cies, it is likely to be superfluous or futile, depending on the good name of the country and its government at that particular time. If the country is generally in favor, then unless the policy is patently wrong-headed, it is likely to be well received by publics and simply needs to be clearly communicated. Little art or skill is required to do this.

If on the other hand the country suffers from a poor or weak reputation, especially in the area relating to the policy, then almost no amount of promo-tional skill or expenditure can cause that policy to be received with enthusi-asm, and it will either be ignored or taken as further proof of whatever evil is currently ascribed to the country. This is why I have often defined brand im-age as the *context in which messages are received,* not the messages themselves.

In synthesis, I think it is helpful to consider public diplomacy as having three distinct stages of evolution or sophistication.

Stage I Public Diplomacy is "pre-Murrow," where public diplomacy offi-cers are simply charged to "sell" whatever policies the administration chooses to implement. A comment from a U.S. government official to a public diplo-macy officer which appeared in John Brown's *Public Diplomacy Press Review* perfectly characterises Stage I Public Diplomacy, "Look, you just forget about policy, that's not your business; we'll make the policy and then you can put it on your damn radios."[1]

Stage II Public Diplomacy is the "post-Murrow" stage, where the func-tion is basically still to "sell" government policies, but public diplomacy offi-cers are "in at the take-offs," and thus have some power to condition the style and indeed the content of foreign policy.

There is a parallel here in the commercial sector when branding be-comes fully represented in the boardroom: here, the marketing function is recognized as the corporation's "eyes and ears on the ground" and its link with the marketplace, not merely informing strategy but actually driving innovation and new product development.

In Stage III, the tools of public diplomacy are used in a different way altogether; one that has seldom been consistently or well used by governments: this is public diplomacy as an *instrument of policy*, rather than as a method of communication. Here, a wide range of non-military methods (which include but are not necessarily limited to communication techniques) are used in order to bring about changes in the behaviors of populations, either in order to cause them to bring about policy changes through democratic influence over their own governments, or even by direct action.

The appeal of such an instrument of "soft power" hardly needs emphasizing. For a country desiring regime change in another country, for example, the prospect of being able to persuade the other country's population to replace their own government is incomparably preferable (not to mention far cheaper) than doing it by direct military intervention. Not surprisingly, there have been numerous attempts in the past to achieve such ends, ranging from deliberate rumour-mongering to fake broadcasting; and some real successes have been achieved through the use of cultural diplomacy, although of course the effectiveness of such methods is notoriously hard to measure as cultural influence is always a slow-burning and indirect influence.

Few now dispute that the deliberate dissemination of American popular culture into the Soviet Union played a part in helping to defeat communism, and many would argue that when the struggle is genuinely an ideological one—as was the case during the Cold War—then cultural diplomacy may well be a more appropriate weapon than warfare. Given that the biggest threats to world peace today are primarily ideological in nature, it seems surprising that the lessons of the Cold War appear not to have been well learned. Where culture is the problem, culture is also likely to be the solution.

In the modern age, it also seems natural that governments should turn to the world of commerce for guidance in this area, since creating wide-scale changes in opinion and behavior through persuasion rather than coercion, through attraction rather than compulsion, is seen to be the essence of branding and marketing. But there's much more to it than simply telling people what you want them to believe, boasting about your attractions and achievements, or instructing people to do what you want them to do.

To "brand" democracy, for example, and thus create widespread "purchase" of the democratic "product" in undemocratic countries, would surely be the least harmful, most cost-effective, and most benign instrument of foreign policy that human ingenuity could devise. It would indeed be a mark of human progress if nations could discover ways of *persuading* each other to change their behaviour—and only when this is necessary for the greater good, of course—the peak of human civilization would occur when such interventions evolved from violent, to peaceful, to non-existent.

But there are many obstacles to such a state of affairs. Conventional commercial branding depends to a large extent on open access to widely-consumed commercial media, a condition that by definition is usually lacking in undemocratic countries; and finding ways to achieve a substantial branding effect *without* the use of media is indeed an interesting challenge. Without the increasing reach of the Internet, this might even seem entirely beyond the realms of possibility.

## Public Diplomacy and National Image

As one ploughs through the ever-increasing quantity of blogs, articles, interviews and academic papers where Competitive Identity or public diplomacy are discussed—and interestingly enough, more and more of them mention both in the same context—one gets a reassuring sense that this important message is finally beginning to permeate the general consciousness: that communications are no substitute for policies, and that altering the image of a country or city may require something a little more substantial than graphic design, advertising or public relations campaigns.

Certainly, one still hears with depressing regularity of national, regional and city governments putting out tenders for "branding agencies" and funding lavish marketing campaigns of one sort or another, yet a rising number of commentators seem to have taken on board the idea that it is deeds which principally create public perceptions, not words and pictures.

Perhaps good sense is at last beginning to prevail; perhaps some policy makers have started to ask themselves when was the last time *they* changed their minds about something they had believed for most of their lives just because an advertisement told them to. Perhaps those same policy makers, seized with an unprecedented academic rigour and a new desire to make their public expenditures accountable and measurable, have even started to search around for properly documented case studies to prove how marketing campaigns have demonstrably and measurably improved the international image of nations, and have failed to find a single one.

Marketing communications, as I explained earlier, are perfectly justifiable when the task is essentially one of selling a product—and the product can just as well be the holiday resorts or investment opportunities of a country as the products of a corporation—but there is no evidence to suggest that using marketing communications to influence international public perceptions of an entire city, region or country is anything other than a vain and foolish waste of taxpayers' money.

In fact, there is even some evidence to suggest the contrary: between 2005 when the Anholt Nation Brands Index was launched and the latest study (now the Anholt-GfK Roper Nation Brands Index$^{SM}$) in 2012, there has been no detectable correlation between changes in national brand value and expenditure on so-called "nation branding campaigns." Several countries which have done no marketing during this period have shown noticeable improvements in their overall images, while others have spent extremely large sums on advertising and public relations campaigns and their brand value has remained stable or even declined.

More research is needed in this area, and a clearer distinction between selling campaigns such as tourism and investment promotion—which may well improve sales within their specific sectors and among their specific audiences, but appear to have little or no effect on the overall image of the country—and so-called nation branding campaigns. Establishing clarity on this point is difficult because remarkably few "nation branding" initiatives appear to include any provision for measuring their impact or effectiveness. Considering that it is usually taxpayers' or donor's money being spent on such campaigns, this is surprising.

Clearly, the reputation of a country's current government may be held in higher or lower esteem than the underlying "brand image" of the nation as a whole, and this is an additional complicating factor for governments attempting to understand how best to manage their international dialogue. When the nation has a better "brand" than its government (a situation which is much more common than the converse), unpopular government policies may do little harm to the country's overall longer-term interests, but it is likely that an internationally unpopular government may over a long period cause damage to the "nation brand" which it is very difficult to undo, as I have argued in a recent book (Anholt & Hildreth, 2005).

The complexity of understanding and managing public (rather than professional) opinion points to one of the key differences between traditional diplomacy and public diplomacy. When the target is a restricted and professional audience such as diplomats and ministers, the background reputation of the country in question, whilst it undoubtedly plays a role in conditioning those individuals' responses to its policies, has only a limited and indirect impact on the way in which they evaluate them. Such professional audiences are more likely to consider policies on their own merits, in detail, and to some degree in isolation of previous policies from the same country or even government.

It is, in fact, one of the fundamental principles of diplomacy to take the fairest, most informed and most balanced view possible of any government's actions and their presumed motivations. Diplomats are, or should be, fully prepared to *change their minds* about any country at any point.

Publics, on the other hand, have neither the expertise, the experience, the habit, or the desire to consider the actions of foreign governments so carefully and in so even-handed a manner, and their responses to governments' policies are likely to be directly and substantially conditioned by their perceptions of the country as a whole. As I have often commented, it is a common tendency of publics to hold on very tightly to a rather simplistic view of countries once it is formed (especially when considering more distant countries or those with which they have no particular connection), and the data from the Anholt-GfK Roper Nation Brands Index$^{SM}$ have invariably confirmed that underlying public perceptions of countries are remarkably stable.

The views of publics are therefore easier to measure and understand, but much harder to alter, whereas the views of governments and their foreign services may be harder to measure and understand, but at least in theory are more susceptible to alteration.

The comparison is analogous to the different ways in which a judge and a jury consider the prisoner in the dock: the trained legal mind will concentrate primarily on the supposed offence and on the evidence, whereas the public will tend to concentrate on the accused, the victim, and on their presumed characters, and may easily be led astray by circumstantial evidence. For this reason considerable thought is given in most democratic countries to *artificial* ways of preventing the jury from taking previous offences into consideration when reaching their verdict. In the court of international public opinion, of course, there can be no such provisions, and governments are thus largely at the mercy of their international reputation, and to a great extent the passive beneficiaries or victims of generations of their predecessors' wisdom or foolishness.

For this reason, public diplomacy is an emasculated discipline unless it has some power to affect the background reputation of the country whose policies it attempts to represent; and since that background reputation can only be significantly altered by policies, not by communications, the critical success factor for public diplomacy is whether its connection to policy making is one-way or two-way.

If there is a two-way mechanism that allows the public diplomacy function to pass back recommendations for policy making, and these recommendations are taken seriously and properly valued by government as critical "market feedback," then public diplomacy has a chance of enhancing the good name of the country, thus ensuring that future policy decisions are received in a more favourable light. It's a virtuous circle because, of course, under these circumstances the policies need far less "selling."

Simply ensuring that the public diplomacy function has an influence over government policies, however, can only have a limited impact on the background reputation of countries. According to my theory of Competitive Identity, it is only when public diplomacy is carried out in coordination with the full complement of national stakeholders as well as the main policy makers, and all are linked through effective brand management to a single, long-term national strategy, that the country has a real chance of affecting its image and making it into a competitive asset rather than an impediment or a liability.

National governments are simply not in control of all of the forces that shape their country's image, and neither is any other single body within the nation. The tourist board cannot control government policies, yet those policies can dramatically affect its business; the success of the investment promotion agency may be influenced by the communications of the tourist board or the cultural institute; institutes of higher education might find that their attempts to attract talent from overseas are affected by the reputation of the products and services exported from the country or the behaviour of prominent athletes or media stars from the same country, and so on.

Who you are, how you are seen, and what you do, are all intimately and perhaps inextricably linked, which is why no state can hope to achieve its aims in the modern world without a mature and sophisticated fusion of public diplomacy and Competitive Identity.

## Public Diplomacy, Power and Perception

Competitive identity is how you build standing, credibility, and soft power; public diplomacy is how you wield it. Of course, there isn't a strict dividing line between the two, and the choice may well depend on how much prior knowledge, trust and esteem there is for the country in the first place—the U.K., for example, needs to do Competitive Identity in China even while doing public diplomacy in Canada. Few governments understand how to build soft power, or at least how to do so quickly and efficiently; and nobody much needs to understand how to wield it, because that becomes an instinct of politicians in countries that have it (although it is remarkable how often they squander it).

Joseph Nye's (2004) celebrated model of soft, hard and smart power is most useful as a simple distinction in this context (and as a means of arguing against the most entrenched hard power positions). The fact is, however, that there are many different types of power, influence, appeal and authority that a country can wield over the public imaginarium and over reality. Most are "soft" (in the sense that they draw people towards them), and perhaps three are truly "hard" (in the sense that they can really be used on people against their will), as I will shortly discuss: but a more sophisticated distinction than this is required in order to understand exactly how more than 200 countries, not to mention countless cities and regions, really compete against each other today for influence and primacy in the world order.

For the sake of simplicity, I distinguish between four major attributes of national standing: morality, aesthetics, strength, and relevance, and they co-exist and overlap in an almost infinite variety of combinations.

*Morality* is concerned with whether we *approve* of the country (which is to say, some combination of its leaders, its population and its commercial and public institutions). Countries like Norway, Holland and Switzerland are able to exert an influence considerably greater than their real size would lead one to expect (i.e., greater than their hard power) as a direct result of their strength on this dynamic, and of the four attributes it is the strongest predictor of overall rank in the Anholt-GfK Roper Nation Brands Index[SM], especially amongst the all-important younger audiences.

One of the reasons why the perception of morality is so significant is because young people tend to be influenced substantially by their moral sense, and are less inclined to cynicism and the corrosive influence of *realpolitik*. And, the older people who form the elites and the individually powerful are in turn influenced by the public opinion of young people. Thus, one of the most effective drivers of positive acceptance (in other words, effective soft power) for any country is a *clearly marked moral position*.

*Aesthetics* is simply a measure of whether the country (in terms of its people, its built and natural environment, products, cultural output, etc.) is regarded as pleasing to the eye—or, in some cases, to the other senses. On the whole, we find it difficult to dislike or disapprove very strongly (or for very long) of beautiful places, people and products—and we have a strong tendency to associate beauty with virtue and wealth. Curiously, the Anholt-GfK Roper Nation Brands Index[SM] showed that many people around the world started to regard the American *landscape* as less beautiful during the second presidential term of George W. Bush; many Muslim respondents had a similar response to the Danish landscape after the publication of the notorious cartoons lampooning the Prophet Mohammad by a Danish newspaper in 2006 (BBC, 2006). Japan and Germany derive much of their huge aesthetic power from product design: each well-designed product from Sony, Bosch, Porsche,

Toyota or Panasonic sold in another country is a tiny ambassador for the aesthetic power of its place of origin.

Aesthetic perception, I would suggest, centres around four categories of perceived "objects." The first, culture, is the broadest, since it also encompasses senses other than visual (taste and hearing in the case of cuisine, music, language and so forth); the natural environment covers both climate and landscape; artefacts embrace made objects in the cultural, commercial and architectural spheres:

- Culture
- Natural environment
- People
- Artefacts

*Strength* is concerned with our perception that a country can wield influence over us or others, irrespectively of the other three attributes. Hard power, as Nye described, is typically military and economic, but to this I would also add media power: the country's ability to force its views on international public opinion via its ownership or influence over a substantial portion of the media messages reaching people. This is almost impossible to synthesize by the use of peripheral techniques such as public relations or lobbying, and really only comes by virtue of channel ownership. The U.S. is of course the category leader here, and is fully capable of what I have in the past called "belligerent branding" of another country using this variety of hard power. It has been doing this to Mexico, as I have argued elsewhere, for several centuries. Soft power tends to be associated more with the first two attributes—moral and aesthetic—but of course this isn't an absolute distinction in any sense.

We may know very little about what a country actually does, makes, or looks like, but we will nonetheless tend to have a fairly strong idea of whether it (or its components, if we know more about it) are good or bad, beautiful or ugly, strong or weak.

Clearly, the combination and balance of moral power and hard power are critical. A country perceived as actively immoral is also perceived to possess strong hard power is likely to create very strong rejection and a strongly negative national image.

*Relevance* is a slightly more complex topic than the previous three. The mistake made by most governments attempting to carry out "nation branding" is to assume that the key to successful image change lies in the persuasive power of the message that they can present to their target audience. Some believe that, as long as the communication is omnipresent and sufficiently attractive and compelling, then surely public opinion will be swayed by the power of emotion. Others take a more rational view and consider that evidence is more potent than charm; so as long as the relevant facts are presented clearly enough, public opinion will bow to the force of reason.

Both are right, and both are wrong: emotion and reason, charm, and proof are all indispensable conditions for the changing of opinions, but they are not sufficient, either singly or in combination. First, the audience needs to be prepared to receive and reconsider. Second, there must be a high degree of consistency in both the charm and the proof, and the assault has to be sustained for much longer than most governments find convenient, before public opinion gradually begins to change.

These two factors are, in fact, closely linked: the less relevant the country is to the target audience, the more powerful, consistent, and sustained the "stream of evidence and emotion" will need to be in order to change the image. On the other hand, the more relevant the country is to the target, the better the conditions for rapid and profound change in their perceptions of that country.

When we hear something new about another country, everything depends on whether we think "this is about me" or "this is about them." A Mexican citizen hearing about the U.S. presidential elections on television, seeing American products in shops, listening to American music, or reading an American book may well think "this affects me," and consequently pay close attention: the object is in the foreground, and has the power to add positive or negative weight to his or her existing image of the United States. However, proportionally, this weight will be quite small, because his or her existing perception of the United States is already substantial: consequently, each new piece of information is likely to have a correspondingly smaller influence on the whole.

The same Mexican citizen hearing about the Indonesian presidential elections, seeing Indonesian products, and so forth, is more likely to think "this is about them," and the new information simply won't stick. However, by the same token, any new information that does stick will be large in relation to the small image he or she has about Indonesia, and will form a more significant proportion of the sum total of his or her beliefs about the country.

The conclusion is a paradoxical one, and underlines the fundamental difficulty of changing people's minds about countries. People who already feel that a country is relevant to their lives are probably more inclined to notice the things that country does or says or makes, but may be less likely to change their minds as a result, whereas people who don't feel a country is relevant are less likely to pay attention, but may be more likely to change their minds.

This model of moral and aesthetic power, strength, and relevance casts many of the traditional instruments of national promotion and presentation in an interesting new light.

*Tourism promotion* is important because (assuming the country possesses sufficiently attractive artefacts, landscapes, and people to show) it is one of the few means that countries wield to deliberately drive up perceptions of aesthetic power in all categories.

*Cultural relations* does this to an even greater degree. If properly managed, it combines influence over aesthetic *and* moral power.

*Public diplomacy*, properly understood, is primarily a tool of moral power. Educational promotion, science diplomacy, talent attraction, and similar sorts of activity are primarily tools of social power.

*Investment promotion* has so little impact on public perceptions anyway (since it is by definition a business-to-business activity), that it really doesn't fit into these categories and is simply an economic instrument. It is undoubtedly a very important one, but it should be understood that, although it is affected by national image, it only affects it very indirectly. (This is quite different from tourism, which is affected by it and affects it in almost equal measure.)

So people's perception of other countries, except where they are formed by personal experience or some other strong form of bias, will basically derive from their view (or perhaps "feeling" is a more accurate term) about whether the country is good or bad; beautiful or ugly; strong or weak; and whether it has anything to do with them or not.

Obviously, if people know or care enough to think about the components of a particular country, then their *overall* assessment of the country on each of these three attributes will be some kind of "average score." For example, if someone knows enough about China to think about its components, they might be happy to rate it as "bad" overall, but might rate its culture, cuisine and landscape as "beautiful" and its people and government as "ugly," and, consequently, lowering the average. It is certainly clear from a close study of the Anholt-GfK Roper Nation Brands Index$^{SM}$ that people are perfectly capable of holding a number of divergent and even strongly contradictory opinions about the same country in their minds at the same time.

## How Competitive Identity Works

It may well be asked why so many countries which practice good governance and a broadly ethical international stance still suffer from a weak or even negative reputation. The fact is that policies alone, even if effectively implemented, are not sufficient to persuade foreign publics to part from their existing prejudices and perceptions, which in the case of national images may prove exceptionally resilient to change. Substance must be coupled with strategy and frequent symbolic actions if it is to result in an enhanced reputation.

*Strategy*, in its simplest terms, is simply knowing *who* a nation is and *where* it stands today (both in reality and according to internal and external perceptions); knowing where it wants to get to; and knowing how it is going to get there. The two main difficulties associated with strategy development are (a) reconciling the needs and desires of a wide range of different national actors into a more or less single direction, and (b) finding a strategic goal that is both inspiring and feasible, since these two requirements are frequently contradictory.

*Substance* is simply the effective execution of that strategy in the form of new economic, legal, political, social, cultural and educational activity: the real innovations, structures, legislation, reforms, investments, institutions and policies which will bring about the desired progress.

*Symbolic actions* are a particular species of substance that happen to have an intrinsic communicative power: they might be innovations, structures, legislation, reforms, investments, institutions or policies which are especially suggestive, remarkable, memorable, picturesque, newsworthy, topical, poetic, touching, surprising or dramatic. Most importantly, they are emblematic of the strategy: they are at the same time a component of the national story and the means of telling it.

Sometimes the symbolic power of such an action cannot be predicted, as its full effect derives from an imponderable fusion of the action itself, the moment and context in which it appears, the mood and culture of the 'audience,' and their perceptions of the place where it originates.

It is clear that new and dedicated structures are required to coordinate, conceive, develop, maintain, and promote such an unbroken chain of proof. None of the traditional apparatus of trade or government is fit for such a purpose—at least not in a way that cuts across all areas of national activity and is capable of sustaining it for the years and decades it takes to enhance, refine or otherwise alter the international image of a nation.

The concept of strategy plus substance plus symbolic actions is a classic "three-legged stool"—an approach that cannot stand up unless all three conditions are met.

Countries, for example, which succeed in developing a strategy and are diligent at creating real *substance* on the basis of this *strategy* but overlook the importance of *symbolic actions,* still run the risk of remaining anonymous, undervalued, or unable to change the long-standing clichés of their international reputation, because strategies are often private and substance is often boring. Without the communicative power of symbolic actions, such countries can remain trapped inside a weak, distorted or outdated brand image for decades, and consequently fail to attract the consumers, talent, media attention, tourists and investors they need in order to build their economies, expand their influence and achieve their aims.

*Substance* without an underlying *strategy* may achieve sporadic and localized economic and social benefits, but it is unlikely to build the country's profile or influence in any substantial way. Even if the substance is accompanied by frequent *symbolic actions*, without an underlying strategic intent the messages will remain fragmented, and no compelling or useful story of the nation's progress will form in the public consciousness.

*Strategy* without *substance* is spin: it is the frequent predicament of weak governments that they make many plans but lack the willpower, the resources, the influence, the expertise or the public support to carry them to fruition.

*Strategy* that is accompanied by *symbolic actions* but no real *substance* is worse still: this is authentic propaganda, a deliberate and schemed manipulation of public opinion designed to make people believe something different from reality. In today's world, where the globalisation of communications has resulted in an environment where no single message can survive unchallenged, propaganda has become virtually impossible, and such an approach will result in the destruction of the country's good name for generations.

Governments that focus purely on *symbolic actions* and fail to provide either *strategy* or real *substance* will soon be recognised as lightweights: carried this way and that by public opinion and intent purely on achieving popularity, they seldom remain in power for long.

Some good examples of symbolic actions are the Slovenian government donating financial aid to their Balkan neighbours in order to prove that Slovenia wasn't part of the Balkans; Spain legalizing single-sex marriages in order to demonstrate that its values had modernized to a point diametrically opposed to the Franco period; the decision of the Irish government to exempt artists, writers and poets from income tax in order to prove the state's respect for creative talent; or the Hague hosting the European Court of Human Rights in order to cement the Netherlands' reputation as a global bastion of the rule of law. Even a building, such as the Guggenheim Museum in Bilbao or the Sydney Opera House, may have a symbolic value for its city and country well beyond its economic "footprint"; and places with no chance of being selected to host major sporting or cultural events often bid for them, apparently just to communicate the fact that they are internationally engaged, ambitious, and proud of their achievements.

Clearly, the deliberate and planned use of symbolic actions can expose governments to the charge of "playing to the gallery" and devising strategies purely or largely in virtue of their impact on national image. Such behavior, it could be argued, is even worse than simple propaganda, as it commits more public resources to the task of creating a certain impression than mere messages do. Each case must be judged on its own merits, but it could be argued that a symbolic action can be defended against the charge of propaganda if it is based on a clear long-term *strategy* and is supported by a substantially larger investment in real *substance*.

In the end, it is largely a matter of quantity that determines such a judgment. If nine out of 10 policies or investments are selected purely on the basis that they benefit the country, and one on the basis that it gets the story across too, government may act not only with a clear conscience, but also in the knowledge that the 10 percent of symbolic actions, by enhancing the reputation of the country, is adding substantial value to the other investments. In this way, they may ultimately contribute even more value to the country then its more weighty but less media-friendly initiatives.

What governments sometimes have difficulty understanding is that the size, ambition, or cost of initiatives is not directly proportional to their symbolic value. Very large buildings, which simply communicate wealth and hubris, may have less power over the popular imagination than very small ones which happen to tell a story.

In the Anholt-GfK Roper City Brands Index[SM], the tiny statue of the *mannekin pis* in Brussels is spontaneously mentioned by 20 times more international respondents than the enormous atomium, or even the gigantic headquarters of the European Commission; the government of Slovenia donating a few hundreds of thousands of euros to Albania, Montenegro and Macedonia is more newsworthy than the U.S. government donating hundreds of millions of dollars to Africa.

The substantial, strategically-informed symbolic actions which help to move national images forward are not to be confused with the symbolic gestures that punctuate the history books—gestures which really have little substance in themselves but are sufficiently symbolic (in other words, media-friendly) to have real impact, memorability, popular appeal, and hence the power to change opinion and even behaviors. For example, British Prime Minister Neville Chamberlain waving his truce with Hitler; Mahatma Gandhi sitting cross-legged at his weaving loom; Japanese Prime Minister Junichiro Koizumi visiting the Yasukuni shrine; the removal of Stalin's body from the Lenin Mausoleum in Moscow's Red Square in 1961; Sir Walter Raleigh laying his cloak over a puddle so that Queen Elizabeth I could keep her shoes dry; or Jesus Christ washing the feet of his disciples. And in fact, there are plenty of examples of equally effective symbols which aren't even gestures but words: Bismarck's "blood and iron," Churchill's "never before in the field of human conflict," Martin Luther King's "I have a dream," and so forth.

Although these gestures and words are, in their own way, powerful "brands," they are in a different category from the symbolic actions described earlier. Some of them only acquire their symbolic power much later through their retelling and the understanding that they crystallized an important turning-point in history; all of them owe most of their power to the highly significant or critical circumstances in which they occurred. In other words, they are good rhetoric, whether this is deliberate or accidental.

Almost any word or gesture can become significant if it is delivered by an important person in a moment of crisis, and this is an important distinction to make when we are speaking of Competitive Identity or nation branding, because the task in hand is usually quite different: the challenge in Competitive Identity is often to attract the attention of an indifferent public in the first place, to create a sense of momentousness when in fact most people are convinced that nothing of interest is going on.

This brings us right back to the original debate about whether nation branding really does have anything to do with branding, or whether the word is being used in a purely metaphorical sense. For this challenge is unquestionably the same one that gives rise to the discipline of marketing in the first place: it's the art or science of obliging people to pay attention to things which they don't believe deserve their attention. Whether they like it or not, countries, cities and regions in the age of global competition all need to market themselves: the most effective methods for doing this may owe little to the art of selling consumer goods, yet the challenge is precisely the same.

But then, didn't the wisest marketers always know that the most important aspect of any marketing initiative was the quality of the product? Good advertising, as Bill Bernbach is supposed to have remarked, can only make a bad product fail faster: and the same is most certainly true of nations.

## Note

1. Cold War U.S. official Paul Nitze (1907–2004) to Gordon Gray, the first director of the Psychological Strategy Board (PSB), established in 1951 by President Truman "to produce unified planning for American psychological operations"; originally cited in Kenneth Osgood, "Total Cold War: Eisenhower's Secret Propaganda Battle at Home and Abroad" (Lawrence, Kansas: University of Kansas Press, 2006), p. 43, p. 45; appeared in *Public Diplomacy Press and Blog Review* for October 19–20, 2006.

## Bibliography

Anholt. S. (1998) Nation-brands of the twenty-first century. *Journal of Brand Management* 5(6), 395–406.

―――. (2007). *Competitive identity: The new brand management for nations, regions and cities.* London: Palgrave Macmillan.

Anholt, S. & Hildreth, J. (2005). *Brand America: The mother of all brands.* London: Cyan Books.

BBC (2006, February 7). Q & A: The Muhammad cartoons row. Retrieved from: http://news.bbc.co.uk/1/hi/4677976.stm

Flanders, L. (2004). *Bushwomen: Tales of a cynical species.* New York: Verso.

Nye Jr., J. S. (2004). *Soft power: The means to success in world politics.* Cambridge, MA: Perseus Books Inc.

# 12. Repairing the "Made-in-China" Image in the U.S. and U.K.: Effects of Government-supported Advertising

KINETA HUNG

There has been a growing awareness among nation-states, large and small, of the importance of their images projected before the world. Seminal works by Anholt and others (Anholt, 2005a; 2005b; 2010; Aronczyk, 2008; Nye, 2004; Szondi, 2008) integrated theory and practice, and examined how nation-states could build and manage their images in an increasingly connected world, the complexity of which is heightened by global events and differential values in international relations (Gilboa, 2008; Nye, 2004). These efforts have led to intense interests in nation branding and prompted the establishment of benchmarking indices to facilitate the comparison of national images over time and across nations (e.g., EAI's soft power index, Anholt-GfK Roper Nation Brands Index). After all, a favorable national image may contribute to preferred treatments both economically (e.g., preferred nation status) and politically (e.g., forestall international embargo).

A nation brand is represented by multi-dimensional perceptions formed by its own people and the international public, including their respective perceptions of a nation's exports, investment, tourism, people, culture, and governance (Anholt, 2005b). Of particular interest are the perceptions of people residing in countries with significant importance to the focal country (e.g., a major trading partner), given the impact these public opinions may exert on their respective governments. Unfortunately, this perception is often stereotypical, formed somewhat passively based on a myriad of direct and indirect sources (Loo and Davies, 2006) mediated by notable events in international affairs (e.g., the U.S.'s "War on Terror," China's rise in economic power). Whereas direct sources such as travels and contacts with local people allow an international public to experience a country first-hand, they are costly and have limited reach. Indirect sources such as word-of-mouth, news reports on a country and its leaders, and government-supported communications, on the other hand, are accessible through the mass media and the internet, making them highly salient tools in nation branding (Golan, 2013).

Among these communicative acts, paid government advertising provides an opportunity for state actors to tailor a message for a target audience. In the aftermath of 9/11, for example, both the American (Kendrick and Fullerton, 2004; Melissen, 2005) and Saudi Arabian governments (Zhang and Benoit, 2004) carried out image restoration campaigns to attempt to dispel concerns in selected international communities and protect their national interests. Whereas these campaigns have achieved varying degrees of success, there is a need for further research to understand the role and impact of paid advertising on nation branding (Fullerton, Kendrick, & Kerr, 2009).

Nation branding denotes a state government's extended efforts to mobilize multiple forces to project a preferred national identity through dialogues with the international public. The process of nation branding often involves *re*-branding, whereby the state actor uses persuasive communication and cultural symbols to generate an effective, credible message to overcome prevailing stereotypes. Kunczik (2001) noted the possible convergence of nation branding, public diplomacy and international public relations as these disciplines share a common core in "the planned and continuous distribution of interest-bound information aimed (mostly) at improving the country's image abroad" (p. 4). These disciplines also employ strategic information exchange to reduce misconceptions and create goodwill to realize the shared objectives of soft power, relation building, and peace (Signitzer and Coombs, 1992; Szondi, 2008).

Unfortunately, the literature on nation branding is primarily anecdotal and ambiguous (Szondi, 2008), with many conceptual and professional challenges remaining to be resolved (Aronczyk, 2008; Loo and Davies, 2006). Recognizing this, the purpose of this chapter is to investigate how paid government advertising could re-brand selected dimensions of a nation. Core tenets including the credibility of message sender, the reduction of receiver stereotype, and effective message tactics will be examined.

There are four parts to the chapter. The first part discusses the salience of nation branding and its consequences, using China exports as the point of discussion. The second part covers relevant theories with an emphasis on country-of-origin and the latest development in changing stereotypes (i.e., reflective-impulsive model). The third part is an illustrative two-country study on a paid advertising campaign aimed at changing the "Made-in-China" stereotype in the U.S. and U.K. This will be followed by a discussion on the findings of the study, including conceptual and managerial insights for the future.

## Salience of Nation Branding and Its Consequences

Governmental concerns regarding a nation's image in an increasingly competitive and resource-stringent world are well founded. Many governments engage themselves in image cultivation and management, with the objective of developing a competitive identity (Anholt, 2008) to attract the "right" kinds of trade, investment, tourism, talents, and export promotion (Szondi, 2008). There are several notable success stories in Asia. First and foremost, Japan reconciled differences among stakeholders to allow policies, people, culture, and businesses to work synergistically. Such efforts created successful corporations that export products under household names such as Toyota, Honda, Sony, Panasonic, and Toshiba that were trusted and desired around the world (Anholt, 2010). Meanwhile, the long-standing "Malaysia Truly Asia" campaign established Malaysia as a major tourist destination (Anholt, 2008). Further, India attracted high-tech investments (Gertner, 2007) while the Seoul Olympics provided sustained economic gains to South Korea, the host country (Kang and Perdue, 1994).

Aside from economic gains in tourism, exports and trade, a nation's image carries intangible benefits, affecting what is said about the country in the media. A country with a poor image may find the media reacting with indifference or even cynicism to even its humanitarian efforts while a well-liked country receives favorable media coverage with much less work (Anholt, 2005a). Thus, a reputable, trusted image functions as a pre-emptive measure that guards a nation against the media, which tends to over-simplify, often unfairly, complex issues in international affairs.

*China as an example.* China as an economic superpower has become increasingly preoccupied with its image as the country extends its global footprint (Tse and Hung, 2014). Considerable developments have been carried out over the past decade to promote the country as an attractive and trusted member of the international community. These efforts included a culture tour across the U.S. that coincided with President Jiang Zemin's historical visit in 2000, rapid expansion of Confucius Institutes since 2004 to nearly 400 branches around the world, contribution of more than 3,000 troops to serve in U.N. peacekeeping operations, participation in multilateral talks, and the hosting of mega events, including the Beijing Olympics and Shanghai Expo in 2008 and 2010, respectively. These efforts, together with concrete steps that align structures and regulations of China's business environment to international norms as outlined in its agreements with the World Trade Organization (Hung, Tse, & Cheng, 2014), attempt to present an open, cultured, and dynamic image of China to the world (Zhang and Cameron, 2003).

Aside from these efforts to boost the country's overall image, China as the world factory (Tse and Hung, 2014) is especially concerned with promoting its exports, an issue heightened by trade deficits with some of its major trading partners. The series of large-scale product recalls in 2007 that ranged from pet food to tires and toys also dealt a heavy blow to Chinese-made products, raising concerns about their quality and safety (Tan and Tse, 2010). Given that it was the first time allegations of product deficiencies were targeted at a country, Wang (2008) questioned the American-led media campaigns that reported disproportionately negative news about Chinese-made products at a time that coincided with the onslaught of the global financial crisis (Elliott, 2011). The events seriously hurt the reputation of the country's exports (Cai, Lee, & Pang, 2009), with China's Nation Index for Products slipping from 24th place in 2005 to 47th place in 2008, making it the third lowest ranking country on the index (Anholt, 2010).

It was against this background that China's Ministry of Commerce commissioned an advertising campaign in 2009 to attempt to bring forth some favorable changes to the perception of its exports. The campaign, masterminded by ad agency DDB Guoan, an affiliate with the Manhattan- (US-) based agency DDB, was entitled "Made in China, Made with the World" (henceforth, Made-with-China ad) (Hung, 2012). The 30-second ad showcased five products embedded in different, yet typical, consumption situations among Caucasian consumers, the presumed target viewers. The products were purported to be made in China with "American sports technology" (footwear); "European styling" (refrigerator); "software from Silicon Valley" (MP3 player); "French designers" (dress); and "engineers from all over the world" (airplane).

## Relevant Theories

### Country-of-Origin Effects

Export is a major component of a nation brand. Its importance is especially salient in export-led economies such as that of China. In discussions of export and consumer acceptability, the country-of-origin effect provides a widely-accepted theoretical approach based on the way people make product judgment and purchase decisions (Anholt, 2010; Szondi, 2008; Loo and Davies, 2006). Rather than evaluating each product and brand on its own merit, consumers often rely on country-based stereotypes such as French wine, German beer and Russian vodka as proxies for quality (Bilkey and Nes, 1982; Shimp and Sharma, 1987), with some willing to pay a premium for these products (Liu and Johnson, 2005). Products made in developed economies generally enjoy favorable country-of-origin effects (Steenkamp, Batra, & Alden, 2003; Tse and Lee, 1993) while products made in emerging economies have to face unfavorable quality images brought on by perceptions of the factories' sweatshop conditions, poor workmanship and product hazard outbreaks.

China as an emerging economy is suffering from such unfavorable stereotypes (Liu and Johnson, 2005). Media coverage on problematic Chinese-made products, trade deficit, product recall and the potential loss of manufacturing jobs to China further intensify these negative perceptions. Interestingly, brand name recognition among even China's best-known brands such as Haier is below 20 percent in developed economies (Tan and Tse, 2010). Thus, many consumers have limited knowledge of Chinese-made products even if they have formed an opinion about their country of origin. The lack of detailed knowledge encourages consumers to use assumptions and predisposed ideas when they evaluate Chinese-made products (Maheswaran, 1994).

## Paid Government Advertising Campaign

To reduce negative country-of-origin effects, products made in emergent economies may carry dual-national origins (Han and Terpstra, 1988), be owned by global brands (Tse and Gorn, 1993), or possess attributes that project a "perceived globalness" image (Steenkamp, Batra, & Alden, 2003). Conceptually, the strategy underlying the "Made-with-China" ad, the focal ad in this chapter, used a related approach. The "made-with" strategy is aimed at decoupling the Made-in-China label into different components, replacing the "100% made-in-China" image with a composite image made up of "designed in France," "manufactured in China," etc. This message strategy also carries a positive connotation of China working "with" other countries to produce the final product. These two effects were intended to improve the "perceived globalness" (Steenkamp, Batra, & Alden, 2003) of Chinese-made products and help reduce their negative stereotypical image.

The "Made-with-China" ad was aired in late 2009 on TV networks among China's major trading partners, including CNN in the U.S. (for a six-week period) and BBC in the U.K (for a five-week period). The ad is also accessible on the Internet for viewing and downloading. The campaign faced a number of challenges in achieving the objective of changing people's perceptions of Chinese-made products in the West. To begin, there is substantial evidence indicating that the country-of-origin cue exerts an

automatic and persistent impact on consumers (Bilkey and Nes, 1982; Verlagh and Steenkamp, 1999), with its valence (positive or negative) difficult
to counterbalance. Also, the ad message may generate counter-arguments.
If an ad message differs from a consumer's preconceptions beyond the latitude of acceptance, it likely would not pass through the perceptual filter
but be ignored or rejected (Hung, 2014). Further, people are motivated
to retain their pre-existing thoughts (Schmader, Johns, & Forbes, 2008).
In particular, consumer ethnocentrism (Shimp and Sharma, 1987) presents a salient defensive mechanism for individuals faced with foreign-made
products. When elicited, it may reduce the acceptability of the focal ad.
These challenges indicate the need for the focal advertisement to project
the intended message without being perceived as a threat to stereotypical
thinking or risk antagonizing the viewers.

## Current Theory on Stereotyping: Reflective and Impulsive Model (RIM)

To understand how the focal ad may operate, this chapter adopts Strack and
Deutsch's (2004) RIM (Reflective and Impulsive Model) to understand the
stereotype changing process that may have been triggered by the focal ad.
RIM posits that human behavior is largely controlled by two interacting systems. The impulsive system provides fast, spontaneous and stereotype-based
responses related to one's emotions and motivational drives. The reflective
system, on the other hand, is dominated by rationality and even virtue (e.g.,
multiculturalism; Fowers and Davidov, 2006) as the guiding principles for human behavior. Individuals engaged in reflective thoughts would process relevant information, perform a reasoned thought process, and derive at a proper
evaluation. Because the two systems are interactive, effects of the impulsive
system, including stereotypes, may be "regulated" by reflective thoughts. The
RIM dual system has been applied to a multitude of consumption contexts,
providing important inputs into the processes underlying consumer regulatory behaviors (Vohs, 2006) such as impulsive buying and eating disorder
(Hofmann, Strack, & Deutsch, 2008; Hofmann, Friese, & Strack, 2009).

## An Illustrative Study on Changing "Made-in-China" Stereotype

The following illustrates an empirical study that assesses the effectiveness of
the Made-with-China ad using RIM. As the elicitation of reflective processes
is central to the focal ad's communicative effectiveness, this study investigates

the ad's ability to stimulate reflective thinking to counter the viewer's impulsive responses such as his/her emotional reactions to the ad and consumer ethnocentrism (Shimp and Sharma, 1987) that may otherwise dominate his/her intent to buy Chinese-made products. Because reflective thinking is effortful and involving, the viewer's interests in the targeted subject are core to stimulating the reflective process to reconsider Chinese-made products. The study purports that the viewer's openness to cultural diversity, a component of multicultural value (Pascarella et al., 1996) may indicate the viewer's propensity to reflect on the focal ad. To summarize, this study examines (a) the viewer's reflective thoughts; (b) openness to cultural diversity; (c) consumer ethnocentrism; and (d) the positive and negative emotional responses to the ad. These processes together are purported to affect (e) the viewer's purchase intent of Chinese-made products, after controlling for the viewers' age, income, and gender.

## *Impulsive Component: Consumer Ethnocentrism*

Made-in-China is a label affixed to products manufactured in China. The label is a legal requirement in countries such as the U.S., where made-in-country information needs to be clearly displayed. From a communication perspective, the label represents a salient, persistent, and difficult to remove quality cue (Bilkey and Nes, 1982; Shimp and Sharma, 1987). According to RIM, a viewer watching the Made-with-China ad will be reminded of the stereotypical image of Chinese-made products. As a result, the encounter may trigger a process where home-country bias plays a central role. Shimp and Sharma (1987) conceptualize this bias as consumer ethnocentrism, the "beliefs held by *American (or other country)* consumers about the appropriateness, indeed morality, of purchasing foreign-made products" (p. 280). Given its motivational nature and its ties with a person's fundamental values, it is postulated that consumer ethnocentrism is an impulsive response when a person considers Chinese-made products. Whereby non-ethnocentric consumers would evaluate products based on their price, quality and other desirable features, ethnocentric consumers distinguish between domestic and foreign products and consider it inappropriate to buy foreign-made products due to their perceptions of loss to the domestic economy (Shankarmahesh, Ford, & LaTour, 2004). Accordingly, a viewer watching the focal ad may be affected by his/her ethnocentric tendencies so that:

**H1**: Consumer ethnocentrism is negatively associated with the focal ad viewers' buying intent of products made in China.

## Impulsive Component: Ad Elicited Emotions

A large body of research has shown that emotional responses are important outcomes of advertising. The elicited emotions, if positive, may attract viewers' attention, enhance their ad and brand liking, and boost their purchase intent (Batra and Ray, 1986). Conversely, the negativity elicited by the ad may be transferred onto the ad message and the brand. Measures of elicited emotions are now commonly included in tests of ad effectiveness in studies. Through the RIM lens, the viewers' emotional responses to an ad may form a component of the impulsive system. In line with previous works and RIM, this study hypothesizes that:

> **H2**: The positive (negative) emotions elicited by the Made-with-China ad would enhance (reduce) the viewers' buying intent of products made in China.

## Reflective Component: Reflective Thoughts

To bring forth a change in one's stereotype, the stimulus needs to entice viewers to engage in salient reflective thoughts to counter the effects brought on by the impulsive system (Strack and Deutsch, 2004). Thus, the Made-with-China ad will need to open up the viewer's mind to reason, think and reflect. During the process, the viewer will recall facts and information relevant to the subject matter and, through multiple iterations of checks-and-balance, to derive a rational evaluation. This process often involves the semantic categorization of facts, planning, mental simulation and more complex relationship estimates (e.g., causality) in addition to simple logical relations (e.g., is, is not) (Strack and Deutsch, 2004). The study purports that the reflective thought process (e.g., think again, think differently) will generate more positive, or more balanced, thoughts on the buying intent for Chinese-made products. Thus it is proposed that:

> **H3**: The reflective thoughts relative to Chinese-made products elicited by the focal ad would enhance the viewers' buying intent of products made in China.

## Reflective Component: Openness to Cultural Diversity

As the most intellective of the Big Five personality traits (Olver and Mooradian, 2003), openness is a critical construct in reducing the influence of stereotypes and prohibiting their formation. The effects of openness and its variants (e.g., openness to others; to diversity; to intellect) have been confirmed in a large body of literature. In a meta-analysis, Sibley and Duckitt (2008) investigated 71 studies that examined various prejudice-related issues (e.g., sexism, racism, anti-foreign attitude) across eight countries. The results confirmed the salient weakening effect of openness on a social dominance orientation, a measure of prejudice. When applied to the "Made-with-China" ad, viewers who are open to cultural diversity are purported to be pre-disposed to engaging in reflective thoughts induced by the focal ad rather than to bypass the effortful task. After all, the information in the focal ad and its main message concern the de-stereotyping of Chinese-made products. It is postulated that:

> **H4**: Viewers open to cultural diversity would be pre-disposed to reflecting on the focal ad, thereby increasing the propensity of a higher buying intent of products made in China.

## Research Methods

The study consists of an online survey of 801 respondents in the U.S. (n = 389) and the U.K. (n = 412). Both countries were among the top 10 destinations for Chinese exports, suffered from trade deficits with China, and were targets for the "Made-with-China" ad. Survey respondents were recruited from Millward Brown's nationally representative e-panel in each country. Millward Brown is a media, advertising, and brand consultancy conglomerate, active in conducting consumer tracking, copy-tests and creative pretests both on- and off-line. The company has 78 offices in 51 countries and is a member of the WPP Group.

*Table 12.1.* Socio-demographic characteristics of country sample.

|  | US | UK |
|---|---|---|
| Age Distribution |  |  |
| 16–24 | 11.83% | 15.53% |
| 25–34 | 16.19% | 19.17% |
| 35–44 | 15.68% | 23.54% |
| 45–54 | 20.57% | 22.09% |
| 55 and over | 35.73% | 19.67% |
| Income Distribution (US$) |  |  |
| < 10,000 | 5.66% | 21.34% |
| 10,001–39,999 | 29.82% | 42.67% |
| 40,000–74,999 | 33.99% | 11.82% |
| 75,000 and more | 28.53% | 24.17% |

|          | US      | UK      |
| -------- | ------- | ------- |
| Gender   |         |         |
| Male     | 53.5%   | 45.1%   |
| Female   | 46.5%   | 54.9%   |

The week-long data collection was carried out in early 2010 as part of Millward Brown's consumer omnibus. As a screening question, the respondents viewed online the focal ad one time and then indicated whether they had watched the ad before. About 4% did and were excluded from the study. Those remaining responded to the survey and received points they could exchange for gifts from the research company. Table 12.1 reports the socio-demographic characteristics of the respondents. In each country, the mean age group is 35–44 and the mean income group is U.S. $10,001–39,999. Compared to the U.K. sample, the U.S. sample includes more men, is slightly older and has higher income.

The majority of the measures were adapted from previous research. The author also worked with researchers at the company to develop and pretest the remaining measures. Reflective Thought and Openness to Cultural Diversity were adapted from Kember and Leung (2000) and Pascarella et al. (1996), respectively. Consumer Ethnocentrism was adapted from Shimp and Sharma (1987). Buying Intent was developed for this study, using a past study that examined Chinese-made products (Tan and Tse, 2010). These constructs were measured on five-point scales (1 = disagree strongly, 5 = agree strongly). Positive and negative emotions were part of Millward Brown's copy-testing metrics and were assessed using two-point scales (0 = no, 1 = yes). Details of the measures can be found in Table 12.2.

*Table 12.2.* Measurement scales and items.

| Items | Scales | α |
| --- | --- | --- |
| Buying Intent | 1. I would try the products from the advertised firms.<br>2. I have confidence in these products.<br>3. With design and technology from around the world, the products offer good value to customers. | 0.90 |
| Reflective Thought | 1. It makes me think again about products made in China.<br>2. It makes me think differently about products made in China.<br>3. It's the sort of advert I'd talk about with friends. | 0.81 |

| Items | Scales | α |
|---|---|---|
| Consumer Ethnocentrism | 1. Regarding British (American)-made products, I feel: <br> 2. UK (US) products, first, last, and foremost. <br> 3. Purchasing foreign-made products is un-British (un-American). <br> 4. It is not right to purchase foreign products because it puts Britons (Americans) out of work. <br> 5. We should purchase products manufactured in the UK (US) instead of allowing other countries to get rich off us. <br> 6. We should buy from foreign countries only those products that we cannot obtain within our own country. | 0.91 |
| Openness to Cultural Diversity | 1. I have a real interest in other cultures or nations. <br> 2. We need to understand the issues in developing countries and appreciate their struggles. <br> 3. I have a real interest in the cultures of developing nations. | 0.84 |
| Positive Emotion | 1. Excited. <br> 2. Attracted. <br> 3. Affectionate. | 0.77 |
| Negative Emotion | 1. Annoyed. <br> 2. Sad. <br> 3. Disappointed. | 0.78 |

## Results

An OLS two-step regression analysis was conducted to test the hypotheses. The dependent variable for the regression analysis was Buying Intent. There were two groups of independent variables, impulsive and reflective systems. The impulsive system included two components: Consumer Ethnocentrism and Emotional Responses (positive, negative) to the focal ad. These variables together with the control variables of Age, Income, and Gender were entered into Step 1 of the regression model. The reflective system also included two components: Reflective Thought and Openness to Cultural Diversity. These variables were entered into Step 2 of the regression model.

Analysis results showed that all the independent variables in Step 1 exerted significant effects in the hypothesized directions, with Consumer Ethnocentrism and Positive Emotion exerting positive effects and Negative Emotion exerting negative effects. The findings provided support for H1 and H2, confirming that the impulsive system exerted significant effects on viewers' Buying Intent of products made in China.

Similar to Step 1, analysis results in Step 2 showed that all the independent variables exerted significant effects in the hypothesized directions.

In addition to the effects exerted by variables under the impulsive system as noted earlier, the variables under the reflective system entered in Step 2, Reflective Thought and Openness to Cultural Diversity, also exerted positive effects, as hypothesized in H3 and H4. Further, compared to the variance in the model explained by variables under the impulsive system (i.e., $R^2$ in Step 1), the $R^2$ change of .16 ($p < .001$) in Step 2 indicates that the variables under the reflective system exerted effects over and above the effects exerted by the impulsive system alone. Thus, the findings provided general support for the proposed two-system model (see Table 12.3).

To provide a stronger test and to validate the proposed model across countries, the above analysis was repeated for each country sub-sample. In both cases, all independent variables exerted significant effects in the hypothesized directions, providing support for H1 to H4 in each country (see Table 12.3). The $R^2$ change in each country sub-sample also showed significant effects, with the components in the reflective system contributing significant improvement in the explanatory power of the model. These findings provided a cross-country validation of the proposed model.

## Country Differences

Although it is not the main objective in this study to examine between-country differences, such an investigation may shed additional insights. To this end, a series of ANOVA (with mean comparisons) was conducted, with Buying

*Table 12.3.* Two-Step Regression Results.

|  | All (n = 1185) | US (n = 389) | UK (n = 412) |
|---|---|---|---|
| Step 1: Impulsive System |  |  |  |
| Consumer Ethnocentrism | -.16*** | -.19*** | -.13** |
| Positive Emotion | .39*** | .36*** | .43*** |
| Negative Emotion | -.31*** | -.36*** | -.19*** |
| $R^2$ | .38 | .44 | .30 |
| Step 2: Impulsive & Reflective Systems |  |  |  |
| *Impulsive System* |  |  |  |
| Consumer Ethnocentrism | -.15*** | -.17*** | -.12** |
| Positive Emotion | .20*** | .21*** | .20*** |
| Negative Emotion | -.27*** | -.30*** | -.14*** |

|  | All<br>(n = 1185) | US<br>(n = 389) | UK<br>(n = 412) |
|---|---|---|---|
| *Reflective System* | | | |
| Reflective Thought | .42*** | .37*** | .51*** |
| Openness to Cultural Diversity | .11*** | .11*** | .10*** |
| $R^2$ | .54 | .57 | .51 |
| $R^2$ Change | .16*** | .13*** | .21*** |

Note: Dependent Variable: Buying Intent; Control Variables: Age, Income, Gender (***p<.001, **p<.01)

Intent, Ethnocentrism, Positive and Negative emotions, Reflective Thought, and Openness to Cultural Diversity as dependent variables; and Country (2 levels: U.S., U.K.) as independent variable. Similar to the regression analysis, Age, Income and Gender were included as control variables in the ANOVA runs.

Research findings showed that all dependent variables, except Positive Emotions, registered significant between-country differences. The U.S. sub-sample scored lower levels of Buying Intent and Openness to Cultural Diversity but higher levels of Ethnocentrism and Negative Emotions. The relatively more negative findings in the U.S. (vs. U.K.) may reflect trade tensions between the two countries given the size of U.S. trade deficits with China (US $143.5 billion in 2009), its dependence on Chinese goods domestically (No. 1 import into U.S.), and the China market for U.S. exports (No. 3). Interestingly, the U.S. sub-sample scored a significantly higher mean value in Reflective Thought. Thus, in spite of trade tension, the focal ad has successfully induced American respondents to reconsider the meanings behind the Made-in-China label.

## Discussion and Conclusion

The current study assessed how the "Made-with-China" ad was perceived by its intended target, (i.e., consumers among China's major trading partners, U.S. and U.K.) and its effectiveness in changing their stereotypical perceptions towards Chinese-made products. The literature suggests that the intended objective may not be easy to achieve. Country-of-origin stereotype is automatic and persistent, and people for the most part select and process information that conforms to their pre-existing thoughts. While the psychological mechanism of decomposing a unified country image into composites has been proposed (Tse and Lee, 1993) and the strategy adopted by some global firms (e.g., some Apple iPhones are labeled "Designed in California, Assembled in China"), there is limited examination of its effectiveness. By adopting RIM as the theoretical framework, the current study provided an empirical examination of the effectiveness of this strategy. Since the hypothesized effects were validated in the full sample and two country sub-samples, the focal ad has achieved its communication objective of stimulating reflective thoughts in the viewers to change a strongly held negative stereotypical perception.

The success of the "Made-with-China" ad poses an interesting question: How did the focal ad trigger reflective thoughts? Whereas an advertising message can be tailor-made, audience receptiveness is not warranted. Viewers are often cynical of advertising and the backing of a foreign government may raise further concerns over the ad's credibility. Take for example the "Shared Values Initiative" campaign sponsored by the U.S. government and directed at Muslim countries after the 9/11 attacks. The campaign featured the "shared values" of faith, family, and education among Americans and Muslims in a series of mini-documentaries that showcased five American Muslims in their day-to-day life. Unfortunately, the portrayal of happy, well-integrated American Muslims in the campaign seemed one-sided and lacked credibility before a skeptical international audience (Kendrick and Fullerton, 2004), thus limiting its effectiveness.

Kates (1998) suggests that, for a political ad to be effective, the information has to be perceived to a significant degree free from bias. Whereas some people have faulted the "Made-with-China" ad for focusing too heavily on China as a manufacturing base and not stressing enough of its innovative potentials (Barr, 2011), the open, suggestive message strategy invites viewers to reconsider Chinese-made products. This gesture may have rendered the ad more credible in the eyes of skeptical viewers than a hard-sell or overly optimistic message strategy. Indeed, the ad is more factual than opinionated, when some companies are already decoupling the country-of-origin label along the value chain into design, assembly, and manufacturing countries. It is also public knowledge that many Chinese exports are made by joint-venture corporations with inputs originated from different countries. Such factual depiction may have rendered the ad message objective and trustworthy, allowing it to fall within the viewers' latitude of acceptance.

## Implications for Nation Branding

As suggested by Manheim (1994), explicit efforts directed at changing people's negative pre-conceptions about a country would be rejected by the public. To facilitate nation branding (or re-branding), the message sender and the message need to be perceived as credible sources of information. China with its authoritarian regime faces an especially difficult credibility issue in its communications with the West (Barr, 2011); yet, the factual approach used in the focal ad allowed the campaign to meet the challenge and potentially improve the image of Chinese-made products in the international market. Given the importance and increased tension in international trade, the campaign may point to the potential of paid government advertising as a genre to moderate pre-conceived public opinions and reduce economic animosity (Klein, Ettenson, & Morris, 1998). Since establishing credibility is of utmost importance in nation branding campaigns, future efforts in this area could adopt similar persuasive message tactics to dispel stereotypes.

Equally important in this study is the delineation of the *reflective system (i.e., reflective thoughts, openness to cultural diversity)* as a response criterion to gauge the public's willingness to reconsider its stereotypical perceptions. A nation brand is often assessed using indices that identify the valence (good, bad), extent (somewhat, extremely positive), and comparative ranking (35th of 50) of its image among other nations. Whereas these summative scores are indicative of the overall cognitive, affective, and evaluative structure of a nation and its soft power in the eyes of the international public (Kunczik, 2001), nation branding efforts are often directed at dispelling specific stereotypes. In such instances, the *reflective system* in general and *reflective thoughts* in particular provide a useful intermediate response criterion to gauge the effectiveness of the campaign. Meanwhile, the public that is *open to cultural diversity* may be targeted first so that they may serve as opinion leaders to facilitate diffusion of the message.

Yet, similar to the Beijing Olympics being just one element in China's sustained nation branding efforts (Anholt, 2010), the "Made-with-China" ad campaign is only a starting point in the country's efforts to build and manage the reputation of Chinese-made products. In spite of the apparent effectiveness of the campaign message, the branding effort needs reinforcement both in the immediate- and long-term. It also needs the infusion of other voices including media coverage, word-of-mouth, and ultimately, the consumer's personal experiences with Chinese-made products. After all, consumers form their product impressions and judgments holistically via a myriad of direct and indirect sources.

International journalism has often been criticized for reporting on non-Western countries with bias (Li and Tang, 2009; Herman and Chomsky, 1988; Zhang and Cameron, 2003). A content analytical study found that during the wave of product recalls in 2007, U.S.-led media blamed Chinese producers most, followed by the Chinese government. The role of American corporations is minimized (Li and Tang, 2009) even though Mattel has publicly acknowledged its sole responsibility in the "lead-tainted" toys crisis, when most of the toys were recalled due to Mattel's faulty design (Story, 2007). Regardless of whether the problem attribution is correctly placed, Chinese producers who are taking the blunt of the blame need to face the social realities and meet the challenges posed by the international press. This includes taking concrete steps to improve the quality of their products and undertaking public relations campaigns to enhance their perceptions. Equally important is the need to build up the reputation of Chinese producers as responsible corporate citizens through corporate social responsibility (CSR) campaigns.

For one, negativity towards Chinese-made products is not restricted to the international market. Consumers in China have expressed similar concerns (Tan and Tse, 2010). This, together with the low price/low quality image associated with products made in emerging economies, has prompted some corporations in China to adopt foreign-sounding brand names such as Chery (automobile), DaVinci (furniture) and Metersbonwe (apparel) to enhance their perceived globalness (Hung, Tse, & Cheng, 2014). Adopting internationally recognized standards such as ISO (International Organization for Standardization) and undertaking IPO (initial public offering) in international exchanges offer other channels for Chinese corporations to take concrete steps towards improving their product quality, corporate image, and transparency to align with international norms. In sum, an overhaul of the Made-in-China label would require coordinated government, media and corporate efforts to resolve hotly-charged issues on problem attribution, job security and trade deficit, and to counter international preconceptions. There remains a long way to go to turn Made-in-China into a trusted and desired brand name.

## Bibliography

Anderson, J. C., & Gerbing, D. W. (1988). Structural equation modeling in practice: A review and recommended two-step approach. *Psychological Bulletin,* 103(3), 411–423.

Anholt, S. (2005a). Editorial: Nation brand as context and reputation. *Place Branding,* 1(3), 224–228.

———. (2005b). Anholt nation brands index: how does the world see America. *Journal of Advertising Research,* 45 (September), 296–304.

———. (2008). Editorial: 'Nation branding' in Asia. *Place Branding and Public Diplomacy,* 4(4), 265–269.

———. (2010). *Places: Identity, Image and Reputation.* New York, NY: Palgrave Macmillan.

Aronczyk, M. (2008). Living the brand: Nationality, globality and the identity strategies of nation branding consultants. *International Journal of Communication*, 2, 41–65.

Barr, M. (2011). *Who's Afraid of China? The Challenge of Chinese Soft Power*. New York: Zed Books.

Batra, R., & Ray, M. L. (1986). Affecting responses mediating acceptance of advertising. *Journal of Consumer Research*, 13(2), 234–249.

Bilkey, W. J., & Nes, E. (1982). Country-of-origin effects on product evaluations. *Journal of International Business Studies*, 13(1), 89–99.

Cai, P., Lee, P. T., & Pang, A. (2009). Managing a nation's image during crisis: A study of the Chinese government's image repair efforts in the "Made in China" controversy. *Public Relations Review*, 35, 213–218.

Elliott, L. (2011, August 7). Global financial crisis: Five key stages 2007–2011. *The Guardian*, Retrieved from http://www.guardian.co.uk/business/2011/aug/07/global-financial-crisis-key-stages

Fowers, B. J., & Davidov, B. J. (2006). The virtue of multiculturalism: personal transformation, character, and openness to the other. *American Psychologist*, 61(6), 581.

Fullerton, J., Kendrick, A., & Kerr, G.F. (2009). Australian student reactions to U.S. tourism advertising: A test of advertising as public diplomacy. *Place Branding and Public Diplomacy*, 5(2), 126–140.

Gertner, D. (2007). Editorial: Place branding: dilemma or reconciliation between political ideology and economic pragmatism. *Place Branding and Public Diplomacy*, 3(3), 3–7.

Gilboa, E. (2008). Searching for a theory of public diplomacy. *ANNALS of the American Academy of Political and Social Science*, 616 (March), 55–77.

Golan, G. (2013). An integrated approach to public diplomacy. *American Behavioral Scientist*, 57 (9), 1251–1255.

Han, C. M., & Terpstra, B. (1988). Country-of-origin effects for uni-national and bi-national products. *Journal of International Business Studies*, 19(2), 235–255.

Herman, E., & Chomsky, N. (1988). *The Political Economy of the Mass Media*. New York: Pantheon Books.

Hofmann, W., Friese, M., & Strack, F. (2009). Impulse and self-control from a dual-systems perspective. *Perspectives on Psychological Science*, 4(2), 162–176.

Hofmann, W., Strack, F., & Deutsch, R. (2008). Free to buy? Explaining self-control and impulse in consumer behavior. *Journal of Consumer Psychology*, 18(1), 22–26.

Hung, K. (2014). Why celebrity sells: A dual entertainment path model of brand endorsement. *Journal of Advertising*, 43 (2), 155–166.

———. (2012).' 携手中国制造'广告效果评估, 公共外交季刊 ["'Made-in-China' Advertising Effects," *Public Diplomacy Quarterly*], 9 (Spring), 110–116

Hung, K., Tse, C. H., & Cheng, S. (2012). Advertising research in the post-WTO decade in China: Meeting the internationalization challenge. *Journal of Advertising*, 41 (fall), 121–146.

Kang, Y., & Perdue, R. (1994). Long-term impact of a mega-event on international tourism to the host country. In M. Uysal (Ed.), *Global Tourist Behavior* (205–226). Binghamton, NY: International Business Press.

Kates, S. (1998). A qualitative exploration into voters' ethical perceptions of political advertising: Discourse, disinformation, and moral boundaries. *Journal of Business Ethics*, 17(16), 1871–1885.

Kember, D., & Leung, D. Y. P. with Jones, A., Loke, A. Y., McKay, J., Sinclair, K., Tse, H., Webb, C., Wong, F. K. Y., Wong, M., & Yeung, E. (2000). Development of a questionnaire to measure the level of reflective thinking. *Assessment and Evaluation in Higher Education*, 25(4), 381–395.

Kendrick, A., & Fullerton, J. (2004). Advertising as public diplomacy: Attitude change among international audiences. *Journal of Advertising Research*, 44 (September), 297–311.

Klein, J. G., Ettenson, R. E., & Morris, M. D. (1998). The animosity model of foreign product purchase: An empirical test in the People's Republic of China. *Journal of Marketing*, 62(1), 89–100.

Kunczik, M. (2001). Globalization: News media, images of nations and the flow of international capital with special reference to the role of rating agencies. Working paper, Deutsches Übersee-Institut.

Lee, S. (2011). The theory and Reality of soft power: Practical approaches in East Asia. In S. J. Lee & J. Melissen (Eds.), *Public diplomacy and soft power in East Asia* (11–32). New York: Palgrave Macmillan.

Li, H., & Tang, L. (2009). The representation of the Chinese product crisis in national and local newspapers in the United States. *Public Relations Review*, 35, 219–225.

Liu, S. S., & Johnson, K. F. (2005). The automatic country-of-origin effects on brand judgments. *Journal of Advertising*, 34(1), 87–97.

Loo, T. & Davies, G. (2006). Branding China: The ultimate challenge in reputation management. *Corporate Reputation Review*, 9(3), 198–210.

Maheswaran, D. (1994). Country of origin as a stereotype: Effects of consumer expertise and attribute strength on product evaluations. *Journal of Consumer Research*, 21(2), 354–365.

Manheim, J. B. (1994), *Strategic public diplomacy and American foreign policy: An Evolution of Influence*, New York: Oxford University Press.

Melissen, J. (2005). The new public diplomacy: Between theory and practice. In J. Melissen (Ed.), *The new public diplomacy* (3–27). New York: Palgrave Macmillan.

Nye, J. (2004). *Soft Power*. New York: Public Affairs.

Olver, J. M., & Mooradian, T. A. (2003). Personality traits and personal values: A conceptual and empirical integration. *Personality and Individual Differences*, 35(1), 109–125.

Pascarella, E. T., Edison, M., Nora, A., Hagedorn, L. S., & Terenzini, P. T. (1996). Influences on students' openness to diversity and challenge in the first year of college. *The Journal of Higher Education*, 67(2), 174–195.

Podsakoff, P. M., and Organ, D. W. (1986). Self-reports in organizational research: Problems and prospects. *Journal of Management*, 12(4), 531–544.

Schmader, T., Johns, M., & Forbes, C. (2008). An integrated process model of stereotype threat effects on performance. *Psychological Review*, 115(2), 336–356.

Shankarmahesh, M. N., Ford, J. B., & LaTour, M. S. (2004). Determinants of satisfaction in sales negotiations with foreign buyers: Perceptions of US export executives. *International Marketing Review*, 21(4/5), 423–446.

Shimp, T. A., & Sharma, S. (1987). Consumer ethnocentrism: Construction and validation of the CETSCALE. *Journal of Marketing Research*, 24(3), 280–289.

Sibley, C. G., & Duckitt, J. (2008). Personality and prejudice: A meta-analysis and theoretical review. *Personality and Social Psychology Review*, 12(3), 248–279.

Signitzer, B. H., & Coombs, T. (1992). Public relations and public diplomacy: Conceptual convergences. *Public Relations Review*, 18(2), 137–147.

Steenkamp, J.-B. E. M., Batra, R., & Alden, D. L. (2003). How perceived brand globalness creates brand value. *Journal of International Business Studies*, 34(1), 53–65.

Story, L. (2007, Sept. 22). Mattel official delivers an apology in China. *New York Times*, http://www.nytimes.com/2007/09/22/business/worldbusiness/22toys.html

Strack, F., & Deutsch, R. (2004). Reflective and impulsive determinants of social behavior. *Personality and Social Psychology Review*, 8(3), 220–247.

Szondi, G. (2008). Public diplomacy and nation branding: Conceptual similarities and differences. In V. Duthoit & E. Huijgh (Eds.), *Discussion Papers in Diplomacy*. Netherlands Institute of International Relations 'Clingendael'.

Tan, P., & Tse, D. K. (2010). Being truly global: Which Chinese brands can succeed in affluent global markets? *Harvard Business Review (China)* (in Chinese).

Tse, D. K., & Gorn, G. J. (1993). An experiment on the salience of country-of-origin in the era of global brands. *Journal of International Marketing*, 1(1), 57–76.

Tse, D. K., & Hung, K. (2014), *Chinese Firms Going Global: Their Impacts, Best Practices, and Implications*, Cambridge, UK: Cambridge University Press.

Tse, D. K., & Lee, W. (1993). Removing negative country images: Effects of decomposition, branding, and product experience. *Journal of International Marketing*, 1(4), 25–48.

Verlagh, P. W. J., & Steenkamp, J.-B. E. M. (1999). A review and meta-analysis of country-of-origin research. *Journal of Economic Psychology*, 20, 521–546.

Vohs, K. D. (2006). Self-regulatory resources power the reflective system: Evidence from five domains. *Journal of Consumer Psychology*, 16(3), 215–221.

Wang, J. (2008). *Brand New China: Advertising, Media, and Commercial Culture*. Cambridge, MA: Harvard University Press.

Zhang, J., & Benoit, W. L. (2004). Message strategies of Saudi Arabia's image restoration campaign after 9/11. *Public Relations Review*, 30(2), 161–167.

Zhang, J., & Cameron, G. T. (2003). China's agenda building and image polishing in the U.S.: Assessing an international public relations campaign. *Public Relations Review*, 29(1), 13–28.

# 13. Taking It to the Streets: The Evolving Use of VNRs as a Public Diplomacy Tool in the Digital Age

COLLEEN CONNOLLY-AHERN & LIAN MA

Seeing, as they say, is believing. Little wonder, then, that governments were quick to realize the value of visual images in support of public diplomacy efforts. The 1930s and 1940s saw widespread efforts by governmental organizations on both sides of the Second World War to gain support for wartime initiatives through the use of newsreel footage for movie-going audiences, for example (Herzstein, 1983). But it was the astounding growth of television audiences in the post-World War II era, combined with the growth of television news as a primary source of information, which spurred the development and use of video news releases, or VNRs, as a public relations tool. Foreign and domestic news outlets offered the possibility of large-scale distribution of public diplomacy information. In return, public relations and public affairs professionals provided news producers with a steady stream of video content – some of it used, but much of it never seen again. Today, with television news audiences dwindling, international governmental initiatives expanding and information distribution channels multiplying and internationalizing, it seems a perfect time to reevaluate the VNR in the practice of public diplomacy, both its current and potential uses.

## Video News Releases: Concept and Controversy

Traditional VNRs are broadcast-ready story segments and/or raw footage distributed to news producers by organizations in the hope that they will be included in news broadcasts. While the use of VNRs in the creation of nightly newscasts is extensive—and appears to be growing—their use by journalists remains controversial. To date, the small body of public relations scholarship about video news releases can be broken into three main areas: media usage, ethics and effects.

While there are no exact figures on the number of video news releases used by news organizations, the Media Education Foundation, a nonprofit organization promoting media literacy, suggests that up to 50% of some U.S. news programming may actually be derived from public relations materials (Media Education Foundation, 2005). But this public relations' involvement in the news is not simply a U.S. phenomenon. Reich (2010) found that journalists' interactions with public relations professionals in Israel gave public relations a significant role in agenda-building.

Two complementary factors appear to be driving the increased use of VNR content in news broadcasts. First, cost-cutting at news operations has decreased news organizations' ability to generate their own footage. Second, expanding newsholes aimed at catching increasingly unpredictable audiences have left news organizations with ever greater amounts of airtime to fill. For cash-strapped news organizations, VNRs represent a nearly endless supply of video content and story ideas. VNR utilization is particularly noticeable at the local level, where smaller budgets make local stations more likely to include video news releases in their newscasts than national broadcasters (Harmon & White, 2001). However, past research indicates that few VNRs are used in their entirety. Instead, they are heavily edited, rewritten, or incorporated as a handy source of B-roll footage (Cameron & Blount, 1996; Harmon & White, 2001). Significantly, VNRs from U.S. government agencies were incorporated into newscasts more often than those from corporations (Harmon & White, 2001), indicating that VNRs are an important—and probably effective—tool in the government's internal public diplomacy efforts.

Theoretically, the use of VNRs has been linked to agenda-building, the process through which news is influenced by public relations or public affairs practitioners, and thus helps shape public opinion. According to Curtin (1999), "as economic pressures on media increase, public relations information subsidies may become more valued by the media, and public relations campaigns employing mass-mediated communication channels may experience enhanced chances for success" (p. 54).

While the use of VNRs in traditional newscasts has been well established, the effects of using VNRs on news consumers remain unclear. Owen and Karrh (1996) showed that corporate information garnered from a VNR was evaluated as more credible than the same information presented in an advertisement. The same study also found that credibility of local news significantly predicted VNR recall, indicating that traditional VNRs may benefit from the news environment in which they are placed to some extent.

A key rationale for the studying the extent of the media's inclusion of VNRs into newscasts is the fact that many scholars believe their use is inherently unethical. Wulfemeyer and Frazier (1992) considered a range of possible ethical problems emanating from the inclusion of VNRs in newscasts, including "providing inaccurate, false, and/or misleading information," "manipulating the channels of communication," "failing to clearly identify a client/sponsor," and "inflating data" (p. 155). Interestingly, none of these ethical issues is specific to the VNR environment, indicating that VNRs share the same ethical concerns of other public relations communication. Likewise, Grunig's (1992) characterization of asymmetrical communication as unethical in his original conceptualization of excellence theory appears to label VNRs as unethical by virtue of their format, regardless of content.

Many ethicists, activists and trade organizations suggest labeling as a prescription for making VNRs more ethical, despite the fact that in the United States there is no legal responsibility to do so. According to White (2012),

> While, current FCC rules do not require labeling for most VNRs, the Public Relations Service Council, The Public Relations Society of America, the National Association of Broadcast Communicators, and the Radio-Television News Directors Association advocate clear identification of the source of VNRs. The onus is on journalists to do so (p. 82).

However, while conventional wisdom assumes that viewers would scrutinize VNR content more closely and view it more skeptically if its origins were known, empirical studies in this area have been mixed.

For example, Connolly-Ahern, Grantham and Cabrera-Baukus (2010) found that labeling VNRs actually increased the perceived expertise for some government-sponsored VNRs. Additionally, results indicated that in the case of VNRs sponsored by U.S. government agencies, an individual's political party affiliation resulted in significant differences in overall perceived credibility of VNRs, while labeling did not result in differences. Similarly, Tewksbury, Jensen and Coe (2011) found that while support for content labeling was strong, exposure to labeling did not increase the perceived bias of news stories. Broaddus, Harmon and Mounts (2012) did find in an Internet-based survey that viewers were only able to identify VNRs correctly about half of the time, thinking they were produced by news organizations. However, that study did not include measures of credibility toward the news organizations, news stories, or products and services featured.

## Public Diplomacy: Evolution of Goals and Tactics

Public diplomacy has historically been associated with facilitating foreign policy goals and advancing national interests. The term "public diplomacy" was formally coined in 1965, when the dean of the Fletcher School of Law and Diplomacy at Tufts University, Edmund Gullion, established the Edward R. Murrow Center for Public Diplomacy (Cull, 2009), although the practice was already established by governments long before that date. According to a Murrow Center brochure, public diplomacy is described as dealing with "the influence of public attitudes on the formation and execution of foreign policies. It encompasses dimensions of international relations beyond traditional diplomacy; the cultivation by governments of public opinion in other countries..." (as cited in Cull, 2009, p. 19). This definition underscores public diplomacy's desire to reach beyond traditional publics (e.g., diplomats and government workers) and conceptualized as expanding beyond the traditional diplomacy, which is limited to government-to-government interactions, by adding the foreign public dimension.

The 1965 description of public diplomacy was meant as an alternative to propaganda, which always carries a negative connotation (Cull, 2009). However, decades later public diplomacy is still regarded by some as little more than a modern variant of the old practice of propaganda (Nichols, 2003), as evidenced by the centrality of persuasion in some definitions. Based on the definition given by the Planning Group for Integration of USIA (1997) "public diplomacy seeks to promote the national interest of the United States through understanding, informing and influencing foreign audiences" (as cited in Public Diplomacy Alumni Association, 2012, paragraph 5). This definition echoes the 1965 description, emphasizing both the persuasion and the national interest dimensions of the practice.

However, some current conceptualizations of public diplomacy have followed public relations scholarship, evolving toward a relationship-building approach. One definition that emphasizes the public dimension describes public diplomacy as "the process by which direct relations are pursued with a country's people to advance the interests and extend the values of those being represented" (Sharp, 2005, p. 106).The relationship-building approach is also moving into practice: a former USIA officer defines public diplomacy as "...not providing information. It is building relationships" (Fitzpatrick, 2010, p. 79).

The study of public diplomacy is hampered by "definitional chaos"(Fitzpatrick, 2010, p. 91). In a study to find a common identity among various definitions of public diplomacy, Fitzpatrick (2009) identified six categories of conceptualizing public diplomacy: 1) advocacy/influence, 2) communication/informational, 3) relational, 4) promotional, 5) warfare/propaganda, and 6) political. In her attempt to organize the various definitions of public diplomacy and find a common identity, Fitzpatrick (2010) uses a four-legged framework to conceptualize public diplomacy: the purpose, actors, targeted publics, and whose interests to be served by public diplomacy.

The definitional challenge reflects the interdisciplinary nature of public diplomacy. Scholars coming from various backgrounds and perspectives have all tried to theorize and advance the study of public diplomacy. As communication scholar Eytan Gilboa (2008) depicts, many disciplines such as political science, sociology, psychology, cultural studies, rhetoric, history, etc. can contribute to the study of public diplomacy (p. 74). For example, from an international relations (IR) theoretical perspective, public diplomacy has been conceptualized in association with three IR theories, namely realism, liberal internationalism, and sociological globalism (Yun & Toth, 2009). From a public relations perspective, scholars have tested the applicability of the excellence theory to the study of public diplomacy on the theoretical and empirical level (Yun, 2006), and adopted the press agentry, public information, two-way asymmetrical communication, and two-way symmetrical communication models (Grunig & Hunt, 1984) to the study of public diplomacy in China's practices (Zhang, 2008).

Although the English language literature of public diplomacy seems to be plentiful, as evidenced by the various scholarly attempts to define and theorize the topic, it is inevitably U.S.-centric (Gilboa, 2008). The lack of a common definition and the interdisciplinary nature of the field, though indicative of an immature stage of development, open up opportunities to include other perspectives on how to conceptualize public diplomacy. For instance, in the context of China, public diplomacy is understood as the external arm of propaganda, which does not have the same negative connotation as it does in the English language context.

In the Chinese language, public diplomacy originates from the concept of xuanchuan (宣传), which is roughly the equivalent of propaganda. In contrast to the pejorative connotation of the word propaganda in English, xuanchuan is a relatively neutral term (Wang, 2008). Xuanchuan as a noun means "benign activities as the release of news, general shaping of ideology, or even advertisement" (Wang, 2008, p. 259). As a verb, it means the act of disseminating and promoting ideas. According to Wang (2008), xuanchuan has two levels: internal and external. Public diplomacy in the Chinese context refers to the external level of xuanchuan, which seeks to promote the Chinese image throughout the world. The idea of external propaganda can be traced back to the Republic of China era. In a historical account of how the Republic of China tried to deal with China's image overseas, Volz (2011) argued that xuanchuan, or international propaganda in the Republic era was considered as "a proper journalistic role" in correcting perceived bias in the foreign press' coverage of China (p. 174). Therefore, propaganda in the Chinese context is not distortion, deception, and disinformation; it is a way to communicate the true image of China (Volz, 2011).

Another Chinese scholar understands public diplomacy as activities initiated by governments, civil society and non-governmental organizations with the purpose of facilitating dialogue among different cultures and promoting peaceful coexistence and harmony (Su, 2011). The two fundamental goals for diplomacy and public diplomacy, according to Su (2011), are zuxin (足信) and qubing (去兵). Zuxin means to build and improve trust and credibility while qubing means to reduce and limit wars. Similar to Su (2011), a former Chinese ambassador argues that conversation and communication among civilizations is the core of public diplomacy (Wu, 2011).

The first Chinese perspective on public diplomacy (i.e., external propaganda) reflects an emphasis on the persuasive dimension reminiscent of the early Cold War formulations of public diplomacy from the U.S. perspective. However, the evolving understanding of public diplomacy from the Chinese perspective suggests that a similar shift toward the relationship-building perspective is currently underway in China as well as in the U.S. Considering that the U.S. and China are arguably the two largest players on the world diplomatic stage, this points to an emerging understanding of the centrality of relationship-building in the emerging scholarship of public diplomacy. Relationship-building, then, and not persuasion, will inform the rest of this chapter, exploring the implementation of audiovisual public diplomacy tools such as VNRs in the digital media environment.

## *Public Diplomacy Tools in the Digital Age*

The definition of public diplomacy is also being reshaped by the advancement of information and communication technologies. For example, the use of the idea of telediplomacy (Ammon, 2001) reflects the impact of global media networks on influencing public opinion. Additionally, with the rise of non-government actors, concepts such as noopolitik, which is coined in contrast to realpolitik (Ronfeldt & Arquilla, 2009) conceptualize public diplomacy as an alternative to the traditional realism and power-based, closed-door diplomacy that took place in secret among and between government officials.

Video news releases represent a significant public diplomacy tool in this mediated environment, giving governments and NGOs a way to introduce foreign publics to conditions outside their borders. Traditional VNRs take advantage of the audiovisual, emotional nature of the television medium to elicit response from publics who might otherwise be unaware of—or at least disinterested—in places, issues or events that may not affect them directly.

Traditionally, audience exposure to VNRs was controlled by television news media. Zoch and Duhé (1997) refer to the traditional media as a "super-public" (p. 16) with the ability to connect an organization with the other publics an organization needs to reach. From the organizational perspective, the "super-public" also functions as a potential "super-gatekeeper," making judgments of newsworthiness and public interest that represent significant barriers to the organization's ability to interact with the news audience—and thereby have an opportunity to help build the public agenda. Even with the expanded news hole created by the 24-hour news cycle, only a small percentage of the VNRs and raw footage offered to news outlets by public relations and public affairs professionals is actually broadcast. And greater sophistication regarding communications among organizational players means an ever-increasing amount of visual material is competing for airtime.

Two public diplomacy trends are emerging in response to the barriers represented by the news media's traditional gatekeeping role regarding VNRs. The first is the creation of pseudo-events or media spectacles that offer news producers both visuals to support their newscasts as well as an identifiable—and sometimes controversial—news hook. The second is the provision of alternate communications channels through which to engage with relevant publics in the social media environment. Two recent examples will serve to illustrate the use of these tactics in allowing governments to help shape the public agenda through relationship building with significant publics outside their borders that might be difficult to reach through traditional media channels.

## A Pseudo-Event Defines Coverage of a "Real" Event

There was little chance that Chinese President Hu Jintao's visit to the United States in 2011 would be ignored by the world's news media. Planned in agonizing detail by diplomats on both sides of the Pacific, the trip would showcase U.S. President Barack Obama's warm greeting of Hu, demonstrate American innovation through a series of corporate visits, and focus on projects of mutual benefit to two of the world's great economic engines. However, beyond the confines of the orchestrated events was China's concern that the

American people continued to misunderstand China, and that American news media might seize on the presidential visit to discuss traditional "hot button" items, emphasizing areas of traditional *disagreements* between China and the U.S.: human rights, currency protection, and job creation. This concern was particularly relevant as the preceding autumn's Congressional elections had seen a number of candidates run on anti-China platforms in response to the U.S.'s lingering economic recession.

The Chinese government responded with "Experience China," a combination national advertising campaign and pseudo-event designed to assure coverage of China's story and "boost China's image among Americans" (Jones & Tze-wei, 2011, p. 4). The 30-second advertisement consisted of a series of famous—and not so famous—Chinese citizens, highlighting China's many accomplishments in the areas of science, business, sports and the arts. For example, one scene ran with the title "Influential Chinese Wealth," and featured Chinese business icons such as Baidu founder Robin Li and NetEase founder Ding Lei (Chao, 2011). The advertisements ran on CNN for about a month around the U.S.-Chinese Summit.

However, it wasn't the advertising campaign that garnered the interest of the U.S. news media. A major portion of the coverage was based on the pseudo-event created by a massive, six-screen display in one of the world's most expensive pieces of advertising real estate: New York City's Times Square. The LCD displays shone traditional Chinese red between the 300 daily showings of the "Experience China" advertisement, dominating one corner of the famed advertising canyon, providing a stunning visual that was picked up by television stations all over the U.S. and around the world, and garnering plenty of attention in print media as well. In fact, the pseudo-event prompted a number of days of coverage, from the installation of the screens to reactions from the crowds of people, New Yorkers and tourists alike, to the display (see, e.g., Barron, 2011; Chen, Li, & Duan, 2011).

Local reaction to the pseudo-event was mixed, and comments on online news stories about the installation ranged from "excited" and "amazed" to downright xenophobic. However, since few of the individuals highlighted in the 30-second commercial were familiar to the U.S. public (basketball player Yao Ming being a notable exception), the use of the striking video by television stations virtually forced discussion of the accomplishments of the featured Chinese citizens. Certainly, the pseudo-event ensured more—and more positive coverage—than would have been garnered by the state visit alone.

Using Fitzpatrick's (2010) four-legged analysis framework, the purpose of the campaign was to increase awareness of China's contributions to the arts, sciences and business. This formed part of an initiative to reframe China as an innovator, as opposed to a manufacturing economy based on the innovations of others. Additionally, it served to "humanize" China, highlighting the country as a possible travel destination for world tourists (Ng, 2011).

The main actors were the China State Information Council Office, who had responsibility for the campaign's creation and placement, and its agency of record, Lintas Shanghai. Other actors included the Chinese citizens who participated in the video, as well as the media companies that custom designed the "Experience China" installation.

While American news viewers might be considered the broadest target for the advertising campaign, the combination of the pseudo-event with the advertisements points to additional groups likely targeted by the campaign. First among these would be members of the American business community. New York City is the commercial heart of the U.S., and many influential members of the business community—those with responsibilities for long-term decisions about investment and outsourcing—were doubtless exposed to the campaign. A second and extremely significant group was the Chinese public. The installation received extensive coverage inside China, and served to underscore China's symbolic arrival on the economic world stage through its placement of its message in one of the most recognizable advertising locations on the planet: Times Square. But the publics targeted went beyond the U.S. and China, with the installation receiving significant attention in other countries around the world, with a slightly different message: China is an ascending world power, a rival to the U.S.'s economic might. Clearly, that is a message that serves the public diplomacy interests of China's business community, but is also a powerful message for the Chinese government to relay as it seeks to build new and stronger relationships in many avenues of global interaction, politically, economically, and socially.

### YouTube and Facebook Build Foreign "Friendships"— and Sometimes Enemies as Well

The Argentine government had repeatedly and unsatisfactorily availed itself of traditional diplomatic channels regarding its ongoing dispute with the U.K. over the islands known in Spanish as Las Malvinas and in English, the Falklands, which sit about 400 miles off Argentina's shores—and some 14,000 miles from England. For example, Argentine President Cristina Fernandez left the 2012 Summit of the Americas before the final meeting when she could not get the body to agree to support Argentina's sovereignty claims over the islands (Merco Press, 2012). Later the same year Fernandez pressed Argentina's claims by addressing the U.N.'s decolonization committee, which resulted in a non-binding resolution requesting that Argentina and Britain enter into talks about the future of the islands (Charbonneau, 2012). However the British government has maintained that it will honor the Falkland Islanders' wishes to remain a territory of Britain, and do not plan to enter into talks.

Traditional diplomatic channels essentially exhausted, the Argentine government, specifically the Casa Rosada, Argentina's executive branch, undertook a multi-pronged public diplomacy effort to focus world attention on an issue it saw as critical, but to which most of the world was indifferent: the sovereignty of Argentina over its natural resources, partially symbolized by the British control of the Falklands. The trigger event for the Argentine government's public diplomacy efforts in the spring of 2012 appears to have been moves by a number of British oil exploration companies to exploit the substantial oil and gas reserves that had recently been discovered around Argentina. In 1993, the Argentine government privatized the country's ailing, state-owned oil company, YPF. A majority stake was later purchased by Spain's leading energy company, Repsol. But with significant shale oil reserves of some one billion barrels announced by YPF in November 2011, Argentina decided to expropriate YPF in April 2012 (Plummer, 2012). The move to gain control of the Falklands formed another part of the country's efforts to gain sovereignty over natural resources that could improve economic conditions in Argentina.

Argentina's public diplomacy efforts were centered on two previously established social networking sites. First was Amigos de Argentina, the official Facebook presence for the government of Argentina. The "About" description calls the page, "A space open to Argentines and our friends from around the world to find out about Argentina and our people" (Amigos de Argentina, n.d.) [translation provided by the authors]. With more than 160,000 followers, the Facebook presence allows Argentina's public affairs professionals to distribute information about cultural and historical events, as well as news and current events to individuals who have already decided to "Like" Argentina on Facebook—presumably a sympathetic audience for the Argentine government, although little is known about why Facebook users "Like" the items they like, or what the impact of those "Likes" are on subsequent attitudes or actions.

Amigos de Argentina content often includes direct links to a second social networking site used in Argentina's public diplomacy efforts, YouTube's Casa Rosada Channel. The original announcement of Argentina's expropriation of YPF appeared on the Amigos de Argentina Facebook page, accompanied by links to Fernandez's press conference explaining the decision, as well as links to a series of slick institutional "spots" entitled "YPF is Argentina," housed on the Casa Rosada Channel. Clearly some time in the making, the spots featured historical and current footage of Argentina's industrial and energy sectors, along with emotional footage of children and families enjoying the good life provided by Argentina's natural resources. The voiceover is taken from the law that restored YPF to Argentine hands, underscoring the critical importance of controlling the country's natural resources, "toward the end of guaranteeing economic and social development, growth in employment, increased competitiveness, and increased education and sustainability" (Casa Rosada, 2012) [translation provided by the authors]. The video link resulted in dozens of comments (both for and against the expropriation), as well as 171 "Likes," and perhaps most importantly, 107 "Shares" by Amigos de Argentina followers to their own Facebook friends. The spot on the Casa Rosada Channel was viewed almost 30,000 times as of July 2012.

While Argentina's expropriation of YPF received plenty of press attention around the world, the institutional videos, completely in Spanish and replete with Argentine symbolism, were not discussed much beyond Argentina. However, with YPF now in Argentine hands, Argentina's next public diplomacy initiative to gain control of its energy reserves provided a controversial news hook that assured its placement in television news segments around the world.

While most of the world was looking forward to the pageantry and sport of the London 2012 Olympics, the event came to serve as a bitter reminder of unfinished business in Argentina. Thirty years after the 10-week war that left the Falkland Islands in British hands, the Argentine government decided to revisit the issue with a controversial advertisement entitled "Homenaje a los caidos y ex combatientes de Malvinas [Tribute to the fallen and veterans of the Malvinas]." The ad featured Argentine Olympian Fernando Zylberberg training at symbolic locations on the Falklands, including a segment with him jumping on a memorial to World War I veterans. The video, posted to the Casa Rosada Channel, finished with the provocative tagline, "To compete on English soil, we train on Argentine soil."

The advertisement, which was filmed secretly on the islands by Young & Rubicam Buenos Aires, a subsidiary of the communications giant WPP, created an immediate stir, engendering more than 650,000 views, almost 4,000 likes (along with nearly 900 dislikes), and more than 1,300 comments. The CEO of WPP repudiated the advertisements, apologized for his company's part in creating them, and asked the government of Argentina to stop airing them (Sweny, 2012). Argentina did not immediately comply with that request.

The video spawned news coverage all over the world. Coverage was mixed, with press reports in the U.K. and in the U.S. focused on the clandestine nature of the video, and the ostensible Argentine desire to politicize the

Olympic Games, while South American reports focused on the issues of colonization and nationalism. Perhaps seeing a commonality with its neighbors, in news coverage subsequent to the airing of the video, Argentina attempted to frame the issue as a "regional one," with the Argentine ambassador to the U.K., Alicia Castro, indicating that by refusing to engage in dialog about the Malvinas, Britain was "turning its back on the South American continent" (Efe, 2012).

Using Fitzpatrick's (2010) four-legged analysis framework, the purpose of Argentina's ongoing public diplomacy efforts was to increase attention to and win support for its fight for sovereignty over the natural resources in its geographic area. The main actors were the executive branch of the Argentine government, including Fernandez herself. Other actors included Y & R Buenos Aires, who conceived of the ad, and the Argentine Olympic athletes who were included in it (although only Zylberberg was included in the final cut of the ad). The British government's strong repudiation of the ad made it a significant actor in the campaign, assuring significant press coverage both in the EU and in the U.S.

While both the "YPF es Argentina" and Olympic ads were first and foremost directed at the people of Argentina, the use of both Facebook and YouTube to deploy the public diplomacy campaign indicates that Argentina was targeting additional audiences for its campaign. In a particular, the government sought to engage citizens from around South America in the discussion. Argentina's failure to secure support for a resolution on Malvinas sovereignty at the 2012 Summit of the Americas was a disappointment, and reframing the issue as a South American energy issue may help its case in the future—in particular if citizens in neighboring South American countries join Argentina's call for a diplomatic solution.

The use of the Amigos de Argentina site on Facebook and the Casa Rosada Channel allowed people from around the world to view the YPF and Olympic videos at will. Many may have been directed to the Casa Rosada site by online news reports. But others were led directly by friends through "Shares" on Facebook. And still others were exposed by subscriptions to the Casa Rosada Channel, because they already had a pre-determined interest in what the government of Argentina is sharing. Therefore the potential audience for the videos was far greater than could be expected from any traditional VNR distribution to news media—and the worldwide press coverage of the Olympic ad provided exposure far greater than any traditional media buy could accomplish. It is important to note, however, that both videos were entirely in Spanish—only the Olympic video included English subtitles. Since the voiceover was particularly important to the understanding of the YPF videos, non-Spanish-speaking publics were not considered in the creation of that campaign.

Clearly, both campaigns serve the interests of the Argentine government. However, since the long-term stability of South America is tied to Argentina as one of its economic engines, the Argentine government is hoping to build relationships with publics throughout South America who have a mutual interest in protecting and benefiting from local resources.

In this case, the campaign to build some relationships has necessarily strained other relationships, in particular with Spain and the U.K. This may be considered an acceptable cost by Argentina, since traditional diplomatic initiatives have yielded no results to date.

## Conclusion

In his Integrated Public Diplomacy Model, Golan (2013) noted "the mediated public diplomacy approach is focused on government-to-citizen engagement that is mediated by a third party—the global news media" (p. 1251). This study adds another dimension to the mediated approach, with VNRs employed in non-traditional media as a new way of garnering attention from news media.

Both of these cases indicate the use of audiovisual materials is likely to play a significant part in ongoing public diplomacy efforts. However, the traditional VNR, distributed to news agencies and aired on traditional news outlets, is only one way to employ this powerful tactic. More eager than ever for control of their message, governments can now circumvent traditional distribution channels and go directly to publics with their messages whenever possible. In some cases, VNRs and B-roll footage have given way to slick advertisements that can both engage multiple audiences and win news coverage. This has both practical and ethical implications for those engaged in those campaigns.

The first implication is that practitioners must carefully evaluate the value and ethics of staging events for public diplomacy purposes. For true relationship building to occur in public diplomacy, the publics targeted by campaigns must perceive some benefit to engagement. Public diplomats must focus on strategies that allow the use of audiovisuals to tell their story to interested publics, while still finding ways to understand the stories of those publics.

The second implication is that governments must be proactive in establishing alternative channels for reaching interested publics. Shaw, McCombs, Weaver, and Hamm (1999) suggest the traditional mass media play a role in helping individuals join groups of common interest by joining agendas, in a process known as agenda melding. In the digital age, Facebook, YouTube, Twitter and a host of other social media forums provide new avenues for individuals to align themselves with agendas beyond their borders. By establishing channels early, governments can have direct access to interested publics when they have a story to tell. In addition to allowing the dissemination of audiovisual materials, the establishment of such channels can be part of a larger relationship building strategy with multiple publics, allowing publics to get answers, ask questions, share information and give feedback.

## *Bibliography*

Amigos de Argentina. (n.d.) About. Retrieved June 15, 2012 from https://www.face book.com/#!/pages/amigos-de-argentina/117990834128

Ammon, R. (2001). *Global television and the shaping of world politics: CNN, telediplomacy, and foreign policy.* Jefferson, NC: McFarland.

Barron, J. (2011, January 18). China's publicity ads arrive in Times Square. *New York Times.* Retrieved from http://www.nytimes.com

Broaddus, M., Harmon, M. D., & Mounts, K. F. (2012). VNRs: Is the news audience deceived? *Journal of Mass Media Ethics, 26*(4), 283–296.

Cameron, G. T., & Blount, D. (1996). VNRs and airchecks: A content analysis of the use of video news releases in television newscasts. *Journalism & Mass Communication Quarterly, 73*(4), 890–904.

Casa Rosada. (2012, April 12). YPF es Argentina. Retrieved June 15, 2012, from http://www.youtube.com/watch?v=H7eniAGIiUA & feature=plcp

Chao, L. (2011, January 16). Pro-China ad debuts in Times Square. *The Wall Street Journal.* Retrieved from http://blogs.wsj.com

Charbonneau, L. (2012, June 14). Argentina's Fernandez takes Falklands claim to U.N. *Reuters.* Retrieved June 15, 2012 from http://www.reuters.com/arti cle/2012/06/14/us-britain-argentina-falklands-un-idUSBRE85D1P220120614

Chen, W., Li, L., & Duan, Y. (2011, January 19). National image lights up Times Square. *China Daily.* Retrieved from http://www.chinadaily.com.cn

Connolly-Ahern, C., Grantham, S., & Cabrera-Baukus, M. (2010). The effects of attribution of VNRs and risk on news viewers' assessments of credibility. *Journal of Public Relations Research, 22*(1), 49–64.

Cull, N. J. (2009). Public diplomacy before Gullion: The evolution of a phrase. In N. Snow & P. M. Taylor (Eds.), *Routledge handbook of public diplomacy* (pp. 19–23). New York, London: Routledge.

Curtin, P. A. (1999). Reevaluating public relations information subsidies: Market-driven journalism and agenda-building theory and practice. *Journal of Public Relations Research, 11*(1), 53–90.

Efe News Service. (2012, May 6). Embajadora argentina: La disputa por las Malvinas es de toda Latinoamérica. Retrieved June 15, 2012 from http://www.lexis.nexis.com

Fitzpatrick, K. R. (2009). Understanding public diplomacy: Toward a common identity. Paper presented at the annual conference of the International Studies Association, New York, New York, February 17, 2009.

Fitzpatrick, K. R. (2010). *The future of U.S. public diplomacy: An uncertain fate.* Leiden; Boston: Brill.

Gilboa, E. (2008). Searching for a theory of public diplomacy. *The ANNALS of the American Academy of Political and Social Science, 616*(1), 55–77.

Golan, G. J. (2013). Introduction: An integrated approach to public diplomacy. *American Behavioral Scientist, 57*(9), 1251–1255.

Grunig, J. E. (1992). *Excellence in public relations and communication management.* Hillsdale, NJ: Lawrence Erlbaum Associates.

Grunig, J. E. & Hunt, T. (1984). *Managing public relations.* New York: Holt, Rinehart and Winston.

Harmon, M. D., & White, C. (2001). How television news programs use video news releases. *Public Relation Review, 27*, 213–222.

Herzstein, R. E. (1983). Crisis on the Eastern Front, 1941–42: A comparative analysis of German and American newsreel coverage. *Film & History, 13*(2), 34–42.

Jones, K., & Tze-wei, N. (2011, January 20). Who's who of great and good mostly blur; China's US image campaign presents positive faces but battles low public recognition [Electronic version]. *South China Morning Post,* p. 4.

Media Education Foundation. (2005). Focus on video news releases. Retrieved June 15, 2012, from http://www.mediaed.org/Handouts/VNRhandout.pdf

Merco Press. (2012, April 15). Cristina Fernandez abandons summit with no declaration on Falklands/Malvinas. Retrieved June 15, 2012, from http://en.merco press.com/2012/04/15/cristina-fernandez-abandons-summit-with-no-declaration-on-falklands-malvinas

Ng, E. (2011, January 19). Red China takes over Times Square. *Marketing-interactive: The art & science of connecting with consumers.* Retrieved March 19, 2012 from http://www.marketing-interactive.com/news/24099

Nichols, J. S. (2003). Propaganda. *Encyclopedia of international media and communications, 3,* 597–606.

Owen, A. R., & Karrh, J. A. (1996). Video news releases: Effects on viewer recall and attitudes. *Public Relations Review, 22*(4), pp. 369–378.

Plummer, R. (2012, April 16). Argentina to expropriate Repsol oil subsidiary YPF. BBC News Business. Retrieved June 15, 2012 from http://www.bbc.co.uk/news/busi ness-17732910

Public Diplomacy Alumni Association.(2012). About U.S. public diplomacy. Retrieved April 30, 2012 from http://publicdiplomacy.org/pages/index.php?page=about-pub lic-diplomacy#2

Reich, Z. (2010). Measuring the impact of PR on published news in increasingly fragmented news environments: A multifaceted approach. *Journalism Studies, 11*(6), 799–816.

Ronfeldt, D. & Arquilla, J. (2009). Noopolitik: A new paradigm for public diplomacy. In N. Snow & P. M. Taylor (Eds.), *Routledge handbook of public diplomacy* (pp. 352–365). New York; London: Routledge.

Sharp, P. (2005).Revolutionary states, outlaw regimes, and the techniques of public diplomacy. In J. Melissen (Eds.), *The new public diplomacy: Soft power in international relations* (pp. 106–123). New York: Palgrave Macmillan.

Shaw, D. L., McCombs, M., Weaver, D. H., & Hamm, B. J. (1999). Individuals, groups, and agenda melding: A theory of social dissonance. *International Journal of Public Opinion Research, 11*(1), 2–24.

Su, C. (2011). Renwen lijie yu wenming duihua: Gonggong waijiao xin neihan [Cultural understanding and dialogue among civilizations: The new meaning of public diplomacy]. *Chinese Social Sciences Today, 160*, 15. Retrieved May 24, 2012 from http://sspress.cass.cn/news/17340.htm

Sweney, M. (2012, May 4). Sir Martin Sorrell condemns Argentinian Falklands Olympics ad. *The Guardian.* Retrieved June 15, 2012, from http://www.guardian.co.uk/media/2012/may/04/sir-martin-sorrell-argentinian-ad

Tewksbury, D., Jensen, J., & Coe, K. (2011). Video news releases and the public: The impact of source labeling on the perceived credibility of television news. *Journal of Communication, 61*, 328–348.

Volz, Y. Z. (2011). China's image management abroad, 1920s–1940s: Origin, justification, and institutionalization. In J. Wang (Eds.), *Soft power in China: Public diplomacy through communication* (pp. 157–179). New York: Palgrave Macmillan.

Wang, Y. (2008). Public diplomacy and the rise of Chinese soft power. *The ANNALS of the American Academy of Political and Social Science, 616*(1), 257–273.

White, C. (2012). Activist efforts of the Center for Media and Democracy to affect FCC policy for video news releases. *Public Relations Review, 38*(1), 76–82.

Wu, S. (2011). Wenming duihua yu jiaoliu shi gonggong waijiao de hexin neirong. [Conversations and communications among civilizations: The core content of public diplomacy]*GonggongWaijiaoJikan* [*Public Diplomacy Quarterly*], 5. Retrieved April 30, 2012 from http://www.china.com.cn/international/pdq/2011-03/01/content_22029518.htm.

Wulfemeyer, K. T., & Frazier, L. (1992). The ethics of video news releases: A qualitative analysis. *Journal of Mass Media Ethics, 7*(3), 151–168.

Yun, S. H., & Toth, E. L. (2009). Future sociological public diplomacy and the role of public relations: Evolution of public diplomacy. *American Behavioral Scientist, 53*(4), 493–503.

Yun, S.-H. (2006). Toward public relations theory-based study of public diplomacy: Testing the applicability of the excellence study. *Journal of Public Relations Research, 18*(4), 287–312.

Zhang, J. (2008). Making sense of the changes in China's public diplomacy: Direction of information flow and messages. *Place Branding and Public Diplomacy, 4*(4), 303–316.

Zoch, L. M., & Duhé, S. (1997). "Feeding the media" during a crisis: A nationwide look. *Public Relations Quarterly, 42*(3), 15–19.

# 14. Conceptualizing International Broadcasting as Information Intervention

Shawn Powers & Tal Samuel-Azran

> "News is a weapon of war. Its purpose is to wage war and
> not to give information."
> —Josef Goebbels, German Minister of Propaganda, 1933–1945.

The production and dissemination of information are at the core of the modern Westphalian nation-state (Braman 2007). Information-communication technologies (ICTs) are an increasingly central element of 21st century statecraft, with adaptive political actors creating and controlling information flows in order to further their interests. At the same time, innovations in ICTs are inevitably described as furthering a universal right to free expression, often connected to the promise of a Kantian (1795) perpetual peace. For example, at the turn of the 20th century, wireless telegraphy mastermind Guglielmo Marconi declared: "communication between peoples widely separated in space and thought is undoubtedly the greatest weapon against the evils of misunderstanding and jealousy" (cited by Hale 1975, xiii). The more connected the world is, the more difficult it is to engage in conflict, or so the thinking goes. Over a century later, US Secretary of State Hillary Clinton (2010) echoed this sentiment, proposing a global right to connect to the World Wide Web: "Information freedom supports the peace and security that provides a foundation for global progress. Historically, asymmetrical access to information is one of the leading causes of interstate conflict." A narrative of *information as peace inducing* is firmly embedded within discourses of communication and technology.

Appealing as the promise of information-driven peace may be, history offers ample evidence for skeptics. Not long after Marconi's radio was adopted by the Western world it was deployed as a tool of war, aiding Nazi aggression and Hitler's genocide of six million European Jews (Doherty 2000). Just six months after Clinton spoke of the need for recognition of a universal right to connect to the World Wide Web, news broke that the U.S. government, in coordination with its Israeli ally, deployed a cyber worm to slow Iran's nuclear program. Despite theorization of an inevitable global village bound by transnational media flows and ubiquitous connectivity (McLuhan 1962), states remain strategic actors, eager to adopt emerging technologies and adapt policy to advance national interests.

Confronted by an increasingly pervasive information society, governments are motivated both to protect their information sovereignty and to intervene into foreign information markets, competing for influence among foreign citizens (Price 2002). Domestic protections and foreign interventions vary in terms of the scope and sophistication. Examples of integrated public diplomacy strategies include the US and Qatar, which invest in emerging information technologies to engage non-traditional audiences in foreign information ecosystems (Powers & Youmans 2012). The governments of North Korea and Bahrain focus instead on controlling and monitoring flows of information within their territories, challenging foreign media by creating barriers to entry and incentivizing nationally grounded media production and consumption. Others, including China, Iran, Russia and Venezuela are active in both arenas.

This chapter focuses on a specific type of information intervention (Metzl 1997): international broadcasting, or "the use of electronic media by one society to shape the opinion of the people and leaders of another" through the use of radio, television and web-based media (Price, Haas & Margolin 2008, pp. 152–153). Conceptualizing international broadcasting as an information intervention requires an explanation as to how strategic actors engage and compete for ideational influence in the international system. While international broadcasting is merely one element of the integrated public diplomacy approach outlined by Golan (2013), it continues to play a crucial part in broader public diplomacy strategy. Drawing from both historical and contemporary material, we outline a model of ideational influence whereby strategic actors utilize policy, law, subsidy and technology to manipulate the market and compete with others attempting to maintain or gain influence among a citizenry (Price 1994). We explore the cases of America's Broadcasting Board of Governors (BBG) and Qatar's Al Jazeera network, identifying how both governments are using new and traditional information technologies to compete for influence, and highlighting both effective and ineffective strategies. To conclude, we discuss the utility of conceptualizing broadcasting as a form of intervention in today's networked markets for loyalty.

## *International Broadcasting in the Market for Loyalties*

Despite its historical importance, and perceived significance in contemporary international politics (Powers 2012), no theory of international broadcasting has gained broad acceptance in policy or academic communities. As a result, international broadcasting is often equated with propaganda, or a "one-way communication system designed to influence belief" (Wood 2000, 25). This model is congruent with "messaging," or non-reflexively explaining the government's policies to foreign audiences (Fitzpatrick 2011, 6). Some practitioners have adapted this into a conflict-oriented approach, resurrecting Cold War-era thinking. Former BBG Chair Walter Isaacson (2010), for example, suggested: "In this new struggle, just like in the old one, one of the most important arrows in our quiver will be the power of a free press in promoting democracy and freedom." Similarly, former BBG member Edward Kaufman (2002, p. 115) argued for thinking of international broadcasting as part of the "modern media war."

Conceptualizing broadcasting as a battalion in combat is of little value. Wartime metaphors may help shore up political support, but they obscure the strategy required for organizing a successful information intervention. War is, at its core, destructive. While deeply geopolitical, information intervention is fundamentally constructive, focusing on cultivating new thinking and relationships. Confusing the two missions decreases the likelihood of a successful intervention.

Practitioners acknowledge a need to move away from propaganda-based models and towards dialogue or network-based approaches to public diplomacy (Glassman 2009; Lord & Lynch 2010; McHale 2009). Emphasizing the importance of non-state actors and listening is instructive for broadcasters adapting to the modern media ecology, but leaves much to be desired from the perspective of building a theory of international broadcasting. How much dialogue is sufficient? How do you measure the quality and effectiveness of a dialogue? How many nodes are needed to constitute a network of influence? Why does being connected to a broad network of actors produce influence only some of the time? Of course, answers to these questions require robust field research and will vary over time, organization and context. Dialogue and networked diplomacy reflect important strategic priorities, but are insufficient for the purpose of policy planning, evaluation and comparative analysis. In practice, they are merely additional tools of influence, operating alongside a variety of tactics states deploy to compete for power in the international system.

Microeconomic theory offers a different approach to conceptualizing international broadcasting, grounding it first and foremost in the context of strategic actors vying for power. Price (1994) suggests that international actors enact policies analogous to a strategic investment aiming to shape the allegiances of foreign audiences in ways that increase the likelihood of an outcome favored by the actor. In this marketplace, international actors (usually governments, but also non-government strategic actors) are the sellers, and audiences are the buyers. Here, the market is deployed as an analogue to analyze and predict the likely success of a policy change (Downs, 1957). We propose using the market for loyalties as a model to analyze international broadcasting.

At a very basic level, international actors are selling information in exchange for the audiences' attention, an increasingly scarce resource given the competitive media markets emerging around the world. Yet actors aren't simply selling information, rather, they are offering stories and identities that in some capacity reflect an ideological perspective. Audiences agree to "buy" what an actor is selling by repeatedly tuning into and engaging with the content, and in return, become increasingly loyal to the underlying narrative and its associated community. Figure 14.1 compares buyers and sellers from a commerce-based market to buyers and sellers in the market for loyalties.

Similar to any marketplace, the more an individual buys (in this case, consumes), the more they have to give (i.e., identify themselves with), and the more loyal they become to the investment's successful outcome and/or popularity. Thus, the more an audience tunes into an actor's medium, the more they will identify with its messages and content, albeit explicit political news opinions (e.g., Al Jazeera Arabic editorial programming) or more subtle cultural or social messages embedded into the plots of cultural programs (e.g., BBC World Service's educational entertainment soap operas). This is not to say that viewing audiences are inevitably "brainwashed" by media content.Rather, given the diversity and plethora of media options available today, if audiences are repeatedly tuning into a particular international broadcaster or YouTube channel, it is because the programming resonates with or fulfills an ideational need of those consumers (Ball-Rokeach 1985). More than ever, content is king.

| | | Commerce | Ideas |
|---|---|---|---|
| **Buyers** | Who: | Individuals, businesses | Citizens, subjects, nationals & consumers |
| | What: | Currency, barter | Attention, identity, loyalty, agency |
| | Why: | Basic needs, shared identity | Connect with others, make sense of lived experience |
| **Sellers** | Who: | Producers, distributors (i.e., cartels) | Governments, businesses, interest groups (i.e., cartels) |
| | What: | Goods & services | Information, propaganda, news & entertainment |
| | Why: | Meet needs, further cartel interests | Meet needs, further cartel interests |

*Figure 14.1.* Comparing commerce and idea-based markets.

Just as in commercial markets, the introduction of new competitors into an ideational market can have significant consequences for individuals and organizations. In Brazil, for example, the adoption of television in rural communities created a more progressive climate for women's rights. Between 1970 and 1990, daily access to television jumped from 10 to 80 percent among Brazilians. Popular *telenovelas* (soap operas), with stories featuring strong, independent, educated, unmarried and ambitious women provided compelling role models in rural areas where women had grown accustomed to a traditional lifestyle of childbearing and housework. Access to television programming, and *telenovelas* in particular, statistically correlated to substantial decreases in the birth rate, a key indicator of development and women's equality (La Ferrara, Chong, & Duryea 2008). Similar results were found in India's rural communities when introduced to television and local soap operas (Jensen & Oster 2009).

To put the example in terms of the ideational marketplace: as communication technology (satellites) decreased the cost of entering the market, a new seller (Globo, the producer of Brazil's *telenovelas*) provided a good (television programs) that was in demand among buyers (Brazil's citizenry). The buyers paid the seller through their loyalty to the programs, talking about the programs with peer groups and consistently tuning in. Large, dedicated and mobilized audiences are valuable to advertisers, thus generating substantial revenue for the seller. The introduction of a new competitor, in this case, altered the marketplace of loyalties through enhanced competition, eventually resulting in changes in consumer behaviors. Policymakers should take note that the introduction of a new competitor itself is not necessarily transformational; rather the new competitor's ability to identify and react to unmet demand shifted loyalties and eventually consumers' leisurely habits.

## Sellers

Why do international actors invest in the market for loyalties? States eager to capitalize on the ways in which altered media ecosystems can transform foreign attitudes, and behaviors and invest in international broadcasting. One clear winner from the current processes of globalization has been the citizen. Governments around the world are increasingly facing activated, mobilized and intelligent citizen groups calling for government reform and accountability. The Arab Spring demonstrated just how powerful these movements are in forcing dramatic change—even revolution—in just a matter of weeks (Edwards 2011). For example, the U.S. government invests in the marketplace of loyalties through its international broadcasting to improve the likely acceptance of its foreign policies and national interests (e.g., democracy in the Middle East). Similar to the plethora of rationales one relies upon when investing in a stock market (e.g., financial profit, ideological support for the corporation's mission, the possibility of undercutting a competitor by investing in its partners, etc.), the precise reasons for any actor's intervention into another's information space vary significantly and over time.

Moreover, as foreign actors appeal to a country's domestic audiences through media technologies, governments are eager to restrict access to content that could negatively impact a citizen's loyalty to the regime, or provide more appealing information (propaganda), favorable economic policy and robust social services to court domestic constituencies. In January 2011, for example, former Egyptian President Mubarak ordered a shutdown of all internet services in an effort to regain control over the flow of information during protests that would eventually force his removal from power. This draconian measure was taken only after weeks of revved-up government propaganda disseminated via terrestrial television and radio services. China, too, is keen to protect its information space from foreign interventions, deploying a mix of censorship, propaganda, and market solutions to increase the amount of web content that strengthens Chinese nationalism.

As economic interests increasingly become interconnected with a state's national interests, governments are moving to regulate international information flows in ways that preserve their national economic advantage. In the U.S., for example, there is growing political interest in expanding the monitoring and regulation of internet traffic not for the purpose of political censorship, but rather to enhance the security of web services (e.g., Google, Facebook, eTrade) and protect intellectual property (e.g., music, movies and television programming) that drives its economic growth (U.S. Department of Commerce 2012). While the motivations and tactics used by Egypt, China and the U.S. are quite diverse, analytically speaking, they are similar in the sense that they represent government efforts to shape the marketplace of information flows for the purpose of national survival.

## *Buyers*

Why do citizens engage in the market for loyalties? Human nature includes an innate fear of social isolation and, early on, we demonstrate the need for acceptance into something greater than the individual self: a community (Noelle-Neumann 1974). Before there were mass media, children were born into a family that would serve as their immediate community, and eventually introduce them to other elements of their collective communities—friends, aunts and uncles, colleagues, and so on and so forth. Today, mass media, and increasingly social media, play an important psycho-social role in establishing community, or shared knowledge, norms and interests.

Ulrich Beck argues that one consequence of rapid globalization is the shattering of traditional means by which community is formed and maintained, both at the level of the hyper local (e.g., family) as well as the societal (e.g., nation) (Beck, 2005). Similar to how a family served as the means by which children were introduced to the local community, on a larger scale, the nation-state was the primary means through which citizens engaged the international community. This, of course, is changing given the nature of modern communications networks. Before commercial satellites, 99 percent of communication occurred within the boundaries of the nation state (Pelton & Oslund 2004). Anderson's conception of the nation as an "imagined community" worked because nation-based media were shared among diverse groups, constituting shared histories, stories and knowledge. As information flows become more difficult to control at the level of the state, and as communication technologies become more mobile, affordable and globally connected, people are able to form their own imagined communities, not based on the established strictures of authority and tradition, but rather on their personal interests, ideas and passions (Castells 1996). Globally connected media offer a more robust market for news, information and entertainment, each of which shapes the modern citizen's loyalties and sense of citizenship.

## Case Studies

To illustrate the operational success and challenges of an information inter-vention in a market for loyalties, we briefly outline two examples: Qatar's Al Jazeera Network and the United States' Middle East Broadcasting Networks (MBN). The success and impact of Al-Jazeera's programming show how a relatively unknown microstate was able to punch above its weight in regional politics as a result of its smart, yet small, investment in an international broad-caster. On the other hand, an analysis of the history of MBN, which manages Alhurra TV, illustrates how adherence to an outdated strategic vision and a misunderstanding of market trends limited its impact early on.[1] Interestingly, the comparison of the results of US and Qatar public diplomacy efforts in-dicates that size and experience are not as important as identifying a specific market gap and strategically targeting resources to provide for unmet demand.

## The Al-Jazeera Network

Qatar launched Al-Jazeera in 1996, at first broadcasting only terrestrially, and for a few hours per day. The emir of Qatar, Sheikh Hamad bin Khal-ifa al-Thani provided the network with an initial grant of $137 million to support its launch, calling for quick transition whereby the organization would operate on a commercial basis. Al-Thani saw the network as part of his broader agenda of political reform, modernization promised to Qatari citizens and the international community soon after he seized power from his father in a bloodless coup. The emir received tentative support from Western governments in part due to his promise of accelerated Westernization. Al-Jazeera was to be the face of Qatar's reform efforts, demonstrating to the world its robust commitment to free and independent media.

Despite intentions to commercialize the broadcaster, Al-Jazeera has been dependent on Qatari government support since its launch and continues to operate with a sizeable public subsidy. When Al-Jazeera failed to generate a profit in 2001, only able to cover 35–40 percent of its costs through advertis-ing revenues (Sharp 2003), the emir extended the loan indefinitely. Accord-ing to *Forbes* magazine, as of 2009 the government of Qatar had invested more than a billion dollars in Al-Jazeera English and covered more than 100 million dollars a year in losses for Al-Jazeera Arabic's operations (Helman 2009). While there is little consensus when it comes to anything about Al-Jazeera, its significance is indisputable. Since its launch, it has dominated the Arab news sector, reaching the widest audiences, and consistently proven able to activate latent political attitudes among Arabs in times of conflict (Lynch, 2006). This success has served Qatar's geopolitical interests in several ways.

First, Qatar can rely on Al-Jazeera to shape the region's news agenda, and encourage certain topics for discussion among Arab publics (i.e., agenda setting). This capacity to control the region's news focus, and with AJE challenge Western news agendas, has significantly enhanced Qatar's political status and recognition in the "global network society" (Castells, 1996).

For example, shortly after the 2003 invasion of Iraq, Al-Jazeera re-broadcast interviews with captured American POWs, taken from Iraq's state TV channel. The Bush administration protested, arguing that content violated the Geneva Conventions, while urging U.S. media to not follow. CBS, CNN, NBC and others disregarded the administration's urging, broadcasting parts of the vitriolic content. Introducing the material, Bob Schieffer (2003), host of CBS' *Face the Nation*, said, "we have just gotten some pictures that have come in from Al-Jazeera. We're told that these are Americans in Iraq. I don't know what else to say about it. Let's just watch." NBC's Chris Jansing (2003) explained the rationale for selectively re-broadcasting Al-Jazeera, translated, to the American public: "we want to continue to give you that perspective so you understand how this is playing out in the Arab world." Networks in the UK and Australia, among America's closest allies, not only re-broadcast the footage, but even refused to pixelate the images, showing the faces of dead soldiers. Not only had Al-Jazeera defined the world's news agenda, but it also shifted established practices of Western journalism.

According to Da Lage (2005), Al-Jazeera's highly critical coverage of the region's despots serves Qatar's "double game," simultaneously appealing to a pan-Arab audience while strengthening ties with the US and Israel. El-Nawawy and Iskandar (2003) and Ayish (2002) argue Al-Jazeera gained its journalistic reputation by criticizing "everybody," from the US to African and Arab regimes for corruption and hypocrisy, raising Qatar's profile as a safe haven for freedom of expression and debate. Yet, the broadcaster rarely provides similarly critical coverage of its host country or government, despite a heavily controlled domestic media sector. By focusing on abuses of power and challenging unpopular authorities elsewhere in the region and world, audiences were steered away from considering Qatar's politics or role in the region's ongoing conflict. While this double game worked well in raising Qatar's profile and generating geopolitical clout, as Qatar's role as a strategic actor in international politics becomes more apparent, audiences are more critical of Al-Jazeera, eager to challenge its credibility.

Related to the first, but distinct is Al-Jazeera's capacity to shape the narrative around current events, priming audiences with certain questions, and portraying victims and heroes (i.e., framing). Leveraging this second function, Qatar gains significant negotiative influence, either by pressuring other governments with a threat of unfavorable media coverage, or by promising to quiet existing criticism in return for a strategic concession. Volkmer (2002, p. 243) found that, despite Qatar's peripheral position in world politics, Al-Jazeera's global reach can "enforce political pressure on national politics and provide a communication realm, which would otherwise not be possible on a national level."

For example, during the Palestinian Intifada, Al-Jazeera broadcast startling images of Muhammad al-Dura, a 12-year-old who was killed in the Gaza Strip during crossfire between Israeli soldiers and Palestinian security forces. Prior to Al-Jazeera's broadcast of actual footage of the event, Israel's domestic media had not reported the death, instead focusing on the official account of the conflict. But Al-Jazeera's broadcast challenged that narrative with graphic, grueling imagery, pushing every news organization to tackle the controversy, asking tough questions about the IDF's ethics and modi operandi (Samuel-Azran 2010; Dor 2001).

Al-Jazeera's role in the navigating relations with Saudi Arabia, Qatar's important neighbor, is illustrative of the negotiative advantage the network provides in diplomatic affairs. After seizing power from his father in 1995, the new Qatari emir al-Thani was concerned by a counter-coup attempt from Saudi Arabia to put his father back in power. Further, the emir faced tremendous ridicule in the Arab press, economically dominated by Saudi interests. Al-Jazeera was launched, in part, to challenge the Arab news status quo and restore the small state's credibility in the eyes of the Arab masses.

Sakr (2002), El Oifi (2005), and Fandy (2007) and contend that the main motive behind the Qatari emir's decision to launch Al-Jazeera was his desire to achieve greater power vis-a-vis rival Gulf countries, particularly Saudi Arabia. The evidence is compelling. During the first 10 years of Al-Jazeera's operation the network jumped at any opportunity to broadcast critical opinions of and embarrassing news for Saudi Arabia. Then, in 2007, after a summit where leaders from Qatari and Saudi met to rejuvenate bilateral ties, Al-Jazeera's tone changed. *The New York Times* (Worth 2008) reported that the chairman of Al-Jazeera's Board of Directors, Sheik Hamad bin Thamer Al-Thani, was present at the historic meeting between the leaders of the two countries, citing off-the record sources at the network concerned by the top-down about-face in Saudi-related news. A diplomatic cable sent from US Ambassador Joseph LeBaron (2009) confirms a shift in Al-Jazeera's coverage of Saudi Arabia at the behest of the Qatari government: "Al Jazeera, the most watched satellite television station in the Middle East, is heavily subsidized by the Qatari government and has proved itself a useful tool for the station's political masters," concluding, "Al Jazeera's more favorable coverage of Saudi Arabia's royal family has facilitated Qatari-Saudi reconciliation over the past year."

Samuel-Azran's (2013) empirical analysis of the interplay between Al-Jazeera's output and Qatar's interests reveals a very strong relationship between the Al-Jazeera tone towards Saudi affairs and Saudi-Qatari relations, with a dramatic rise in the frequency of articles criticizing Saudi Arabia for human rights violations and support of terrorism during diplomatic conflict, and a dramatic decline after the 2007 bi-lateral agreement. He suggests that Al-Jazeera's popularity among Saudis brought substantial pressure to bear on the Saudi kingdom to make concessions to its tiny neighbor and end the conflict.

Finally, the launch of Al-Jazeera English (AJE) enables more direct engagement with public opinion leaders in West, and the US in particular, increasing its capacity to challenge America's national news agenda. Al-Jazeera first reached out to English-speaking audiences on the eve of the war in Iraq—February 16, 2003—launching a separate English-language website to provide news about the war from a non-Western perspective. The global launch of an English-language TV channel followed three years later, broadcasting its first program on November 15, 2006. AJE mission is to give a voice to the voiceless, challenging Western news narratives and allowing for greater cross-cultural knowledge and dialogue (Powers 2012).

The network went to great lengths to ensure the success of dialogue with English-speaking viewers. First, AJE distinguished itself from Al-Jazeera Arabic. HaLevi (2007) found Al-Jazeera Arabic to be much more aggressive in its reporting of US affairs than the "sanitized" English version, as the "Arabic version included the language of a terror organization, while the English version was cleaned with changes and omissions, including changes to the language of direct quotes" (HaLevi 2007; see also similar arguments in Abdul-Mageed & Herring 2008; Kraidy 2008). Prior to the 2006 launch of its TV channel, the Al-Jazeera network published a Code of Ethics, promising the channel's commitment to Western norms of journalism.[2]

To appeal to its US viewers, AJE executives recruited senior, well-known journalists with experience at other popular news networks, including Sir David Frost (BBC) and Riz Khan (CNN and BBC). Acknowledging its brand was severely tarnished among American audiences, AJE's executives recruited a major Manhattan-based public relations firm and launched a high-profile "Demand Al-Jazeera" campaign to persuade potential viewers in North America to "give the network a fair chance."[3] Indeed, in early 2012 a group of activists gathered over 23,000 signatures demanding that Comcast, one of the biggest American cable companies, provide Al-Jazeera to all its customers. It is, however, important to note that these endeavors have faced strong resistance from conservative groups in North America and Israel. Since its launch, many US cable and satellite providers have refused to carry AJE, and providers that did carry AJE in several cities faced opposition and threats (Samuel-Azran 2010).

The success of these efforts is confirmed by statistics that show that the majority (81.4 percent) of the website's English-language users are located in the United States and other Western countries (cf. Fahmy and Al-Emad 2011). Studies illustrate that several niche audiences are more likely than others to watch Al-Jazeera. On the web, Azran (2006) found that left-wing bloggers often imported stories from AJE to compensate for what they saw as biased coverage of the "war on terror" on Fox and CNN. Similarly, Johnson and Fahmy's (2009) study revealed that Westerners who visited Arab nations were more likely to perceive that AJE is a credible news source.

The network achieved tremendous success during the 2011 Arab Spring, with its global viewership spiking by 2500 percent, the majority of whom were Americans. As demonstrations grew and Egyptians turned out in droves to protest 29 years of President Mubarak's heavy-handed corruption, American news networks were slow to shift their cameras towards Egypt. Compared to the startling images AJE broadcast from Cairo, Alexandria, Suez and other major Egyptian cities, the American domestic news networks fell flat. Even as American networks refocused their gaze towards the Middle East, AJE continued to be the place to go to for breaking, real-time news about the ongoing situation. While the Al-Jazeera Network deployed seven teams of journalists in Egypt, CNN International relied on just two of its star journalists to cover events on the ground. The main American broadcast news networks—NBC, ABC and CBS—didn't get feet on the ground for days.

Demonstrating the significance of AJE's coverage among US policymakers, President Obama and his foreign policy staff were found keeping a close eye on the network's coverage. When Egyptian authorities closed Al-Jazeera's Egypt office, revoking its journalists' press credentials and arresting six of its journalists, Hillary Clinton intervened and secured their quick and safe release (Powers 2012). Since, the American print media, including the *New York Times*, the *Wall Street Journal* and the *Los Angeles Times*, as well as notable bloggers (such as Jeff Jarvis) have recoiled at the state of American television news, calling for the addition of AJE to the cornucopia of channels offered by subscription cable providers.

In 2013, Qatar made another major step in its quest to conquer US citizens' hearts and minds, acquiring Al Gore's failed liberal news channel Current TV in order to gain its distribution network accessing 47 million US homes. It renamed the channel Al-Jazeera America to further increase its appeal to US viewers.

Overall, although Al-Jazeera is still fighting to gain distribution and credibility among conservative groups in the West, since its launch, it has significantly advanced Qatari foreign policy interests. These include applying pressure on Qatar's geopolitical rivals during political conflicts, advancing Qatar's ability to shape news about and from the Arab world, and by promoting Arab perspectives within various influential sectors in the West.

## U.S.-International Broadcasting in the Middle East

At the end of the Cold War, the importance of US propaganda efforts declined. In 1990, all US government international broadcasting services began to work more closely together and the VOA, Worldnet Television and Film Service, and Radio and TV Martí were consolidated under one umbrella. In 1999, as a result of the Foreign Affairs Reform and Restructuring Act of 1998, USIA was shut, and international broadcasting responsibilities were moved to a newly created independent agency, the Broadcasting Board of Governors (BBG). However, in the wake of the events of September 11, 2001 and the ensuing "war on terror," international broadcasting re-emerged as a means of promoting pro-American news and sentiment, particularly in Arab regions.

Congress, via the BBG, began funding MBN in 2003, which in turn launched Radio Sawa, an Arabic-language radio for Arab League countries; Alhurra, a satellite TV channel for Arab League countries; and Alhurra-Iraq, a terrestrial TV station targeting Iraqis. Headquartered in Virginia and operating on an annual $110.3 million budget, MBN broadcasters reach a combined 35.5 million viewers and listeners weekly. While Alhurra's audience share is dwarfed by Al-Jazeera and Saudi Arabia-funded Al-Arabiya, its reach is greater than comparable Arab-speaking Western stations such as BBC Arabic and CNN Arabic. Less encouraging are the findings of the 2008 University of Maryland/Zogby poll conducted in Jordan, Lebanon, Morocco, Saudi Arabia, and the United Arab Emirates, which found that only 2 percent of respondents listed Alhurra as their primary source of news. When Egyptian respondents were added to the poll in 2009, the audience shrank to just 1 percent (Telhami 2009).

Several other empirical studies similarly indicate that MBN's broadcast initiatives faced difficulties early on. El-Nawawy's (2006) analysis of the reception of Alhurra and Radio Sawa in Kuwait, United Arab Emirates, Jordan, Palestine, and Morocco found no correlation between the respondents' frequency of listening to Radio Sawa and the credibility they attributed to its news; in fact students had become slightly less supportive of US foreign policy since the station's launch. A survey in seven Lebanese universities also confirmed that Alhurra viewership and credibility are considerably lower compared to Al-Jazeera and Al-Arabiya, and that Alhurra viewership did not predict a positive attitude toward the USA. Similarly, results of quantitative analyses found negligible influence on pro-US attitudes in Morocco (Douai 2009) and Egypt (Clark and Christie 2006).

According to Lynch (2007), MBN's main mistake is the presumption that Arabs are deprived of free public debate, and therefore the state-sponsored stations should operate in a similar manner to the Cold War stations. In reality, however, Arabs are "drowning" in multiple sources of information. Further, he notes that its U.S. government funding significantly reduces chances of success. For example, while Alhurra at times censored controversial material (including speeches by Hizbollah leader Nasrallah) due to Congressional pressure, other Arab networks showcased the content. Such disparities naturally raise questions of political bias in its reporting.

A review of BBG's recent reports reflects an acknowledgment of the various challenges it has faced. Its 2012–2016 strategic plan notes the struggle against the fierce competition for audiences in the various regions BBG-funded stations operate: "Those brands—Voice of America, Radio Free Europe/Radio Liberty, Alhurra TV and Radio Sawa, Radio Free Asia, and Radio and TV Martí—face intense competition from an ever-expanding universe of emerging media choices as well as the challenges of censorship and extremist voices."[4] BBG's 2013 budget request also acknowledges the challenges to keep up with the various delivery methods (i.e., smartphones, various tablets) of information in comparison to its competitors:

> BBG has struggled to fully keep pace with changes in the way that audiences choose to consume media. Maintaining heavy investments in delivery platforms that are fast declining in media use limits BBG's ability to adapt to the newer technologies that increasingly represent the media platforms of choice.[5]

Despite the broader challenges American international broadcasting has faced, there are several productive examples of US public diplomacy in the Middle East. Christie and Clark (2011) found Radio Sawa was effective in promoting pro-US sentiment in the United Arab Emirates (UAE). Christie and Clark note that this might be due to the fact UAE is a rich country with an affinity to Western culture, traits that are uncommon in the region. In an interview with Snow (2010), Alhurra staff stated that they perceive that the station has a high chance of success due to the 2009 launch of *Alyoum*, a show focusing on human interest stories that gained a wide audience base. The the success of Alhurra-Iraq, which is more popular than Al-Jazeera and the fifth most popular station in the Iraqi television market, is another sign of MBN's maturation (BBG 2010).

Alhurra's viewership also skyrocketed during the 2011 Egyptian uprising. Amidst growing protests and insecurity, 25 percent of Egyptians turned to Al-hurra for breaking news. Nine percent of Egyptians reported that they watched Alhurra more than any other channel, including Al-Jazeera, BBC and CNN. It turns out, when the country went into crisis, viewers trusted Al-Jazeera less and less due to its one-sided, activist coverage of the protests, turning to foreign channels seeking more reliable information. Al-Arabiya, a Saudi-funded news network, also saw a huge spike in its Egyptian audience, with viewers explaining they were tuning in for a perspective that could only be found from a safe distance from Cairo (Broadcasting Board of Governors, 2011).

Finally, another surprising success is the growing popularity of the Persian-language satire show, *Parazit*, that mocks Iran's political culture and is broadcast on VOA's PNN. The program, modeled on *The Daily Show* with John Stewart, is popular both in Iran and among Iranian expatriates worldwide. Although VOA does not have exact numbers of people listening to the show, *Parazit's* Facebook page has close to one million followers and its videos received close to 10 million views on YouTube, indicating its huge popularity. According to Semati (2012), the show's success reflects viewers' pro-active attempts to resist the Iranian government's censorship of information that contradict its "Islamic state" vision.

## Implications

Traditionally, credibility has been considered the key factor upon which international broadcasters succeed or fail. Most metrics focus on audience reach and perceptions of trustworthiness, assuming that beyond providing credible news that reaches large portions of a target population, there is little more a broadcaster could do to ensure its impact in a given context. In the cases of Alhurra and Al-Jazeera, both broadcasters are concerned first and foremost with audience reach—literally, how many viewers tune in on a weekly basis—as a marker of impact. This holds true despite a dearth of evidence that reach and reach alone, even when a broadcaster is considered credible, shapes attitudes and behaviors. What does a citizen tuning into a broadcaster at least once in the past week really tell us about its possible significance? Absolutely nothing.

At the same time, despite insufficient metrics, these two case studies indicate that international broadcasters have had an impact on audiences in certain circumstances, even in cases where they were not established as credible sources of information. AJE was effective during the Egyptian uprising, with American citizens, journalists and policymakers all relying on its real-time coverage to keep pace with Egypt's transformation from autocratic oppression to, potentially, a young, flourishing democracy. This is despite a flurry of criticism and suspicion surrounding the network, with the majority of Americans unsupportive of Al-Jazeera's entrance into the U.S. market. During the same crisis, Egyptians shunned the beloved Al-Jazeera and turned to Alhurra for information that would help place the ongoing protests in a regional and global context. This is despite recent surveys showing Egyptians unsatisfied with Alhurra's news coverage. So what gives?

In a marketplace, a seller has power when it has something that buyers want and can't get elsewhere, and buyers are powerful in a saturated marketplace. In the ideational marketplace, the typical American's informational needs are met sufficiently by domestic commercial broadcasters and organizations. Without a crisis in the Middle East, there is little need for what Al-Jazeera English's programming is selling: real-time, graphic, high quality stories from the region. The same logic holds true for the average Egyptian, too.The Middle East news market is saturated, and on a typical day, one's news needs are easily satisfied through a plethora of domestic and regional sources of news. Alhurra's goods simply not in demand. But with a country in crisis, and domestic and regional news sources faltering, the value of Alhurra's news increased substantially, providing a perspective and context on current events that could not be offered by others. Informational needs drive demand, and successful international broadcasters focus on meeting unmet demand, especially that created through market disruptions. The other successes outlined above, including VOA's *Parazit* and Al-Jazeera's Arabic-language programming, are best explained using this model too.

What does this mean for international broadcasters? First and foremost, identify unmet demand. With freedom of the press indicators signaling a decline in free expression around the world, there is ample opportunity for successful information interventions. But what about intervening into an already saturated market, where there is little unmet demand? Microeconomic theory says that, in a saturated market, the key to increasing market share is to identify: (1) latent markets, comprised of potential buyers who would buy if an offer better matched their exacting needs; (2) ignored markets, or willing buyers who are considered non-strategic and thus ignored by existing sellers; and (3) lost markets, or potential buyers lost due to a combination of price, differentiation and focus. International broadcasters would be best served by adapting their strategies from Cold War models of information dissemination and moving towards a market for loyalties, whereby market-based analysis can effectively craft a path towards success in even the most saturated of markets.

## Notes

1. MBN has substantially adapted the strategies behind both Alhurra TV and Radio Sawa and, as a result, increasingly connecting with audiences in meaningful ways.
2. See: Al-Jazeera Network Code of Ethics: www.alJazeera.com/aboutus/2006/11/2008525185733692771.html
3. See: http://www.aljazeera.com/demandaljazeera
4. http://www.bbgstrategy.com/2012/02/bbg-strategic-plan-2012–2016-full-text/
5. http://www.bbg.gov/wp-content/media/2012/02/FY-2013-BBG-Congressional-Budget-Request-FINAL-2-9–12-Small.pdf

## Bibliography

Abdul-Mageed, M. M., & Herring, S. C. (2008). Arabic and English news coverage on AlJazeera.net. In *Proceedings of Cultural Attitudes Towards Technology and Communication 2008* (CATaC'08), Nîmes, France, June 24–27. F. Sudweeks, H. Hrachovec, & C. Ess. (Eds.). Murdoch, Australia: Murdoch University Press.

Anderson, B. (1983). *Imagined Communities*. New York, NY: Verso.

Ayish, M. I. (2002). Political communication on Arab world television: Evolving patterns. *Political Communication* 19(2), 137–154.

Azran, T. (2006). From Osama Bin-Laden's mouthpiece to the darling of the alternative media websites: The representation of English Aljazeera.Net in the West. In R. Berenger (Ed.) *Cybermedia Go to War* (pp. 103–114). Spokane, WA: Marquette Books.

Ball-Rokeach, S. J. (1985). The origins of individual media-system dependency. *Communication Research* 12(4), 485–510.

Beck, U. (2005). *Power in the Global Age*. Cambridge, MA: Polity Press.

Black, G. D., & Koppes, C. (1977). "What to show the world: The Office of War Information and Hollywood, 1942–1945." *The Journal of American History* 64: 87–105.

Braman, S. (2007). *Change of State*. Cambridge, MA: MIT Press.

Broadcasting Board of Governors. (2010). Broadcasting Board of Governors fiscal year 2010 budget request. Retrieved from www.docstoc.com/docs/53963939/Broadcasting-Board-of-Governors-Fiscal-Year-2010-Budget-Request

Broadcasting Board of Governors. (2011, February 14). Media consumption during the uprising in Egypt. Research Memorandum. IBB Office of Research.

Carruthers, S. L. (2000). *The Media at War*. New York, NY: St. Martin's Press.

Castells, M. (1996). *The Rise of the Network Society*. Malden, MA: Blackwell Publishers.

Christie, T. B., & Clark, A. M. (2011). Believe it or not: Understanding the credibility and effectiveness of Radio Sawa in the UAE. *International Communication Gazette*, 73(4), 359–371.

Clark, A. M., & Christie, T. B. (2006). Molding Public Opinion in the Middle East: Understanding the credibility and effectiveness of Radio Sawa and Television Alhurra among audiences in Egypt. *Journal of Middle East Media* 1(2), 23–36.

Clinton, H. R. (2010, January 21). Remarks on internet freedom. U.S. Department of State. Retrieved from http://www.state.gov/secretary/rm/2010/01/135519.htm

Da Lage, O. (2005). The politics of Al Jazeera or the diplomacy of Doha. In M. Zayani (Ed.), *The Al Jazeera Phenomenon: Critical Perspectives on New Arab Media* (pp. 171–82). London, England: Pluto.

Dale, H. (2012). *Why America Has Trouble Reaching Iran: VOA's Persian News Network in Dire Need of Reform*. Washington, DC: The Heritage Foundation. Retrieved from www.heritage.org/research/reports/2012/03/why-america-has-trouble-reaching-iran-voas-persian-news-network-in-dire-need-of-reform

Doherty, M. (2000). *Nazi Wireless Propaganda: Lord Haw-Haw and British Public Opinion*. Edinburgh: Edinburgh University Press.

Dor, D. (2001). *Newspapers under the Influence*. Tel-Aviv: Babel (Hebrew).

Dorfman, A., & Mattelart, A. (1975). *How to Read Donald Duck*. New York, NY: International General.

Douai, A. (2009). International broadcasting and the management of foreign public opinion: The case of Al-Hurra television in the "Arab Street." Doctoral Dissertation in the College of Communications at Pennsylvania State University.

Downs, A. (1957). An economic theory of political action in a democracy. *Journal of Political Economy, 65*(2), 135–150.

Edwards, H. (2011, September 30). Former Al Jazeera Head on Quitting, the Arab Spring, and Qatar's Role. *The Atlantic*. Accessed online at: http://www.theatlantic.com/international/archive/2011/09/former-al-jazeera-head-on-quitting-the-arab-spring-and-qatars-role/245932/?single_page=true

El-Nawawy, M. (2006). US public diplomacy in the Arab world: The news credibility of Radio Sawa and Television Alhurra in five countries. *Global Media and Communication* 2(2), 183–203.

El-Nawawy, M., & Iskandar, A. (2003). *Al-Jazeera*. Cambridge, MA: Perseus Book Group.

El Oifi, M. (2005). Influence without power: Al Jazeera and the Arab public sphere. In M. Zayani (Ed.), *The Al Jazeera Phenomenon* (pp. 171–82). London: Pluto.

Fahmy, S., & Al-Emad, M. (2011). Al-Jazeera vs Al-Jazeera: A comparison of the network's English and Arabic online coverage of the US/Al Qaeda conflict. *International Communication Gazette* 73(3), 216–232.

Fandy, M. (2007). *(Un)Civil War of Words*. Santa Barbara, CA: Praeger Security International.

Fitzpatrick, K. (2011). *U.S. Public Diplomacy in a Post-9/11 World: From Messaging to Mutuality*. Los Angeles, CA: Figueroa Press.

Gallup. (2002, February 26). Gallup Poll of the Islamic world. Retrieved from www.gallup.com/poll/5380/gallup-poll-islamic-world.aspx

Glassman, J. K. (2009, September 1). It's not about us. *Foreign Policy*. Retrieved from www.foreignpolicy.com/articles/2009/09/01/its_not_about_us

Golan, G. J. (2013). Introduction: An integrated approach to public diplomacy. *American Behavioral Scientist*. 57(9), 1251–1255.

Hale, J. A. S. (1975). *Radio Power*. Philadelphia, PA: Temple University Press.

HaLevi, E. (2007). Arabic News Service sanitizes English Translations. *Arutz Sheva*. Retrieved from www.israelnationalnews.com/News/News.aspx/121712#.UC1BmqCNiTg

Helman, C. (2009, July 13). Will Americans tune to Al Jazeera? *Forbes*.

Isaacson, W. (2010, September 28). America's voice must be credible and must be heard. Celebrating 60 years of RFE. Retrieved from http://docs.rferl.org/en-US/2010/09/29/100928%20rferl-isaacson.pdf

Jansing, C. (2003, March 21). [Transcript]. Target Iraq: 4:00 AM. NBC News.

Jensen, R., & Oster, E. (2009). The power of TV: Cable Television and Women's Status in India. *The Quarterly Journal of Economics* 124(3), 1057–1094.

Johnson, T., & Fahmy, S. (2009). See no evil, hear no evil, judge as evil? Examining whether Al-Jazeera English-language website users transfer credibility to its satellite network. In G. Golan (Ed.), *International Communication in a Global Age* (pp. 241–60). Philadelphia, PA: Routledge/Lawrence Erlbaum.

Kant, I. (1983). *Perpetual Peace, and Other Essays on Politics, History, and Morals.* (T. Humphrey Trans.). Hackett Pub Co. (Reprinted from 1795).

Kaufman, E. (2002). A broadcasting strategy to win media wars. *The Washington Quarterly*, 25(2), 115–127.

Kraidy, M. M. (2008). Al-Jazeera and Al-Jazeera English: A comparative institutional analysis. In M. Kugelman (Ed.), *Kuala Lumpur Calling: Al-Jazeera English in Asia* (pp. 23–30). Washington, DC: Woodrow Wilson International Center for Scholars.

La Ferrara, E., Chong A., & Duryea S. (2008, March). Soap operas and fertility: Evidence from Brazil. Working Paper, No. 172. Bureau for Research and Economic Analysis of Development.

LeBaron, J. (2009, July 1). Embassy Doha's analysis of Qatari prime minister's Al Jazeera interview. Confidential section 01 of 05. Doha 000432 SIPDIS EO 12958. Retrieved from www.guardian.co.uk/world/us-embassy-cables-documents/214776

Lord, K. N., & Lynch, M. (2010). *America's Extended Hand: Assessing the Obama Administration's Global Engagement Policy.* Washington, DC: Center for a New American Security.

Lynch, M. (2006). *Voices of the New Arab Public.* New York, NY: Columbia University Press.

Lynch, M. (2007). The Alhurra Project: Radio Marti of the Middle East. *Arab Media & Society*, 2. Retrieved from www.arabmediasociety.com/?article=268

Mahtani, S. (2012, May 17). Asia's lighter taxes provide a lure. *The Wall Street Journal*, C3.

Mattelart, A. (2000). *Networking the World, 1794–2000.* (L. Carey-Libbrecht & J. A. Cohen., Trans.). Minneapolis, MN: University of Minnesota Press.

McHale, M. (2009, May 13). [Testimony]. Senate Foreign Relations Committee confirmation hearing. Retrieved from www.state.gov/r/remarks/124155.htm

McLuhan, M. (1962). *The Gutenberg Galaxy.* Toronto: University of Toronto Press.

Metzl, J. F. (1997). Information intervention. *Foreign Affairs* 76(6), 15–20.

Nisbet, E. C., & Myer, T. A. (2011). Anti-American sentiment as a media effect? Arab media, political identity, and public opinion in the Middle East. *Communication Research* 38(5), 684–709.

Noelle-Neumann, E. (1974). The spiral of silence: A theory of public opinion. *Journal of Communication* 24(2), 43–51.

Pelton, J. N., & Oslund, R.J. (2004). *Communications Satellites.* New York, NY: Psychology Press.

Powers, S. (2012). From broadcast to networked journalism: The case of Al-Jazeera English. In N. Brugger & M. Burns (Eds.), *Histories of Public Service Broadcasters Online.* New York, NY: Peter Lang Publishing.

Powers, S. & Youmans, W. L. (2012). A new purpose for international broadcasting: Subsidizing deliberative technologies in non-transitioning states. *Journal of Public Deliberation* 8(1). Online access only, available at http://www.publicdeliberation.net/jpd/vol8/iss1/art13

Price, M. E. (2002). *Media and Sovereignty.* Cambridge, MA: MIT Press.

Price, M. E. (1994). The market for loyalties. *The Yale Law Journal* 104:3, 667–705.

Price, M. E., Haas, S., & Margolin, D. (2008). New technologies and international broadcasting: Reflections on adaptations and transformations. *The ANNALS of the American Academy of Political and Social Science* 616(1), 150–172.

Reagan, R. (1983, September 10). Radio address to the nation on American International broadcasting, Retrieved from www.reagan.utexas.edu/archives/speeches/1983/91083a.htm

Sakr, N. (2002). *Satellite Realms.* London: I.B. Tauris.

Samuel-Azran, T. (2010). *Al-Jazeera and US War Coverage.* New York, NY: Peter Lang.

Samuel-Azran, T. (2013). Al-Jazeera, Qatar, and new tactics in state-sponsored media diplomacy. *American Behavioral Scientist* 57(9), 1293–1311.

Schieffer, B. (2003, March 23). Secretary Donald Rumsfeld discusses the war in Iraq. [Transcript]. *Face the Nation.* CBS News.

Schiller, H. (1976). *Communication and Cultural Duration.* White Plains, NY: International Arts and Sciences Press.

Semati, M. (2012). The geopolitics of *Parazit,* the Iranian televisual sphere, and the global infrastructure of political humor. *Popular Communication* 10(1–2), 119–130.

Sharp, J. M. (2003). The Al-Jazeera News network. CRS Report for Congress: Middle East Policy Analyst.

Snow, N. (2010). Alhurra to Al Youm: The maturation of U.S. television broadcasting in the Middle East. The Luce Foundation.

Telhami, S. (2009). 2009 Annual Arab Public Opinion Survey. University of Maryland/Zogby International. Retrieved from www.brookings.edu/~/media/events/2009/5/19%20arab%20opinion/2009_arab_public_opinion_poll

Tommasi, M. & Ierull, K. (1995). *The New Economics of Human Behavior.* New York, NY: Cambridge University Press.

U.S. Department of Commerce. (2012, April 10). Intellectual Property and the U.S. Economy: Industries in Focus. Retrieved from www.esa.doc.gov/Reports/intellectual-property-and-us-economy-industries-focus.

U.S. Information Agency. (1998). Overview. Retrieved from dosfan.lib.uic.edu/usia/usiahome/oldoview.htm#overview

Volkmer, I. (2002). Journalism and political crises in the global network society. In B. Zelizer & S. Allan (Eds.). *Journalism After September 11* (pp. 235–46). London and New York, NY: Routledge.

Wood, J. (1992). *The History of International Broadcasting.* London: The Institution for Engineering and Technology.

Wood, J. (2000). *The history of international broadcasting.* London: The Institution for Engineering and Technology.

Worth, R. F. (2008, January 4). Al Jazeera no longer nips at Saudis. *The New York Times.*

Youmans, W. L., & Powers, S. (2012). Remote negotiations: International broadcasting as bargaining in the information age. *The International Journal of Communication* 6, 2149–2172.

Zayani, M., & Sofiane, S. (2007). *The Culture of Al Jazeera.* Jefferson, NC: McFarland.

*Engaging Domestic and Foreign Publics*

# 15. *Contextual Meaning*

BRUCE W. DAYTON & DENNIS F. KINSEY

Effective communication in public diplomacy depends on a solid understanding of the point of view of the people with whom you are communicating. Therefore, one of the first steps in a strategic approach to public diplomacy is to determine the perceptions of the people you are trying to reach. That is, to understand what the concepts or ideas that you are interested in communicating or promoting "mean" to those you are talking with. What is the contextual meaning?

Adhering to a principle of two-way communication, or what we think of as dialogue, helps to open doors of communication and to build positive relationships. If you aren't listening or if you have little knowledge about the views of your target public, then your communication is fundamentally one-way. One-way communication is not generally effective for building positive relationships because it leaves the attributions applied by each side to the other unchallenged, misses opportunities for learning and change, and is more likely to damage than to build long-term relationships. The power of dialogue, in contrast, lies in its ability to have participants explore the assumptions, beliefs, and worldviews which are central to their assertions. In so doing, dialogue processes can transform the outlook of participants such that new perspectives on a particular topic are jointly formed (Dayton, 2010).

## *Public Relations in Public Diplomacy*

Like public diplomacy, public relations has changed over the years in terms of its understanding of communication. Early public relations models of communication were primarily one-way. These one-way models of communication are still used today, however, more sophisticated models are driving effective public relations. For example, in its simplest form PR communication can be classified into four types or models: press agentry, public information, two-way asymmetrical and two-way symmetrical (Grunig, 1993; Grunig and Hunt, 1984). The first two are one-way models. There is no attempt in one-way models of communication to understand the target public or any contextual meaning. That is, no research is conducted or referenced on the perceptions of the target public in one-way communication. The goal is to simply pump out information in the hopes of getting media coverage (in the press agentry model) or to "inform" the public (in the public information model).

The practice of two-way asymmetrical and two-way symmetrical communication puts more focus on discovering and understanding the point of view of the target audience. Incorporating knowledge of the target public into message construction will allow messages to be more powerful. Messages that reflect the views or contextual meaning of the target public will strike a responsive chord and be more persuasive because they address what is important to your audience. You understand them, and in two-way symmetrical communication, they understand you.

The public relations tenets of understanding your target public have direct relevance to public diplomacy (Gilboa, 2008; Snow, 2009; Wang, 2006; Yun, 2006). Cull argues that "listening" or the "collecting and collating data about publics and their opinions" precedes all successful public diplomacy (Cull, 2008, p. 32). Fisher believes that listening not only precedes all public diplomacy, but is public diplomacy, "Consciously and publicly listening to the perceptions of others can be a PD [public diplomacy] act in itself" (Fisher, 2009).

Kruckeberg and Vujnovic (2005) argue that the practice of "true" public diplomacy must rely on communication models of public relations such as two-way symmetrical communication (Grunig, 1993; Grunig and Hunt, 1984) and community-building (Kruckeberg and Starck, 1988) that start with the task of understanding the people you are communicating with because it is fundamental to building successful relationships.

Signitzer and Wamser (2006) see the strategic dimension of two-way communication, found in public relations, as especially useful to public diplomacy: "...public relations can help public diplomacy in developing its scope and in advancing—not only in theory, but also in practice—from one-way information models to more two-way communication models" (p. 454).

## An Example: Contextual Meaning of Democracy

The only reliable way for public relations and public diplomacy practitioners to understand those they are trying to communicate with is through research. Here, studies that examine the different meanings of democracy are particularly useful to students of public diplomacy. For example, some scholars have recently revealed contextual meaning by examining the under-explored area of visual communication in public diplomacy (Kinsey & Zatepilina, 2010; Lord, 2006; Nye, 2005). In their content analysis of 120 videos focused on the meaning of democracy, for instance, Seo and Kinsey (2012) examined how citizens around the world represent their ideas and understanding of democracy in videos produced for the Democracy Video Challenge (U.S. Department of State, 2008). Videos from Africa and Europe or Eurasia emphasize popular participation in their meaning of democracy. Videos from the Near East put greater emphasis on diversity, while videos from the Western Hemisphere hold freedom of speech and freedom of press as part of the meaning of democracy.

Former Under Secretary of State for Public Diplomacy and Public Affairs James K. Glassman explains the significance of discovering and understanding what democracy means to disparate audiences:

> We in the State Department...are not trying to define democracy for young people around the world. Rather, the Challenge [Democracy Video Challenge] asks participants to share their visions of what democracy means. If the Challenge can generate thought and debate about democracy, on the medium of choice for young people, we'll have achieved success. (U.S. Department of State, 2008).

Much academic research has been conducted recently to examine the barriers to democratization in the Near East and to better understand why efforts to promote democracy within traditional societies are sometimes viewed suspiciously by both leaders and citizens of those countries (Anderson, 1991; Hudson, 1996; Albrecht and Schlumberger, 2004; Lust-Okar, 2005). Among the barriers being considered is the way that the concept of democracy is understood in the Near East and how that understanding may be at odds with understandings of democracy held in the West. Here the argument is that democracy is itself a contested term, subject to various interpretations, and rife with contention over the processes, pathways, value of creating societies where individuals are in charge of their own political future.

A few years ago, the United States Department of State initiated the Leaders for Democracy Fellows Program (LDF). This was a new visitor program destined to improve public diplomacy efforts in the Near East and to encourage democracy in this area.

The idea was to bring opinion leaders from countries in the Near East to the United States so that they could directly experience life in the US, participate in open communication with US citizens and see "Democracy" at work. The hope then is that on return to their individual countries these LDF participants will be better prepared and motivated to encourage democratic development in their own countries.

Yet democracy as a term has many meanings. It describes a method of governance, a normative ideal, a relationship between citizens and their leaders, and a historical movement. As a concept it also entails an ambiguous balance between individual rights and communal responsibility, or 'thin' verses 'strong' democratic ideals, a tension that has been particularly salient throughout the modern usage of the word in the United States (Smith, 1987).The question, then, is how can programs such as LDF 'work' without understanding how participants themselves understand the process? By pushing a view of democracy that doesn't incorporate aspects of the target public you are using one-way communication and talking "at" instead of "with."

The participation of 25 civil society leaders from the Near East in Syracuse University Maxwell School's Leaders for Democracy Fellowship Program presented us with a unique opportunity to engage in this exploration with elites from the area. In March of 2007 we engaged with the Democracy Fellows in an effort to better understand how they see democracy, democratic transition, and the relationship between Islam and democracy. This example outlines a particularly well-suited methodology to gain access to deeply held views of your target public.

## *Methodology*

Our study used Q Methodology as a tool for analyzing the subjective beliefs of the Leaders for Democracy Fellows. Introduced to the social science community by the psychologist William Stephenson (1978), Q methodology has now extended its reach beyond psychology to fields as diverse as education, communication, and philosophy. In political science, Q methodology has been used to investigate various aspects of public opinion, meanings of democracy (Dryzek & Berejikian, 1993), elite attitudes (Durning & Edwards, 1992), voter decision-making (Thomas, Sigelman, & Baas, 1984), and environmental beliefs (Peritore, 1993; Dayton, 2000), among other issues. The goal of Q methodology is to reveal patterns of beliefs about political and social issues within a given discourse domain, in effect, to model the 'flow of communicability' or concourse of ideas present in a policy discourse.

The Q technique typically proceeds in two phases. In the first phase researchers present individuals with a range of stimuli about social and political issues—culled from any number of sources such as texts, opinion pieces, interviews, cartoons, etc.—and ask them to sort these statements, pictures, or even sound recordings according to a specified condition of instruction (e.g., most like my point of view to most unlike my point of view). Statistical tools are then used to generate factors which link similar perspectives, attitudes, and beliefs together to reveal distinct viewpoints about the topic under investigation. In the second phase of the technique, the factors resulting from the statistical analysis of each individual's 'Q sort' are interpreted in order to give the researcher a window to the range, the content and the character of the viewpoints that underlie the issue under debate.

## *Procedure*

Our first study used Q methodology to study the typologies of beliefs about democracy and democratization that exist within the Democracy Fellows who visited the Syracuse University in the spring of 2007. The research procedure took place in three phases. First, a Q sample consisting of statements of belief about democracy was selected out of the written material about democracy in general and democracy and the Near East in particular. Source materials included academic books and articles, speeches by policy makers, texts of major works in democratic theory, and press releases from government agencies. This pool of statements was then narrowed down to a final 35 statements based on Fisher's experimental design principles (Brown, 1980) whereby statements are initially placed into similar groups and then most similar statements within each group are eliminated until the desired number of statements is achieved. A five-cell typology into which all initial statements were placed and then narrowed to the final 35 statements is presented in Table 15.1.

*Table 15.1.* Q Sample Structure.

| Statement Design Categories | |
| --- | --- |
| 1. | Meaning of Democracy / Essential Elements of Democracy (7 statements) |
| 2. | Means to Achieve Democracy (7 statements) |
| 3. | Impediments and Barriers to Democracy (7 statements) |
| 4. | Advantages and Disadvantages of Democracy and Democratic Systems (7 statements) |
| 5. | Democracy and the Near East / Democracy and Islam (7 statements) |

Second, participants in the Leaders for Democracy Project were brought together for a two-hour workshop where participants were asked to sort all thirty-five statements according to a scale running from "most like my point of view" to "most unlike my point of view." Finally, the resulting Q sorts were correlated and then factor analyzed. Centroid extraction with varimax rotation was performed through the PCQ software program (Stricklin, 1987–1996).

## Results

Results of this study reveal two distinct discourses about democracy within the group studied. These are listed on Table 15.2 below with 'A' representing factor one and 'B' representing factor two. The number beneath each factor

Table 15.2. Factor Arrays.

| Scores | | |
|---|---|---|
| A | B | |
| 3 | 4 | 1. In a democracy, government authority flows from the people and is based upon their consent. |
| 0 | -1 | 2. The spread of democracy is the best guarantor of both domestic and international peace. |
| 0 | 3 | 3. Wealth concentrated in the hands of the few is a clear barrier to the emergence of a democracy. |
| -4 | -1 | 5. Islam is incompatible with a democratic form of government. |
| 0 | -1 | 6. Democracies are guided by a system of meritocracy, where those most capable of ruling do so. |
| 4 | 2 | 7. Freedom of speech, including a free press and media, is an essential element to any democracy. |
| 1 | -4 | 8. Free market capitalism and democracy go hand in hand. |
| 2 | 3 | 9. In principle, in a democracy everyone has an equal shot at achieving wealth. |
| -2 | -3 | 10. Democracies are less likely to support terrorists or threaten the world with weapons of mass murder. |
| -1 | -2 | 11. Democratic societies are peaceful societies. |
| 3 | 1 | 12. Democracy requires that members of society tolerate opposing points of view. |
| -1 | -2 | 13. Some cultural and social norms are inherently incompatible with democracy. |
| 0 | 0 | 14. Democracy simply substitutes election by incompetent masses for appointment by corrupt elites. |
| -4 | -3 | 15. Those against America are against democracy/freedom. |
| 4 | -2 | 16. Democracy requires of all of its citizens a willingness to make commitments and sacrifices for the general interest |
| 2 | 0 | 17. Civil society deters the state's power and increases prospects for democratization. |

| Scores | | |
|---|---|---|
| A | B | |
| 0 | 1 | 18. Secrecy and a free democratic government don't mix. |
| -1 | 0 | 19. Democracies in the Near East will look very different from democracies in the West. |
| -3 | 0 | 20. Democracy is simply a dictatorship of the majority. |
| 3 | 4 | 21. In a democracy, everyone must be allowed to express any opinion and join any political, religious, or civil groups of their choice without fear of persecution. |
| 1 | -3 | 22. Democracy is best established "top-down," through the establishment of strong government institutions that respect the rule of law and rights of citizens. |
| 0 | -1 | 23. An impediment to democracy is the failure to separate religion and the state. |
| -2 | 3 | 24. Democracies are no better at eliminating government corruption than any other form of government. |
| -1 | 0 | 25. To separate belief in Islam from its connectedness to the state is blasphemous. |
| 1 | 0 | 26. Democracy cannot be imposed on any country from outside parties. |
| -3 | -4 | 27. The use of violence may be necessary in order to achieve democracy. |
| 1 | 2 | 28. Bribery is a fundamental impediment to the emergence of healthy democracy. |
| 2 | 1 | 29. Democracies encourage the competition of ideas and therefore strengthen societies. |
| 0 | 2 | 30. Imam Ali would endorse and advocate for a democracy over an Imamate. |
| -2 | 0 | 31. Democracy is the only form of social order that is consistent with justice. |
| -1 | 1 | 32. Democracies provide an incentive for groups of similar people to band together and promote their own political agenda over a common national agenda. |
| 1 | 1 | 33. The 4 caliphs would advocate for democracy rather than the caliphate. |
| -3 | 2 | 34. All of the main alternatives to democracy in the world have either disappeared or lost their legitimacy as forms of political organization. |
| -2 | -2 | 35. Authoritarian systems have some notable advantages over democratic ones. |

column indicates where each statement appeared on the final factor array with -4 being 'most unlike my point of view' and +4 being 'most like my point of view' and '0' representing a neutral stance on the statement.

## Discussion

### Areas of Consensus

The two factors (hereafter perspective A and perspective B) are of note as much for what they have in common as well as how much they differ. Each perspective appears to lean on a common discourse about democracy that revolves around the ability of democracy to establish societies where political and social freedom, tolerance, and equality of opportunity are dominant. These values are reflected most directly in statements 7, 21, 9, and 1 (scores in parenthesis are for perspectives A and B).

7. Freedom of speech, including a free press and media, is an essential element to any democracy. (+4, +2).
21. In a democracy, everyone must be allowed to express any opinion and join any political, religious, or civil group of their choice without fear of persecution. (+3, +4)
9. In principle, in a democracy everyone has an equal shot at achieving wealth. (+2, +3)
1. In a democracy, government authority flows from the people and is based upon their consent (+3, +4).

Interestingly, however, is that central to this dominant perspective on democracy is a *rejection* of what has been termed 'democratic peace theory'; that is, the belief that democracies are inherently more peaceful than non-democracies. Simply put, it would appear that the subjects interviewed feel that democracies are no more likely to be peace-loving than non-democracies.

10. Democracies are less likely to support terrorists or threaten the world with weapons of mass murder. (-2, -3)
11. Democratic societies are peaceful societies. (-1, -2)

Also notable as an item of cross-perspective continuity is the high salience of statement 15.

15. Those against America are against democracy and freedom. (-4, -3).

Both groups appear to strongly believe that being 'against' American policy does not make them anti-democratic. Finally, members of both perspectives are unified in their rejection of the notion that democratic change should ever be achieved via violent means.

27. The use of violence may be necessary in order to achieve democracy (-3, -4).

## Areas of Cleavage

Areas of cross-factor agreement should not, however, be overstated. Several areas of cross-factor cleavage also emerged in the analysis of the Q sort interviews. Perspective A, for instance, takes a bottom-up approach to the building of democratic societies, suggesting that citizen participation is key to strong democracy and that top-down approaches to democracy building do not work. By contrast, perspective B rejects these claims, holding instead that top-down approaches do hold some merit for establishing democratic rule and that vigorous citizenship and civic participation is *not* essential for the establishment of a functioning democracy.

16. Democracy requires of all of its citizens a willingness to make commitments and sacrifices for the general interest. (+4, -2).
22. Democracy is best established top-down, through the establishment of strong government institutions that respect the rule of law and the rights of citizens (+1, -3).

Perspective A is also distinct in its strong rejection of the notion that Islam and democracy are incompatible and its relative support of the notion that other forms of social order are equally consistent with justice as democracy.

5. Islam is incompatible with a democratic form of government. (-4, -1)
31. Democracy is the only form of social order that is consistent with justice. (-1, +1)

On the relationship between free markets and democracy we also find strong areas of disagreement between each perspective. One of the most salient items to those clustered under Perspective B was the notion that free market capitalism and democracy go hand-in-hand.

8. Free market capitalism and democracy go hand in hand. (+1, -4)

This coupled with their support of statements 3 and 24, suggests a strong concern with economic justice within Perspective B that is not felt within Perspective A.

3. Wealth concentrated in the hands of the few is a clear barrier to the emergence of a democracy. (0, +3)
24. Democracies are no better at eliminating government corruption than any other form of government. (-2, 3)

Finally, an interesting cleavage appears with item cluster of items 34, 31 and 5. Here we see that Perspective A *rejects* the notion that democracy is the only viable system of political order, that justice can be achieved without democratic institutions being present. Indeed, Perspective A seems to be arguing that democracy is not the 'only game in town' and that other forms of social organization are just as legitimate while Perspective B, by contrast, agrees that democracy is the only legitimate form of political organization left in the world.

5. Islam is incompatible with a democratic form of government. (-4, -1)
34. All of the main alternatives to democracy in the world have either disappeared or lost their legitimacy as forms of political organization. (-3, +2)
31. Democracy is the only form of social order that is consistent with justice. (-2, 0)

## Next Steps: Further Evaluation of Democracy and Impacts of the Leaders for Democracy Project

This brief study of the meaning of democracy to the Leaders for Democracy Fellows shows how Q methodology can be employed to profile the 'stories' about democracy and the contextual meaning of democracy that underlie democracy-building in the Near East. While the two factors uncovered by this study are similar in their overall view of the value of democracy, they do have significant differences when it comes to alternatives to democracy, the relationship between free markets and democracy, and the degree to which active citizenship is essential to democratic transition.

The factors generated and explained during this study can be used in the first of a time-series research project to evaluate the impact of public diplomacy projects on Near Eastern elites in general. The Fellows subject pool can be interviewed using the same sample of statements about democracy and democratization at several points in time over the course of their interaction. In this way the effects of the program can be assessed by looking at changes in the way that participants organize their views. Similarly, progressive groups of Leaders for Democracy Fellows that visit the Maxwell School in future years can also perform the Q-sort so that their perspectives enrich the analysis done this year. Alternatively, a new set of statements related to democracy that better reflects the goals of the Democracy Fellows program can be selected for inclusion in future studies of Leaders for Democracy Fellows in years to come. Finally, the Q-sorts performed by the Democracy Fellows can also be performed by other subjects such as the academic leaders of the Democracy Fellows Program as well as staff in the US Department of State so that an even broader set of meanings behind the concept of democracy are revealed.

## *Bibliography*

Albrecht, H. & Schlumberger, O. (2004). Waiting for Godot: Regime change without democratization in the Near East, *International Political Science Review, 25*(4), 371–392.

Anderson, L. (1991). Absolutism and the resilience of monarchy in the Near East, *Political Science Quarterly 106*(1), 1–15.

Brown, S. R. (1980). *Political subjectivity: Applications of Q methodology in political science.* New Haven, CT: Yale University Press.

Cull, N. J. (2008). Public diplomacy: Taxonomies and histories. *The ANNALS of the American Academy of Political and Social Science, 616(1),* 31–54.

Dayton, B. (2000). Policy frames, policy making and the global climate change discourse In H. Addams & J. Proops, (Eds.). *Social discourse and environmental policy* (pp. 71–99). Cheltenham: Edward Elgar.

Dayton, Bruce W. (2010). Dialogue Processes. *International encyclopedia of peace,* ed. by Nigel Young. Oxford: Oxford University Press, 171–182.

Dryzek, J. & Berejikian, J. (1993). Reconstructive democratic theory. *American Political Science Review,* 87, 48–60.

Durning, D. & Edwards, D. (1992). The attitudes of consolidation elites, Southeastern. *Political Review,* 20, 355–383.

Fisher, A. (2009). Four seasons in one day: The crowded house of public diplomacy in the UK. In N. Snow & P. M. Taylor (Eds.), *Routledge handbook of public diplomacy* (pp. 251–261). New York: Routledge Taylor and Francis Group.

Gilboa, E. (2008). Searching for a theory of public diplomacy. *The ANNALS of the American Academy of Political and Social Science, 616*(1), 55–77.

Grunig, J. E. (1993). Public relations and international affairs: Effects, ethics and responsibility. *Journal of International Affairs,* 47(1), 137–161.

Grunig, J. E., & Hunt, T. (1984). *Managing public relations.* New York: Holt, Rinehart and Winston.

Hudson, M. (1996). Obstacles to democratization in the Near East. *Contention*, 5, 81–105

Kinsey, D. F., & Zatepilina, O. (2010). The impact of visual images on non-U.S. citizens' attitudes about the United States: A Q study in visual public diplomacy. *Exchange: The Journal of Public Diplomacy, 1,* 25–32.

Kruckeberg, D. & Starck, K. (1988). *Public relations and community: A reconstructed theory.* Praeger, New York.

Kruckeberg, D. & Vujnovic, M. (2005). Public relations, not propaganda, for US public diplomacy in a post-9/11 world: Challenges and opportunities. *Journal of Communication Management, 9,* 296–304.

Lord, C. (2006). *Losing hearts and minds: Public diplomacy and strategic influence in the age of terror.* Westport, CT, London: Praeger Security International.

Lust-Okar, E. (2005). *Structuring conflict in the Arab world: Incumbents, opponents, and institutions.* Cambridge University Press: Cambridge, United Kingdom.

Nye, J. S. (2005). *Soft power: The means to success in world politics.* New York: Public Affairs.

Peritore, N. (1993). Environmental attitudes of Indian elites. *Asian Survey*, 33, 804–818.

Seo, H. & Kinsey D. F. (2012). Meaning of democracy around the world: A thematic and structural analysis of videos defining democracy. *Visual Communication Quarterly, 19:*2, 94–107.

Signitzer, B., & Wamser, C. (2006). Public diplomacy: A specific government public relations function. In C. H. Botan & V. Hazelton, (Eds.), *Public relations theory II* (pp. 435–464). Mahwah, NJ: Lawrence Erlbaum Associates.

Smith, R. M., (1997). Civic ideals: *Conflicting visions of citizenship in U.S. history.* New Haven: Yale University Press.

Snow, N. (2009). Rethinking public diplomacy. In N. Snow & P. M. Taylor (Eds.), *Routledge Handbook of public diplomacy* (pp. 3–11). New York: Routledge Taylor & Francis Group.

Stephenson, W. (1978). Concourse theory of communication, *Communication* 3, 21–41.

Stricklin, M. (1987–1996). PCQ Factor analysis programs for Q-technique [Computer software]. Lincoln, NE: Michael Stricklin.

Thomas D., Sigelman, L. & Baas, L. R. (1984). Public evaluations of the president. *Political Psychology*, 5, 531–542.

U.S. Department of State. (2008). Video contest launched at UN to promote dialogue on democracy [Press release]. Retrieved from http://www.videochallenge.america.gov/press_archive/release3.html.

Wang, J. (2006). Managing national reputation and international relations in the global era: Public diplomacy revisited. *Public Relations Review, 32,* 91–96.

Yun, S.-H. (2006). Toward public relations theory-based study of public diplomacy: Testing the applicability of the excellence study. *Journal of Public Relations Research, 18*(4), 287–312.

# 16. The Importance of Diaspora Communities as Key Publics for National Governments Around the World

VANESSA BRAVO

Diaspora communities in host countries are increasingly regarded as key stakeholders or strategic publics for home governments all around the world. The relationship-building efforts developed by home governments to establish or nurture state-diaspora relations can be categorized as public diplomacy strategies and, as many scholars argue, can be studied through the lens of the global public relations perspective (Fitzpatrick, 2007; Signitzer & Coombs, 1992; Signitzer & Wamser, 2006; Zaharna, 2009).

This chapter explains why diaspora communities have gained relevance as key stakeholders for many home-governments in recent years, what are the political and economic factors that explain this stronger connection between some home nation states and their diasporas, and why diaspora communities in host countries can be considered both as home publics located abroad and abroad publics residing at home. The chapter ends by presenting an exemplary case of state-diaspora relations in Latin America: Mexico and its relationship with Mexican migrants in the United States.

## Diaspora and Transnational Communities

Diasporas have been defined as "the movement, migration, or scattering of a people away from an established or ancestral homeland," as "people settled far from their ancestral homelands," and as "the place where these people live" (Merriam Webster Online Dictionary, 2014). Diasporas have existed for centuries, but recent changes in communication technologies, migration patterns and political processes have allowed many home governments to connect to their diasporas in closer ways than before (Koslowski, 2005a).

Diaspora members share a national origin; either by birth or by a sense of belonging to a certain homeland, but the level of connection of each diaspora member to the home country varies widely; from little or no contact with the home country to strong bonds with the homeland. As Vertovec (2005) explains, "not all diasporas are transnational communities, but transnational communities arise within diasporas" (p. 4). And even though, as indicated before, the levels of connection of the diaspora members to the home country fluctuate from person to person, and those connections are fluid through space and time, there has been a definite increase in the interest of many nation states around the world to better interact/communicate with their transnational communities.

Transnational communities are the communities that form when migrants integrate both their home country's and host country's social environments into a single unit (Basch, Schiller, & Szanton Blanc, 1994), maintaining social relationships and networks that cross national borders (Lessinger, 1995). "Rather than moving out of an old society and into a new one, they participate simultaneously in several social arenas located in several different parts of the world" (Lessinger, 1995, p. 88). For example, migrants live and work in the host country, but in many cases they send remittances home; they invest in their communities of origin; they pay taxes in both countries; they travel back and forth if their legal status and economic situation allow it, and, in some cases, they even contribute to retirement funds or have health coverage in both environments. For the purpose of this chapter, although there are conceptual differences, the concepts of diaspora communities and transnational communities are used interchangeably.

These communities, and the relationships they maintain with their home nation states, had been overlooked in the migration studies' literature, and in the public diplomacy and global public relations literature, until recently. The literature on international migration, in the 20th century, mainly emphasized the study of this phenomenon in the receiving countries (Østergaard-Nielsen, 2003a). The stream of research had been less profuse and less concerned, until the last couple of decades, with analyzing the "policies of sending countries (and homelands) towards their nationals abroad" (Østergaard-Nielsen, 2003b, p. 3).

State-diaspora studies, especially in the last 15 years, have rapidly emerged to try to understand and explain the ties that form between diaspora groups and their home governments (Koslowski, 2005a), the reasons why these ties form and develop (Gamlen, 2008), and the ways in which different governments have used these relationship-building processes to "win the hearts and minds" of their citizens abroad. In this regard, as Levitt and de la Dehesa (2003), indicate, citizenship and/or membership is seen as a de-territorialized experience, as a process of belonging to a homeland no matter where the person is geographically located. Why has this interest in studying state-diaspora relations emerged? Several factors are involved.

## *Domestic Politics Abroad*

Authors such as Portes and Rumbaut (2006), Koslowski (2005a), Øster-gaard-Nielsen (2003b), and Levitt and de la Dehesa (2003), among others, have contributed to a theoretical framework in the field of migration studies that suggests that the increased interest of home nation-states in building ties with their diaspora communities lies in the increasing participation of these communities in home politics. This process has been possible thanks to technological advancements, the growth of international migration in the last three decades, and the granting of several transnational political rights, such as dual citizenship, representation of some diaspora communities in Congress (the right to run for public office at home) and, in some instances, the right to absentee vote in home elections.This phenomenon, which Koslowski (2005b) labeled "the globalization of domestic politics" (p. 25), has allowed migrant-sending countries to establish stronger ties with their diasporas in the United States, to obtain "a multitude of political and economic gains" (Yun, 2012, p. 2203) and, at the same time, has forced the home governments to offer diaspora communities "a more formal, powerful gate" (Yun, 2012, p. 2203) to influence homeland politics, especially when it comes to democratization efforts (Yun, 2012).

Koslowski (2005b) explains that "the combination of international migration, advances in transportation and communications technology, and spreading democratization fosters a globalization of the domestic politics of many States that is similar to the globalization of national economies" (p. 5). Koslowski (2005b) argues:

> When the domestic politics of one state actually takes place in several states, it is a dimension of politics that is neither within the individual states nor between several states. In that this political practice is not captured by state-centric international relations theories that conceptualize the world in terms of international anarchy in contrast to domestic hierarchy, the globalization of domestic politics challenges traditional conceptualizations of world politics. (pp. 5–6)

Two other relevant factors—besides the stronger participation of transnational communities in home politics—that explain the interest of nation states in building relationships with their diaspora communities are the economic impact of remittances and migrants' direct investments in the home country and the growing trend of nation states of "giving back" to their diasporas by defending their human rights abroad (González Gutiérrez, 1999, 2006; Koslowski, 2005a; Smith, 2005; Levitt & de la Dehesa, 2003; Østergaard-Nielsen, 2003a, 2003b, 2003c).

Regarding migrants' remittances and investments, in countries such as El Salvador, Honduras, and Haiti, this money accounts for more income for the home country than the one the home economy obtains from foreign direct investment or foreign aid (World Bank, 2011). For thousands of families from certain communities of origin, this money also means the difference between living below or above the home country's poverty line (Gonzalez Gutiérrez, 1999, 2006; Délano, 2010). Furthermore, migrants with legal status in the host country and with means to travel back and forth also bring money to the home country through tourism (Gonzalez Gutiérrez, 1999, 2006). This economic impact from remittances, investments and tourism translates into diaspora groups' political strength at home (Koslowski, 2005a).

The "giving back" trend has grown thanks to the size and social capital that some diaspora communities have achieved, motivating some home countries to respond by defending the migrants' human rights in host countries (González Gutiérrez, 2006; Koslowski, 2005a; Smith, 2005). Some home countries place a stronger emphasis in this task than others, depending on the power leverage they have with the host countries, whether or not there are international agreements between them, the home country's desire to follow modern international norms of international relations, and how serious the home country is in defending its nationals' human rights abroad (Østergaard-Nielsen, 2003a, 2003b; Levitt & de la Dehesa, 2003).

## Contextual Factors at Home

While the migration trends of recent decades, the advancements in communications and transportation technology, and the democratization processes occurring in several nations around the globe are seen as the structural conditions that have led to stronger connections between certain transnational communities and their home countries, there are also contextual factors or conditions at the home-country level that explain why some home countries have been more aggressive or proactive than others in engaging their diasporas. These contextual factors also explain why the relationship-building styles have been so different from country to country, even among countries with similar migration patterns.

For example, through single and collective case studies, authors such as Délano (2010); Gamlen (2008); Margheritis (2007); Koslowski (2005a); Østergaard-Nielsen (2003c); Levitt and de la Dehesa (2003); and González Gutiérrez (1999, 2006) have compiled a list of reasons why some governments engage—or don't engage—their diaspora communities, and why the governments' strategies and tactics vary so much. Some contextual conditions include the following:

- The characteristics of a particular migrant community (Margheritis, 2007); for example, the migrants' "level of engagement, their sense of commitment and their confidence in local and national authorities" (Østergaard-Nielsen, 2003b, p. 6), and the migrants' context of exit from the home country and context of reception in the host country (Portes & Rumbaut, 2006)
- The specific political goals the state wants to achieve by engaging the diaspora community (González Gutiérrez, 1999, 2006); for example, the desire of the Mexican state to create a "diasporic identity" among Mexican migrants in the United States (González Gutiérrez, 1999, 2006), or the Argentinian state goal of stopping or slowing down the "brain drain" of Argentinians moving to Spain (Margheritis, 2007)
- The role of domestic actors, specifically the role of the home nation's president, in promoting this relationship-building process, especially for governments with highly centralized presidential systems (Margheritis, 2007)
- The costs-versus-benefits analysis of political parties regarding the pros and cons of involving the transnational community as voters and active participants in home politics (Levitt & de la Dehesa, 2003; Østergaard-Nielsen, 2003b)
- The existence and nature of international agreements between home and host countries (Margheritis, 2007; Østergaard-Nielsen, 2003b, 2003c); for example, Mexico sought the approval of its diaspora, intensely, when trying to gain support to sign NAFTA, the North American Free Trade Agreement between Mexico, the United States, and Canada (Østergaard-Nielsen, 2003c)
- The home country's interest in following international norms (Levitt & de la Dehesa, 2003)
- The availability of resources to support this relationship-building strategy (Levitt & de la Dehesa, 2003; Østergaard-Nielsen, 2003b)

No matter what objectives a nation state wants to accomplish with its diaspora, scholars in the fields of public relations, public diplomacy, and migration studies agree that the strategies and tactics undertaken by the state will be effective only to the degree that the diaspora community feels that there is a win-win situation in the process and in the outcomes. This relates to the main indicators of relationship quality in relationship-cultivation theory (also known as organization-public relationship theory, OPR) in public relations, such as satisfaction with, commitment to, control mutuality of, and trust in the relationship (Ferguson, 1984; L. Grunig, J. Grunig & Ehling, 1992; Huang, 1997, 2001; Ledingham & Bruning, 1998; Hon & J. Grunig, 1999; Bruning & Ledingham, 2000; Kim, 2001; Bruning & Galloway, 2003; Jo, 2006). It also relates to the notion of fairness. In this regard, Østergaard-Nielsen (2003b) argues:

> While sending countries are quick to call for their expatriate population's economic and political contribution to development in the country of origin, it is clear that most expatriates and their representative organizations expect this to be a two-way deal. Emigrants want their country of origin to support their struggle for equal rights and against discrimination in the labour market. More established migrant and diaspora groups demand more transparency and good governance in order to feel that their remittances and foreign direct investment are spent in the best possible way. And if migrants are expected to be good representatives and to do some lobbying for their country of origin abroad, then they would often like some influence on the homeland policies that they are expected to represent. (pp. 4–5)

## The "Governmentality" Perspective and the Diaspora

Some political science scholars use the "governmentality" approach to explain how and why different nation-states are changing their conceptualization of and discourse about their diaspora communities, and why some nation states are also changing the way they conceptualize themselves, their functions in society, and their political reach, particularly in terms of how they can govern their citizens located outside geographical boundaries (Ragazzi, 2009; Kunz, 2008).

Using Michel Foucault's "governmentality" perspective as a theoretical base, Ragazzi (2009) and Kunz (2008) have indicated that some nation states, especially the ones experiencing moments of crisis, are increasingly sharing their authority with non-state actors, such as their diaspora communities, as part of a neoliberal "governmentality" that involves reducing the size of the state, decentralizing its power, weakening its welfare, and encouraging non-state actors to take responsibility and contribute to the well being of their country. This encompasses involving different non-state "members" through a de-territorialized perspective, where belonging and membership are not based on geographical location.

As a logical next step, nation states have started to create mechanisms to give diasporas a certain identity, to turn diasporas into political subjects, and to govern these new political subjects (Ragazzi, 2009). In return, the state has had to develop mechanisms to protect its diaspora's human rights in the host environments, and in the in-transit path to the host country, which constitutes a challenge in the context of neoliberal restructuring and securitization of borders (Margheritis, 2010). It also creates a challenge for the state to develop creative, flexible styles of governing over a population, not just over a territory (Iskander, 2010; Varadarajan, 2010; Ragazzi, 2009; Kunz, 2008; Gamlen, 2008).

## *Redefining Migrants as Heroes, Agents of Development and Ambassadors*

At the discourse level, several states have re-conceptualized their migrants as heroes, key participants in the home country's reconstruction, agents of development, and citizens worthy of defense of their human rights while in this new environment and while in transit (Cohen, 1996; Martínez-Saldaña, 2003; Fitzgerald, 2006). In some countries, migrants have gone from being the forgotten, the neglected, or even "the traitors" to being the heroes (Martínez-Saldaña, 2003).

Another way in which diaspora members have been labeled is as "ambassadors" of the home country in the host countries, acting as resources for the home country public diplomacy efforts. In the fields of public relations and public diplomacy, the references to this concept of "diaspora diplomacy" have been relatively scarce (Leonard, 2002; Leonard, Small & Rose, 2005; Fiske de Gouveia, 2006; Gilboa, 2008; Zaharna, 2009). Contrarily, in migration studies, more authors have theorized about the relevance of diaspora members as image builders of the home country in the host countries, and also as intermediaries of the host country in the home country, in what could be called "reverse diaspora diplomacy." For example, regarding diaspora diplomacy, Agunias (2009) and Newland (2010) have indicated that diaspora members can help home governments, in collaborative efforts or independently, to raise the profile and reputation of the home country through cultural interactions. In this respect, Newland (2010) said:

Diasporas share the heritage of their countries of origin through art, music, films, literature, photography, cuisine, crafts, and other cultural artifacts. Actively promoting these—and at times using them as tools of protest—is a form of cultural diplomacy or advocacy. Exposure to the culture of a country through its diaspora may serve as a portal through which people in a host country develop a broader interest in the diaspora's homeland—including its political and economic circumstances (p. 12).

Similarly, Hernández Joseph (2012) has said that the Mexican diaspora community in the United States has gained empowerment and constitutes a venue for public diplomacy in the United States. "Its agenda is not always in line with the diplomatic bilateral agenda of Mexico, and in that sense the diaspora is not always a venue of public diplomacy. There are other circumstances, however, in which interests meet, and it could be argued that the Mexican diaspora serves to promote many of the positive aspects of Mexican culture and their contribution to the development in the United States" (Hernández Joseph, 2012, p. 234).

In terms of "reverse diaspora diplomacy," or the possibility of having diaspora communities collaborate with public diplomacy efforts of the host country in the diaspora's home country, Leonard et al. (2005) suggested that host countries that partner with diaspora communities can acquire "much needed language skills, cultural knowledge, political insight, and human intelligence, though they can also provide partisan views, dated interpretations and political engagements—all of which need to be taken carefully into account" (p. 45).

One specific example of diasporic networks collaborating with host countries to advance public diplomacy efforts in the home country is that of the Muslim communities in the United Kingdom. Different delegations of UK-Muslims tour the Islamic world "lecturing, debating, engaging with the media—with the purpose of educating people about the diversity of UK society, and particularly, for example, the freedom of worship" (Fiske de Gouveia, 2006, p. 7).

In this regard, Yun (2012) mentioned Shain's (1999) and Naim's (2002) perspectives about the capability of diasporas to become instruments of democracy and transmitters of U.S. values and ideologies (for instance, democracy, pluralism, capitalist entrepreneurship) at home, although not all diaspora groups will behave in this way, as some diasporas are not necessarily "heralds of democratic values in their home politics" (Yun, 2010, p. 2203). Furthermore, through dual citizenship, diaspora communities have the capability to establish a two-way flow of political influence, both at home and in the host environment (Yun, 2012).

In summary, diaspora communities can become allies and contribute both to the home country's public diplomacy in the host country, and to the public diplomacy of the host country in the migrants' home country. For example, in terms of "diaspora diplomacy," through their activism and support, groups from a home country—such as, say, Mexico, South Korea, or El Salvador—can help their countries improve their image in the United States, especially when there are collaborative efforts of the diaspora community with its government at home. Cultural activities, educational exchanges and daily interactions are possible routes to achieve results.

At the same time, these communities of Mexicans, South Koreans, or Salvadorans can help improve the image of the United States in their countries of origin through the conversations and other interactions that these migrants might have with relatives, friends, and even government officials at home. If these migrants have been treated well in the United States, have found opportunities in the host country, and have acquired new perspectives about issues such as the value of democracy, human rights, entrepreneurism, and basic freedoms while living in the new environment, these perspectives can find their way back and permeate the home country, influencing the population—and possibly the government—in the migrant's home country. This process of "reverse diaspora diplomacy" can translate into changes of attitude about some of those issues mentioned before, and it can also facilitate technology transfer, educational shifts, and democratization advancements, for example.

Going back to the concept of "diaspora diplomacy," in return for the aforementioned home-government efforts to re-conceptualize migrants as heroes, agents of development, key participants, and informal ambassadors of the home country (and of the host country, in certain cases), the home nation states have made it clear that diaspora members are expected to contribute to the home country's recovery (Kunz, 2008). The result has been the emergence of the field of diaspora politics, which tries to turn diaspora communities into active subjects of politics at home (Ragazzi, 2009). At the communication level, different nation states have developed a wide array of informational and relational strategies and tactics to engage or "court" the diaspora (Ragazzi, 2009; Kunz, 2008; Margheritis, 2010). Some typologies and descriptions of informational and relational state-led efforts toward diasporas can be found in Zaharna (2009), Gamlen (2008), González Gutiérrez (2006), Levitt and de la Dehesa (2003), Bravo (2011), and De Moya and Bravo (2013).

## Diasporas as Foreign Publics at Home

Diaspora communities are generally regarded as "abroad publics" for home-country governments, but they can also be considered foreign publics at home, in the host country. As Fiske de Gouveia (2006) explains and illustrates:

> Foreign policy is no longer something which needs only to be conducted abroad, often the abroad itself is at home. This is something that both the UK and Dutch governments have adjusted to in the last few years as a consequence of the July 2005 bombings in London, and the murder of Pym Fortuyn and Theo Van Gogh in Amsterdam. Following the London bombings, specialised working groups on Preventing Extremism were assembled to respond to the new internal threat. Their work certainly hasn't been perfect or free of controversy but it is emblematic of an inevitable trend in public diplomacy. The UK Foreign Office is now looking, for example, at specific means of engaging better with marginalised UK-based African communities -and it makes absolute sense to do so-. ...In a globalised world where more and more of us are migrating to live in each other's countries, it makes sense for foreign ministries to seek to engage not just with foreign publics abroad but foreign publics at home (pp. 7–8).

"U.S. ethnic lobbying" has been studied throughout the 20th century in the United States as the efforts of different ethnic groups to "sway U.S. foreign policy in the interests of their homelands" (Yun, 2012, p. 2202)—for example, the political activities of the Jewish, the Irish and the Greek diasporas in the United States in the first half of the 20th century and, since the 1980s, the activism of new groups such as Mexicans, Indians, or Koreans. Despite this, the field of public diplomacy has still to embrace the study of ethnic lobbying in a more holistic way, to achieve the engagement of these ethnic communities by the host government. As Yun (2012) argues, U.S. ethnic lobbying has been relegated to the field of comparative American politics but, in reality, it actually best "complements the workings of public diplomacy" and "is a sociological model of public diplomacy" (p. 2202).

## Final Remarks: Understand Your Audience

Increasingly, countries all around the world are acknowledging the importance of diaspora communities as key publics of the public diplomacy strategies or government global public relations efforts of home governments abroad (diaspora diplomacy abroad), and of home governments at home (diaspora diplomacy at home). Yet, for these efforts to be truly successful, it is necessary to remember and consider that diaspora communities are complex publics, remarkably heterogeneous in composition, affected not only by the context of exit of the home country and the context of reception in the host country, but also impacted by the characteristics of the migrant community itself, by time and space (Bravo, 2011).

In this regard, diasporas should not be seen as monolithic audiences, even less as segmented stakeholders who can easily be placed in Western-centric typologies of publics, but as diverse groups with changing circumstances, identities, discourses and needs. Within that framework, diasporas can better be analyzed not through rigid excellence models, but through cultural-economic models of public relations (Curtin & Gaither, 2007), where publics are not seen as segments or groups, but as communities where identities overlap, shift and flow.

Besides, the relationship-building process that gets established between nation states and diaspora communities in host countries can be better understood through the lens of the integrated public diplomacy approach, that takes into consideration not one but three layers of public diplomacy: relational public diplomacy (for instance, soft-power programs), mediated public diplomacy (the use of global news media and social media for public diplomacy purposes), and nation branding and country reputation strategies (Golan, 2013).

## Mexico: An Exemplary Case of State-Diaspora Relations

To analyze the case of the state-diaspora relations established and stewarded by the government of Mexico with the millions of Mexicans who live in the United States, this section follows the categories used by Levitt and de la Dehesa (2003) to describe Mexico's efforts. These include: "1) ministerial or consular reforms; 2) investment policies which seek to attract or channel migrant remittances; 3) extension of political rights in the form of dual citizenship or nationality, the right to vote from overseas, or the right to run for public office; 4) the extension of State protections or services to nationals living abroad that go beyond traditional consular services; and 5) the implementation of symbolic policies designed to reinforce emigrants' sense of enduring membership" (pp. 589–590).

Mexico was selected as a case study for this chapter because it is considered a pioneer and a leader of strong state-diaspora relations in the continent. Mexico was the first Latin American country to establish sustained strategic efforts to create and maintain long-term interactions with its diaspora community (Hernández Joseph, 2012; Félix, 2010; Délano, 2010; González Gutiérrez, 1999, 2006; Smith, 2005; Martínez-Saldaña, 2003; Massey, Durand & Malone, 2002; Goldring, 2002). There are documented efforts of Mexico's state-led transnationalism since the 1970s (González Gutiérrez, 1999, 2006), with one of the most significant efforts happening in 1990, when Mexico created its General Directorate for Mexican Communities Abroad (Levitt & de la Dehesa, 2003; González Gutiérrez, 1999, 2006). This action helped to create the necessary structural conditions to serve this population.

## Ministerial or Consular Reforms

Mexico, over the years, has created the institutional structure it requires to serve its diaspora communities. The General Directorate for Mexican Communities Abroad, part of Mexico's Secretariat of Foreign Affairs, was created in 1990 (González Gutiérrez, 1999, 2006; Levitt & de la Dehesa, 2003). In 2001, the Presidential Office for Mexicans Abroad was founded as well but, as it duplicated some of the functions of the General Directorate, both entities were merged in 2002 under the National Council for Mexican Communities Abroad (NCMCA), which is part of the Secretariat of Foreign Affairs (Levitt & de la Dehesa, 2003).

Along with this structure, the Mexican consulates play a key role in the relationship-building process with the diaspora communities. The Mexican consulates provide a wide variety of services, from the most traditional (i.e., issuing passports, ID cards and birth certificates) to the most sui-generis (i.e., repatriation of cadavers or translation services to non-Spanish-speaking migrants from indigenous communities, to name a few) (Hernández Joseph, 2012), and everything in between. Consulates also connect migrants to their state and municipal authorities, promote productive investments in the communities of origin, organize business events, back the efforts of migrant-run organizations, and recognize migrants as valid spokespeople for the Mexican community abroad (González Gutiérrez, 1999, 2006). Also, the consulates are trying to show respect to migrants by making consular processes more efficient.

As of 2011, Mexico had the world's strongest consular concentration in the United States, with 50 of its 67 worldwide consulates located in the United States alone. Additionally, 53 percent of Mexico's foreign-service personnel worked in consular activities (Hernández Joseph, 2012). This makes sense, considering that Mexico borders the United States, has roughly 12 million Mexican migrants there, and has about 20 million more people of Mexican descent who are U.S. citizens (Hernández Joseph, 2012).

## Investment Policies to Attract or Channel Migrant Remittances

Remittances are such an important source of foreign currency in Latin America that, in 2010, in seven Latin American countries (Honduras, Guyana, El

Salvador, Haiti, Jamaica, Nicaragua, and Guatemala) the money sent home by migrants accounted for at least 10% of the country's GDP (World Bank, 2011). This factor helps to explain the relevance of the efforts that different nation states in the region make to attract those remittances to the home country.

Mexico is also aware of the importance of remittances for certain migrants' communities of origin in Mexican territory, although remittances only constitute about 2.6% of Mexico's GDP. Yet, since 2007, remittances to Mexico have steadily remained above $20 billion annually (Hernandez Joseph, 2010), certainly a considerable figure. Thus, Mexico has implemented several measures to channel this money. For example, since the 1990s, the Mexican government developed matching-fund programs to support public work projects in Mexican communities that are sponsored or led by migrants in the United States (Levitt & de la Dehesa, 2003). The "tres por uno" (three for one) federal program, for example, adds one federal dollar and one state dollar to every dollar donated by migrants to fund public work projects (Félix, 2010). Mexican authorities have also negotiated favorable rates with remittance-sending agencies (such as Western Union) for money transfers sent by Mexicans in the United States back to Mexico (Levitt & de la Dehesa, 2003).

## Extension of Political Rights

Since 1996, Mexico offers dual nationality and dual citizenship, and, since 2006, Mexican migrants can vote through absentee vote/ballot in national elections and can hold office in Mexico (Levitt & de la Dehesa, 2003; Felix, 2010). These rights have increased the political participation of Mexicans in domestic politics since 2006.

## Extension of State Protections or Services

Beyond consular services, Mexico has also aggressively extended state protections and services to its diaspora. Some of these services include mobile consulates, primary and secondary schooling for adults, health and education campaigns, book donations, teacher trainings, document processing so that students can pass from one country's educational system to the other without having to repeat grades, health insurance packages for the migrant's relatives in Mexico, legal counseling, etc. (Hernández Joseph, 2012; González Gutiérrez, 1999, 2006; Levitt & de la Dehesa, 2003). As part of the state protections, the Mexican embassy and its consulates use various communication strategies and tactics (i.e., news conferences and speeches) to condemn human rights abuses against Mexican migrants in the United States.

## Symbolic Policies to Reinforce the Diasporic Identity

Mexico uses communication and relationship-building strategies and tactics to keep the diasporic identity alive, for example, through visits of Mexican American delegations to Mexico, meetings between migrant clubs and migrant organizational leaders with Mexican authorities in Mexico and in the United States, sports activities such as soccer tournaments, youth encounters, folklore and art exhibitions, holiday celebrations, art contests, pilgrimages, and more (González Gutiérrez, 1999). It also utilizes websites (such as the one belonging to the Instituto de los Mexicanos en el Exterior) and social media to connect with the Mexican diaspora.

## Other Cases

The Mexican case has served as an example of best practices to other countries around the world about the kind of actions and decisions that different governments can make to strengthen their relations and interactions with their diaspora communities in the short and long term. Some countries such as El Salvador have followed the Mexican model to implement some of the actions the Mexican government started decades ago in their own public diplomacy strategies. In this regard, the Mexican example has relevance to the practice of public diplomacy and transnational public relations in other nations.

It is beyond the scope of this chapter to describe in detail other examples of state-diaspora relations in Latin America or the rest of the world, but, certainly, other countries are establishing similar strategies and tactics in their public diplomacy efforts with their diaspora communities. Evidently, different countries achieve different levels of success and face different structural and contextual factors that limit and shape those state-led transnational initiatives.

Among others, some cases studies of state-led diaspora relations have been developed by different scholars for countries such as the Dominican Republic (Howard, 2003), Haiti (Levitt & de la Dehesa, 2003), Brazil (Levitt & de la Dehesa, 2003), Argentina (Margheritis, 2007), Ecuador (Margheritis, 2010), Jamaica (Sives, 2012), Turkey (Ögelman, 2005), Israel (Lahav & Arian, 2005), China (Freedman, 2005), India (Kurien, 2005), Russia (Saunders, 2005), the Kurds in Germany (Lyon & Ucarer, 2005), El Salvador (Bravo, 2011) and Costa Rica (Bravo, 2011).

## Bibliography

Agunias, D. R. (Ed.). (2009). *Closing the distance: How governments strengthen ties with their diasporas.* Washington, D.C.: Migration Policy Institute.

Basch, L. G., Schiller, N. G., & Szanton Blanc, C. (1994). *Nations unbound: Transnational projects, postcolonial predicaments, and deterritorialized nation-states.* New York: Gordon and Breach.

Bravo, V. (2011). *Conceptualization of diaspora relations from the government viewpoint: An exploratory qualitative study of diaspora relations in the cases of Costa Rica and El Salvador.* Unpublished doctoral dissertation. University of Florida, Gainesville.

Bruning, S. D., & Galloway, T. (2003). Expanding the organization-public relationship scale: Exploring the role that structural and personal commitment play in organization-public relationships. *Public Relations Review, 29*(3), 309–319.

Bruning, S. D. & Ledingham, J. A. (2000). Perceptions of relationships and evaluations of satisfaction: An exploration of interaction. *Public Relations Review*, 26 (1), 85–95.

Cohen, R. (1996). Diasporas and the nation-state: From victims to challengers. *International Affairs, 72*, 507–520.

Curtin, P. & Gaither, K. (2007). *International public relations: Negotiating culture, identity and power.* Thousand Oaks: SaGE Publications.

Délano, A. (2010). Immigrant integration vs. transnational ties? The role of the sending state. *Social Research, 77* (1), 237–268.

De Moya, M. & Bravo, V. (2013, June). *Communicating the homeland's relationship with its diaspora community: The cases of El Salvador and Colombia.* Paper presented at the International Communication Association (ICA) 63st Annual Conference. Global Communication and Social Change Division. London, England, June 17–21.

diaspora (n.d.). In *Merriam-Webster Online Dictionary.* Retrieved January 15, 2014 from http://www.merriam-webster.com/ dictionary/diaspora

Felix, A. (2010). *Latino Politics.* Guest lecture presented on October 5, 2010, to the Latino Culture in the United States course at the Center for Latin American Studies, University of Florida.

Ferguson. M. A. (1984, August). *Building theory in public relations: Interorganizational relationships.* Paper presented at the convention of the Association for Education in Journalism and Mass Communication, Gainesville, FL.

Fiske de Gouveia, P. F. (2006). The future of public diplomacy. *The present and future of public diplomacy: A European perspective.* The 2006 Madrid Conference on Public Diplomacy. Retrieved September 1, 2012, from http://www.realinstitutoelcano.org/

Fitzgerald, D. (2006). Inside the sending state: The politics of Mexican emigration control. *International Migration Review, 40* (2), 259–293.

Fitzpatrick, K. R. (2007). Advancing the new public diplomacy: A public relations perspective. *The Hague Journal of Diplomacy, 2*(3), 187–211.

Freedman, A. L. (2005). Politics from outside: Chinese overseas and political and economic change in China. In R. Koslowski (Ed.), *International migration and the globalization of domestic politics* (130–147). Transnationalism. London: Routledge.

Gamlen, A. (2008). The emigration state and the modern geopolitical imagination. *Political Geography*, 27, 840–856.

Gilboa, E. (2008). Searching for a theory of public diplomacy. *The Annals of the American Academy of Political and Social Science, 616* (1), 55–77.

Golan, G. J. (2013). Introduction: An Integrated Approach to Public Diplomacy. *American Behavioral Scientist*, *57* (9), 1251–1255.

Goldring, L. (2002). The Mexican state and transmigrant organizations: Negotiating the boundaries of membership and participation. *Latin American Research Review*, 37(3), 55–99.

González Gutiérrez, C. (1999). Fostering identities: Mexico´s relations with its diaspora. *The Journal of American History*, 86 (2), pp. 545–567.

———. (2006). Del acercamiento a la inclusión institucional: La experiencia del Instituto de los Mexicanos en el Exterior. In C. González Gutiérrez (Coord.), *Relaciones Estado Diáspora: Aproximaciones Desde Cuatro Continentes* (181–220). México: Porrúa.

Grunig, L. A., Grunig, J. E. & Ehling, W. P. (1992). What is an effective organization? In J. E. Grunig (Ed.), *Excellence in Public Relations and Communication Management* (65–90). Hillsdale, NJ: Lawrence Erlbaum Associates.

Hernández Joseph, D. (2012). Mexico´s concentration on consular services in the United States. *The Hague Journal of Diplomacy 7*, 227–236.

Hon, L. & Grunig, J. E. (1999). *Guidelines for measuring relationships in public relations.* Gainesville, FL: Institute for Public Relations.

Howard, D. (2003). Dominicans abroad: Impacts and responses in a transnational society. In E. Østergaard-Nielsen (Ed.), *International migration and sending countries: Perceptions, policies, and transnational relations* (57–76). Basingstoke, Hampshire: Palgrave Macmillan.

Huang, Y. (1997). *Public relations strategies, relational outcomes, and conflict management strategies.* Unpublished doctoral dissertation, University of Maryland, College Park, MD.

———. (2001). OPRA: A cross-cultural, multiple-item scale for measuring organization-public relationships. *Journal of Public Relations Research*, *13*(1), 61–90.

Iskander, N. (2010). Creative State. *Forty Years of Migration and Development Policy in Morocco and Mexico*. Ithaca, NY: Cornell University Press.

Jo, S. (2006). Measurement of organization–public relationships: Validation of measurement using a manufacturer relationship. *Journal of Public Relations Research, 18* (3), 225–248.

Kim, Y. (2001). Searching for the organization-public relationship: A valid and reliable instrument. *Journalism and Mass Communication Quarterly, 78* (4), 799–816.

Koslowski, R. (2005a). *International migration and the globalization of domestic politics.* Transnationalism. London: Routledge.

———. (2005b). International migration and the globalization of domestic politics: A conceptual framework. In R. Koslowski (Ed.), *International migration and the globalization of domestic politics* (5–32). Transnationalism. London: Routledge.

Kunz, R. (2008). Mobilising diasporas: A governmentality analysis of the case of Mexico. *Working Paper Series "Glocal Governance and Democracy" 03*, 1–23.

Kurien, P. (2005). Opposing constructions and agendas: The politics of Hindu and Muslim Indian-American organizations. In R. Koslowski (Ed.), *International migration and the globalization of domestic politics* (148–172). Transnationalism. London: Routledge.

Lahav, G. & Arian, A. (2005). Israelis in a Jewish diaspora: The dilemmas of a globalized group. In R. Koslowski (Ed.), *International migration and the globalization of domestic politics* (83–104). Transnationalism. London: Routledge.

Ledingham, J. A., & Bruning, S. D. (1998). Relationship management in public relations: Dimensions of an organization-public relationship. *Public Relations Review,* 24(1), 55.

Leonard, M. (2002). Diplomacy by other means. *Foreign Policy,* 132 (Sept-Oct), 48–56.

Leonard, M., Small, A., & Rose, M. (2005, February). *British public diplomacy in the age of schisms.* London: The Foreign Policy Centre. Retrieved September 1, 2012, from http://fpc.org.uk/fsblob/407.pdf

Lessinger, J. (1995). *From the Ganges to the Hudson: Indian immigrants in New York City.* The new immigrants series. Boston: Allyn and Bacon.

Levitt, P. & de la Dehesa, R. (2003).Transnational migration and the redefinition of the state: Variations and explanations. *Ethnic and Racial Studies, 26* (4), 587–611.

Lyon, A. J. & Ucarer, E. M. (2005). Mobilizing ethnic conflict: Kurdish separatism in Germany and the PKK. In R. Koslowski (Ed.), *International migration and the globalization of domestic politics* (pp. 62–82). Transnationalism. London: Routledge.

Margheritis, A. (2007). State-led transnationalism and migration: Reaching out to the Argentine community in Spain. *Global Networks, 7* (1), 87–106.

Margheritis, A. (2011). "Todos Somos Migrantes" (We Are All Migrants): The Paradoxes of Innovative State-led Transnationalism in Ecuador1. *International Political Sociology, 5*(2), 198–217.

Martínez-Saldaña, J. (2003). *Los olvidados* become heroes: The evolution of Mexico's policies towards citizens abroad. In E. Østergaard-Nielsen (Ed.), *International migration and sending countries: Perceptions, policies, and transnational relations* (pp. 33–56). Basingstoke, Hampshire: Palgrave Macmillan.

Massey, D. S., Durand, J., & Malone, N. J. (2002). *Beyond smoke and mirrors: Mexican immigration in an era of economic integration.* New York: Russell Sage.

Naim, M. (2002). The new diaspora: New links between emigrés and their home countries can become a powerful force for economic development. *Foreign Policy, 131* (96–99).

Newland, K. (2010, November). *Voice after exit: Diaspora advocacy.* Washington, D.C.: Migration Policy Institute.

Ögelman, N. (2005). Immigrant organizations and the globalization of Turkey's domestic politics. In R. Koslowski (Ed.), *International migration and the globalization of domestic politics* (pp. 33–61). Transnationalism. London: Routledge.

Østergaard-Nielsen, E. (2003a). *International migration and sending countries: Perceptions, policies, and transnational relations.* Basingstoke, Hampshire: Palgrave Macmillan.

———. (2003b). International migration and sending countries: Key issues and themes. In E. Østergaard-Nielsen (Ed.), *International migration and sending countries: Perceptions, policies, and transnational relations* (pp. 3–32). Basingstoke, Hampshire: Palgrave Macmillan.

———. (2003c). Continuities and changes in sending country perceptions, policies and transnational relations with nationals abroad. In E. Østergaard-Nielsen (Ed.), *International migration and sending countries: Perceptions, policies, and transnational relations* (pp. 209–224). Basingstoke, Hampshire: Palgrave Macmillan.

Portes, A., & Rumbaut, R. G. (2006). *Immigrant America: A portrait.* Berkeley: University of California Press.

Ragazzi, F. (2009). Governing diasporas. *International Political Sociology 3,* 378–397.

Saunders, R. A. (2005). A marooned diaspora: Ethnic Russians in the near abroad and their impact on Russia´s foreign policy and domestic politics. In R. Koslowski (Ed.), *International migration and the globalization of domestic politics* (pp. 173–194). Transnationalism. London: Routledge.

Shain, Y. (1999). *Marketing the American creed abroad: Diasporas in the US and their homelands.* Cambridge University Press.

Signitzer, B. H., & Coombs, T. (1992). Public relations and public diplomacy: Conceptual covergences. *Public Relations Review, 18*(2), 137–147.

Signitzer, B., & Wamser, C. (2006). Public diplomacy: A specific governmental public relations function. *Public relations theory II,* 435–464.

Sives, A. (2012). Formalizing diaspora-state relations: Processes and tensions in the Jamaican case. *International Migration, 50 (1),* 113–128.

Smith, R. C. (2005). Migrant membership as an instituted process: Transnationalization, the state and the extra-territorial conduct of Mexican politics. In R. Koslowski (Ed.), *International migration and the globalization of domestic politics* (pp. 105–129). Transnationalism. London: Routledge.

Varadarajan, L. (2010). *The domestic abroad. Diasporas in international relations.* New York: Oxford University Press.

Vertovec, S. (2005). *The political importance of diasporas. Working Paper No. 15.* Centre on Migration, Policy and Society. University of Oxford. Retrieved September 3, 2012, fromhttp://www.compas.ox.ac.uk/publications/working-papers/wp-05-13/

World Bank (2011). *Migration and remittances factbook 2011.* Second edition. Washington, D.C.: The International Bank for Reconstruction and Development/The World Bank.

Yun, S-H. (2012). Relational public diplomacy: The perspective of sociological globalism. *International Journal of Communication 6,* 2199–2219.

Zaharna, R. S. (2009). Mapping out a spectrum of public diplomacy initiatives: Information and relational communication frameworks. In N. Snow & P. M. Taylor (Eds.), *Routledge handbook of public diplomacy* (pp. 86–100). New York: Routledge.

# 17. Soft Power, NGOs and Virtual Communication Networks: New Strategies and Directions for Public Diplomacy

AIMEI YANG

During the Cold War, public diplomacy was used as a tool for image cultivation, propaganda and other activities aimed at influencing public opinions in foreign lands (Leonard, 2002; Tuch, 1990). The end of the Cold War spread democracy and its values into many countries and increased people's access to international information (Sriramesh & Verčič, 2009). Nye (2004) coined the term "soft power" to refer to nations' power of influence that is largely based on perceived value, social norms and image. Public diplomacy is crucial for nations to enhance their soft power. Additionally, as nations increasingly become interdependent, diplomats recognized that the effective implementation of public diplomacy requires new approaches such as an integrated approach to public diplomacy that considers short, medium and long term effects of diplomatic strategies (Golan, 2013).

In recent decades, one common thread connecting different public diplomatic strategies is the emphasis on public perception (Albritton & Manheim, 1985; Brookings Institution, 2004). As Leonard (2002) noted, "the last decade is rife with examples of popular perceptions, rather than governments, setting the pace for international diplomacy" (p. 48). Nations have realized that different perceptions held by foreign publics can create an enabling or a disabling environment that has influence on nations' activities (Foreign Policy Centre, 2002).

To effectively engage broad foreign publics and shape perceived image, value and norms, public diplomacy relies on, among other things, trustworthy messengers and effective media of communication (Dizard, 2004; Signitzer

& Coombs, 1992; Wang, 2006). Traditional approaches to public diplomacy such as cultural festivals, seminars, promotion, or polity advocacy are often imprinted with the mark of foreign governments. The suspicion surrounding the motives for these foreign governments' activities often leads audiences to be leery or skeptical of the received information. Leonard (2002) argues that NGOs are one of the best messengers of public diplomacy campaigns because they have credibility, expertise and extensive networks in foreign countries. In addition, information technology and new media may also alter public diplomatic strategies. An integrated approach to public diplomacy requires different media. New media may be particularly valuable to carry out public diplomatic campaigns as dialogues targeting different publics, especially the younger generation (Gilboa, 2004). Nevertheless, Wang (2006) noted that in the field of public relations, "there is a glaring absence of efforts devoted to studying the role of the Internet and other new communication technologies in public diplomacy" (p. 94).

Golan (2013) proposed the concept of integrated public diplomacy, which encompasses three approaches to public diplomacy: the short- to medium-termed mediated public diplomacy, national brandings that aim at medium- to long-termed effects; and the long-termed relational public diplomacy. This Chapter assesses the potential value of NGOs as partners of nation states' public diplomatic campaigns for the integrated approach to public diplomacy. This Chapter also examines the role of new media in NGOs' global networks, and studies a group of NGOs' new media use patterns and how NGOs reach worldwide publics via the Internet. This study also provides empirical evidence to illustrate the diplomatic values of partnership with NGOs and offers suggestions for diplomats to form effective public diplomacy strategies.

This study examines international NGOs (INGOs) that have membership in multiple countries because of their capacity to influence foreign publics. Given the large scope of international civil society, this study focuses on a representative segment of INGOs, those working in the field of environmental protection. Environmental INGOs are among the most active NGOs in the international arena (Castells, 2009). Additionally, environmental INGOs are often perceived as independent and critical of powerful social institutions (Castells, 2008). The study demonstrates that environmental INGOs' websites can effectively attract millions of visitors around the world. Furthermore, INGOs have built a global network with distinctive structural features. INGOs' global influence can be considered as valuable public diplomatic assets. In the following sections, the tradition and recent developments in public diplomacy are briefly introduced, followed by a review of the role of NGOs and new media in public diplomacy. Results are presented and major findings discussed.

## Public Diplomacy: Tradition and New Development

### Traditional Approach to Public Diplomacy

Traditionally, public diplomacy mainly refers to countries' official communication aimed at foreign publics (Dizard, 2004). Although the practice of public diplomacy has existed for thousands of years, the term emerged during the initial years of the Cold War (Arquilla & Ronfeldt, 1999). The formidable destructive power of nuclear weapons forced the two superpowers of that era, the U.S. and Soviet Union, to seek alternative weapons, such as information and persuasion campaigns, to fight their ideological and strategic battles. Public diplomacy can help nations create favorable images of their policies, actions, and political and economic systems (Foreign Policy Centre, 2002). Public diplomacy can also facilitate domestic pressure on foreign governments to modify hostile policies or even smooth the progress of regime change and nation building (Taylor & Doerfel, 2003; Taylor & Kent, 2000).

Conventionally, mass communication, cultural and academic exchanges, participation in exhibitions, building cultural centers, language education and establishing local friendship leagues and trade associations are major tools of public diplomacy (Vickers, 2004). Those tools are supposed to help nations cultivate positive images and serve as propaganda tools (Brookings Institution, 2004). Among those tools, mass communication is mainly used to inform publics about current affairs; other cultural channels are designed to shape long-term perceptions. The most active agents of public diplomacy in the traditional approach are nation states. As noted by Gilboa (2008), this limited view of agents of public diplomacy leads to the dearth of "research on public diplomacy programs and activities of countries other than the United States and of new international actors such as NGOs, civil society groups and individuals" (p. 56).

### New Development in Public Diplomacy

Three current forces—globalization, the multipolar international system, and new information and communication technology—present challenges to the traditional public diplomacy approach (Gilboa, 2008; Leonard, 2002; Yang, Klyueva, & Taylor, 2012). In recent decades, the academic community started to reconsider the nature of public diplomacy. For example, Nye (2004) argues that power refers not only to nations' ability to force others into certain actions, as reflected by the concept of "hard power" (e.g., military power, economic power, etc.), but also refers to states' ability to influence the opinions, norms and behaviors of others to yield desirable outcomes (soft power). The major difference between soft and hard power is that soft power arises from the persuasiveness of a nation's values, culture and policies; nations exercise soft power through cooperation rather than coercion. According to Nye (2004), in the postmodern international relations era, countries that are more likely to be powerful are those that have the ability to frame issues; those whose culture and ideas are closer to prevailing international norms and those whose credibility abroad is reinforced by their values and policies. Furthermore, when policies and positions of states or non-state actors have moral authority, or are seen as legitimate in the eyes of others, their soft power is increased.

Nye's (2004) concept of soft power has been further developed and linked with public diplomacy. Batora (2005) argues that actions of public diplomacy pursued by both state and non-state actors contribute to the maintenance and promotion of a nation's soft power. Arquilla and Ronfeldt (1999) apply Nye's soft power to national strategic thinking. They coined the term, 'noopolitik' to describe strategies that are different from the traditional, hard-power driven 'realpolitik' approach. Noopolitik adapts to the information age and emphasizes the primary role of ideas, values, norms, standards, laws and ethics in international relationships.

The emphasis on soft power and noopolitik advocates for a dialogic approach to public diplomacy (Gilboa, 2004; 2008). The dialogic approach is aimed at creating a communication system that facilitates dialogue among multiple publics. This approach goes beyond image cultivation (Yang, Klyueva, & Taylor, 2012). It fosters a shared understanding and action. To effectively carry out dialogic public diplomacy, it requires a novel understanding of active agencies. Nations are no longer the sole agency of public diplomacy. Non-state actors, such as individuals, corporations, media networks, international organizations and NGOs should also be considered as indispensable actors. Furthermore, to reach broad publics and publics that are not targets of traditional public diplomacy (e.g., younger generations), new channels of communication should be involved. The need to adapt to the changing practice suggests that it may be valuable to involve NGOs and new media in diplomatic strategies. The following sections discuss these NGOs' strategic values more specifically.

*NGOs and public diplomacy.* NGOs are not-for-profit and private organizations pursuing issues of societal and even global influence (Yang, 2012; Castells, 2004). These organizations are highly diverse and heterogeneous. Together, they form an important part of civil society (Alexander, 2006). In recent years, NGOs have attracted considerable academic attention, and are studied in multiple disciplines and through various perspectives (Boli & Thomas, 1997; Castells, 2008; DeMars, 2005; Kaldor, 2005).

In general, NGOs are often seen as possessing a significant amount of knowledge and information, but with limited institutional, military or financial power (Boli & Thomas, 1997). The process of globalization allows NGOs to exert more influence through domestic and transnational networks (DeMars, 2005). NGOs have also demonstrated that they are particularly adept at influencing foreign publics (Castells, 2008). For example, Ayres (2003) found that NGOs can effectively influence the reform of institutions of global trade governance.In addition, some have observed converging interests among states and NGOs (Beckfield, 2003).This chapter argues that for nations to create dialogues that engage broader societies in foreign countries, it is beneficial for diplomats to collaborate with non-governmental agents.

The value of involving NGOs in public diplomacy efforts arises from NGOs' unique credibility, expertise, and access. First, in reality, it is often difficult to communicate with publics in foreign countries, especially when there are great cultural or ideological differences between countries (e.g., Western countries and Mid East countries). Diplomats sometimes find that it is hard for them to communicate in a culturally appropriate or engaging manner. In addition, it is also difficult to ensure information is received in the way that it was intended, which is far from easy as people are inclined to be suspicious of foreign officials' motives. In contrast, NGOs often have credibility among foreign publics. For example, a Canadian polling company found that 65 percent of participants in a large survey trusted NGOs to work in the best interest of society, while only 45 percent believed governments would do the same (Leonard, 2002). Therefore, collaborating with NGOs will allow diplomatic messages to be sent by credible messengers.

Second, NGOs are often formed by experts in certain areas (Boli & Thomas, 1997). Their expertise makes them relevant and credible in many areas. For example, Boli and Thomas (1997) found that in 1988, one quarter of all international INGOs were industry or trade organizations. And, about one third of INGOs were based on scientific or technology fields. These two types of INGOs account for about 60 percent of INGOs. When the situation involves specific knowledge (e.g., oil spread, landmine explosion, child labor, etc.), people are more likely to turn to experts for information than to diplomats. Therefore, working with NGOs will help diplomatic messages to be sent by perceived experts and, hence, encourage greater acceptance.

Third, it is difficult for nation states to gain access to local networks or media channels in foreign countries. NGOs, however, often have existing relationships with their local counterparts because of shared missions or interests (Castells, 2009). NGOs may also have established networks to influence local legislators or other activists because of their advocacy needs (DeMars, 2005). Those existing connections offer NGOs access to diverse local networks. NGOs' networks help them to communicate with foreign publics more efficiently and effectively. Involving NGOs in diplomatic efforts, therefore, would help diplomats to gain access to these valuable networks and thus gain access to different national publics.

In sum, the literature suggests that, while diplomats retain an important role in engaging other governments and political elites, they are often not the ideal agents for engaging with broader foreign publics. Civil actors such as NGOs may be better agents to reach broader foreign publics because of their credibility, expertise and access. Another new development in public diplomatic practice is the influence of new media on international information flow.

***New media and public diplomacy.*** In modern society, media are important forums of public sphere because media construct a large amount of public narratives and symbols (Cozier & Witmer, 2001; Gilboa, 2000; Signitzer & Coombs, 1992). New media such as the Internet radically reduce the costs and increase the speed of communication, and allow a broad range of new actors to participate in the debate over, and implementation of, foreign policy (Gilboa, 2004). New media make new actors of international relationships, such as international corporations, NGOs, and less formal groupings of citizens, increasingly visible in the practice of public diplomacy. Not only do new media allow these new actors to communicate and collaborate more efficiently, but they also open up alternative sources of information (Yang & Taylor, 2010). Virtual participation and information allow new actors to become well informed on key policy issues and geo-political developments. New media have become a major platform for information dissemination and offer opportunities for cyber public diplomacy. For example, many states and non-state actors currently maintain websites to present their history, policies, values, culture and other achievements. Websites provide opportunities for these actors to present themselves in a way that cultivates positive support or even neutralizes or attacks opponents (Conway, 2005). To explore the diplomatic value of INGOs' websites and the structural features of the virtual networks among these websites, the following two research questions are proposed to guide the analysis:

RQ1: Do INGOs' websites reach a global public?
RQ2: What are the basic structural features of INGOs' networks among their websites?

Based on the previous discussion, this study examines how INGOs have used new media to engage international publics and how INGOs form networks in the cyberspace. Information gathered from this study provides valuable insight for public diplomatic strategy and policy making. To study structural features of INGOs' virtual networks, this study employs hyperlink network analysis to study how activists develop relationships online.

## Hyperlink Network Analysis

A hyperlink is one of basic building blocks of the Internet and guides Internet users' online navigation (Park & Thelwall, 2003; Shumate & Lipp 2008). The amount of hyperlinks a website receives affects the searchability of the site (Thelwall, 2009). Further, Shumate and Lipp (2008) conceptualized hyperlink networks as "a set of inter-organizational links that enable members and nonmembers to reach a homogenous set of like-minded organizations in order to enhance the visibility of the network's goals" (p. 179). Therefore, the study of hyperlink networks helps to illustrate organizations' choices of online allies.

NGOs' hyperlink networks have unique features. Research suggests that NGOs focused on similar issues tend to cluster together and use their virtual networks to represent their alliances. For instance, Bae and Choi (2000) studied the hyperlinks among human rights NGOs and found that most organizations link to others with similar goals. Shumate and Lipp (2008) found that NGOs' goals and missions also play a key role in influencing NGOs' virtual connections. Shumate and O' Connor (2010) conceptualized hyperlink network alliance building as a form of symbolic action, and found organizations used hyperlinks to signify their stands on social issues. In other words,organizations often make an active and selective choice about which other organizations to form alliances with. Yang (2012) found that in China, Northern NGOs and indigenous Chinese NGOs demonstrated distinctive and different hyperlink network formation patterns.

Recently, in the field of communication research, there has been an increasing interest in hyperlink network analysis (HNA) (Bae & Choi 2000; Park & Thelwall 2003; Shumate & Lipp, 2008). HNA has been applied to topics such as the structure of international hyperlinks and information flow (Barnett & Sung, 2005), the reproduction of world systems in international cyberspace (Himelboim, Chang, & McCreery, 2010), ideological landscape (Himelboim, McCreery, & Smith, 2013), and inter-organizational communication (Shumate & Dewitt; 2008). Studies have found that HNA provides a robust quantitative approach to study the Web network structure. In this study, HNA and secondary data analysis are combined to address research questions.

## Methods

### Sampling

This study seeks to provide a comprehensive description of environment INGO websites' diplomatic values. To achieve this goal, the researcher first obtained a list of all identifiable environmental INGOs in the world. Any INGO that met the following criteria was included: 1) had membership in more than one country; 2) mainly focused on environmental protections as suggested by mission statements; 3) the organization is an INGO. Information about INGOs can be obtained from *The Yearbook of International Organizations* (Union of International Associations), which is the most comprehensive source on INGOs (Beckfield, 2003).

### Data Collection

A list of these INGOs' websites was fed into LexiURL Searcher. LexiURL Searcher is a web crawler that draws hyperlinks among these civil actors' sites. This crawler automatically collects hyperlink data through the applications' programming interfaces (APIs) provided by major search engines such as Yahoo! and Google (Mayr & Tosques, 2006). The obtained data are edited and are developed into a directional network matrix for further analysis.

## Results

Overall, 509 INGOs were identified. These INGOs focused on environmental protection; they have offices or memberships in at least two countries and they are not founded by any government. These INGOs have headquarters in 86 different countries and regions, which suggests that environmental INGOs have representations and influences in a large part of the world. People from many nations were involved in founding and organizing environmental INGOs, offering access to broad publics, which is valuable for diplomatic purposes.

Among these 509 INGOs, the majority originate from Western countries such as the United States (21.0%), United Kingdom (9.6%), France (7.3%) and Belgium (6.3%). A smaller number of organizations are located in developing countries. If the number of connections with NGOs reflects a country's soft power, then this finding indicates that Western countries tend to have more soft power than developing countries. Among these INGOs, 32.0% are networks of smaller NGOs operating in different countries. A significant number of those organizations (46.0%) include individual-based member-ships and recruit individual members from all over the world. On average, these INGOs attract members from about 29 countries. The majority (60%) draw members from about 20 countries, and a few organizations (3.8%) draw members from more than 100 countries. It is clear that some of these INGOs can reach a global public.

In terms of the languages used by INGOs, overwhelmingly, English is the dominant language. Among these INGOs, 69.9% use English as the sole working language and 23.5% use English in combination with other languages. Besides English, French is the second (11.6%) and Spanish is the third most used language (7.5%). This finding may be due to the fact that most of these environmental INGOs operate at the international level and, to communicate with a globally diverse audience, English may be the ideal language. Overall, these INGOs seem to have achieved global influence. Most of the INGOs have memberships in multiple nations, and therefore have existing networks with local publics. The following two sections discuss how INGOs have used new media and the structural features of INGOs' virtual networks.

## INGO Websites' Global Reach

For RQ1, it was found that the majority of these INGOs have functioning organizational websites (89.8%), and only 10.2% either have bad links or do not have organizational websites. These sites help INGOs to communicate with a globally diverse public. According to the data mining results, many of these sites attract visitors from more than one country (46.4%), and some websites even attract visitors from more than 10 countries (25.8%). For example, the website of Greenpeace attracts visitors from 33 countries. On average, these websites attract about .004 (SD = .018) of global Internet us-ers. Given the huge population of global Internet users (about 2.7 billion) (World Bank, 2011), these websites have a large number of visitors. On average, visitors spend 2 minutes and 35 seconds (SD = 137.8 seconds) on these websites. Interestingly, the study found that visitors from the United States are most likely to visit an INGO's website. In comparison to websites, fewer INGOs have adopted social media tools such as Facebook, Twitter, LinkedIn, Myspace and YouTube (54.8%). For those using social media, Facebook is the most popular choice (37.5%). Only 9% have adopted more than one type of social media and a few (5.6%) have adopted more than five types.

## Structural Features of INGOs' Global Virtual Network

RQ2 directs attention to structural features of INGOs' networks. For this study, 455 unique websites were found. The analysis identified a basically connected virtual network. This network indicated that there are cooperative relationships among those INGOs outside of their traditional headquarters-subunit structure. Such a transnational network helps connect different locales into a global sphere (See Figure 17.1).

The density of a binary network is the proportion of all possible ties that are present (Wasserman & Faust, 1994). About 1% of all the possible ties are present in this network. In comparison to the mean, the standard deviation is large, suggesting that some areas within the network are denser than others. As can be observed from Figure 17.1, a group of actors positioned in the center are well connected and are surrounded by a group of less well-connected actors. Far away from the center, there are some isolated actors that are not connected with any others.

In terms of hyperlinks, geodesic distance means the smallest number of websites one visitor needs to pass through should the visitor wish to navigate from website A to website B. In this network, to reach from one random site to another, a visitor may pass through an average of three websites. Given the fact that in society, it has been suggested that six degrees of separation was rather common (Granovetter, 1973), it can be argued that this geodesic distance is relatively short and it is relatively easy for a visitor to navigate from one INGO site to another.

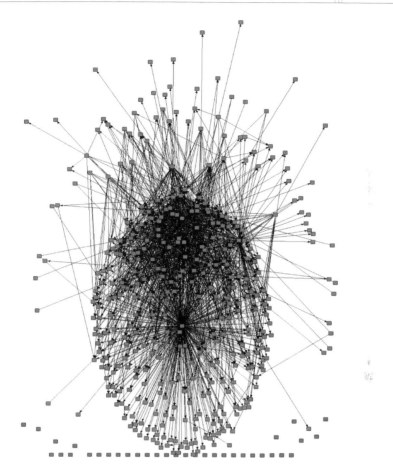

*Figure 17.1.* The Overall Network Structure of Environmental INGOs.

Reciprocity indicates the percentage of all possible ties as parts of a reciprocal structure (Bae & Choi, 2000). Reciprocity is an important measure for the study of civil society. According to Putnam (1993), "social trust in complex modern settings can arise from two related sources—norms of reciprocity and networks of civic engagement" (p. 171). In a network with a high level of heterogeneity (such as the global civil society), reciprocity facilitates long-term relationship building (Wasserman & Faust, 1994). For this network, 4.45% of ties were reciprocated. Furthermore, 9% of the actors are involved in reciprocal relationships. Scholars have suggested that networks demonstrate an equilibrium tendency toward dyadic relationships to be either null (no ties exist) or reciprocated and that asymmetric ties may be unstable (Hanneman

& Riddle, 2011). For a network to maintain a high level asymmetry, of either there exists a hierarchy in the network to prevent the development of reciprocal relationships, or more changes will emerge from the network. This study found that the majority of INGOs do not have reciprocal ties. This finding suggests that this network is neither a stable nor an equal network. Based on this finding, it can be argued that either there exists a hierarchical structure in this network, or this is an evolving network.

In large networks, it is often observed that groups of actors are clustered into tight neighborhoods. These sub-groups are loosely connected by only a few ties (Milgram, 1967). For this network, when an actor is embedded in a cluster, it is often a highly dense cluster with 79.3% of all possible ties present. The weighted overall clustering coefficient was 0.118, which means there are some well-connected clusters existing in this network but many actors are not part of such clusters. A close examination suggested that a small number of sites are embedded in highly dense clusters and many sites are not embedded in any clusters.

In sum, this study found a relatively large network with a relatively low density, which suggests the possibility for INGOs to further develop hyperlink relationships. Further, the density is not evenly distributed. A group of INGOs are extremely well-connected; the majority are connected; and some actors are isolated. Findings revealed that the average distance between two random actors is relatively small. In combination, these measures suggest that a considerable number of INGOs engage in developing reciprocal relationships that lead to some high density clusters. The existence of high density clusters did not contribute to a higher overall density, which suggests that many tie-building actions happen within clusters rather than among clusters.

## Discussion

Engaging with broader foreign publics requires a totally different mindset of public diplomacy than targeting political elites. The traditional, state-centered approach is limited in terms of credibility, expertise and diversity of networks in foreign countries. In addition, international relationships, a realm previously occupied by diplomats is increasingly participated in by NGOs (especially INGOs), private enterprises, activists, academics and other groups. This study suggests that INGOs and new media may provide new opportunities for public diplomacy. Specifically, for diplomatic considerations, INGOs and their new media based networks could offer global reach, serve as credible sources and provide access to diverse networks around the globe. NGOs have value as messengers of mediated public diplomacy campaigns; add credibility to national branding campaigns; and facilitate nations' long-termed relationship building with foreign publics. Each of the aforementioned values is discussed in the following sections.

## INGOs' Capacity to Reach Global Publics

The analysis illustrates that INGOs have the capacity to reach a broad global public both online and offline. The study found that INGOs often have membership in multiple countries. Many of these members have different social backgrounds. INGOs' members are brought together by shared mission or common interests and they could potentially help INGOs reach the local communities. In the cyberspace, findings also suggest that the Internet provides a useful portal to reach diverse publics living in different countries. As argued by Nye (2004), the soft power of a state is created through activities of multiple actors and organizations. The ability to reach and involve a much broader group of people than political elites may qualify as an effective public diplomatic effort. Therefore, INGOs' capacity to disseminate information and maintain relationships with a diverse global public can be valuable assets for public diplomatic purposes.

When implementing public diplomatic campaigns, if the goal is to reach and engage a broad public that is concerned with specific issues, diplomats should consider involving INGOs that share the public's concerns. Such an approach may allow diplomats to effectively disseminate information through INGOs' networks.

## INGOs' Websites as Credible Information Sources

New media are less constrained by geographic boundaries and therefore offer new opportunities for public diplomatic efforts. New media allow large publics around the world to be informed of important issues in other countries. In such an environment, states face the challenge to make themselves attractive and relevant. Therefore, the identification of an information source that global publics consider valuable and credible is crucial for public diplomatic purposes.

This study found that millions of visitors have visited INGOs' websites or have become fans of INGOs' social media. When visitors visited those sites, they spent time on consuming the content. It is likely visitors browse through INGOs' websites to seek relevant information because of INGOs' perceived specialty and authority. Since no government or organization can force so many people from different countries to visit INGOs' websites and spend time consuming the content, it is possible that INGOs are perceived as credible sources of information by many around the world. The perceived high credibility of INGOs' websites is consistent with findings of other studies (Yang & Taylor, 2010). For diplomatic purposes, it is important that messages are delivered by credible messengers. When advocating for specific purposes, diplomats can involve respected INGOs with relevant specialty.

## INGOs' Transnational Network

One of the effects of globalization and the communication revolution is the intensification of global networks that transcend national boundaries and the rise of a more interconnected civil society. This study identifies a set of INGOs' network structural features. First, surrounding the commonly shared mission, environmental protection, a virtual network of INGOs was formed at the global level. INGOs in this network are relatively close to each other and their connections transcend geographic boundaries and cultural differences. These INGOs actively build relationships with strategic allies that share their passion and missions. The fundamental importance of mission is unique to activists' strategic relationship building. For corporations that operate following a capitalist logic, their collaborations are often based on resource dependency or calculations of interests. When establishing collaborative relationship with INGOs, diplomats should offer INGOs opportunities that serve their missions.

Second, this study found that some INGOs are engaged in building reciprocal ties, and they are members of highly dense clusters. This network structure revealed a pattern of relationships that exists in the global civil sphere. In other words, INGOs tend to focus on in-group relationship building rather than out-group relationship building. A potential effect of such a relationship structure is that, over time, INGOs may be increasingly limited by their close allies. Their close allies may continue to offer them support and resources. However, they may lose contact with broader international communities and therefore become isolated circles.

When collaborating with INGOs, diplomats should be aware of this relationship pattern. Diplomats should selectively involve INGOs whose missions are consistent with the goals of a public diplomatic campaign, because relevant actors are more likely to offer diplomats connections to a relevant network. Further, when the goal of a campaign is to reach diverse publics, diplomats should identify and collaborate with INGOs that could reach different networks, and avoid only working with INGOs belonging to the same cluster. By understanding INGOs' network structural features, and involving civil partners strategically, diplomats can enjoy the tight connection and support of INGOs' clusters and, at the same time, avoid limitations inherited in NGOs' tendency to focus on in-group relationships.

## Existing Issues

In addition to the aforementioned NGOs' diplomatic values, the analysis did reveal several issues. First, the finding suggests a Western dominance in the global civil society. The majority of INGOs included in this study have Western roots. On one hand, this finding suggests that developing countries may have overlooked the value of INGOs in diplomatic efforts and failed to establish or sponsor NGOs to advocate for their values and cultures. Roberts and Parks (2007) found that although the INGO sector has been explored over the past a few decades, the trend has not been adopted in some countries. Beckfield (2003) found that while countries are more equal with regard to their participation in international governmental organizations (IGOs), there is a great deal of inequality among countries in terms of their ties to INGOs. The inequality in terms of connection with INGOs may limit the sophistication level of developing countries' diplomatic strategies, and further limit their development of soft power. On the other hand, the obvious Western dominance may harm INGOs' legitimacy in the long run. As noted by Dutta-Bergman (2005), the level of legitimacy for Western INGOs to represent interests of the Global South is questionable. When implementing public diplomacy strategies, diplomats from Western countries should consider involving NGOs from the Global South.

The dominance of English as the official language also presents problems because, in many countries, the majority of the population does not speak English. The current situation may become a barrier for INGOs to reach more people in countries where English is not the local residents' native language. When collaborating with INGOs, diplomats should be aware of this limitation. It is advisable to incorporate multiple languages in public diplomatic campaigns.

## Conclusion

As international relations increasingly operate, not at a single interstate level but through complex, multi-level and interdependent networks, governments and their diplomats must learn to operate in these networks. Ham (2002) contends there is a profound shift from the modern world of geopolitics and hard power towards a postmodern world of images and soft power. This study maintains the importance of INGOs and new media and accords them significant roles and functions in public diplomacy. Findings suggest that the engagement of agents from the broader civil society, reinforced by the effective use of new media, may help nation states better achieve their public diplomacy goals. The involvement of INGOs in public diplomatic campaigns allows nations to go beyond image building, but to shape ideas and values and build broader relationships with foreign publics.

## Bibliography

Albritton, R. B., & Manheim, J. B. (1985). Public relations efforts for the Third World: Images in the news. *Journal of Communication, 35*(1), 43–59.

Alexander, J. C. (2006). *The civil sphere*. Oxford: Oxford University Press.

Arquilla, J. & Ronfeldt, D. (1999).*The emergence of Noopolitik: Toward an American information strategy*. Los Angeles: Rand.

Ayres, J. M. (2003). Global governance and civil society collective action. *International Journal of Political Economy, 33*(4), 84–100.

Bae, S., & Choi, J. H. (2000). Cyberlinks between human rights NGOs: A network analysis. Paper presented to the 58th annual national meeting of the Midwest Political Science Association, Chicago.

Barnett, G. A., & Sung, E. (2005). Culture and the structure of the international hyperlink network. *Journal of Computer-Mediated Communication, 11*(1). Retrieved September 3, 2010, from http://jcmc.indiana.edu/vol11/issue1/barnett.html

Batora, J. (2005). *Public diplomacy in small and medium-sized states: Norway and Canada*. Netherlands: University of Warwick.

Beckfield, J. (2003). Inequality in the world polity: The structure of international organization. *American Sociological Review, 68,* 401–424.

Boli, J., & Thomas, G. M. (1997). World culture in the world polity: A century of international non-governmental organization. *American Sociological Review, 62,* 171–190.

Brookings Institution. (2004). *The need to communicate: How to improve U.S. public diplomacy with the Islamic world*. Washington, DC: The Saban Center for Middle East Policy at the Brookings Institution.

Burt, R. S. (1992). *Structural holes: The social structure of competition*. Cambridge, MA: Harvard University Press.

Castells, M. (2004). *Informationalism, networks, and the network society: A theoretical blueprint*. Northampton, MA: Edward Elgar.

———. (2008). The new public sphere: Global civil society, communication networks, and global governance. *The ANNALS of the American Academy of Political and Social Science, 616,* 78–93.

———. (2009). *Communication Power*. New York: Oxford University Press.

Conway, M. (2005). Terrorist websites: Their content, functioning and effectiveness. In P. Seib (Ed.), *Media and conflict in the twenty-first century* (pp. 185–215). New York.

Cozier, Z. R., & Witmer, D. F. (2001).The development of a structuration analysis of new publics in an electronic environment.In R. L. Heath (Ed.), *Handbook of public relations* (pp. 615–623). Thousand Oaks, CA: Sage.

DeMars, W. E. (2005). *NGOs and transnational networks: Wild cards in world politics*. London: Pluto Press.

Dizard, W. P. (2004). *Inventing public diplomacy: The story of the U.S. Information Agency*. Boulder, CO: Lynne Rienner Publishers.

Dutta-Bergman, M. J. (2005). Civil society and public relations: Not so civil after all. *Journal of Public Relations Research, 17*(3), 267–289.

Foreign Policy Centre. (2002). *Public diplomacy*. London: The Foreign Policy Centre.

Gilboa, E. (2000). Mass communication and diplomacy.*Communication Theory, 10*, 290–294.

———. (2004). Diplomacy in the media age: Three models of uses and effects. In C. Jonsson & R. Langhorne (Eds.), *Diplomacy*, Vol. III (pp. 96–119). London.

———. (2008). Searching for a theory of public diplomacy. *The ANNALS of the American Academy of Political and Social Science, 616*, 55–77.

Golan, G. J. (2013). Introduction: An integrated approach to public diplomacy. *American Behavioral Scientist, 20*(10), 1–5. DOI: 10.1177/0002764213487711

Granovetter, M. S. (1973). The strength of weak ties. *American Journal of Sociology, 78*(6), 1360–1380.

Grunig, J. E. (1993). Public relations and international affairs. *Journal of International Affairs, 47*, 137–162.

Ham, P. V. (2002). Branding territory: Inside the wonderful worlds of PR and IR theory. *Millennium, 31*(2): 249–269.

Hanneman, R. A., & Riddle, M. (2011). Concepts and measures for basic network analysis. In J. Scott, & P. J. Carrington (Eds.), *The Sage handbook of social network analysis* (pp. 340–369). Thousand Oaks, CA: Sage Publications.

Himelboim, I., Chang, T. K., & McCreery, S. (2010). International network of foreign news coverage: Old global hierarchies in a new online world. *Journalism & Mass Communication Quarterly, 87*(2), 297–314.

Himelboim, I., McCreery, S., & Smith, M. (2013). Birds of a feather tweet together: Integrating network and content analyses to examine cross-ideology exposure on Twitter. *Journal of Computer-Mediated Communication, 18*, 154–174.

Kaldor, M. (2005).The idea of global civil society. In G. Baker & D. Chandler (Eds.), *Global civil society: Contested futures* (pp. 103–112). New York: Routledge.

Leonard, M. (2002). Diplomacy by other means. *Foreign Policy, 132*, 48–56.

Mayr, P., & Tosques, F. (2006). Google Web APIs: An instrument for Webometric analyses? Accessed from http://arxiv.org/abs/cs/0601103

Milgram, S. (1967). The small world problem. *Psychology Today, 2*, 60–67.

Nye, J. S. (2004). *Soft power: The means to success in world politics*. New York: Public Affairs.

Park, H. W., & Thelwall, M. (2003). Hyperlink analyses of the World Wide Web: A review. *Journal of Computer Mediated Communication, 6*. Paper retrieved on August 12, 2011, from http://jcmc.indiana.edu/vol8/issue4/park.html

Putnam, R. (1993). *Making democracy work*. Princeton: Princeton University Press.

Roberts, J. T., & Parks, B. C. (2007). *A climate of injustice: Global inequality, North-South politics, and climate policy*. Cambridge, MA: MIT Press.

Shumate, M., & Dewitt, L. (2008). The north/south divide in NGO hyperlink networks. *Journal of Computer Mediated Communication, 13*, 405–428.

Shumate, M., & Lipp, J. (2008). Connective collective action online: An examination of the hyperlink network structure of an NGO issue network. *Journal of Computer Mediated Communication, 14*, 178–201.

Shumate, M., & O' Connor, A. (2010). Corporate reporting of cross-sector alliances: The portfolio of NGO partners communicated on corporate websites. *Communication Monographs, 77*(2), 207–230.

Signitzer, B. H. & Coombs, T. (1992). Public relations and public diplomacy: Conceptual convergence. *Public Relations Review, 18*(2), 137–147.

Sriramesh, K. & Verčič, D. (2009). *The global public relations handbook: Theory, research, and practice* (2nd Ed.). New York: Routledge.

Taylor, M., & Doerfel, M. L. (2003). Building inter-organizational relationships that build nations. *Human Communication Research, 29* (2), 153–181.

Taylor, M., & Kent, M. L. (2000). Media transitions in Bosnia: From propagandist past to uncertain future. *Gazette, 62*, 355–378.

Thelwall, M. (2009) *Introduction to Webometrics: Quantitative Web Research for the Social Sciences*. San Rafael, CA: Morgan & Claypool Publishers.

Tuch, H. N. (1990). *Communicating with the world: U.S. public diplomacy overseas*. New York: St. Martin's Press.

Union of International Associations (2011). *Yearbook of international organizations*. Accessed online athttp://www.uia.be/login

Vickers, R. (2004). The new public diplomacy: Britain and Canada compared. *British Journal of Politics and International Relations, 6*, 151–168.

Wang, J. (2006). Managing national reputation and international relations in the global era: Pubic diplomacy revisited. Public Relations Review, 32, 91–96.

Wasserman, S., & Faust, K. (1994) *Social network analysis: Methods and applications*. New York: Cambridge University Press.

World Bank. (2011). *World development indicators* (CD-ROM). Washington, DC: World Bank.

Yang, A. (2012). When transnational civil network meets local context: An exploratory hyperlink network analysis of Northern/ Southern NGOs' virtual network in China. *Journal of International & Intercultural Communication, 5*(3), 40–60.

Yang, A., Klyueva, A., & Taylor, M. (2012). A relational approach to public diplomacy in a multipolar world: Building public relations theory by analyzing the U.S.-Russia-China relationship. *Public Relations Review, 38*(5), 652–664.

Yang, A., & Taylor, M. (2010). Relationship-building by Chinese ENGOs' websites: Education, not activation. *Public Relations Review, 36* (4), 342–351.

# 18. Live Tweeting at Work: The Use of Social Media in Public Diplomacy

Juyan Zhang & Shahira Fahmy

The use of social media for the purpose of public diplomacy has increasingly drawn the attention of U.S. public diplomacy professionals, observers, and political analysts. In fact, as one of the post-Sept. 11 public diplomacy initiatives series, the U.S. government launched its Public Diplomacy 2.0 program in 2009 initially aimed to engage directly with citizens in the Middle East (Khatib, Dutton, & Thelwall, 2011). The program attempted to integrate social networking, blogging and information aggregating tools to nurture individual expression and the competition of ideas in the world (Glassman, 2008), which could be considered as a sign of the emergence of integrated public diplomacy (IPD) (Golan, 2013). Currently the White House has its Facebook account (http://www.facebook. com/WhiteHouse) and Twitter account (http://twitter.com/WhiteHouse). In 2009, the U.S. Department of State also announced a pilot program that would award up to $5 million in grants to expand the use of social networking technologies in the Middle East, with the goal of increasing citizen engagement and civic participation (U.S. Department of State, 2009). U.S. embassies also started using Twitter feeds, Facebook Groups, and blogs (Fouts, 2009).

In recent years social media has been increasingly used in other parts of the world, as well. Twitter helped mobilize protesters in the mass protests in Moldova in 2009 (Cohen, 2009). In Iran, it was the essential tool for the opposition protests to appeal to the support of the world public opinion in 2009 by helping dissidents plan rallies and spread first-person accounts of the protest movement. In one speech, the U.S. Secretary of State Hillary Clinton credited social media's role in Iran's case by stating that "Their protestors also used websites to organize. A video taken by cell phone showed a young woman named Neda killed by a member of the paramilitary forces, and within hours, that video was being watched by people everywhere." (Clinton, 2011) Further, about 100,000 people on Facebook befriended the opposition leader Mir Hussein Mousavi (Last, 2009). In Israel, a blog reported that the Israeli Foreign Ministry announced its plans to embrace social media such as Twitter and Facebook. The Israeli government explained it would focus less on Palestinian issues and more on the Iranian threat (Israel Politik, 2009). In March 7, 2012, Israeli President Shimon Peres visited Facebook Inc.'s headquarters in Silicon Valley and praised Facebook as a vehicle for social change. He reportedly told a Facebook engineer, "What you are doing is convincing people they don't have reason to hate" (Guynn, 2012).

Overall, the U.S. government and foreign policy analysts have shown great interest and enthusiasm in exploring how to increase the efficiency of using social media for more effective public diplomacy. However, scholarly studies on the issue have been rare. Such a scholarly gap is inconsistent with the rapid adoption and use of this powerful media genre. Thus, the adoption and impact of social media, the perceptions, attitudes and behaviors of their users, and the way to integrate these technologies into the existing practice of public diplomacy, among other issues, are all in need of systematic analysis. This study thus represents an attempt to fill this gap by exploring factors affecting the use of social media by public diplomacy specialists.

Based on a survey of foreign embassies in the United States, this study specifically examined foreign public diplomacy specialists' adoption of social media for public diplomacy purposes. It explored whether the following—effort and performance expectancy, social influence and attitudes, facilitating conditions, and perceived credibility—might have influenced the adoption of social media in public diplomacy practice. Further, it examined whether gender, age, or level of national income have a moderating effect on the adoption of these media technologies. We hope that, with an analytic charting of the behaviors in the use of social media by public diplomacy specialists, this study could guide future research on the effects of using social media in public diplomacy.

## Literature Review

### Social Media and Public Relations

Social media is a group of Internet-based applications that allow the creation and exchange of User Generated Content (UGC) (Kaplan & Haenlein,

2010). These applications present tremendous opportunities for networking, collaborating, sharing best practices, communicating, and connecting to a nearly unlimited pool of people with similar needs and desires (Patton, 2009). The new genre of media is based on Web 2.0, a term used to describe a new way in which software developers and end-users use the World Wide Web as a platform where content and applications are continuously modified by all users in a participatory and collaborative fashion (Kaplan & Haenlein, 2010).

Large corporations are increasingly adopting social media to communicate both internally and externally. However, there are reservations about the risks these activities might represent. For example, nearly half the communicators who responded to a survey felt that employees discussing their organization online posed a significant risk to the company's reputation (Hathi, 2009). Eyrich, Padman, and Sweetser (2008) surveyed the adoption of social media by U.S. public relations practitioners. They found that practitioners adopted the more established and institutional tools, but they were slower to integrate the more technologically complicated tools that cater to a niche audience.

Not surprisingly then, the literature suggests organizations with defined public relations departments are more likely to adopt social media. Further, public relations practitioners are more likely to use social media tools particularly if they perceive them as credible. Steyn, Salehi-Sangari, Pitt, Parent and Berthon (2010) observed that the Social Media Release (SMR) is emerging as a potentially powerful public relations tool in the world of social networking, specifically when targeted at influential bloggers. Further, in the nonprofit sector, Curtis and colleagues (2009) found that social media are becoming beneficial communication tools for public relations practitioners in the nonprofit sector.

## Social Media and Public Diplomacy

In 2006, then Secretary of State Condoleezza Rice declared her intention to set up "virtual posts," where people could visit a website and chat online with U.S. diplomats (Stockman, 2006). The first State Department blog entry was posted in 2007. Then the State Department officially launched its own blog, "Dipnote," on public diplomacy. In 2007, the U.S. government launched its public diplomacy portal America.gov, which is a platform for a whole host of interactive media—webcasts, blogs, videos, YouTube, Twitter, Facebook, and even Second Life (a 3-D virtual world where users can socialize with free voice and text chat). More recently, one of the State Department's latest new media ventures is Co.Nx, a Web conferencing program that connects U.S. experts in a variety of fields with foreign audiences as well as U.S. embassies. More recently the U.S. Department of State's Bureau of Educational and Cultural Affairs launched its social media platform, http://connect.state.gov/.

Most discussions on use of social media in public diplomacy are found in policy analysis, reports, and blogs by public diplomacy practitioners. For example, public diplomacy expert Dale (2010) notes there are limited data to quantify and analyze the U.S. government's new media effectiveness and impact. She argues that, without a national communications strategy and in the absence of a capacity to measure the impact of various communications platforms, the new media's effectiveness for public diplomacy will remain limited. Other analysts are more optimistic, however. Matt C. Armstrong (2009) explains social media has the capacity to break through geographical, cultural and even linguistic barriers, democratizing the access to, and distribution of information. In a blog post at the Center of Public Diplomacy (CPD) at the University of Southern California (USC), Abeer Al-Najjar (2009) notes that social media are placing more power in the hands of citizens; and therefore governments should take a more pro-active approach in conducting their public diplomacy campaigns and efforts.

Scholars have shown increasing interest in use of social media in diplomacy and public diplomacy. Ciolek (2010) observed that the U.S. Embassy in Jakarta, Indonesia, has effectively integrated Facebook into its public diplomacy efforts. She argued that social media tools will likely remain part of U.S. public diplomacy efforts for the foreseeable future, and its contribution to public diplomacy occurs when it creates potential for continued engagement and dialogue. Comor and Bean (2012) argued that the Obama administration's dominant concept in public diplomacy is "engagement," which essentially aims to leverage social media and related technologies to persuade skeptical audiences to empathize with American policies. Potter (2008) explains that governments need to be very selective about their online representation, however. Hayden (2011) suggests that the confluence of President Obama's personal communication efforts and policy strategy and the global context of ubiquitous social media technologies indicate a productive moment for U.S. public diplomacy planners and policy advocates to capitalize on the president's popularity through a reinvigorated strategy of engagement. Researchers have observed that new media, including social media tools such as Facebook and Twitter, took center stage in broadcasting the protests in North Africa and the Middle East in 2011 (Leight, Walton, Ananian, Cruz-enriquez & Jarwa-harlal, 2011).

## Public Diplomacy, Credibility and Internet

The practice of public diplomacy must attach great importance to building and maintaining credibility (Gass & Seiter, 2009). In fact, the failure of public diplomacy is often equated with a loss of credibility (Goodall, Trethewey & McDonald, 2006), which was articulated by the former USIA director Edward R. Murrow, "To be persuasive, we must be believable; to be believable, we must be credible; to be credible, we must be truthful." When unbelievable messages are used in public diplomacy, they only raise the adversary's morale (Gass & Seiter, 2009). Smart public diplomacy requires an understanding of the roles of credibility, self-criticism, and civil society in generating soft power (Nye, 2008). Credibility of public diplomacy has many dimensions, including primary dimensions such as expertise of source, trustworthiness, goodwill, and numerous secondary dimensions such as composure and dynamism of the source (Pratkanis, 2009).

With regard to credibility and social media, past studies have shown mixed results. Early studies indicated that the Web information was perceived less credible than traditional news media because the internet is rife with rumors and misinformation (Kiousis, 2001), while other studies showed that users of social media, such as blogs, rated blogs as more credible than traditional sources (Johnson & Kaye, 2004). In this study, we examine whether perceived credibility is a factor motivating public diplomacy specialists to use social media. For this purpose, we applied the key constructs outlined by the Unified Theory of Acceptance & Use of Technology (UTAUT).

## Unified Theory of Acceptance and Use of Technology (UTAUT)

This research adapts Venkatesh, Morris, Davis and Davis (2003) Unified Theory of Acceptance and Use of Technology (UTAUT) model to examine foreign nations' adoption of social media for public diplomacy purposes. The model incorporates elements of previous major theories that predict user intentions to use an information system and subsequent usage behavior.[1] It explains as much as 70 percent of the variance in intention to use technology and, thus, outperforms the previous models presented in the literature (Venkatesh et al., 2003).

This model theorizes that four constructs play a significant role as direct determinants of user acceptance and usage behavior: 1) performance expectancy, 2) effort expectancy, 3) social influence, and 4) facilitating conditions. According to Venkatesh and colleagues (2003), *performance expectancy* is the degree to which an individual believes that using the system will help him or her to attain gains in job performance. *Effort expectancy* is defined as the degree of ease associated with use of the system. *Social influence* refers to the degree to which an individual perceives that others believe he or she should use the new system. *Facilitating condition* is the degree to which an individual believes that an organizational and technical infrastructure exists to support the use of the system (pp. 450–52). Moreover, gender, age, experience, and voluntary of use were found to impact the four key constructs on usage intention and behavior (Venkatesh et al., 2003, p. 453). The present study added one more variable: *perceived credibility*. The goal is to explore an additional factor affecting user acceptance of social media (See Yeow & Loo, 2009), which is defined as a person's psychological state with regard to his or her voluntary use and intention to use a technology (Dillon & Morris, 1996).

Based on above, in this research we intended to find out what types of social media are mostly used by public diplomacy practitioners. We also hope to find out whether gender, age, and level of country development will be significant moderators for use of social media in public diplomacy. Finally, we also want to know if performance expectancy, effort expectancy, social influence, facilitating conditions and perceived credibility have positive influence on use of social media in public diplomacy.

## Method

### Defining Social Media

According to the Organization for Economic Co-operation and Development (OECD, 2007), social media means user-generated content that is produced by users to be published either on a publicly accessible website or on a social networking site that is accessible to a selected group of people. The content needs to show a certain amount of creative effort and to have been created outside of professional routines and practices. Social media include a wide range of tools: blogs, intranets, podcasts, video sharing (e.g., YouTube), photo sharing (e.g., Shutterbug, Flickr), social networks, wikis (e.g., Wikipedia), gaming, virtual worlds (i.e., Second Life), micro-blogging/presence applications (e.g., Twitter, Pownce, Plurk), text messaging, videoconferencing, PDAs, instant message chat, social event/calendar systems (e.g., Upcoming, Eventful), social bookmarking (e.g., Delicious), news aggregation/RSS, and e-mail ( See Eyrich et al., 2008). For the purpose of this research, we narrowed down the definition of social media by eliminating email.

## The Survey Instrument

The data come from a hybrid survey combining online and telephone survey conducted on June 26, 2010 through Nov. 15, 2010 with foreign diplomats in Washington, D.C. The questionnaire was adapted from one used by Curtis et al. (2009). Their questionnaire examined the adoption of social media by U.S. non-profit organizations. We revised their instrument to better adapt it to the international context and the purpose of this study. For example, we changed "your public relations department" into "your embassy." We also added questions regarding the (GNI) and the level of country development to measure the impact of national development on use of social media in public diplomacy.

## Data Collection

To compile a list of embassies and consulates present in the United States, we consulted the U.S. Department of State (2009)[2] and identified 194 independent states. The list included contact information for most of the foreign embassies in the United States. We excluded countries that do not have diplomatic missions in the United States and a list of 178 countries was compiled. Personalized e-mails were then sent to cultural and media attachés of the diplomatic missions and directing them to a web-based questionnaire. The online questionnaire was posted at www.surveymonkey.com. Participation was voluntary and all of the responses remained anonymous. Four weeks later, a personalized letters was sent to non-respondents requesting their participation. Finally, we made phone calls two months later to encourage more participation if the parties had not responded to earlier call. A total of 83 respondents completed the survey by the second week of November, with a response rate of 46.6%.

## Measures

**Use of social media.** The main dependent variable for this study was the actual use of social media. Many researchers (e.g. Compeau & Higgins, 1995; Venkatesh & Davis, 2000) have used intention to use or actual usage as a dependent variable. We asked respondents to check 17 types of social media that their organizations have used. The list of social media types was adapted from Curtins and colleagues' study (2009) instead of Eyrich et al.'s (2008) list because the former is more up-to-date. It included blogs, events (Upcoming.org), instant messaging, internet hosted video games (World of Warcraft, etc.), intranets, news aggregation (Digg, Reddit, Stumbleupon), PDA, photo sharing (Flickr, Zoomer), podcast, presence applications (Twitter), Second Life (or another virtual world), social bookmarking (del.icio.us), social networks (Myspace, Facebook, etc.), text messaging, videoconferencing, video sharing (YouTube, Vimeo, etc.), Wiki. Data on use of the social media were then summed to form the dependent variable *Use of Social Media*.

*Performance expectancy.* One of the main independent variables for this study was the degree to which an individual believes that using the system will help him or her attain gains in job performance. The index included these items: "My organization would find social media useful"; "Using social media enables my organization to accomplish tasks more quickly"; "Using social media increases my organization's productivity;" and "If my organization uses social media, it will increase my chances of getting a raise." Possible responses ranged from "strongly agree" to "strongly disagree". The four variables were then summed to form a *Performance Expectancy* index.

*Effort expectancy.* The second independent variable is defined as the degree of ease associated with the use of a system. The index included the following items: "It would be easy for my organization to become skillful at using social media"; "My organization would find social media easy to use"; and "Learning to operate social media is easy for my organization." Possible response categories again ranged from "strongly agree" to "strongly disagree." The three variables were then summed to form an *Effort Expectancy* index.

*Social influence and attitudes.* The third independent variable for this study referred to the degree to which an individual perceives that others believe he or she should use the new system. The index included the following items: "Using social media is a good idea"; "Social media make work more interesting"; "Working with social media is fun"; "My organization likes working with social media"; "People who influence my unit/department behavior think that we should use social media"; "People who are important to my unit/department think that we should use social media"; "The senior management of this business has been helpful in the use of social media"; and "In general, my organization has supported the use of social media". Possible response categories again ranged from "strongly agree" to "strongly disagree". The eight variables were then summed to form a *Social Influence and Attitudes* index.

*Facilitating conditions.* The fourth independent variable for this study referred to the degree to which an individual believes that an organizational and technical infrastructure exists to support the use of the system. The index included the following items: "My organization has the resources necessary to use social media"; "My organization has the knowledge necessary to use social media"; "Social media are not compatible with other technologies my organization uses"; "A specific person (or group) is available for assistance with social media difficulties"; "My organization could complete a job or task using social media if there was no one around to tell us what to do as we go"; "My organization could complete a job or task using social media if we could call someone for help if we got stuck"; "My organization could complete a job or task using social media if we had a lot of time to complete the job"; and "My organization could complete a job or task using social media if we had just online help for assistance." Response categories also ranged from "strongly agree" to "strongly disagree." The eight variables were then summed to form a *Facilitating Conditions* index.

*Perceived credibility.* The fifth independent variable that referred to perceptions of credibility of social media, used the same response categories as mentioned above. The index included the following six variables: "believability," "fairness," "accuracy," "depth," "trustworthiness," and "expertise."

*Demographic variables.* A set of background questions used for descriptive and comparison purposes was used. This study specifically examined associations between the adoption of social media and level of country development, age and gender. Respondents were asked to choose categories for their countries' GNI per capita based on the World Bank Atlas method. Response categories included: low income (US$975 or less); lower middle income (US$976–$3,855); upper middle income (US$3,856–$11,905); and high income (US$11,906 or more). Respondents were also asked to report their age and gender.

*Data analysis.* The data were analyzed using descriptive statistics and other statistic tools such as multiple linear regression, t-test and ANOVA test.

## Results

### Respondents' Characteristics

A total of 83 usable responses from foreign diplomats were analyzed for this study. A majority of the respondents were women (58.3%) with an average age of 28 years. With regards to level of GNI per capita, almost half of the respondents (46.5%) represented low-income (US$975 or less) and lower-middle income (US$976–US$3855) nations. More than one-fourth (27.4%) represented high-income nations (US$11,906 or more) and 16.7 percent represented upper-middle income nations (US$3,856–US$11,905).

*Types of social media used.* The first research question asked about the types of social media used by public diplomacy practitioners. All of the respondents indicated they used different types of social media. Diplomats reported using an average of six different types of social media. As shown in Table 18.1, the most used were social networks (Myspace, Facebook, etc.) followed by video sharing sites, intranet, blogs, video conferencing, text messaging and Wiki. The least used were Second Life (or another virtual world) and social bookmarking.

*Perceived credibility and influences of UTAUT factors on use of social media.* The five indices were transformed into five predictors for multiple linear regression analysis, namely, effort expectancy, performance expectancy, social influence and attitudes, facilitating conditions, and perceived credibility. In the regression analysis, the five variables explain about 40 percent of the variance in using social media for public diplomacy. This means that effort expectancy, performance expectancy, social influence and attitudes, facilitating conditions and perceived credibility have significant influence upon intention to use social media.

*Perceived credibility and influence of country development, gender and age.* We are interested in finding out whether the level of GNI per capita, gender and age have moderating effects on the adoption of social media in the context of public diplomacy. Statistics show that gender has a moderating effect on three of the predictors, respectively: facilitating conditions, perceived credibility, and effort expectancy. Age on the other hand has a moderating effect on social influence and facilitating factors. Level of GNI has a moderating effect on social influence, perceived credibility, and effort expectancy.

Further, results showed that more women reported the use of social media than males, but on average, men used more types of social media than their female counterparts. Further, findings suggest that there is a significant difference between how men and women perceive credibility of social media. Men tend to perceive social media as more credible than women do. Thus the results showed that level of GNI per capita, gender, and age could influence the adoption of social media in public diplomacy.

*Table 18.1.* Percentage and types of social media used by foreign diplomats ( $N = 83$ ).

| Social Media | Percentage |
| --- | --- |
| Social Networks (Myspace, Facebook, etc.) | 78.6 |
| Intranet | 54.8 |
| Video Sharing (YouTube, Vimeo, etc.) | 63.1 |
| Blogs | 50 |
| Videoconferencing | 50 |
| Text Messaging | 33 |

| Social Media | Percentage |
|---|---|
| Wiki | 40.5 |
| Instant Messaging | 39.3 |
| Presence Applications (Twitter) | 38.1 |
| Photo sharing (Flickr, Zoomer) | 32.1 |
| Events (Upcoming events.org) | 31 |
| Podcast | 23.8 |
| PDA | 20.2 |
| News Aggregation (Digg, Reddit, Stumbleupon) | 11.9 |
| Internet Hosted Video Games (World of Warcraft, etc.) | 10.7 |
| Social Bookmarking (del.icio.us) | 8.3 |
| Second Life (or another virtual world) | 4.8 |

## *Discussion and Conclusion*

In this research we examined the factors that might influence the adoption of social media in public diplomacy practice by foreign diplomatic missions in the United States. Results of our study revealed some interesting characteristics regarding the use of social media by public diplomacy specialists. Social influence and attitudes and perceived credibility ranked highest in predicting the use of social media, suggesting that public diplomacy specialists attach great importance to the credibility of social media when they decide to use them. Also, pressure and expectation from society greatly affected their decisions to use social media. Effort expectancy, however, weighed least in predicting use of social media, suggesting that social media as a technology are not an intimidating factor to public diplomacy specialists. Our results further showed that gender, age and status of country development have moderating effects for use of social media in public diplomacy.

Gender, for example, has a moderating effect on three of the predictors: facilitating conditions, perceived credibility, and effort expectancy. Moreover, our study found that more women reported the use of social media than men, but on average, men used more different types of social media than their female counterparts. Further, men tended to perceive social media as more credible than women did. This might explain why men use more types of social media. The level of GNI per capita appeared to have moderating effects on social influence and attitudes, perceived credibility, and effort expectancy. This suggests that specialists from countries with different levels of development have different perceptions of credibility of social media, effort expectancy and social influence. Finally, age appeared to have a moderating effect on social influence and facilitating factors. However, compared to the moderating effects of gender and level of GNI, age appears to have the most limited moderating effects on adoption of social media. This is not surprising because most of the respondents were born during the 80s, and, thus, they all grew up at the same time during the dissemination, and the booming of the Internet and the birth of varying social media tools.

In terms of types of social media, public diplomacy practitioners in this study indicated they mostly used social networks (Myspace, Facebook, etc.) followed by video sharing sites, intranet, blogs, video conferencing, text messaging and Wiki. The least used were Second Life (or another virtual world) and social bookmarking. This is largely consistent with the ranking of top social networking sites in 2009, in which Facebook and Myspace, respectively, ranked number one and number two among 25 sites (Kazeniac, 2009). Twitter however ranked eighth, which is much lower than the ranking in the 2009 survey, in which Twitter ranked third (Kazeniac, 2009). This is interesting given that Twitter has reportedly played significant roles in the recent citizen upheavals in the Middle East and North Africa. This could be due to the relay-chat nature of Twitter that does not exceed 140 characters. Public diplomacy specialists seem to prefer the use of other social media tools that can disseminate longer messages.

As previous studies (e.g., Comor & Bean, 2012) indicated, use of social media in public diplomacy is the key characteristic of the "engagement" doctrine of the Obama administration's public diplomacy strategy. In fact, the concept of "engagement" represents the essence of the two-way symmetrical communication that was proposed by Grunig (2001) as the most ethical and most effective practice of public relations. Some marketing specialists summarized the characteristics of engagement marketing as the following: transparency, interactivity, immediacy, facilitation, engagement, co-creation, collaboration, experience and trust, all of which become possible in the social media era. In this sense, use of social media in public diplomacy is not merely application of a new communication tool. Instead, it could represent a paradigm shift in the practice of public diplomacy. In this process, some of the generic principles identified by the Excellence Theory to determine excellence in strategic communication practice, such as gender and level of development (Khamis & Toth, 2009), are still relevant and need to be addressed if they become a problem. In addition, perceived credibility as a prediction factor on adoption of social media indicates that in the social media era public diplomacy should be practiced in a candid, honest and truthful manner since as every individual social media user could become an investigative journalist and a critical participant in the sphere of public opinions. Effective public diplomacy in such a media environment has to embrace the core spirit of engagement, namely, collaboration, authentic partnerships, mutual respect, active, inclusive participation, power sharing and equity and mutual benefit (Tindana, Singh, Tracy, Upshur, Daar, Singer, Frohlich & Lavery, 2007).

## Notes

1. The previous theories include Theory of Reasoned Action, Technology Acceptance Model, Motivational Model, Theory of Planned Behavior, a Combined Theory of Planned Behavior/Technology Acceptance Model, Model of Personal Computer Utilization, Innovation Diffusion Theory, and Social Cognitive Theory.
2. In testing the applicability of the Excellence Study of public relations to developing the study of public diplomacy, Yun (2006) collected data from 113 embassies in Washington, D.C., through mail survey and interviews. In another study, Yun (2007) explored a new sampling strategy of using embassies as cultural enclaves for large-scale cross-national research in testing the generic status of individual excellence principles in the normative theory of global public relations. These studies showed that a survey of foreign embassies in Washington, D.C., to examine their public relations practice is a feasible and a realistic method.

## Bibliography

Al-Najjar, A. (2009). Kaust and social networking: The new face of Saudi Arabia. Retrieved on February 24, 2010 at: http://uscpublicdiplomacy.org/index.php/ newswire/cpdblog_detail/kaust_and_social_networking_the_new_face_of_saudi_arabia/.

Anonymous. (2010). White House preserves social media content. *Information Management Journal,* 44 (1), 7.

Armstrong, M. C. (2009). Social media as public diplomacy. Perspectives, 1(2). Retrieved on November 20, 2009 at http://www.layaline.tv/publications/Perspectives/ MattArmstrong.html.

Baron, R. M., & Kenny, D. A. (1986). The moderator-mediator variable distinction in social psychological research: Conceptual, strategic and statistical considerations. *Journal of Personality and Social Psychology,* 51, 1173–1182.

Ciolek, M. (2010). Understanding social media's contribution to public diplomacy: How Embassy Jakarta's Facebook Outreach Illuminates the Limitations and Potential for the State Department's Use of Social Media. *CPD Prize for Best Student Paper, CPD Research & Publications.* Retrieved on June 10, 2012 from http://uscpublicdiplomacy.org/index.php/research/paper_award_2010/

Clinton, H. (2011). Internet rights and wrongs: Choices and challenges in a networked world. U.S. Department of State, February 15. Retrieved on June 6, 2012 from: http://www.state.gov/secretary/rm/2011/02/156619.htm

Cohen, N. (2009). Twitter on the Barricades: Six lessons learned. *The New York Times*, June 20, 2009. Retrieved on February 18, 2010 from http://www.nytimes.com/2009/06/21/weekinreview/21cohenweb.html?ref=weekinreview

Comor, E., & Bean, H. (2012). Americas engagement delusion: Critiquing a public diplomacy consensus. *The International Communication Gazette, 74*(3), 203.

Compeau, D. R., & Higgins, C. A. (1995). Application of social cognitive theory to training for computer skills. *Information Systems Research*, 6(2), 118–143.

Curtis, L., Edwards, C., Fraser, K., Gudelsky, S., Holmquist, J., Thornton, K., Sweetser, K. (2009). Adoption of social media for public relations by nonprofit organizations. *Public Relations Review*, 36, 90–92.

Dale, H. (2010). Public diplomacy 2.0: Where the U.S. government meets "new media." *Home page of Heritage Foundation*. Retrieved on February 20, 2010. http://www.heritage.org/research/publicdiplomacy/bg2346.cfm

Department of State (2009). Independent states in the world. Retrieved on March 10, 2010 at: http://www.state.gov/s/inr/rls/4250.htm

Dillon, A. & Morris, M. (1996). User acceptance of information technology: Theories and models. *Annual Review of Information Science and Technology:* p. 3–32. Medford NJ: Information Today, Inc.

Eyrich, N., Padman, M. L., & Sweetser, K. D. (2008). PR practitioners' use of social media tools and communication technology. *Public Relations Review*, 34, 412–414.

Fouts, J. (2009). Social media, virtual worlds and public diplomacy. *World Politics Review*. Retrieved on February 24, 2010 at: http://www.worldpoliticsreview.com/article.aspx?id=4440

Gass, R., & Seiter, J. (2009). Credibility and public diplomacy. *Routledge handbook of public diplomacy*. Routledge, New York, 162.

Glassman, J. (2008). Public diplomacy 2.0. *Policy Innovations*. Retrieved on February 18, 2010 from http://www.policyinnovations.org/ideas/media/video/data/000094.

Golan, G. (2013). Introduction: An integrated approach to public diplomacy. *American Behavioral Scientist*, 57(9), 1251–1255.

Goodall, H. L., Trethewey, A., & McDonald, K. (2006). Strategic ambiguity, communication, and public diplomacy in an uncertain world: Principles and practices. Retrieved at: http://www.comops.org/article/116.pdf

Grunig, J. E. (2001). Two-way symmetrical public relations: Past, present, and future. In R. L. Heath (Ed.), *Handbook of public relations* (pp. 11–30). Thousand Oaks, CA: Sage.

Guynn, J. (2012). Israeli President Peres visits Facebook during Silicon Valley tour. Los Angeles Times, March 7. Retrieved at: http://articles.latimes.com/2012/mar/07/business/la-fi-facebook-peres-20120307

Hathi, S. (2007). Study reveals social media use. *Strategic Communication Management*, 11(3),.9.

Hayden, C. (2011). Beyond the "Obama Effect": Refining the instruments of engagement through U.S. public diplomacy. *American Behavioral Scientist*, 55, 784–802.

Israel Politik (2009). Israel FM embraces social media in public diplomacy. Retrieved on February 24, 2010 at: http://www.transracial.net/2009/07/09/israels-foreign-ministry-less-palestinians-more-facebook/

Johnson, T. J., & Kaye, B. K. (2004).Wag the blog: How reliance on traditional media and the Internet influence credibility perceptions of weblogs among blog users. *Journalism & Mass Communication Quarterly, 81*, 622–642.

Kaplan, A., & Haenlein, M. (2010). Users of the world, unite! The challeneges and opportunies of social media. *Business Horizons*, 53, 59–68.

Kazeniac, A. (2009). Social Networks: Facebook Takes Over Top Spot, Twitter Climbs. Retrieved on February 2011 at: http://blog.compete.com/2009/02/09/facebook-myspace-twitter-social-network/

Khamis, S., & Toth, E. L. (2009). International public relations: An American perspective. *Trípodos*, 24, 31–40.

Khatib, L., Dutton, W., & Thelwall, M. (2011). Public diplomacy 2.0: An exploratory case study of the US Digital Outreach Team. Center on Democracy, Development, and The Rule of Law (CDDTRL) Working Papers, 120. Retrieved on June 12, 2012 from: http://iis-db.stanford.edu/pubs/23084/No.120-_Public_Diplomacy_2.0.pdf

Kiousis, S. (2001). Public trust or mistrust? Perceptions of media credibility in the information age. *Mass Communication & Society* 4 (fall 2001): 381–403.

Last, J. (2009). Tweeting while Tehran burns: How many divisions does Twitter have? *Weekly Standard 14*(45). Retrieved from http://www.weeklystandard.com/Content/Public/Articles/000/000/016/818fosdl.asp

Leight, N., Walton, S. B., Ananian, T., Cruz-enriquez, M., & Jarwaharlal, K. (2011). PDiN quarterly—trends in public diplomacy: January, February and March 2011. *Place Branding and Public Diplomacy*, 7(2), 136–149.

Nunnaly, J. (1978). *Psychometric theory.* New York: McGraw-Hill.

Nye, J. (2008). Public diplomacy and soft power. The ANNALS of the American Academy of *Political and Social Science*, 616, 94–109.

OECD. (2007). Participative web and user-created content: Web 2.0, wikis, and social networking. *Paris: Organisation for Economic Co-operation and Development*. Retrieved on April 12, 2010 at: http://www.oecd.org/document/ 40/0,3746,en_215 71361_38620013_39428648_1_1_1_1,00.html.

Patton, C. (2009). The social networking express. *Professional Safety*, 54(11), 5.

Potter, E. H. (2008). Web 2.0 and the new public diplomacy: Impact and opportunities. In Jolyon Welsh and Daniel Fearn (eds.), *Engagement. Public Diplomacy in a Globalised World*. London, UK: Foreign and Commonwealth Office.

Pratkanis, A. (2009). Public diplomacy in international conflicts: A social influence analysis. *Routledge Handbook of Public Diplomacy*. New York: Routledge 111.

Steyn, P., Salehi-Sangari, E., Pitt, L., Parent, M., & Berthon, P. (2010). The social media release as a public relations tool: Intentions to use among B2B bloggers. *Public Relations Review*, 36, 87–89.

Stockman, F. (2006). US plans to shift diplomats to developing countries . Other-news. info, January 19. Retrieved on June 5, 2012 from: http://www.other-news. info/2006/01/us-plans-to-shift-diplomats-to-developing-countries/

Tindana, P., Singh, J., Tracy, C., Upshur, R., Daar, A., Singer, P., Frohlich, J. and Lavery, J. (2007). Grand challenges in global health: Community engagement in research in developing countries. PLoS Med, 4(9): e273. doi:10.1371/journal.pmed.0040273. Accessed on November 20, 2011.

U.S. Department of State (2009). Funding Opportunity Title: New Empowerment Com-
    munication Technologies: Opportunities in the Middle East and North Africa. Re-
    trieved on February 24, 2010 at: http://mepi.state.gov/opportunities/129624.htm
Venkatesh, V., & Davis, F. (2000). A theoretical extension of the Technology Acceptance
    Model: Four longitudinal field studies. *Management Science*, 46(2), 186–204.
Venkatesh, V., M. G. Morris, G. B. Davis, & F. D. Davis. (2003). User acceptance of infor-
    mation technology: Toward a unified view. *MIS Quarterly*, 27(3), 425–478.
Yeow, P., & Loo, W. (2009). Applications embedded in multipurpose smart identity card:
    An exploratory study in Malaysia. *International Journal of Electronic Government Re-
    search*, 5(2), 37–56.
Yun, S. H. (2006). Toward public relations theory-based study of public diplomacy: Test-
    ing the applicability of the Excellence Theory. *Journal of Public Relations Research*,
    18(4), 287–312.
———. (2007). Exploring the embassy sampling strategy for large-scale cross-national
    study in replicating the normative theory of global public relations. *Public Relations
    Review*, 33(2), 224–226.

*Global Issues & Challenges*

# 19. The Public Relations of Populism: An International Perspective of Public Diplomacy Trends

Jiska Engelbert & Jacob Groshek

On April 30, 2012, Dutch parliamentarian and head of the right-wing Party for Freedom, Geert Wilders, gave a speech in the Four Seasons Hotel in New York that was entitled *Stifling Free Speech in Europe*. By invitation of the conservative U.S. think tank, the Gatestone Institute, and against the background of a large Dutch flag, Wilders presented his four strategies on how "we" ought to "defeat Islam" (Wilders, 2012). Although this language signals both Wilders' and Gatestone's shared vision on freedom of speech in the context of criticizing Islam, it also seems to imply a broader alliance of countries:

> We must reassert our national identities. The nation-state enables self-government and self-determination. This insight led the Zionists to establish Israel as the homeland of the Jews. Zionism teaches us one of the most important lessons which the modern world needs today. Theodor Herzl argued that a Jewish state would facilitate "a new blossoming of the Jewish spirit." Today, we need our own respective nation-states to preside over a new blossoming of our own Western spirit. Our nations are the homes in which freedom and democracy prospers [*sic*]. This is true for the Netherlands. This is true for America. This is true for Israel.

Wilders, however, was not in New York as an official or formal representative of the Dutch government. In fact, only nine days earlier his Party for Freedom (Partijvoor de Vrijheid; PVV) had officially withdrawn its support of the minority government, a cabinet that had existed only by virtue of the Party for Freedom's assured endorsement. Rather, Wilders' speech coincided with the U.S. release of his autobiography, *Marked for Death: Islam's War against the West and Me*. This book does not reflect any official Dutch stance on foreign policy or internal affairs, but documents the innate juncture between Wilders' private and political life as his views on Islam have led to death threats and Wilders living under permanent protection. Indeed, when Wilders was interviewed on *Fox News* by Sean Hannity about his book the following day, he was introduced there as "a marked man."

Wilders' visit to the U.S. was made in a personal capacity and by private invitation. Yet, his parliamentary affiliation and governmental position suggest that his U.S.-targeted book, New York speech, and *Fox* interview inexorably have ramifications for perceptions of "The Netherlands" or, more specifically, of the Dutch government's position in the field of international politics and affairs as it is publicly known.

Additional international speaking engagements featuring Wilders further illustrate the role of media platforms and international alliances in the dissemination of his political vision for the Netherlands that are at odds with official Dutch policy, particularly in the areas of foreign affairs and immigration. As examples, in 2009, Wilders gave a speech to the Danish Free Press Society, where he outlined his version of a two-state solution for the Middle East conflict, namely, "one Jewish state called Israel including Judea and Samaria and one Palestinian state called Jordan" (Wilders, 2009), and where he called for a boycott of the U.N. Human Rights Council. Also in 2010, after having been denied entry to the United Kingdom the year before, Wilders controversially addressed the House of Lords in London, by invitation of Lord Malcolm Pearson, who is a peer from the U.K. Independence Party. Wilders asserted there that, "[…] *we* will have to end and get rid of cultural relativism" (Wilders, 2010a, emphasis added). When Wilders was in Berlin in 2010 by invitation of *die Freiheit* [the Freedom], the German counterpart to the PVV, he stated, "I am here because Germany matters to *the Netherlands* and the rest of the world" (Wilders, 2010b, emphasis added). And on Sept. 11, 2010, at a much anticipated speech at the 9/11 Remembrance Rally, Wilders argued,

> […] *we, we* will not betray those who died on 9/11. For their sakes we cannot tolerate a mosque on or near Ground Zero. For their sakes loud and clear *we* say: No mosque here! […] So that New York, rooted in Dutch tolerance, will never become New Mecca (Wilders, 2010c, emphasis added).

Wilders' performances on these international stages are typically controversial. They, consequently, attract extensive national and international media coverage. Wilders can thereby capitalize on the strategic public relations potential of these platforms, on which he is consistently seen to explicitly contend with government voices and stances on foreign policy, immigration politics and international affairs. Although Wilders' actions may be primarily rhetoric and polemic in intent, they explicitly *claim a diplomatic entitlement* and may thus have very real diplomatic consequences.

Importantly, Geert Wilders' case is not idiosyncratic, but emblematic of an emerging kind of actor that ought to be considered for its diplomatic ramifications. These typically populist agents are not to be mistaken for incumbent populist leaders and governments that deploy anti-elitist tactics in their approaches to foreign policy and management of international relations (McPherson, 2007). Instead, the actors focused on here are self-positioned as political outsiders who, because of explicit ties with state institutions, have demonstrated (potential) access to political power; are explicitly opposed to federalism, centralism, and to political institutions and symbols associated with it; advocate nationalist and anti-immigration politics; and operate in international networks that are influential in both domestic electoral behavior and diplomatic relationships between nation states. Most interesting, however, is that they do and convey almost all of the above through strategically benefiting from the workings and economy of mainstream media in conjunction with the affordances of online and social media. Key contemporary examples of this growing phenomenon, which this chapter terms the 'contesting public diplomat,' are Nigel Farage, leader of the increasingly popular anti-Europe and anti-immigrant UKIP party in Britain; Marine Le Pen, party leader for the French National Front; Sarah Palin, former senator and one of the symbolic leaders of the Tea Party movement in the United States, but also Silvio Berlusconi, who is currently out of political office but continues to disseminate his vision for Italy through domestic and international mainstream media.

The "contesting public diplomat" described is increasingly visible in the arena of international politics and public diplomacy. This shift is certainly related to the surge of neo-populism in Europe and North America but also shaped by the increasingly widespread use of both mass and personal media as a space (Castells, 1997) for performing politics and mobilizing support. The aim of this chapter is therefore to provide a starting point for understanding the diplomatic impact of populist practices in other international contexts. By drawing on Geert Wilders and particular instances of mediated controversy surrounding him, this chapter explores the broader strategic significance and diplomatic consequences of neo-populists positioning themselves as contending non-state actors or as contesting public diplomats. The chapter concludes its empirical exploration with a reflection on the broad repercussions of contesting public diplomats for our thinking about the relationship between the realms of strategic public relations and public diplomacy (Signitzer

& Coombs, 1992; Gilboa, 2008), particularly in the governmental pursuit of an integrated public diplomacy (Golan, 2013). This reflection specifically considers how strategic communication in all three layers of an integrated approach to public diplomacy may actively anticipate and aptly respond to populist public relations.

## *Populists as Contending Non-State Actors*

Put somewhat briefly, in 2004 Wilders clashed with the leaders of his own Dutch Liberal Party (VVD), which led to him leaving that party in order establish his own political movement, the Party for Freedom (PVV). This impasse needs to be considered in the context of what Prins (2002) termed "new realism" as hegemonic discourse that candidly considers non-Western and Muslim migrants for their economic and cultural-ideological risks to traditional Dutch national culture, identity, and society. The essence of Wilders' conflict with the VVD—his explicit objection to the party's support for Turkey's proposed ascension to full membership in the European Union—highlights a perception of (global) society as individuals, institutions, and nation states classified and evaluated along an us / them-axis.

Moreover, the Wilders controversy signals how in neo-populist movements, ranging from the PVV in the Netherlands to the Tea Party in the United States, xenophobia is inextricably entwined with foreign policy stances. Populists often challenge stances of incumbent governments or explicitly propose the contours of their own foreign policy. Both their challenge and alternative entail calls to restrict immigration and to reduce or withdraw from particular supra-national and centralist alliances, such as the European Union (EU).

The close connection between state nationalism and international politics is already acknowledged in political science scholarship (cf. McCartney, 2004), for example, through the idea of a "dialectical relationship" mediating national identity and foreign policy (Prizel, 1998). In addition, foreign policy is perceived as a key national security resource (Campbell, 1998) and, in the particular context of populism, adopting a nationalist foreign policy stance enables the practical convergence of populists' two central adversaries: elitism and pluralism (Mudde, 2004; Jagers & Walgrave, 2007). Specifically, this adoption allows for subsequently attacking the political left for embracing a cultural relativism, which, according to Wilders in his 2012 New York speech, "[…] refuse[s] to stand for liberty and prefer[s] to appease Islam." Yet, what is left underexplored is if and how neo-populists' explicitly anti-state and anti-elite pronouncements and performances, in relation to foreign policy, affect the field and future of public diplomacy.

Contemporary approaches to diplomacy, under the banner of "the New Public Diplomacy" (Melissen, 2005a, 2005b), have extended the kind of practices and the nature of actors that can qualify as potentially diplomatic, even if some actors do not evidently have a "working relationship" (Melissen, 2011, p. 3) with the state (Leonard 2002; Ross, 2003). Still, such work has not necessarily been able to make full sense of the public diplomatic impacts of agents that explicitly resist such affiliations.

Public diplomacy should, of course, always be considered in the realm of those practices that set out to ensure national interests by, ultimately, promoting government policies abroad, for example, through nation branding or place branding (Anholt & Hildreth, 2005; Anholt, 2006). This conceptualization, however, does not fully consider perceptions of neo-populists without formal government representation in *any* diplomatic capacity, even as counter-public diplomacy. After all, neo-populists *too* equally claim to aspire to safeguarding national interest, and they extensively do so by engaging in cultural and strategic public relations activities that are increasingly international in orientation and impact. In exploring the case of Geert Wilders, the conceptual territory of public diplomacy should thus be expanded through the notion of "double differentiation."

## *Double Differentiation and Accredited Representation*

In his empirical exploration of how alleged Dutch populists in the post-Fortuyn era relate to "ideal type" populists, Vossen asserts the complexity of assessing Geert Wilders. Vossen argues that Wilders does not "match the populist archetype of the 'reluctant politicians' with a strong dislike for politics and politicians" (2010, p. 34), referring to Wilders' long-standing political ties with established governmental bodies. Yet, the populist prototype does not acknowledge that, increasingly, the "reluctant politician" (Taggart, 2000) or "anti-party party" (Mudde, 1996) can also be understood as a discursive achievement. Explorations of parliamentary ties and government alliances of the regional Lega Nord in Italy (McDonnell, 2006), the national Dansk Folkeparti in Denmark (Rydgren, 2004), or the European UKIP in the United Kingdom (Hayton, 2010) emphasize anti-establishment identities as rhetorical resources rather than actual prerequisites for populist parties.

The salience of performance in populism can therefore be situated through the concept of double differentiation (Kriesi, 2011). Double differentiation considers as characteristic for contemporary (European) populist actors the ability to distance themselves from the political establishment, while simultaneously displaying a potential to work within and exert influence in the political order. Groshek and Engelbert (2012) extended Kriesi's concept in a comparative study of populist movements in the United States and the Netherlands. They found leaders in both groups use self-representational and online media to "both negotiate and reconcile the potential conflict between their anti-establishment image and their (past, current, and potential) political affiliation" (Groshek & Engelbert, 2012, p. 198–199).

Here, Wilders' distinct political style of being able to operate within the very center of power he also challenges is essentially something he intentionally constructs and keeps alive (cf. Fairlcough, 2000; Ankersmit, 2003). As is typical for the rhetoric of so many neo-populist movements (Vossen, 2011), expressions of nationalism and xenophobia are pervasive in the performance of Wilders' political style and, consequently, of issues that typically concern the realm of foreign policy (be they international trade, immigration or the sovereignty of Europe). Consequently, double differentiation is a practice that emphasizes the performative dimensions to populism and public diplomacy. As such, populists' performances inevitably entail, and indeed, encourage a push-and-pull-struggle with formal state representatives over who is best equipped to not only protect but also direct national interests amid fluid globalization processes.

Paradoxically, Wilders takes that struggle over national preservation to media platforms that are available to or specifically targeted at international audiences. As could readily be observed in the extract of Wilders' New York speech, he does so through laying out what is ultimately a vision for protecting (Dutch) national interest as a vision for international solidarity between nation-states that are similarly facing the "challenges" of immigration, Islam, and the consequences of centralization and globalization. Wilders consequently constructs the Netherlands as an object for international identification and tool for ideological exclusion. He thereby engages in what displays a striking resemblance with the Cold War diplomatic practice of ideological warfare (Kennedy & Lucas, 2005). In fact, Wilders' purpose in addressing international issues and managing international relations, but, specifically, his perceived entitlement to address and manage these issues, seems to pertain to the broader practice of public diplomacy.

Characteristic of Wilders' populist style, then, is his explicitly *claimed* entitlement to being the "accredited representative" (Melissen, 2005b, p. 4), who is to safeguard Dutch national interest both home and abroad. He is permitted to do so not by virtue of the state, but by popular appointment. Consequently, in Wilders' alternative version of public diplomacy two acts converge: aligning international audiences and swaying national publics. This convergence of international orientation and nationalism is indeed paradoxical: it shows the ambiguous conceptual boundary (Signitzer & Coombs, 1992) or "intricate relationship" (Melissen, 2005b, p. 9) between the realms of public diplomacy and public affairs.

Altogether, contesting public diplomacy as a mode of strategic public relations management is a significant element of the performative dimension to populism. First, it ensures a focus on populist vanguards, such as immigration, Islam, and Europe. Second, it provides an apt stage for double differentiation; enabling populists to challenge the very political institutions they operate in or with which they are associated. It, finally, constitutes an excellent opportunity to simultaneously display cultural and political leadership. There is yet an additional advantage to engaging in contesting public diplomacy: it is enabled by online and social media, the economy of mass news media, and, not in the least, by populists' sophisticated integration of these.

## *From Media Populism to Media Politik*

In February 2012, Wilders' opposition against EU enlargement and policy emerged in a quintessential example of double differentiation when he launched the *Meldpunt Midden- en Oost-Europeanen* [Central and Eastern European Register] (MOE). The MOE was an online and social media space, originally embedded within the PVV website, where individuals could register their complaints against CEE citizens living and working in the Netherlands. The site contextualizes this particular group in the light of "problems" caused by "mass labour immigration," which involve "nuisance, pollution, repression [of the Dutch] on the labour market and integration and housing issues" (Partij voor de Vrijheid, 2012). The MOE thus extends the anti-Islam discourse so typically deployed by Wilders in problematizing the cultural consequences of non-Western migrants. Moreover, the MOE articulates and reinforces the familiar Wilders discourse of migration as a tidal wave or "tsunami" (De Landtsheer, Kalkhoven & Broen, 2011).

When Wilders' party launched the MOE on Feb. 8, 2012, the PVV was still bound by the construction of providing secured support to the government of Liberal Prime Minister Mark Rutte. The MOE exposes tension and conflict within this political arrangement but also provokes and discriminates against nationals from the CEE countries. The MOE thereby meets two important criteria—sensation and scandal (Arsenault & Castells, 2008, p. 507)—that make for a controversial and thereby commercially viable news story in increasingly competitive and market-oriented media systems (cf. Curran, 2011).

The launch of the MOE is thus commercially viable for the news agency and for its clients' news outlets because it allows for emphasizing and capitalizing *the conflict* potentially affected by the register (cf. Semetko & Valkenburg, 2000). Interestingly, a press release from the national news agency ANP already makes this potential explicit by presenting as part of the news event the responses of Dutch parliamentarians and Polish government representatives:

> The PVV has established a website where people can leave complaints about CEE citizens in our country. They are Poles and people from other countries in Central and Eastern-Europe [...]. Are you bothered by CEE citizens? Or have you lost your job to a Pole, Bulgarian, Romanian or other Central- or Eastern European? We like to hear from you," the website states. The PVV intends to present all complaints to Henk Kamp, the Minister for Social Affairs. A spokesperson of the Polish embassy has expressed his sorrow in *Algemeen Dagblad* [a major national newspaper]: "Offensive party initiatives do not contribute to thoughtful debate." Jolanda Sap [leader of the Green Party] was furious: "The PVV has acquired a new toy by bombarding Eastern Europeans into new enemies. Problems and nuisance should be seriously tackled, just as the exploitation of Eastern Europeans for their cheap labor should. But this register does not contribute to this. This is mere rabble-rousing" (ANP, 2012).

However, journalistic attention for the MOE signals more than a media economy that is characterized by "an intensified focus on political celebrity and political gossip and scandal" (Corner, 2007, p. 216). It again points to the significant performative dimension to successful populism that can be repurposed in the international arena by these actors in staking out public diplomatic efforts. Populism, then, is more than what is commonly referred to as "media populism" (Mazzoleni, 2002; Waisbord, 2002) and shares essential features with what Peri (2004) terms "media politik," a social practice that is only possible because of its mediation. With the example of MOE provided here, as a platform that allows and invites citizens to put a name to issues that would have been systematically tabooed by the political elite, the PVV created a key opportunity to enact its political identity. Without the actual online media infrastructure itself, but crucially without media performances and journalistic attention, this potential would not have been actualized.

Controversy and provocation are thus equally as important to the survival and success of media institutions as they are to that of populist movements. From this perspective, the MOE is an example of how Geert Wilders attempts to create opportunities for himself and his party to double differentiate in relation to the *national* political establishment. Yet, the MOE also brings to the fore how Wilders' "national media politik" and the opportunities for local double differentiation increasingly have repercussions for international perceptions of the Netherlands abroad.

## Something Old, Something New

When pressed by parliamentarians, ambassadors, and other officials to condemn the MOE days after it was launched, Dutch Prime Minister Mark Rutte instead classified it as a "performance of political parties" (Rutte, 2012). This reaction signals the increasingly influential position of populist movements in, especially, Europe, either through their contribution to actual governments (for example, in the Netherlands and Denmark) or through their influence in shaping the agenda of mainstream politics (for example, in Finland and France). Accordingly, neo-populists, like Wilders, can more easily *claim* to be speaking on behalf of national and political majorities. The major repercussion of this consensual self-accreditation—consensual in the sense that governments are increasingly impaired to openly criticize populists' behavior—is that something like the MOE risks being interpreted as representative of a government stance or, at least, as a voice to be reckoned or diplomatically battled with.

This confluence of trends means that Wilders' actions—be it the MOE, his calls to pull out of and disband the European Union, his protest against Turkey's proposed EU membership, his particular two-state solution for the Middle East Conflict, or the release of his controversial anti-Islam film *Fitna*—are not incidents that need to be anticipated and responded to through formal diplomacy (Melissen, 2008). Rather, in order to grasp the international consequences of a national media politik, the actions themselves need to be understood in a public diplomatic capacity, even if these actions appear explicitly anti-diplomatic, undermine former long-standing diplomatic efforts, or directly threaten the status quo of international relations.

At the same time, however, Wilders is actively pursuing new international alliances. In the case of the MOE—but similarly in all of Wilders' actions aimed *against* the values, aspiration and symbols of a European Union—the alternative international community would reject the values and aspirations of *any* global, supra-national or federal body to which the nation state is to delegate sovereignty. Similarly, it would reject *any* development that may threaten the supremacy of national culture, such as immigration or multiculturalism. And, finally, the community *could* look at the Netherlands, and the PVV in particular, for cultural and political leadership in pursuing this ideological program through double differentiation, though Wilders is willing to share that leadership with countries with which he ideologically aligns.

Importantly, the "imagined community" of Wilders, or the partnership with whom he is to engage diplomatically, then, is not bound by the borders of the European Union. Rather, his community is an international one, in which a shared concern over very particular national interests constitutes the prerequisite *and* currency for diplomatic exchange. This is how, in his New York Speech for the Gatestone interview in April 2012, Wilders was able to ideologically align with 'the' United States over his own anti-Europe politics:

> [...] previous Dutch governments [...] have signed away a significant part of our own sovereignty to the EU, the European Union, a supranational institution run by unelected and undemocratic bureaucrats. [...] We are now heading for elections [...] Our electoral campaign will focus on the need to restore our national sovereignty, because without our sovereignty we cannot defend our identity and fight against Islamization. *My friends, we continue our efforts.*[...] *One of my favourite presidents Ronald Reagan once said: "The future doesn't belong to the fainthearted." Reagan was right. The future belongs to us* (Wilders, 2012, emphasis added).

In sum, Wilders' strategic public relations can be considered as an act of contesting public diplomacy in the sense that it condemns, problematizes and tries to break down existing allegiances, policy stances and values whilst it concurrently creates an alternative international community with its own set of ideological beliefs and aspirations. The realm of public diplomacy, then, is accessed by Wilders through strategic public relations efforts. Equally, the realm of international public diplomacy, because of the controversy that accessing it permits and the opportunity for "frame fighting" (Entman, 2004) it provides, constitutes a key resource for populist opposition "in the domestic debate about the right thing to do" (Gilboa, 2008, p. 65). The final section of this chapter considers the broader implications and relevance of this contingent relationship between populists' strategic public relations and (integrated) public diplomacy.

## Conclusion

This chapter has attempted to construct a framework for exploring the significance and consequences of populist actors who explicitly promote values in the field of foreign affairs, immigration politics and international relations that challenge and even compromise those of a national government. These populist actors were conceptualized as contending non-state actors and as contesting public diplomats given their claimed entitlement to represent national interest on mediated international platforms. More specifically, the performance of contesting public diplomacy was argued to constitute a mode of strategic public relations management, which, in turn, allows populists to *double differentiate*; to distance themselves from the very political institutions and established practices they are in fact a part of, whilst simultaneously displaying political and cultural leadership.

Populists thus draw on political repertoires of foreign policy and public diplomacy and are increasingly international in orientation, whereas they are in fact attending to domestic conflict with the political establishment. Though double differentiation highlights the performative dimension to populism, its ramifications for the realm of public diplomacy and international relations may be very real. This chapter considered these consequences as inevitably shaped by particular national political configurations, such as a minority government that is directly bound by populist support or more indirectly shaped by the hegemony of populist discourse. Furthermore, diplomatic consequences should be considered in terms of existing allegiances that are compromised and new international and ideological alliances that are actively created.

A framework built around a particular case, embedded within its own nation-specific political culture, can, of course, never be readily transported into another context. Yet, the central mechanism of the framework (the ceaseless frame fight over domestic politics and national interest) and its conceptual core (populists' strategic management of public relations provides access to the realm of public diplomacy) allow for an application to those national contexts in which the populist forces are increasingly evident, either by means of formal political representation or symbolic opposition.

For example, considering briefly the United States, the populist Tea Party emerged in early 2009 as a reaction to the financial "bailout" programs administered by the Obama administration. Since that time, the Tea Party has been instrumental in the outcome of the 2010 U.S. midterm elections, where Republicans—particularly those farther right—won back or took over previously, Democratic-held positions at the Congressional, gubernatorial, and state levels. While the differences between the non-hierarchical Tea Party and the leader-as-party PVV are clear (cf. Groshek & Engelbert, 2012), what is transcendent about populist public diplomacy is that it pushes local, state, and national issues into the international arena where opinions about a nation and its policies are formed by foreign audiences.

In this manner, the mantle of Tea Party values regarding reductions in government spending and taxes, as well as smaller government are reflected by a stance toward American exceptionalism and relatively isolationist attitudes (Mead, 2011). These outward foreign policy positions—some being outlined by Tea Party representatives such as Ron Paul who assume the inadvertent role of the contesting public diplomat (cf. Paul, 2011)—thus exert a similar, if more diffuse effect that changes not only the national political reality, but also the *perceived* shift of American politics towards conservatism on issues such as global warming, gay marriage, immigration, and Christian religiousness (Campbell & Putnam, 2011).

Altogether, there is a certain similarity of Wilders' performative practices of double differentiation being carried out in the United States by Tea Party politicians, in both instances of formal or informal endorsements (Jonsson, 2011). Though the "imagined communities" of these actors are likely far less international in intent, their impact eventually becomes writ large on the stage of public diplomacy, often through a strategic melding of mass and online media.

Given the upsurge in contesting, neo-populist public diplomats in Europe and North America, like Geert Wilders, Marine Le Pen, Silvio Berlusconi, Sarah Palin and Nigel Farage—who can all count on extensive coverage in international mainstream media and further dissemination through social media spaces—governments cannot but actively *be seen to* anticipate and respond to the alternative international solidarities, alliances and country reputations established by these contenders. Yet, while the diplomatic threat may be so intricate because it comes from *within*, new integrated models of and approaches to public diplomacy are more than ever equipped to deal with this challenge. That is, given their reliance on the doxa and economies of mainstream media, performativity and cultural exchange, contesting public diplomats can be repudiated in their claimed diplomatic entitlement through the very differentiated (soft power) dimensions that integrated public diplomacy offers. With mediated public diplomacy, nation branding, reputation management and relational public diplomacy at its core (Golan, 2013, p. 1252), integrated public diplomacy is particularly well resourced to 'disintegrate' the contesting neo-populist diplomat.

## *Bibliography*

Anholt, S. (2006). Public diplomacy and place branding: Where's the link? *Place Branding*, 2 (4), 271–275.

Anholt, S., & Hildreth, J. (2005). *Brand America: The mother of all brands*. London: Cyan Communications.

Ankersmit, F. (2003). Democracy's inner voice: Political style as unintended consequence of political action. In: J. Corner & D. Pels (Eds.), *Media and the restyling of politics: Consumerism, celebrity and cynicism* (pp. 18–40). London: Sage.

ANP (2012, February 8). PVV verzamelt klachten over Polen voor Kamp. ANP. Retrieved from http://www.nu.nl/politiek/2735933/pvv-verzamelt-klachten-polen-kamp.html.

Arsenault, A., & Castells, M. (2008). Switching power. Rupert Murdoch and the global business of media politics: A sociological analysis. *International Sociology*, 23 (4), 488–513.

Campbell, D. (1998). *Writing identity: United States foreign policy and the politics of identity*. Minneapolis, MN: University of Minnesota Press.

Campbell, D. E., & Putnam, R. D. (August 16, 2011). Crashing the Tea Party. *The New York Times*.

Castells, M. (1997). *The power of identity*. Malden, MA: Blackwell.

Corner, J. (2007). Media, power and political culture. In: E. Devereux (Ed.), *Media studies: Key issues and debates* (pp. 211–230). London: Sage.

Curran, J. (2011). *Media and democracy*. London: Routledge.

De Landtsheer, C., Kalkhoven, L., & Broen, L. (2011). De beeldspraak van Geert Wilders: Een Tsunami over Nederland? *Tijdschrift voor Communicatiewetenschap*, 39 (4), 5–20.

Entman, R. (2004). *Projections of power: Framing news, public opinion, and U.S. foreign policy*. Chicago: University of Chicago Press.

Fairclough, N. (2000). *New Labour, new language?* London: Routledge.

Gilboa, E. (2008). Searching for a theory of public diplomacy. *The ANNALS of the American Academy of Political and Social Science*, 616 (1), 55–77.

Golan, G. J. (2013). An integrated approach to public diplomacy. *American Behavioral Scientist*, 57 (9), 1251–1255.

Groshek, J., & Engelbert, J. (2012). Double differentiation in a cross-national comparison of populist political movements and online media uses in the United States and the Netherlands. *New Media & Society*, 15(2), 183–202.

Hayton, R. (2010). Towards the mainstream? UKIP and the 2009 elections to the European Parliament. *Politics*, 30 (1), 26–35.

Jagers, J., & Walgrave, S. (2007). Populism as political communication style: An empirical study of political parties' discourse in Belgium. *European Journal of Political Research*, 46 (3), 319–345.

Jonsson P. (2011). Tea Party fuels rise of Herman Cain. So how can it be racist? *The Christian Science Monitor*, 13 October. Available at: www.csmonitor.com/USA/Elections/Tea-Party-Tally/2011/1013/Tea-party-fuels-rise-of-Herman-Cain.-So-how-can-it-be-racist.

Kennedy, L., & Lucas, S. (2005). Enduring freedom: Public diplomacy and U.S. foreign policy. *American Quarterly*, 57 (2), 309–33.

Kriesi, H. (2011). The changing political preconditions for political communication: The forces that shape the political elites' ability to control the citizen public. Keynote speech presented at the *Conference on Political Communication in Europe: Changing Contexts, Changing Contents*. Amsterdam, January 7.

Leonard, M. (2002). Diplomacy by Other Means. *Foreign Policy*, 13 (9), 48–56.

Mazzoleni, G. (2002). The media and neo-populism: A contemporary comparative analysis. In: G.J. Mazzoleni & B. Horsefield (Eds.), *The media and neo-populism: A contemporary comparative analysis* (pp. 1–21). Westport, CT: Praeger.

McCartney, P. T. (2004). American nationalism and U.S. foreign policy from September 11 to the Iraq War. *Political Science Quarterly*, 119 (3), 399–423.

McDonnell, D. (2006). A weekend in Padania: Regionalist populism and the Lega Nord. *Politics*, 26 (2), 126–132.

McPherson, A. (2007) The limits of populist diplomacy: Fidel Castro's April 1959 trip to North America. *Diplomacy & Statecraft*, 18 (1), 237–269.

Mead, W. R. (March/April, 2011). The Tea Party and American foreign policy: What populism means for globalism. *Foreign Affairs*, 28–44.

Melissen, J. (Ed.) (2005a). *The new public diplomacy: Soft power in international relations.* London: Palgrave Macmillan.

———. (2005b). Wielding Soft Power: The new public diplomacy. *Clingendael Diplomacy Papers*, 2.

———. (2008, March 14). Why the Dutch Must Win Hearts and Minds. *Clingendael Commentary.* Retrieved from http://62–177–195–230.dsl.bbeyond.nl/publica tions/2008/20080314_clingendael_commentary_1_melissen.pdf.

———. (2011). Beyond the New Public Diplomacy. *Clingendael Diplomacy Papers*, 2.

Mudde, C. (1996). The paradox of the Anti-Party Party: Insights from the extreme right. *Party Politics*, 2 (2), 265–276.

Mudde, C. (2004). The populist Zeitgeist. *Government and Opposition*, 39 (4), 542–563.

Partij voor de Vrijheid. (2012). Meldpunt Midden en Oost Europeanen. Retrieved from http://www.meldpuntmiddenenoosteuropeanen.nl/.

Paul, R. (August 27, 2010). A Tea Party Foreign Policy. *Foreign Policy.*

Peri, Y. (2004). *Telepopulism: Media and politics in Israel.* Stanford, CA: Stanford University Press.

Prins, B. (2002). The nerve to break taboos: New realism in the Dutch discourse on multiculturalism. *Journal of International Migration and Integration*, 3 (3–4), 363–379.

Prizel, I. (2008). National identity and foreign policy: Nationalism and leadership in Poland, Russia and Ukraine. Cambridge: Cambridge University Press.

Ross, C. (2003). Pillars of Public Diplomacy: Grappling with international public opinion. *Harvard International Review*, 25 (2), 22–28.

Rutte, M. (2012, February 14). Vragen van het lid Schouw aan de minister-president, minister van Algemene Zaken over het oordeel van de Europese Commissie over het "Polenmeldpunt" van de PVV [Prime Minister Question Time]. Retrieved from https://zoek.officielebekendmakingen.nl.

Rydgren, J. (2004). Explaining the emergence of radical right-wing populist parties: The case of Denmark. *West European Politics*, 27 (3), 474–502.

Semetko, H.A., & Valkenburg, P. (2000). Framing European politics: A content analysis of press and television news. *Journal of Communication*, 50 (2), 93–109.

Signitzer, B.H., & Coombs, T. (1992). Public relations and public diplomacy: Conceptual convergences. *Public Relations Review*, 18 (2) 137–147.

Taggart, P. (2000). *Populism.* Buckingham: Open University Press.

Vossen, K. (2010). Populism in the Netherlands after Fortuyn: Rita Verdonk and Geert Wilders compared. *Perspectives on European Politics and Society*, 11 (1), 22–38.

Vossen, K. (2011). Classifying Wilders: The ideological development of Geert Wilders and his Party for Freedom. *Politics*, 31 (3), 179–189.

Waisbord, S. (2002). Media populism: Neo-Populism in Latin America. In: G.J. Mazzoleni, & B. Horsefield (Eds.), *The media and neo-populism: A contemporary comparative analysis* (pp. 197–216). Westport, CT: Praeger.

Wilders, G. (2009). Speech at the Danish Free Speech Society. Copenhagen. June 15. Retrieved from http://www.pvv.nl/index.php?option=com_content&task=view & id=2045 & Itemid=1.

———. (2010a). Speech at the House of Lords. London. March, 5. Retrieved from http://www.geertwilders.nl/index.php?option=com_content&task=view&id=1662&Itemid=1.

———. (2010b). Speech at *die Freiheit*. Berlin. October 2. Retrieved from http://www.pvv.nl/index.php/component/content/article/36-geert-wilders/3586-speech-geert-wilders-berlijn.html.

———. (2010c). Speech at 9/11 Remembrance Rally. New York. September 11. Retrieved from http://www.geertwilders.nl/index.php?option=com_content&task=view&id=1712.

———. (2012). Stifling free speech in Europe. Speech at the Gatestone Institute. New York, April 30. Retrieved from http://www.geertwilders.nl/index.php/in-english-mainmenu-98/in-the-press-mainmenu-101/77-in-the-press/1781-speech-geert-wilders-new-york-april-30.

# 20. Presidents, Approval Ratings, and Standing: Assessing Leaders' Reputations

Margaret G. Hermann

Pundits have likened political leadership to standing on a moving sidewalk with fire at either end while trying to juggle a number of problems with people pushing and shoving their positions at you from each side. At issue is remaining standing and continuing to move toward a set of goals while at the same time developing and maintaining a relationship with those for whom the current issue is also salient. It involves persuasion in the service of setting an agenda, building networks and coalitions, and accomplishing things. Thus defined, leadership is more than leaders; it is composed of a set of ingredients, each of which is important to understanding what is happening at any point in time and to knowledge about an incumbent's standing.

Indeed, we do not have leaders without some sort of followers, constituents, or supporters. Even someone who appears to have complete control of his government like Kim Jong Il did in North Korea is responsive to certain others who keep him in power and in his position—in Kim Jong Il's case, the million person military. In the US, many believe that the president is always in campaign mode, working to forge a consensus among disparate interest groups, the attentive elite, and the general public in his own country as well as other world leaders and the opinion leaders in other countries. Consider in Afghanistan, the US and some constituencies are supporting one leader while other constituencies are being pushed and pulled by potential leaders to engage in violence in an attempt to seize authority and assert leadership.

The relationship between leaders and their constituents is also important to leadership. Often we measure the nature of this relationship through approval ratings. Note how the approval rating of a US president affects what he can and cannot do, how much scrutiny his policies receive, and how much latitude he has in negotiating with other leaders both within and outside his borders. The desires and expectations of a leader's constituents are important determinants of this relationship as are the leader's skills in accomplishing things of relevance to these constituents.

Leaders and constituents work together in a particular context. In effect, the nature of the context can facilitate or hinder a leader being selected or the development of the relationship between the leader and those led. Research tells us that constituents select different types of leaders in times of crisis than in times of peace, in democracies versus more authoritarian political systems, in times of plenty as opposed to periods of recession, to lead revolutionary movements versus to institutionalize change, and when developing a vision is critical in contrast to when maintaining stability is the name of the game (for an overview of this literature, see Hermann 2014).

This chapter builds on this conceptualization of political leadership. It is going to take US presidents as an example and explore the impact that their images at home and abroad have on their reputations as reflected in their approval ratings. How does knowledge about approval ratings provide us with information about the president's standing both domestically and internationally? Do such ratings suggest what constituencies the president is having problems with and where the relationship is working well? How do presidents use foreign policy to deal with their appraisal of their own approval ratings? And whose positions count when it comes to approval ratings? Of interest here is how important assessing leaders' approval ratings is to understanding a country's standing and reputation.

## Approval Ratings— Here and Abroad

Research on the interactions between domestic and international politics has emphasized the Janus-faced nature of what is required of leaders such as US presidents as they seek to implement policy. They participate in a two-level game where they work to balance what is happening domestically with what is occurring abroad. Presidential standing appears to influence how well and in what way they engage in this game. As Robert Putnam (1988, 451–452) observed when first discussing the nature of this two-level game, a president "whose political standing at home is high can more easily win ratification of his foreign initiatives" and "America's negotiating partners have reason for concern whenever the American president is domestically weakened." Approval ratings are often used as a surrogate measure for standing both at home and abroad. Such ratings have been regularly collected on US presidents since the late 1930s. Although begun by George Gallup, there are currently 15 such polls conducted on a weekly basis.

The relevance of approval ratings as an indicator of standing is evident in Shibley Telhami's (1999, 282) analysis of Arab-Israeli negotiations when he notes in discussing the Madrid Conference in 1991 that "the problem for the Shamir [Israeli] government, who came to Madrid reluctantly, was that the Bush Administration came out of the Gulf War with great popularity, with President Bush enjoying 90 percent approval ratings in opinion polls." They could ill afford not to do what was requested. George Edwards (1997, 113–114), a noted presidential scholar, has observed that there is "virtual unanimity" among advisors, members of the bureaucracy, and participants in the legislative process concerning the importance of approval ratings as an indicator of "the president's public standing" and "an important source of presidential power."

Approval ratings are generated based on the responses of a representative sample of the general public to the following question. "Which of the following best describes your opinion of the things President [Name] has done: strongly approve, somewhat approve, somewhat disapprove, strongly disapprove, or no opinion/undecided." Generally the strongly and somewhat approve categories are summed together to generate the rating. High approval ratings are viewed as providing political capital to a president and facilitating movement on his agenda. Indeed, Andrew Barrett and Matthew Eshbaugh-Soha (2007) have found that the higher the president's approval rating, the better his bargaining position with Congress and the more likely he is to see much of what he wants enacted into law.

Checking on the policy congruence between approval ratings more generally and approval ratings by issue (is the current administration spending too much, too little, or about the right amount of time on a particular issue?), Brandice Canes-Wrone and Kenneth Shotts (2004) showed that presidents who were highly popular or highly unpopular paid less attention to issues of importance to the public than those who were average in popularity, particularly in the second half of their first term. These scholars argue that presidents with average approval ratings at this point in their term realize that they could be in for a tight reelection race and begin pushing issues important to the public regardless of their own agendas. In line with much writing on the presidency, foreign policy and defense issues showed the least policy congruence between general approval ratings and those for particular issues. Presidents are thought to have more flexibility in areas associated with these issues than on domestic, "doorstep" issues that are more salient to the public—they can engage in policy leadership rather than in "pandering" to the public. But they, then, "own" the policy and bear the brunt of what happens should the issue become a media "hot potato" and engage the public later on.

In the past decade, something similar to approval ratings has begun to appear on American presidents in countries other than the United States. The Pew Global Attitudes Program, World Public Opinion, and the BBC, for example, have surveyed opinion yearly in 20 to 44 countries, asking about peoples' confidence in the US president, that is, their confidence that the president will do the "right thing in world affairs." Questions have also been raised regarding their approval of his policies and their expectations regarding what he is likely to do. Consider that when Obama became president of the United States in 2009, he had the highest approval rating among world leaders at that time (e.g., Brown, Merkel, Hu Jin-tao, Putin, Ahmadinejad) with on average 61% of those responding across 22 countries indicating a lot or some confidence he would do the right thing in world affairs; the only policy where disapproval exceeded approval was with regard to sending more troops to Afghanistan (see worldpublicopinion.org June 29, 2009). Contrast these data with those in 2008 which showed that George W. Bush as president triggered the least confidence on average in the likelihood he would do the right thing in world affairs—on average 67% of respondents had little or no confidence in him. Indeed, there was a 37 point difference on average in Obama's favor when the confidence ratings between Bush and Obama were compared across countries from 2008 to 2009 (see pewglobal.org July 23, 2009). In some senses, the data indicated that in these publics' minds Obama could do little wrong and Bush could do little right. By the end of his first administration, confidence in Obama continued to be high in Europe, Japan, and Brazil, but overall confidence in his leadership had dropped by six percentage points or more in most countries (pewglobal.org June 13, 2012).

At issue is what these two indicators imply for American standing in the world. One could postulate that these two types of approval ratings provide us with an assessment of the general publics' perceptions of how well a particular administration is doing—its current credibility with the American public and the esteem with which its leader is held abroad. In effect, these indicators suggest the predisposition of the publics both in the United States and abroad to give the benefit of the doubt to the president and his presidency or to expect the worst of him. The indicators provide us with the lens through which others are viewing the current president and suggest how much leeway they are willing to allow him and the nature as well as the strength of their expectations concerning the direction of American foreign policy. The global indicators do not translate one-to-one into favorability ratings for the United States, but they do appear to bear some relation to such ratings. Consider that US favorability ratings increased on average 10 points across 22 countries between 2008 and 2009 in the transition from Bush to Obama (pewglobal.org July 23, 2009) and in 50% of these countries remained the same or increased slightly during Obama's first administration (pewglobal.org June 13, 2012).

Both presidential approval ratings at home and abroad, however, are ephemeral and responsive to changes in the political context, thus their usefulness in keeping us abreast of the twists and turns in standing. Consider the 90% approval rating that George W. Bush received 10 days after September 11 as compared to his average overall approval rating of 49% (gallup.com/ poll/116500/Presidental-Approval-Ratings-George-Bush.aspx). Events such as 9/11 and his father's leadership in the liberation of Kuwait (yielding an 89% approval rating) are suggestive of the event-driven nature of such ratings. Also consider the observation that "presidential standing" in the first six months does not forecast how a president is likely to do across his first term in office but does suggest the ability he will have to push his policies in the second six months. Similar kinds of twists and turns appear in the global approval ratings as well. Survey results comparing respondents in the Palestinian Territories and Israel who were interviewed before and after Obama's Cairo speech in which he talked directly to the Muslim community show a decline of 11% in the confidence Israelis had in Obama after the speech and an increase of 5% in the confidence of those in the Palestinian Territories. Perhaps more important for standing with regard to the Palestinians, there was a 12% increase in the number of respondents who answered that Obama would consider their interests after the speech than before (see pewglobal.org July 23, 2009). Moreover, there appears to be a difference in standing between a president using words and a government engaging in actions. While majorities in 24 countries were generally optimistic when Obama assumed office that he would lead the United States in a more multilateral fashion, similar majorities did not see evidence of any change in the country's behavior by summer 2009 (see pewglobal.org July 23, 2009).

To this point we have been describing how others see the president and rate his behavior. Another way of going at the question is to ask how does the president view such approval ratings and use public opinion. Two types of literatures have played around with trying to answer this question. One has explored how presidents use foreign policy to work on improving their approval ratings. The other has examined how presidents engage public opinion and approval ratings and whose opinions count.

## *Using Foreign Policy to Change Approval Ratings*

There have been a number of studies across the past several decades focused on presidents' use of foreign policy to counter vulnerability or low standing domestically. Some (e.g., Downs and Rocke 1994; Smith 1996) have called it the "gamble for resurrection in the eyes of the voters." Others (e.g., Ostrom and Job 1985; James and Oneal 1991; Morgan and Bickers 1992; Richards et al. 1993; DeRouen 1995) have reported a diversionary use of force internationally in response to a decline in public approval at home. Then there is the "rally round the flag" phenomenon which provides an incentive to presidents with domestic political problems to see a fast increase in their approval ratings with an international crisis (e.g., Mueller 1973; MacKuen 1983; Baker and Oneal 2001; Chapman and Reiter 2004). Still others (e.g., Miller 1995; Gelpi 1997; Brule 2006) have proposed a "policy availability" notion that focuses on the use of foreign policy as a substitute when other avenues are closed to the president. And some (e.g., Leeds and Davis 1997; Miller 1999; Fordham 2005) have posed a strategic interaction argument, finding that "potential targets of diversionary behavior are less likely to initiate disputes with states experiencing incentives to divert" (Brule 2008, 352)—"leaders take into account not only their own domestic political conditions but the domestic political situation of their rivals" (Leeds and Davis 1997, 831).

A recent study by David Brule (2008) tries to unravel several of the propositions raised above. He argues that the relations between the president and Congress help us understand when foreign policy becomes a focus of attention for a president and, in particular, the use of force. An "uncooperative Congress reduces the number of remedial policies available…compelling the president to look beyond the domestic arena for opportunities to demonstrate his competence" (Brule 2008, 353). Thus, the president turns to foreign policy and a place to demonstrate his capabilities where constitutionally he has a greater capacity to act without Congressional approval. Brule contends, and finds, that presidents do, indeed, initiate disputes internationally when the president's approval rating is low and Congress is unsupportive of his policies. In effect, there is a 93% increase in the likelihood of the initiation of a dispute when the president's approval rating is low and his success in Congress is minimal. Presidents can apparently still focus on domestic policy and deal with lower approval ratings if they are having legislative success.

Interestingly, the Brule study and those described above do not explore when foreign policy might be used in a more positive or cooperative manner in response to vulnerability and decreasing approval ratings at home. Consider, for instance, the fact that the year 1998 in which Clinton traveled abroad the most was the same year as the Monica Lewinsky scandal broke at home and that Nixon engaged in the most foreign travel of his presidency during 1974 at the height of the Watergate scandal (Berthoud and Brady 2001). As Reagan's staffers admitted regarding one of his trips to Europe: "Because the polls were showing a drop in the president's popularity, which made him vulnerable in Washington, we decided that conferring on location with European heads of state would be good for his image as a leader" (Kernell 1986, 96). In a systematic study of these travels and summits—these presidential dramas, David Burbach (2003) found that if elite opinion concerning the travel was positive, and there was at least a story a day in the *New York Times* about what was happening for up to two weeks, approval ratings increased as much as 5% as matched to a 6% rise when the president engaged in the use of force. In effect, as Paul Brace and Barbara Hinckley (1992) have argued, most foreign travel of US presidents is strategic and reactive and timed closely with conditions affecting a president's support at home.

Some have also observed an increase in presidents' approval ratings after peace-making ventures (e.g., MacKuen 1983; Burbach 2003). For instance, Jimmy Carter's approval rating went up 12 points with the announcement of the Camp David Accords and the peace agreement between Egypt and Israel. Similarly Richard Nixon's approval rating increased 15 points with the announcement of the formal end to the Vietnam War. And, as observed above, Bush, Sr. had his highest approval rating (89%) following the end of the Gulf War and the liberation of Kuwait. As James Baker is reported to have commented: Why shouldn't the public rally round the flag for positive, non-crisis events in the same way that they do for incidents involving conflict and tension? In either case, we know that such rally events have an effect on approval ratings for a limited period of time even though while present they may help mask periods of vulnerability in the president's, government's, or country's life.

There is little or no research yet examining how presidents' behavior can affect the approval of mass publics in other countries since the gathering of such data is relatively new. But it is interesting to note how some of those with more negative views of the United States were already trying to "Bushify" Obama as he took office, painting him as nothing more than a clone of Bush—as noted at the time, a "campaign to rebrand a new US president who is inconveniently popular by those who need to have a perpetual enemy in the White House" (Naim 2009, 1). We can also examine data in the World Public Opinion polls regarding how different world leaders are viewed across the globe and consider how particular leaders are viewed in their own countries versus in the United States or a majority of the 22 other countries that are sampled. Take, for example, the World Public Opinion poll data for 2009 (see worldpublicopinion. org June 29, 2009). Such an examination shows some 82% of the Russian public had confidence in Putin, their prime minister, to do the right thing in world affairs while only 27% of the American public had such a view. Moreover, a majority of the publics in the 22 (15 out of 22 or 69%) other countries studied agreed with the US public. While having standing at home, Putin was viewed warily abroad. Hu Jin-tao, then Chinese president, had more countries with a majority of the public having confidence in what he was likely to do than Putin (10 to 7 of the 22 countries); these majorities at 50% or higher occurred in 7 of the 8 countries (88%) in Asia that were polled. In effect, the data suggest that Hu Jin-tao appeared to have standing in the Asian region. An examination of the data on Obama showed 8 countries where less than 50% of the public had confidence in what he was likely to do in world affairs—and 5 of these countries were those where US foreign policy was under threat (Russia, Turkey, Iraq, Palestinian Territories, and Pakistan). From the very start of his administration, Obama was viewed as having to prove himself in these countries— these were countries where Obama was already "Bushified."The data suggest that there is a complex interaction between approval at home and that abroad and the notion of standing.

### *How Presidents View Approval Ratings and Whose Count*

What are American presidents' perspectives on the role that public opinion and approval ratings play in foreign policymaking? Where does standing "stand" with them? Research suggests that their perspectives differ on just how and when such public opinion should be taken into account. Douglas Foyle (1999), for example, examined presidents' beliefs about the relevance of public opinion in the foreign policymaking process and the necessity of having public support for foreign policy decisions once made. Contrasting these beliefs produced the two by two matrix found in Table 20.1.

*Table 20.1.* Presidents' Beliefs about the Relevance of Public Opinion to Policymaking. Is public support of foreign policy necessary once decisions are made?

| Is it desirable to consider public opinion in making foreign policy decisions? | Yes | No |
|---|---|---|
| Yes | **Delegate** (Clinton) Public opinion should shape the evaluation of policy options and partially define what is viewed as correct policy. | **Executor** (Carter) Public opinion should shape the evaluation of policy options. |
| No | **Pragmatist** (Eisenhower, Kennedy, Nixon, Ford, H.W. Bush) Public opinion becomes the rationalization used to justify a decision. | **Guardian** (Truman, Johnson, Reagan) Believe should do what is "right" regardless of public support, the public can be educated. |

Adapted from Foyle (1999).

For all but those having the Guardian belief system noted in Table 20.1, public opinion is important to foreign policymaking in the formation of policy options and/or in garnering support for the final policy. For presidents with the Delegate belief system, public opinion comes into play throughout the foreign policymaking process. The belief systems in the table suggest adherence to the various roles that democratic theory has suggested elected politicians can play from being a representative of the people to being a delegate for what they want to being a trustee for the public—that is, going from including to excluding the public and their opinions/wants/interests from foreign policymaking as well as moving from trusting that the public is informed enough about foreign policy to justify having their ideas taken into account to assuming they are not that well informed. Digging into archival data and doing a series of case studies, Foyle was able to classify the belief systems of presidents from Truman through Clinton based on what they said about public opinion and its importance as well as how they acted in a set of national security crises. According to his exploration, American presidents are more likely to differ on the necessity of getting the public on board once decisions are made than in including their views in the policymaking process—6 of these 10 presidents (60%) viewed getting the public's support for a decision once made as necessary while 4 (40%) did not. In other words, for six presidents public opinion and the notion of how they stood with the public acted as a constraint on their foreign policymaking.

Perhaps of even more interest, Foyle found that it was not the "actual" public opinion data that drove these presidents but their expectations regarding what the public wanted as well as their views regarding whether or not their approval ratings were declining or increasing that shaped their foreign policy. The particular policy chosen and how well they were doing were based on anticipation of others' responses. Indeed, "when public opinion affected foreign policy choices, it was because the president feared losing the public's support of either the policy or the administration" (Foyle 1999, 266). Beliefs about public opinion and their interpretations of the meaning of the data shaped these six presidents' views on standing and its importance. For the four presidents who, themselves, knew the "right" foreign policy action to take without consideration of the nature of public support, they took actions with the view that they could, if necessary, educate the public about the appropriateness of their agendas and gain such support.

Foyle's (1999) study as well as those of others (e.g., Graham 1994; Powlick 1995; Powlick and Katz 1998) have suggested that presidents' expectations about public opinion are often tempered by the perceptions of their advisers and their interactions with members of Congress. Indeed, the question can be raised as to when the public even becomes aware of what is happening—in effect, when their opinion is sought. Is it when there is dissensus between the Congress and the president and the media pick up on it, conflict among bureaucracies, events occur abroad? If such is the case, then presidents can expect approval ratings to be ephemeral and that the public is indicating its support or lack thereof on information that is generally negative in nature and calls forth their own optimism or pessimism and beliefs about the American government's ability to have any control over what is happening. And, if such is the case, it is probably no wonder Foyle indicates—as noted above—that presidents who consider public opinion focus on it when they fear they are losing support for a particular policy or their administration.

At issue is who gets to define standing—the public through their approval ratings, Congress through legislation or lack there of, events that are happening abroad, or the president. Remember that leadership, and in our example here the presidency, involves moving toward the government's goals while at the same time working on developing and maintaining a semblance of a consensus among those involved in the process. The research just discussed suggests that presidents build their expectations regarding their standing by assessing who can affect their policies and their continuation in office (or legacy) the most at a particular point in time. Sometimes—particularly around election times—it may be the public that influences such expectations. But at other times it could be the Congress, leaders in specific other countries, powerful interest groups, or some combination thereof that shapes their expectations. Most of the research to date uses objective as opposed to subjective data in exploring the effects of approval ratings and public support on actions of presidents. Foyle's study pushes us to consider ascertaining how presidents themselves are viewing their standing and whose opinions are counting for them in specific situations.

Determining whose positions count for presidents becomes even more relevant and complicated when we discover the differences in opinion that often exist between those in the general public and those in the political elite as well as the differences in opinion that are found among the general publics and political elites in other countries. Consider the fact that while 76% of the US public in a recent poll were concerned about the large amount of US debt held by China, only on average 22% of political elites and experts indicated such concern (pewglobal.org September 18, 2012). And US policies are viewed more favorably by "younger, wealthier, well-educated, and urban Chinese" than by the general Chinese public (pewglobal.org October 16, 2012).

## *In Conclusion*

Suffice it to say this discussion is meant as an initial attempt to stimulate thinking about what is involved in the relationship between standing and political leadership using as an illustration the American presidency. Much remains to be done. The research reported does suggest some avenues that might prove interesting for future study and different types of data and information that are needed to more effectively study if there is a relationship between leadership, standing, and reputation. The study of public diplomacy can only gain with such information.

## *Bibliography*

Baker, W. D. & Oneal, J. R. (2001). Patriotism or opinion leadership: The nature and origins of the "rally 'round the flag" effect. *Journal of Conflict Resolution,45* (5), 661–687.

Barrett, A. W. & Eshbaugh-Soha, M. (2007). Presidential success on the substance of legislation. *Political Research Quarterly, 60* (1), 100–112.

Berthoud, J. & Demian Brady. (2001) Detailed review of presidential travel crowns Bill Clinton Harlem's honorary globetrotter. Retrieved August 19, 2009 from: ntu.org

Brace, P. & Hinckley, B. (1992). *Follow the leader: Opinion polls and the modern presidency.* New York: Basic Books.

Brule, D. (2006). Congressional opposition, the economy, and US dispute initiation, 1946–2000. *Journal of Conflict Resolution, 50,* 463–483.

———. (2008). Congress, presidential approval, and US dispute initiation. *Foreign Policy Analysis, 4,* 349–370.

Burbach, D. T. (2003). Wagging the doves: Peace-promoting actions as a source of presidential support. Proceedings from the annual meeting of the American Political Science Association. Philadelphia, PA, August 23.

Canes-Wrone, B. & Shotts, K. W. (2004). The conditional nature of presidential responsiveness to public opinion. *Journal of Political Science, 48* (4), 690–706.

Chapman, T. L. & Reiter, D. (2004).The United Nations Security Council and the rally 'round the flag effect. *Journal of Conflict Resolution, 48* (6), 886–909.

DeRouen, K. (1995). The indirect link: Politics, the economy, and the use of force. *Journal of Conflict Resolution 39,* 671–695.

Downs, G. W. & Rocke, D. M. (1994). Conflict, agency, and gambling for resurrection: The principal-agent problem goes to war. *American Journal of Political Science, 38,* 362–380.

Edwards Jr., G. C. (1997). Aligning tests with theory: Presidential approval as a source of influence in Congress. *Congress and the Presidency, 24,* 113–130.

Fordham, B. (2005). Strategic conflict avoidance and the diversionary use of force. *Journal of Politics, 67,* 132–153.

Foyle, D. C. (1999). *Counting the Public In: Presidents, Public Opinion, and Foreign Policy.* New York: Columbia University Press.

Gelpi, C. (1997). Democratic diversions: Governmental structure and the externalization of domestic conflict. *Journal of Conflict Resolution, 41,* 255–282.

Graham, T. W. (1994). Public opinion and US Foreign policy decision making. In D. A. Deese (Ed.), *The New Politics of American Foreign Policy.* New York: St. Martin's Press.

Hermann, M. G. (2014). Political psychology and the study of political leadership. In P. Hart & R. Rhodes (Eds.), *Oxford Handbook of Political Leadership.* Oxford: Oxford University Press.

James, P. & Oneal, J. R. (1991). The influence of domestic and international politics on the president's use of force. *Journal of Conflict Resolution, 35,* 307–332.

Kernell, S. (1986). *Going Public.* Washington, DC: Congressional Quarterly Press.

Leeds, B. A. & Davis, D. R. (1997). Domestic political vulnerability and international disputes. *Journal of Conflict Resolution, 41* (6), 814–834.

MacKuen, M. B. (1993). Political drama, economic conditions, and the dynamics of presidential popularity. *American Journal of Political Science, 27,* 165–192.

Miller, R. A. (1995). Domestic structure and the diversionary use of force. *American Journal of Political Science, 39,* 760–785.

———. (1999). Regime type, strategic interaction, and the diversionary use of force. *Journal of Conflict Resolution, 46* (3), 388–402.

Morgan, T. C. & Bickers, K. (1992). Domestic discontent and the external use of force. *Journal of Conflict Resolution,36,* 25–52.

Mueller, J. (1973).*War, presidents, and public opinion.* New York: Wiley & Sons.

Naim, M. (2009, January). "The Bushification of Barack Obama." Retrieved August 19, 2009 from: ForeignPolicy.com.

Ostrom, C. & Job, B. (1985).The president and the political use of force. *American Political Science Review 79,* 541–566.

Pew Research Center (2009, July 23). Confidence in Obama lifts US image around the world. Retrieved August 15, 2012 from: Pewglobal.org

———. (2012, June 13). Global opinion of Obama slips, international policies faulted. Retrieved October 18, 2012 from: Pewglobal.org

———. (2012, September 18). US public, experts differ on China policies. Retrieved October 18, 2012 from: Pewglobal.org

———. (2012, October 16). Growing concerns in China about inequality, corruption. Retrieved October 18, 2012 from: Pewglobal.org

Powlick, P. J. (1995). The sources of public opinion for American foreign policy officials. *International Studies Quarterly, 39*, 327–452.

Powlick, P. J. & Katz, A. Z. (1998) Defining the American public opinion/foreign policy nexus. *Mershon International Studies Review, 42*, 29–61.

Putnam, R. D. (1988). Diplomacy and Domestic Politics: The Logic of Two-Level Games. *International Organization, 42*, 427–460.

Richards, D., Morgan, T. C., Wilson, R. C., Schwebach, V., & Young G. D. (1993). Good times, bad times, and the diversionary use of force: A tale of some not so free agents. *Journal of Conflict Resolution, 37*, 504–535.

Smith, A. (1996). Diversionary foreign policy in democratic systems. *International Studies Quarterly, 40*, 133–153.

Telhami, S. (1999) From Camp David to Wye: Changing assumptions in Arab-Israeli negotiations. *Middle East Journal, 53*(3), 379–392.

Worldpublicopinion.org. "Obama rockets to top of poll on global leaders." June 29, 2009. Retrieved August 15, 2012 from Worldpublicopinion.org

# 21. A Contextualized Interpretation of PD Evaluation

JAMES PAMMENT

While the term public diplomacy (PD) has undergone a major revival in the early 21st century, the evaluation of PD programs has not been given anywhere near the same level of attention. The number of studies which consider either the methods used for the evaluation of PD campaigns or the theoretical grounds of PD evaluation methodologies remain few compared to the number which discuss PD policy or campaign outputs (see Banks, 2011 for an extensive overview). When describing what PD programs *do*, scholars quite understandably tend to make assumptions based on the goals or outputs of the program rather than on the basis of reliable, empirical data on the results. Yet, clearly it is only once the effects of a campaign have been measured and the results compared and analyzed that we can say with any certainty what a campaign has *done*.

There are at least three explanations for why evaluation has not been given the consideration it deserves in PD research. First, scholars have tended to agree with practitioners on the idea that the 'contents' or processes of the campaign should be the focus of analysis (Heath & Coombs 2006, pp. 184–187). Evaluation has invariably been considered distinct from the campaign as a body of empirical materials. Second, carrying out independent evaluations of somebody else's PD campaigns, without their consent and full transparency, is impractical if not impossible. Unless practitioners provide access to their data, scholars can only analyze the media artefacts from a campaign, which places the focus of evaluation once again on outputs and processes. Third, scholars who have looked more closely at evaluation have quickly realized that "measuring the effectiveness of public diplomacy is universally recognized as a very difficult task." This is because "the multiple factors—both objective and subjective—involved in achieving goals and influencing outcomes make any rigid application of a cause-and-effect rationale injudicious" (Pahlavi, 2007, p. 274). In other words, scholars have assumed that evaluation of PD campaigns is more or less impossible.

Establishing how PD programs function and what impact they have has, therefore, been a thankless task. Yet, the question has become increasingly pressing within government circles in recent years. *Objectives, outcomes, impact, accountability* and *efficiency* have become buzzwords within foreign ministry communication departments. PD practitioners are now expected to be able to demonstrate the relevance of their campaigns to diplomatic priorities, the efficacy and value-for-money of their methods, and their concrete impact upon target groups. This means that the traditional ad-hoc measures used by press officers at overseas posts—such as calculating the advertising equivalent costs of a binder full of media clippings—are less credible now than they were five or ten years ago. An academic study from 2007, noting the subjective nature of PD measurement at the time, concluded:

> Examination of major PD programmes reveals that, broadly speaking, these programmes are centred on immeasurable goals, tend to consider out*puts* rather than out*comes*, concentrate on the wrong indicators, and suffer from a lack of appropriate methods for conducting audience analysis (Pahlavi, 2007, p. 256).

Based on evaluation data from the first five years or so of the 21$^{st}$ century, there is ample evidence to support this view. Evaluation has been an afterthought, a secondary concern subservient to the personal judgement of those working in the field. The key themes for this chapter take their point of departure from Pahlavi's 2007 analysis. I will argue here there are sufficient examples in recent years of innovation in the field of PD evaluation to suggest that things have moved on in quite significant ways. In fact, the development of an evaluation culture is fundamentally changing how PD is theorized, planned, and executed. Evaluation is not just emerging as a niche area of interest: *it is changing the entire culture of public diplomacy.* My principal argument is that if scholars wish to understand how and why PD campaigns take the forms they do, they will need to develop an appreciation for the *cultures of accountability and evaluation* at PD institutions.

This chapter draws upon examples from the recent evaluation methods of a number of national-level PD actors in the U.S. and Europe. Based on the findings of this research, I make three important arguments regarding PD evaluation. First, I make the point that methods of PD communication are tending towards convergence. By this, I mean that the traditional components of PD such as listening, advocacy, cultural diplomacy, exchange diplomacy, international broadcasting, and information operations have, in a number of cases, become less diverse in their choices of communication methods (cf Cull, 2008). The unique styles of communication once associated with political lobbying or cultural exchange have, for a number of reasons, tended towards convergence. Perhaps the most important of these reasons is the imposition of evaluation cultures across different kinds of PD activities. This culture of evaluation has reduced diversity and increased standardization of PD campaigns.

Second, I present a framework in support of the idea that there are, broadly speaking, four major approaches to evaluation used to assess these increasingly convergent PD styles. These hinge upon evaluating outputs, outcomes, perceptions or networks. However, it is important to observe that these approaches do not simply measure PD, but are bound to implicit understandings of the purpose of PD, how communication influences attitudes or behavior, and the ways in which influence becomes tangible. Adoption of a certain style and methodology of evaluation is implicitly connected to preconceived ideas of PD's purpose and what it can and should do.

Finally, I argue that the choice of evaluation method reflects national and institutional cultures with regard to accountability and transparency; it is a result of management trails and cultures of public scrutiny. I propose that these approaches to evaluation should not simply be treated as methodologies for data collection, but as paradigms intimately linked to implicit theories of what PD is, does, and how it is accounted for in the context of each institution. In this sense, selection of evaluation tools is not merely a question of finding the most effective data collection methods, but of reinforcing expectations and ideologies of the role of PD within the expectation of results expected by stakeholders. Choice over methods, and the overall hierarchies in which results are placed, is first and foremost a decision drawing upon a prior understanding of the purpose and goals of PD, heavily influenced by the institutional need for reporting results.

## *The Story So Far: Evaluation as Convergence*

In his 2007 article in the *Hague Journal of Diplomacy*, Pahlavi recognized that a key shift had occurred in PD during the mid-2000s; namely, the increased interest by government decision-makers in PD's "concrete utility" to foreign policy. These interests could be seen in three indicators of change: 1) the adoption of "measurable objectives" surrounding campaign design; 2) the closer integration of funding approval processes and planning/reporting processes; and 3) in "the promotion of a professional culture of evaluation" (Pahlavi 2007, pp. 279–280). Although this article contains a great deal of relevant information and analysis, and perhaps remains the most important interjection in the field, it tends toward trying to discover the best evaluation method. Like others since (e.g., Fitzpatrick, 2010), it seeks to improve evaluation activities by identifying best practices from normative scientific, rather than sociological, principles. However, I argue that more consideration needs to be given to how and why evaluation practices look a certain way; to interpret and explain within individual contexts rather than provide a single model for improvement.

In my subsequent survey of PD evaluation in the first decade of the 21st century, I found ample data from the U.S., U.K. and Sweden to support the thrust of Pahlavi's analysis (Pamment, 2011a). Huge efforts had been made to improve objective-setting so as to provide a firm basis for evaluating outcomes. Resources were increasingly allocated based on strategic importance to the organization as a whole rather than on traditional patterns of behavior. Together, these shifts contributed to an overwhelming sense in which evaluation work was indeed being professionalized. Foreign and cultural ministries in these three countries designed and implemented global management databases, trackers and spreadsheets to capture and standardize various types of data about their PD campaigns. They recorded a wide variety of variables, connecting diverse measures such as overarching strategic priorities, specific objectives, allocated resources and campaign outputs, the perceptions of those involved, and any notable impacts upon their environment. Most, but certainly not all of these systems had the capacity to be plugged into decision-making and accounting chains, thereby directly contributing to the rationalization of PD funding.

In two follow-up discussions, I further considered the impact of these changes upon the PD field (Pamment, 2012; 2013). I argue that this period of reorganization, inspired by notions of a "new" PD, could be characterized by increased introspection within PD organizations. The clear pattern across these cases was that a focus upon objective-setting, strategy, and evaluation had substantially changed how PD was being carried out. Instead of looking *outwards* to the target groups and target cultures of PD, organizations were instead looking *inwards* at what they wanted from PD, what resources they were prepared to allocate to it, and what impact PD was having on their business priority areas.

Emerging evaluation cultures have focused upon the effects of PD campaigns, using the goals of the organization as the yardstick. Attempts to understand foreign cultures, perceptions and attitudes have been rearticulated within these goals, where the concept of *outcomes*—simply put, whether the things "we" did seemed to contribute to the results "we" wanted—has subsumed all other measures into supporting the organization's objectives (Pamment, 2013, pp. 127–128).

Rather than attempting to capture all the possible direct and indirect effects of a PD campaign, evaluation had taken a far more pragmatic direction, which primarily hinged on the achievement of each organization's objectives. The impact of this on different kinds of organizations was striking. In cultural bodies like the British Council and Swedish Institute, which traditionally considered their work to consist of longer-term relationship-building distinct from the government's immediate political objectives (as pursued by foreign ministries), the increased interest in accountability meant that they were now expected to report the results of their efforts annually. Data were often logged immediately following an event, indicating in some sense at least that the lifespan of PD activities had changed in line with accounting needs. The traditional distinctions between the promotional, cultural, advocacy, and informational components of PD were in practice blurred, in part because of changing expectations of how PD activities should be evaluated.

I will argue here that four distinct approaches to PD evaluation have emerged during this period, and that each holds implicit views of how PD *works*. The four approaches are *output analysis, outcome analysis, perception analysis* and *network analysis*. Each introduction below outlines their main data collection methodologies, some of their general underlying theoretical considerations, and a summary of what they attempt to evaluate.

## Output Analysis

PD evaluation since the late 1990s has been heavily contingent upon public relations' (PR) evaluation methods. Yet within PR, there is little consensus on how to best measure *influence*. "There is no one, simple, all-encompassing research tool, technique or methodology that can be relied on to measure and evaluate PR effectiveness. Usually, a combination of different measurement techniques are needed." These techniques might include measuring column inches or airtime, polls, surveys, focus groups, in-depth interviews, media content analysis, headcounts at events, participant observation, and Internet tracking to name but a few (Lindenmann, 2003, p. 4). The problem in many respects is that these approaches, taken individually, tend to measure the activities of a campaign rather than its outcomes. This is termed *process evaluation*, in which what you do during the campaign is the focus of evaluation. However, PR scholars tend to see evaluations of campaign outputs as flawed, since they describe and confirm the process of PR, not the outcomes (Heath & Coombs, 2006, pp. 184–185).

These ad hoc methods measure a range of attributes from exposure and reach to attitudes and perceptions. Perhaps the most common ad hoc measurement is "clip counting," the number of press clippings generated during a campaign (Watson, 2000). This is also (negatively) referred to as the "thud factor," to express the impact made when a binder full of press clippings lands on a table. Critics contend that this approach is "usually short-term and surface," and "the analysis contains no insights, discussion or interpretation" (Michaelson & Griffin, 2005, pp. 2–3; Lindenmann, 2003, p. 4). Clip counting analysis is often supplemented by circulation and demographic data in order to establish the potential number of "impressions" or exposures to the story. Other measurements, such as the overall size of the article (column inches), its prominence, the number of spokesperson quotes or times core messages are quoted, and photos, may also be included (Lindenmann, 2003, pp. 5–6; Michaelson & Griffin, 2005, p. 5). This can also include rudimentary content analysis such as the coding of certain types of information in order to quantify their frequency and favorability. However, "This method accurately represents only what is actually written. Intended messages or specific items of information that are not included in the codes or do not appear in the articles are not included in the analysis" (Michaelson & Griffin, 2005, p. 4; see also Lindenmann, 2003, pp. 9–11).

Measurements of campaign outputs such as these are often supplemented by estimations of *advertising value equivalence*. This involves the conversion of editorial space into the equivalent daily cost of purchasing advertisement space. An ambitious press or public affairs officer at an embassy might use such a calculation as proof of the campaign's—and their personal—value to the mission. However, "This approach is generally discredited by public relations practitioners as well as by leading researchers" (Michaelson & Griffin, 2005, p. 3). Furthermore, some measurements artificially multiply the advertising cost on the basis that editorial space is of greater value than an advert. "Most reputable researchers view such arbitrary 'weighting' schemes aimed at enhancing the alleged value of editorial coverage as unethical, dishonest, and not at all supported by the research literature" (Lindenmann, 2003, pp. 9–11).

As Pahlavi noted in 2007, these methods have fallen into disrepute in recent years. Yet, if the reporting chains of a given PD institution are focused primarily on the activities of staff, it could be argued that measurement of their processes and outputs can provide valid evidence of productivity. Furthermore, it is important to note that most of the ambitious evaluation approaches that have been developed over the past decade or so still rely on these individual methods to some degree. The difference is that they are rearticulated within an overall strategy for evaluation based around expectations of what PD *is* and *does*, and what results are required by the PD institution within their culture of accountability.

## Outcome Analysis

Perhaps the most prevalent approach to evaluation—and the one which is frequently identified as *the best*—is that which emphasizes the outcomes of a PD campaign. Outcome-based methods compare different sources of information in order to establish a "bottom-line" perspective on a campaign's impact. These bottom-line outcomes are then assessed against the organization's objectives in order to determine whether the campaign contributed to the organization's overall purpose. These approaches build upon *logic models*, which are well established within PR literature as an essential basis for campaign evaluation. Logic models integrate the four steps of influence campaigns into an outcomes-based approach: assessment of the situation, planning of the campaign, conducting the campaigns, and evaluating its impact. Since the outcomes determine the overall success or failure of the campaign, they must be linked to objectives. This means that the organization needs to fully understand its own intentions and expectations of what PD can achieve; for example increasing awareness about an issue or changing attitudes or behaviour. A well-defined objective is key to being able to evaluate results (Heath & Coombs, 2006, pp. 185–187).

Organizational priorities are used to contextualize measurements in terms of the overall needs of the communicator, so that the effectiveness of specific campaigns is benchmarked against an actor's strategy. The first step is, therefore, to set objectives that are achievable and measurable. The second is to assess the activities and processes involved in the campaign, such as the resources allocated, the outputs produced, and what participants learned following exposure to the campaign. "Outcomes" refer to the extensive analysis of all of these elements and further analyses of changes to the environment or in behavior over the long-term. This builds on the principle that multiple "weak signals" gathered from a number of sources, though insufficient in themselves, can be aggregated to build a picture of the overall impact of PD strategy. Finally, these results should be reassessed in terms of the organizational priorities outlined in the first step to see if resources have been appropriately allocated (Michaelson & Griffin, 2005; Lindenmann, 2003, pp. 5–8; Spence 2007, pp. 8–9). The aim is not to assess all possible results from a PD campaign, but rather only those relevant to the organization's business objectives. In this sense, it conducts a measurement of an organization's efficacy in producing PD to achieve results, not of the PD in and of itself.

Theories that support this approach emphasize the real-world impact of communication activities, and hence may be found in the *realist* paradigm of international relations. Realism, though diverse and with many iterations, tends to interpret international affairs on the basis of power relations, access to material resources, and the inter-balance between areas of international affairs (e.g. Lebow, 2007; Mearsheimer, 2007; and Elman, 2007). In the field of PD, Joseph Nye's (1990) notion of soft power provides an influential realist interpretation of the role of communication. Soft power arises from "intangible power resources such a culture, ideology, and institutions," and is defined as "the ability to affect what other countries want" (pp. 165–166). Pahlavi (2007) defines the goal of PD evaluation from this perspective as attempting to understand the *hard effects* of *soft diplomacy* (p. 272). Outcome-based approaches want to know what concrete changes occurred in the policy area as a result of the communication campaign. Therefore, they are also closely linked to attempts to rationalize institutions' activities, for which PD has been allocated resources, and the efficacy of resource allocation is tested.

For example, the U.S. State Department recently introduced an online database called the *Mission Activity Tracker* (MAT) which allows embassies to record their PD activities and link campaign objectives to accounting chains, resources deployed, events and outputs, and any observed results. MAT was developed to articulate PD activities at posts within the federal government's accountability system, PART (Program Assessment Rating Tool). This means that U.S. PD activities are evaluated using the same standardized accountability processes as most other areas of governmental activity. Each of the variables collected are rearticulated within objectives which are related to the overall priorities and budget headings of the State Department or other relevant actors. Hence, the focus is on outcome analysis established out of organizational goals which are motivated by the broader culture of accountability within the federal government (Pamment, 2013).

## Perception Analysis

While outcome analysis is ultimately interested in determining whether the concrete outcomes desired by the PD organization were achieved, other alternative (and at times complementary) approaches are used. A widely-used alternative method is to collect data on the attitudes and opinions of foreign citizens in order to understand whether policies or campaigns change how people think. The goal is not to evaluate concrete social change or an organization's capacity to deliver results, but rather to evaluate the knowledge and values which motivate change. Opinion polls such as those conducted by Pew and Gallup are probably the best known measures of attitudes, although they are too general to say much about specific PD campaigns, and practitioners tend to consider such surveys useful for researching the context of a campaign rather than for evaluating its results (http://pewglobal.org/about/; http://

www.gallup.com). PD organizations, therefore, conduct their own surveys of specialized target groups; for example, the State Department conducts the bi-annual *Public Diplomacy Impact* project (PDI), a series of opinion surveys and focus groups comparing the views of PD participants to those of equivalent non-participants (Pamment, 2013). The data are then used as a complement to outcomes-based approaches.

There can be little doubt that, with the introduction of marketing and branding techniques to PD from the late-1990s onward, methods inspired by PR have heavily influenced this approach to PD. The *Nation Brands Index* (NBI), for example, has been fully integrated into the development of PD strategies in regions like the Nordics, where Sweden, Denmark, Norway and Finland each adopted a nation branding approach when they redesigned their PD setups between 2005 and 2010 (see, for example, Pamment, 2011b). Initiated in 2005 by Simon Anholt, the NBI measures the reputations of 50 countries in subjects such as tourism, culture, and governance, and produces an overall ranking of the national image. Although it lacks the sense of cause-and-effect created around organizational goals in outcome analysis, perception analysis links to longer-term values, norms and stereotypes with which some styles of PD engage.

The theory of *nation brands* is one of the more important underlying themes behind perceptions analysis in contemporary PD. The term originates from the context of Tony Blair's strategic communication initiatives in the late 1990s, and British practitioners Simon Anholt, Mark Leonard, and Wally Olins can claim to have contributed to its earliest definitions. The approach focuses on self-representation, and uses values and ideas as a means of manipulating image. Mark Leonard (1997), for example, based his argument around nation-states being "relatively recent and deliberately constructed creations" which, like all constructions, require the occasional face lift (pp. 18–20). This supposes a kind of discursive or semiotic sphere in which symbols and values interact and transfer ideas between nations, goods, and peoples (Anholt, 1998, p. 395). Scholars attracted to the notion of ideas as a dominant force in international affairs have gone so far as to state that, "Favorable image and reputation around the world, achieved through attraction and persuasion, have become more important than territory, access, and raw materials" (Gilboa, 2008, p. 56).

In other words, the importance of influence over hearts and minds in the era of nation brands provides an alternative to realist conceptions of international relations. From this perspective, the goal of PD is to affect perceptions, ideas and beliefs, and not necessarily (or directly) the distribution of material resources. Bush's War on Terror discourse certainly contributed to this view, although in branding exercises the indirect goals of such campaigns are often to produce "concrete" changes (e.g., boosting tourism and trade). Much like with commercial brands, the focus on perceptions allows for the measurement of how people think and feel about a potential purchase, but evaluation does not stretch to considering whether that purchase was actually made (buying behaviour). Rather, the focus is on how a given actor is represented within a battle of ideas, as earlier attempts to link the PR and PD fields emphasized (e.g. Signitzer & Coombs, 1992). The coordination and cooperation of domestic actors in helping shape and promote a consistent brand image are considered absolutely essential (Anholt, 2007). A similar perception-based theoretical approach has been termed *noopolitik*; the idea that a radical new international society is emerging based on boundary-spanning information processing and structuring systems and consisting of cosmopolitan ideas, values, and norms. Approaches such as these explicitly link information and opinions to power, indeed to the idea that international public opinion has become a new superpower (Ronfeldt & Arquilla, 1999, 2009).

Consider, for example, the case of Finland. As a small country on the fringe of Europe, with Russia as an immediate neighbor, Finland focused its Cold War PD on promoting its neutrality, primarily through press relations. Since 1995, it has shifted focus to pursue a political and economic agenda through EU institutions. Finnish PD is currently coordinated by the Finland Promotion Board under the Ministry for Foreign Affairs and involves the collaboration of approximately a dozen actors with an interest in overseas promotion. PD underwent major restructuring in 2008 and is still in a process of evolution. Whereas previously seven different units were involved in areas of international communication and promotion, this is now reduced to two within the Foreign Ministry, which coordinates all areas of activity. The first focuses on PD, and particularly its longer-term aspects such as campaign design, interaction with embassies, and coordination. The second deals with the shorter-term aspects of daily news management and coordinates press conferences, media monitoring, and rapid reaction to news events.

Within this evolving structure, there is little consensus about how evaluation should take place. The Foreign Ministry rejects ad hoc measures such as press clippings since they are considered too subjective, and the ministry does not want to allocate resources based on misleading figures. Since there are so many actors involved in overseas promotion, coordination is a major issue and they are exploring the construction of a common database for coordinating information about campaigns. Evaluation is considered a costly luxury, and the focus has instead been placed on producing and coordinating a unified Finnish brand. The limited budget means that the Foreign Ministry only makes use of NBI data every three or four years. The principal indicator of success is, therefore, unified messages across all the players: "We're sure the public perceptions will come after this" (T. Heino, Director for PD at the MFA, personal communication, 16 September 2011). There is very little consideration of outcomes; rather, the focus is on domestic coordination, and the expectation is that positive changes in perceptions of Finland will occur as a result of better coordination. PD is seen as a coordinated means of influencing public opinion in order to boost exports (see Country Brand Delegation, 2010).

This approach underscores the notion that self-representation, through the cultivation of associated ideas, symbols, and values, is a central purpose of contemporary PD. Evaluation methods are diverse and can capture a range of data through questionnaires, before-and-after surveys, focus groups and qualitative interviews. The emphasis is usually placed on the effects of exposure to policies or values in the minds of target groups, and in the interaction between how a place or idea should be represented according to the PD actor and how others perceive it. A consequence of this is that domestic coordination, ensuring all overseas promotional actors use the same image, is important. Individual perspectives are usually aggregated and presented as statistics (e.g., as a favorability percentage). Therefore, diverse groups are aggregated together as a single statistical mass, which lacks nuance. The approach is usually asymmetrical, with the aim of self-promotion rather than dialogue (Signitzer & Coombs, 1992, pp. 143–144). The emphasis is limited to the realm of ideas, which can lead to ambiguous or presumptuous interpretations of the relationship between information, perceptions and power. Nonetheless, it represents a clearly distinct approach to PD activities aimed at influencing perceptions, where the focus of evaluation is on engaging with opinions, values, beliefs, ideas, attitudes and reputations within an overall paradigm of self-promotion.

## Network Analysis

Network analysis is a second alternative to outcome analysis and probably represents the least well-established approach both in PD literature and among practitioners. Traditional diplomacy is based on a careful understanding and cultivation of relationships in foreign countries, including networking strategies for incorporating like-minded people into policy objectives or influencing key individuals in civil society. PD strategies seek to identify "key influencers," "multipliers," or "agents of change"—individuals who, usually on the basis of a leadership position in their respective social sphere, act as "hubs" with access to a large number of "nodes" in a network. These individuals redistribute core messages in their own voices, which can help shift public opinion. To give a very simplistic example, a typical PD campaign might identify a friendly or like-minded journalist in a specialist magazine about climate change and provide that journalist with favored expert interviewees and other prepared content (information subsidy). From a network perspective, the PD actor has employed a single "multiplier" or "hub" to potentially reach and influence thousands of target "nodes" and additional "hubs" within that policy network.

However, simplistic models of "information transfer" through networks have come into question in recent years, and this kind of PD activity would nowadays most likely be evaluated within an outcome model. The challenge for this approach is to engage with networks while acknowledging that "relationship building" is becoming increasingly central to all "new" PD activities (Zaharna, 2009, pp. 95–97). This draws heavily on the notion of *relationship management*, which emerged in the mid-1980s and has become one of the single most important aspects of PR theory. Relationship management builds on a symmetrical model of communication in which influence flows in both directions and relationships are considered mutually beneficial. This development parallels the notion of *new public diplomacy*, which emphasizes dialogue and mutuality (Fitzpatrick, 2010, pp. 115–127; Melissen, 2005; and Signitzer & Coombs, 1992). PD networks are now more typically characterized as decentralized and multilateral, with multifaceted agendas and multidirectional flows of information (Hocking, 2002).

The position of PD within this phenomenon has not been particularly well developed, although it is telling that Manuel Castells, who has published extensively on the role of networks in globalization, has more recently turned his attention to PD (Castells, 1996/2000, 2008). Castells (2008) argues that the purpose of PD, in difference to traditional diplomacy, "is not to assert power or to negotiate a rearrangement of power relationships. It is to induce a communication space in which a new, common language could emerge as a precondition for diplomacy" (p. 91). In Castells's sense, PD lays the groundwork for the common understandings of issues necessary for contemporary multilateral diplomacy. The emphasis is not on material outcomes, but on managing different perspectives and interests within complex and decentered policy networks. PD's role is, therefore, to build relationships and to understand and engage with the perspectives held by different interests within those relationships as a precondition for formal diplomatic negotiation. It involves all sides adapting to others in order to build a common starting point for engaging with a shared issue (Evans & Steven, 2008).

Traditionally, information transfer through networks is evaluated either through outputs (the number of articles or events and their reach) or on an ad hoc basis as the personal judgement of the PD practitioner, such as through informal feedback from contacts. The evaluation of relationships is a relatively young field in PR, with the focus resting upon perceptions of the relationship through surveys, interviews and focus groups. Measures can assess before-and-after changes, the content of communication, and any outcomes or results. Issues such as trust, satisfaction, commitment and control mutuality (who has the rightful power to influence the other in which areas) are central to evaluation of perceptions within relationships. The notion that relationships can be measured outside of perceptions such as through linkages, exchanges and patterns of interaction has also been explored (Fitzpatrick, 2010, pp. 198–201; Broom, Casey, & Ritchey, 2000; and Lindenmann, 1999). Particularly in social and online media, tools can be used to reveal hub points for the linking of information between networks, including data on locations, activities, groupings of friends, and topics engaged (Fisher, 2010). One of the major challenges for evaluating PD based upon mutuality and consensus-building is to find a sufficiently defined sense of purpose so as to avoid rearticulating analysis within a self-interested, outcome-based approach. Here, the disconnect between PD (and particularly "new" PD) theory and practice is pronounced (Pamment, 2013).

An example may be seen in the British Council project *The Network Effect*, which Ali Fisher (2010) has discussed in detail. This project analyzed the ways in which event participants remained in contact professionally and socially, including before-and-after surveys and graphical representations of how relationships developed. Such an approach enabled analysis of how participants were using the network, its evolution over time, and the development of key hubs, such as individuals who maintained their contact lists, joined them with others, and initiated new conversations and meetings.

Network analysis is, at its core, a means of understanding diverse individual perspectives within a complex array of relationships. It can be used for mapping where key "nodes" develop and which parts of the network they relate to and impact. It captures power relationships and the ways in which information flows interact, reinforce, or challenge them. It helps explain how common conceptions of geopolitical issues emerge as a basis for traditional diplomacy, and how technology can challenge national boundaries and debates. However, the conceptual basis for this approach is still at an early stage, and its goals of symmetrical engagement are in sharp contradiction to the objectives of many national forms of PD.

## Conclusion: Evaluation Within Cultures of Accountability

These four approaches to PD evaluation are highly significant insofar as they imply underlying understandings of the role of PD. Output analysis suggests that PD is essentially about the activities of press officers, and that the success of PD may be judged on the basis of getting a message "out there." Outcome analysis suggests that PD is about concrete change, and it functions by transforming communication activities into desired goals. Perception analysis suggests that PD is essentially about moving hearts and minds through coordinated self-representation, with influence taking part in the battleground of values and ideas. Finally, network analysis suggests that PD is about symmetrical engagement with multilateral actors via key hubs, with influence moving in both directions. An overview of these approaches may be seen in Table 21.1.

*Table 21.1.* Overview of PD evaluation approaches.

| Evaluation Method | Methods | PD theory | Anticipated results |
| --- | --- | --- | --- |
| Output analysis | Ad hoc, Press clippings, AVE, OTS | PD as outputs | Proof of labor/ reach/volume |
| Outcome analysis | Logic models, Impact measurements | Soft power = Hard effects | Proof organization is effective/ efficient |
| Perception analysis | Surveys, attitudes, favorability | Reputation management | Proof of influence over ideas & values |
| Network analysis | Hubs & multipliers, forming alliances | Relationship management | Proof of attention to relationships |

My principal argument here is that no single approach is "better" or "more effective" than the others. On the contrary, the relevance and validity of each approach must be considered within the context of insitutional needs, national cultures of accountability, and how they influence the manner in which PD is conducted. Evaluation must be considered within the context of how and why actors employ PD. The ways in which PD is conducted must be considered within the context of cultures of accountability and evaluation.

These brief analyses help establish how varied evaluation cultures can be in different institutional contexts. For this reason, I consider it inappropriate to argue normatively for how evaluation should be conducted. Rather, the relationship between evaluation and cultures of accountability helps explain how and why PD is conducted in certain ways. As researchers, students and practitioners of PD, it is essential that we integrate a contextualized understanding of evaluation cultures into our analyses of PD activities. These four approaches provide conceptual tools for approaching different cultures of accountability which can help us better understand how and why PD takes the form it does.

For a more detailed elaboration of this argument, including its theoretical grounds, position within PD theory and additional case studies, see Pamment (2014).

## *Bibliography*

Anholt, S. (1998). Nation-brands of the twenty-first century. *The Journal of Brand Management*, 5(6), 395–406.

———. (2007). *Competitive identity: The new brand management for nations, cities and regions.* New Hampshire: Palgrave MacMillan

———. (2008). The importance of national reputation. In J. Welsh & D. Fearn (Eds.), *Engagement: Public diplomacy in a globalised world* (31–32). London: Foreign & Commonwealth Office.

Banks, R. (2011). *A resource guide to public diplomacy evaluation* (CPD Perspectives on Public Diplomacy 9/2011). Los Angeles: Figueroa Press.

Broom, G. M., Casey, S. & Ritchey, J. (2000). Concept and theory of organization-public relationships. In J. A. Ledingham & S. D. Bruning (Eds.), *Public relations as relationship management* (pp. 3–22). Mahwah, NJ: Lawrence Erlbaum Publishers.

Castells, M. (2000). *The rise of the network society* (2nd Edition). Oxford: Blackwell Publishing.

———. (2008). The new public sphere: Global civil society, communication networks, and global governance. *The ANNALS of the American Academy of Political and Social Science*, *616*, 78–93.

Country Brand Delegation. (2010, November 25). *Mission for Finland! How Finland will solve the world's most wicked problems. Consider it solved!* Country Brand Report.

Cull, N. J. (2008). *The Cold War and the United States Information Agency: American propaganda and public diplomacy.* Cambridge: Cambridge University Press.

Elman, C. (2007). Realism. In M. Griffiths (Ed.), *International relations theory for the twenty-first century* (11–20). London & New York: Routledge.

Evans, A. & Steven, D. (2008). Towards a theory of influence for twenty-first century foreign policy: Public diplomacy in a globalized world. In J. Welsh & D. Fearn (Eds.), *Engagement: Public diplomacy in a globalised world* (44–61). London: Foreign & Commonwealth Office.

Fisher, A. (2010). *Mapping the Great Beyond: Identifying meaningful networks in public diplomacy: CPD perspectives on public diplomacy.* Los Angeles: Figueroa Press

Fitzpatrick, K. R. (2010). *The future of U.S. public diplomacy: An uncertain fate.* Leiden: Martinus Nijhoff Publishers

Gilboa, E. (2008). Searching for a theory of public diplomacy. *The ANNALS of the American Academy of Political and Social Science*, *616*, 55–77.

Heath, R. L. & Coombs, W. T. (2006) *Today's public relations: An introduction.* Sage.

Hocking, B. (2002). Introduction: Gatekeepers and boundary-spanners– Thinking about foreign ministries in the European Union. In B. Hocking & D. Spence (Eds.) *Foreign ministries in the European Union: Integrating diplomats* (1–17). Basingstoke, UK: Palgrave Macmillan.

Jentleson, B. W. (2007). *American foreign policy: The dynamics of choice in the 21st century, third edition.* London: W.W. Norton & Company.

Lebow, R. N. (2007). Classical realism. In T. Dunne, M. Kurki, & S. Smith (Eds.), *International relations theories: Discipline and diversity*. Oxford: Oxford University Press.

Leonard, M. (1997). *Britain™: Renewing our identity*. London: Demos

Lindenmann, W. K. (2003). *Guidelines for measuring the effectiveness of PR programs and activities*. Institute for Public Relations. http://www.instituteforpr.org/files/uploads/2002_measuringprograms_1.pdf

Mearsheimer, J. J. (2007). Structural realism. In T. Dunne, M. Kurki, & S. Smith (Eds.), *International relations theories: Discipline and diversity*. Oxford: Oxford University Press.

Melissen, J. (2005). *The new public diplomacy: Soft power in international relations*. London: Palgrave Macmillan.

Michaelson, D. & Griffin, T. L. (2005). *A new model for media content analysis*. Institute for Public Relations. http://www.instituteforpr.org/files/uploads/2002_measuring programs_1.pdf

Nye Jr., J. S. (1990). Soft Power. *Foreign Policy, 80*, 152–171.

Pahlavi, P. C. (2007). Evaluating public diplomacy programmes. *The Hague Journal of Diplomacy, 2*, 255–281.

Pamment, J. (2011a). *The limits of the new public diplomacy: Strategic communication and evaluation at the Foreign & Commonwealth Office, British Council, U.S. State Department, Swedish Foreign Ministry & Swedish Institute* (Doctoral dissertation). Retrieved from Stockholm University: http://urn.kb.se/resolve?urn=urn:nbn:se:-su:diva-55021

———. (2011b). Innovations in public diplomacy & nation brands: Inside the House of Sweden. *Journal of Place Branding and Public Diplomacy, 7*(2), 127–135.

———. (2012). What became of the new public diplomacy? Recent developments in British, U.S. & Swedish public diplomacy policy and evaluation methods. *The Hague Journal of Diplomacy, 7*(3), 313–336.

———. (2013). *New Public Diplomacy in the 21ˢᵗ Century: Evaluating Policy and Practice*. Oxford: Routledge.

———. (2014). Articulating influence: Toward a research agenda for interpreting the evaluation of soft power, public diplomacy and nation brands. *Public Relations Review, 40*, 50–59.

Ronfeldt, D. & Arquilla, J. (1999). *The emergence of Noopolitik: Toward an American information strategy*. RAND: MR-1033-OSD

———. (2009). Noopolitik: A new paradigm for public diplomacy. In N. Snow & P. M. Taylor (Eds), *Routledge handbook of public diplomacy* (352–366). London & New York: Routledge.

Signitzer, B. H. & Coombs, T. (1992). Public Relations & Public Diplomacy: Conceptual Convergences. *Public Relations Review, 18*(2), 127–147.

Spence, J. (2007). The future of public diplomacy. *Report on Wilton Park Conference (WP842), March 1–3, 2007*. Retrieved from: https://www.wiltonpark.org.uk/re ports/

Watson, T. (2000). Integrating planning and evaluation. In R. L. Heath (Eds.), *Handbook of public relations* (259–268). Thousand Oaks, CA: Sage Publications.

Zaharna, R. S. (2009). Mapping out a spectrum of public diplomacy initiatives: Information and relational communication frameworks. In N. Snow & P. M. Taylor (Eds), *Routledge handbook of public diplomacy* (86–100). London & New York: Routledge.

## 22. Tenets of Diversity: Building a Strategy for Social Justice in Public Diplomacy

BRENDA WRIGLEY

Diversity makes people nervous. We're afraid we'll make a mistake, say the wrong thing, create an awkward situation, or even spark an international incident. This makes diversity a highly charged, fascinating, and controversial topic. Definitions are difficult and agreement on scope and application is fraught with contention. Nonetheless, diversity poses one of the most opportune frames for furthering Public Diplomacy efforts and increasing understanding across cultures, borders and continents. An agency professional describes it this way:

> It's just smart for a lot of reasons. The world is changing a lot. We take the whole global economy and global community seriously. And, most of the world isn't White. You have got to be diverse if you are going to speak to diverse audiences. (Hon & Brunner, 2000, p. 327)

This chapter proposes a set of tenets to move communication efforts toward achieving social justice, applying theories of Public Relations, Public Diplomacy, diversity, and a host of other organizational and social science theories that, taken together, can begin to examine the complex nature of relationships, the foundation for both Public Relations and Public Diplomacy.

Social scientists working in Public Relations and Public Diplomacy often explore theories from other disciplines. Indeed, our understanding of Public Relations begins with organizational theory and sociology. Our understanding of relationships emerged from theories of interpersonal communication. Even our understanding of adoption of new ideas or persuasion, more commonly known in communications theory circles as *Diffusion of Innovations Theory*, started with studies in agriculture of how farmers came to adopt new strains of corn (McQuail, 2010). It can be argued that Public Relations and Public Diplomacy have really come up with very little "original" theory.

That being said, this blending of theories from studying other fields has many benefits. Particularly in the area of diversity, little research has been conducted in Public Relations; indeed, prior to the 1970s, there was almost no research about diversity. Early studies focused primarily on gender and Public Relations. Seminal scholars like Elizabeth Toth, Larissa Grunig, Judy Turk, Carolyn Cline, Lana Rakow and others made gender a primary focus of their research agendas. Kern-Foxworth (1989) was the only theorist to tackle issues of race in Public Relations during the early days (i.e., the 1980s). This lack of focus on diversity issues in Public Relations can be attributed to several reasons/factors:

1. Until very recently, getting tenure was difficult with a research agenda in diversity or gender.
2. The field in the U.S. is heavily populated with women, but became increasingly "non-diverse" in terms of gender representation as we progressed through the 1980s and 1990s. Women now represent 80% of all practitioners in the U.S. Their numbers are growing in many other parts of the world, although they are not the majority of the practitioners in many countries. A similar lack of diversity exists in terms of race, ethnicity and social class in U.S. Public Relations.
3. Until recently, few researchers were able to parlay a gender or diversity research agenda into a viable consulting practice.

Still other researchers felt there was not sufficient "prestige" in establishing a research agenda that focused on gender or diversity. Indeed, because much of the early work—and even more recent publications—are qualitative, some felt this stream of research was not sufficiently scholarly.

Public Relations, and by extension, Public Diplomacy, has suffered because of this lack of focus. This chapter is meant to spark discussion and offer strategies to consider, rather than offer concrete solutions. Because there is so much we do not know about diversity and the larger issue of social justice, discussion is the place to begin.

## Concepts for the Framework

### Diversity

Webster's defines diversity as "1. the condition of having or being composed of differing elements: *variety*; *especially*; the inclusion of different types of people (as people of different races or cultures) in a group or organization "programs intended to promote *diversity* in schools." 2. an instance of being composed of differing elements or qualities: an instance of being *diverse* "a *diversity* of opinion."

Therefore, diversity as a purely descriptive term is fairly easy for most of us to grasp. It is when we attempt to enact diversity, deal with issues of difference and misunderstanding, or wrestle with competing interests that the conversation becomes much more complicated. And what do we really mean by "diversity"? Is it gender, race, class, sexual orientation, religion, political framework, disability? By creating this short list, we have likely left out significant areas of diversity. Even gender, a concept many view as simple and dichotomous, has evolved in the research into a much more complex area of study; now we often see the term "gender expression," which can mean a continuum of gender from masculine to feminine. Are we talking about gender expression? Biological sex? Sexual behavior and attraction? You can see how it becomes much more complicated than we first thought.

Diversity for diversity's sake alone does not translate to understanding. Nor does it address the tensions and inequities that result from lack of inclusion, tokenism or stereotypes. Indeed, we must have a sort of "mental shorthand" for dealing with those who are different from us, but these shortcuts become problematic when they engrain devaluation and diminishment due to lack of effort in getting to know others, form relationships with them, or build understanding.

## Diversity and Gender

In the Public Relations field, it was thought that the increasing numbers of female practitioners would erase the inequities for women that a lack of diversity may have created. Such has not been the case:

> Some leaders in public relations, too, have pronounced that "the work" has been done and the gaps narrowed to insignificance. However, statistical data have contradicted that rhetoric. Women in public relations have continued to earn substantially less than men, as documented by such trade publications as *pr reporter* and the *Public Relations Journal* as early as 1988 and by the International Association of Business Communicators biannual trend studies between 1998 and 1997....Although attractive salaries have brought women to the field of public relations, these women have found themselves segregated within the lower paying technical positions (Grunig, L. A., Toth & Hon, 2001, pp. 49–50.)

Ferguson (1990) calls the assumption that women are doing well, given their large numbers in the field, "the feminist fallacy." We see many women in

Public Relations and communications in the United States, for example, and assume they are able to rise to positions of influence and management, earn pay comparable to their male counterparts in similar roles, and enjoy the benefits of inclusion. Such has not been the case.

Such assertions provoke strong reactions. Singularly successful women in Public Relations belie the notion that they are not treated fairly. Denial of the problem persists. The author contends that similar, misguided assumptions also persist when we talk about other aspects of diversity and inclusion in Public Relations and communications management. Tokens here and there, particularly visible ones, do not further true efforts toward diversity and inclusion. They merely mask the problem.

Therefore, our first tenet is: *Diversity in Public Relations and communications management and, by extension, in Public Diplomacy, is not only lacking, but it is misunderstood. The result is that efforts toward inclusion have stalled. And, despite efforts by various organizations and professional societies to "tackle" the issue of diversity, our own assumptions and denials prevent us from moving forward in any measurable way.*

## Public Relations as Relationship Building and Relationship Management

James Grunig readily admits that some of his ideas for the famous Four Models of Public Relations came from examination of theories in other disciplines. The Four Models include Press Agentry, Public Information, Two-Way Asymmetrical and Two-Way Symmetrical Communications (Grunig, Grunig, Sriramesh, Huang, & Lyra, 1995). The models are listed in order of chronological development, with early persuasive approaches giving way to more collaborative means of building dialogue and understanding. These later, balanced approaches have been demonstrated to be much more effective in creating relationships that have mutual benefit for organizations and publics (Grunig, J. E., 2001). Still, we cannot assume that the classic four models work in all international settings. For example, Grunig et al. found craft public relations (i.e., the "personal influence model" and "cultural translation") were predominant in India, Greece and Taiwan. (Grunig et al., 1995, pp. 163–164).

Building relationships becomes increasingly more complicated by perceived and actual differences between organizations (in this case, governments) and their publics. Even within particular diverse publics, there can often be a lack of homogeneity. Assumptions about "all Latinas/Latinos," for example, can trip up even the most sincere communicator.

At the core of recognizing, incorporating and embracing diversity as communicators we must remember that relationships and relationship building are our primary charge; mediated or traditional nation branding efforts alone will not be sufficient. James Grunig and Sung-Un Yang concluded that organization-public *relationship outcomes* had a greater impact on perceived organizational performance than did organizational *reputation* (J. Grunig, 2006).

Thus, in building a model for diversity in Public Diplomacy, the/our second tenet is: *Relationships form the foundation of any successful Public Relations and Public Diplomacy efforts. Understanding how they are developed, nurtured and grown is critical in building successful communications programs for diverse audiences.*

## Individual and Social Identity & Intersectionality

When we talk about identity, what first comes to mind is *individual identity*. Most see this as largely self-created, as a result of social, economic, educational, religious, and other individual experiences and characteristics. *Standpoint theory* (Hartsock, 1983) "posits a series of levels of reality in which the deeper level both includes and explains the surface or appearance" (p. 292). Social scientists use *standpoint epistemology* as a tool to understand the life experiences of their research participants, valuing the lived experience of those individuals as the best way of "knowing" their own worlds. Feminist scholarship has drawn heavily on standpoint epistemology, rejecting male-centered research as not being representative of women's lived experience.

Standpoint epistemology in feminist scholarship, "research conducted by women for women" (Olesen, 2003, pp. 332–297), is grounded in three basic assumptions:

1. Women's standpoints in society and knowledge are different from men's.
2. Women's knowledge has not been considered equal in most official, legitimized social systems.
3. Women's knowledge has been relegated to a very few sites within society, such as the home and around children, rather than in public sites (Acker, Barry & Esseveld, 1983; Reinharz, 1992)

This approach is also referred to as *situated knowledge.*

Critical scholars push identity beyond its individual boundaries to examine the concept of *social identity*. This is formed based on public discourse and interactions. What results is a much more complicated understanding of how an individual's identity is formed: the *dialogic self:*

> ...an identity theory that provides useful tools for studying *intersectionality* (italics added). In terms of the dialogical self, the formation of identity is a process of orchestrating voices within the self that speak from different I-positions. Such voices are embedded in field-specific repertoires of practices, characters, discourses and power relations specific to the various groups to which individuals simultaneously belong (Buitelaar, M., 2006, p. 259).

As research in diversity has evolved, this concept of *intersectionality* provides a greater understanding of the complexity of identity and its formation through social discourse and interaction:

> ...each individual is believed to have multiple, intersecting identities that necessarily impact their lives in different ways, whether these identities are privileged or oppressed. These intersections have been identified as vital influences upon our identities and actions, as well as the ways in which we interpret the identities and actions of others...the body of work that makes up intersectionality theory must be expanded beyond that of the individual (Baldwin-Philippi, J., 1 January, 2009, p. 1).

Why is intersectionality important? Intersectionality theory provides both an opportunity and a challenge to build relationships that take diversity into account in a much more holistic way:

> Intersectionality examines how some individuals and communities exist at the convergence where oppressions take on a cascading, multiplying effect. In other words, to some individuals and communities, race, gender, class, sexuality, or disability are not the only identities on which people are oppressed by systemic power, nor do any of these identities exist within a vacuum. Instead systemic oppressions can happen simultaneously, in an interlocking way, thereby creating a web of inequality (Zinn & Dill, 1996 in Vardeman-Winter & Tindall, 2010, pp. 223–224).

At the center of this theoretical approach are some assumptions:

1. That there is no one identity that suffices to describe a person or a group; homogeneity among race, gender, or any other characteristic is overly simplistic and does not capture the complexity of a person's identity.
2. It would be naïve to assume that there is an additive effect when characteristics such as race and gender are present in the same individual; this also ignores the complexity of identity and the social and cultural implications of intersectionality.

3. Communicators must understand and accept a concept such as intersectionality; otherwise, their efforts stall at the beginning when only race, only religion, only gender, and only other identities are assumed to be drivers of motivation, markers of lived experience, and patterns of behavior.

Just as feminist scholarship has recognized *power* as an integral part of understanding gender and social identity, so too does power have a role in intersectionality and diversity contexts.

*Power* dictates the allocation of scarce resources, the division of labor, the control of decision-making bodies and a host of other activities that determine how diverse people will be served in a national or global context. Joseph Nye's framework for *softpower* (vs. *hard power* or force) advocates for use of approaches that are often synonymous with Public Diplomacy efforts:

> A country may obtain the outcomes it wants in world politics because other countries—admiring values, emulating its example, aspiring to its level of prosperity and openness—want to follow it (Nye, 2004, p. 175).

This approach goes beyond traditional nation branding to help shape perceptions of countries and their intentions toward others. Government actors using cultural diplomacy, NGOs (Non-Governmental Organizations) performing charitable, cultural and environmental roles, and others making connections around the world often use relational or *soft power* to build relationships and understanding. Those in Public Relations and Public Diplomacy are well situated to play a key role in such relationship building, but to do so, they must understand the cultural complexities at work. Intersectionality theory provides the framework for such understanding. It must be combined with a more expansive and less ethnocentric worldview than has been at work in past U.S. Public Diplomacy efforts.

This brings us to the/our third tenet: *Understanding diversity requires an intersectional lens through which we view those with whom we wish to form relationships. Without this application of multiplicity in identity, we are left with an inadequate understanding of diversity, which limits our ability to form optimal relationships.*

## Trust in Relationship

In *relationship measurement theory* (Hon & Grunig, 1999), the strength of relationships is measured by a number of variables:

- Control Mutuality
- Satisfaction Commitment
- Exchange vs. communal
- Trust

They define trust as a degree of openness between parties in a relationship; this is based on integrity (fairness and justice), dependability (degree to which a party can deliver on promises) and competence (capability to perform). Trust is a complex concept in relationship measurement and requires a skilled communications professional to recognize how to do research and conduct programs that take the multidimensional elements of trust into account (Hon & J. Grunig, 1999).

While all of the dimensions of relationship measurement are important, in matters relating to diversity, *trust* is the one which has the potential to create the greatest opportunities for building and maintaining relationships. Without trust, none of the other relationship elements would be possible.

To build trust, a perception of fairness and justice must be established. This brings us to our fourth tenet: *Understanding that fairness and justice form the foundation for trust in relationships, those in Public Relations and Public Diplomacy must be the keepers of trust in helping to build relationships with diverse publics.*

## Organizational Justice

Critical to any discussion of diversity is a further examination of fairness and justice. Both are relative terms, perceived based on one's individual and social identity and shaped by the intersectionality effect we discussed previously. For purposes of this discussion, the author views the terms fairness and justice as being synonymous. When we talk about diversity issues, we often speak of fairness and justice for those whose differences have caused them oppression, discrimination, or denial of rights.

*Organizational justice* is defined as "the extent to which people perceive organizational events as being fair" (Colquitt & Greenberg, 2003, p. 166). There are three types of organizational justice:

1. *Distributive Justice*—This refers to the allocation of resources in an organization and the perceived fairness of allocations such as pay, benefits, perks or privileges.
2. *Procedural Justice*—This refers to the extent to which decision-making and procedural activities are perceived to be fair, consistent and free of bias.

3. *Interactional Justice*—This relates to communication of decisions and policies on an interpersonal and informational basis and the perception that there is sufficient information, delivered timely and honestly (Kim, H-S, 2007, pp. 167–197).

Kim (2005) notes the importance of symmetrical communication combined with fair treatment by an organization in determining successful relationship outcomes. Publics will decide whether they are being treated justly based on their perception of fairness, commitment, trust, control mutuality and satisfaction in relationships with organizations. While Kim's study examined the antecedents to successful relationships in organizational settings relative to employees, we can reasonably assume that successful relationships between countries and diverse publics require the same elements to be present. The greater the values proximity for these elements, the more likely integrated approaches to public diplomacy will be successful (Golan, 2013).

Hamilton and Knouse (2011) propose an experience-focused model of ethical action, which builds on earlier work in organizational justice. The researchers explain why it is important to refine the theory:

> We propose an experience-focused framework in order to map the relationships among ethical processes that individuals can recognize based on *lived experiences* [emphasis added]…processes that indicate *what* happens when an individual acts ethically rather than *how* it happens (Hamilton & Knouse, 2011, p. 231)

This approach recognizes the need to conduct research prior to enacting communication campaigns or instituting public diplomacy initiatives, since the perception of publics based on their personal, lived experience will determine how those publics respond to such initiatives. Studies of employee/management relationships and organizational justice show that fairness is at the core of these perceptions:

> …equity sensitivity has an indirect effect on perceived organizational justice. More specifically, we found that perceived organizational trust mediated the relationship between an employee's equity sensitivity and their perceptions of procedural justice, justice and social accounts. (Kickul, Gundry, & Posig, 2005, p. 206)

This brings the discussion of diversity and organizational justice full circle, since trust is a key predictor of perception of organizational justice. Mistrust can result from a refusal to take organizational justice elements into account when dealing with diverse publics. If diverse publics perceive that procedural, distributive or interactional justice falls short, they will be less likely to support the initiatives of public diplomacy actors.

## Perception and Co-orientation

There is a common understanding among Public Relations professionals that "perception is reality" for publics. In other words, how audiences or publics perceive a situation is much more a predictor of attitudes and opinions than factual information or even the perception of the organizational communicator. Before communicating, organizational actors need to conduct research to determine states of *co-orientation*.

> Broom (2007) referred to the mutual attempts of two or more parties to orient to each other and the common aspects of their environments. This involves the congruence, accuracy, understanding, and agreement that each party has to the other and to the issue confronting them (Springston & Keyton, 2001, p. 121).

Co-orientation theory examines agreement, accuracy of perceiving agreement or disagreement, shared agreement or shared disagreement, and understanding. Imagine the confusion and the potential for misunderstanding if communicators dealing with other cultures disregard the need for research regarding co-orientation. A government might assume, for example, that citizens in another country welcome economic development and infusion of capital into the host country, but citizens may perceive such actions as intervention or even manipulation of markets, threats to environmental concerns, paternalistic dominance of well-established industries and practices, or a host of other perceptions. Without research, communicators are whistling in the dark and risk offending, mobilizing and alienating diverse publics. Thus, the/ our fifth tenet: *In international communication, research is essential to determine public opinion and states of co-orientation before programs are created and enacted. Only with this formative research can communications attempt to promote organizational and social justice.* Co-orientation needs to examine values proximity for maximum benefit in mediated, nation branding and relational public diplomacy efforts (Golan, 2013).

## Diversity Strategies

Earlier in the chapter, the disproportionate number of women in U.S. Public Relations was mentioned, but it was noted that such is not the case internationally (i.e., in countries where women are discouraged or prevented from assuming work roles because of local laws or cultural barriers, it is more difficult to have a gender-diverse workforce):

> ...women in some countries have been able to enhance economic development, effect political change, and improve the lives of all. In other settings, the traditional cultural, social, economic, and political forces continue to silence

women's voices (L. Grunig, Toth & Hon, 2001, p. 143 citing Newsom and Carrell, 1995).

At a recent DiversityInc event, panelists proposed strategies for developing female talent in international organizations:

1. Provide a peer support system for women to help keep top performers in the workforce.
2. Promote diversity and inclusion in the workplace with respect for local laws.
3. Gain cultural competence and understanding for local barriers to gender equality.
4. Provide opportunities for global assignments to challenge and engage employees.
5. Understand special issues facing women with strong family demands and devise culturally competent solutions.
6. Adopt flexible workplace practices and educate managers about the value of flexibility.
7. Use alumni/networking connections to encourage loyalty from female talent.
8. Get senior-level managers on board with gender-intelligence training.
9. Assign diversity champions in select countries to promote diversity-and-inclusion initiatives and help reduce gender bias. (www.diversity inc.com)

An understanding of other cultures and cultural norms and practices is essential not only for the inclusion of women, but also for the inclusion of other forms of diversity in international relations and Public Diplomacy efforts. This leads us to the concepts of *culture and cultural competency.*

## Culture

Our understanding of culture has evolved with advancements in technology and communication, expansion of international commerce, and a host of other trends (Wang, 2008). Early research of culture could never have imagined these phenomena, and, instead, viewed culture within the confines of a country or region.

Tylor (1871) defined *culture* as:

…that complex whole which includes knowledge, belief, art, morals, custom, and any other capabilities and habits acquired by man as a member of society.

Kroeber and Kluckhohn's (1952) definition of culture:

> …a set of attributes and products of human societies, and therewith of mankind, which are extrasomatic and transmissible by mechanisms other than biological heredity (p. 145).

One researcher who has been prominent in cultural studies is Geert Hofstede, who defines culture as "mental software" to deal with the way people learn how to think, feel and act in a particular setting. Hofstede's original four dimensions of social culture are:

> *Power distance*: Social inequality, including the relationship with authority.

> *Individualism/Collectivism*: The relationship between the individual and the group.

> *Masculinity/Femininity:* The social implications of having been born as a boy or a girl.

> *Uncertainty avoidance*: Ways of dealing with uncertainty, relating to the control of aggression and the expression of emotions (Minkov & Hofstede, 2011, p. 12).

Hofstede (1991) added a fifth dimension, first referred to as *Confucian dynamism* and later, *long-term orientation*. With Hofstede's dimensions of culture, researchers and practitioners alike have a way of examining culture that seems much more manageable than tackling culture as one amorphous and unwieldy phenomenon that defies description/definition. While not perfect, Hofstede's cultural dimensions theory provides a solid framework for cultural understanding.

Because individual countries differ, it is important to do further research:

> The field would benefit from having empirical evidence about the nexus between the specific cultural idiosyncrasies of individual countries and public relations practice before we can move toward globalizing some of the cultural principles (Sriramesh, 2003, p. 515).

Jones believes global human rights can be balanced with local cultural norms by allowing for "diverse ethical perspectives, which may justify rights on some basis other than individual equality or may impose social responsibilities along with individual rights" (in Caney & Jones, 2001, pp. 1–173). (See also Pollis & Schwab, 2000).

Sotshangane posits that cultural identity is the determinant of a country's position in world affairs:

> In this new world of globalization, however, cultural identity is the central factor shaping a country's association and antagonism. The question, 'Which side are you on?' has been replaced by the much more fundamental one, 'Who are you?'

Every state has to have an answer. An answer would be aligned with a cultural identity and defining the state's place in world politics, its friends, and its enemies (2002, p. 225).

## Cultural Competency

Cultural competency is an important concept in the practice of diverse communications:

> Some think of cultural competency as affirmative action, multiculturalism, diversity training, equal employment opportunity, political correctness, or other methods and laws used to increase diversity in organizations. However, it is a much broader concept that begins with the dominant culture becoming self-aware of its own customs and then being responsive to and understanding of the cultural differences of other people within a system (Benavides & Hernández, 2007, p. 15).

Ethnocentrism is the enemy of cultural competency. It negates an appreciation for difference and diversity and limits the possibilities of developing strong relationships with diverse publics. Thus, our sixth tenet is: *Considerations regarding culture and cultural competency must be a part of any planned communication program to enhance relationships with diverse audiences.*

One of Public Diplomacy's most important contributions may be in establishing cross-cultural conversations, a means to getting started in bridging the gap between a "one world" viewpoint and a distinctly separate culture's perspective. Balslev (2003) predicts that world conflict will develop chiefly because of cultural issues.

## *Summary: Diversity and Social Justice as an Ethical Imperative*

This chapter has drawn theories from several disciplines with one goal in mind: to spur international communicators to consider the complexity of communications in a global environment and to urge them to develop programs that are grounded in such theories, taking into account diversity as an intersectional concept.

The importance of diversity in international Public Relations cannot be overstated:

> ...it is not only the 'international public relations professional' who needs to be aware of the differences in cultures, political philosophies, and economic systems, but this knowledge needs to be a part of the repertoire of every public relations professional...to become a multicultural communicator in an ever globalizing world (Sriramesh, 2003, p. 505).

Public Diplomacy communicators cannot conduct sophisticated research prior to every communications effort. The success of such communications, however, will depend upon the extent to which diversity, in all its complexity, is made part of strategy. There is no magic process for incorporating diversity in communications campaigns, but awareness of the tenets put forth here will help international communicators make fewer mistakes, enjoy more widespread support for relationship development, and enhance understanding among international actors using both mediated and traditional diplomacy approaches. If, as we have proposed here, the core of Public Relations and Public Diplomacy practice is relationship development and relationship management, then making diversity a priority in such endeavors not only strengthens relationships, but also serves as an ethical imperative.

Social justice demands moving beyond transactional relationships. The longer view, one of symmetrical balance in relationships, while impossible to achieve in every culture in every situation, still provides a framework for valuing all points of view and achieving greater harmony between governments and publics. These concepts can form the foundation for the integrated approach to public diplomacy, and a values proximity analysis can guide successful programs in mediated, nation building and cultural diplomacy efforts (Golan, 2013).

When considering the adoption of universal human rights standards as a way to achieve the goals of social justice, the incorporation of cultural diversity is complicated, at best:

> While cultural diversity undoubtedly contributes to the rich tapestry of our world, granting too much authority to cultural groups, particularly without discriminating between those that respect the human rights of their members and those that do not, risks sending us down the slippery slope of cultural relativism (Eckert, 2002, p. 6).

The danger of ethnocentrism also cannot be overstated:

> ...the truth is that all cultures are equal, and no single one of them has the right to judge and interpret the others in its own terms. This view concerns the specific claim that the equality of cultures must be recognized. Even when there are conflicts of cultures, there are no right answers in a conflict of cultures because people look at the world in different ways (Sotshangane, 2002, p. 220).

Much is at stake in determining a pathway for respecting diversity in culture and values in global human rights policy. But doing so requires using culture as the foundation for such work:

All human rights are universal, indivisible and interdependent and interrelated. The international community must treat human rights globally in a fair and equal manner, on the same footing, and with the same emphasis. While the significance of national and regional particularities and various historical, cultural and religious backgrounds must be borne in mind, it is the duty of States, regardless of their political, economic and cultural systems, to promote and protect all human rights and fundamental freedoms (United Nations, 1993).

The six tenets put forth in this chapter are a starting point for discussion and debate. Thinking theorists do not follow in lock-step behind those who are widely published and frequently cited. The best theorists spark debate and ideas which push the theory forward, taking into account the impact of shifting demographics, dizzying changes in technology and digital communication, global reach of media and business, and a host of other trends that demand that theory be dynamic and relevant.

If Public Relations professionals are the "ethical compass" for organizations, the last stop before poor decisions are made, then diversity serves as a strong ethical imperative for future international practice.

Sriramesh and White (1992) perhaps said it best:

> ...we foresee an era in which public relations will undergo fundamental changes and become enriched as a profession...to succeed in their effort to communicate to [with] their publics in a global marketplace, public relations practitioners will have to sensitize themselves to the cultural heterogeneity of their audiences....The result will be the growth of a culturally richer profession (Sriramesh & White, 1992, pp. 597–614).

## *Appendix A*

The six tenets of diversity in Public Relations and Public Diplomacy communications practice are:

1. Diversity in Public Relations and communications management and, by extension, in Public Diplomacy, is not only lacking, but it is misunderstood. The result is that efforts toward inclusion have stalled. And, despite efforts by various organizations and professional societies to "tackle" the issue of diversity, our own assumptions and denials prevent us from moving forward in any measurable way.

2. Relationships form the foundation of any successful Public Relations and Public Diplomacy efforts. Understanding how they are developed, nurtured and grown is critical in building successful communications programs for diverse audiences.

3. Understanding diversity requires an intersectional lens through which we view those with whom we wish to form relationships. Without this application of multiplicity in identity, we are left with an inadequate understanding of diversity which limits our ability to form optimal relationships.

4. Understanding that fairness and justice form the foundation for trust in relationships, those in Public Relations and Public Diplomacy must be the keepers of trust in helping to build relationships with diverse publics.

5. In international communication, research is essential to determine public opinion and states of co-orientation before programs are created and enacted. Only with this formative research can communications attempt to promote organizational and social justice.

6. Considerations regarding culture and cultural competency must be a part of any planned communication program to enhance relationships with diverse audiences.

## *Bibliography*

Baldwin-Philippi, J. (2009, January 1). The role of public discourse in intersectionality theory: Navigating flexible and static identity formation. Paper presented at the National Communication Association.

Balslev, A. (2003). Philosophy and the question of cultural diversity in the new millennium. *World Affairs, 7*(1), 1–4. Retrieved [date] from: http://www.ciaonet.org/olj/wa/wa_jan03_baa01.html

Benavides, A. D. & Hernández, J.C.T. (2007). Serving diverse communities—Cultural competency. *Public Management, 89*(6), 14–18.

Buitelaar, M. (2006). "I am the ultimate challenge:" Accounts of intersectionality in the life-story of a well-known daughter of Moroccan migrant workers in the Netherlands. *European Journal of Women's Studies,* 13 (3), pp. 259–276.

Caney, S., & Jones, P. (Eds.) (2001). *Human rights and global diversity.* Portland, OR: Frank Cass & Co.

Colquitt, J. A., & Greenberg, J. (2003). Organizational justice: A fair assessment of the state of the literature. In J. Greenberg (Ed.), *Organizational behavior: The state of the science* (pp. 165–210). Mahwah, NJ: Erlbaum.

Eckert, A. (2002). The global and the local: Reconciling universal human rights and cultural diversity. *Human rights and human welfare,* 2(2), 1–7. Retrieved from: www.ciaonet.org/olj/hrhw/apr2002/hrhw_apr2002a.pdf

Ferguson, M. (1990). Images of power and the feminist fallacy. *Critical Studies in Mass Communication,* 7(3), 215–230.

Golan, G. (2013). Introduction: An integrated approach to public diplomacy. *American Behavioral Scientist, 57,* no. 9, 1251–1255.

Grunig, J. E., Grunig, L. A., Sriramesh, K., Huang, Y-H., & Lyra, A. (1995). Models of public relations in an international setting. *Journal of Public Relations Research,* 7 (3), 163–186.

Grunig, J. E. (2001). Two-way symmetrical public relations: Past, present and future. In R.L. Heath (Ed.), *Handbook of public relations* (pp. 11–30). Thousand Oaks, CA: Sage.

———. (2006). Decomposing organizational reputation: The effects of organization-public relationship outcomes on cognitive representations of organizations and evaluations of organizational performance. *Journal of Communication Management,* 305–325.

Grunig, L. A., Toth, E. L., & Hon, L. C. (2001). *Women in public relations: How gender influences practice.* New York: The Guilford Press.

Hamilton, J. B. III, & Knouse, S. B. (2011). The experience-focused model of ethical action: A conceptual foundation for ethics and organizational justice research. In S. W. Gilliland, D. D. Steiner and D. P. Skarlicki (Eds.), *Emerging perspectives on organizational justice and ethics.* Charlotte: Information Age Publishing, Inc.

Hartsock, N.C.M. (1983). *Money, sex and power: Toward a feminist historical materialism.* Boston: Northeastern University Press.

Hofstede, G. (1991). *Culture and organization: Software of the mind.* London: McGraw-Hill.

Hon, L. C., & Brunner, B. (2000). Diversity issues and public relations. *Journal of Public Relations Research,* 12(4), 309–340.

Hon, L. C., & Grunig, J. E. (1999). *Guidelines from measuring relationships in public relations.* (pp. 1–40). Gainesville, FL: Institute for Public Relations.

Kern-Foxworth, M. (1989). Status and roles of minority PR practitioners. *Public Relations Review,* 15 (3), pp. 89–97.

Kickul, J., Gundry, L. K., & Posig, M. (2005). Does trust matter? The relationship between equity sensitivity and perceived organizational justice. *Journal of Business Ethics,* 56: 205–218.

Kim, H-S. (2005). Organizational structure and internal communication as antecedents of employee-organization relationships in the context of organizational justice: A multilevel analysis. Unpublished doctoral dissertation. University of Maryland, College Park.

———. (2007). A multi-level study of antecedents and a mediator of employee-organization relationships. *Journal of Public Relations Research,* 19 (2), pp. 167–197.

Kroeber, A. L. & Kluckhohn, C. (1952). Culture: A critical review of concepts and definitions. *Papers of the Peabody Museum of American Archeology and Ethnology,* 47(1). Cambridge, MA: Harvard University Press.

McQuail, D. (2010). *McQuail's mass communication theory* (6th Edition). Los Angeles: Sage.

Merriam-Webster Dictionary. (8 August, 2012). Diversity. Retrieved from: http://www.merriam-webster.com/dictionary/diversity

Minkov, M. & Hofstede, G. (2011). The evolution of Hofstede's doctrine. *Cross Cultural Management,* 18(1), 10–20.

Newsom, D. A., & Carrell, B. J. (Eds.). (1995). *Silent voices.* Lanham, MD: University Press of America.

Nye, J. S. (2004). *Soft power: The means to success in world politics.* New York: Public Affairs.

Olesen, V. L. (2003). Feminisms and qualitative research at and into the millennium. In N. K. Denzin & Y. S. Lincoln (Eds.), *The landscape of qualitative research: Theories and issues* (2nd edition) (pp. 332–397).Thousand Oaks, CA: Sage.

Pollis, A., & Schwab, P. (Eds.). (2000). *Human rights: New perspectives, new realities.* Boulder, CO: Lynne Rienner.

Sotshangane, N. (2002). What impact globalization has on cultural diversity? *Alternatives: Turkish Journal of International Relations,* 1(4), 214–231.

Springston, J. K. & Keyton, J. (2001). Public relations field dynamics. In R. L. Heath (Ed.), *Handbook of public relations* (pp. 115–126). Thousand Oaks: Sage Publications, Inc.

Sriramesh, K. (2003). The missing link: Multiculturalism and public relations education. In K. Sriramesh & D. Verčič (Eds.), *The global public relations handbook: Theory, research and practice.* Mahwah, NJ: Lawrence Erlbaum Associates.

Sriramesh, K., & White, J. (1992). Societal culture and public relations.In J. E. Grunig (Ed.), *Excellence in public relations and communication management* (pp. 597–614). Hillsdale, NJ: Lawrence Erlbaum Associates.

Tylor, E. B. (1871). *Primitive culture.* London: Murray.

United Nations. (1993). *Vienna Declaration on Human Rights.* UN Doc. A/CONF.157/23, 12 July 1993, paragraph 5.

Vardeman-Winter, J., & Tindall, N. T. J. (2010). "If it's a woman's issue, I pay attention to it": Gendered and intersectional complications in The Heart Truth media campaign. *PRism,* 7(4). http://www.prismjournal.org

Wang, J. (2008). Toward a critical perspective of culture: Contrast or compare rhetorics. *Journal of Technical Writing and Communication,* 38 (2), 133–148.

## 23. Public Diplomacy, Public Relations, and the Middle East: A Culture-Centered Approach to Power in Global Contexts

Mohan J. Dutta

The culture-centered approach to public diplomacy critically interrogates the embodiment of power in communication activities, specifically rendering impure the claims of democracy, civil society, and participation that serve as markers of neoliberal expansionism, rooted in taken-for-granted linkages between the market, state, and notions of democracy (Dutta-Bergman, 2005, 2006). The task of cultural centering is one that locates claims of public diplomacy amid the materiality of international relations practices and activities of nation states, situating specific practices of public diplomacy amid the dialectical relationship between the symbolic and the material, constituted amid relationships of power (Cloud, 2004; Dutta, 2009, 2011). An orientation toward dialogue and listening creates an opening for mutually-directed cultural understanding through co-construction, simultaneously foregrounding the terrains of power that define the public diplomacy initiatives carried out by powerful nation states (Dutta, 2011). Culturally-centered public diplomacy enables the opportunity for foregrounding alternative cultural logics of organizing economic and political systems, which in turn then create new openings for conceptualizing international relationships grounded in principles of dialogue (Dutta, 2011).

In this chapter, I will work through the culture-centered approach as a framework for reading US public diplomacy efforts in the Middle East in the context of US invasions of Iraq and Afghanistan. Given the strategic importance of public diplomacy in the wake of US invasion of Iraq and Afghanistan and the global criticism of the US in the post-invasion period, the US sought to reinvent its public diplomacy through an emphasis on transformational diplomacy (US Department of State, 2006a, 2006b). The public diplomacy targeted at the Middle East played a vital role in the backdrop of the strongly growing negative public opinion toward the US in the Middle East (see US Department of State, 2006b). The culturally-centered critique of public diplomacy efforts is guided by the question: What are the specific articulations of power that are carried out through US efforts of public diplomacy and how do these articulations serve neoimperial/neoliberal goals?

## Culture-Centered Approach to Public Diplomacy

The culture-centered approach to communication suggests that communication itself is a culturally-derived activity, immersed within shifting cultural contexts and culturally-rooted value frames, and constituted amid relationships of power (Dutta-Bergman, 2005, 2006). Public diplomacy works within this framework of discursively constructing specific materialities, circulating assigned interpretive frames disseminated by dominant global actors, with the agenda of asserting global imperial control, simultaneously erasing, obfuscating or backgrounding other interpretive frames (Dutta-Bergman, 2006). For instance, erased from hegemonic discursive spaces of democracy promotion are empirically-grounded interpretations of projects of democracy promotion that have resulted in large scale oppressions, colonialism, and subversion of popular movements (Dutta-Bergman, 2005). The culture-centered approach attends to the material dominance of discursive spaces of international relationships by Western (read US) ideals, achieved through the elevation of Western values as universally accepted, dissociating these ideals from their cultural roots and simultaneously leveraging these ideals toward achieving the interests of the powerful global actors.

Of specific relevance is the articulation of neoliberalism, encapsulated in liberalization, promotion of the free market, privatization and minimization of tariffs, as a global frame for organizing international relationships (Dutta, 2011; Kim, Millen, Irwin, & Gershman, 2000). The culture-centered approach therefore suggests that public diplomacy works toward these dominant goals of market promotion, leveraging the powerful role of the imperial state (US) in achieving specific market goals for US-based transnational corporations (TNCs). Public diplomacy therefore needs to be looked at as a specific form of public relations function carried out by the nation state, working hand in hand with the interests of capital. The state, rather than being independent from the market, is integral to the functioning of the market and to serving the interests of transnational hegemony.

In this essay, based on close reading of US public diplomacy narratives in the Middle East between 2003 and 2009 in the backdrop of the US imperial invasions of Iraq and Afghanistan, I propose the argument that US public diplomacy in the Middle East serves precisely as a method for disseminating US-backed neoliberal values, complementing top-down military interventions with symbolic narratives that exert the hegemony of neoliberalism (Pal & Dutta, 2008a, 2008b). Furthermore, the establishment of the neoliberal order on a global scale serves as the justification of forms of power and control that carry out the agendas of transnational hegemony (Kim, 2008; Kim, Millen, Irwin, & Gershman, 2000; Pal, 2008). Culture-centered theorizing of public diplomacy foregrounds the powerful role of strategic communication in obfuscating the powerful agendas of the state, reframing state aggression in the language of democracy, liberty, and economic opportunity (Kim, 2008; Pal, 2008).

## Critically interrogating language: Strategic inversion

The strategic function of public diplomacy is often grounded in top-down messaging strategies directed at image building that often runs counter to a listening-based approach to relational communication. Even as the US invaded Iraq and Afghanistan through the use of military force, it did so by using the languages of freedom, democracy, and liberty. The language of transforming democracy therefore is also the language of new imperialism, depicting the linkages between the state and the market. Through the instruments of public diplomacy, imperialism is reframed to serve the interests of neoliberal governance (read "free market" expansionism), strategically using the languages of democracy, participation, and shared governance (Dutta-Bergman, 2005). The effectiveness of the logic of neoliberal expansionism lies precisely in the creative circulation of the language of democracy that obfuscates the materiality of exploitation and oppression perpetuated by imperial invasion. Consider for instance the following statement on "transformational diplomacy" by the US Department of State Website (US Department of State, nd):

> The Secretary's objective of transformational diplomacy (US Department of State, 2006b) is to "work with our many partners around the world to build and sustain democratic, well-governed states that will respond to the needs of their people—and conduct themselves responsibly in the international system....Transformational diplomacy is rooted in partnership, not paternalism—in doing things with other people, not for them. We seek to use America's diplomatic power to help foreign citizens to better their own lives, and to build their own nations, and to transform their own futures....Now, to advance transformational diplomacy all around the world, we in the State Department must rise to answer a new historic

calling. We must begin to lay new diplomatic foundations to secure a future of
freedom for all people. Like the great changes of the past, the new efforts we undertake today will not be completed tomorrow. Transforming the State Department is the work of a generation. But it is urgent work that cannot be deferred."

The interplay of democracy and governance consolidates power in the
hands of transnational capital to carry out neoliberal economic reforms.
Worth noting here is the emergence of the rhetoric of transformational diplomacy amid the imperial occupation of Iraq and Afghanistan by the United States through the top-down use of force. Our culture-centered reading
therefore renders visible the role of diplomacy as a political tool in the hands
of power structures. For instance, the communication of democracy promotion happens in the very midst of the undemocratic use of top-down force
in international relations by the US. Similarly, the language of partnership is
invoked amid material practices that are a far cry from partnership.

The freedom for all people is rhetorically positioned as an objective amid
the imperial occupation of nation states and their people. The language of
improving lives of foreign citizens and fostering transformational opportunities for self-determination are articulated precisely amid top-down neoliberal
reforms in Iraq and Afghanistan that singlehandedly use the power of imperial control to turn these colonies into sites of neoliberal governance. For
instance, in the case of Iraq, the US utilized the window of opportunity to
experiment with neoliberal reforms in the country, contracting out resources
and opportunities in Iraq to primarily US-based TNCs. Also worth noting
is the rhetorical framing of these communicative discrepancies as efforts of
promoting truth, specifically then depicting the underlying functions of top-
down propaganda that are couched under the chador of democracy promotion and global transformational leadership. In the very same introduction to
the archives, here is the opening sentence, "Secretary Rice recognizes that in
its fight for freedom, the U.S. must increase exchanges with the rest of the
world—confronting hate, dispelling dangerous myths, and getting out the
truth" (US Department of State, nd).

The emergence of transformation diplomacy between 2003 and 2009
was constituted amid a top-down global climate of economic and governmental reforms that were being carried out by the US through its access to
the international financial institutions (IFIs) and through the use of military power such as in the cases of Iraq and Afghanistan (Dutta, 2011). The
rhetorical emphasis on popular participation, democracy, and people-driven
change are situated in opposition to US-led efforts in shaping the world in
the image of the free market. The role of the US state in securing freedom for
all people is embedded in the neoliberal ideology of freeing up the market,

which is framed as a marker of freedom in the global marketplace. Freedom as understood in the principles of the market operates on the basis of thwarting the opportunities of recognition, representation, and participation among the public. As depicted in critical interrogations of democracy promotion initiatives promoted by the US in the global South, market-driven notions of freedom and democracy are often rooted in top-down and exploitative manipulations of national governments in order to create opportunities for wealth accumulation for the elite classes in collusion with TNCs rooted in elite nation states (such as the US and UK) in the form of development and democracy promotion initiatives.

## *Top-down interventions couched in language of democracy*

Although the notions of diplomacy are framed in the language of participation and partnership, embedded in US public diplomacy missions are top-down agendas that are tied to the top-down US interventions carried out in the Middle East. Critical interrogations of public diplomacy discourses reveal the underlying thread of US exceptionalism, married to rhetorical frames of democracy and capitalism. The top-down framework of public diplomacy embedded in notions of US superiority is evident in the following statement made by Secretary Condoleezza Rice at Iraq neighbors conference held on May 4, 2007 (Rice, 2007a):

> I would like to close with a word about the United States and what the United States sees as its role in helping to bring about a stable and democratic Iraq, to lay that foundation. And here, I just have to say something about history. Several colleagues have cited, I think quite rightly, the progress that Iraq has made from the days of the governing council to the elections which then established a constitution on the basis of which a democratically elected government is before us here today.

> But let's remember this wouldn't have happened if Iraq had not been liberated from Saddam Hussein. The United States is very proud of the fact that it participated in the liberation of Iraq from Saddam Hussein. The United States, the United Kingdom, other members of the coalition gave blood and treasure to liberate Iraq, and frankly, to liberate the region from a dictator who had caused two wars in the matter of a little more than a decade, a million lives in two countries. And so we are very proud to have participated in the liberation of Iraq.

Note the reference to the pivotal role of the US in bringing about democracy in Iraq. The conceptual definitions of terms such as stability and democracy are rooted in US-driven value frames that redefine the role of the US as the savior of Iraqi freedom, celebrating the US invasion as an intervention of liberty. The pride of the US is tied to the role played by the US in liberating the Iraqi people and the region from a dictator. Obfuscated from the articulation of Dr. Rice is the imperial invasion of Iraq by the US. Absent are references to global resistance against what is often seen in the global community as the imperial invasion of Iraq for economic and geostrategic reasons. Also absent are the voices of the Iraqi people and opportunities for their genuine participation in defining the frames of meaning in a discursive frame celebrating democracy, participation, and liberation.

In the context of Iraq, the top-down mission of invasion also becomes apparent in the following excerpt from Secretary Condoleezza Rice's remarks to US mission personnel in Iraq (Rice, 2007b):

> First of all, this is an essential mission for the security and well-being of the United States of America. I know we talk a great deal about helping the Iraqi people to find their way out of violence, out of tyranny, to democracy and to living together in peace and prosperity. And that's a noble cause, and America has always been at its best when it uses its power for noble causes. But this mission, bringing a stable and secure Iraq, is also essential for the security of the United States of America. Because on September 11th when those 19 men drove our own airplanes into the Pentagon and into the World Trade Center and would have driven it into the Capitol in Washington, we realized that we were no longer isolated from danger and terror, that the great oceans that had protected us for almost 200 years were no barrier to fear and destruction on our own territory, and we recognized at that point that we were going to have to come to the source of the problem, that we were going to have to go on the offense, that no matter how well we tried to defend America with port security and airport security, we couldn't play defense because the terrorists only have to be right once and we have to be right 100 percent of the time.

> And that's an unfair fight, and therefore we decided we had to go on the offense. And that meant coming to the source of the problem here in the Middle East and trying nothing more grand than trying to actually bring about a different kind of Middle East. And a different kind of Iraq, an Iraq freed of Saddam Hussein, an Iraq freed of the tyranny that was a part of this land for so long, that's the different kind of Iraq that can be a pillar of that different kind of Middle East.

Evident here is the linkage of public diplomacy to the geostrategic and security interests of the Middle East, also depicting the contradiction between the liberating Iraq frame and the US interests frame. In spite of the absence of evidence that connected Iraq with the terrorist attacks on September 11, the secretary refers back to the terror frame to justify the occupation of Iraq. Securing Iraq is connected to question of security and embedded within the 9/11 frame that has strong resonance among Americans. Iraq is identified as the source of the problem in spite of the absence of evidence that connects the terror attacks to Iraq or to weapons of mass destruction.

Underlying the articulations of public diplomacy is the role of the US as a source of global values, attempting to shape the world through its hegemonic access to power. These global values which are framed as universals are juxtaposed in the backdrop of the portrayals of the Middle East as backward and under-developed. In a *Washington Post* op-ed written by the US Secretary of State, this becomes apparent (Rice, 2005):

> The "freedom deficit" in the broader Middle East provides fertile ground for the growth of an ideology of hatred so vicious and virulent that it leads people to strap suicide bombs to their bodies and fly airplanes into buildings. When the citizens of this region cannot advance their interests and redress their grievances through an open political process, they retreat hopelessly into the shadows to be preyed upon by evil men with violent designs. In these societies, it is illusory to encourage economic reform by itself and hope that the freedom deficit will work itself out over time.

The Middle East is broadly homogenized into a monolith by the secretary, being portrayed in terms of its "freedom deficit." The ideology in the Middle East is portrayed as vicious and virulent and as the basis for terror. Absent from the discursive frame is acknowledgment of the violent role of the US in the Middle East, the history of US imperialism, and US strategic use of force in the region. The articulation further goes on to depict suicide bombers and evil men with violent designs in Orientalist terms, building and bolstering the frame of the backward Middle East as a backdrop for the justification of US invasions in the region. Economic reform is constituted in the logics of development, framed in relationship to the portrayal of a primitive Middle East. The Orientalist frame further continues (Rice, 2005):

> Though the broader Middle East has no history of democracy, this is not an excuse for doing nothing. If every action required a precedent, there would be no firsts. We are confident that democracy will succeed in this region not simply because we have faith in our principles but because the basic human longing for liberty and democratic rights has transformed our world. Dogmatic cynics and cultural determinists were once certain that "Asian values," or Latin culture, or Slavic despotism, or African tribalism would each render democracy impossible. But they were wrong, and our statecraft must now be guided by the undeniable truth that democracy is the only assurance of lasting peace and security between states, because it is the only guarantee of freedom and justice within states.

That Middle East has no history of democracy is a discursive statement that emerges within the framework of the primitive Middle East. Broad generalizations and denigration of the history of the Middle East are utilized in order to create a frame that justifies US imperial invasion in the region through the US of force. The notions of basic human longing for liberty and democracy are framed as justifications. US statecraft emerges as the solution within the frame, as the guarantor of freedom and justice within states. The framing of US-style democracy as the only solution is embedded within imperial maneuverings of the democracy frame to justify fundamentally undemocratic imperial invasions and other non-transparent democracy promotion initiatives globally directed at subverting the fundamental sovereignty of people.

The hypocrisy of such top-down public diplomacy discourse becomes further evident in the following articulation (Rice, 2005):

> Implicit within the goals of our statecraft are the limits of our power and the reasons for our humility. Unlike tyranny, democracy by its very nature is never imposed. Citizens of conviction must choose it—and not just in one election. The work of democracy is a daily process to build the institutions of democracy: the rule of law, an independent judiciary, free media and property rights, among others....Our power gains its greatest legitimacy when we support the natural right of all people, even those who disagree with us, to govern themselves in liberty.

Observe the fundamental divergence between the representation of democracy as never imposed and the top-down US imperial aggressions in Iraq and Afghanistan. Although references are made to the fostering of democratic spaces where people can govern themselves in liberty, such constructions of liberty are constituted within the very use of force and the undermining of sovereignty of the people of the invaded nation states. Democracy then becomes the rhetorical justification for neocolonial invasion, reinvented in the language of liberty to fundamentally undermine the sovereignty and liberty of the people of Iraq and Afghanistan (Rice, 2005).

> After all, who truly believes, after the attacks of Sept. 11, 2001, that the status quo in the Middle East was stable, beneficial and worth defending? How could it have been prudent to preserve the state of affairs in a region that was incubating and exporting terrorism; where the proliferation of deadly weapons was getting worse, not better; where authoritarian regimes were projecting their failures onto innocent nations and peoples; where Lebanon suffered under the boot heel of Syrian occupation; where a corrupt Palestinian Authority cared more for its own preservation than for its people's aspirations; and where a tyrant such as Saddam Hussein was free to slaughter his citizens, destabilize his neighbors and undermine the hope of peace between Israelis and Palestinians? It is sheer fantasy to assume that the Middle East was just peachy before America disrupted its alleged stability. Had we believed this, and had we done nothing, consider all that we would have missed in just the past year: ...And, of course, an Iraq that in the face of a horrific insurgency has held historic elections, drafted and ratified a new national charter, and will go to the polls again in coming days to elect a new constitutional government.

Freedom ironically emerges as the justification for imperial invasion. The US is framed as the liberator of people in the Middle East and its military invasions are justified as catalysts of liberty and democracy. The intersections between public diplomacy and imperial invasion become apparent, working together to bring about US-style free market democracy (Rice, 2005):

> ...in times of unprecedented change, the traditional diplomacy of crisis management is insufficient. Instead, we must transcend the doctrines and debates of the past and transform volatile status quos that no longer serve our interests. What is needed is a realistic statecraft for a transformed world...President Bush outlined the vision for it in his second inaugural address: "It is the policy of the United States to seek and support the growth of democratic movements and institutions in every nation and culture, with the ultimate goal of ending tyranny in our world."

The work of freeing the world from tyranny is achieved through the tyrannical invasion of nation states through the use of imperial aggression. The paradox of public diplomacy during the Bush regime lies precisely in the usage of terms such as democracy, liberty, and freedom to fundamentally undermine the freedom and liberty of invaded nation states.

## *The economic question*

US public diplomacy works as a global propaganda machine for rendering commonsensical the basic tenets of neoliberalism that tie in ideas of democracy and participation with the notions of the market. Consider for instance the following statement on the Middle East Partnership Initiative promoting partnership between US and Middle East Universities (US Department of State, 2006):

> The Department of State's Middle East Partnership Initiative (MEPI) is supporting greater freedom and opportunity for students in the region with four new grants totaling $1,160,000 for partnerships between colleges and universities in the United States and the Middle East.... The Middle East Partnership Initiative provides tangible support to reformers in the region so democracy can spread, education can thrive, economies can grow, and women can be empowered. The initiative has invested more than $293 million in four years in more than 350 programs in 16 countries and the Palestinian territories.

The partnership then becomes a framework for top-down dissemination of US values. Education emerges as a key site for disseminating these values, utilizing the languages of capacity strengthening and improving access to foster channels for the dissemination and circulation of neoliberal ideals.

Rather than fostering opportunities for listening to the voices of those in the Middle East, efforts of building educational initiatives become top-down frames for diffusing US-style values. The idea of creating opportunities for children in the Middle East is constituted within the spreading of neoliberal values of US-style democracy, rooted in the concept of the market. The language of freedom of opportunity is constituted amid the economics of neoliberal trade; the escalation of terms such as democracy, freedom, and opportunity to universal terms obfuscates the fundamentally cultural and Eurocentric roots of these terms. The notion of informed citizenry is intrinsically connected with the implied notions of building a pro-free-market citizenry aligned with the interventionist agendas of the US in the Middle East.

Here is another example, excerpted from the statement made by Condoleezza Rice at the launching of an US-Palestine public-private partnership (Rice, 2007c):

> The United States is making an unprecedented effort to increase opportunity for Palestinians. Last month, as we blocked funds to Hamas, our financial assistance to the Palestinian people actually increased....The peace and security that we seek in the Middle East requires the active engagement of private citizens, civil society groups, and the business community. And that is where each and every one of you can make a real impact through this new public-private partnership. Focusing this partnership on projects that reach young Palestinians directly, that prepare them for responsibilities of citizenship and leadership can have an enormous, positive impact...I want to demonstrate that America writ large, not just the government, but our entire nation and our citizenry will welcome the Palestinian people into the community of nations and will help them to develop a stake in the global economy. Mobilizing investment and generating jobs will be key to the success of this initiative.

Note the paradox inherent in a framework of public diplomacy that on one hand discusses the notion of partnership and on the other hand, does so through top-down notions of global organizing rooted in US-centric neoliberal thought. The possibilities of partnership are embodied in US-centric ideals of governance, conceptualizing private citizenship, civil society and business community as mechanisms of governance, embodied in private-public partnerships. The privatized notions of citizenship are rooted in US-centric notions of neoliberal forms of governance that privilege private property-bearing citizens as participating subjects of democracies. Participation is framed in economic terms, in terms of investment and participation in the global market.

The economic agenda of US public diplomacy constituted within its top-down role in opening up markets is evident in the following remark by

Condoleezza Rice to the international compact with Iraq ministerial (Rice, 2007d):

> Under the Compact, Iraq has undertaken important steps for advanced economic reforms and good governance—including priority goals: reforming fuel subsidies, restructuring the hydrocarbon sector, and sharing oil revenues fairly among all Iraqis. In return, Iraq's Compact partners have agreed to help Iraq by providing substantial debt relief, along with significant financial and technical assistance....While the goals of the Compact are economic in nature, they extend much further—providing powerful incentives for the Iraqi Government to function more effectively and to achieve its broader national goals of political reconciliation and security for all Iraqis. In turn, this will help to build the Iraqi people's faith and confidence in their new democratic public institutions.... Another goal of the Compact is to promote Iraq's economic integration in the region and the world. This is absolutely vital to Iraq's success, but it is also a goal that will benefit all of us...The United States has been and will continue to be a partner for the Iraqi people and for Iraq's democratic government. We will continue our efforts to help the Iraqi people to develop their economy and to achieve economic self-reliance.

Once again, public diplomacy is framed within the neoliberal reforms that are pushed into the Middle East through the opening up of markets in Iraq. Reforming the hydrocarbon sector and reforming fuel subsidies, elements of sovereign decision-making, emerge as top-down agendas carried out by the US through its imperial invasion of Iraq. The language of democracy promotion and liberation is located within the economic agendas of the US in imposing a top-down economic reform agenda in Iraq, and this becomes evident in the above excerpt. The notions of leveraging the full economic promise of Iraq and building a new relationship with the world become the avenues for carrying our neoliberal reforms across Iraq. Furthermore, diplomacy emerges then as a strategic device for the economic reforms carried out in Iraq, couching these reforms in the languages of democracy and liberation. Note the disconnection between the description of transformation diplomacy as a dialogic partnership with other nation states, and the specifics of public diplomacy efforts that continue to embody top-down principles of neoliberal reforms that are driven by the essential privileging of the market. Here is another statement highlighting the economic logic as Secretary Rice outlines the Iraq strategy to the House Foreign Affairs Committee: "I would note that we have an international compact which is a bargain between the international community and the Iraqis. The Iraqis would agree to do certain things, an oil law, fight corruption, certain other activities, and the international community would promise support. It seems to me that this is something that could have a positive effect on support for Iraq, but also a positive effect on developments for reform in Iraq" (Rice, 2007e).

## Strategies of co-optation

In her articulations, Secretary Rice outlines several efforts that are positioned as strategies for leading globally, depicting the communication strategies that are directed at achieving US interests in the Middle East. One such strategy is to utilize the Internet to reach out to the youth. Consider the following depiction in the position statement on *"Transformational diplomacy"*: "Programs are being developed to enhance America's presence through a medium that young people worldwide increasingly rely upon for their information. Café USA/Seoul and other programs being developed will reach young people through interactive, online discussions" (US Department of State, 2006). Note the use of the language of dialogue and participation within the broader agendas of the US to shape public opinion among youth through top-down strategies. Culture-centered interrogations of public diplomacy practices specifically draw attention to the ways in which the language of dialogue and participation is framed within broader top-down agendas of neoliberalism that exert power through co-optation.

In an interview with Radio Sawa describing US public diplomacy in the Middle East, Secretary Rice notes (Rice, 2007f): "I hope that in the Middle East we can make real progress on helping the forces of moderation in the Middle East, helping democratic forces in the Middle East. You know, the Middle East is a wonderful region with energetic people, people who are proud, people who want the best for their children. They don't want to live in a world in which young people are encouraged to be suicide bombers. I believe that the people of the Middle East want a better and more prosperous future." The understanding of the people of the Middle East and their desire for US style notions of democracy and liberty are embedded within US-centric agendas and understandings of democracy and liberty.

In a similar sense, the US invasion of Iraq is narrated in the language of democracy and freedom. In addressing the Iraqi reconstruction team in November 2005, Secretary Rice notes the following (Rice, 2005):

> In that way, as we help the Iraqi people secure their freedoms, we indeed secure our own. Because if Iraq does not succeed and should Iraq become a place of despair, generations of Americans would also be condemned to fear and to insecurity. And so our fates and our futures are very much linked ...But I want to close with where I started. We—Americans and our coalition partners, civilian and military, government organizations from the State Department, from Justice,

from other parts of our government—are helping to create conditions in Iraq that the Iraqi people will seize to secure their future.

The invasion of Iraq is defined as the freedom of the Iraqi people. The language of freedom and democracy becomes the cornerstone for justifying the continued US occupation of Iraq, disregarding the strong and consistent resistance offered to the US presence in Iraq by the Iraqi people. In this sense, public diplomacy emerges as propaganda, as one-way communication that narrates a particular version of truth and simultaneously ignores the realities on the ground. When discussing elections held in Iraq and the electoral processes, Secretary Rice ignores the consistent struggles and resistance of the Iraqi people. Consider further the democracy drumbeating in the following excerpt (Rice, 2005):

> And there is a reason that we should have great confidence in their ability to do that. I have watched in amazement over the last couple of years as the Iraqi people have emerged from one of the most brutal tyrannies of the 20th century, 20th and 21st century, as they have repeatedly cast their lot with their political process, as they went to the polls 8.5 million strong in January of this year and almost 10 million strong just a few weeks ago, to cast their ballots despite the threats of terrorists, despite the violence that they have experienced on a daily basis, despite the fact that people have sacrificed family members in order to just try and secure the blessings of liberty that we have long enjoyed.

To celebrate the markers of democracy in the elections, local resistance is labeled as terrorism and as threat. The frame of liberty is superimposed to write over the localized forms of challenge continually being offered by Iraqi people. Consider for instance the reference to people sacrificing their family members in order to secure the blessings of liberty. The framing of US-style liberty as the sacred cow writes over the very oppressive nature of the occupation that has been carried out in the name of liberty. Public diplomacy thus becomes a propaganda device for reframing the realm of the symbolic, for reframing occupation as liberation, and for continuing to recirculate that frame to various stakeholders.

## *Discussion*

Throughout this chapter, the examination of US public diplomacy efforts in the Middle East in the midst of US invasions in Iraq and Afghanistan depicts the flows of power through which the terms of public diplomacy are dictated as instruments of neo-imperial communication. Finding continuity with the early roots of public relations as public diplomacy directed at promoting an image (Nelson & Izadi, 2009), public diplomacy emerges as one-way communication that utilizes the languages of listening, participation, and dialogue to push top-down agendas. The rhetoric of freedom, democracy, and liberty is embedded within US agendas of transforming Iraq into a neoliberal experiment (Harvey, 2005). Inherent in frames of public diplomacy circulated by the US is the paradox in the use of democracy as a rhetorical device to achieve and justify undemocratic ends (in this case the military invasion of Iraq and Afghanistan). The language of democracy gets continually circulated in a neo-imperial invasion that in essence undermines the sovereign rights of the people of Afghanistan and Iraq, depicting the hypocrisies inherent in US-style democracy promotion efforts abroad as instruments of colonial expansion. Democracy and liberty become buzzwords for justifying the imperial control of spaces in the Middle East, constituted within US economic agendas.

Even as the US invaded Iraq and Afghanistan, the language of democracy became the framework for the invasion, and public diplomacy played a vital role in organizing this shift through the continual references to democracy and liberation in depictions of Iraq and Afghanistan. Thus, US public diplomacy served as the cornerstone of US imperialism, drawing upon notions of liberty and freedom to justify invasion and occupation. The hypocrisy of the liberal tradition in justifying and perpetuating the oppressions carried out by the European-American center as a means for civilizing the savage other is well evident in the racist writings of John Stuart Mill (1972), referring to colonial control as a means of civilizing the "other":

> Despotism is a legitimate mode of government in dealing with barbarians, provided the end be their improvement, and the means justified by actually effecting that end. Liberty, a principle, has no application to any state of things anterior to the time when mankind have become capable of being improved by free and equal discussion. Until then, there is nothing for them but implicit obedience to an Akbar or a Charlemagne, if they are so fortunate as to find one (p. 73)

The "transformational diplomacy" framework introduced in the backdrop of the US invasions in the Middle East continued to embody concealed strategic action (Habermas, 1987), utilizing public diplomacy as a strategic tool for managing an image communicating the spirit of dialogue and listening although the nature of communication itself was top-down, strategic, and guided by US economic interests in the Middle East amid neo-imperial invasions of the Middle East.

The public diplomacy efforts of the US targeted toward the Middle East continue to reiterate the age-old top-down frames of a primitive Middle East grounded in notions of US superiority, in spite of the language of participation and listening foregrounded in the narrative of "transformational diplomacy."

Grounded in the Habermasian (1987) notion of communicative action, to truly listen, culturally-centered public diplomacy seeks to co-create discursive spaces for cultural understanding through which policies and programs can be established through co-participation of multiple stakeholders in discursive processes (Dutta-Bergman, 2006). A culturally-centered stance of listening would guide the US toward participating in meaningful conversations with communities in the Middle East, which would therefore create openings for policy changes in the US as well as in the Middle East (serving as an impetus for transforming the Empire and its neoimperial practices). To be dialogic, communication needs to be grounded in a dialectical relationship with the material, connecting the symbolic and the material in guiding mutual understanding (Dutta-Bergman, 2006). The roles of relationship processes are centered on listening, bringing together various stakeholder groups across national boundaries to generate dialogues, that in turn create entry points for mutual understanding. In such a framework, the emphasis of public diplomacy as public relations is not on developing messaging strategies directed at changing public opinion or on selling, but rather on fostering spaces for honest conversations among various stakeholder groups across national boundaries, grounded in the search for truth. In the context of Iraq then, culturally-centered public diplomacy would foreground participation guided by truth, and would work on developing new understandings through dialogues among various stakeholders, creating conversational entry points among various forms of social and cultural organizing. Bringing Iraqi communities in conversations with various local US communities would foster forms of understanding that can create meaningful entry points for communities in both Iraq and US, attending to discussions of lived experiences, struggles, and engagement with materiality. Such a framework moves away from offering image strategies to shape public opinion to engaging stakeholders in a mutually enriching journey of understanding, grounded in honest and open dialogues that attend to the realities of the lived experiences of various stakeholders.

Moreover, the spirit of dialogue in public diplomacy therefore would need to work at the upstream of international relations efforts, with a commitment to building authentic relationships through dialogue (Dutta-Bergman, 2005, 2006). A culturally-centered commitment to dialogue seeks to foster spaces of communicative action by foregrounding authenticity, truth, and debate, grounded in materiality (Habermas, 1987). Aligned with calls for two-way symmetrical public diplomacy (Nelson & Izadi, 2009), culturally-centered public diplomacy attends to the inequities of power that render impossible the opportunities for dialogue, and then works through these terrains of inequalities in distribution of power to co-construct possibilities of dialogue. Through culturally-centered public diplomacy, dialogue becomes possible in the processes of questioning the taken-for-granted assumptions about governance and social organizing as circulated within the hegemonic structures, as well as in the foregrounding of the hypocrisies and violence that are embedded within liberal models of public diplomacy. Instead, spaces are opened up for inviting diverse worldviews, understandings, and interpretations, attending to the lived experiences at the margins of global spaces (Bakhtin, 1981). The engagement of various state and non-state actors and publics in these processes of dialogues also foster opportunities for transforming the ways in which states are organized. Public diplomacy thus emerges as a way of organizing global spaces through mutually constitutive communication rather than being used as a top-down public relations tool directed at circulating strategic images of the nation state to achieve certain hidden imperial agendas.

## References

Bakhtin, M. M. (1981). *The dialogic imagination: Four essays by M. M. Bakhtin* (M. Holquist, Ed.; C. Emerson & M. Holquist, Trans.). Austin: University of Texas Press

Cloud, D. (2004). "To veil the threat of terror": Afghan women and the "clash of civilization" in the imagery of the U.S. war on terrorism. *Quarterly Journal of Speech, 90,* 285–306.

Dutta, M. (2009). Theorizing resistance: Applying Gayatri Chakravorty Spivak in public relations. In Ø. Ihlen, B. van Ruler, & M. Fredriksson (Eds.), *Social theory on public relations.* New York: Routledge.

Dutta, M. (2011). *Communicating social change: Structure, culture, agency.* New York: Routledge.

Dutta-Bergman, M. J. (2005). Civil society and public relations. Not so civil after all. *Journal of Public Relations Research, 17,* 267–289.

Dutta-Bergman, M. J. (2006). US public diplomacy in the Middle East: A critical cultural approach. *Journal of Communication Inquiry, 30,* 102–124.

Habermas, J. (1987). *The theory of communicative action. Vol 2. Life world and system: A critique of functionalist reason* (T. McCarthy, Trans.). Boston: Beacon Press.

Harvey, D. (2005). *A brief history of neoliberalism.* London: Oxford University Press.

Hegel, G. W. F. (1991). *Elements of the philosophy of right* (H. B. Nisbet, Trans.) Cambridge: Cambridge University Press. (Original work published in 1820).

Kim, I. (2008). *Voices from the margin: A culture-centered look at public relations of resistance.* Unpublished doctoral dissertation, Purdue University, West Lafayette, IN.

Kim, J., Millen, J., Irwin, A., & Gershman, J. (Eds.). (2000). *Dying for growth: Global inequality and the health of the poor.* Monroe, ME: Common Courage Press.

Mill, J. S. (1972) *Utilitarianism, on liberty, and considerations on representative government.* London: Dent.

Nelson, R., & Izadi, F. (2009). Ethics and social issues in public diplomacy. In N. Snow & P. Taylor (Eds.), *Routledge Handbook of Public Diplomacy* (pp. 334–351). New York: Routledge.

Pal, M., & Dutta, M. (2008a). Public relations in a global context: The relevance of critical modernism as a theoretical lens. *Journal of Public Relations Research, 20,* 159–179.

Pal, M., & Dutta, M. (2008b). Theorizing resistance in a global context: Processes, strategies and tactics in communication scholarship. *Communication Yearbook, 32,* 41–87.

Rice, C. (2005). Remarks at the construction of the provincial reconstruction team. Retrieved from http://2001–2009.state.gov/secretary/rm/2005/56794.htm on May 1, 2013.

Rice, C. (December 11, 2005). The promise of democratic peace. *The Washington Post* (op-ed). Retrieved from http://2001–2009.state.gov/secretary/rm/2005/57888.htm on May 1, 2013.

Rice, C. (2007a). Remarks from the intervention at Iraq neighbors conference. Retrieved from http://2001–2009.state.gov/secretary/rm/2007/may/84292.htm on May 1, 2013.

Rice, C. (2007b). Remarks to U.S, mission personnel in Iraq. Retrieved from http://2001–2009.state.gov/secretary/rm/2007/feb/80645.htm on May 1, 2013.

Rice, C. (2007c). Retrieved from http://2001–2009.state.gov/secretary/rm/2007/12/96142.htm on May 1, 2013.

Rice, C. (2007d). Remarks at the international compact with Iraq ministerial. Retrieved from http://2001–2009.state.gov/secretary/rm/2007/may/84210.htm on May 1, 2013.

Rice, C. (2007e). Iraq: a new way forward. Retrieved from http://2001–2009.state.gov/secretary/rm/2007/78640.htm on May 1, 2013.

Rice, C. (2007f). Interview on Radio Sawa with Samir Nader. Retrieved from http://2001–2009.state.gov/secretary/rm/2007/89330.htm on May 1, 2013.

US Department of State. (n.d.). Secretary of State Condoleezza Rice. Retrieved from http://2001-2009.state.gov/secretary/ on September 1, 2014.

U.S. Department of State. (2001). *What the secretary has been saying.* Retrieved from http://2001–2009.state.gov/secretary/rm/index.htm on May 1, 2012.

U.S. Department of State. (2006a). Middle East Partnership Initiative providing more than $1.1 million for US-Middle East University Partnerships. Retrieved from http://2001–2009.state.gov/r/pa/prs/ps/2006/76455.htm on May 1, 2013.

U.S. Department of State. (2006b). Transformational diplomacy. Retrieved from http://2001–2009.state.gov/r/pa/prs/ps/2006/59339.htm on May 1, 2013.

*Conclusion*

# 24. An Integrated Approach to Public Diplomacy

Guy J. Golan

The current book aimed to synthesize the wide body of literature regarding the conceptual similarities between international public relations and public diplomacy scholarship. Based on the integrated public diplomacy approach (Golan, 2013), authors discussed strategic communication programs, reputation management and long-term relational engagement dimensions that bridge the two disciplines. A multitude of definitions were presented in the book regarding what public diplomacy actually means and how it relates to international public relations.

I believe that public diplomacy is a subset of political public relations (see Stromach and Kiousis, 2011) with an emphasis on government as the primary organization and foreign publics as the primary publics. My definition of public diplomacy is government based and may not be consistent with those of scholars who argue for a wider definition that includes government, corporations and even citizen-to-citizen diplomacy (Gregory, 2008; Seib, 2009).

Recognizing the many conceptual similarities between public diplomacy and international public relations, several of the book chapters argue for the appropriateness of mass communication and public relations theoretical perspectives on the study of public diplomacy.

While dozens of peer-reviewed academic studies have examined the many facets of public diplomacy, the field is continuously undermined by its underdeveloped theoretical approach. Inspired by various disciplines, such as international relations, political science and mass communication, public diplomacy scholarship draws upon many discipline-related theories but lacks a guiding theoretical framework that allows scholars to make predictions regarding international engagement outcomes. The field's largely theoretical nature represents a key limitation, as pointed to by various scholars (See

Entman, 2008; Gilboa, 2008). A review of two decades' worth of public diplomacy literature does, however, point to an oft-cited, common key concept: Joseph Nye's (1990) soft power. While soft power may be useful in explaining the logic behind government engagement of foreign publics, it in itself is not a social scientific theory as it does not include the key criteria required of a positivist theory (Shoemaker et al., 2004).

Gilboa (2000) provides one of the only theoretical models for the study of public diplomacy and of the complex interaction between media, government and public opinion. His model includes six separate elements. The first three focus on traditional diplomacy: secret diplomacy, closed-door diplomacy and open diplomacy. The second three focus on public diplomacy, media diplomacy and media-brokered diplomacy. Overall, Gilboa's model is useful as a taxonomy, but it falls short of providing the sort of predictive attributes required of a social scientific theory.

As noted by Entman (2008), public opinion, both domestic and global, involves a complex interaction between government, elites, the news media and the public. He claims that scholars lack a full understanding of this interaction and, therefore, cannot easily predict public diplomacy programs and their impact on global public opinion outcomes. Building upon his previous scholarship (Entman, 2004), he argues for the applicability of the cascade activation model as a theoretical framework for public diplomacy research. There is much promise in Entman's model, yet it largely applies to the mediated public diplomacy approach and is less applicable for research on country reputation or relational public diplomacy.

In a recent publication, I introduce the integrated public diplomacy model (Golan, 2013) as a useful approach for analyzing government/ foreign public engagement. Based on a strategic planning perspective, the integrated public diplomacy model identifies three levels of engagement.

## Mediated Public Diplomacy

The first level deals with integrated public diplomacy. Here, the focus is on strategic media frame building by governments who actively aim to influence foreign media coverage (Entman, 2008; Sheafer & Shenhav, 2009) as a part of a global communication competition between nations (Schafer & Gabay, 2009). As the foreign public engagement process is filtered through the channels of global mass communication, governments must recognize that public diplomacy does not occur inside a vacuum. While a variety of educational and cultural exchanges may be useful in highlighting a nation's soft power, the majority of foreign citizens will never be exposed or participate in them.

Rather, as supported by dozens of previous studies, most people get their information about any nation from mass media outlets (Bennett et al., 1994; Golan, 2006). It is because of this fact that the fundamental relationship between any government and foreign public occur, first and foremost, through mass media channels. As an intervening public (see Carroll and McCombs, 2003), mass media channels are not only central in the dissemination of news and information regarding a nation, but they also play a key role in interpreting the meaning of the news (Scheufele, 1999; Borah, 2011).

Ultimately, mediated public diplomacy scholarship focuses on the strategic management of the content of foreign news coverage. As such, mass communication and international public relations-based theories can provide an appropriate theoretical framework for this field of research. Agenda-setting theory (McCombs & Shaw, 1972) and agenda-building literature (Kiousis et al., 2006, 2007) provides robust theoretical underpinnings for studying the transfer of issue and attribute salience from the government agenda to the media agenda (Weaver & Elliott, 1985; McCombs, 1997) and potentially the public agenda (Kiousis et al., 2009).

The centrality of the media as a mediator between governments and foreign citizens is best understood through the mediatization prism (Kepplinger, 2006; Strömbäck, 2008). As explained by this area of scholarship, news media organizations no longer simply cover international politics but may in fact be active participants in global political processes. For this exact reason, many nations around the world are allocating large amounts of money towards international broadcasting channels (see Powers and Samuel-Azran).

As noted by Entman (2008), the concept of mediated public diplomacy does not simply refer to the use of the news media by governments in an attempt to increase support of its policies by foreign publics. Rather, he defines mediated public diplomacy as "the organized attempts by a president and his foreign policy apparatus to exert as much control as possible over the framing of...policy in foreign media" (p. 89). As such, Entman's definition directly relates to agenda-building research that focuses on organizational attempts to promote the saliency of certain organizational issues and attributes while downplaying others (Kiousis, Mitrook, Wu, & Seltzer, 2006; Kiousis, Popescu & Mitrook, 2007; Sweetser & Brown, 2008). The key difference between mediated public diplomacy and traditional agenda-building research is found in the type of organization and its target stakeholders.

It is important to note that governmental attempts to influence foreign media coverage can be best understood in the context of international relations. Nations and non-nation actors often compete over media framing of salient events, not only with one another but also with a variety of third party interests (Sheafer & Gabay, 2009). Examples include frame-building at times of international conflict (Fahmy, 2007; Kothari, 2010), territorial disputes (Maoz, 2006; Rogers & Ben-David, 2010) and contention over foreign policy (Bonomi & Pan, 2013). As such, it is often the case that mediated public diplomacy efforts occur in response to international crisis. For this reason, I argue that crisis communication literature (Coombs & Holladay, 2004; Coombs 2007; Jin & Liu, 2014) can provide scholars and practitioners alike with a theoretical perspective as well as real life best practices to follow.

The importance of successfully shaping foreign media framing of salient international events is further magnified when considering its potential outcome. The successful promotion of salient frames will likely transfer to the saliency of issues and attributes in the foreign public agenda as predicted by second level agenda-setting (Wanta, Golan & Lee, 2004; Kiousis & Wu, 2008), resulting in improved public opinion and potentially influence on foreign elites (Sheafer & Shenhav, 2009).

## *Nation Brands / Reputation Level*

The second level of the integrated public diplomacy model (Golan, 2013) focuses on nation branding and country reputation. A review of public diplomacy scholarship points to dozens of studies focused on such branding efforts as nation branding (Molleda & Suarez, 2006; 2005; Taylor & Kent, 2006) or country-of-origin advertising campaigns (Kunczick, 1997; Peterson & Jolibert, 1995). The current book also included several chapters that deal with similar tactics (see Hung, Connolly-Ahern & Ma). While a rich body of literature details nation branding and country reputation management efforts, the research field, as a whole, is partially undermined by a lack of theoretical grounding. As argued in Anholt's chapter, foreign public perceptions of nations are a product of a complex set of variables. It is important to note that many international branding and/or reputation management campaigns are reactive rather than proactive. Unable to successfully engage in mediated public diplomacy efforts, governments are often seduced by the promises of advertising and marketing professionals. However, I argue that those efforts to engage in branding are unlikely to succeed during times when nations are not successfully managing their overall foreign media strategy. The integrated public diplomacy model (Golan, 2013) suggests that successful mediated public diplomacy efforts are a prerequisite for successful nation-branding or country reputation management efforts. I further argue that no nation can likely succeed in long-term relationship building via government engagement and/or track two diplomacy unless they fulfill the first two requirements of the model. For example, despite sophisticated research-based, image-building efforts, the nation of Israel—which actively aims to position itself as a start-up nation or as the Middle East's only true democracy—is unable to make significant changes in foreign public opinion largely due to the consistent framing of the nation within the context of the Israeli-Palestinian conflict. Another example is the continent of Africa. Despite many positive developments in the field of economics, technology, and civil society, the African continent receives limited media coverage in the West and, when it is covered, frames tend to focus on conflict, corruption and natural disasters (Fair, 1993; Golan, 2008). It is therefore my contention that gaining favorable media coverage is a prerequisite for all public diplomacy efforts. As long as global media coverage is unfavorable to the nation, it is unlikely to gain the necessary credibility with foreign publics that is required for successful relationship-building. It is important to note that many nations around the world do not need to focus on the mediated public diplomacy level. These nations can, therefore, focus on nation-branding and relational diplomacy efforts. For example, the Netherlands is not engaged in hostile media competition with international rivals who aim to discredit it, nor does international media coverage of the nation focus on negative media frames such as war and conflict. Therefore, the Dutch nation can focus international communication efforts on bicycle diplomacy and/or its international aid efforts. However, nations involved in international disputes or conflict consistently face an attempt by their rivals to define and often discredit their foreign policy (Sheafer & Shenhav, 2009). Those nations operate within the context of crisis communication and, therefore, must successfully engage in active frame-building promotion in order to strategically position themselves within the international community. The failure of the American Shared Values campaign provides a good case study of the inability to brand a nation at a time when it was discredited and undermined by its rival in the global media. The inability to manage a nation's reputation at times of crises is also exemplified by recent attempts by Mexico to promote tourism in response to global media coverage of its drug wars or India's attempt to brand itself as an innovative nation while international audiences were exposed to horrid tales of sexual violence against women.

The integrated public diplomacy model views the nation branding stage as a medium- to long-term effort. Ineffective nation-branding campaigns may discredit the international standing of a nation or simply waste its financial resources. However, successful nation-branding campaigns may provide a strong foundation to the third level of the integrated public diplomacy model: relational diplomacy.

## The Relational Level

A review of public diplomacy literature identifies Nye's (1990) soft power approach as the key conceptual framework for the majority of published public diplomacy studies.

As argued by Nye (1990), soft power occurs "when one country gets another country to want what it wants" (p. 166). Nye (2008) further explains: "The soft power of a country rests primarily on three resources: its culture (in places where it is attractive to others), its political values (when it lives up to them at home and abroad), and its foreign policies (when they are seen as legitimate and having moral authority)" (p. 96). Gilboa (2008) further contextualizes the soft power idea and its applicability to the field of public diplomacy: "Power is the ability to alter the behavior of others to get what you want. To achieve this outcome, an actor may employ two elements of hard power—coercion (sticks) and payments (carrots)—and/or attraction (soft power). Soft power arises from the attractiveness of a nation's values, culture, and policies (Nye 2004). It causes people to act through cooperation rather than coercion. When policies and positions of states or nonstate actors have moral authority, or are seen as legitimate in the eyes of others, their soft power is increased." (p. 61).

As noted, the soft power approach is largely based on the assumption that using soft power assets such as culture, political values and foreign policy, governments can achieve desirable international relations outcomes through global cooperation rather than by military force. The soft power approach has been widely adopted by public diplomacy scholars and often has been applied as a theoretical construct in research focused on soft power programs. Furthermore, soft power serves as the intellectual justification behind many of the American government's global public diplomacy programs. Focused largely on the relationship management function of public diplomacy, I argue that scholars have much to learn from public relationships scholarship. A variety of public relations theoretical perspectives such as relationship management theory (Ledingham, 2003), contingency theory (Cancel, Cameron, Sallot, and Mitrook, 1997), excellence theory (Grunig, 1992), and the situational theory of publics (Grunig, 1997) can guide public diplomacy scholarship at the relational level of my model.

## Soft Power Programs

Many of the so-called soft power programs are based on a liberalist assumption, which posits that international relations between nations can be best understood through a prism of international cooperation between international players all aimed at achieving mutually beneficial outcomes.[1] This soft power approach promotes government-to-citizen as well as citizen-to-citizen diplomacy and promotes long-term relationship building. This approach will be discussed in the current chapter as the relational approach to public diplomacy. Programs aimed at achieving these goals through citizen engagement, including exchange, aid and language instruction programs will be referred to as soft power programs. Based on the relational approach, the United States government allocates a large amount of funds towards the sponsorship and support of public diplomacy soft power programs such as educational exchanges, cultural exchanges, aid diplomacy, English-language instruction, and American spaces and libraries abroad.

The centrality of such programs to America's global public diplomacy outreach was best summarized by the remarks of former Under Secretary of Public Diplomacy James Glassman (2008, January), who remarked: "Another way to counter the ideas of the extremists is personal engagement through educational and cultural exchange programs. Funding for these programs has more than doubled since fiscal 2003[14]—and with good reason. Exchanges are the crown jewels of public diplomacy." It has been widely argued that participants in such educational exchange programs as the Fulbright program or the Lincoln Study Abroad Fellowship Program yield positive public opinion outcomes regarding the United States by foreign citizens. This sentiment was echoed by Secretary of State Condoleezza Rice (2006) who argued that: "Every foreign student attending one of our universities represents an opportunity to enhance democracy in America and to strengthen the cause of freedom abroad." In a different speech, Secretary Rice further argued:

> We define the success of transformational diplomacy as a new kind of engagement among peoples, new and ever more public diplomacy. This is not and cannot be the job of just American diplomats. It's a mission for the American people. That is why we are dramatically increasing our people-to-people engagement to connect students and journalists and scholars of the world. That is why we issued more student and exchange visas last year than at any other time in our history.

Scott-Smith (2009) further explains: "Whereas propaganda refers to the deliberate manipulation of information to achieve a desired result, exchanges are (ideally) the most two-way form of public diplomacy, opening up spaces for dialogue and the interchange of alternative viewpoints" (p. 51). A similar logic is applied to arts and cultural exchanges which are viewed as citizen diplomacy programs likely to result in mutual understanding and cooperation. Brown (2009) notes: that: "Art creates powerful impressions that are often remembered forever. At the very least, arts diplomacy can make people abroad associate America with the kind of unique moments that make our lives worth living" (p. 59).

While no single soft power program alone can account for positive outcomes in the form of improved public opinion of the United States abroad, they holistically aim to build bridges between citizens and establish mutually beneficial long-term relationships between Americans and foreign publics. A key assumption behind many of the soft power programs is the notion that they produce favorable sentiments by program participants who may in turn transfer those sentiments to other people in their home nation (Scott-Smith, 2008).

Under Secretary of Public Diplomacy Judith McHale (2009) argued that "the goal of this kind of person-to-person engagement has always been to form lasting relationships. This is now a foundation of our communications strategy as well. In a crowded media environment, relationships offer a way to break through the clutter." Similar thoughts were echoed by Under Secretary of Public Diplomacy Tara Sonenshine (personal communication, October 18, 2012): "21$^{st}$ century statecraft is about reaching out to the biggest table we can imagine. We have to reach and teach."

## Soft Power and Public Opinion

Recognizing the potential impact of citizen diplomacy and soft power programs on cultivating relationships between citizens of different nations, many in government and academia place an emphasis on these programs as key components of public diplomacy. Such emphasis is widely supported by budget allocation towards soft power programs. While this focus makes sense intuitively, it is difficult to assess the direct influence that soft power programs have on global public opinion in both the short, medium and long term. The challenge of linking soft power programs to outcomes was highlighted by Under Secretary Sonenshine (2012) as she explained that

> Congress these days, wants to know what the facts are. What do we really get from bringing all the students here? And for a long time, you would try to explain it as the way we would to get positive cultural and educational transformation. But now they want to get a little finer detail, like some quantitative diametrics. So we've gone out and looked at what international students contribute to a local economy. In this state, in one year, the presence of international students have contributed two-and-a-half-billion dollars to New York....Across the United States, last year, the presence of 775,000 international students generated 20 billion dollars in this country. Can you imagine if we shut that off?

While the under secretary's argument is convincing, public diplomacy programs by design are not meant to serve as engines of economic growth, but rather, they are ultimately aimed at promoting positive sentiments towards the host nations in terms of influencing participant opinion. However, there is little evidence that exchange programs can achieve such goals. Rather, they are likely to sustain status quo or reinforce opinions (Scott-Smith, 2009). The key limitation of soft power programs is the inherent difficulty in measuring and evaluating their success and in arguing for their causality. Pahlavi (2007) underlined the complexity of soft power program evaluation. He argued that "the multiple factors—both objective and subjective—involved in achieving goals and influencing outcomes make any rigid application of a cause-and-effect rationale injudicious."

It is important to note that no nation around the world will have the same exact public diplomacy goals and objectives as another. While some nations will focus their engagement efforts on attracting tourism or foreign investments, other nations may deal with more short-term international relations crises.

The American case study is worthy of examination due to both its failures and successes. Revamped after the attacks of September 11, 2001, the United States focused its public diplomacy efforts on the goal of reducing anti-American sentiments around the world.

## Anti-Americanism on the Rise

As noted by Goldsmith, Horiuchi and Inoguchi (2005), global public opinion is a complex construct that is shaped and influenced by various predictors. Indeed, Tai, Petersen and Gurr (1973) explained that "issues identified in past studies as contributing to anti-American attitudes range from disagreement with U.S. policies to rejection of western values and ideals to resentment and/or fear of U.S. power and influence to scapegoating, or blaming America for a nation's own problems" (p. 155). Chiozza (2009) further details the complex nature of global public opinion: "The disaggregated, multidimensional nature of popular attitudes towards the United States implies that anti-Americanism is not a single policy problem that calls for a single policy response" (p. 201).

A growing body of research on anti-Americanism has identified a multitude of variables, such as media exposure (Nisbet et al., 2004; Nisbet & Shanahan, 2008), evaluations of the American president (Dragojlovic, 2011; Golan & Yang, 2013) and of his policies (el-Nawawy, 2006; Johnston & Stockmann, 2007; Lynch, 2007), political identity (Nisbet & Myers, 2010), evaluations of American values (DeFleur & DeFleur, 2003; Graber, 2009), and education (Gentzkow & Shapiro, 2004) as predictors of global public opinion.

One key criticism of soft power programs is the inability to directly demonstrate their impact on global public opinion. However, because so many variables impact foreign public opinion of the United States, no soft power program, no matter how effective, can alone account for changes in international public opinion. This paradox may answer criticisms of soft power programs but, at the same time, it may raise questions regarding their effectiveness and their return on investment.

Based on statements made by American government officials, the desired outcomes of American public diplomacy are to reduce anti-Americanism, reduce support for extremism and gain increased favorability in global attitudes towards the United States. As noted by Van Ham (2003): "Public diplomacy has become an essential 'soft power' tool in the U.S. war on terrorism. The U.S.-led war on Iraq has made it imperative to garner public support for the U.S. and its policies, but it has also proven more difficult to do so" (p. 441). Over the past decade, the United States has invested billions of dollars in the development and reconstruction of Iraq and Afghanistan, where it built schools, factories and hospitals. It expanded its educational and cultural exchanges with citizens of the Muslim world. It established American spaces all around its Near East embassies and established Twitter and social media accounts in Farsi, Arabic, Urdu, and Turkish. Consistent in their belief that public diplomacy programs can reduce anti-Americanism and support for terror by highlighting America's values, both the Bush and Obama administrations have argued for the potential necessity of public diplomacy in the war on terror.

During the administration of Under Secretary of Public Diplomacy Charlotte Beers, the United States spent more than five million dollars on its "Shared Values Initiative" advertising campaign. These advertisements were placed around the Muslim world with the clear purpose of convincing the Muslim world that America was not waging a war on Islam (see Kendrick and Fullerton, 2004). Under Secretary Karen Hughes (2006) explained:

> Our second strategic imperative is to isolate and marginalize the violent extremists and confront their ideology of tyranny and hate. We must undermine their efforts. They want to portray the West as in conflict with Islam. That's the window into which they recruit. We have to undermine those by providing platforms for debate, by empowering mainstream voices and by demonstrating respect for Muslim cultures and contributions to our society and to world society.

Two years later, Under Secretary Glassman (2008, October) identified the goal of public diplomacy:

> Our mission today in the war of ideas is highly focused. It is to use the tools of ideological engagement, words, images, and deeds to create an environment hostile to violent extremism. We want to break the linkages between groups like al-Qaida and their target audiences. Indeed, in the war of ideas, our core task is not how to fix foreigners' perceptions of the United States, but how to isolate and reduce the threat of violent extremism. Our task is not to build our brand, but to destroy theirs.

Furthermore, Secretary Rice (2008) explained:

> Leading security experts are increasingly thinking about the war on terrorism as a kind of global counterinsurgency. What that means is that the center of gravity in this conflict is not just the terrorists themselves, but the populations they seek to influence and radicalize and in many cases, terrorize.

As a strategy, the replacement of USIA-style persuasion efforts in favor of citizen-to-citizen diplomacy justifies large scale investments and support for programs based on the assumption that soft power programs will increase support for the U.S. in the Muslim world and reduce support for terrorism. Pointing to a long term strategy of citizen engagement, the establishment and support of institutions of democracy and offering an alternative to radicalization, U.S. public diplomats have made the case for desired public diplomacy outcomes. Secretary of State Hillary Clinton (2010) explained:

> Our diplomats and development experts are helping to build institutions, expand economic opportunities, and provide meaningful alternatives for insurgents ready to renounce violence and join their fellow Afghans in the pursuit of peace.... In Pakistan, our request includes $3.2 billion to combat extremism, promote economic development, strengthen democratic institutions, and build a long-term relationship with the Pakistani people.

As demonstrated, public diplomats in both the Bush and Obama administrations have argued for the allocation of large sums of funds towards soft power programs aimed at gaining favorable public opinion of the United States in the Muslim world and at reducing support for the global Al-Qaeda network. Based on such arguments, public diplomacy budgets have drastically increased over the past decade. For example, congressional budget appropriations for educational and cultural exchange programs more than tripled, going from 204 million dollars in 2000 to 635 million in 2010 (Department of State Budget, 2012). According to the 2013 State/USAID budgetary fact sheet, more than two billion dollars were directly allocated to public diplomacy programs, and hundreds of millions invested in public diplomacy programs in Pakistan, Sudan, Palestine, Jordan, Egypt, and Indonesia.

Despite these investments, longitudinal data indicate that despite America's best efforts, the investment in soft power programs in the Muslim world did not result in the desired outcomes. As noted by Zaharna (2007): "So far, U.S. public diplomacy attempts to wield its soft power have proved frustrating, as public perception of the U.S. remains overwhelmingly negative, particularly in the Arab and Islamic world—the primary target of U.S. intensive public diplomacy efforts" (p. 214).

An analysis of longitudinal data from the Pew Global Attitude Project indicates that favorability ratings of the United States in much of the Arab and Muslim world remained consistently low throughout the 2000s (Pew Research Center, 2010). For example, a Pew Global Attitudes poll (2003) indicates that in Pakistan, the second largest Muslim nation in the world and a key ally in America's global war on terror, more than 69% of people have an unfavorable view of the United States. In the years following 9/11, the United States provided Pakistan with more than 20 billion dollars in direct aid, about half of which was military assistance (Epstein & Kronstadt, 2012). Yet, despite this meaningful aid, public opinion polls showed that the majority of Pakistanis held unfavorable views of the United States, ranging from lows of 56% following the 2006 earthquake in Pakistan to highs of 75% in 2011 (Wike, 2012).

Similarly, public opinion polls following 9/11 pointed to general disapproval of the United States amongst the majority of respondents across the Arab world (Newport, 2002). Recognizing this problem, the United States provided key Arab allies such as Egypt, Jordan, Lebanon, and Iraq with significant sums of foreign aid during the following decade. Both the Bush and Obama Administrations appropriated hundreds of millions of dollars through USAID and into such soft power initiatives as The Millennium Challenge Account, The Middle East Partnership Initiative, The Foundation for the Future, and The Near East Regional Democracy Program. In addition, the United States allocated billions of dollars in economic and military aid to the governments of key Arab allies (Sharp, 2010). Yet, despite these high appropriations, longitudinal public opinion surveys point to persistent disapproval of the United States amongst the majority of people in Egypt, Jordan, Lebanon, and the Palestinian Authority (Telhami, 2010).

In terms of simple evaluation, American public diplomacy programs have failed to produce increased pro-American sentiments in much of the Arab and Muslim world despite the allocation of large budgets toward public diplomacy programs. As argued by Nye (2004): "Anti-Americanism has increased in recent years, and the United States' soft power—its ability to attract others by the legitimacy of U.S. policies and the values that underlie them—is in decline as a result" (p. 16). Based on global public opinion data (see Pew 2012), these sentiments are just as relevant nearly ten years later. Beyond global public opinion, the Al-Qaeda global network has endured and even expanded its global base of operations and is successfully recruiting members all around the Muslim world (see Braniff and Moghadam, 2011; Celso, 2012) while support for Al-Qaeda remains in the double digits in such key nations as Pakistan, Egypt, Jordan, and Tunisia (Pew, 2012).

As noted, America's expensive global outreach based on the soft power approach failed to meet the stated outcomes of improving Muslim public opinion, reducing anti-Americanism and curbing Al-Qaeda's recruitment. One can argue that soft power program outcomes cannot be evaluated in the short term. Perhaps such stated outcomes will bear fruit in the years—or even decades—to come. Such arguments for the potential success of public diplomacy programs over the long run may be supported by the case study of America's efforts in the former Soviet Union during the Cold War.

On the other hand, some will argue that a decade's worth of data fails to support the notion that traditional soft power programs are successful instruments of improving global public opinion. Could it be that America's leading public diplomats got it wrong? Is it possible that educational exchanges and citizen diplomacy are not effective tools in America's global war on terror? This chapter argues that soft power programs alone cannot achieve their stated outcomes as articulated by American public diplomats. Rather, I argue for the integration of traditional relational public diplomacy programs (those programs that I referred to as soft power programs) with the mediated public diplomacy approach.

## Losing the Media War

It is difficult to account for the conflicting research findings regarding the relationship between American soft power outreach programs and the consistent negative evaluations of the United States in the Muslim world. As previously noted, a variety of independent variables such as scapegoating, disapproval of U.S. regional policies, disapproval of American values, perceptions of the United States as a hegemon, and education are all interconnected in accounting for anti-Americanism in the Muslim world.

One key factor that may account for the wide scale negative perceptions of American policies and values is their representation in the pan-Arab news media. Since individual citizens are not privy to the intimate details of foreign policy, they often depend on mass media for interpretation and analysis. According to a Zogby (2011) poll, the majority of Arab respondents identified such pan-Arab satellite news channels as Al Jazeera, Al Arabiya and MBC as their main source of news regarding foreign affairs.

The significant relationship between the consumption of pan-Arab and satellite channels and anti-American sentiments (Nisbet et al., 2004; Nisbet & Myers, 2011) has raised concern among academics and American government officials (see Powers and Samuel-Azran chapter). Ubiquitous pan-Arab news coverage tends to highlight themes of Arab and Muslim victimization while often misrepresenting American policy and values (Sharp, 2003; Kai, 2005). This chapter argues that the relational diplomacy approach focused on soft power programs cannot succeed without a short-term media strategy that will focus on issue management and on crisis communication. Regardless of foreign policy, any nation is unlikely to gain support among foreign publics if it consistently loses the media wars.

## America's Media Strategy

The worrisome impact of negative Arab media coverage of the United States and its potential behavior consequences have raised concern among government officials. Under Secretary Hughes (2005) explained:

> I'm concerned that a lot of what I see is—in the press in this area and in the region of the Middle East where there's been an explosion of Pan-Arab stations and satellite stations and a number of other stations that I'd hoped that I would like to challenge the press to—and not just here, but across the world, to seek to enlighten people rather than incite and to try to work to help build understandings among—to help build understanding of the issues.

Hughes's sentiments exemplify the attempts by governments all around the world to influence the manner in which foreign media cover stories relating to their nations. Indeed, several scholars investigated government employment of global public relations counsel in an attempt to build and influence the global media agenda (Manheim & Albritton, 1984; Zhang & Benoit, 2004; Kiousis & Wu, 2008). Recent scholarship on public diplomacy has shifted attention away from traditional relational diplomacy and towards the subfield of mediated public diplomacy.

Traditionally, American public diplomacy attempted to communicate American values to foreign publics. This effort was largely focused on such interpersonal communication venues as exchanges, English-language instruction programs and other soft power programs that promoted citizen-to-citizen diplomacy. While research indicates that messages communicated through interpersonal channels are more likely to be perceived as credible and therefore more persuasive (Eveland & Shah, 2003), one cannot ignore the limitation of interpersonal communication as compared to mass communication channels. Nor should people forget that interpersonal discussion of political matters is often influenced by exposure to mass communication channels.

Annually, more than 700,000 foreign students study in American institutions of higher learning (Open Doors, 2012). More than 40,000 of these students receive grants from the Department of State's Bureau of Educational and Cultural Affairs as a part of the Fulbright public diplomacy initiative. While impressive, these numbers pale in comparison to Al Jazeera's global audience of more than 150 million viewers who learn about the United States and its policies through the channel's particular perspective (Seib, 2008). While the interpersonal channels may yield desirable message outcomes, they do so on a limited scale and do not necessarily offer consistency of message or message repetition, both of which are key elements of persuasive communication (Benoit et al. 2011).

The political campaign perspective based on the integrated public diplomacy approach does not dismiss the importance of exchange, language or any other type of a soft power program but rather argues that such programs should be focused and consistent. To maximize their impact, soft power programs should be aligned with the strategic communication efforts designated at influencing key foreign publics based on macro campaign objectives.

As identified by Entman (2008), there are a variety of moderating factors that may shape the success or failure of governments in impacting foreign media coverage of salient issues. Chief among these moderators is cultural congruence (Sheafer & Gabay, 2008; Sheafer & Shenhav, 2009). As such, nations that share cultural values with the target media publics are more likely to successfully shape a/the foreign media agenda.

The failure of the United States in shaping its coverage in the Pan-Arab media may be explained by the lack of cultural congruence. However, one could also argue that this failure stems from a lack of an overall mediated public diplomacy strategy. A clear example of this strategic shortcoming is demonstrated in America's global broadcasting strategy in the Arab and Muslim media markets. Much has been written about the Broadcast Board of Governors, its various communication platforms and its programing objectives. Key criticisms regarding American broadcasting in the Middle East and the Muslim world are often focused on its Middle East broadcasting networks, Radio Sawa and Alhurra Television (see chapters by Powers & Samuel-Azran and Schneider in the current book). Focusing on the promotion of free speech and journalism as a part of its congressional mandate along with an attempt to gain credibility amongst target publics, BBG platforms have often failed to serve a strategic function in America's overall public diplomacy strategy.

The limitations of the Broadcast Board of Governors are not the fault of the administrators, who are all highly competent and dedicated public servants. Rather, I argue that the BBG's limitations are a product of the absence of central leadership command. Housed in a multitude of departments and agencies, American public diplomacy programs run parallel to one another, often lacking coordination. While some foreign engagement efforts are overseen by the Department of State, others are directed by the Department of Defense or directly through the White House. The key question that I present is: who is in charge of American public diplomacy? Currently, there is no clear answer to this question. While some will argue that America's public diplomacy strategy should be crafted by the secretary of state, others may point to the president, who is not only the commander in chief but also the chief diplomat. Furthermore, it is important to note that the establishment of the position of under secretary of public diplomacy and public affairs did little to clear the confusion.

Since its establishment in 1999, eight different individuals have served in the position of under secretary. Each individual brought with them a unique set of skill sets as well as diverse perspectives regarding the role and priorities of the under secretary. In addition, the under secretaries have served under three different presidents, each of whom had different public diplomacy goals and priorities during different periods of their presidential tenure.

*Table 24.1.* Under secretaries of state for public diplomacy and public affairs[2]

| Name | Assumed Office | Left Office | Served Under |
|---|---|---|---|
| Evelyn Lieberman | October 1, 1999 | January 19, 2001 | Bill Clinton |
| Charlotte Beers | October 2, 2001 | March 28, 2003 | George W. Bush |
| Margaret D. Tutwiler | December 16, 2003 | June 30, 2004 | George W. Bush |
| Karen Hughes | September 9, 2005 | December 14, 2007 | George W. Bush |
| James K. Glassman | June 10, 2008 | January 15, 2009 | George W. Bush |
| Judith McHale | May 26, 2009 | July 2011 | Barack Obama |
| Kathleen Stephens | February 6, 2012 | April 4, 2012 | Barack Obama |
| Tara D. Sonenshine | April 5, 2012 | July 1, 2013 | Barack Obama |
| Richard Stengel | February 14, 2014 | Current | Barack Obama |

While all of the under secretaries were highly qualified individuals and, for the most part, had substantial professional experience in the field of strategic communications, there is little evidence that any of them focused their tenure on devising and implementing a strategic communication plan that will allow the United States to successfully communicate with key target publics.

The exception was Under Secretary Beers, who attempted to rebrand the United States in the Muslim world through a specific marketing effort. Her expensive fifteen million dollar "Shared Values" global advertising campaign failed to shift global public opinion and was widely assessed as a failure (Hayden, 2007; Seib, 2008).

Tasked with the short-, medium- and long-termed outcomes of America's public diplomacy, it seems that the under secretary role is over-tasked and underfunded. As reflected by the past itineraries of most under secretaries, it appears that they largely serve as cheerleaders for soft power programs as opposed to serving as the strategic leaders of America's global communication effort, a responsibility that is neither defined nor allocated by the president to the under secretary. The nonexistence of a clearly defined mandate for the under secretary position continues to undermine the success of the office and its various functions. Based on the core assumptions of the mediated public diplomacy model (Golan, 2013), I argue that America's foreign engagement effort can only succeed if it is approached from the political campaign war room perspective. This will include defined leadership, specific program objectives, and a research-based campaign messaging and programming strategy that will be evaluated on a regular basis. Much like in political campaigns, a nation's public diplomacy strategy must identify priorities in terms of its key target publics, key rivals and key allies. Ultimately, each country around the world will devise a unique public diplomacy strategy depending on its overall foreign policy aims and perspectives. As such, any one-size-fits-all approach to public diplomacy is doomed to fail.

I point to the United States' Center for Strategic Counterterrorism Communications as a good example of a integrated, inter-agency organization that largely follows the political war room model. Focused on a strategic research based approach rather than normative theoretical assumptions, the political campaign war room approach based on the integrated public diplomacy model is likely to provide nations with a real return on investment.

This edited book provides an overview of the many convergences between international public relations and public diplomacy scholarship. Both disciplines embody a wide range of subtopics and strategic communication functions. While some chapters focused on government to foreign public engagement, others focused on corporate, not-for-profit, citizen-to-citizen track two diplomacy. Recognizing that there is no one-size-fits-all formula for global relationship building efforts, the book points to the various opportunities and challenges that face scholars and practitioners in this area of research. It is the hope of the book editors that the integrated public diplomacy model will be of use to future scholars who aim to understand the complex and multi-dimensional nature of this field. As the globalization and mediatization phenomena continue to evolve, we hope that international public relations and mass communication theories will provide a sound framework for understanding global communications.

## Notes

1. For more information about liberalism as a key theoretical perspective in international relations, read Kegley, C. W., Jr. 1995. *Controversies in International Relations Theory: Realism and the Neoliberal Challenge.* St. Martin's Press; Latham, R. 1997. *The Liberal Moment: Modernity, Security, and the Making of Postwar International Order.* New York, NY: Columbia University Press; Long, D. 1996. *Toward a New Liberal Internationalism: The International Theory of J. A.Hobson.* New York, NY: Cambridge University Press.
2. Table copied from Wikipedia.com. All information verified for accuracy.

## Bibliography

Bennett, W. L., & Paletz, D. L. (Eds.) (1994). *Taken by Storm: The Media, Public Opinion, and US Foreign Policy in the Gulf War.* University of Chicago Press.

Benoit, W. L., Glantz, M. J., Phillips, A. L., Rill, L. A., Davis, C. B., Henson, J. R., & Sudbrock, L. A. (2011). Staying "on message": Consistency in content of presidential primary campaign messages across media. *American Behavioral Scientist, 55,* 457–468.

Bonomi, V., & Pan, P. L. (2013). Framing of the US-Venezuela diplomatic relationship in major US newspapers. *Journal of International Communication, 19*(2), 235–251.

Borah, P. (2011). Conceptual issues in framing theory: A systematic examination of a decade's literature. *Journal of Communication, 61*(2), 246–263.

Braniff, B., & Moghadam, A. (2011). Towards global Jihadism: Al-Qaeda's strategic, ideological and structural adaptations since 9/11. *Perspectives on Terrorism, 5*(2).

Brown, J. (2009). Arts diplomacy: The neglected aspect of cultural diplomacy. In N. Snow & P. M. Taylor (Eds.), *Routledge Handbook of Public Diplomacy* (57–59). New York: Routledge.

Cancel, A. E., Cameron, G. T., Sallot, L. M., & Mitrook, M. A. (1997). It depends: A contingency theory of accommodation in public relations. *Journal of Public Relations Research, 9,* 33.

Carroll, C. E., & McCombs, M. (2003). Agenda-setting effects of business news on the public's images and opinions about major corporations. *Corporate Reputation Review, 6*(1), 36–46.

Celso, A. N. (2012). Al Qaeda's post–9/11 organizational structure and strategy: The role of Islamist regional affiliates. *Mediterranean Quarterly, 23*(2), 30–41.

Chiozza, G. (2009). *Anti-Americanism and the American world order.* Baltimore, MD: Johns Hopkins University Press.

Clinton, H. (2010, February 24). Statement made to Committee on Foreign Relations. Washington, DC. http://www.gpo.gov/fdsys/pkg/CHRG-111shrg63232/html/CHRG-111shrg63232.htm

Connolly-Ahern, C., & Ma, L. (2014). Taking it to the streets: The evolving use of VNRs as a public diplomacy tool in the digital age. In G. J. Golan (Ed.), *The Handbook of Strategic Public Diplomacy.* Bern: Peter Lang.

Coombs, W. T. (2007). Protecting organization reputations during a crisis: The development and application of situational crisis communication theory. *Corporate Reputation Review, 10*(3), 163–176.

Coombs, W. T., & Holladay, S. J. (2004). Reasoned action in crisis communication: An attribution theory-based approach to crisis management. In D. P. Millar & R. L. Heath (Eds.), *Responding to Crisis: A Rhetorical Approach to Crisis Communication* (95–115). Mahwah, NJ: Lawrence Erlbaum Associates.

DeFleur, M. H. and DeFleur, M. L. (2003). *Learning to Hate Americans: How US Media Shape Negative Attitudes Among Teenagers in Twelve Countries.* Spokane, WA: Marquette Books.

Dragojlovic, N. I. (2011). Priming and the Obama effect on public evaluations of the United States. *Political Psychology, 32*(6), 989–1006.

el-Nawawy, M. (2006). US public diplomacy in the Arab world: The new credibility of Radio Sawa and Television Alhurra in five countries. *Global Media and Communication, 2*(2), 183–203.

Entman, R. M. (2008). Theorizing mediated public diplomacy: The US case. *The International Journal of Press/Politics, 13*(2), 87–102.

Entman, R. M. (2004). *Projections of Power: Framing News, Public Opinion, and U.S. Foreign Policy.* Chicago: University of Chicago Press.

Epstein, S. B. & Kronstadt, K. A. (2012). Pakistan: U.S. foreign aid conditions, restrictions, and reporting requirements. *Congressional Research Service*, Washington, DC. Retrieved from http://www.fas.org/sgp/crs/row/R42116.pdf

Eveland Jr, W. P., & Shah, D. V. (2003). The impact of individual and interpersonal factors on perceived news media bias. *Political Psychology, 24*(1), 101–117.

Fahmy, S. (2007). "They took it down": Exploring determinants of visual reporting in the toppling of the Saddam statue in national and international newspapers. *Mass Communication & Society, 10*(2), 143–170.

Fair, J. E. (1993). War, famine, and poverty: Race in the construction of Africa's media image. *Journal of Communication Inquiry, 17*(2), 5–22.

Gentzkow, M. A., & Shapiro, J. (2004). Media, education and anti-Americanism in the Muslim world. *Journal of Economic Perspectives, 18*(3), 117–133.

Gilboa, E. (2000). Mass communication and diplomacy: A theoretical framework. *Communication Theory, 10*(3), 275–309.

Gilboa, E. (2008). Searching for a theory of public diplomacy. *The ANNALS of the American Academy of Political and Social Science, 616*, 55–77.

Glassman, J. (2008, July 8). *Winning the war of ideas.* Speech presented at the Washington Institute's Special Policy Forum, Washington, DC.

Glassman, J. (2008, January 30). *Opening statement of James K. Glassman*. Speech presented to the Senate Foreign Relations Committee, Washington, DC. Retrieved from http://www.aei.org/speech/society-and-culture/opening-statement-of-james-k-glassman/

Golan, G. J. (2006). Inter-media agenda setting and global news coverage: Assessing the influence of *The New York Times* on three network television evening news programs. *Journalism Studies, 7*(2), 323–333.

Golan, G. J. (2008). Where in the world is Africa? Predicting coverage of Africa by US television networks. *International Communication Gazette, 70*(1), 41–57.

Golan, G. J. (2013). An integrated approach to public diplomacy. *American Behavioral Scientist, 57*(9), 1251–1255.

Golan, G. J. & Yang, S. U. (2013). Diplomat in chief? Assessing the influence of presidential evaluations on public diplomacy outcomes among foreign publics. *American Behavioral Scientist, 57*(9), 1277–1292.

Goldsmith, B. E., Horiuchi, Y., & Inoguchi, T. (2005). American foreign policy and global opinion who supported the war in Afghanistan? *Journal of Conflict Resolution, 49*(3), 408–429.

Graber, D. A. (2009). Looking at the United States through distorted lenses: Entertainment television versus public diplomacy themes. *American Behavioral Scientist, 52*(5), 735–754.

Gregory, B. (2008). Public diplomacy: Sunrise of an academic field. *The ANNALS of the American Academy of Political and Social Science, 616*(1), 274–290.

Grunig, J. E. (1992). What is excellence in management. *Excellence in Public Relations and Communication Management*, 219–250.

Grunig, J. E. (1997). A situational theory of publics: Conceptual history, recent challenges, and new research. In D. Moss, T. MacManus, & D. Verčič (Eds.), *Public Relations Research: An International Perspective* (pp. 3–48). London: International Thomson Business Press.

Grunig, J. E. (Ed.) (2013). *Excellence in Public Relations and Communication Management*. New York, NY: Routledge.

Grunig, J. E., & Grunig, L. A. (2008). Excellence theory in public relations: Past, present, and future. *Public Relations Research*, 327–347.

Hayden, C. A. (2007). Maintaining the digital hub: Locating the community technology center in a communication infrastructure. *New Media & Society, 9*(2), 235–257.

Hughes K. (2006, March 29). *Remarks on the Shell distinguished lecture series*. Speech presented at the Baker Institute for Public Policy, Houston, TX. Retrieved from http://2001-2009.state.gov/r/us/64106.htm

Hughes, K. (2005, September 27). *Discussion with students at Dar al-Hekma College*. Speech presented at Dar al-Hekma College, Jeddah, Saudi Arabia. Retrieved from http://2001-2009.state.gov/r/us/2005/54722.htm

Jin, Y., & Liu, B. F. (2010). The blog-mediated crisis communication model: Recommendations for responding to influential external blogs. *Journal of Public Relations Research, 22*(4), 429–455.

Johnston, A. I., & Stockmann, D. (2007). Chinese attitudes toward the United States and Americans. In P. J. Katzenstein & R. O. Keohane (Eds.), *Anti-Americanisms in World Politics*, 157–195. Ithaca: Cornell University Press.

Kai, H. (2005). Arab satellite broadcasting: Democracy without political parties. *Transnational Broadcasting Studies, 15.* Retrieved July 15, 2010 from http://www.tbsjournal.com/Archives/Fall05/Hafez.html

Kendrick, A., & Fullerton, J. A. (2004). Advertising as public diplomacy: Attitude change among international audiences. *Journal of Advertising Research, 44*(3), 297–311.

Kepplinger, H. M. (2006). Mediatization of politics: Theory and data. *Journal of Communication, 52*(4), 972–986.

Kiousis, S., Kim, S. Y., McDevitt, M., & Ostrowski, A. (2009). Competing for attention: Information subsidy influence in agenda building during election campaigns. *Journalism & Mass Communication Quarterly, 86*(3), 545–562.

Kiousis, S., Mitrook, M., Wu, X., & Seltzer, T. (2006). First-and second-level agenda-building and agenda-setting effects: Exploring the linkages among candidate news releases, media coverage, and public opinion during the 2002 Florida gubernatorial election. *Journal of Public Relations Research, 18*(3), 265–285.

Kiousis, S., Popescu, C., & Mitrook, M. (2007). Understanding influence on corporate reputation: An examination of public relations efforts, media coverage, public opinion, and financial performance from an agenda-building and agenda-setting perspective. *Journal of Public Relations Research, 19*(2), 147–165.

Kiousis, S., & Wu, X. (2008). International agenda-building and agenda-setting: Exploring the influence of public relations counsel on US news media and public perceptions of foreign nations. *International Communication Gazette, 70,* 58–75.

Kothari, A. (2010). The framing of the Darfur conflict in *The New York Times:* 2003–2006. *Journalism Studies, 11*(2), 209–224.

Kunczick, M. (1997). *Images of Nations and International Public Relations.* Mahwah, NJ: Lawrence Erlbaum Associates.

Ledingham, J. A. (2003). Explicating relationship management as a general theory of public relations. *Journal of Public Relations Research, 15*(2), 181–198

Lynch, M. (2007). Anti-Americanisms in the Arab world. In P. J. Katzenstein & R. O. Keohane (Eds.), *Anti-Americanisms in World Politics,* 196–224. Ithaca: Cornell University Press.

Manheim, J. B., & Albritton, R. B. (1984). Changing national images: International public relations and media agenda setting. *The American Political Science Review,* 641–657.

Maoz, I. (2006). The effect of news coverage concerning the opponents' reaction to a concession on its evaluation in the Israeli-Palestinian conflict. *The Harvard International Journal of Press/Politics, 11*(4), 70–88.

McCombs, M. (1997). Building consensus: The news media's agenda-setting roles. *Political Communication, 14*(4), 433–443.

McCombs, M. & Shaw, D. (1972). The agenda-setting function of mass media. *Public Opinion Quarterly, 36*(2), 176–187.

McHale, J. A. (2009, June 11). *Public diplomacy: A national security imperative.* Speech presented at the Center for a New American Society, Washington, DC. Retrieved from http://www.state.gov/r/remarks/2009/124640.htm

Molleda, J. C. & Suarez, A. M. (2006). Engaging Colombian coffee growers in dialogue: Social reports campaign of the department of committee of Antioquia. In M. G. Parkinson & De. Ekachai (Eds.), *International and Intercultural Public Relations: A Campaign Case Approach* (306–319). Boston: Pearson Education, Inc.

Molleda. J. C. & Suarez, A. M. (2005). Challenges in Colombia for public relations professionals: A qualitative assessment of the economic and political environments. *Public Relations Review*, *31*, 21–29.

Newport, F. (2002). Gallup poll of the Islamic world. *The Gallup Poll*. Retrieved from: http://www.gallup.com/poll/5380/gallup-poll-islamic-world.aspx

Nisbet, E. C., & Myers, T. A. (2010). Challenging the state: Transnational TV and political identity in the Middle East. *Political Communication*, *27*(4), 347–366.

Nisbet, E. C., & Myers, T. A. (2011). Anti-American sentiment as a media effect? Arab media, political identity, and public opinion in the Middle East. *Communication Research*, *38*(5), 684–709.

Nisbet, E. C., Nisbet, M. C., Scheufele, D. A., & Shanahan, J. E. (2004). Public diplomacy, television news, and Muslim opinion. *Journal of Press/Politics*, *9*(2), 11–37.

Nisbet, E., & Shanahan, J. (2008). Anti-Americanism as a communication problem? Foreign media and public opinion toward the United States in Europe and the Middle East. *American Journal of Media Psychology*, *1*, 7–35.

Nye Jr., J. S. (1990). Soft power. *Foreign Policy*, *80*, 153–171.

Nye Jr., J. S. (2004). *Soft Power: The Means to Success in World Politics*. New York, NY: Public Affairs.

Nye Jr., J. S. (2008). Public diplomacy and soft power. *The ANNALS of the American Academy of Political and Social Science*, *616*(1), 94–109.

Open Doors (2012). International student enrollment increased by 6 percent [Press Release]. Retrieved from: http://www.iie.org/Who-We-Are/News-and-Events/Press-Center/Press-Releases/2012/2012-11-13-Open-Doors-International-Students

Pahlavi, P. C. (2007). Evaluating public diplomacy programmes. *The Hague Journal of Diplomacy*, *2*(3), 255–281.

Peterson, R. A. & Jolibert, A. P. (1995). A meta-analysis of country-of-origin effects. *Journal of International Business Studies*, *26*, 883–900.

Pew Research Center (2012). Most Muslims want democracy, personal freedoms, and Islam in political life. *Pew Research Global Attitudes Project*. Retrieved from http://www.pewglobal.org/2012/07/10/most-muslims-want-democracy-personal-freedoms-and-islam-in-political-life/

Pew Research Center (2010). Chapter 1. Views of the U.S. and American foreign policy. *Pew Research Global Attitudes Project*. Retrieved from http://www.pewglobal.org/2010/06/17/chapter-1-views-of-the-u-s-and-american-foreign-policy-3/

Pew Research Center (2003). Views of a changing world 2003. *Pew Research Global Attitudes Project*. Retrieved from http://www.pewglobal.org/2003/06/03/views-of-a-changing-world-2003/

*President's Proposed Budget Request for RY2011 for Department of State and Foreign Operations*: Hearing before the Senate Appropriations Subcommittee on State, Foreign Operations, and Related Programs, *U.S. Senate*, 112th Cong. (2010). (Testimony of Hillary R. Clinton). Retrieved from: http://m.state.gov/md137227.htm

Rice, C. (2006, February 12). *Remarks on Transformational Diplomacy*. Speech presented at Georgetown University, Washington, DC. Retrieved from http://2001–2009.state.gov/secretary/rm/2006/59306.htm

Rice, C. (2008, February 12). Remarks on Transformational Diplomacy. Speech presented at Georgetown University, Washington, DC.

Rogers, R., & Ben-David, A. (2010). Coming to terms: A conflict analysis of the usage, in official and unofficial sources, of 'security fence,' 'apartheid wall,' and other terms for the structure between Israel and the Palestinian territories. *Media, War & Conflict*, 3(2), 202–229.

Scheufele, D. A. (1999). Framing as a theory of media effects. *Journal of Communication*, 49(1), 103–122.

Scott-Smith, G. (2009, March 1). Curbing the Pentagon. *De Volkskrant*. Retrieved from http://depot.knaw.nl/5560/2/Volkskrant_-_Pentagon.pdf

Seib, P. (Ed.). (2009). *Toward a New Public Diplomacy*. Palgrave Macmillan.

Seib, P. (2008a). *The Al-Jazeera Effect: How the New Global Media are Reshaping World Politics*. Dulles, VA: Potomac Books

Seib, P. (2008b). Hegemonic no more: Western media, the rise of Al-Jazeera, and the influence of diverse voices. *International Studies Review*, 7, 601–615

Sharp, J. M. (2010, June 15). *U.S. foreign assistance to the Middle East: Historical background, recent trends, and the FY2011 request* (CRS Report No. RL32260). Washington, DC. Retrieved from Congressional Research Service: http://www.fas.org/sgp/crs/mideast/RL32260.pdf

Sharp, J. M. (2003, July 23). *The Al-Jazeera news network: Opportunity or challenge for U.S. foreign policy in the Middle East*. (CRS Report No. RL31889). Washington, DC. Retrieved from Congressional Research Service http://fpc.state.gov/documents/organization/23002.pdf

Sheafer, T., & Gabay, I. (2009). Mediated public diplomacy: A strategic contest over international agenda building and frame building. *Political Communication*, 26(4), 447–467.

Sheafer, T., & Shenhav, S. R. (2009). Mediated public diplomacy in a new era of warfare. *The Communication Review*, 12(3), 272–283.

Shoemaker, P. J., Tankard, J. W., & Lasorsa, D. L. (2004). *How to Build Social Science Theories*. London: Sage Publications.

Sonenshine, T. (2012, October 18).

Strömbäck, J. (2008). Four phases of mediatization: An analysis of the mediatization of politics. *The International Journal of Press/Politics*, 13(3), 228–246.

Strömbäck, J., & Kiousis, S. (Eds.) (2011). *Political public relations. Principles and applications*. New York, NY: Routledge.

Sweetser, K. D., & Brown, C. W. (2008). Information subsidies and agenda-building during the Israel-Lebanon crisis. *Public Relations Review*, 34(4), 359–366.

Tai, C. S., Peterson, E. J., & Gurr, T. R. (1973). Internal versus external sources of anti-Americanism: Two comparative studies. *Journal of Conflict Resolution*, 17(3), 455–488.

Taylor, M. & Kent, M. L. (2006). Public relations theory and practice in nation building. In C. Botan & V. Hazelton (Eds.) *Public Relations Theory II* (pp. 341–359). Mahwah, NJ: Lawrence Erlbaum Associates.

Telhami, S. (2010). Annual Arab public opinion survey. Retrieved from http://www.brookings.edu/~/media/research/files/reports/2010/8/05%20arab%20opinion%20poll%20telhami/0805_arabic_opinion_poll_telhami.pdf

U.S. Department of State. (2012, February 13). *State and USAID—FY 2013 budget*. Washington, DC. Retrieved from http://www.state.gov/r/pa/prs/ps/2012/02/183808.htm

Van Ham, P. (2003). War, lies, and videotape: Public diplomacy and the USA's War on Terrorism. *Security Dialogue, 34*(4), 427–444.

Wanta, W., Golan, G., & Lee, C. (2004). Agenda setting and international news: Media influence on public perceptions of foreign nations. *Journalism & Mass Communication Quarterly, 81*(2), 364–377.

Weaver, D., & Elliott, S. N. (1985). Who sets the agenda for the media? A study of local agenda-building. *Journalism Quarterly, 62*(1), 87–94.

Wike, R. (2012, March 6). Does humanitarian aid improve America's image? Retrieved from http://pewresearch.org/pubs/2213/united-states-humanitarian-aid-disaster-relief-pakistan-indonesia-japan-tsunami-earthquake

Zaharna, R. S. (2007). The soft power differential: Network communication and mass communication in public diplomacy. *The Hague Journal of Diplomacy, 2*(3), 213–228.

Zhang, J., & Benoit, W. L. (2004). Message strategies of Saudi Arabia's image restoration campaign after 9/11. *Public Relations Review, 30*(2), 161–167.

Zogby, J. (2011). Iraq: The war, its consequences & the future. *Zogby Research Services* Retrieved from http://b.3cdn.net/aai/da8812cad12eb3cda2_4tm6vtlg7.pdf

# Contributors

## EDITORS

**Guy J. Golan** (Ph.D., University of Florida) is an associate professor of Public Relations and Public Diplomacy at the S.I. Newhouse School of Public Communications, Syracuse University. His research focuses on mediated public diplomacy and international public relations. Golan has published more than two dozen peer reviewed journal articles, including articles in such journals as *Communication Research, Journalism and Mass Communication Quarterly, Mass Communication and Society, The Journal of Computer-Mediated Communication, Journal of Public Relations Research*, and the *Journal of Interactive Advertising*.

**Dennis F. Kinsey** (Ph.D., Stanford University) is the director of Public Diplomacy and professor of Public Relations at the S. I. Newhouse School of Public Communications, Syracuse University. He has published in *Corporate Reputation Review, Exchange: The Journal of Public Diplomacy*, the *Journal of Advertising Research, Journal of Marketing for Higher Education, Journalism Educator, Political Communication, Political Psychology, Public Relations Review, Operant Subjectivity* and *Visual Communication Quarterly*. Kinsey serves on the editorial board of the *Journal of Political Marketing*.

**Sung-Un Yang** (Ph.D., University of Maryland) is an Associate Professor in the Department of Journalism at The Media School, Indiana University. He was a tenured associate professor and the former Newhouse Endowed Chair of Public Communications in the S. I. Newhouse School of Public Communications, Syracuse University. His research agenda includes (a) public relationship and organizational reputation management; (b) public diplomacy; and (c) social/digital media and communication effectiveness. Sung-Un authored or coauthored numerous articles in leading refereed journals in his field, including *Communication Research, Journal of Public Relations Research, American Behavioral Scientist, Public Relations Review, Journal of*

*Communication Management, Corporate Reputation Review, International Journal of Strategic Communication, Higher Education,* and *Asian Journal of Communication,* among others.

## AUTHORS

**Simon Anholt** is an independent policy advisor to numerous heads of state and heads of government and a professor of Political Science at the University of East Anglia. He is the publisher of the Anholt-GfK Roper Nation Brands Index, and founder and editor Emeritus of the journal *Place Branding and Public Diplomacy.* He was vice chairman of the UK Foreign Office's Public Diplomacy Board between 2002 and 2008. He was awarded the Nobel Colloquia Prize in 2009 by a jury of 25 Nobel economists.

**Vanessa Bravo** (Ph.D., University of Florida) is an assistant professor of strategic communications in the School of Communications at Elon University. Her research interests include the study of diaspora communities as strategic publics, government-diaspora relationship-building processes, transnational communications, ethnic public relations, immigration, and the contributions of Latinos to the United States. Her work has been published in journals such as *Public Relations Review, The Hague Journal of Diplomacy, International Journal of Communications, Global Media Journal* (American Edition), *Revista Internacional de Relaciones Públicas* (Spain), and *Palabra Clave* (Colombia). She also authored a chapter in the book *Communication and Community.* She has fifteen years of professional experience as a journalist, editor, and public relations practitioner, mainly in Costa Rica.

**Colleen Connolly-Ahern** (Ph.D., University of Florida) is an associate professor of Advertising and Public Relations at the College of Communications at Penn State University. Her research interests include political advertising as well as culture, framing and media access issues. Her work has been published in a wide range of academic journals, including *Journalism and Mass Communication Quarterly, The Journal of Public Relations Research, The Communication Review,* and *Communication, Culture & Critique.* Connolly-Ahern sits on the editorial boards of the *Journal of Public Relations Research* and the upcoming *Journal of Entertainment and Media Studies.*

**Bruce W. Dayton** (Ph.D., Syracuse) is the associate director at the Moynihan Institute of Global Affairs and an Assistant Research Professor of Political Science at the Maxwell School of Syracuse University. His work focuses on understanding and modeling leadership decision making in times of crisis and conflict. Dayton has published articles related to crises and conflict processes in the *International Studies Perspective*, the *International Studies Review*, the *Journal of Contingencies and Crisis Management*, and the *Oxford Encyclopedia of Peace*. He has two books on conflict management processes: *Constructive Conflicts: From Escalation to Resolution* (2012); and *Peacebuilding and Conflict Transformation* (2009), both co-authored with Louis Kriesberg.

**Mohan J. Dutta** is Provost's Chair Professor and Head of the Department of Communications and New Media at the National University of Singapore, and Courtesy Professor of Communication at Purdue University. At NUS, he is the Founding Director of the Center for Culture-Centered Approach to Research and Evaluation (CARE), directing research on culturally-centered, community-based projects of social change. He teaches and conducts research in international communication, critical cultural theory, subaltern studies and dialogue, and public policy and social change.

**Jiska Engelbert** (Ph.D., Aberystwyth University) is an assistant professor in the Erasmus School of History, Culture and Communication at Erasmus University, Rotterdam. Her research explores the discourse of politics and the politics of discourse, which has resulted in research projects and publications on the discourse of New Labour and reformed social democracy; populists' self-presentation in online spaces; the discourse of public value, and discourses on diversity and pluralism in media policy. Recent publications feature in *Critical Discourse Studies, Journal of Language and Politics* and *New Media & Society*.

**Shahira Fahmy** (Ph.D., Missouri-Columbia) is a tenured associate professor in the School of Journalism at the University of Arizona. She holds an adjunct/courtesy joint appointment with the Department of Communication and another one in the School of Middle Eastern & North African Studies (MENAS) and works closely with the Center for Middle Eastern Studies (CMES). She is also an affiliated member with the National Institute for Civil Discourse (NICD). With native fluency in four languages combined with Middle Eastern, European and US citizenships, she has served as an international guest editor, international keynote speaker and lectured on global reporting and visual journalism in Western European cities. Currently she is on the board of more than a dozen scholarly journals on the national and international levels. She has been the associate editor for *Mass Communication*

*& Society* and has written almost 140 scholarly books, journal articles, special issues and conference presentations on the national and international levels. Her work has appeared in journals such as *Journalism & Mass Communication Quarterly, Mass Communication & Society, American Behavioral Scientist, Journal of Broadcasting & Electronic Media, International Communication Gazette, Media, War & Conflict,* and *Visual Communication Quarterly.*

**Kristi S. Gilmore**, APR (Ph.D., Syracuse University), is an assistant professor of Public Relations in the College of Media and Communications at Texas Tech University. She spent 20 years as a public relations professional with experience in corporate communications, crisis management, nonprofit communications, strategic public relations and corporate social responsibility. Her research interests are in the areas of crisis communications and corporate reputation, as well as the evolution of corporate public relations.

**Jacob Groshek** (Ph.D., Indiana University) is an assistant professor at Boston University in the newly formed Division of Emerging Media Studies. His research interests include the democratic utility of communication technologies and the ways in which the structure, content and uses of online and mobile media may influence political change. Additional research pursuits include applied econometric analyses, data mining, public diplomacy, and media ethics. He has over 20 peer-reviewed publications and recent work is featured in *Journal of Communication, New Media & Society, International Communication Gazette,* and *Journalism,* among others. He sits on the editorial board of *Communication Yearbook* and regularly reviews for more than a dozen journals.

**Margaret G. Hermann** (Ph.D., Northwestern University) is the Daphna and Gerald Cramer Professor of Global Affairs and Director of the Moynihan Institute of Global Affairs at the Maxwell School of Syracuse University. Her research focuses on the study of political leadership, decision making, crisis management, and the comparative approach to foreign policymaking. She has published widely in such journals as *Political Psychology, International Studies Quarterly, Journal of Conflict Resolution, Leadership Quarterly,* and *Dynamics of Asymmetric Conflict.* She has been president of the International Society of Political Psychology and the International Studies Association.

**Kineta Hung** (Ph.D., York University) is a professor and head of the Department of Communications Studies, Hong Kong Baptist University. Her research interests include celebrity endorsement, communication engagement, and advertising in China. Her works have appeared in *Journal of Advertising*, *Journal of Marketing*, *Journal of International Business Studies*, and *Journal of Advertising Research*. Professor Hung serves on the Research Committee of the Advertising Academy of Advertising and has given academic and executive talks on various advertising topics in Hong Kong, China and overseas. She is the recipient of multiple competitive research grants and awards including the Emerald Management Reviews Citations of Excellence.

**Hua Jiang** (Ph.D., University of Maryland, College Park) is an assistant professor in the Department of Public Relations at the S. I. Newhouse School of Public Communications, Syracuse University. Her research interests include relationship management in public relations, employee engagement, social media and public relations leadership, and work, life, and gender issues of public relations practitioners. Her works appear in *Journal of Public Relations Research*, *Public Relations Review*, *Journal of Applied Communication Research*, *Journal of Health Communication*, *Asian Journal of Communication*, and *International Journal of Strategic Communication*, among others. Hua Jiang currently serves as Chair of PRSA's Work, Life and Gender Committee.

**Eyun-Jung Ki** (Ph.D., University of Florida) is an associate professor of Department of Advertising and Public Relations at The University of Alabama. Her research interests focus on 1) Developing measurement scales 2) Testing models linking crisis, relationship, attitudes, and behaviors, 3) Examining new technologies in public relations, 4) Evaluating ethics in the public relations, and 5) organization sustainability communication. Her works appear in *Journal of Communication*, *Journal of Public Relations Research*, *Journalism & Mass Communication Quarterly*, *Journal of Business Ethics*, and *Public Relations Reviews* among many others. She is a lead editor of the second volume of *Public Relations as Relationship Management: Relational Approach to the Study and Practice of Public Relations*.

**Jangyul Robert Kim** (Ph.D., University of Florida) is an associate professor in the Department of Journalism and Technical Communication at Colorado State University. His research interests include 1) application of public relations theories to public diplomacy from issues and crisis communication perspective, and 2) application of political and persuasion theories to public relations. His works appear in *Journal of Public Relations Research*, *Public Relations Review*, *Asia Pacific Public Relations Journal*, and several other journals.

**Jeong-Nam Kim** (Ph.D., University of Maryland) is associate professor at the Brian Lamb School of Communication at Purdue University, Indiana. His specialties are communication theory, strategic management of public relations, public behavior and its social consequences, information behaviors and problem solving. Jeong-Nam Kim has constructed a communication theory called the situational theory of problem solving with James E. Grunig, which explains causes and processes of information behaviors in problematic life situations. The situational theory has been applied to public relations, public diplomacy, corporate communication, health communication, risk communication, science communication, and employee communication.

**Sarabdeep K. Kochhar** (Ph.D., University of Florida) is the Director of Research at the Institute for Public Relations (IPR). She also holds the position of Associate Director of Measurement and Analytics at APCO Worldwide. At APCO, Sarab serves as a strategic counsel for clients on measurement and evaluation. At IPR, she is the chief research strategist, advising and leading the Institute on priorities and research programs. Sarab has several years of professional work experience in both public and private sectors. She has authored book chapters and refereed conference papers, received the top paper award from PRSA Educators Academy, the Chester Burger Award for Excellence in Public Relations from PRSA, and the Ketchum Public Relations Research Award from IPR.

**Lian Ma** is a Ph.D. candidate in the College of Communications at Penn State University. Her research interests include public diplomacy, nation branding, framing and international communication. She is particularly interested in how China is being constructed in the global media. Her work has been published in *International Relations of the Asia-Pacific* and *Ecquid Novi: African Journalism Studies.*

**Juan-Carlos Molleda** (Ph.D., University of South Carolina) is Professor and Chair of the Department of Public Relations and Director of the online MAMC Global Strategic Communication of the College of Journalism and Communications, University of Florida. He is also an affiliate faculty of the UF Center for Latin American Studies and a Fulbright Senior Specialist. Molleda is a member of the Institute for Public Relations' Board of Trustees and a founding member of its Commission on Global Public Relations. Research. He holds a bachelor's degree from Universidad del Zulia (Venezuela), a master's degree from Radford University, and a Ph.D. degree from University of South Carolina.

**James Pamment** (Ph.D., Stockholm University) is post-doc at the University of Texas at Austin and assistant professor at Karlstad University, Sweden. He is author of *New Public Diplomacy in the 21st Century* (Routledge New Diplomacy Series), a comparative study of public diplomacy policy, practice and evaluation in Sweden, the United Kingdom and the United States. Pamment is also a research fellow at the Center on Public Diplomacy, University of Southern California (2013–2015) and at the Department of International Development at Oxford University (2014).

**Shawn Powers** (Ph.D., University of Southern California) is an assistant professor in the Department of Communication at Georgia State University. His research specializes in international political communication with particular attention to the geopolitics of information and technology policy. Powers is a faculty affiliate of GSU's Transcultural Violence and Conflict initiative and co-leads its British Council and U.S. Institute of Peace funded project on Civic Approaches to Religious Conflict. Powers is also an associate director at the Center for International Media Education, where he co-directs an Open Society Foundations sponsored project on Critical Thinking in Iraqi Higher Education. In 2010, Powers helped launch GSU's Global Business & Media program in Istanbul, Turkey and continues to oversee the initiative as co-director.

**Tal Samuel-Azran** (Ph.D., University of Melbourne) is the head of the international school at the Sammy Ofer School of Communications at the Interdisciplinary Center in Herzliya, Israel. His main fields of research are political communication, new media and media globalization. His book *Al-Jazeera and the US Media* was published in 2010 (Peter Lang). In 2008, he co-edited the book *New Media and Innovative Technologies* (Ben-Gurion University Press) with Professor Dan Caspi. He has lectured at New York University, The University of Melbourne, Victoria University (Melbourne, Australia), the Hebrew University and Tel Aviv University.

**Michael D. Schneider** (Ph.D., American University) is the Director of the Washington Public Diplomacy Program of the Maxwell School, Syracuse University. Previously, he directed the Maxwell in Washington Program, and served abroad and in Washington, D.C. with the U.S. Information Agency and State Department. He authored studies on "The Future of U.S. Broadcasting" and "Fulbright at Fifty," and conducted an analysis of competition for international students, "Others Open Doors." He is past president of the PDA—Association of Public Diplomacy Professionals and a member of the Public Diplomacy Council.

**Nancy Snow** (Ph.D., American University) is an advisor at Langley Esquire, a leading public affairs firm in Tokyo, Japan. Snow is Professor Emeritus at Cal State Fullerton and a longtime Adjunct Professor in the USC Annenberg School. Her books include the forthcoming *Routledge Handbook of Critical Public Relations* and the *Routledge Handbook of Public Diplomacy* with Philip M. Taylor. A former USIA and Department of State official, Snow has been a visiting professor in China, Japan, Malaysia, and Israel and in the S.I. Newhouse School at Syracuse University, where she was Associate Professor of Public Diplomacy. Snow was an SSRC Abe Fellow and Visiting Professor at Keio University in Tokyo, where she completed research for a book on Japan's nation brand image since 3/11.

**Kelly Vibber** (Ph.D., Purdue University) is an assistant professor in Public Relations at the University of Dayton. Her research interests include public diplomacy, development communication, nation branding, and international public relations. Her work has been published in the *International Journal of Strategic Communication* and *PRism*.

**Richard D. Waters** (Ph.D., University of Florida) is an associate professor and interim director of the Master of Nonprofit Administration program at the University of San Francisco. The author of more than 70 peer-reviewed journal articles and book chapters, his research focuses on nonprofit organizations' use of technology, fundraising, and stakeholder relations. He is the associate editor of *Case Studies in Strategic Communication* and a member of the editorial review board for *Journal of Public Relations Research, Public Relations Review*, and *Journal of Nonprofit and Public Sector Marketing*.

**Brenda J. Wrigley** (Ph.D., Syracuse University) is an associate professor of Public Relations in the Department of Marketing Communication at Emerson College, Boston. She has published more than 20 peer-reviewed journal articles and book chapters on gender, diversity, crisis communications, and public relations. She is currently studying diversity in U.S. public relations firms and the use of public relations in furthering the LGBT civil rights movement.

**Aimei Yang** (Ph.D., University of Oklahoma), is an assistant professor of public relations in the Annenberg School for Communication and Journalism at the University of Southern California. Yang's work focuses on international public relations, public diplomacy, global activism studies, and social network research. Yang has received research awards from both the International

Communication Association and National Communication Association. Yang has published over thirty journal articles and book chapters in leading refereed journals in her field, including *Communication Theory, Journalism and Mass Communication Quarterly, Public Relations Review, Journal of International & Intercultural Communication, Mass Communication and Society,* and *Computers in Human Behavior,* among others.

**Olga Zatepilina-Monacell** (Ph.D., Syracuse University) is an assistant professor of Communication at Appalachian State University in Boone, NC. She joined the academy after a twelve-year career in communications and international development. Zatepilina-Monacell has published in peer-reviewed journals such as *Corporate Reputation Review, Journal of Nonprofit & Public Sector Marketing, Place Branding and Public Diplomacy,* and *Public Relations Review.*

**Juyan Zhang** (Ph.D., University of Missouri-Columbia) is an associate professor of Communication at the University of Texas at San Antonio (UTSA). He is also a Contributing Scholar at the USC Center on Public Diplomacy. His research interests include public diplomacy, strategic communication, and international communication. He has published in journals such as *Public Relations Review, Place Branding and Public Diplomacy,* and *International Journal of Communication.*

# *Index*